Knowledge Management for Corporate Social Responsibility

Gregorio Martín-de Castro
Complutense University of Madrid, Spain

Jaime Juan González-Masip
Rey Juan Carlos University, Spain

IGI Global
PUBLISHER of TIMELY KNOWLEDGE

A volume in the Advances in Business Strategy and Competitive Advantage (ABSCA) Book Series

Published in the United States of America by
IGI Global
Business Science Reference (an imprint of IGI Global)
701 E. Chocolate Avenue
Hershey PA, USA 17033
Tel: 717-533-8845
Fax: 717-533-8661
E-mail: cust@igi-global.com
Web site: http://www.igi-global.com

Library of Congress Cataloging-in-Publication Data

Names: Martín de Castro, Gregorio, 1972- editor. | González-Masip, Jaime Juan, 1977- editor.
Title: Knowledge management for corporate social responsibility / Gregorio Martín-de Castro and Jaime Juan González-Masip, editors.
Description: Hershey : Business Science Reference, 2020. | Includes bibliographical references and index. | Summary: "This book explores the theoretical and practical aspects of linking firm profitability, social development, and natural environment in respect to business management practices"-- Provided by publisher.
Identifiers: LCCN 2020001201 (print) | LCCN 2020001202 (ebook) | ISBN 9781799848332 (hardcover) | ISBN 9781799852735 (paperback) | ISBN 9781799848349 (ebook)
Subjects: LCSH: Knowledge management. | Social responsibility of business.
Classification: LCC HD30.2 .K62976 2020 (print) | LCC HD30.2 (ebook) | DDC 658.4/038--dc23
LC record available at https://lccn.loc.gov/2020001201
LC ebook record available at https://lccn.loc.gov/2020001202

This book is published in the IGI Global book series Advances in Business Strategy and Competitive Advantage (ABSCA) (ISSN: 2327-3429; eISSN: 2327-3437)

British Cataloguing in Publication Data
A Cataloguing in Publication record for this book is available from the British Library.

For electronic access to this publication, please contact: eresources@igi-global.com.

Advances in Business Strategy and Competitive Advantage (ABSCA) Book Series

Patricia Ordóñez de Pablos
Universidad de Oviedo, Spain

ISSN:2327-3429
EISSN:2327-3437

Mission

Business entities are constantly seeking new ways through which to gain advantage over their competitors and strengthen their position within the business environment. With competition at an all-time high due to technological advancements allowing for competition on a global scale, firms continue to seek new ways through which to improve and strengthen their business processes, procedures, and profitability.

The **Advances in Business Strategy and Competitive Advantage (ABSCA) Book Series** is a timely series responding to the high demand for state-of-the-art research on how business strategies are created, implemented and re-designed to meet the demands of globalized competitive markets. With a focus on local and global challenges, business opportunities and the needs of society, the **ABSCA** encourages scientific discourse on doing business and managing information technologies for the creation of sustainable competitive advantage.

Coverage

- Economies of Scale
- Tacit Knowledge
- Strategic Management
- Differentiation Strategy
- Strategic Alliances
- Outsourcing
- Small and Medium Enterprises
- Cost Leadership Strategy
- Balanced Scorecard
- Business Models

IGI Global is currently accepting manuscripts for publication within this series. To submit a proposal for a volume in this series, please contact our Acquisition Editors at Acquisitions@igi-global.com or visit: http://www.igi-global.com/publish/.

The Advances in Business Strategy and Competitive Advantage (ABSCA) Book Series (ISSN 2327-3429) is published by IGI Global, 701 E. Chocolate Avenue, Hershey, PA 17033-1240, USA, www.igi-global.com. This series is composed of titles available for purchase individually; each title is edited to be contextually exclusive from any other title within the series. For pricing and ordering information please visit http://www.igi-global.com/book-series/advances-business-strategy-competitive-advantage/73672. Postmaster: Send all address changes to above address.

Titles in this Series

For a list of additional titles in this series, please visit:
http://www.igi-global.com/book-series/advances-business-strategy-competitive-advantage/73672

Applications of Soft Systems Methodology for Organizational Change
Maryam Ebrahimi (Independent Researcher, Germany)
Business Science Reference • © 2021 • 236pp • H/C (ISBN: 9781799845041) • US $195.00

Handbook of Research on Multidisciplinary Approaches to Entrepreneurship, Innovation, and ICTs
Luísa Cagica Carvalho (Instituto Politécnico de Setúbal, Portugal & CEFAGE, Universidade de Évora, Portugal) Leonilde Reis (Instituto Politécnico de Setúbal, Portugal) Alcina Prata (Instituto Polytechnic of Setúbal, Portugal) and Raquel Pereira (Instituto Polytechnic of Setúbal, Portugal)
Business Science Reference • © 2021 • 455pp • H/C (ISBN: 9781799840992) • US $295.00

Ethical Standards and Practice in Managerial and Financial Accounting
Ionica Oncioiu (Titu Maiorescu University, Romania)
Business Science Reference • © 2021 • 300pp • H/C (ISBN: 9781799840121) • US $195.00

Sustainability Reporting, Ethics, and Strategic Management Strategies for Modern Organizations
Ionica Oncioiu (Titu Maiorescu University, Romania) Sorinel Căpuşneanu (Titu Maiorescu University, Romania) Dan Ioan Topor (1 Decembrie 1918 University, Romania) and Dana Maria (Oprea) Constantin (University of Bucharest, Romania)
Business Science Reference • © 2021 • 320pp • H/C (ISBN: 9781799846376) • US $195.00

International Perspectives on the Youth Labor Market Emerging Research and Opportunities
Samir Amine (Université du Québec en Outaouais, Canada)
Business Science Reference • © 2020 • 217pp • H/C (ISBN: 9781799827795) • US $170.00

Open and Innovative Trade Opportunities for Latin America and the Caribbean
Pablo Alberto Baisotti (University of Costa Rica, Costa Rica)
Business Science Reference • © 2020 • 255pp • H/C (ISBN: 9781799835035) • US $215.00

Cases on Performance Improvement Innovation
Darlene M. Van Tiem (Capella University, USA & University of Michigan – Dearborn, USA) and Nancy Crain Burns (Crain Burns Associates LLC, USA)
Business Science Reference • © 2020 • 377pp • H/C (ISBN: 9781799836735) • US $195.00

IGI Global
PUBLISHER of TIMELY KNOWLEDGE

701 East Chocolate Avenue, Hershey, PA 17033, USA
Tel: 717-533-8845 x100 • Fax: 717-533-8661
E-Mail: cust@igi-global.com • www.igi-global.com

Table of Contents

Detailed Table of Contents

The concept of corporate social responsibility continues in a state of lack of academic consensus, which makes it difficult to propose new research proposals on the company's social and environmental commitment. With the aim of facilitating research tasks, this chapter systematically compiles a list of definitions of the concept and lists a set of dimensions or drivers that are either present in these definitions or can be considered as fundamental elements or perspectives for the study of corporate social responsibility. As conclusions, the most relevant ideas presented in the chapter are compiled. The incorporation, in academic studies, of perspectives based on impacts of business activity rather than principles of action is also proposed, since they present a possible greater operability. These concepts are corporate social performance or corporate sustainability.

The European Commission 2011 defines social responsibility as the responsibility of companies for their impacts on society, so it is a complex concept that the authors will define, not only theoretically to give content to this activity but also practical to get to understand the advantages that can be used to use corporate social responsibility, not only at the image level but also at the economic level. Organizations can carry out different types of actions with social responsibility; stations with some advantages can even become a competitive advantage. But not all are advantages for companies when CRS policies are made; there are also disadvantages that must be known by marketing managers. In this chapter they will be developed. Finally, the conclusions of all the above will be presented.

Despite the high academic and business interest in corporate sustainability and everything related to the

Developing the pathways that lead to sustainable innovation in SMEs represents an important aspect of the business world and society. The aim of this chapter is to verify the relations and pathways that lead to sustainable product innovation performance while considering all three pillars of the triple bottom line approach. This study proposed a mixed methods approach to identify the antecedents of sustainable product innovation performance. The model was used to measure the effects of the three pillars of the triple bottom line: economic, social, and environmental developments. The model was also designed to account for the firm's type (public limited companies vs. general partnerships). The authors determined whether a firm's type moderates the effects of the three pillars. They identified alternative configurations of conditions and determined those that are likely to lead to sustainable product innovation performance. The findings show that social and environmental developments are two important antecedents for product innovation performance, and they contribute to different pathways.

The chapter looks to contribute in a theoretical way to the measurement of the concepts of CSR (corporate social responsibility), good governance, and reputation in SMEs, since they are concepts of great importance in business management and are related. Social responsibility actions through the exercise of good governance means that SMEs can obtain a solid reputation. The purpose of the chapter is to develop how companies that incorporate social responsibility into their business model achieve a better image in the eyes of their stakeholders. Codes of ethics play an important role as an instrument of good governance. As a result, the chapter proposes measurement indicators to be used in future empirical research to verify the effects of causality. They can be a valuable tool for knowledge management as a source of innovation for SMEs.

The conceptual model proposed in this study is used to serve a guide for Industry 4.0 to understand the effect of GIC (green intellectual capital) and GKM (green knowledge management) on sustainability. Green challenge in Industry 4.0 has increasingly become a hot topic in both academia and practice. Among the Industry 4.0 topics, digital chain monitoring has a great impact on the performance of the company. The study of the industrial digital chain is a great green challenge in the 21st century in order

The objective of this chapter is to deepen into the association between corporate governance and the adoption of environmentally proactive strategies. The theoretical approach used is the knowledge-based view. This chapter explains how the environmentally proactive strategies could be enhanced by the director interlocks, who help the company to acquire environmental knowledge. The concept of the environmental absorptive capacity is used to inquire how the knowledge from the director interlocks is utilized to improve the company's environmental responsiveness. The results of the analysis conducted indicates that the main contribution of the director interlocks is to help companies to acquire resources and environmental knowledge, useful to deploy environmentally proactive strategies. This study is of particular importance for firms, establishing environmentally proactive strategies. The study invites investors, CEOs, and managers to consider the director interlocks to renew the environmental capacities and comply the most stringent requirement of stakeholders.

This chapter introduces readers to the micro-foundation framework in corporate sustainability. Traditionally, strategic management and corporate sustainability research have explained why firms become more sustainable from a macro-level perspective. In recent years, new research has focused on the micro-level mechanism at the individual or group level. This research stream is known as the micro-foundations movement and tries to highlight individual characteristics, knowledge, background, etc. when firms decide to become more sustainable. Through the literature review, the authors tried to identify the studies published in top journals about the micro-foundation framework. Therefore, the aim of this chapter is to give a primary introduction and an overview of the micro-foundations framework in corporate sustainability and identify what mechanisms have been found at the micro-level that explain why firms become more sustainable.

Preface

KNOWLEDGE MANAGEMENT FOR CORPORATE SOCIAL RESPONSIBILITY: NEW INSIGHTS AND FUTURE RESEARCH DIRECTIONS

Introduction

In a Knowledge Economy and Society, knowledge, intellectual capital and innovation are the key drivers of firm's sustainable competitive advantage and performance (Martín-de Castro, Delgado-Verde, López-Sáez, & Navas-López, 2011).

Furthermore, in a changing and complex environment currently facing the main challenge of sustainable development, the effective management of knowledge, and intellectual assets, intra and inter-organizational learning and talent management are the basis for social innovation and new ways of competition under the framework of sustainable development (Hart, 1995) paradigm, where firm profitability, environmental respect and social development can be jointly achieved.

In that sense, management and business practice are gradually incorporating social and environmental demands made by all types of internal and external stakeholders in strategy and business decisions. Thus, and despite of the growing relevance of corporate social responsibility (CSR), partially due to its inclusion in the SDGs as part of the global initiative for sustainability, the concept of CSR is still broad and relatively ambiguous (Matten & Moon, 2008; Van Marrewijk, 2003). It is a cross-company discipline that analyzes the strategic way (McWilliams, Siegel, & Wright, 2006; McWilliams & Siegel, 2011) in which the firm relates to its environment through its stakeholders and manages its economic, social and environmental impacts (Carroll, 1991).

It covers traditional and new strategic and managerial perspectives of study, such as Stakeholder Management (Freeman, 1984; Martín-de Castro, Amores-Salvadó, & Navas-López, 2016), Business Ethics (Goodpaster, 1991), Triple Bottom Line and Sustainable Development (Elkington, 1997; Hart, 1995), Corporate Sustainability (Montiel, 2008), Reputation and Legitimacy (Brammer & Pavelin, 2006; Du & Vieira, 2012; Fombrun, 2005; Martín-de Castro et al., 2016), Corporate Governance (Jamali, Safieddine, & Rabbath, 2008), Accountability and Corporate Citizenship (Valor, 2005), or Talent Management (González-Masip, Martín-de Castro, & Hernández, 2019), among others.

In order to understand the complexity of CSR in the current business models, this research monography offers fifteen contributions around five main current hot topic that are presented and organized in the following section.

CSR is closely related to innovation processes (Halme & Laurila, 2009), systematic dialogue with stakeholders (O'riordan & Fairbrass, 2008; Pedersen, 2006) and preferential access to talent by attracting highly qualified workers (Bhattacharya, Sen, & Korschun, 2008; Greening & Turban, 2000). In addition, companies that carry out CSR practices must maintain, to meet the expectations of their stakeholders (Dawkins & Lewis, 2003), high levels of transparency, through accountability for their results and non-financial impacts (Gray, Owen, & Maunders, 1988; Michelon, Pilonato, & Ricceri, 2015). All these circumstances and initiatives are an intense source of knowledge for the company, generating virtuous circles and attractive competitive advantages.

MAIN CONTRIBUTIONS AND NEW INSIGHTS

This book makes a compilation of those aspects from a cross-fertilized perspective in which a Knowledge-Based View is the main frame to understand and advance new avenues for an effective management of Corporate Social Responsibility, by linking firm profitability, social development and natural environment respect. CSR practices (Gjølberg, 2009) show business intentions, can be evaluated by stakeholders, and affect many aspects of the firm, with Knowledge Management and Intellectual Capital being ones of them. More importantly, social and environmental innovation are knowledge-intensive processes that require, from a Strategic Management perspective, a Knowledge-Based and Intellectual Capital View of the Firm (Martín-de Castro, 2020).

This book introduces the concepts of Strategic Management, Knowledge and Innovation Management and Corporate Social Responsibility and Sustainability to undergraduate and post graduate students as well as researchers, and scenarios in which those concepts combine to generate sustainable competitive advantages, generating from a triple bottom line, with economic, social and environmental values. It is also relevant to practitioners, small business owners, entrepreneurs, non-profit organizations and policy makers.

This book contains 14 contributions from different perspectives and frameworks that jointly offer some recent advances in order to understand the phenomenon of corporate social responsibility in the organization. More specifically, they can be organized around five main topics:

1. Conceptual analysis of corporate social responsibility, its nature, characteristics, and related concepts. As Durand, Grand and Madsen (2017) remarked, the excessive fragmentation of the field and the proliferation of multitude concepts and labels, in what can be named 'terminological jungle' impedes its advancement and consolidation as a coherent and mature field of research. In this sense, new efforts in construct delimitation and characterization are welcome. In this vein, the following three chapters contribute to this aim.

The first contribution on this topic is made by González-Masip on the concept of corporate social responsibility including a compilation of CSR definitions and identifying a set of dimensions and drivers that are either present in these definitions or can be considered as fundamental elements or perspectives for the study of Corporate Social Responsibility.

From a global perspective, Zapata-Agüera analyses in her chapter, CSR in organizations, its advantages and drawbacks. As a complex concept, its definition, both theoretically and in practical terms, lead us to understand the advantages that can be taking into account when managing corporate social responsibility, not only at the image level but also at the economic level. Organizations can carry out different types of actions with social responsibility, implying some advantages but also drawbacks, that must be known specially by marketing managers.

The so-called 'terminological jungle' existing around CSR and related issues, such as corporate and business sustainability, is the aim of the third chapter on this topic by González-Masip. As he remarks, despite the high academic and business interest in corporate sustainability and everything related to the impact of organizations on their social and environmental environment, there is still a notable confusion between the concepts of corporate social responsibility, corporate sustainability and even business sustainability. This chapter helps to identify common aspects and differentiating elements between these concepts, which allow researchers and practitioners to understand the existing literature on the topic and to propose lines of work and research in an appropriate manner, according to its objectives and analysis perspectives.

2. The phenomena of corporate social responsibility and sustainability is SME, innovation, and entrepreneurial activity, which includes five contributions.

In the chapter entitled "An Entrepreneur Sees the Reward: The Importance of Intellectual Capital and CSR in a Company", Professor Merve Ünal aims to advance the understanding of how social entrepreneurs analyze and apply intellectual capital and corporate social responsibility within their companies. Based on literature review, the broad definitions of intellectual capital and corporate social responsibility, the measurement models and the management of intellectual capital and the development process of corporate social responsibility were identified. In order to develop holistic understanding, the relationship between intellectual capital and corporate social responsibility on the basis of entrepreneur were analyzed. The understanding of the intellectual capital and corporate social responsibility in companies were shed light by theoretical framework of resource-based view, dynamic capabilities, stakeholder theory and legitimacy theory.

The second contribution co-authored by Professors Valle-Mestre, García-Pérez and Jiménez-Jimenez studies the effects of social entrepreneurship on organizational performance and the mediating role of CSR practices. This study empirically analyzes the effects of social entrepreneurship on organizational performance, as well as the indirect effect through CSR. Based on data collected from 213 Social Economy companies, structural equations models have been used to verify the research hypotheses. The results obtained confirm the positive effect of social entrepreneurship on economic performance and announce the existence of the mediatory effect of the practices of corporate social responsibility.

The third chapter under this topic written by Professors Muñoz-Pascual and Galende about the impact of the triple bottom line on sustainable product innovation explores the pathways that lead to sustainable innovation in SMEs. The aim of this chapter is to verify the relations and pathways that lead to sustainable product innovation performance while considering all three pillars of the Triple Bottom Line. This study proposed a mixed methods approach to identify the antecedents of sustainable product innovation performance. The findings show that social and environmental developments are two important antecedents for product innovation performance, and they contribute to different pathways.

In the four contribution on this research topic, Professors Rubio-Andrés, Ramos-González and Sastre-Castillo explore in the links between CSR, good governance practices and corporate reputation in the context of SMEs, offering a proposal of indicators. The objective of this chapter is focused on highlighting the relevance of good governance in socially responsible SMEs, so that a positive effect on their image and business reputation is generated.

Finally, Professor Martín Rubio in her chapter on challenges in green intellectual capital and knowledge management in sustainability and industry 4.0 identifies that green innovation needs more environmental knowledge than traditional innovations due to its complexity and costs. Also, the industry 4.0 paradigm includes new topics of analysis, such as digital chain monitoring. All in all, a wide discussion and debates about the corporate sustainability, green intellectual capital and knowledge management are integrated in a conceptual model proposed that serves as a practical guide for companies managing this complexity.

3. Clusters, geographic agglomeration, and corporate social responsibility. The phenomenon of CSR at cluster level is one of the most promising avenues of research with direct implications for both business practitioners and policy makers. Understanding how CSR practices are developed and transferred among firms belonging to clusters or its implications for competitiveness and corpore image are some research questions of interest. This topic includes two chapters.

The first chapter, entitled "Corporate Social Responsibility and the Local Community Effect: Insights From the Spanish Footwear Cluster" and written by Professors Díez-Vial, Belso-Martínez and López-Sánchez, explores, from a multilevel perspective, how CSR practices are developed inside a cluster. The aim is to describe how CSR practices are developed comparing both firm's characteristics and local interactions inside the cluster. In particular, they analyze how internal dynamics of the cluster, defined by the networks of relationships that are developed with supporting organizations, along with leading firms in the cluster shape a new institutional framework that locally legitimates CSR practices.

The second contribution on this issue is the work entitled "CSR in the Spotlight: Location and Gender as Drivers of Its Development", written by Professors Claver-Cortés, Marco-Laraja and Poveda-Pareja. This study analyzes the existence of relationship between Corporate Social Responsibility and two factors, namely: business location; and managers' gender. The Industrial District (ID) theory serves as the basis to demonstrate the possible influence of location on this type of environment with an improved implementation of social practices. Also, they consider the possible influence of internationalization within the cluster on CSR development since, globalization itself can further favor the implementation of CSR practices. The study additionally examines the role that the variable 'directors' gender', and more precisely, women directors, can play as a key factor in the development of such practices.

4. Corporate social responsibility and stakeholders' engagement and collaboration is a fundamental issue to a fully understanding of most proactive CSR practices, which imply in-depth cooperation with both internal and external stakeholders (Martín-de Castro et al., 2016). In this topic, three chapters analyses specific issues of it.

From an external perspective, the first contribution analyses the relevance of CSR going beyond traditional organizational limits, engaging external stakeholders and especially in vertical relationships, as an emerging hot topic. That is what Professor Tobaruela explores in his chapter entitled "Suppliers Social Responsibility: Auditing vs. Engagement in a Relational Capital Reference". From a relational perspective, he studies how companies implement CSR practices along their supply chains to fulfil stakeholder requirements, exploring supplier engagement to compliance with CSR framework and the relationship firm-stakeholder. The chapter introduces an exploratory study about practices and attitudes of stakeholders and knowledge sharing in a collaborative environment of relational capital.

The second chapter from an external perspective entitled "University Social Responsibility: A Framework That Places Them as Strategic Partners to an European Digital Single Market" by Stratu-Strelet, López-Hernández, Guerola-Navarro, Gil-Gómez and Oltra-Badenes highlights the role of technology-based universities in Public-Private Partnerships to strengthen and deploy the Digital Single Market strategy. Moreover, it analyzes how these collaboration channels have used knowledge management as an effective tool for sustainable collaboration.

From an internal perspective, the third chapter on the topic is co-authored by Professors Hendrickson, Baumann and Thompson and entitled "Understanding Relationships Between CSR, Organizational Identification, and Ethical Behavior: USVI Retail Employees' Perceptions". It examines the predictive relationships of retail employees' perceptions of corporate social responsibility (PCSR) and organizational identification (POI) on their perceptions of ethical organizational behavior (PEOB). One hundred and eighteen retail employees from 20 companies, in the United States Virgin Islands, participated in an online survey. The findings of this study identified significant relationships between retail employees PCSR, POI and perceived ethical organizational behavior PEOB.

5. The environmental dimension of CSR. Climate change and emergency constitutes one of the main challenges that firms have to face in current times. Due to this fact, proactive corporate environmentalism (Hart, 1995) is an issue of increasing relevance for managers and policy makers. In that sense, two chapters are presented.

The chapter entitled "Environmentally Proactive Strategies and Absorptive Capacity: The Role of the Directors Interlock", has been written by González-Zubieta and Professor Amores-Salvadó. It seeks to shed some light in the interplay between corporate governance, knowledge management, and the adoption of environmentally proactive strategies by firms. This chapter explains how the environmentally proactive strategies could be enhanced by the director interlocks, who help the company to acquire environmental knowledge. Under this framework, the main contribution of the director interlocks is to help companies to acquire resources and environmental knowledge, useful to deploy environmentally proactive strategies.

Finally, the second chapter on environmental topic is framed under recent theoretical developments in strategic thinking such as the Micro-Foundations. Professors Balarezo-Núñez and Corcuera explore the micro-foundations of corporate sustainability. Traditionally, strategic management and corporate sustainability research have explained why firms become more sustainable from a macro-level perspective. In recent years, new research has focused on the micro-level mechanism at the individual or group level. This research stream is known as the micro-foundations movement and tries to highlight individual characteristics, knowledge, background, etc. when firms decide to become more sustainable. Through the literature review in business source complete we tried to identify the studies published in top journals about the micro-foundation framework. in the last years.

CONCLUSION AND SOME AVENUES OF FUTURE RESEARCH

Researchers, business practitioners and policy makers can be benefited from this research monography that under the title "Knowledge Management for Corporate Social Responsibility" contains fifteen pieces of theoretical and empirical research focused on the understanding the phenomena of corporate social responsibility and business sustainability in the current society and economy (Burke & Logsdon, 1996; Porter & Kramer, 2006).

Triple bottom line and the United Nations Sustainable Development Objectives Agenda 2030, jointly with Climate Change and Emergency are forcing companies to adopt CSR principles and environmental respect, emerging as a key management agenda and a business priority to firm survival and sustained competitive advantage (Hart, 1995).

Under the complexity of CSR management in the business arena, research contributions have been organized around five main topics of analysis, which constitutes current hot topics of debate and for sure, future avenues of fruitful research and business developments. Thus, the main focus of analysis in this book with five contributions has been the analysis of CSR in the context of SMEs, innovation and entrepreneurial activities. Certainly, although there is abundant literature on CSR in large corporations, SME represents the majority of economic activity, and the nature, role and contribution of CSR to these types of business models and their competitive implications have been less studied. Also, this monography put the accent in the increasing role of social and green entrepreneurship as key driver of sustainable business models.

The second topic addressed in this book focuses in the definitional landscape of corporate social responsibility. As a current hot topic in Management, many definitions, characterizations, typologies, and related issues, such as corporate sustainability or social performance has appeared in recent years. This variety of definitions, similar concepts and measurement methods generates confusion among researchers and managers when designing concrete work plans and policies (Montiel & Delgado-Ceballos, 2014). In this vein, three contributions try to shed some light in this issue.

So interesting for academics, business practitioners and policy makers is the topic about clusters, industrial districts and CSR. In this sense, two interesting researches explore the nature, diffusion level and competitiveness effects of CSR practices and models in companies belonging to clusters and industrial districts, giving useful tools for managing CSR in those ecosystems.

At the heart of CSR, the fourth topic of this monography focuses on internal and external stakeholders' engagement and collaboration as effective mechanism to implement successful CSR practices in companies and institutions. In this vein, three chapters explores, both from internal and external stakeholders' engagement

Finally, the last topic highlights the environmental dimension of corporate social responsibility. Climate change, the loss of biodiversity, pollution, etc., implies -jointly with social issues- one of the main challenges for nations, economies and business of XXI century. How companies can adapt, and even reinvent, their business models toward sustainability implies deep changes in all organizational members and activities. Two contributions of this monography explore the complexities and main challenges.

All in all, the five main topics and the related fifteen contributions constitute a current state-of-the-art of corporate social responsibility and the firm under the Strategy and Management frameworks of Knowledge Management and Intellectual Capital-Based Views give a very interesting perspective of current hot topics of research and business practice constituting starting points to develop new fruitful avenues of research on the topic.

Gregorio Martín-de Castro
Complutense University of Madrid, Spain

Jaime González-Masip
Rey Juan Carlos University, Spain

REFERENCES

Bhattacharya, C. B., Sen, S., & Korschun, D. (2008). Using corporate social responsibility to win the war for talent. *MIT Sloan Management Review*, *49*(2), 37–44.

Brammer, S. J., & Pavelin, S. (2006). Corporate reputation and social performance: The importance of fit. *Journal of Management Studies*, *43*(3), 435–455. doi:10.1111/j.1467-6486.2006.00597.x

Burke, L., & Logsdon, J. M. (1996). How corporate social responsibility pays off. *Long Range Planning*, *29*(4), 495–502. doi:10.1016/0024-6301(96)00041-6

Carroll, A. B. (1991). The pyramid of corporate social responsibility: Toward the moral management of organizational stakeholders. *Business Horizons*, *34*(4), 39–48. doi:10.1016/0007-6813(91)90005-G

Dawkins, J., & Lewis, S. (2003). CSR in stakeholder expectations: And their implication for company strategy. *Journal of Business Ethics*, *44*(2-3), 185–193. doi:10.1023/A:1023399732720

Du, S., & Vieira, E. T. Jr. (2012). Striving for legitimacy through corporate social responsibility: Insights from oil companies. *Journal of Business Ethics*, *110*(4), 413–427. doi:10.100710551-012-1490-4

Durand, R., Grant, R. M., & Madsen, T. L. (2017). The expanding domain of strategic management research and the quest for integration. *Strategic Management Journal*, *38*(1), 4–16. doi:10.1002mj.2607

Elkington, J. (1997). *Cannibals with forks*. Capstone.

Fombrun, C. J. (2005). A world of reputation research, analysis and thinking—building corporate reputation through CSR initiatives: Evolving standards. *Corporate Reputation Review*, *8*(1), 7–12. doi:10.1057/palgrave.crr.1540235

Freeman, R. E. (1984). *Strategic management: A stakeholder approach*. Pittman.

Gjølberg, M. (2009). Measuring the immeasurable? Constructing an index of CSR practices and CSR performance in 20 countries. *Scandinavian Journal of Management*, *25*(1), 10–22. doi:10.1016/j.scaman.2008.10.003

González-Masip, J., Martín-de Castro, G., & Hernández, A. (2019). Inter-organisational knowledge spillovers: Attracting talent in science and technology parks and corporate social responsibility practices. *Journal of Knowledge Management*.

Goodpaster, K. E. (1991). Business ethics and stakeholder analysis. *Business Ethics Quarterly*, *1*(1), 53–73.

Gray, R., Owen, D., & Maunders, K. (1988). Corporate social reporting: Emerging trends in accountability and the social contract. *Accounting, Auditing & Accountability Journal*, *1*(1), 6–20. doi:10.1108/EUM0000000004617

Greening, D. W., & Turban, D. B. (2000). Corporate social performance as a competitive advantage in attracting a quality workforce. *Business & Society*, *39*(3), 254–280. doi:10.1177/000765030003900302

Halme, M., & Laurila, J. (2009). Philanthropy, integration or innovation? exploring the financial and societal outcomes of different types of corporate responsibility. *Journal of Business Ethics*, *84*(3), 325–339. doi:10.100710551-008-9712-5

Hart, S. L. (1995). A natural-resource-based view of the firm. *Academy of Management Review*, *20*(4), 986–1014. doi:10.5465/amr.1995.9512280033

Jamali, D., Safieddine, A. M., & Rabbath, M. (2008). Corporate governance and corporate social responsibility synergies and interrelationships. *Corporate Governance*, *16*(5), 443–459. doi:10.1111/j.1467-8683.2008.00702.x

Martín de Castro, G. (2020). (in press). Exploring the market side of corporate environmentalism: Reputation, legitimacy and stakeholders' engagement. *Industrial Marketing Management*. Advance online publication. doi:10.1016/j.indmarman.2020.05.010

Martín-de Castro, G., Amores-Salvadó, J., & Navas-López, J. E. (2016). Environmental management systems and firm performance: Improving firm environmental policy through stakeholder engagement. *Corporate Social Responsibility and Environmental Management*, *23*(4), 243–256. doi:10.1002/csr.1377

Martín-de Castro, G., Delgado-Verde, M., López-Sáez, P., & Navas-López, J. E. (2011). Towards 'an intellectual capital-based view of the firm': Origins and nature. *Journal of Business Ethics*, *98*(4), 649–662. doi:10.100710551-010-0644-5

Matten, D., & Moon, J. (2008). Implicit' and 'explicit' CSR: A conceptual framework for a comparative understanding of corporate social responsibility. *Academy of Management Review*, *33*(2), 404–424. doi:10.5465/amr.2008.31193458

McWilliams, A., & Siegel, D. S. (2011). Creating and capturing value: Strategic corporate social responsibility, resource-based theory, and sustainable competitive advantage. *Journal of Management*, *37*(5), 1480–1495. doi:10.1177/0149206310385696

McWilliams, A., Siegel, D. S., & Wright, P. M. (2006). Corporate social responsibility: Strategic implications. *Journal of Management Studies*, *43*(1), 1–18. doi:10.1111/j.1467-6486.2006.00580.x

Michelon, G., Pilonato, S., & Ricceri, F. (2015). CSR reporting practices and the quality of disclosure: An empirical analysis. *Critical Perspectives on Accounting*, *33*, 59–78. doi:10.1016/j.cpa.2014.10.003

Montiel, I. (2008). Corporate social responsibility and corporate sustainability: Separate pasts, common futures. *Organization & Environment*, *21*(3), 245–269. doi:10.1177/1086026608321329

Montiel, I., & Delgado-Ceballos, J. (2014). Defining and measuring corporate sustainability: Are we there yet? *Organization & Environment*, *27*(2), 113–139. doi:10.1177/1086026614526413

O'riordan, L., & Fairbrass, J. (2008). Corporate social responsibility (CSR): Models and theories in stakeholder dialogue. *Journal of Business Ethics*, *83*(4), 745–758. doi:10.100710551-008-9662-y

Pedersen, E. R. (2006). Making corporate social responsibility (CSR) operable: How companies translate stakeholder dialogue into practice. *Business and Society Review*, *111*(2), 137–163. doi:10.1111/j.1467-8594.2006.00265.x

Porter, M. E., & Kramer, M. R. (2006). Strategy & society: The link between competitive advantage and corporate social responsibility. *Harvard Business Review*, *84*(12), 78–92. PMID:17183795

Valor, C. (2005). Corporate social responsibility and corporate citizenship: Towards corporate accountability. *Business and Society Review*, *110*(2), 191–212. doi:10.1111/j.0045-3609.2005.00011.x

Van Marrewijk, M. (2003). Concepts and definitions of CSR and corporate sustainability: Between agency and communion. *Journal of Business Ethics*, *44*(2/3), 95–105. doi:10.1023/A:1023331212247

Chapter 1
The Concept of Corporate Social Responsibility:
Study Perspectives Proposal

Jaime González-Masip
Rey Juan Carlos University, Spain

ABSTRACT

The concept of corporate social responsibility continues in a state of lack of academic consensus, which makes it difficult to propose new research proposals on the company's social and environmental commitment. With the aim of facilitating research tasks, this chapter systematically compiles a list of definitions of the concept and lists a set of dimensions or drivers that are either present in these definitions or can be considered as fundamental elements or perspectives for the study of corporate social responsibility. As conclusions, the most relevant ideas presented in the chapter are compiled. The incorporation, in academic studies, of perspectives based on impacts of business activity rather than principles of action is also proposed, since they present a possible greater operability. These concepts are corporate social performance or corporate sustainability.

INTRODUCTION

When considering an investigation on CSR, in general, two possible points of view can be adopted. The first is to consider that there is a definition of this concept that is valid and useful for the research objectives and, moreover, is universal. A second, more prudent, point of view is to assume that such a definition does not exist and that the investigation could be non-generalizable since it is impossible to find a universally valid definition of CSR. It seems reasonable to opt for the second option, since it happens that academics, professionals and managers still do not reach a consensus regarding a single, clear and simple definition of CSR, thus generating a certain degree of confusion (Aguilera, Rupp, Williams, & Ganapathi, 2007; Aguinis & Glavas, 2012; Bauman & Skitka, 2012; Dahlsrud, 2008; Garriga & Melé, 2004; McWilliams, Siegel, & Wright, 2006; Sheehy, 2015; Van Marrewijk, 2003).

DOI: 10.4018/978-1-7998-4833-2.ch001

The apparent state of eternal development of CSR and its wide range of definitions reflects the ambiguous nature of possible interpretations of CSR, causes divergence in approaches to the concept and contributes to its lack of attractiveness among professionals and entrepreneurs (Lindgreen & Swaen, 2010), as they find it difficult to put it into practice. This vagueness in the definition of the concept, on the one hand, makes research work difficult, since it is necessary to consider different approaches and the variables necessary for the studies and, on the other hand, causes companies to prefer the approach that best suits to their circumstances and gives them greater utility for the business (Van Marrewijk, 2003), misrepresenting the nature of the concept. And it is that, ultimately, corporate social responsibility can mean different things to different people (Lyon & Maxwell, 2008), and some of the reasons are discussed in this chapter.

The objective of this chapter is to offer new perspectives on the limitations existing in the academic literature for the creation of a universal definition of CSR, based on the analysis of different approaches and approaches found on it. As a conclusion to the chapter, the conflicts and ambiguities detected in the bibliographic review of the concept of CSR are reviewed, offering suggestions and guidelines on how to deal with future research on this matter. The main contributions of the chapter are, first, the compilation, systematic review and analysis of various definitions of CSR existing in the academic literature, and second, the realization of a series of proposals that can be considered by researchers of the concept of CSR in their work to avoid planning errors or uncomfortable theoretical biases.

The chapter is structured as follows. First, a review of definitions of stakeholder concept is shown, closely related to CSR. In the same section, below, a systematic review of definitions of the concept of Corporate Social Responsibility is included, which serves to review the diversity of approaches and observable concepts or dimensions in said list of definitions. The following section reviews various types of motivations that condition companies to implement CSR initiatives that can be considered in studies on the subject. Finally, a chapter of conclusions compiles the main ideas presented in the chapter, highlighting various possible scenarios of study on the concept of CSR that may be of interest to the researcher.

BACKGROUND

This chapter analyzes the concept of corporate social responsibility by going to its origins, reviewing a long list of definitions of it, and raising a series of questions related to the way it has been defined and ambiguities and gaps that generate possible disadvantages for the research on the subject. The chapter also reviews the concept of stakeholders due to their importance regarding CSR.

Origins of the CSR Concept

To analyze the concept of corporate social responsibility (CSR), it is interesting to start by reviewing some of the authors who used it in their publications as early as the first half of the 20th century. For example, Dodd (1932) already mentioned the responsibility of the directors of organizations towards society as a whole, going beyond the demands of shareholders, replicating the argument present in the legal regulation that understands that companies can act for the benefit they bring to society as a whole (Dodd, 1932, in Cochran, 2007). Bowen (1953), Davis (1960) y Frederick (1960) also included the responsibilities of the company's management, and its power, with respect to society. The first of them specifically mentioned the term *social responsibility*. The second recognized their ability to arbitrarily affect or influence the company's workforce and the honesty of the company's actions. The third author attributed to the board of directors the ethical approach of the company's performance, its role in society and the creation of social value, not only economic. Boulding (1956) also advanced a different perspective of the non-economic activity of companies, which is their impact on the environment, referring to the equivalent of the so-called corporate social performance (see below in the Conclusions section).

The era of CSR as we know it today begins in the 1950s (Carroll, 1999) and gained prominence from the 1960s (Wang, Tong, Takeuchi, & George, 2016). Since then, interest in the concept has grown throughout the second half of the 20th century (Garriga & Melé, 2004), suffering a notable increase throughout the 21st century (Montiel & Delgado-Ceballos, 2014). Among others, the reason for this incremental interest in alternatives to classical business management is that it focuses specifically on economic returns, and therefore shows itself as an outdated model, and it is necessary to adopt other different models that moderate the negative impacts on society and the environment.

The Stakeholder Concept

Although there is no agreed definition of stakeholders (see Table 1), it can be said that the stakeholders are those individuals, grouped by interests or motivations and kind of interaction they have with an organization, who have some type of capacity or legitimacy to influence, modify and channel the relationships of companies with their social, economic and environmental context, as well as the impact they generate. The interaction can be passive or active for both the corporation and the stakeholders, and the impact generated can be internal or external to the organization. The value provided by each group of stakeholders is specific and independent of others (they are disjoint groups). As Donaldson & Preston (1995, p.67) said, "The interests of all stakeholders are of intrinsic value. That is, each group of stakeholders merits consideration for its own sake and not merely because of its ability to further the interests of some other group, such as the shareowners."

According to the approach of the Stakeholders Theory, "the objectives of the firm should be derived by balancing the conflicting claims of the various stakeholders in the firm" (Freeman & Reed, 1983, p.89). Thanks to the interest groups, it happens that the correct behavior of the company is evaluated through these groups and the social demands on companies include moral justification and legitimacy (Whetten, Rands, & Godfrey, 2002). Thus, the search for this general good for society through the performance of CSR practices is feasible through the deep involvement of a broad set of interest groups in its approach (Barnett, 2007). Thus, having as reference the classic business strategy approaches, CSR is a means of creating value (Hussain, 1999), including the value generated up to society as a whole, and considers relations with stakeholders as a means to achieve the goals.

The Concept of Corporate Social Responsibility in Management

The foundation of the concept of CSR is found in the relationships that companies establish with society, taking into account that it has expectations placed on it, on their behavior and results (Wood, 1991). Society wants companies to meet social responsibilities, regardless of the economic interests of the profit activity and always above a simple compliance with the legal framework (Carroll, 1979). Behind this approach, there is the idea that company and society are connected and interrelated entities. The relationship they establish is valued in terms of rights, justice, and impact on human well-being (Bauman & Skitka, 2012). In this way, an adequate CSR approach would seek to positively affect both the

Table 1. Definitions of the concept of stakeholders

Author/s	Definitions of stakeholders
Stanford Research Institute (1963), cited in Freeman & Reed (1983, p.89)[1]	"The word *stakeholder* [...] refers to those groups without whose support the organization would cease to exist."
Rhenman (1968, p.25)	"Stakeholders in an organization are the individuals or groups dependent on the company for the realization of their personal goals and on whom the company is dependent for its existence."
Freeman & Reed (1983:91)	"Any identifiable group or individual who can affect the achievement of an organization's objectives." (*Wide Sense of Stakeholder*: includes contractually related groups, groups that are not closely related to the company and hostile groups.)
Freeman & Reed (1983, p.91)	"Any identifiable group or individual on which the organization is dependent for its continued survival." (*Narrow Sense of Stakeholder*: includes those groups directly or contractually related to the organization.)
Freeman (1984, p.46)	"A stakeholder is (by definition) any group or individual who can affect or is affected by the achievement of the organization's objectives"
Clarkson (1994, p.5), in Mitchell, Agle, & Wood (1997, pp.856-857)	"Voluntary stakeholders bear some form of risk as a result of having invested some form of capital, human or financial, something of value, in a firm. Involuntary stakeholders are placed at risk as a result of a firm's activities. But without the element of risk there is no stake"
Clarkson (1995, p.106)	"Stakeholders are persons or groups that have, or claim, ownership, rights or interests in a corporation and its activities, past, present or future. Such claimed rights or interests are the result of transactions with, or actions taken by, the corporation, and may be legal or moral, individual or collective."
Donaldson & Preston (1995, p.67)	"Stakeholders are persons or groups with legitimate interests in procedural and/or substantive aspects of corporate activity. Stakeholders are identified by their interests in the corporation, whether the corporation has any corresponding functional interest in them."
Phillips (1999, p.32), citing Clarkson (1994)	Stakeholders are those having something in risk in the firm.
Garriga & Melé (2004, p.59)	"[...] people who affect or are affected by corporate policies and practices."
Garriga & Melé (2004, p.60), citing Freeman (1984)	"[...] those groups who have a stake in or claim on the firm (suppliers, customers, employees, stockholders, and the local community)."
Werther & Chandler (2010, p.4)	"[...] a firm's stakeholders include those individuals and groups that have a stake in the firm's operations."

Source: own elaboration.

well-being of society as a whole and the interests of the organization (Davis & Blomstrom, 1966, p.5). Also, we have to consider that a corporation is defined as an entity created and empowered by a state charter to act as an individual giving the corporation "the right to own, buy, and sell property, to enter into contracts, to sue and be sued, and to have legal accountability for damages and debt only to the limit of the stockholders' investment" (Kilcullen & Kooistra, 1999, p.159). Since it is convenient to review existing definitions in the academic literature of the concept of Corporate Social Responsibility, Table 2 compiles an exhaustive review of them.

An identifiable pattern in the definitions of CSR is the existence of a regulatory framework, different from the legal, imposed or voluntarily self-imposed in companies (Sheehy, 2015). According to S. Rahman (2011), there are dimensions in the CSR definitions that guide a possible generic interpretation of the concept. These dimensions are: improvement of the quality of life, economic development, obligation towards society, involvement of interest groups, business ethics, compliance with the law, volunteering,

Table 2. Definitions of the concept of corporate social responsibility

Author/s	Definitions and Concept of CSR
Bowen (1953:6)	"The term *social responsibilities of businessmen* [...] refers to the obligations of businessmen to pursue those policies, to make those decisions, or to follow those lines of action which are desirable in terms of the objectives and values of our society."
Heald (1957, p.375)	"*Corporate conscience,* [is] a recognition on the part management of an obligation to the society it serves not only for maximum economic performance but for humane and constructive social policies as well."
Davis (1960, p.70)	"Social responsibility [...] within a management context [...] refer[s] to businessmen's decisions and actions taken for reasons at least partially beyond the form's direct economic or technical interest."
Frederick (1960, p.60)	"[...] when we invoke the phrase *the social responsibilities of the businessmen*, we mean that businessmen should oversee the operation of an economic system that fulfils the expectations of the public. And this means in turn that the economy's means of production should be employed in such a way that production and distribution should enhance total socio-economic welfare."
Friedman (1963, p.133)	"[...] there is one and only one social responsibility of business—to use its resources and engage in activities designed to increase its profits so long as it stays within the rules of the game, which is to say, engages in open and free competition without deception or fraud." "Few trends could so thoroughly the very foundations of our free society as the acceptance by corporate officials of a social responsibility other than to make as much money for their shareholders as possible."
McGuire (1963, p.144)	"The idea of *social responsibilities* supposes that the corporation has not only economic and legal obligations, but also certain responsibilities to society which extends beyond these obligations."
Davis & Blomstrom (1966, p.12)	"Social responsibility [...] refers to a person's obligation to consider the effects of his decisions and actions on the whole social system. Businessmen apply social responsibility when they consider the needs and interests of others who may be affected by business actions. In so doing, they look beyond their firm's narrow economic and technical interests."
Walton (1967, p.18)	"[...] the new concept of social responsibility recognizes the intimacy of the relationships between the corporation and society and realizes that such relationships must be kept in mind by top managers as the corporation and the related groups pursue their respective goals."
Johnson (1971)	"A socially responsible firm is one whose managerial staff balances a multiplicity of interests. Instead of striving only for larger profits for its stockholders, a responsible enterprise also takes into account employees, suppliers, dealers, local communities, and the nation" (p.50). "[...] social responsibility states that businesses carry out social programs to add profits to their organization" (p.54). "A socially responsible entrepreneur or manager is one who [...] is interested not only in his own well-being but also in that of the other members of the enterprise and that of his fellow citizens" (p.68).
Davis (1973, pp.312-313)	"The concept of social responsibility [...] refers to the firm's consideration of, and response to, issues beyond the narrow economic, technical, and legal requirements of the firm. It is the firm's obligation to evaluate in its decision-making process the effects of its decisions on the external social system in a manner that will accomplish social benefits along with the traditional economic gains which the firm seeks."
Eilbirt & Parket (1973, p.7)	"Perhaps the best way to understand social responsibility is to think of it as *Good neighborliness*. The concept involves two phases. On one hand, it means not doing things that spoil the neighborhood. On the other, it may be expressed as the voluntary assumption of the obligation to help solve neighborhood problems. Those who find neighborliness an awkward or coy concept may substitute the idea that social responsibility means the commitment of a business or Business, in general, to an active role in the solution of broad social problems, such as racial discrimination, pollution, transportation, or urban decay."
Sethi (1975, p.62)	"[...] social responsibility implies bringing corporate behavior up to a level where it is congruent with the prevailing social norms, values, and expectation of performance."
Fitch (1976, p.38)	"Corporate social responsibility is defined as the serious attempt to solve social problems caused wholly or in part by the corporation."
Carroll (1979, p.500)	"The social responsibility of business encompasses the economic, legal, ethical, and discretionary expectations that society has of organizations at a given point in time."
Jones (1980)	"Corporate social responsibility is the notion that corporations have an obligation to constituent groups in society other than stockholders and beyond that prescribed by law or union contract" (pp. 59-60). "First, the obligation must be voluntary adopted; behavior influenced by coercive forces of law or union contract is not voluntary. Second, the obligation is a broad one, extending beyond the traditional duty to shareholders to other societal groups such as customers, employees, suppliers, and neighboring communities" (p. 60).
Carroll (1983, p.604)	"CSR involves the conduct of a business so that is economically profitable, law abiding, ethical, and socially supportive. To be socially responsible [...] then means that profitability and obedience to the law are foremost conditions to discussing the firm's ethics and the extend to which it supports the society in which it exists with contributions of money, time and talent. Thus, CSR is comprised in four parts: economic, legal, ethical and voluntary or philanthropic."
Drucker (1984, p.62)	"*Social responsibility* is to tame the dragon, that is to turn a social problem into economic opportunity and economic benefit, into productive capacity, into human competence, into well-paid jobs, and into wealth."
Murray & Montanari (1986, p.816)	Since business receives its legitimation from society, the definition [...] is: a socially responsible firm is one that accomplishes - and is perceived to accomplish – the desired ends of society in terms of moral, economic, legal, ethical, and discretionary expectations.
Epstein (1987, p.107)	"Discernment of specific issues. Problems, expectations and claims upon business organizations and their leaders regarding the consequences of organizational policies and behavior on both internal and externa stakeholders. The focus is upon the *products* of corporate action."
Reder (1994, p.5)	"An all-encompassing notion, social responsibility refers to both the way a company conducts its internal operations, including the way it treats its work force, and its impact on the world around it."
Robbins (1994, p.123)	"Social responsibility is an obligation, beyond that required by the law and economics, for a firm to pursue long-term goals that are good for society."
Boone y Kurtz (1994, p.54), in Coldwell, Billsberry, Van Meurs, & Mars (2008, p.612)	"Social responsibility is management's acceptance of the obligation to consider profit, consumer satisfaction and societal wellbeing of equal value in evaluating the firm's performance."
Maclagan (1998, p.147)	"Corporate Social Responsibility may be viewed as a process in which managers take responsibility for identifying and accommodating the interests of those affected by the organization's actions"
Kilcullen & Kooistra (1999, p.158)	"Corporate Social Responsibility is the degree of moral obligation that may be ascribed to corporations beyond simple obedience to the laws of the state."
Watts & Holme (1999, p.3)	"Corporate social responsibility is the continuing commitment by business to behave ethically and contribute to economic development while improving the quality of life of the workforce and their families as well as of the local community and society at large."

continued on following page

Table 1. Continued

Author/s	Definitions and Concept of CSR
Watts & Holme (2000, p.10)	"Corporate social responsibility is the commitment of business to contribute to sustainable economic development, working with employees, their families, the local community and society at large to improve their quality of life."
European Commission (2001, p.6)	"[…] concept whereby companies integrate social and environmental concerns in their business operations and in their interaction with their stakeholders on a voluntary basis."
Foran (2001, p.1)	"CSR can be defined as the set of practices and behaviors that firms adopt towards their labor force, towards the environment in which their operations are embedded, towards authority, and towards civil society. This definition of CSR focuses primarily on what firms actually do in these domains (as opposed to what ought they ought to do). Corporate social responsibility is the product of ongoing interactions between the state, firms, and other civil society actors."
Kok, van der Wiele, McKenna & Alan Brown (2001, p.287)	"Corporate social responsibility is the obligation of the firm to use its resources in ways to benefit society, through committed participation as a member of society, taking into account the society at large, and improving welfare of society at large independently of direct gains of the company."
McWilliams & Siegel (2001, p.117)	"Here we define CRS as actions that appear to further some social good, beyond the interests of the firm and that which is required by law."
Whetten et al. (2002, p.374)	"Societal expectations of corporate behavior, a behavior that is alleged by a stakeholder to be expected by society or morally required and is therefore justifiably demanded of a business."
Hopkins (2003, p.1)	"CSR is concerned with treating the stakeholders of the firm ethically or in a responsible manner." "Ethically or responsible means treating stakeholders in a manner deemed acceptable by society. Social includes economic responsibility. Stakeholders exist both within a firm and outside – the natural environment is an stakeholder. The wider aim of social responsibility is to create higher and higher standards of living, while preserving the profitability of the corporation, for peoples both within and outside the corporation."
Van Marrewijk (2003, p.102)	"In general, corporate sustainability and, [sic] CSR refer to company activities – voluntary by definition – demonstrating the inclusion of social and environmental concerns in business operations and in interactions with stakeholders. This is the broad – some would say *vague* – definition of corporate sustainability and CSR."
Castka, Balzarova, Bamber, & Sharp (2004, p.148)	"CSR is a concept to run organizations profitably yet in a socially and environmentally responsible way in order to achieve business sustainability and stakeholder satisfaction."
Elhauge (2005)	"Sacrificing corporate profits in the public interest" (p.733). "[…] any corporate conduct that goes beyond legal compliance even if it is profit-maximizing" (p.744). "To make the concept meaningful, such a definition must implicitly be limited to conduct that exceeds legal compliance in some socially desirable way. But such a limit just begs the question of what legal conduct is socially desirable and deprives the definition of its supposed advantage in clarity" (p.745).
Kotler y Lee (2005, p.3)	"Corporate social responsibility is a commitment to improve community well-being through discretionary business practices and contributions of corporate resources."
Portney (2005, p.108)	"CSR [is] a consistent pattern, at the very least, of private firms doing more than they are required to do under applicable laws and regulations governing the environment, worker safety and health, and investments in the communities in which they operate."
Barnett (2007, p.801)	"CSR may be more narrowly defined as a discretionary allocation of corporate resources to improving social welfare that serves as means of enhancing relationships with key stakeholders."
Matten y Moon (2008, p.405)	"CSR (and its synonyms) empirically consists of clearly articulated and communicated policies and practices of corporations that reflect business responsibility for some of the wider societal good."
Basu & Palazzo (2008, p.124)	"[…] we can define CSR as the process by which managers within an organization think about and discuss relationships with stakeholders as well as their roles in relation to the common good, along with their behavioral disposition with respect to the fulfillment and achievement of these roles and relationships."
Werther Jr. & Chandler (2010, p.5)	"A view of the corporation and its view in society that assumes a responsibility among firms to pursue goals in addition to profit maximization and a responsibility among firm's stakeholders to hold the firm accountable for its actions."
Aguinis (2011, p.855) in Aguinis & Glavas (2012, p.933)	"Context-specific organizational actions and policies that take into account stakeholders' expectations and the triple bottom line of economic, social, and environmental performance."
Hansen, Dunford, Boss, Boss, & Angermeier (2011, p.30)	"CSR has been defined as the voluntary activities or policies that organizations engage in for the purpose of causing positive social change and environmental sustainability."
Business for Social Responsibility (BSR), quoted in Iqbal. Ahmad, Sheeraz, & Bashir (2012, p.78)	"[…] corporate social responsibility is defined as *accomplishing commercial achievement in ways that credit ethical values and respect people, communities, and the natural environment.*"
Lin, Baruch, & Shih (2012, p.167)	"Corporate social responsibility (CSR)—also known as corporate citizenship, responsible business, corporate responsibility, and social performance—is a form of corporate self-regulation integrated into business and organizational models."
Park y Levy (2014, p.333-334)	"Although there are many definitions of CSR exist, they commonly refer to the relationship between businesses and society, which denotes firms' actions to balance financial performance, impacts on society and the environment."
Sheehy (2015, p.639)	"CSR is a type of international private law and can be defined as a socio-political movement which generates private self-regulatory initiatives, incorporating public and private international law norms seeking to ameliorate and mitigate the social harms of and to promote public good by industrial organisations. A shortened definition would be international private business self-regulation."

Source: own elaboration.

human rights, protection of the environment, as well as practices of transparency and accountability. Analyzing the definitions on a temporary basis, it is observed that in the 1950s the interpretation of "obligation towards society" predominates, in the 1960s the focus on "relationship between corporation and society", and in the 1970s legal and philosophical, as well as the relationship of interest groups.

The Environmental Dimension

Within the different dimensions identified in the definition of the concept of CSR, the environmental dimension, or the protection of the environment, has been consolidated as part of CSR since the work of Carroll (1999) in the first decade of the 21st century (Dahlsrud, 2008). Some authors affirm that the environment is a component within the responsibility of the company towards its social environment (and therefore of its corporate social responsibility), for other authors, the environmental dimension has its own and independent identity, according to which social responsibility affects specifically to people and not to the environment. The first scenario fits the definition of CSR (see Table 2) provided by the European Commission (2001:6). The second scenario allows us to independently identify the so-called Corporate Environmental Responsibility (CER), which is the one that focuses on business activities, both restrictive and preventive, which limit the adverse effect of business activities on the environment (N. Rahman & Post, 2012). These theoretical approaches may consider the natural environment as one more interest group to which the company must be held accountable (Lynes & Andrachuk, 2008). In general, it can be said that currently, when CSR is mentioned, CER is assumed as an integral part of CSR, and that CER is only mentioned when you want to work or research specifically on it.

Problems of Ambiguity in Interpretations

Certain perspectives in various disciplines of business management may fit within the CSR approaches, as is the case with Quality Management, Marketing, Communication, Finance, Engineering or Human Resources Management, and this causes CSR to be interpreted according to interests. and the objectives of each specific discipline (Van Marrewijk, 2003). This diversity allows definitions to be found that very adequately justify certain business actions or research as within the scope of CSR (Dahlsrud, 2008). On the other hand, research oriented to practical aspects of CSR tends to provide definitions that show application guidelines, simplicity and utility (which would be a more instrumental approach), while academic research is characterized by holistic, complex approaches. and ethical or philosophical (Montiel & Delgado-Ceballos, 2014). This ambiguity in the definition of the concept forces researchers to assess different approaches and contexts in their studies (which makes work difficult), and opens the door for companies, possibly interested, to choose the most appropriate approach to their circumstances. or that gives them greater utility according to their objectives (Van Marrewijk, 2003).

In the late 1960s, McGuire (1969) identified four lines of study on the concept of CSR that make it easier to raise questions for their understanding: *traditional* (a neoclassical approach that states that CSR has no place in business), *liberal* (CSR It is a useful tool for the company itself), *responsible* (CSR is morally correct, what a company should do although it may not compensate), and a last approach that he calls *confusing* (according to which ethics justifies CSR, since through this the company obtains compensation in an unclear way). The *traditional* approach coincides with the assertions that defend that the social work of the company should be only the creation of economic wealth that will later be distributed in society. The *liberal* approach defends the use of CSR for strategic purposes, since its presence facilitates the improvement of business results, and opposes the *responsible* approach, which defends the moral obligation of the company to adopt CSR to act correctly and with legitimacy. It is the ethical perspective that generates the greatest confusion even today, since it does not allow to clearly identify the mechanisms that relate competitiveness, business results and ethical issues in decision-making, needing to go to philosophical or social foundations far from the usual approaches of Research in Management.

DRIVERS FOR CHOOSING CSR STRATEGIES

The decision of the companies on the adoption of CSR practices and their mode of implementation finds its origin in several drivers that are analyzed in this section. Among others, these drives are: the existing regulatory frameworks, the voluntary or forced adoption of standards or certificates of responsible operations and the ethics or voluntariness of the company's performance, and the impacts it generates. Finally, the duality in the company's motivations to adopt responsible actions is analyzed, differentiating between a moral approach that seeks to do the right thing (normative approach), from the search for economic benefits as the origin of the company's responsible action (instrumental approach).

Regulatory Frameworks

Regulatory frameworks determine minimum social action levels from which social business initiatives begin to be considered voluntary and, therefore, CSR. When these frameworks are strict, they can limit the potential for companies to act, both in market and non-market environments, which may affect their competitiveness. In this regard, the voluntary nature of CSR makes it possible to add competitiveness to companies without the need for excessively demanding regulatory frameworks and encourages imitation behavior among them (Orlitzky, Schmidt, & Rynes, 2003). However, it happens that in contexts of weak normative or regulatory pressures, companies sometimes opt for a minimum "opportunistic compliance" with the legal requirements (Schwartz & Carroll, 2003:511), so the existence of an adequate balance in the regulatory requirements that ensure a minimum scenario of mandatory compliance is recommended.

Standards and Certifications

Another important driver for the adoption of CSR practices by companies are the standards and certifications in terms of social or environmental responsibility. Obtaining these certificates leads company managers to meet their requirements, albeit sometimes minimally or symbolically (Christmann & Taylor, 2006; Tenbrunsel, Wade-Benzoni, Messick, & Bazerman, 2000). Sometimes certification is an essential requirement to establish business relationships with public or private organizations, these contracting agencies acting as prescribers who force their suppliers to ensure and justify a minimum of social or environmental responsibility in their business operations.

Ethics and Voluntariness

There are classic opinions that defend that companies should be exclusively concerned with generating economic profit, leaving social issues aside as it is not their responsibility (Friedman, 1970; Levitt, 1958). However, an updated and increasingly widespread vision of the role of the company in socio-economic systems defends that companies must compensate and even internalize the possible negative effects that their operations may cause in the environment (Auld, Bernstein, & Cashore, 2008). CSR is a tool that guides companies towards objectives that condition their performance, directing them to generate, in a more or less normative way, beneficial rather than adverse effects on related interest groups (Epstein, 1987:104). This normative CSR perspective is related to the design of high-level business strategies that include ethical approaches to their participation in the economy and society (Knudsen, 2013). This implies considering again its voluntary or commitment nature (related to that kind of self-regulatory framework for companies) that is based on a series of practices that are considered recommended compliance (Sheehy, 2015). The ethics of business action is based on the corporate values that are set out in the design of the business strategy in each case.

Instrumental and Normative Approaches

CSR acts as a set of principles (Wood, 2010) on which, as a basis or model and for each specific case, companies build policies, processes and generate results. A principle is a basic value, a belief considered true, that motivates people to act (Wood, 1991). In general, the reasons that companies have or the objectives that they pursue with the adoption of CSR practices can be grouped (without considering the descriptive approach) into two study perspectives: instrumental or normative, existing between both perspectives a continuous spectrum with different combinations of factors (Garriga & Melé, 2004). The first corresponds to interests of a strategic nature, such as defensive strategies of the company, and the second has an altruistic or philanthropic nature (Vogel, 2006). When talking about CSR, we usually refer to the altruistic approach, which does not pursue economic results as the main objective, while when mentioning *CSR strategy*, we usually refer to initiatives that seek profitability (Baron, 2001).

The instrumental motivation or perspective has a mainly economic focus, and understands CSR as a means or strategy, devoid of moral responsibility, that the company can use to achieve or improve its own results (McWilliams et al., 2006) and the existing relationships between the company and society, improving mainly in reputation and legitimacy (Dhanesh, 2012). Therefore, CSR strategy can be defined as "voluntary CSR actions that improve competitiveness and reputation", generating an improvement in the economic and financial performance of the company (Orlitzky, Siegel, & Waldman, 2011, p. 6). Proponents of this approach argue that the company's social actions should be limited exclusively to maximizing the benefits of its owners and investors, interacting with other stakeholders only to reinforce the above (Friedman, 1970; Goodpaster, 1991). The forced (or reactive) adoption of CSR practices in the company due to pressures from society or regulatory frameworks is usually considered instrumental (Aguinis & Glavas, 2012).

The normative motivation or perspective is opposite to the previous one, and has an important moral and ethical component in its foundations to explain the type of activity of the company (Lindgreen & Swaen, 2010). At its core, it refers to "what companies should or should not do" (Swanson, 1999, p. 506), and how they should be. Taking as a reference the moral evaluation and the habitual judgment on the activity of the human being, it is understood that every company has the moral or ethical obligations attributable to any member of society (Bauman & Skitka, 2012). Thus, companies have an inescapable responsibility to provide economic goods and services while creating social welfare. The Stakeholders Theory (Freeman, 1984) states that the company must attend to the claims and demands of a wide set of stakeholders, beyond those specifically related to economic and financial aspects of the company (Jones, 1995). To achieve the benefit of society and interest groups as a whole, the company must coordinate the interests of the different stakeholders (Donaldson & Preston, 1995). Note that the voluntary nature of companies in adopting CSR initiatives (proactively) does not specifically imply ethical or moral motivations, since they can do so either with instrumental economic objectives or with normative ethical or moral motives (Aguinis & Glavas, 2012). While the instrumental perspective considers priority economic principles, the normative perspective shifts the economic component from its main position to the last one in degree of importance within the principles that motivate CSR in the company (see Kang & Wood, 1995).

FUTURE RESEARCH DIRECTIONS

To consolidate a definitive approach to studying CSR, it would be necessary to consider a definition of CSR as unique and definitive, but it seems difficult. The presence of one and the other dimensions in the various definitions of the concept (S. Rahman, 2011) is puzzling for researchers, while making its use in different settings more flexible. The wide range of definitions reflects the ambiguous nature of the perspectives of CSR studies.

A specific case is the study of the company's environmental responsibility. It can be said that all activities carried out by the company affect the environment in some way and therefore that environmental management, understood as the company's proposal regarding its environmental impact, can always be analyzed, even if it is absent (Waddock, 2004). In general, environmental responsibility is a kind of environmental agenda for the company and its results, the principles of which seek to reduce negative impacts on the environment and increase positive ones (Post, Rahman, & Rubow, 2011). They highlight the problems in deciding on the inclusion of the environmental dimension within CSR, starting with the semantic questions themselves that can lead to confusion. This confusion allows the coexistence in academic literature of scenarios in which social responsibility includes environmental responsibility, and others in which it does not. In any case, the two options are not clearly differentiated, since a dependency or interaction between the social and environmental dimensions is always assumed, whether the latter is independent of CSR or not. Thus, the distinction between the two scenarios is based on the researcher's preferences or the most appropriate perspective for the study in question, but not on a general academic consensus.

It is also interesting that the issues raised by McGuire (1969) are not yet fully resolved. Mainly that related to finding out the mechanisms by which companies should or should not implement CSR strategies and how they obtain benefits in return. This classification derives in the dichotomy of considering CSR from an instrumental or normative perspective (Garriga & Melé, 2004), which is probably one of the greatest challenges for the researcher. The instrumental approach seems the easiest to analyze, since the business benefits are mainly manifested in economic format. But how to analyze the results of the normative approach? Perhaps the fulfillment of the demands of the interest groups could be a frame of reference, but the question remains of seeking balance with the other dimensions of CSR. And even more difficult, how is it possible to assess the ethical or moral aspects of companies' CSR initiatives? In general, it is easy to analyze the existence of certain types of activities carried out by companies, understood as part of the catalog of social responsibility initiatives. However, it is much more difficult to assess, and especially to measure, the intentions of companies when developing them, which leads us to consider the concept of principles and values existing in the company (Carroll, 1979).

In general, it would seem easier and more reasonable to assess the actions and the impacts generated by the companies, regardless of their intentions. For this reason, during the 80s and 90s other concepts were developed, alternative or derived from CSR, such as corporate social responsiveness and corporate social performance. The corporate social responsiveness is defined as "The processes by which these outcomes are produced, monitored, evaluated, compensated and rectified (or not) [in relation to impacts and results in society, stakeholders and the company]" (Wood, 2010, p. 54). It describes how organizations actively interact and manage their environments (Swanson, 1999), encompassing their processes and social issues management, and their capacity (what they can do), actions and response to social demands (Brammer & Pavelin, 2006; Carroll, 1979; Frederick, 1994).

On the other hand, corporate social performance can be defined as "a set of descriptive categorizations of business activity, focusing on the impacts and outcomes for society, stakeholders and the firm" (Wood, 2010, p. 54). It is equivalent to the capture at a specific moment of the aggregate of the social performance of a company (Barnett, 2007), referring to the amount of resources dedicated to it, and especially to the quality of said performance. It allows identifying, promulgating and evaluating company responsibilities, as well as specific duties faced, defined processes, results obtained and impacts generated on stakeholders, society and the company itself (Wood, 2010). In general, corporate social performance makes it easier to resolve the issue of CSR measurement. However, if the focus on impact measurement is sought, it is inevitable to consider the use of the concept of corporate sustainability, defined as "Corporations' taking into consideration their environmental and social impacts in concert with their economic objectives" (Strand, 2014, p.688). It seems that corporate sustainability could be an option to assess, from a practical point of view, the social and environmental impacts of the company, without assessing, as key pieces, the motivations or principles that originated said actions.

In this chapter, the concept of CSR has been developed, as well as several analytical perspectives that can help researchers to conveniently approach their studies on the subject. The text details aspects that may suggest scenarios of suitability of different approaches and perspectives, their degree of practicality, as well as aspects in favor or against their usefulness to demonstrate certain types of hypotheses. Although the ideas remain open, it can be considered that the text raises a possible research agenda on those aspects of CSR that are still far from being understood unambiguously. That is why the reader is encouraged to continue with the work of studying CSR, and thus contribute to social and environmental well-being in general, something of great value in current and future society.

REFERENCES

Aguilera, R. V., Rupp, D. E., Williams, C. A., & Ganapathi, J. (2007). Putting the S back in corporate social responsibility: A multilevel theory of social change in organizations. *Academy of Management. Academy of Management Review*, *32*(3), 836–863. doi:10.5465/amr.2007.25275678

Aguinis, H. (2011). Organizational responsibility: Doing good and doing well. In S. Zedeck (Ed.), *APA handbook of industrial and organizational psychology* (pp. 855–879). American Psychological Association. doi:10.1037/12171-024

Aguinis, H., & Glavas, A. (2012). What we know and don't know about corporate social responsibility: A review and research agenda. *Journal of Management*, *38*(4), 932–968. doi:10.1177/0149206311436079

Auld, G., Bernstein, S., & Cashore, B. (2008). The new corporate social responsibility. *Annual Review of Environment and Resources*, *33*(1), 413–435. doi:10.1146/annurev.environ.32.053006.141106

Barnett, M. L. (2007). Stakeholder influence capacity and the variability of financial returns to corporate social responsibility. *Academy of Management Review*, *32*(3), 794–816. doi:10.5465/amr.2007.25275520

Baron, D. P. (2001). Private politics, corporate social responsibility, and integrated strategy. *Journal of Economics & Management Strategy*, *10*(1), 7–45. doi:10.1162/105864001300122548

Basu, K., & Palazzo, G. (2008). Corporate social responsibility: A process model of sensemaking. *Academy of Management Review*, *33*(1), 122–136. doi:10.5465/amr.2008.27745504

Bauman, C. W., & Skitka, L. J. (2012). Corporate social responsibility as a source of employee satisfaction. *Research in Organizational Behavior, 32*, 63–86. doi:10.1016/j.riob.2012.11.002

Boone, L. E., & Kurtz, D. L. (1994). *Business and society*. Harper Collins.

Boulding, K. E. (1956). General systems theory—The skeleton of science. *Management Science, 2*(3), 197–208. doi:10.1287/mnsc.2.3.197

Bowen, H. R. (1953). *Social responsibilities of the businessman*. Harper.

Brammer, S. J., & Pavelin, S. (2006). Corporate reputation and social performance: The importance of fit. *Journal of Management Studies, 43*(3), 435–455. doi:10.1111/j.1467-6486.2006.00597.x

Carroll, A. B. (1979). A three-dimensional conceptual model of corporate performance. *Academy of Management. Academy of Management Review, 4*(4), 497–505. doi:10.5465/amr.1979.4498296

Carroll, A. B. (1983). Corporate social responsibility. *Vital Speeches of the Day, 49*(19), 604.

Carroll, A. B. (1999). Corporate social responsibility. *Business & Society, 38*(3), 268–295. doi:10.1177/000765039903800303

Castka, P., Balzarova, M. A., Bamber, C. J., & Sharp, J. M. (2004). How can SMEs effectively implement the CSR agenda? A UK case study perspective. *Corporate Social Responsibility and Environmental Management, 11*(3), 140–149. doi:10.1002/csr.62

Christmann, P., & Taylor, G. (2006). Firm self-regulation through international certifiable standards: Determinants of symbolic versus substantive implementation. *Journal of International Business Studies, 37*(6), 863–878. doi:10.1057/palgrave.jibs.8400231

Clarkson, M. (1994). A risk based model of stakeholder theory. *Proceedings of the Second Toronto Conference on Stakeholder Theory*, 18-19.

Clarkson, M. B. E. (1995). A stakeholder framework for analyzing and evaluating corporate social performance. *Academy of Management Review, 20*(1), 92–117. doi:10.5465/amr.1995.9503271994

Cochran, P. L. (2007). The evolution of corporate social responsibility. *Business Horizons, 50*(6), 449–454. doi:10.1016/j.bushor.2007.06.004

Coldwell, D. A., Billsberry, J., Van Meurs, N., & Marsh, P. J. G. (2008). The effects of person-organization ethical fit on employee attraction and retention: Towards a testable explanatory model. *Journal of Business Ethics, 78*(4), 611–622. doi:10.100710551-007-9371-y

Dahlsrud, A. (2008). How corporate social responsibility is defined: An analysis of 37 definitions. *Corporate Social Responsibility and Environmental Management, 15*(1), 1–13. doi:10.1002/csr.132

Davis, K. (1960). Can business afford to ignore social responsibilities? *California Management Review, 2*(3), 70.

Davis, K. (1973). The case for and against business assumption of social responsibilities. *Academy of Management Journal, 16*(2), 312.

Davis, K., & Blomstrom, R. L. (1966). *Business and society: Environment and responsibility*. McGraw-Hill.

Dhanesh, G. S. (2012). The view from within: Internal publics and CSR. *Journal of Communication Management (London), 16*(1), 39–58. doi:10.1108/13632541211197987

Dodd, E. M. (1932). For whom are corporate managers trustees? *Harvard Law Review, 45*(7), 1145–1163. doi:10.2307/1331697

Donaldson, T., & Preston, L. E. (1995). The stakeholder theory of the corporation: Concepts, evidence, and implications. *Academy of Management. Academy of Management Review, 20*(1), 65 91. doi:10.5465/amr.1995.9503271992

Drucker, P. F. (1984). Converting social problems into business opportunities: The new meaning of corporate social responsibility. *California Management Review, 26*(2), 53.

Eilbirt, H., & Parket, I. R. (1973). The practice of business: The current status of corporate social responsibility. *Business Horizons, 16*(4), 5–14. doi:10.1016/0007-6813(73)90043-8

Elhauge, E. (2005). Sacrificing corporate profits in the public interest. *New York University Law Review, 80*(3), 733; 733.

Epstein, E. M. (1987). The corporate social policy process: Beyond business ethics, corporate social responsibility, and corporate social responsiveness. *California Management Review, 29*(3), 99–114. doi:10.2307/41165254

European Commission. (2001). *Green paper. Promoting a European framework for corporate social responsibility*. European Commission.

Fitch, H. G. (1976). Achieving corporate social responsibility. *Academy of Management Review, 1*(1), 38–46. doi:10.5465/amr.1976.4408754

Foran, T. (2001). *Corporate social responsibility at nine multinational electronics firms in Thailand: A preliminary analysis, report to the California global corporate accountability project*. Nautilus Institute for Security and Sustainable Development.

Frederick, W. C. (1960). The growing concern over business responsibility. *California Management Review, 2*(4), 54.

Frederick, W. C. (1994). From CSR1 to CSR2 the maturing of business-and-society thought. *Business & Society, 33*(2), 150–164. doi:10.1177/000765039403300202

Freeman, R. E. (1984). *Strategic management: A stakeholder approach*. Pittman.

Freeman, R. E., & Reed, D. L. (1983). Stockholders and stakeholders: A new perspective on corporate governance. *California Management Review, 25*(3), 88–106. doi:10.2307/41165018

Friedman, M. (1963). *Capitalism and freedom*. University of Chicago Press.

Friedman, M. (1970). The social responsibility of business is to increase its profits. *The New York Times Magazine*.

Garriga, E., & Melé, D. (2004). Corporate social responsibility theories: Mapping the territory. *Journal of Business Ethics, 53*(1-2), 51–71.

Goodpaster, K. E. (1991). Business ethics and stakeholder analysis. *Business Ethics Quarterly*, *1*(01), 53–73. doi:10.2307/3857592

Hansen, S. D., Dunford, B. B., Boss, A. D., Boss, R. W., & Angermeier, I. (2011). Corporate social responsibility and the benefits of employee trust: A cross-disciplinary perspective. *Journal of Business Ethics*, *102*(1), 29–45. doi:10.100710551-011-0903-0

Heald, M. (1957). Management's responsibility to society: The growth of an idea. *Business History Review*, *31*(4), 375–384. doi:10.2307/3111413

Hopkins, M. (2003). *The planetary bargain: CSR matters*. Earthscan.

Hussain, S. S. (1999). The ethics of 'going green': The corporate social responsibility debate. *Business Strategy and the Environment*, *8*(4), 203–210. doi:10.1002/(SICI)1099-0836(199907/08)8:4<203::AID-BSE204>3.0.CO;2-I

Iqbal, N., Ahmad, N., Sheeraz, M., & Bashir, N. A. (2012). The impact of perceived corporate social responsibility (CSR) on job attitude and performance of internal stakeholders. *International Journal of Human Resource Studies*, *2*(4), 77. Doi:10.5296/ijhrs.v2i4.2272

Johnson, H. L. (1971). *Business in contemporary society: Framework and issues*. Wadsworth Pub. Co.

Jones, T. M. (1980). Corporate social responsibility revisited, redefined. *California Management Review*, *22*(3), 59.

Jones, T. M. (1995). Instrumental stakeholder theory: A synthesis of ethics and economics. *Academy of Management. Academy of Management Review*, *20*(2), 404–437. doi:10.5465/amr.1995.9507312924

Kang, Y., & Wood, D. J. (1995). Before-profit social responsibility: Turning the economic paradigm upside down. *Proceedings of the International Association for Business and Society*, *6*, 809-829. 10.5840/iabsproc1995672

Kilcullen, M., & Kooistra, J. O. (1999). At least do no harm: Sources on the changing role of business ethics and corporate social responsibility. *RSR. Reference Services Review*, *27*(2), 158–178. doi:10.1108/00907329910275150

Knudsen, J. S. (2013). The integration of corporate social responsibility (CSR) initiatives into business activities: Can lessons be learnt from gender diversity programmes? *International Journal of Business Governance and Ethics*, *8*(3), 210. doi:10.1504/IJBGE.2013.057376

Kok, P., van der Wiele, T., McKenna, R., & Brown, A. (2001). A corporate social responsibility audit within a quality management framework. *Journal of Business Ethics*, *31*(4), 285–297. doi:10.1023/A:1010767001610

Kotler, P., & Lee, N. (2005). *Corporate social responsibility: Doing the most good for your company and your cause*. Wiley.

Levitt, T. (1958). The dangers of social-responsibility. *Harvard Business Review*, *36*(5), 41–50.

Lin, C., Baruch, Y., & Shih, W. (2012). Corporate social responsibility and team performance: The mediating role of team efficacy and team self-esteem. *Journal of Business Ethics*, *108*(2), 167–180. doi:10.100710551-011-1068-6

Lindgreen, A., & Swaen, V. (2010). Corporate social responsibility. *International Journal of Management Reviews*, *12*(1), 1–7. doi:10.1111/j.1468-2370.2009.00277.x

Lynes, J. K., & Andrachuk, M. (2008). Motivations for corporate social and environmental responsibility: A case study of Scandinavian airlines. *Journal of International Management*, *14*(4), 377–390. doi:10.1016/j.intman.2007.09.004

Lyon, T. P., & Maxwell, J. W. (2008). Corporate social responsibility and the environment: A theoretical perspective. *Review of Environmental Economics and Policy*, *2*(2), 240–260. doi:10.1093/reep/ren004

Maclagan, P. (1998). *Management and morality*. Sage.

Matten, D., & Moon, J. (2008). Implicit' and 'explicit' CSR: A conceptual framework for a comparative understanding of corporate social responsibility. *Academy of Management Review*, *33*(2), 404–424. doi:10.5465/amr.2008.31193458

McGuire, J. W. (1963). *Business and society*. McGraw-Hill.

McGuire, J. W. (1969). The changing nature of business responsibilities. *Journal of Risk and Insurance*, *36*(1), 55.

McWilliams, A., & Siegel, D. (2001). Corporate social responsibility: A theory of the firm perspective. *Academy of Management. Academy of Management Review*, *26*(1), 117–127. doi:10.5465/amr.2001.4011987

McWilliams, A., Siegel, D. S., & Wright, P. M. (2006). Corporate social responsibility: Strategic implications. *Journal of Management Studies*, *43*(1), 1–18. doi:10.1111/j.1467-6486.2006.00580.x

Mitchell, R. K., Agle, B. R., & Wood, D. J. (1997). Toward a theory of stakeholder identification and salience: Defining the principle of who and what really counts. *Academy of Management.the Academy of Management Review*, *22*(4), 853–886. doi:10.5465/amr.1997.9711022105

Montiel, I., & Delgado-Ceballos, J. (2014). Defining and measuring corporate sustainability: Are we there yet? *Organization & Environment*, *27*(2), 113–139. doi:10.1177/1086026614526413

Murray, K. B., & Montanari, J. B. (1986). Strategic management of the socially responsible firm: Integrating management and marketing theory. *Academy of Management Review*, *11*(4), 815–827. doi:10.5465/amr.1986.4284013

Orlitzky, M., Schmidt, F. L., & Rynes, S. L. (2003). Corporate social and financial performance: A meta-analysis. *Organization Studies*, *24*(3), 403–441. doi:10.1177/0170840603024003910

Orlitzky, M., Siegel, D. S., & Waldman, D. A. (2011). Strategic corporate social responsibility and environmental sustainability. *Business & Society*, *50*(1), 6–27. doi:10.1177/0007650310394323

Park, S., & Levy, S. E. (2014). Corporate social responsibility: Perspectives of hotel frontline employees. *International Journal of Contemporary Hospitality Management*, *26*(3), 332–348. doi:10.1108/IJCHM-01-2013-0034

Phillips, R. (1999). On stakeholder delimitation. *Business & Society, 38*(1), 32–34.

Portney, P. R. (2005). Corporate social responsibility: An economic and policy perspective. In B. L. Hay, R. N. Stavins, & R. K. Vietor (Eds.), *Environmental protection and the social responsibility of firms* (pp. 107–131). Resources for the Future.

Post, C., Rahman, N., & Rubow, E. (2011). Green governance: Boards of directors' composition and environmental corporate social responsibility. *Business & Society, 50*(1), 189–223. doi:10.1177/0007650310394642

Rahman, N., & Post, C. (2012). Measurement issues in environmental corporate social responsibility (ECSR): Toward a transparent, reliable, and construct valid instrument. *Journal of Business Ethics, 105*(3), 307–319. doi:10.100710551-011-0967-x

Rahman, S. (2011). Evaluation of definitions: Ten dimensions of corporate social responsibility. *World Review of Business Research, 1*(1), 166–176.

Reder, A. (1994). *In pursuit of profit and principle: Business success through social responsibility*. GP Putnam's Sons.

Rhenman, E. (1968). *Industrial democracy and industrial management*. Tavistock Publications.

Robbins, S. P. (1994). *Management*. Prentice-Hall.

Schwartz, M. S., & Carroll, A. B. (2003). Corporate social responsibility: A three-domain approach. *Business Ethics Quarterly, 13*(4), 503–530. doi:10.5840/beq200313435

Sethi, S. P. (1975). Dimensions of corporate social performance: An analytical framework. *California Management Review, 17*(3), 58.

Sheehy, B. (2015). Defining CSR: Problems and solutions. *Journal of Business Ethics, 131*(3), 625–648. doi:10.100710551-014-2281-x

Strand, R. (2014). Strategic leadership of corporate sustainability. *Journal of Business Ethics, 123*(4), 687–706. doi:10.100710551-013-2017-3

Swanson, D. L. (1999). Toward an integrative theory of business and society: A research strategy for corporate social performance. *Academy of Management Review, 24*(3), 506–521. doi:10.5465/amr.1999.2202134

Tenbrunsel, A. E., Wade-Benzoni, K. A., Messick, D. M., & Bazerman, M. H. (2000). Understanding the influence of environmental standards on judgments and choices. *Academy of Management Journal, 43*(5), 854–866.

Van Marrewijk, M. (2003). Concepts and definitions of CSR and corporate sustainability: Between agency and communion. *Journal of Business Ethics, 44*(2/3), 95–105. doi:10.1023/A:1023331212247

Vogel, D. (2006). *The market for virtue: The potential and limits of corporate social responsibility* (2nd ed.). Brookings Institution Press. Retrieved from http://www.jstor.org/stable/10.7864/j.ctt6wpg2c

Waddock, S. (2004). Parallel universes: Companies, academics, and the progress of corporate citizenship. *Business and Society Review: Journal of the Center for Business Ethics at Bentley College, 109*(1), 5–42. doi:10.1111/j.0045-3609.2004.00002.x

Walton, C. C. (1967). *Corporate social responsibilities*. Wadsworth Publishing Company.

Wang, H., Tong, L., Takeuchi, R., & George, G. (2016). Corporate social responsibility: An overview and new research directions. *Academy of Management Journal, 59*(2), 534–544. doi:10.5465/amj.2016.5001

Watts, P., & Holme, L. (1999). *Corporate social responsibility. Meeting changing expectations*. World Business Council for Sustainable Development.

Watts, P., & Holme, L. (2000). *Corporate social responsibility: Making good business sense*. World Business Council for Sustainable Development.

Werther, W. B. Jr, & Chandler, D. (2010). Strategic corporate social responsibility: Stakeholders in a global environment. *Sage (Atlanta, Ga.)*.

Whetten, D. A., Rands, G., & Godfrey, P. (2002). What are the responsibilities of business to society? In A. Pettigrew, H. Thomas, & R. Whittington (Eds.), *Handbook of strategy and management* (pp. 373–408). Sage.

Wood, D. J. (1991). Corporate social performance revisited. *Academy of Management. Academy of Management Review, 16*(4), 691–718. doi:10.5465/amr.1991.4279616

Wood, D. J. (2010). Measuring corporate social performance: A review. *International Journal of Management Reviews, 12*(1), 50–84. doi:10.1111/j.1468-2370.2009.00274.x

ENDNOTE

1 The authors cite the source as "an international memorandum at the Stanford Research Institute in 1963". However, they do not indicate a reference that would facilitate locating said document for consultation. For these reasons, it is not possible to include in the references section of this chapter the detail of the original document. However, many authors consider this reference with the original seed of the concept of stakeholders and that is why it is mentioned in Table 1. Freeman (1984, p.34) later explains that "The term was meant to generalize the notion of stockholder as the only group to whom management need be responsive".

Chapter 2
Corporate Social Responsibility in Organizations:
A Global Perspective – Types, Advantages, and Disadvantages

María de la Soledad Zapata Agüera
https://orcid.org/0000-0001-6153-969X
Universidad Politécnica de Cartagena, Spain

ABSTRACT

The European Commission 2011 defines social responsibility as the responsibility of companies for their impacts on society, so it is a complex concept that the authors will define, not only theoretically to give content to this activity but also practical to get to understand the advantages that can be used to use corporate social responsibility, not only at the image level but also at the economic level. Organizations can carry out different types of actions with social responsibility; stations with some advantages can even become a competitive advantage. But not all are advantages for companies when CRS policies are made; there are also disadvantages that must be known by marketing managers. In this chapter they will be developed. Finally, the conclusions of all the above will be presented.

INTRODUCTION

Companies have begun to introduce into their vocabulary the concepts of transparency, ethics, training, protection of human rights, financial and social inclusion or sustainability, even priorities within their corporate culture.

Also, having a positive impact on society, companies want to generate trust among both their employees and their clients, thus fostering a sense of belonging. It is demonstrated by the figures, according to Nielsen (2015), four out of ten consumers would be willing to pay more for products manufactured by companies with corporate social responsibility. The international report called: "Consumer versus Corporate Social Responsibility of Brands," was carried out 2015, with the participation of more than

DOI: 10.4018/978-1-7998-4833-2.ch002

30,000 consumers from 60 Asian countries Pacific, Europe, Latin America, Middle East, Africa, and North America, which have had a child in the last five years. It is Figure 1.

However, in addition to price and quality, for about one in three, it is also decisive when buying the brands' social commitments.

In particular, it takes into account aspects such as the company known for its social values (36%) and its commitment to its community (36%). The environmental factor is decisive for 35% of consumers because the brand is known for its commitment to the environment or its environmentally friendly packaging. (Nielsen, 2015). This practice is why organizations need to use socially responsible causes, as a profound change is taking place in society.

This chapter tries to define which is a CRS, types, factors to consider, developing the objectives to be achieved by the organizations, as well as the models used by them. Also, the use of corporate social responsibility has advantages and disadvantages for those who use them, and in the end, conclusions will drawed from the above.

CORPORATE SOCIAL RESPONSIBILITY

This section will develop the evolution and the corporate social responsibility concept, as well as the impact that this tool has had in the marketing world.

Evolution and Concept of CRS

Evolution

For Chaffee (2017), the origins of the social part in company behavior will be derived back to the traditional Roman Laws. It might saw in entities like asylums, homes for the poor and previous, hospitals, and orphanages. "Modern corporate law largely grew out of English law governing universities, municipalities, and religious institutions during the Middle Ages" (Chaffee, 2017, p. 352). Later, it distended into the sixteenth and seventeenth centuries with the influence of the English Crown, which saw companies as Associate in Nursing instrument for social development (Chaffee 2017).

During the late 1800's and early 1900s, the creation of welfare schemes took a paternal approach geared toward protective and retentive workers, and a few corporations even looked into up their quality of life (Carroll, 2008; Heald, 1970).

In the years 1920's and early 1930's, business managers began with the social seeking a balance between their benefits and service to the community, maintaining equilibrium with the strain of their purchasers, their labor, and the community (Carroll, 2008). This semiconductor diode to managers viewed as trustees for the various sets of external relations with the corporation, that successively translated into social and economic responsibilities adopted by companies (Carroll, 2008; Heald, 1970).

According to the organization Joined Hands (2016)[1], CSR emerged in the United States in the late 1950s and early 1960s, following the Vietnam War and other world conflicts, such as apartheid. It is of interest to citizens who are beginning to believe that, through their work, companies by purchasing certain products, are collaborating with the maintenance of specific political regimes or with politically or economically questionable practices.

In 1953, Howard R. Bowen first coined the concept of Corporate Social Responsibility (CSR) in his work "Social Responsibilities of Entrepreneurs," in which the author requested that corporate social responsibility used to produce not only goods and services., to somehow return to society something of what it had provided. It is precisely from this moment, in the sixties and seventies, that the debate on business objectives reaches the academic world. (García, 2016).

Already in the '80s, have begun to use the corporate social responsibility in the strategic direction, and it is Freeman (1984) that through the Theory of the Stakeholders, who proposes that the organization should take into account the groups that can contribute to the company's achievements and identifies them as clients, society or employees.

In the 1990s, corporate social responsibility was no longer seen as an isolated phenomenon within the company but was used transversely by the different areas that make up the organization. In this vein, Peter Drucker in 1996 stated that: "each organization must assume full responsibility for the effect it has on its employees, on the environment, on customers and on anyone or anything it touches. That is social responsibility". The dates more important are in Figure 2.

Concept of CSR

The term "corporation" derives from the Latin term "corpus," which means "body of the people," although these organizations under Roman law known by other names, including "collegium" and "Universitas" (Chaffee, 2017).

Corporate social responsibility (CSR) outlined in many alternative ways in which. Corporate social liability is defined by Kotler and Lee (2005) as a commitment to improving the well-being of the community through business practices and contributions from resources corporate.

Corporate social responsibility is the set of business practices open and transparent, based on ethical values and respect for employees, communities, and the environment.

According to Cowan et al. (2011) may be a basic that means of the term because the selections created and activities performed by companies in areas of worker safety, product position, and natural environmental protection that exceed the necessities of the laws applicable to businesses and organizations. For other authors, the CSR as a compassionate act performed by a corporation (Sarkis, 2012).

In all the concepts presented here is the ethical component that has allowed the established company to evolve from an entity that generates economic benefits to a much more complex structure that also seeks the creation of value for all groups affected by the activity carried out by the organization.

The term responsibility is broad since it encompasses both responsibilities in itself with society and, on the other hand, economic benefits about shareholders. In 1971, Harold Johnson established four visions of the concept it can be complementary in practice and that focus equitably on the realization of economic benefits through the implementation of socially responsible actions:

- **Vision 1:** Knowledge of the environment in which the company operates.
- **Vision 2:** Implementation of social programs to obtain higher profits
- **Vision 3:** The main interest of the company is to obtain benefits, both economic and social.
- **Vision 4:** Knowledge of and relationships with interest groups to gain wealth.
- Chaffee (2017) suggests that there are different currents or theories which propose the purpose of organizations in society:

- *The artificial entity theory,* or concession theory because it is usually better-known, suggests that firms are artificial entities that owe their existence entirely to the government.
- *Real entity theory,* sometimes reference is made to the theory of natural entity, it is another of the theories proposed in this field that are important. Every corporation has an associate identity and existence from its owners and managers.
- *The aggregate theory,* also known as the theory of the nexus of contracts, which proposes that the organization is the sum of the people who compose it, they organize, operate and have obligations between them. Some authors go further, arguing that the corporation also includes creditors, clients, and the public as well as managers, employees, and shareholders. But in this case, the identity of the organization is not different from those who organize, operate, and own it. (King, 1996).

Two key concepts to consider are the distinction made by Porter and Kramer in 2006, differentiating between CSR (corporate social responsibility) and CSV (creating shared value).

CRS is only within the interests of rising name through such actions as being a decent company national, attuning to the evolving social considerations of stakeholders, and mitigating existing or anticipated adverse effects from business activities. From a company perspective, responsive CSR may be a price, a constraint, or a charitable deed. Therefore, its impact is kind of restricted and offers a minimal basis for achieving semi-permanent objectives. For this reason, corporations read CSR as providing minimal strategic benefit for his or her business, focuses on both social and business interests. Therefore it moves beyond good corporate citizenship. It involves both firm and society working in tandem.

CSV: Porter and Kramer (2011) additional explored strategic CSR and developed the conception of CSV by characteristic the following 3 points:

1. CSV is to reinforce the core competitiveness of a corporation, whereas at the same time advancing the economic and social conditions.
2. CSR activities tend to be more disconnected from the business objective, whereas CSV activities are additionally connected by reconceiving the intersection between society and company performance.
3. CSR activities don't seem to be about sharing; however, a lot of centered on redistributing profits that were already generated by corporations. In contrast, CSV activities create communities healthily and prosperous, and also the groups with offer firms. (See the differences in Table 1).

On the other hand, it is necessary to distinguish between 3 concepts that are related but that are not equal between social marketing, cause-related marketing, and CSR. In this regard, it can conclude that "social marketing, Philanthropy or patronage, are the company's understandings of the problems that affect the society from a specific perspective. In contrast, the CSR is a long-term commitment undertaken by the company, and it has growing implications on the design of the corporate strategy" (Marín 2004, p. 49)

In this sense, Kotler and Lee (2005, p. 23), differentiate between "social initiatives" devised in referring to:

1. **Cause Promotion:** A corporation provides funds, in-kind contributions, or other corporate resources to increase awareness or concern on a social issue,
2. **Cause-Related Marketing:** A corporation commits to donating a percentage of revenues to a specific cause based on product sales,

3. **Corporate Social Marketing:** A corporation supports the development and implementation of a behavior change campaign intended to improve public health, safety, environmental, or community well-being.
4. **Corporate Philanthropy:** A corporation makes a direct contribution to a charity or cause, and most often in the form of cash grants, donations, or in-kind services.
5. **Community Volunteering**: A corporation encourages employees, retail partners, or franchise members to volunteer their time in support of local community organizations and causes.
6. **Socially Responsible Business Practices:** A corporation adopts and conducts discretionary business practices and investments that support social causes to improve community well-being and protect the environment.

As a result, CSR has evolved over the years as explained by Marrewijk (2002), who maintains that there are three fundamental elements for the development of corporate social responsibility: corporate, State, and social and civil; and that the relationship between them has changed as can be seen in Figure 3. Businesses have a crucial link with the State and civil society. Usually, the State is responsible for creating and preserving legislation (control). On the other hand, companies produce the wealth necessary for collaboration and cooperation in the market. Finally, civil society, through collective action and the structure of participation, shapes culture. According to Swart (2002), civil society has gained importance since the government and companies must answer to social groups, religion, and, in particular, to NGOs. All this makes organizations take special care in applying sustainability in their business.

The Impact of CSR in Marketing

The idea of social responsibility holds that companies must be sensitive citizens, leveling their operations to obtain economic benefits with activities that benefit society, be it on a local, national, or global scale. The promotion of social responsibility has involved focusing efforts on attracting buyers. The U.N. agency, for example, needs to create a definite distinction by making its purchases. Several corporations have adopted socially responsible components in their forms of promotion as a way to help a community through useful services and products.

In fact, in the study carried out by Forrester in 2017, entitled "The power of a strategy based on values," it is highlighted that 52% of consumers in the USA. In the U.S., the value when making buying certain brands moves their beliefs and values actively. "Corporate responsibility must base on the commercial strategy by conviction, we should not make the programs look good, but because it is part of the base of the company," Callol (2018)[2]. This author concluded, reminding the attendees that, in the end, sustainability is everyone's responsibility, and that we must work in our day to day to improve the environment and the society.

All this implies the development of business management practices, strategies, and systems, which is why it can say that a company is socially responsible. When in its decision-making process, it evaluates the impact of its actions on society, workers, and the environment in a real and practical way (Torreblanca, 2017). The organizations' increases, another concept called Organizational Social Responsibility, can reach in acronym RSO, which comprehensively covers different interest groups such as companies, unions, universities, NGOs, political parties, public administrations, employers, media, etc.

At figure 3, the elements that come into play in the marketing strategy to carry out CSR find.

TYPES OF CORPORATE SOCIAL RESPONSIBILITY. DEFINITIONS AND EXAMPLES

In this section, the types of CSR will develop through their definitions and illustrative examples.

Individual Social Responsibility

It achieves from learned in the environment family, the value of things, and the repercussions that the actions of everyone have on society. The first step for CSR to be successful, as individually, the community must be aware of its responsibility and, therefore, of the burden of others.

For example, this is the case of many celebrities who ally with social causes, either through their image, giving visibility to some common issues in the world, or through donations of money such as the case of Madonna, who contributes 910 million dollars for the set "Raising Malawi Foundation." In collaboration with Michael Berg in 2006, the Queen of Pop is working to help the thousands of children in Malawi who have been orphaned by the AIDS epidemic, through medical and educational programs (Acosta, 2016).

Corporate Social Responsibility

It refers to the actions carried out by companies or corporations, and that has repercussions in society; it is also known as CSR. This type of liability is directly related to productivity, cost reduction, and profit-making without exploiting or negatively affecting the environment.

According to Deloitee (2018), there are critical commitments of socially responsible companies, which are:

- Provide legitimate goods and services to society.
- Carry out a responsible tax system.
- Promote actions aimed at fighting fraud and the shadow economy.
- Develop transparency, integrity, and anti-corruption programs.
- Establish more transparent payment systems.
- Promote diversity within the workforce and the presence of women on the board of directors.
- Create and maintain quality employment.
- Facilitate the reconciliation of personal, family, and work life.
- Take care and respect the environment and the human capital of their environment.

The Reputation Institute conducted a study; this organization was founded in 1997 and had been measuring reputation for over 20 years. The study included more than 7,000 companies per year in 40 countries, 25 different industries, and more than 1,000,000 annual ratings. Figure 4are the top ten companies with the best reputation in CRS.

There are five new companies in the top 10: Natura, Novo Nordisk, Canon, Michelin, and IKEA. Google returns to number 1 after ranking third in 2017, exchanging its position with The LEGO Group. Only two companies manage to maintain a strong CRS position. BMW, Intel, Cisco, Rolls-Royce Aerospace, and Colgate-Palmolive fell out of the Top 10 (Global CR RepTrak® 100, 2018). Figure 4 shows the positions of the Top Ten organizations in 2018 in C.R.

The company Google is the first in the ranking, there are many reasons, such as:

- The score obtained in Google's C.R. is mainly due to its performance in the workplace: It is the only company that has a solid rating in the place and a leader in equal opportunity, wellness, and employee rewards.
- Google's CEO, Sundar Pichai, lives our corporate values and speaks out regarding DACA lobby and employee memo actions.
- Google is also #1 in citizenship: 72.3

Public or Government Social Responsibility

Social responsibility is something all share. However, public or governmental social responsibility is that of the institutions and administrations responsible for designing and implementing public policies. The actions of these organizations, which concretized in laws, decrees, regulations, etc., have a significant impact, and very direct, on the natural and social environment of their jurisdiction (Oxfam Intermon, 2017).

The social responsibility of public bodies is twofold:

1. First, by regulating the activities of individuals, organizations, companies, etc., which are under its administrative umbrella.
2. Second, its responsibility must be carried out internally in the management of its activity (Oxfam Intermon, 2017).

In this sense, to understand the dimensions of social responsibility in the administration has been based on Puig et al. (2008), and it's observing Figure 6. On the left can follows by all the necessary policies, both promotion and of control in the State, to foster social responsibility. On the right side, strategies to be implemented by the public administration, both general and specific strategies

FACTORS TO CONSIDER IN CORPORATE SOCIAL RESPONSIBILITY

This section will develop the most important theories that include the determining factors in CSR. Still, first, it's essential to must distinguish from corporate social responsibility from Philanthropy and com munity investment because sometimes it can confuse each other. According to Kiran and Sharma (2011), the differences between the two elements are:

Pyramid of CRA by Carroll (1991)

Carroll in 1991 created the "Pyramid of Responsibilities" was included four classes that correspond to the four responsibilities: economic, legal, ethical, and philanthropic, which enabled managers to understand the varying sorts of obligation and, therefore, the continual tensions between them. Carroll (1991, p.40) "acknowledged that none of the four responsibilities were new to the CSR concept, but argued that it was only recently that the significance of the ethical and philanthropical functions had assumed prominence." It observes in Figure 7.

- **Economic Responsibilities:** It forms the basis of the pyramid and understands as the production of goods and services that consumers need and want. As compensation for the delivery of these goods and services, the company must make an acceptable profit in the process.
- **Legal Responsibilities:** They have to do with compliance with the law and state regulations, as well as with the basic rules according to which businesses must operate.
- **Ethical Responsibilities:** They refer to the obligation to do what is right, fair, and reasonable, as well as to avoid or minimize harm to the groups with which the enterprise relates. This type of responsibility involves activities and practices that society expects, as well as avoiding those that its members reject, even if they not prohibited by law.
- **Philanthropic Responsibilities:** They include those corporate actions that respond to social expectations about good corporate citizenship. These behaviors include the active involvement of companies in activities or programs that promote social welfare and improve the quality of life of the population. The difference between ethical and philanthropic responsibilities arises because the company wants to comply with the ethical standards of society; These expected standards are not in an ethical or moral sense, since it is a voluntary activity by companies, taking into account that there is always a social expectation. In short, according to the pyramid theory, CSR implies the simultaneous fulfillment of economic, legal, ethical, and philanthropic responsibilities. In other words, CSR must lead the company to profit, obey the law, be moral, and behaves like a good corporate citizen.

Two Dimensional Model of Corporate Social Responsibility by Quazi and O'Brien (2000)

The vertical axis represents two extremes in terms of the consequences of social perception. The action on the part of companies, namely the costs of social involvement and the benefits of social commitment; that is, the primary consideration take into account, in this case, is the short-term expenses arising from the exercise of social responsibility. The positive side of the vertical axis represents those companies evaluate the long-term benefits resulting from the social action and perceives that the potential gains derived from such work in the long term exceed the costs that can obtain from it.

Thus the model proposed by Quazi and O'Brien (2000) defines four quadrants, each of which can be called as follows and defined by Balaguer, Fernández, and Muñoz (2007):

- **The Classic View:** Corresponds to the CSR's initial vision. Companies do not aim for anything other than maximizing profit and consider that social involvement generates a net cost and a real benefit.
- **The Socioeconomic View:** It represents a reduced vision of the CSR. Still, it accepts that adopting some degree of social responsibility will provide net benefits to the company in terms of, for example, avoiding costly legislation, build good relationships with customers and suppliers or establish collaborative networks. This vision can simultaneously develop a dual function of profit maximization and service to social demands.
- **The Philanthropic View:** It draws a broad view of the CSR, according to which companies are willing to make donations, even if these perceive as a net cost to the company. This attitude can come from altruistic or ethical behavior, which prompts them to do something for society.

- **The Modern View:** It is from a perspective in which the company maintains a broad relationship with society and obtains net long-term and short-term benefits from corporate social involvement; This vision also includes the views of interest groups. (See at the Figure 8)

Three Dimensional Model of CSR by Scwartz and Carroll (2003)

This model proposes a set schema, which allows overlapping, generating seven categories in which the CSR can conceptualize. The dimensions of this model are:

- **Purely Economic:** This concentrates on those business activities that have directly or indirectly a beneficial impact of the organization.
- **Purely Legal:** Is the corporate response to the legitimate expectations established by society through the different jurisdictions. The legality of a company can understand according to three categories: law enforcement, avoidance of lawsuits and litigation, and anticipation of the law.
- **Purely Ethical:** Ethical responsibility of the business, as expected by the community in general and for interest groups in particular. The model proposes three types of ethical standards: conventional, consequential, and deontological; these distinguish from each other according to the philosophy that supports every kind of standard.The intersecting dimensions, as well as the areas that compete with the three dimensions in its purest manifestation, represent business situations that managers face in constant decision-making.From a regulatory point of view, the company must be at the central point containing the overlap of the three dimensions.

Two of the three models contain Philanthropy, while the Swartz and Carroll model (2003) includes a dimension called ethics purely, where we find three types of ethics: conventional, consequential, and deontological, but Philanthropy is not recovering as such. This concept generally designates love for the human species, and all that humanity is concerned with, expressed in selfless help to others (Wikipedia). Therefore, the Philanthropy of the model has removed, replacing it with the ethics that are most related to the business world.

MODELS USED BY COMPANIES

In the previous section, the most noted models of CSR-related have been collected, which have been generated by the authors theoretically and then be able to use them practically. In this section will develop the models that companies or organizations use today to improve their Corporate Social Responsibility program. It can see in Table 3.

Global Reporting Initiative (GRI)

It is an independent institution that created the first global standard for the development of sustainability reports for those companies that wish to evaluate their economic, environmental, and social performance. It is an official collaboration center of the United Nations Environment Programme. From its inception in 1997 to 2002, the GRI was a joint project between UNEP and CERES: Coalition for Environmentally Responsible Economies. It conceives to increase the quality of the sustainability production reports, to equate them with financial summary in terms of comparative, rigor, credibility, periodicity, and integrity. Since 2016, the GRI index table also includes references to the U.N. Sustainable Development Goals (SDGs). (Total, 2019)[3]The summary of all the standards used by GRI includes Figure 11.

How does this program work? It is going to be developed, according to Zamudio (2018), THE GRI standards divide into modules:

1. Universal Standards:
   a. **Basics (101)** applicable to any organization that prepares a sustainability report:
   b. *Section one* of this standard presents the Reporting Principles for defining report content and report quality.
   c. Section two explains the necessary process of using the GRI Standards for sustainability reporting. This section includes fundamental requirements for applying the Reporting Principles, and for identifying and reporting on material topics.
   d. *Section three* sets out the ways that the GRI Standards can use and the specific claims, or statements of use, which require for organizations using the Standards. The topics are in Table 4.
   e. **General Declarations (102)** addresses all aspects of the company that allows the reader to build a profile on it and include the organizational profile, strategy, and governance of the organization.
   f. **Management Approach (103)** This Standard includes general requirements and disclosures for reporting the management approach for material topics.
2. Topics specific standards:
   a. **Economic (200),** used to report information on an organization's material impacts related to economic issues.
   b. **Environmental (300)** used to summarize information on an organization's tangible effects associated with environmental topics.
   c. **Social (400)** used to report information on an organization's material impacts linked to social issues like employment, Labor/Management Relations, etc[4].

Next, the reporting principles report content and quality, which can overstate in Table 3.

1. Reporting principles for defining report content are:

The reporting organization shall identify its *stakeholders* and explain how it has responded to their reasonable expectations and interests.

The underlying question of *sustainability* coverage is, however, a company contributes or aims to provide within the future, to the development or deterioration of economic, environmental, and social conditions at the native, regional, or world level.

>*Materiality* is the principle that determines that relevant topic's area unit ample vital that it's essential to report on them. Not all material topics area units of equal importance and the emphasis inside a report predicted to mirror their relative priority.

>*Completeness* can also consult with practices in info assortment (for example, ensuring that compiled knowledge includes results from all entities wherever the impacts occur) and whether or not the

presentation of data is cheap and appropriate. Problems besides are associated with report quality and are addressed in more extensive detail of the principles of Accuracy and Balance.

2. Reporting principles for defining report quality:

   a. **Accuracy:** This principle intends to mirror the fact that information may express in many various ways in which, from qualitative responses to elaborate quantitative measurements.
   b. **Balance:** According to info, shall reflect positive and negative aspects of the reporting organization's performance to change a reasoned assessment of overall performance.
   c. **Clarity:** The report anticipates to gift information in a very approach that is understandable, accessible, and usable by the organization's vary of stakeholders, whether or not in print form or through different channels.
   d. Comparability: It is crucial for evaluating performance. Stakeholders must be able to compare information on the organization's current economic, environmental, and social performance against the organization's past performance, its objectives, and, to the degree doable, against the performance of different organizations.
   e. **Reliability:** The reporting organization shall gather, record, compile, analyze, and report info and processes utilized in the preparation of the report in a manner that they'll be subject to examination, and that establishes the quality and materiality of the data.
   f. Timeliness: Refers to the regularity with which the reports make as well as the impact described in it

An Example

A company that uses GRI to be an organization that aligns with Corporate Social Responsibility standards is the "Total" is an integrated energy group and one of the world's largest, through its international presence and its activities. Total's goal is to make its development a vehicle of progress that benefits as many people as possible (Total 2019).

SGE 21 (Ethically and Socially Responsible Management System, in Europe)

It is the first European standard to implement, audit, and certify an ethically and socially responsible management system. It is a vital tool for the integration of environmental, social, and good governance (ASG) aspects in the management of companies and organizations of all kinds. SGE 21 develops the requirements that allow the ethical and socially conscientious management system, proposed by Forética[5], to be established, implemented, and evaluated in organizations. Implementing this system is a conviction for the management of the organization of its ability to generate responsible leadership (SGE 21 2019).

The SGE 21 standards established nine management areas that correspond to the main stakeholders and address the critical social, environmental, and ethical governance aspects for the company or organization. For each of these areas, several requirements establish that must meet.

The management areas covered by this standard list in Figure 2

The evaluation can do in two ways:

1. Conformity assessment: The evaluation made by the Forética application level of the Standard requirements in an organization through a documentary review and collection of evidence in the public information of that entity. Through the process, a validation of the use methodology management proposed by the standard at a given time obtain.

The conformity assessment process is carried out by Forética through approved professionals according to the following considerations:

a. It is a documentary review of the information provided by the company (self-declaration) and evidence obtained through the public knowledge of that entity.
b. It includes the nine management areas considered by SGE 21 (Included in Figure 2)
c. It does not imply a thorough assessment of every single requirement of the standard, but it does allow for a first approximation of the degree of development of the RSS in the organization, taking as a reference this international standard (Forética 2018)
    2. Certification: The certification process is carried out exclusively through Foretica-approved certification bodies in three-year certification cycles (initial audit in the first year and follow-up audits in the following two years). List of Forética certification entities: ADOK; APPLUS + Certificación; Bureau Veritas Certificación; Cámara Certifica; DNV Business Assurance; Instituto de Certificación CDQ; OCA Instituto de Certificación; SGS; TÜV Rheinland Ibérica.

The entity that passes the audits receives a certificate proves it on behalf of the certification authority has performed the inspection and Forética.

This option is especially interesting for those organizations with a purpose of continuous improvement through management systems and for which obtaining a certification in the SGE 21 standards are an element of differentiation and recognition. (Forética 2018)

An Example

A typical example is a family business call Pàver, which is a four-group company with 120 employees in total. Dedicated to metal stamping and the construction of dies and tools intended mainly for automotive, for years in family reconciliation, flexibility with the staff and family aids have earned him official recognition (Cincodías 2017).

It also recognizes for its environmental work. "We were the first company in Catalonia to certify sustainability actions," says Javier Vera, representative of the second generation of the family in Pàver. Its environmental commitment and the management it carries out, which began in the early 2000s, is endorsed by the certification of ISO 14001 and EMAS III implemented by the European Commission.

This company is a clear example of the CSR; it goes beyond what regulations require it, also serves us to demonstrate how public administration. Moreover, engages in Corporative Social Responsibility, which has already explained above, is one of the elements fundamental to being able to carry out these policies. Another example of CSR compliance is the granting of certification IATF 16949:2016 is the international standard for quality management systems in the automotive industry for Páve.

OBJECTIVES OF CORPORATE SOCIAL RESPONSIBILITY

According to Responsabilidad Social Corporativa (2019), betting on Corporate Social Responsibility in organizations carries the following general benefits/objectives:

- **Increased Productivity:** Through better conditions for the internal customer leading, to best talent retention, and thus lower turnover rates.
- **Customer Loyalty:** Meeting your needs, starting with providing you with a place where you can convey your needs and complaints. In addition to quality and price, customers begin to demand information on the conditions of production and outsourcing, the certifications that the product or service has, among others.
- **Market Access:** For compliance with standards and certifications required by external actors, including consumers.
- **Credibility:** The company that is respectful of people, communities, the environment, and society as a whole, projects a reputation guarantees finer sustainability over time, reducing risks, anticipating situations that can affect greater agility to react and adapt to change, and generating confidence. As can observe Figure 13, according to Foretica study (2018), companies looking for different objectives to achieve through the use of the CSR, from 2012 to 2017. The goals have changed, for example, the aim in 2017 most persecuted is: "aligning our objectives, mission and values" with 48%, the second objective pursued by organizations is: "build, maintain or improve reputation" with 32%. However, in 2012 the aim is pursued with 35%. It should note that the objective complies with the rules of the industry is only continued with 15%, although it is true that in 2012, it was just 6%. Therefore, it leads us to infer that companies seek to be ethical and responsible with their environment, and improve their image. For example, Coca-Cola conducted a significant global stakeholder consultation with local experts from all their countries of operation. Based on this interactive dialogue, Coca-Cola identified several material issues. Organized them into seven commitment areas and developed qualitative and quantitative targets for each one[6]. In Figure 3 are collected the objectives of Coca-Cola, the goals are related to education, poverty, equality, and the environment; some of the targets most pursued by organizations.

ADVANTAGES OF CRS FOR COMPANIES

Corporate social responsibility focuses, in this vein, on three aspects: care for the environment, the working conditions of its workers, and support for humanitarian causes (Barragán, 2017).

Figure 5 can see all the benefits companies can gain when using CSR.

For Employees

- *Create more self-sufficient employees* with more capacity to solve problems themselves. The overnight pyramid-steering structure gives way to the organization by self-managed teams. Improves working climate and productivity (Barragan 2017)Along with talent recruitment and retention, a good RSC strategy has very positive effects on the degree of satisfaction and commitment of workers to the company. The implementation of corporate volunteer programs offers many advantages. Improves workers' motivation, skills, and self-esteem; fosters pride to be part of the company and reinforces the involvement of employees and their commitment to it. (RSE, 2018)

- *Millennials will be the bulk of the job of the future*. It project to account for 75% of workers by 2020. For millennials, work is not a burden, but an area of enjoyment and fulfillment. When they value a job, the economic factor loses weight against variables such as the suitability of it to their life project. They seek to adhere to causes, prefer companies committed to society and the environment, and value environments that promote multiculturalism and diversity. In this scenario, the CRS helps design and offer novel and attractive proposals for this new profile of 21st-century workers (RSE, 2018).
- *According to Half (2019), Offering opportunities for corporate volunteerism can*:
    - Increase employee loyalty and job satisfaction
    - Boost employee engagement
    - Create a knock-on effect that improves productivity
    - Give employees the chance to develop new skills
    - Improve morale and motivation

For Society

- **Improves Energy Efficiency:** The environmental objectives that companies assume as part of their RSC actions include energy efficiency measures, recycling, and other initiatives to reduce the consumption of natural resources. In doing so, in addition to minimizing their negative impacts on the environment, they achieve significant savings in economic terms (RSE, 2018)-*Society as well as benefits from a better quality of products*. Corporations' efforts to obey CSR rules make them eliminate all the defects at the production stage, resulting in diminishing the amount of complaints and increasing customer satisfaction (Mullerat, 2010). *CSR actions about health increase awareness in society* and influence its behavior, convincing people to go to their medical examinations and teaching them that prevention is always better than treating. These activities result in a healthier and better-educated society (Arnold, 2010).

For Business

- Improved reputation for collaborating with these types of charitable causes
- Worker involvement and motivation
- Recognition of the company's work by consumers
- Free advertising by organizations
- Rebate for collaborating financially with such partnerships
    - **Increases Consumer and Customer Loyalty:** Consumers admire those companies that value their employees, develop social projects, care about the environment, and invest anti-corruption efforts. Social responsibility is, therefore, an essential factor in ensuring consumer loyalty. An upward trend, taking into account the new consumption habits of generations to come. (RSE, 2018)
- *Social responsibility of companies led them to develop new technologies*, innovations, and infrastructure that can be used by every member of society (Carrol and Buchholtz,2008).

CSR values may result in developing better relations with governments. Thanks to this cooperation, both sides can discover a better way to serve society and provide it with higher than before economic development opportunities (Arnold, 2010).

For Nonprofits

Learn from companies to better control the temporary development of projects to achieve their objectives more effectively begin to have resources provided by the company for some of their projects.

POSSIBLE DISADVANTAGES OF CRS FOR COMPANIES

Corporate social responsibility, or CSR, can cause some problems unless companies engage in this with care and planning. the following are the potential disadvantages of use by CSR companies, according to Hartman (2019):

- **Cost:** One of the main drawbacks of a corporate social responsibility program is the cost that this entails. Efforts such as event sponsorship, charitable donations, product donations, and voluntary commitment to environmental standards cost money that a company is unlikely to recover in the short term. Despite the long-term positive effects of an improved corporate image, companies can't be able to measure the value of corporate responsibility, rather than to take their cost to make a profit.
- **Justice:** Companies are free to invest in the social causes deem. Still, it may not generate the desired visibility or that there will be a diversion of the NGO's funds to purposes that are not those specified, and this harms the image of the company.
- **Unintended Consequences:** Social responsibility can have unintended and unexpected consequences for businesses, regardless of how or where they spend their money. This situation occurs when a company tries to exercise social responsibility to resolve conflicts alongside the government's efforts by doing the same, confusing members of the public, offering a new, and perhaps temporary, option to solve a problem social-specific. This type of social responsibility can cause taxpayers to resent the government for providing a service and also paying a private company to do the same. A different kind of unintended consequence is an investment in social responsibility in a program or organization that turns out to be inefficient or illegitimate.
- **Increased Scrutiny:** A company that conducts a social responsibility course falls under greater scrutiny from critics, customers, and competitors. For example, if a company invests in energy-efficient manufacturing methods and a public awareness campaign to promote recycling, competitors may try to discredit behavior by pointing out other parts of the operation of the business that are less environmentally beneficial

CONCLUSION

- As has been seen through the chapter, companies increasingly incorporated the use of CSRs into their policies, due to:
- In the business world, responsible behavior translates into priority and better results. Following the trend of years, this phenomenon continues to move forward with the population, maintaining the importance and the added value of an Authentic CRS (Forética, 2018).
- Consumers are more aware of the care of the environment, and value companies that are careful with it. New lifestyles have been developed based on more sustainable and healthy practices, which are acquiring significant value in consumers. These are consumers who manifest unique needs in their day-to-day life, which therefore reflect in their consumption styles. Businesses should position themselves close to this new consumer and be able to respond to the new demands has.
- Society demands that companies devaluate some of what they get from it.
- Workers, as part of society, environmentally responsible value companies that carry out volunteer policies, etc., this makes them better workers.
- Stakeholders, make a profit because the company's use of the CSR produces a return on investment, there is a growing interest in non-financial information such as commitment to the environment, with society and with good governance practices.
- Today, it cannot understand that a company does not take CSR shares, as CSR makes the difference between companies in the market.

REFERENCES

Acosta, C. (2016). *Son famosos y millonarios, pero ¿son responsables?* Retrieved from: https://www.expoknews.com/son-famosos-y-millonarios-pero-son-responsables/

Arnold, M. F. (2010). Competitive Advantage from CSR Programmes. In C. Louche, S. O. Idowu, & W. L. Filho (Eds.), *Innovative CSR: From Risk Management to Value Creation*. Greenleaf Publishing Limited. doi:10.9774/GLEAF.978-1-907643-26-2_7

Balaguer, M., Fernández, M., & Muñoz, M. (2007). *La responsabilidad social de la empresa. Relaciones entre la performance social, financiera y bursátil*. Conselleria de Empresa, Universidad y Ciencia. Generalitat Valenciana.

Barragán. (2017). *Ventajas de la Responsabilidad Social*. Retrieved from: http://www.pymerang.com/direccion-de-negocios/1035-aplicando-el-design-thinking-para-resolver-problemas-de-negocio-cuando-su-mente-se-ha-bloqueado

Carroll, A. B. (1991). The pyramid of corporate social responsibility: Toward the moral management of organizational stakeholders. *Business Horizons*, *34*(4), 39–4. doi:10.1016/0007-6813(91)90005-G

Carroll, A. B. (2008). A history of corporate social responsibility: concepts and practices. In A. M. Andrew Crane, D. Matten, J. Moon, & D. Siegel (Eds.), *The Oxford handbook of corporate social responsibility* (pp. 19–46). Oxford University Press.

Carroll, A. B., & Buchholtz, A. K. (2008). *Business and Society: Ethics, Sustainability, and Stakeholder Management* (9th ed.). Cengage Learning.

Casa de Bolsa Monex. (2018). *Conoce los tres tipos de responsabilidad social: individual, empresarial y pública.* Retrieved from: https://blog.monex.com.mx/conoce-los-tres-tipos-responsabilidad-social-individual-empresarial-publica

Chaffee, E. C. (2017). The origins of corporate social responsibility. *University of Cincinnati Law Review*, *85*, 347–373.

Cowan, A., Welch, S., & Welch, O. (2011). *An empirical investigation of the link between performance and Corporate Social Responsibility in the oil and gas industry.* Midwest Finance Association, Annual Meetings Paper. 10.2139srn.1929113

Deloitte. (2018). *Responsabilidad Social y Gobierno Corporativo.* Retrieved from: https://www2.deloitte.com/es/es/pages/governance-risk-and-compliance/articles/responsabilidad-social-y-gobierno-corporativo.html

Dimson, E., Karakaş, O., Li, X., & Ownership, A. (2015). *Review of Financial Studies.* Available at SSRN: https://ssrn.com/abstract=2154724

Drucker, P. F. (1996). *La gestión en tiempos de grandes cambios.* Ediciones Gestión 2000 S.A.

Forética. (2018). *INFORME FORÉTICA 2018 sobre la evolución de la RSE y Sostenibilidad. La recompensa del optimista.* Retrieved from: https://www.foretica.org/informe_foretica_2018.pdf

Forrester. (2017). *The Power Of A Values-Based Strategy.* Retrieved from: https://go.forrester.com/what-it-means/ep15-values-based-strategy/

Freeman, R. E. (1994). The politics of stakeholder theory: Some future directions. *Business Ethics Quarterly*, *4*(4), 409–421. doi:10.2307/3857340

García, Q. (2016). *Historia de la RSC.* Retrieved from: https://mansunides.org/es/rsc/responsabilidad-social-corporativa/historia-rsc

Half, R. (2019). *4 little known benefits of CSR for any company.* Retrieved from: https://www.roberthalf.com.hk/blog/employers/4-little-known-benefits-csr-any-company

Hartman, D. (2019). *Desventajas de una empresa socialmente responsable.* Retrieved from: https://www.cuidatudinero.com/13102036/desventajas-de-una-empresa-socialmente-responsable

Heald, M. (1970). *The social responsibilities of business: company and community 1900–1960.* Pr. of Case Western Reserve Univ.

Intermon, O. (2017). *Los diferentes tipos de responsabilidad social: del ámbito individual a las acciones gubernamentales*. Retrieved from: https://blog.oxfamintermon.org/los-diferentes-tipos-de-responsabilidad-social-del-ambito-individual-a-la-acciones-gubernamentales/?gclid=Cj0KCQiA0ZHwBRCRARIsAK0Tr-p6cDAHhJR-qypw3uOwNf_OaOFGXsoXi0DMOXCQos4XFDx9LWuBDWkaAs-9EALw_wcB

Johnson, H. (1971). *Business in contemporary society: framework and issues*. Wadsworth Pub.

King, B. (1996). The Use of Supermajority Voting Rules in Corporate America: Majority Rule, Corporate Legitimacy, and Minority Shareholder Protection, Delaware. *The Journal of Corporation Law*, *21*(3), 895.

Kiran & Sharma. (2011). Corporate Social Responsibility: A Corporate Vision. *International Journal of Contemporary Business Studies*, *2*(3), 58–67.

Kotler, P., & Lee, N. (2005). *Corporate social responsibility. Doing the most good for your company and your cause*. John Wiley & Sons, Inc.

Księżak, P. (2016). The Benefits from CSR for a Company and Society. *Journal of Corporate Responsibility and Leadership Contemporary Challenges in Corporate Social Responsibility*, *3*(4), 53–65.

Marín, A. (2004). Del Marketing con causa a la responsabilidad social de la empresa. *Research and Marketing*, *85*, 48–51.

Marrewijk, M. (2013). *Concepts and definitions of CSR and corporate sustainability: Between agency and communion*. Doi:10.1007/978-94-007-4126-3_32

Moon, H.-C. H., & Parc, J. (2019). Shifting corporate social responsibility to corporate social opportunity through creating shared value. *Strategic Change*, *28*(2), 115–122. doi:10.1002/jsc.2252

Nielsen. (2015). *Consumer versus Corporate Social Responsibility of Brands*. Retrieved from: https://www.nielsen.com/es/es/press-releases/2015/Cuatro-de-cada-diez-consumidores-pagarias-mas-por-prodcutos-de-empresas-socialmente-comprometidas/

Prince of Wales Business Leadership Forum. (n.d.). *Website Resources, CSR Themes*. www.pwblf.org

Puig, M., & Martínez, A. (2008). *La responsabilidad social en la administración pública. Un reto para el s.XXI.* Diputación de Barcelona. Retrieved from: https://www1.diba.cat/uliep/pdf/39527.pdf

Quazi, A. M., & O'Brien, D. (2000). An Empirical Test of Cross-National Model of Corporate Social Responsibility. *Journal of Business Ethics*, *25*(1), 33–51. doi:10.1023/A:1006305111122

Reputation Institute. (2018). *Global CR RepTrak® 100*. Retrieved from: https://ri.reputationinstitute.com/hubfs/_PDF/RepTrak/2018_Global_CR_100.pdf

Responsabilidad Social Corporativa. (2019). *La responsabilidad social empresarial*. Retrieved from: https://responsabilidad-social-corporativa.com/la-responsabilidad-social-empresarial/

Rodríguez, N. (2010). *Responsabilidad social y ONG*. Retrieved from: http://www.eexcellence.es/index.php/expertos-en-gestion/responsabilidad-social-y-ong

RSE. (2018). *10 ventajas de la RSE para las compañías*. Retrieved from: http://rse.elsalvador.com/articulos/10-ventajas-de-la-rse-para-las-companias/

Sarkis, J. (2012). Models for Compassionate Operations. *International Journal of Production Economics, 139*(2), 359–365. doi:10.1016/j.ijpe.2012.06.018

Schwartz, M. S., & Carroll, A. B. (2003). Corporate social responsibility: A three domain approach. *Business Ethics Quarterly, 13*(4), 503–530. doi:10.5840/beq200313435

Torreblanca, F. (2017). *Responsabilidad social corporativa en la estrategia de marketing*. Retrieved from: https://franciscotorreblanca.es/responsabilidad-social-corporativa-marketing/

van der Zwart, A. (2002). *Reputatie mechanisme in beweging: doelstreffend bij issues aan MVO?* (Master thesis). Erasmus University Rotterdam.

Zamudio, M. (2018). *Global Reporting Initiative (GRI): el lenguaje universal de la sostenibilidad*. Retrieved from: https://www.esan.edu.pe/conexion/actualidad/2018/08/20/global-reporting-initiative-gri-el-lenguaje-universal-de-la-sostenibilidad/

ENDNOTES

1 Article realized by García, Q.. Retrieved from: https://mansunides.org/es/rsc/responsabilidad-social-corporativa/historia-rsc

2 VP Public Affairs & Communications de Coca-Cola European Partners. The Future Brand Index 2018": Ponencia de Ana Callol, de Coca-Cola, retrieved from: https://www.marketingdirecto.com/marketing-general/marketing/responsabilidad-social-corporativa-un-punto-clave-para-la-reputacion-de-marca

3 GLOBAL REPORTING INITIATIVE (GRI), Retrieved from: https://www.sustainable-performance.total.com/en/reporting/reporting-standards/global-reporting-initiative-gri

4 All the standards can be found at: GRI STANDARDS DOWNLOAD CENTER. Retrieved from: https://www.globalreporting.org/standards/gri-standards-download-center

5 Forética is the leading organization in sustainability and corporate social responsibility. Its mission is to integrate the social, environmental and good governance aspects in the strategy and management of companies and organizations. It currently consists of more than 240 partners, including 43% of the companies listed on IBEX 35, as well as subsidiaries of multinationals, small and medium-sized enterprises, reference NGOs and personal partners.Forética is the representative of the World Business Council for Sustainable Development (WBCSD) in Spain and therefore the Spanish Business Council for Sustainable Development. In Europe, Forética is a national partner of CSR Europe. In addition, it is part of the State Council of SERS in Spain.Forética was born in 1999. It subsequently launched SGE 21, the first ethically and socially responsible management system. Today, more than 150 companies and organizations are certified with the Standard in Spain and Latin America. (Forética.org).

6 SIX PRACTICAL STEPS FOR A GOOD CSR STRATEGY AND COMMUNICATIONS, Retrieved from: https://www.sustainabilityconsult.com/downloads-blanks/our-work/62-csr-strategy-and-communications-report-2013-six-practical-steps-for-a-good-csr-strategy-and-communications/file

APPENDIX

Table 1. Comparison between CSR and CSV

		CRS	CSV
Motivation	Reputation, external pressure, etc.	X	
Relation to business	Disconnected	x	
	Connected		x
Beneficiary	Society	x	
	Corporation		x
Overall	Zero-sum	x	
	Positive-sum		x

Source: Moon and Park (2019)

Table 2. Factors influencing Corporate Social Responsibility

Factors	CSR & Multinationals	Philanthropy & Community Investments
Enhanced reputation	Experimentation	Improved
Alliance with Business partner	Futuristic	New Opportunities
Better Stakeholder relationship	Quick Decisions	Better Decisions
Attractive employer	High	Moderate
Customer satisfaction-loyalty	HIgh	Considerable
New business opportunity	Strategic	Tactical
Cost savings	HIgh	Moderate
Minimize risks	Quantitative	Quantitative & Qualitative
Reduce Regulatory interventions	Relatively Difficult	Easy

Source: Kiran and Sharma (2011)

Table 3. First to adopt CSR

YEAR	COUNTRY	ORGANIZATION	TOOL
1995	United Kingdom	Accountability	Standard AA1000
1997	Global	Global Reporting Initiative	Guide G1-GRI
	United States	Social Accountability International	Standar SA 8000
1999	Switzerland	Sustainable Asset Management	Index Dow Jones Sustainabiity
	Spain	Forética	Standard SGE 21

Source: Forética (2018).

Table 4. Types of reporting principles of 101

Reporting Principles for defining report content	Reporting Principles for defining report quality
•Stakeholder Inclusiveness •Sustainability Context •Materiality •Completeness	•Accuracy •Balance •Clarity •Comparability •Reliability •Timeliness

Source: GRI (2019)

Figure 1. Consumption data related to CRS organizations
Source: Nielsen (2015)

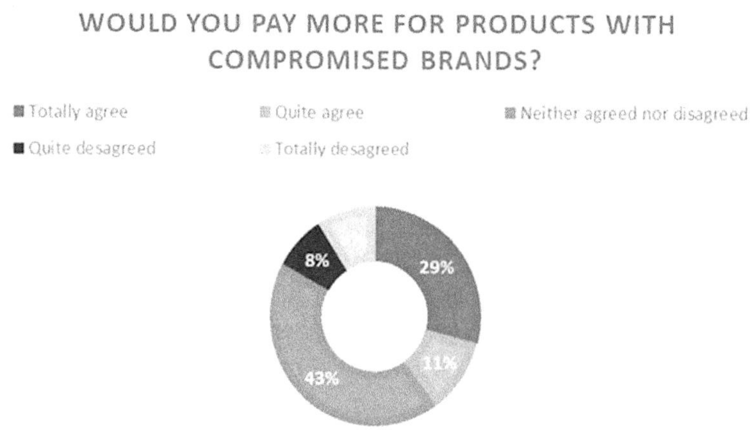

Figure 2. Evolution of Corporate Social Responsibility
Source: Own elaboration

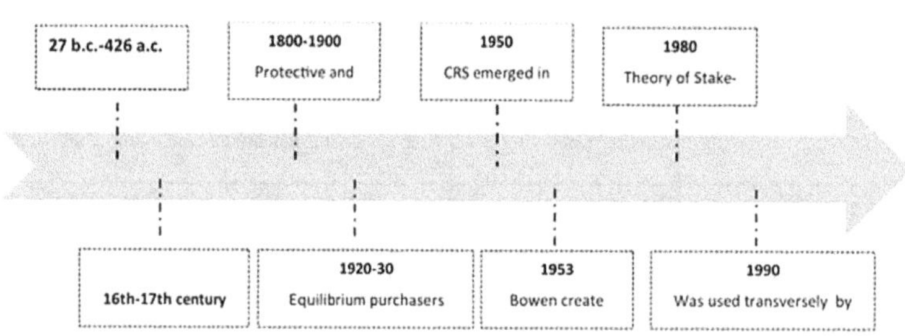

Figure 3. Evolution of the relationship between organizations, government and civil society in CSR
Source: Marrewijk (2002)

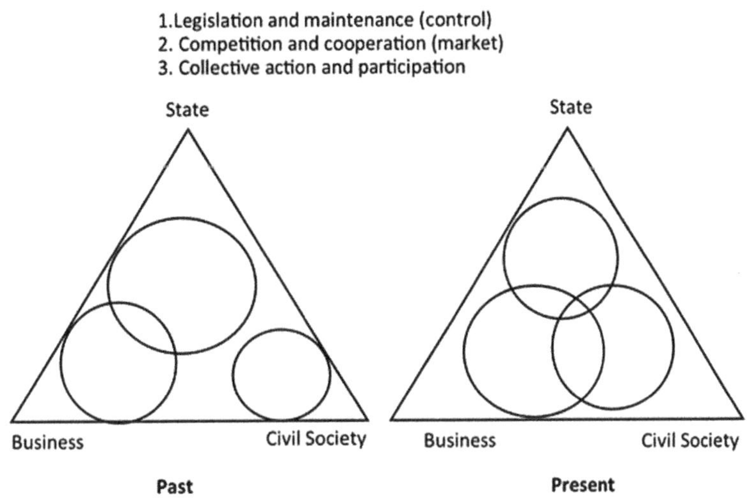

Figure 4. Corporate social responsibility in marketing strategy
Source: Torreblanca (2017)

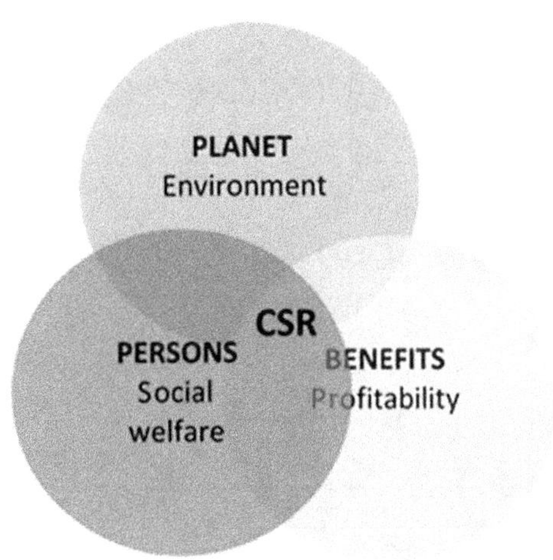

Figure 5. 2018 Global CR RepTrak® Top 10 Companies
Source; Global CR RepTrak® 100 (2018)

Rank	Home	2018	Score
1	United States	Google	71.9 ↑
2	United States	The Walt Disney Company	69.5 ↑
3	Denmark	LEGO	69.4 ↓
4	Brazil	natura	69.4
5	Denmark		68.7
6	United States	Microsoft	68.1 ↓
7	Germany	BOSCH	68.1
8	Japan	Canon	67.6 ↑
9	France	MICHELIN	67.6 ↑
10	Sweden	IKEA	67.2 ↑

Figure 6. Dimensions of public social responsibility: public policies and social responsibility of administrations
Source: Puig et al. (2008)

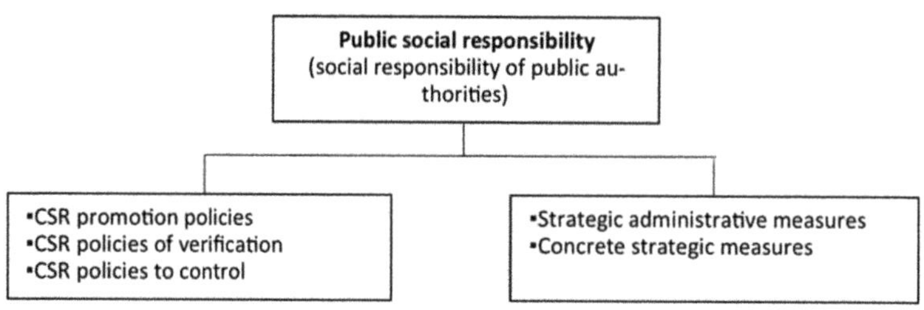

Figure 7. Pyramid model of CSR by Carroll, 1991
Source: Carroll, 1991

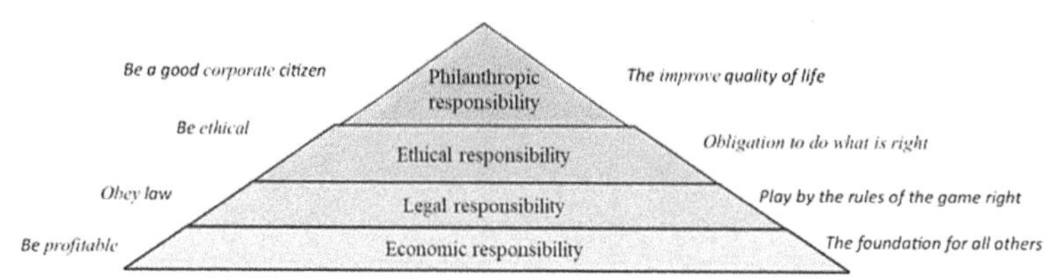

Figure 8. The two-dimensional model of Quazi and O'Brien (2000)
Source: Quazi and O'Brien (2000)

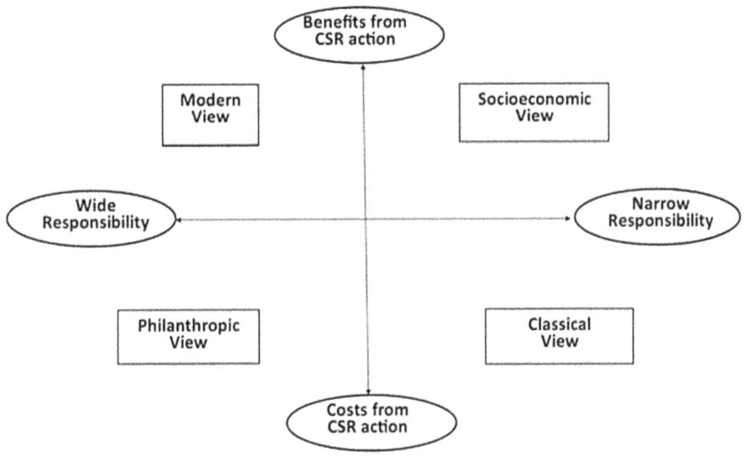

Figure 9. Three-dimensional model of CSR by Schwartz and Carroll (2003)
Source: Schwartz and Carroll (2003)

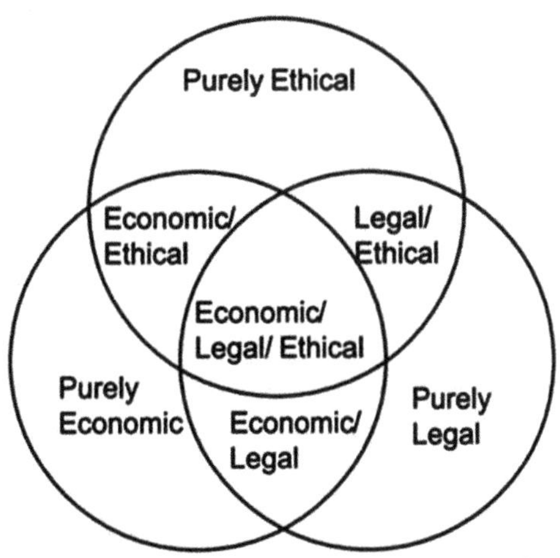

Figure 10. Standards GRI
Source: GRI (2019)

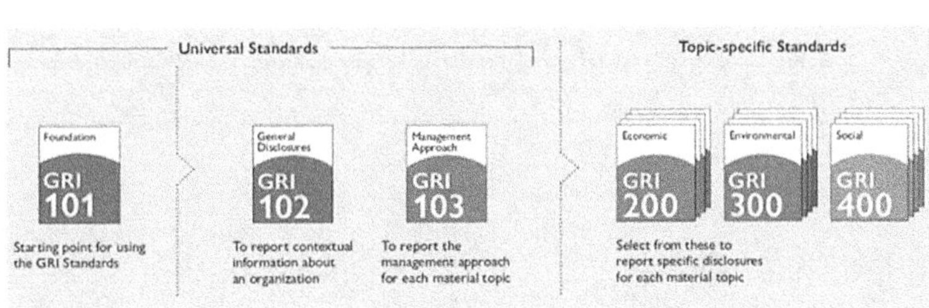

Figure 11. Actions for CSR's total company
Source: www.Total.com

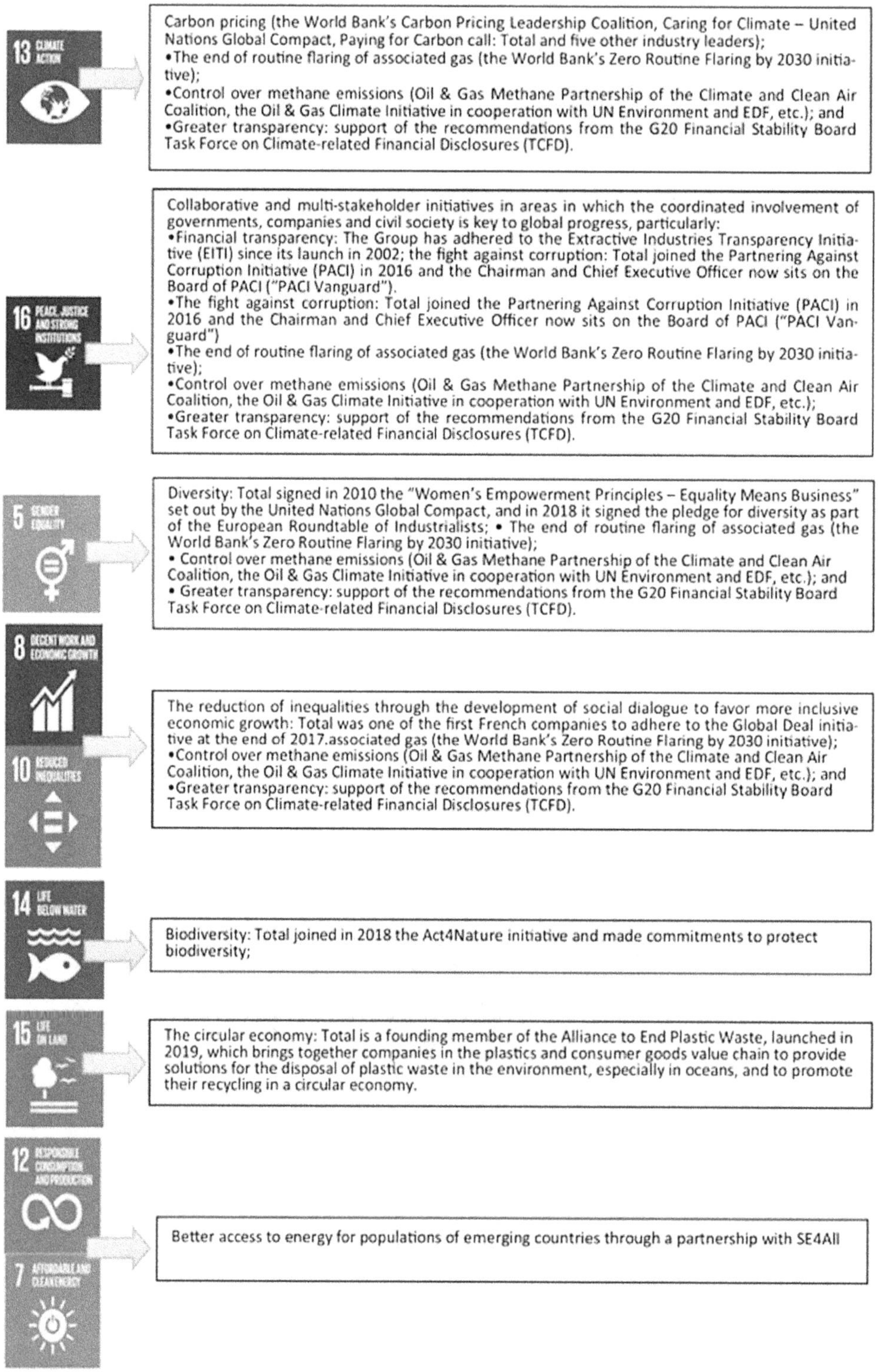

Figure 12. Management areas covered by SGE21
Source: Own elaboration

Figure 13. Example of Páves's environmental actions
Source: www.Páves.es (2019)

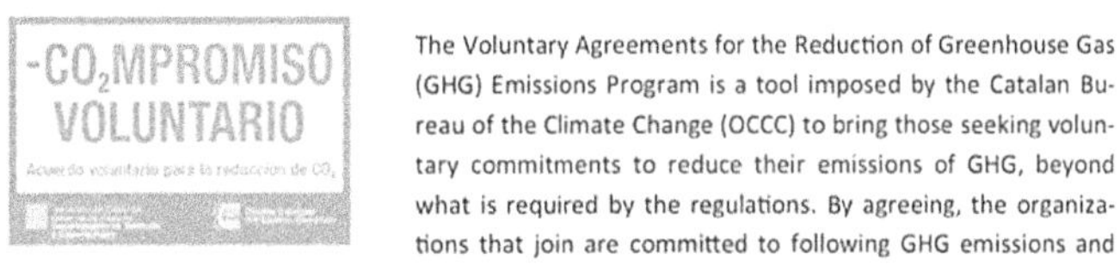

Figure 14. Coca-Cola's goals sustainable development
Source: Coca-Cola sustainability report 2018

Figure 15. The benefits of CSR for the company
Source: Księżak (2016)

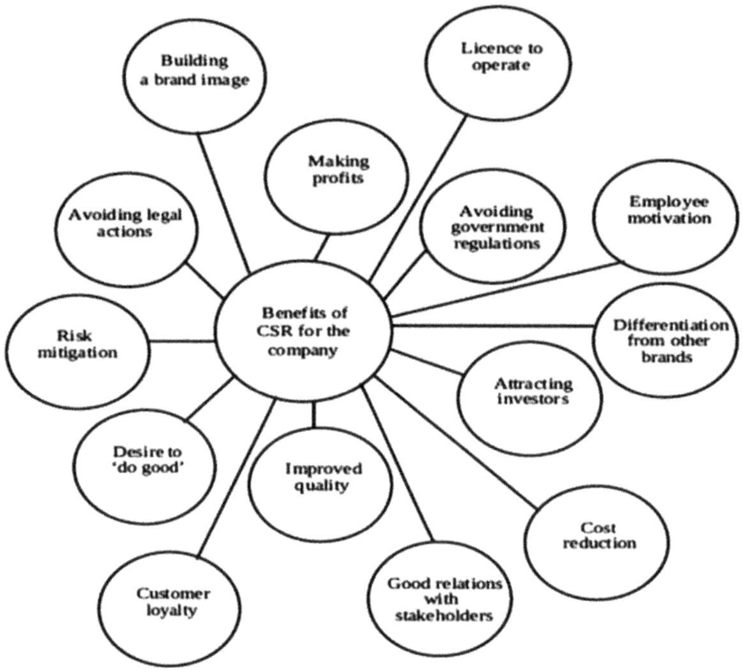

Chapter 3
Corporate Sustainability, Business Sustainability, or Corporate Social Responsibility
Some Relevant Criteria for Choosing the Right One

Jaime González-Masip
Rey Juan Carlos University, Spain

ABSTRACT

Despite the high academic and business interest in corporate sustainability and everything related to the impact of organizations on their social and environmental environment, there is still a notable confusion between the concepts of corporate social responsibility, corporate sustainability, and even business sustainability. This chapter helps to identify common aspects and differentiating elements between these concepts, which allow researchers and practitioners to understand the existing literature on the topic and to propose lines of work and research in an appropriate manner, according to its objectives and analysis perspectives. The text includes a review of the concept of corporate sustainability and a set of criteria and recommendations to make an appropriate choice and contribute to a more logical convergence in the use of the terms.

INTRODUCTION

There is a clear academic urgency in all issues related to the social impact of organizations (Gond & Crane, 2010). The literature dedicated to business and society navigates in a changing and undefined sea of concepts and theories that maintain these lines of research in a "continuing state of emergence" (Lockett, Moon, & Visser, 2006, p.133). Among them, corporate sustainability (CS) "has emerged as the theme of the 21st century" (Ng & Rezaee, 2015, p.128). Due to its link with sustainable development,

DOI: 10.4018/978-1-7998-4833-2.ch003

and its focus on socially and ecologically sustainable economic development, corporate sustainability (CS) has become "a key issue as we move forward" (Curran, 2009, p.10).

The concept of CS has evolved historically as a result of economic growth, environmental regulations, and a growing interest in social justice and equity (Christofi, Christofi, & Sisaye, 2012). However, it is evident the lack of a common definition and method of measurement, which forces researchers and managers to move in a kind of "sustainability jungle" (Montiel & Delgado-Ceballos, 2014). It seems clear that corporate sustainability is a megatrend (Lubin & Esty, 2010), but there are still numerous visions and interpretations of the concept and its implementation. Sustainability is a growing concern for organizations which, in addition to being economically beneficial, must now also be environmentally and socially responsible. Just this expression creates confusion: should companies be sustainable or socially responsible? The lack of clarity on the concept of CS makes it difficult to understand how companies can effectively incorporate these practices into their activities (Meuer, Koelbel, & Hoffmann, 2019). Managers, as individuals and as part of a management team, can understand CS and how it is implemented differently. It depends on whether this is addressed as something fundamental, as an opportunity, a possible risk, as a mere administrative formality to comply with, or as a nuisance to combat (Schaltegger & Burritt, 2010).

This situation also makes it difficult to set up research scenarios on the subject. The academic community is clear that "[…] while corporate sustainability recognizes that corporate growth and profitability are important, it also requires the corporation to pursue societal goals, specifically those relating to sustainable development - environmental protection, social justice and equity, and economic development" (Wilson, 2003, p.1). But this approach looks like very similar, if not the same, to corporate social responsibility (CSR). Then, one question can arise in the mind of someone interested in this matter which is "What is the difference between corporate social responsibility, business sustainability and corporate sustainability if they seem to be the same thing?"

The relationship between the concepts CSR and CS remains unclear (Bansal & Song, 2017), since the definitions of both, and other sister concepts, are not consensual. Currently the CS approach, as well as other approaches linked more or less with sustainable development such as CSR, include the social dimension for the achievement of the strategic objectives of organizations in the long term (Watts & Holme, 2000). To differentiate scenarios, some authors propose that when talking about CS, CSR refers specifically to the scope of people and organizations (Van Marrewijk, 2003). Not all authors respect this criterion. As Huang and Watson (2015, p.2) say, "Corporate social responsibility is closely related to corporate sustainability", and many companies use the concepts interchangeably in their non-financial performance reports, but there are details that differentiate the two concepts. It seems clear that, although both concepts are sometimes considered similar, it is necessary to consider the essential differences between them (Van Marrewijk, 2003).

As we said, both companies and practitioners are overwhelmed and confused by the diversity of approaches to the concepts, without understanding which to choose or how to define their own approach, which can lead to complexity and implementation costs that they cannot afford (Van den Brink & van der Woerd, 2004). To improve this scenario, the objective of this chapter is to compile and compare a number of characteristics that will make it easier for researchers, on the one hand, to properly understand and interpret existing literature on this topic and, on the other hand, to identify and choose between CSR, CS and business sustainability (BS) according to the objectives and approaches of their research on business and society. Also, the text helps to avoid the increase of confusion in the literature by facilitating the authors the design of constructs and the definition of their scope, and generate approaches that contributes to make those concepts more homogeneous.

The chapter is structured in three parts. First, the concept of corporate sustainability is reviewed, identifying its key aspects. Second, common aspects between CSR and CS that contribute to confusion in the literature are developed. Third, and as a main contribution of the chapter, it presents a set of criteria that could make the choice of CS, BS or CSR easier, differentiating elements between these concepts.

BACKGROUND

Interest in corporate sustainability (CS) has increased significantly over the past two decades, to the point where a high percentage of managers surveyed indicate the importance of this issue in their businesses, although there is still much ambiguity in the nature of the concept (Meuer et al., 2019). Corporate motivations for engaging in sustainability are, among others, the need to meet stakeholder requirements, improved image and reputation, cost savings, improved employee motivation, improved competitiveness, and reduced risk (Searcy, 2012), as well as just addressing environmental or social issues, from the normative perspective of doing the right thing.

The Concept of Corporate Sustainability

Corporate sustainability, apparently, can have two main approaches that academics handle in a differentiated way: one that combines economic, environmental and social factors, and another that emphasizes the environmental aspect, referring to the environment in general, in which case it would be closer to the concept of *ecological sustainability* (Montiel, 2008). The Table 1 shows some definitions of CS, in which we can observe a certain diversity of perspectives and approaches that exist in the use of the concept among different authors. Note also that the concept itself evolute and acquires different interpretations that are discussed later in this chapter.

The Triple Bottom Line in Corporate Sustainability

Taking as a reference the concept of triple-bottom-line, introduced by Elkington (1997), according to which companies harmonize their efforts and resources to obtain economically viable results, while at the same time being socially and environmentally responsible, it is assumed that "in the long run sustainability requires all three dimensions to be satisfied simultaneously" (Dyllick & Hockerts, 2002, p.132). These dimensions show causal interrelations among them and synergistic effects, which make it necessary to consider the performance of all in a set, and not in an isolated way, also including a fourth dimension called *governance* (Budsaratragoon & Jitmaneeroj, 2019). The CS definitions shown in Table 1 indicate the importance of considering these three dimensions in the concept, and the interdependence between them. Table 2 shows an interpretation of what it is like for a company to be sustainable in each of the dimensions of triple-bottom-line.

Table 1. Definitions of corporate sustainability

Authors	Corporate Sustainability Definitions
Deloitte & Touche, ISSD[1] (1992), in Labuschagne et al. (2005)	''Adopting business strategies and activities that meet the needs of the enterprise and its stakeholders today while protecting, sustaining and enhancing the human and natural resources that will be needed in the future.''
Dyllick and Hockerts (2002, p.131-132)	"[...] meeting the needs of a firm's direct and indirect stakeholders (such as shareholders, employees, clients, pressure groups, communities etc), without compromising its ability to meet the needs of future stakeholders as well. Towards this goal, firms have to maintain and grow their economic, social and environmental capital base while actively contributing to sustainability in the political domain."
Van Marrewijk (2003, p.103)	"[...] company activities - voluntary by definition - demonstrating the inclusion of social and environmental concerns in business operations and in interactions with stakeholders."
Bansal & DesJardine (2014, p.71)	Business sustainability[2] [not *corporate sustainability*] is "[...] the ability of firms to respond to their short-term financial needs without compromising their (or others') ability to meet their future needs."
Strand (2014, p.688)	"Corporations' taking into consideration their environmental and social impacts in concert with their economic objectives."
Budsaratragoon & Jitmaneeroj (2019)	"[...] firm's contribution to environmental, social, governance and economic activities" (p.1). "[...] an integration of environmental, social, governance and economic performance, often called the quadruple bottom line (QBL) sustainability" (p.2).

Source: Own elaboration

The Link Between Business Sustainability and Corporate Sustainability

The literature shows that the concept of business sustainability (BS) can refer to two issues. First, with a market approach, it refers to the ability of a company to maintain economic returns over time, that is, a profit that is not sustainable but sustained over time, and thus endures. It mainly refers to the viability of companies and their business models to generate positive financial results. A second approach, close to "sustainable business" (see Montiel & Delgado-Ceballos, 2014), incorporates the creation of value in the social and environmental dimensions, being an interpretation approximating, or equivalent, to corporate sustainability. In this second case, when academics prefer the use of business sustainability in their publications rather than corporate sustainability, the special importance of the economic or market dimension as the main driver of the business is perceived, being non-financial ones a support for the

Table 2. Corporate sustainability criteria according to the triple baseline

Economically Sustainable Companies	Ecologically Sustainable Companies	Socially Sustainable Companies
"They guarantee at any time cashflow sufficient to ensure liquidity while producing a persistent above average return to their shareholders" (p.133).	"They use only natural resources that are consumed at a rate below the natural reproduction, or at a rate below the development of substitutes. They do not cause emissions that accumulate in the environment at a rate beyond the capacity of the natural system to absorb and assimilate these emissions. Finally they do not engage in activity that degrades eco-system services" (p.133).	"They add value to the communities within which they operate by increasing the human capital of individual partners as well as furthering the societal capital of these communities. They manage social capital in such a way that stakeholders can understand its motivations and can broadly agree with the company's value system" (p.134).

Source: Dyllick and Hockerts (2002)

achievement of the strategic objectives and a justification for the necessary investments. For example, Pojasek (2007, p.81) says that "Business sustainability seeks to create long-term shareholder value by embracing the opportunities and managing the risks that result from an organization's economic, environmental, and social responsibilities. Business sustainability must meet the needs of the organization and its stakeholders today while also protecting, sustaining, and enhancing the environmental, social, and economic resources needed for the future." This statement reflects the intention to consider the claims of stakeholders, as well as the preservation of sustainable development resources, with the intention of improving value creation for shareholders. This situation suggests an instrumental use of CS as a business strategy.

In an intermediate position, Rezaee (2016, p.49) states that "[business] sustainability focuses on activities that generate financial economic sustainability performance and nonfinancial ESG (environmental, social and governance) sustainability performance through maximizing corporate governance effectiveness and business opportunities and minimizing environmental and social harms, and, above all, securing long-term success in creating stakeholder value". The author, with this approach, incorporates two components of sustainable performance: (1) financial economic sustainability performance, focused on achieving long-term financial performance to create shareholder value, and (2) non-financial sustainability performance (environmental, social and governance) in protecting interests of non-shareholding stakeholders. As a reference, it can be understood that the socially responsible investing (SRI) indexes consider this approach as the desired one for the global investors and their analysis, since it grants a specific and relevant value to the economic performance.

Importance of the Environmental Dimension and the Sustainable Development

A researcher familiar with the concept of CS knows that it is closely linked to the concept of sustainable development (Sharma & Henriques, 2005). The origin of the CS concept is related to the Brundtland Report's (World Commission on Environment and Development, 1987) definition of sustainable development (Montiel & Delgado-Ceballos, 2014), sharing the growth perspective, the temporary component (especially the long term) and the environment.

Sustainable development "cannot be pursued without the active involvement of companies and organizations that have the resources, skills, and motivation to engage in more sustainable societies" (Simões & Sebastiani, 2017, p.424). Also, Labuschagne et al. (2005, p.373) affirm that "Business sustainability entails the incorporation of the objectives of sustainable development, namely social equity, economic efficiency and environmental performance, into a company's operational practices". In other words, CS is linked to how companies can contribute to sustainable development (Meuer et al., 2019).

As well as sustainable development, corporate sustainability shows a markedly eco-centrist approach (Gladwin, Kennelly, & Krause, 1995) incorporating the environment as an intrinsic value in the model that acts as a complementary (not accessory) dimension to the rest of dimensions (Montiel, 2008). In those ideas related to sustainability, the environment stops being something external to the model to be one of the central aspects, or just the central element, to consider (Cai, Cui, & Jo, 2016). In this context, eco-efficiency is defined as "a concept according to which improving the way resources are used can reduce environmental damage and reduce costs" (European Commission, 2001, p.24). That are the reasons because traditionally CS has been considered strongly attached to the environmental dimension of the triple bottom line.

THE SHARED ASPECTS BETWEEN THE CONCEPTS

It is common to find in academic literature authors who equate the concepts of corporate social responsibility and corporate sustainability (e.g., Curran, 2009). In that line, the terms CS, CSR and BS have been interchangeably used in the literature frequently (Rezaee, 2016). One of the reasons can be, to start with, the fact that there are no standard definitions for them (Montiel & Delgado-Ceballos, 2014).

Bansal and Song (2017) affirm that CSR in its origins is based on the morality of business management, evolving in a second stage towards considering the social impact of the activity of the company in relation to its economic benefit. On the other hand, CS, which was originally based on the limits of growth, evolved in a second stage towards considering the environmental impact of the company in relation to its economic benefit. However, at present, there is a strong conceptual convergence partly due to the following reasons:

1. Both concepts now consider the economic, social and environmental dimensions as key elements in business strategy. Therefore, constructs associated with responsibility and sustainability, in certain research contexts, are interchangeable and perceived as equivalent.
2. In both cases the relationship between the company and the society is considered, analyzing the issues for which the company is responsible.
3. They agree on the importance of assessing the non-financial performance of the company, the role of senior management in responsible and sustainable business practices and the need to be accountable to stakeholders and the social context.
4. The measures used to investigate both concepts are usually very similar (although, perhaps by trajectory, CSR gives more relevance to the variables of the social dimension and CS to those of the environmental dimension).

Stakeholders have an important participation in the construction of CSR related initiatives as well as in the creation of CS initiatives. The demands of stakeholders on companies, such as good corporate governance, transparency on the origin of products and their production process, responsibilities on the impact on society and the environment, or reporting on environmental impact, are related to how companies "aligning their activities with the principles of sustainable development" (Keeble, Topiol, & Berkeley, 2003, p.149). Thus, for CS to be part of sustainable development, it is necessary to involve in the decisions of the organization, not only the external stakeholders, but also the management of the company, so that they can create value correctly and develop a suitable business strategy (Schaltegger & Wagner, 2006). In the end, this is because the sustainable development agenda includes a large number of aspects for which the company is responsible (Keeble et al., 2003).

But, apart from the relationship with stakeholders, is CSR also related to achieving sustainable development? As it turns out, some authors use the concept of CSR as a business tool to contribute to sustainable development (e.g., Korhonen, 2003; Larssaether & Nijhof, 2009) making both concepts equivalent in this aspect. However, although both the concept of CSR and that of CS intend to implement the vision of sustainable development at the corporate level, it seems that the second is more appropriate for that mission (Kleine & von Hauff, 2009).

CRITERIA FOR CHOOSING BETWEEN THE CONCEPTS

There are important aspects to consider that allow identifying differences between CSR and CS (Van Marrewijk, 2003). In this section we will analyze these differences to guide the reader on the main keys that make it easier to choose between them. The study of the differences in these concepts, and because they have common elements, will lead to identifying relationships that include complementarity, belonging or divergence between them.

The Environment Dimensions

First of all, CS has been considered in academia traditionally linked to the environmental dimension to a greater extent than CSR. In cases where the concept of CS is discussed, CSR often refers specifically to the area of people and organizations (Van Marrewijk, 2003). Montiel and Delgado-Ceballos (2014, p.6), talking about the uses of CS, indicate that "in top academic journals, 62% of the articles used the CS-related terms to refer to the environmental dimension of sustainability while only 26% refer to CS to include both social and environmental issues. Among articles published in practitioner outlets, we found that 33% of the articles were about environmental sustainability while 60% of them include both social and environmental aspects". However, they note that "Articles analyzing solely social sustainability issues were more rare: 12% in top academic journals, 6% in practitioner journals, and 15% in specialized SEM journals" (p.6). In other words, in CS studies, the environmental dimension tends to always be present, accompanied or not by the social dimension. On the other hand, it seems that CS is seldom intended to deal with the social dimension alone (as it could happen with CSR), but, at least, accompanied by the environmental dimension.

Adaptive Capacity and Long-Term Survival

While companies must ensure short-term economic performance, sustainable practices ensure long-term survival. Therefore, some authors present a relationship between CS and the concept of sustainability as the company's capacity to last (Marsden, 2000). CS can be considered a CSR approach derived from sustainable development, which expands the scope of environmental action, in addition to including the social dimension, as inseparable for the achievement of the company's long-term objectives (Watts & Holme, 2000). Thus, it can be said that the CS is an adaptation of the CSR especially oriented to the paradigm of sustainable development and allows to add, to the scenario drawn by CSR, the variable of continuity in the long term. For example, analyzing the definition of CS provided by Dyllick and Hockerts (2002), which appears in Table 1, the authors Kleine and von Hauff (2009, p.520) state that "corporate sustainability may be regarded explicitly as a sustainability-driven, sub-concept of CSR", so "corporate sustainability should start with the three dimensions of sustainability (economic, ecologic, and social) rather than with the traditional ethical categories such as justice or discourse with stakeholders".

We could say that CS serve to fit environmental and social concerns into the company's operations and its relations with stakeholders by affecting the ability of companies to endure and generate long-term profits (Van Marrewijk, 2003), since it allows the company to strategically adapt to changes in the environment and to consider the complexity of its social context. This would suggest that the part of CSR focused on environmental and social performance is actually a subset of CS (Budsaratragoon & Jitmaneeroj, 2019). According to that, if we assume that CS adds dimensions to CSR to make companies be able to survive in the long term, we can also say that CS is an umbrella concept or construct that covers other related concepts, such as CSR, or also corporate citizenship, ethics, stakeholder, triple bottom line, or stewardship (Gond & Crane, 2010; Strand, 2014). As can be seen in Figure 2, the so-called "main business impacts" of the CS has a greater scope than in the other terms, and may encompass the impacts generated by the other concepts (the concept of *corporate social performance* is described below in this chapter). In the relationships between these concepts, from the perspective of adaptation, CS would be in the highest positions, encompassing the rest.

Stakeholder Management

According to van Marrewijk (2003), (2003, p.102), CRS is related to phenomena such as transparency, stakeholder dialogue and sustainability reporting (the term CSR would have to be reformulated as *corporate social accountability)*, while CS focuses on value creation, environmental management, environmental friendly production systems, human capital management and so forth". In that way, according to stakeholder theory, managers should take into consideration effects and benefits of different stakeholders when making business decisions such as the design of business strategies or action plans (Ng & Rezaee, 2015). CSR promotes policies, according to which, through governance structures and processes for CSR, companies can or should better incorporate stakeholders' interests and requests into their decision-making model, monitor, manage and report on its progress towards better corporate sustainability (Klettner, Clarke, & Boersma, 2014). (Ng y Rezaee, 2015). In other words, CSR is about the commitment of companies with the interaction between company and stakeholders. As Larssaether and Nijhof (2009, p.234) affirm, "responsibility is negotiated in actor networks that may cross the borders between organizations and sectors in society".

However, as Schaltegger and Wagner (2006) say, an excessively oriented approach to meet the expectations of stakeholders in society as a priority objective of CSR could lead to building a parallel organization, separating business interests from external interests, which are non-economic problems and measures non-economic aspects of performance. This parallel or satellite organization is liable to disappear in times of deteriorating economic performance in the company. On the other hand, the CS also makes corporations deal with differing stakeholder demands, continually shifting priorities, and a multitude of alternatives to address sustainability challenges (Searcy, 2012, p.250), which ultimately consist of modulating the impacts that the company generates and its contribution to sustainable development.

Responsibility and Principles of Action vs. Impacts

CSR is related to the way in which companies choose to incorporate the demands of stakeholders in their strategies, and therefore with their principles of action. In other words, "CSR may be concerned with what corporations should do" (Gond & Crane, 2010, p.681). Responsibility and principles affect the entire process, before and after the performance of the company. On the other hand, CS is related as the management and preservation of economic, social and environmental capital (Kleine & von Hauff, 2009), which implies a direct relationship with the management of positive or negative impacts (improvements or deterioration). While CSR principles allow companies to incorporate defensive or reactive strategies that facilitate the increase of regulatory compliance and resource efficiency, "the more progressive stages of corporate sustainability involve strategic proactivity and transformation into a truly sustaining corporation" (Klettner et al., 2014, p.147).

It can be understood that CSR is in the foundations of business initiatives in each company, and that ultimately derive in its impacts. It is linked to the moral principles that underpin the decisions of companies, that is, with the origin of the actions of companies and the impacts that generate or, in other words, it is the ethical motivation and legitimacy to address sustainability issues (Schaltegger & Burritt, 2010). According to this statement, CSR would be integrated into the early stages of the CS process, and CS is the final result or desired objectives for the company. As Curran (2009, p,.8) mentions, "Sustainable practices [...] allow for satisfactory outcomes for humans and the environment while fulfilling the social and economic needs of current and future generations." It seems reasonable to assess, beyond the intentions of the companies, the actions and the results of them. CS means having a record of the impacts generated, and therefore of all externalities caused by the firm, and that affect sustainable development, through a full-cost accounting (Atkinson, 2000). This vision of the management of CS is not compatible with the creation of parallel structures as was proposed for the case of CSR, since the externalities generated in terms of sustainability cannot be compensated in the company, but must be avoided or internalized. In the CS, responsibility appears all along the business process, accounting for the results.

Figure 1. Balance between dimensions in sustainability
Source: Curran (2009, p.8)

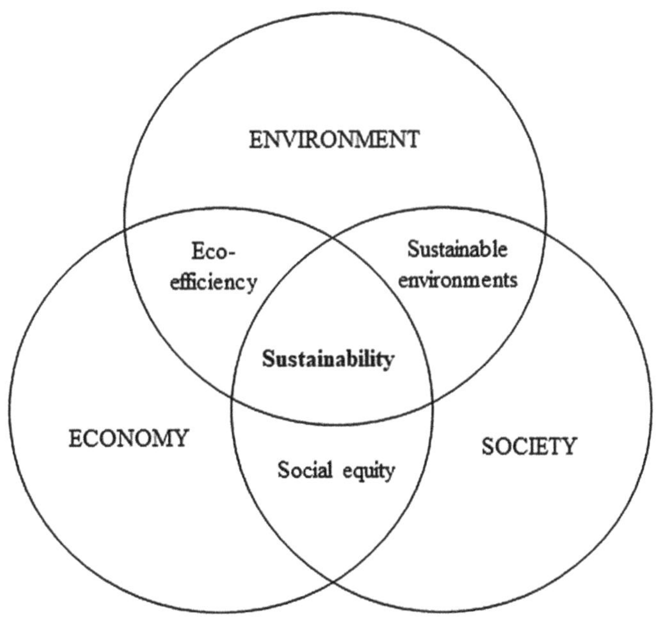

In order to solve in CSR what is related to the impacts generated, during the decade of the eighties and nineties the concepts social responsiveness and corporate social performance (CSP) were developed. The CSP is a concept related to what companies actually do, not what they pose or propose, and the degree to which they do so, i.e., a capture of the actions, the social role and the societal impacts of corporations (Gond & Crane, 2010). It can be defined as "a set of descriptive categorizations of business activity, focusing on the impacts and outcomes for society, stakeholders and the firm" (Wood, 2010, p.54). It is equivalent to the capture at a point in time of the aggregate of the social performance of a company (Barnett, 2007). Conceptually, it refers to both the volume of effort devoted to achieving socially responsible performance and the quality of that performance. This concept comes to compensate for the vacuum (which the CS does resolve), since it gives the CSR a structure, allowing to identify and evaluate the responsibilities of the company, and test results obtained and impacts generated in individuals, stakeholders, company and the company itself (Wood, 2010). In short, it makes it easier to solve the question of the measurement of CSR, which is difficult to measure because it consists of a set of principles or motivation for the social performance of companies (Carroll, 1979). It is striking that academically it has been necessary to identify an accessory concept to CSR to cover the aspects of impacts generated that CS itself already considers.

The Systemic Approach

Due to the approach of satisfaction of different stakeholder groups, researchers in CSR or corporate social performance (CSP) typically analyze the social outcome (including or not the environmental dimension) and the economic outcome separately, while in the case of CS there is an interrelationship between its three components (economic, environmental and social). It can be said that, in those studies on CSR in which a balance between its social and environmental dimensions is analyzed (see Figure 1), the approach used is CS (Montiel, 2008). CS considers the company's ability to interact with its environment, as embedded in a system. Therefore, research in CS implies questioning growth as an objective of the company, considering the existing natural limits to such growth, what leads to the argument that the economic results do not make sense if the company does not respect the system in which it is included (Bansal & Song, 2017). In short, investigating CS involves investigating how firms contribute to outcomes at the level of the systems in which they are nested" (Meuer et al., 2019, p.3).

Criteria for Choosing the Right Concept

Bansal and DesJardine (2014) list some differences that they identify between CSR and CS, and that position the latter as, apparently, the desirable option. The first is that the CS is proposed as an investment that requires a return or compensation in the long term, while the CRS consists of good shares for society and the company, which make the latter a *good business* that generates shared value and wins-wins situations between the company and the society, without expecting compensation. Second, the CSR comes from the combination of, sometimes, conflicting demands from different stakeholders, internal and external, based on moral and ethical aspects, and that can generate lines of action that are far from the company's strategy. The CS considers the interactions in the system that includes the company and the macro system, without moral imperatives (right or wrong), but from a perspective of quantitative analysis and consequences. Third, the CSR encourages business to reconcile economic and social objectives, but the pursuit of social legitimacy can sometimes lead to superficial measures that seek to compensate in some way for insurmountable social or environmental impacts generated by business activity (such as environmental degradation or changes in social customs). In addition, the search for shared value, with possibly accelerated returns to generate social well-being, can put at risk the long-term sustainability of the system, accelerating also its deterioration. In fact, actions of, for example, philanthropy or donations do not ensure the sustainability of systems in the long term as they do not solve the basic problems or pose continuity over time. In contrast, sustainable practices align organizations with

Figure 2. Concept map linking CSR, CSP, CS and BS
Source: Own elaboration

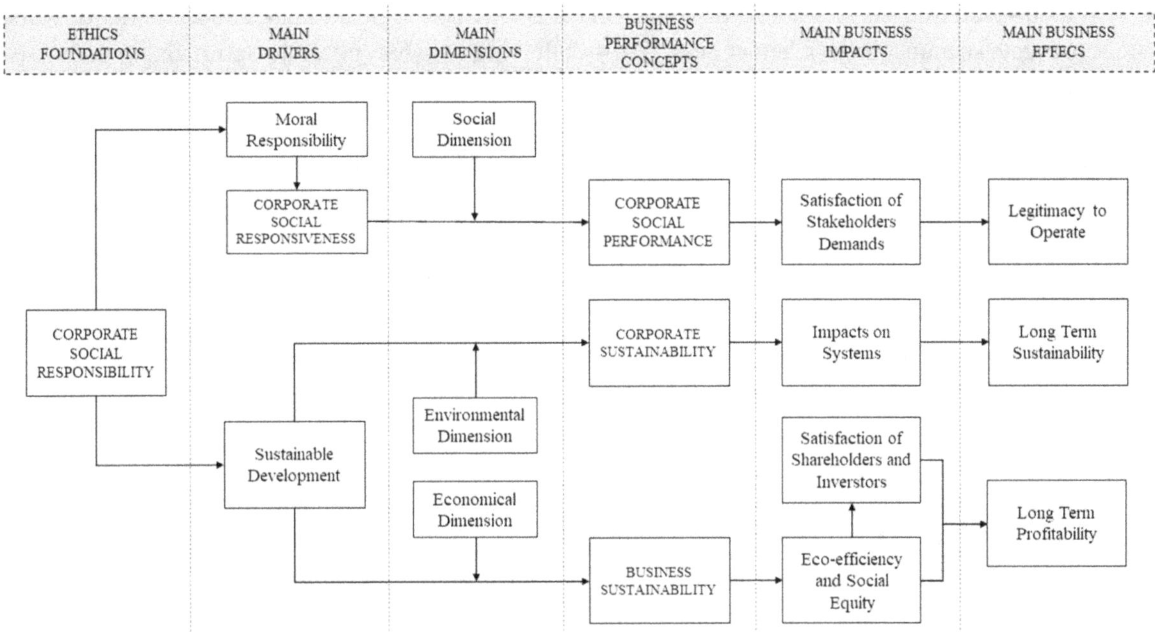

their systems over time. These practices are often flexible and modular, so the company can adapt more quickly to environmental change.

Table 3. Key questions depending on the approach

Responsibility Based on Ethical Principles	Sustainability Based on Systems Science
What is the purpose of business?	What is sustainability across different levels of analysis?
How should business pursue this purpose?	How can systems remain stable, while permitting change?
How do business choose?	What triggers systems disruptions?

Source: Bansal y Song (2017)

Table 3 shows some questions that clearly depend on the research approach desired. That guide the researcher on which to choose, between responsibility and sustainability, depending on the type of questions he or she wants to ask. Beyond these issues, the following are some aspects of CS that could justify that choice:

- CS further entails a long-term and, somehow, endless perspective (Kiron, Kruschwitz, Haanaes, & Reeves, 2015).
- It is a more progressive concept, and involves proactivity and real transformation in the company (Klettner et al., 2014).

- Gives a greater and indisputable value to the environmental dimension, eliminating the doubt about its inclusion in the studies to be carried out.
- It focuses on impacts and not on principles. That is why it is logical to talk about a better or worse corporate sustainability (Klettner et al., 2014), allowing to assess possible optimization processes.
- It is a final goal that CS seeks a balance in the Triple Bottom Line, considering CSR as an initial or intermediate stage of the process (Van Marrewijk, 2003).
- It values future effects, linked to the concept of sustainable development (Van Marrewijk, 2003), meeting the needs of the present without compromising the ability of future generations to meet their own needs (World Commission on Environment and Development, 1987).
- Allows to consider a fourth dimension related to corporate governance (Budsaratragoon & Jitmaneeroj, 2019; Ng & Rezaee, 2015).
- Due to the contribution to sustainable development, it is understood that there is a linkage with a larger set of stakeholders due to the potential impact of business performance (Ng & Rezaee, 2015).

The benefits generated by CS are related to economic results, while considering the ethical or moral arguments of CSR in decision-making. This includes benefits derived from compliance, industry reputation, freedom of action, the improvement of corporate performance and corporate competitiveness and fit within the sustainable development of the economy and society. That requires an accounting system (Schaltegger & Burritt, 2010). It can be said, therefore, that CSR is embedded in the core of CS, while the latter focuses on impacts and profits generated by the company: they would be two sides of the same coin. In a middle point between ethical principles and impacts on the sustainable development of the system, one can find the instrumental perspective of the concept of business sustainability (BS), focused on the optimization of business results and long-term survival. The Table 4 shows important aspects to consider in order to understand the role of these three concepts in the academic literature and to choose with more criteria the most appropriate approach depending on the type of research to be carried out.

Figure 3 shows the relative positioning of these three concepts taking as a reference the systemic approach to impacts (Bansal & Song, 2017) in the dimensions of the triple bottom line perspective. The CS appears as an umbrella concept (Strand, 2014) that encompasses both the BS (with a more economic orientation) and the CSR (with an orientation towards accountability to the societal environment). In the most extreme positions appear, on one hand, companies that seek profit maximization as the main means of societal contribution (see Friedman, 1963), as well as, on the other hand, entities of a philanthropic nature, such as non-profit entities, for which economic results are not objective. The RSC can encompass, in certain circumstances, philanthropic-type initiatives (e.g., Amaeshi et al., 2016), which move away from the search for balances in the three dimensions and which can lead to the existence of the parallel structures inside companies, as mentioned above (Schaltegger & Wagner, 2006). The BS can be used as an instrumental means to achieve better financial results in the company (Pojasek, 2007), and its initiatives may disappear if the companies perceive that they do not generate an economic benefit for the companies.

Table 4. Criteria for choosing the right concept

		Corporate Social Responsibility	Business Sustainability	Corporative Sustainability
Origins and foundations	Roots of the concept	Ethical: Moral obligations of business and managers.	Economics: find the balance that optimizes profits.	Scientific: Managing systems for sustainable development.
	Foundational dimensions	Economic and social	Economic, social and environmental	Economic and environmental
	Theoretical home	Moral theory, welfare economics, theology	Environmental and social management	Ecology, development economics
Structure	Economic dimension is	Balanced with social and environmental ones	A dimension separated from the others	Embedded as part of the benefits of sustainability
	Contribution to sustainable development	Considered through some stakeholders.	Conditioned by economic performance	Essential at all levels.
	Priority stakeholders	Wide range of stakeholders	Shareholders	Shareholders and other stakeholders
Business management decisions	Management approaches	Deciding proper morale (principles and motivation)	Balance impacts to ensure economic outcomes	Assess the appropriate level of impact and performance (tools and processes)
	Management foundation	Good intentions (principles)	Profitability in long-term (survival)	Good impacts (results)
	Main police	Incorporating economic, legal, ethical, and philanthropic responsibilities into decision making	Adopt corporate sustainability standards to optimize the value of the company (attract investment) and financial results	Minimize negative impacts and maximize positive to survive over time
Actual and future research orientations	Research purpose	Justifying, prescribing	Predicting, identifying causality	Describing, explaining.
	Relevant literature	Normative stakeholder theory	Instrumental stakeholder theory, resource-based view	Paradox, systems theory, descriptive stakeholder theory
	Study perspective	Ethics/moral and principles of action	Resources and capabilities	Impacts on the system
	Level of study	Individuals, stakeholders, corporations	Stakeholders, corporations	Corporations
	Assumptions in researching	The company must meet the requirements of stakeholders: corporate profits are to serve society	The incorporation of sustainable paradigms in the company improves its economic performance	The company must take care of the three types of performance: systems are interconnected, so every system impacts on the others
	Research question	What is the moral responsibility of managers and firms to society and environment?	What are the strategic decisions in social and environmental aspects that improve company's outcomes?	What are the connections and interdependencies of economics, society and environment?

Source: Own elaboration, based on Bansal y Song (2017)

CONCLUSION

The lack of clarity on the concept of CS makes it difficult to understand how companies can incorporate these practices effectively in their activities (Meuer et al., 2019), as well as proposing appropriate research on the subject. But beyond understanding the concept, the differences between it and the concept of CSR, intimately related with CS in recent decades, must be clear. The level of relationship between the two is so strong that for some academics they are considered equivalent concepts.

In this chapter we have analyzed the fundamental differences in the academic use and understanding of the concepts of CSR, CS and also BS. Figure 2 summarizes the most important relationships between these terms. This figure allows, visually, to understand the proposal according to which CSR is at the origin of the development process of the other concepts, which derive in different types of impacts and business results. Table 4 collects the most important features of these concepts and organizes it in a schematic manner to facilitate their understanding and application for designing a research plan. Both main concepts, CS and CSR, allow research on the triple balance between the social, economic and environmental dimensions. The choice of one or the other depends on the approach to be taken in each study and the aspects to be incorporated into it. Choosing an appropriate theoretical framework is an important starting point. For example, CS focus mainly on the evaluation of the impacts of business activ-

Figure 3. Positioning map according to the type of impacts
Source: Own elaboration

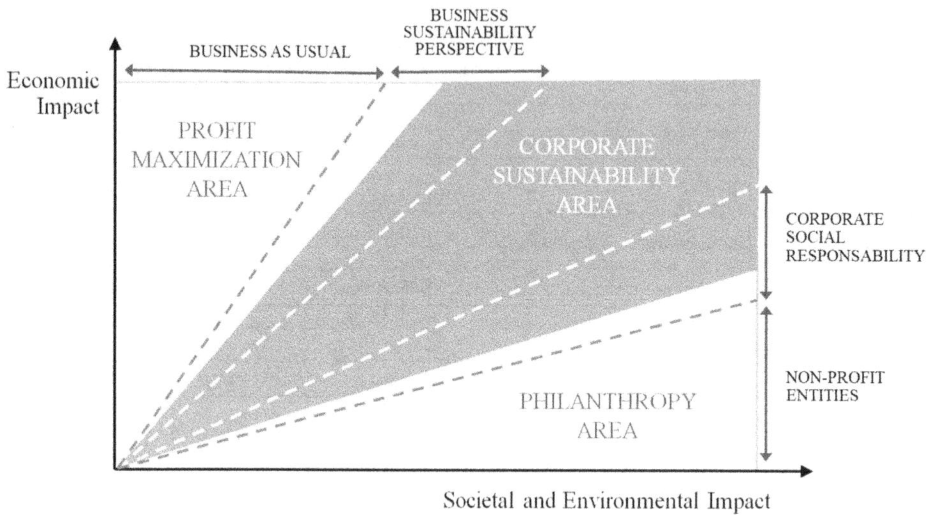

ity on the systems in which it operates and its focus is mainly descriptive from a scientific perspective. However, a possible and excessive corporate approach on efficient lean operations that save materials, energy, and money, from a production or operations point of view (closer to the concept of business or financial sustainability), it would justify the usefulness of CSR in the guiding principles that channel the companies' lines of action for "integrating the environmental, economic, and social imperatives of their activities, resembling the concept of the triple bottom line" (Curran, 2009, p.10). In many scenarios of analysis, both concepts could be presented as complementary.

If a researcher want to focus on only one of the three dimensions, from the perspective of CS, specific labels that identify the dimension considered, such as "corporate environmental sustainability", "corporate social sustainability" or "corporate economic sustainability", can help to minimize ambiguity in the use of terms (Montiel & Delgado-Ceballos, 2014). The use of "corporate social sustainability" could be particularly confusing. Researchers should be especially careful in the description of the scope of the term, since, as discussed above, the analysis of the exclusive social dimension seems something traditionally characteristic of CSR.

The choice of CS or CSR should take into account the nature of the sustainability, especially oriented to system impacts and effects over time, or of the responsibility, ethically oriented and the inclusion of stakeholders in business strategy decision-making. A special interest in analyzing the economic results of the application of sustainable paradigms in business strategy, would be more oriented to the BS approach and its instrumental perspective. In terms of business management and practitioners' publications, the scenario can be even more confusing. For example, SRI rating agencies use sustainability information provided by companies (through reports) to conduct comparative analyses of the sustainability performance of companies, which in most cases are listed on the stock markets. This information is of interest to investors and shareholders. By means of best practice benchmarks by sector, these analyses serve to assign companies a *sustainability score*, which can improve the valuation of its shares and determine their potential financial performance (Van den Brink & van der Woerd, 2004). In these cases, reporting is related to corporate governance and accountability, and corporate transparency mechanisms (Brennan

& Solomon, 2008). The key is to identify the type of stakeholders to which the company is accountable (in this case mainly investors and shareholders).

Managers had agency, and their decisions influence the way the company will create and distribute value, affecting aspects such as labor standards, product quality, human rights, society welfare, and even exploitation or not of indigenous people (Bansal & Song, 2017). CSR emphasizes the moral responsibilities of companies and the rules that guide their behavior (Meuer et al., 2019). The corporate social performance (CSP) construct, very close conceptually to CSR and which incorporates aspects of business impacts, was shifted in theoretical debates as well as in empirical work, while CSR has once more become the predominant concept in the field (De Bakker, Groenewegen, & Den Hond, 2005). Gond and Crane (2010, p.691) stated that "with CSP at such a critical juncture in its development, is it possible that it can be reformulated in a more constructive, durable, and researchable way, or is any such attempt ultimately doomed?" The disappearance of interest in the CSP may be because everything related to business impacts on society and the environment became linked exclusively to the concept of CS, the latter becoming an object of attention. The industry probably boosted the use of the term by the best reception it had among its stakeholders, notably sensitized by the environmental crisis so present in the current social agenda. Another aspect that probably has boosted the adoption of CS in the industry is the greater facility to propose measurement instruments that visualize the corporate performance in terms of impacts (e.g. GRI). That can be reflected in comparative reports and rankings of sustainable business performance (e.g. SRI indexes) that do not take into account the ethical motivations or values that underpin the impacts.

In short, although a key aspect in the differentiation between corporate social responsibility and corporate sustainability can be the orientation towards ethics or impacts respectively, the researchers choosing between the two concepts should take into account other issues. This chapter compiles, in a comparative way, a large number of them. It also considers business sustainability as another specific concept which creates confusion in the literature that studies the impact and relationship of the company with its environment. It looks like that, when considering instrumental perspectives, the possibility of using the BS approach comes into play. This text helps authors to properly specify the scope and perspectives of the construct to be used, contributing to a more efficient approach to research. It can also help stop the increasing confusion in the literature about the use and understanding of all these terms.

REFERENCES

Amaeshi, K., Adegbite, E., Ogbechie, C., Idemudia, U., Kan, K. A. S., Issa, M., & Anakwue, O. I. (2016). Corporate social responsibility in SMEs: A shift from philanthropy to institutional works? *Journal of Business Ethics*, *138*(2), 385–400. doi:10.100710551-015-2633-1

Atkinson, G. (2000). Measuring corporate sustainability. *Journal of Environmental Planning and Management*, *43*(2), 235–252. doi:10.1080/09640560010694

Bansal, P., & DesJardine, M. R. (2014). Business sustainability: It is about time. *Strategic Organization*, *12*(1), 70–78. doi:10.1177/1476127013520265

Bansal, P., & Song, H. (2017). Similar but not the same: Differentiating corporate sustainability from corporate responsibility. *The Academy of Management Annals*, *11*(1), 105–149. doi:10.5465/annals.2015.0095

Barnett, M. L. (2007). Stakeholder influence capacity and the variability of financial returns to corporate social responsibility. *Academy of Management Review*, *32*(3), 794–816. doi:10.5465/amr.2007.25275520

Brennan, N. M., & Solomon, J. (2008). Corporate governance, accountability and mechanisms of accountability: An overview. *Accounting, Auditing & Accountability Journal*, *21*(7), 885–906. doi:10.1108/09513570810907401

Budsaratragoon, P., & Jitmaneeroj, B. (2019). Measuring causal relations and identifying critical drivers for corporate sustainability: The quadruple bottom line approach. *Measuring Business Excellence*.

Cai, L., Cui, J., & Jo, H. (2016). Corporate environmental responsibility and firm risk. *Journal of Business Ethics*, *139*(3), 563–594. doi:10.100710551-015-2630-4

Carroll, A. B. (1979). A three-dimensional conceptual model of corporate performance. *Academy of Management. the Academy of Management Review*, *4*(4), 497–505. doi:10.5465/amr.1979.4498296

Christofi, A., Christofi, P., & Sisaye, S. (2012). Corporate sustainability: Historical development and reporting practices. *Management Research Review*.

Curran, M. A. (2009). Wrapping our brains around sustainability. *Sustainability*, *1*(1), 5–13.

De Bakker, F. G., Groenewegen, P., & Den Hond, F. (2005). A bibliometric analysis of 30 years of research and theory on corporate social responsibility and corporate social performance. *Business & Society*, *44*(3), 283–317. doi:10.1177/0007650305278086

Deloitte & Touche. (1992). Business strategy for sustainable development: Leadership and accountability for the 90s. IISD.

Dyllick, T., & Hockerts, K. (2002). Beyond the business case for corporate sustainability. *Business Strategy and the Environment*, *11*(2), 130–141. doi:10.1002/bse.323

Elkington, J. (1997). *Cannibals with forks*. Capstone.

European Commission. (2001). *Green paper. promoting a european framework for corporate social responsibility*. European Commission.

Friedman, M. (1963). *Capitalism and freedom*. University of Chicago Press.

Gladwin, T. N., Kennelly, J. J., & Krause, T. (1995). Shifting paradigms for sustainable development: Implications for management theory and research. *Academy of Management Review*, *20*(4), 874–907. doi:10.5465/amr.1995.9512280024

Gond, J., & Crane, A. (2010). Corporate social performance disoriented: Saving the lost paradigm? *Business & Society*, *49*(4), 677–703. doi:10.1177/0007650308315510

Huang, X., & Watson, L. (2015). Corporate social responsibility research in accounting. *Journal of Accounting Literature*, *34*, 1–16. doi:10.1016/j.acclit.2015.03.001

Keeble, J. J., Topiol, S., & Berkeley, S. (2003). Using indicators to measure sustainability performance at a corporate and project level. *Journal of Business Ethics*, *44*(2-3), 149–158. doi:10.1023/A:1023343614973

Kiron, D., Kruschwitz, N., Haanaes, K., & Reeves, M. (2015). Joining forces: Collaboration and leadership for sustainability. *MIT Sloan Management Review*, *56*(3).

Kleine, A., & von Hauff, M. (2009). Sustainability-driven implementation of corporate social responsibility: Application of the integrative sustainability triangle. *Journal of Business Ethics*, *85*(S3), 517–533. doi:10.100710551-009-0212-z

Klettner, A., Clarke, T., & Boersma, M. (2014). The governance of corporate sustainability: Empirical insights into the development, leadership and implementation of responsible business strategy. *Journal of Business Ethics*, *122*(1), 145–165. doi:10.100710551-013-1750-y

Korhonen, J. (2003). Should we measure corporate social responsibility? *Corporate Social Responsibility and Environmental Management*, *10*(1), 25–39. doi:10.1002/csr.27

Labuschagne, C., Brent, A. C., & Van Erck, R. P. (2005). Assessing the sustainability performances of industries. *Journal of Cleaner Production*, *13*(4), 373–385. doi:10.1016/j.jclepro.2003.10.007

Larssaether, S., & Nijhof, A. (2009). Moral landscapes–understanding agency in corporate responsibility initiatives. *Corporate Social Responsibility and Environmental Management*, *16*(4), 228–236. doi:10.1002/csr.205

Lockett, A., Moon, J., & Visser, W. (2006). Corporate social responsibility in management research: Focus, nature, salience and sources of influence. *Journal of Management Studies*, *43*(1), 115–136. doi:10.1111/j.1467-6486.2006.00585.x

Lubin, D. A., & Esty, D. C. (2010). The sustainability imperative. *Harvard Business Review*, *88*(5), 42–50.

Marsden, C. (2000). The new corporate citizenship of big business: Part of the solution to sustainability? *Business and Society Review*, *105*(1), 8–25. doi:10.1111/0045-3609.00062

Meuer, J., Koelbel, J., & Hoffmann, V. H. (2019). On the nature of corporate sustainability. *Organization & Environment*, *33*(3), 319–341. doi:10.1177/1086026619850180

Montiel, I. (2008). Corporate social responsibility and corporate sustainability: Separate pasts, common futures. *Organization & Environment*, *21*(3), 245–269. doi:10.1177/1086026608321329

Montiel, I., & Delgado-Ceballos, J. (2014). Defining and measuring corporate sustainability: Are we there yet? *Organization & Environment*, *27*(2), 113–139. doi:10.1177/1086026614526413

Ng, A. C., & Rezaee, Z. (2015). Business sustainability performance and cost of equity capital. *Journal of Corporate Finance*, *34*, 128–149. doi:10.1016/j.jcorpfin.2015.08.003

Pojasek, R. B. (2007). A framework for business sustainability. *Environmental Quality Management*, *17*(2), 81–88. doi:10.1002/tqem.20168

Rezaee, Z. (2016). Business sustainability research: A theoretical and integrated perspective. *Journal of Accounting Literature*, *36*, 48–64. doi:10.1016/j.acclit.2016.05.003

Schaltegger, S., & Burritt, R. L. (2010). Sustainability accounting for companies: Catchphrase or decision support for business leaders? *Journal of World Business*, *45*(4), 375–384. doi:10.1016/j.jwb.2009.08.002

Schaltegger, S., & Wagner, M. (2006). Integrative management of sustainability performance, measurement and reporting. *International Journal of Accounting. Auditing and Performance Evaluation*, *3*(1), 1–19. doi:10.1504/IJAAPE.2006.010098

Searcy, C. (2012). Corporate sustainability performance measurement systems: A review and research agenda. *Journal of Business Ethics*, *107*(3), 239–253. doi:10.100710551-011-1038-z

Sharma, S., & Henriques, I. (2005). Stakeholder influences on sustainability practices in the canadian forest products industry. *Strategic Management Journal*, *26*(2), 159–180. doi:10.1002mj.439

Simões, C., & Sebastiani, R. (2017). The nature of the relationship between corporate identity and corporate sustainability: Evidence from the retail industry. *Business Ethics Quarterly*, *27*(3), 423–453. doi:10.1017/beq.2017.15

Strand, R. (2014). Strategic leadership of corporate sustainability. *Journal of Business Ethics*, *123*(4), 687–706. doi:10.100710551-013-2017-3

Van den Brink, T. W. M., & van der Woerd, F. (2004). Industry specific sustainability benchmarks: An ECSF pilot bridging corporate sustainability with social responsible investments. *Journal of Business Ethics*, *55*(2), 187–203. doi:10.100710551-004-1901-2

Van Marrewijk, M. (2003). Concepts and definitions of CSR and corporate sustainability: Between agency and communion. *Journal of Business Ethics*, *44*(2/3), 95–105. doi:10.1023/A:1023331212247

Watts, P., & Holme, L. (2000). *Corporate social responsibility: Making good business sense.* World Business Council for Sustainable Development.

Wilson, M. (2003). Corporate sustainability: What is it and where does it come from. *Ivey Business Journal*, *67*(6), 1–5.

Wood, D. J. (2010). Measuring corporate social performance: A review. *International Journal of Management Reviews*, *12*(1), 50–84. doi:10.1111/j.1468-2370.2009.00274.x

World Commission on Environment and Development. (1987). *Our common future*. United Nations.

ENDNOTES

1 The authors do not indicate the page where the quotation is located.

2 In this case, the authors consider the concepts of business sustainability and corporate sustainability as equivalent concepts.

Chapter 4
An Entrepreneur Sees the Reward:
The Importance of Intellectual Capital and Corporate Social Responsibility in a Company

Zeynep Merve Ünal
https://orcid.org/0000-0003-4927-3117
Istanbul Gelisim University, Turkey

ABSTRACT

The aim of this chapter is to advance the understanding of how social entrepreneurs analyze and apply intellectual capital and corporate social responsibility within their companies. From the extensive literature review, the broad definitions of intellectual capital, and corporate social responsibility, the measurement models and the management of intellectual capital and the development process of corporate social responsibility were identified. Modern, socio-economic, philanthropic, and classical views were taken into consideration to explain corporate social responsibility in detail. In order to develop holistic understanding, the relationship between intellectual capital and corporate social responsibility on the basis of entrepreneur were analyzed. The understanding of the intellectual capital and corporate social responsibility in companies were shown by theoretical framework of resource-based view, dynamic capabilities, stakeholder theory, and legitimacy theory.

INTRODUCTION

In today's business life, creativity and innovation are two superior necessities that every organization must have. These two factors are seen as basic needs for entrepreneurs to compete and create quality in market. One of the most important characteristics of entrepreneurs is creativity embraces knowledge, personal equipment and competency. Knowledge is perceived as inevitable need for organizations rather than solely a data. This need has turned information-based capital into crucial topic when organizations

DOI: 10.4018/978-1-7998-4833-2.ch004

has realized the power of knowledge and its return on investment. It can be said that there is a chain relationship between information and knowledge. In order to understand this relation there is a classic noise example. The noises such as noise of the wind or patter of rain that someone hears are data, but meaning can be given to those noises through information. Structured and organized information generate knowledge that is laid up at the cognitive system of individuals. Knowledge is considered as the basis value creation. The success of using knowledge might be measured by its own contribution. Within an organization perspective, knowledge is analyzed as a dimension of intellectual capital. Intellectual capital can be defined as the value of intangible assets and their added value create dynamic factor that they do not take a part in organization's balance sheet. Dynamic ability of an organization and intellectual capital are significantly related (Teece, Pisano & Shuen, 1997; Eisenhardt & Martin, 2000).

Human being has been making an effort to fulfill their needs and to master nature since its existence. Through the occurrence of this effort, the fulfillment of individual needs and demand saturation have been actualized. In addition to meeting the customer demands, the quality of goods and services or customer satisfaction, community service or contribution are purposes of entrepreneurs. These purposes might be divided into two parts: community service and consumer service. While community service contributes to the financial and social development of community; consumer service focuses on needs fulfillment of consumer segment. Corporate social responsibility focuses on the certain voluntarily behaviors or actions to meet various stakeholders' needs or expectations (Peloza & Shang, 2011). For example, CEO Elon Musk declared that Tesla Inc. would allow individuals and organizations in order to use its patents in 2014. This action reflects benefiting from projects that include advanced technologies.

Social responsibilities that focalizes social benefit make significant contribution to organizations for being highly competitive, having good image and reputation, having loyal customers, committed employees, recruitment of competent candidates, government incentives and cost reduction. Within the social sector, social entrepreneurship has gained attention in several countries. Primarily, they adopt to serve a social mission (Luke & Chu, 2013) and are appeared in the bipolar of the hybrid structure as follows non-profit (i.e., public) and for-profit (i.e., private) organizations. While public sector organization focuses on the benefits of public, private sector organization prioritizes the forces of market to increase their return on investment. Since social entrepreneurship does not fit the arrangements between public and private organizations, social entrepreneurs suggest a hybrid organizational structure as a prime example (Pache & Santos, 2012). The justification of hybrid structure is guided by the social impact as well as financial gain. Social enterprises survive through transactions to financially sustain their mission activities.

Organizations has engaged attention that human does not only contribute physically but also mentally to organizations that they work in. The impacts of knowledge and resource-based views (RBV) showed that organizations have valuable and rare resources that are hard to imitate and substitute (Barney, 1991). The resources are *all assets, capabilities, organizational processes, firm attributes, information, and knowledge controlled by firms* (Barney, 1991, p. 101). These resources generate competitive advantage for the organizations where intellectual capital, organizational performance and values are created. RBV is a theoretical model to explain the competitive advantage of resources. The availability of resources eases the product and service development through strategic management of the companies. The RBV embraces the relationship between company's strategy and its internal sources relying on *value, rareness, imperfect imitability, non-substitutability* (VRIN) framework. *Value* indicates the creative power of tangible and intangible assets on sustainable value. *Rareness* refers to resources that are unique and hardly accessible. *Imperfect imitability* arises when inimitable resources accomplish one or combinations of three circumstances: (a) resource obtaining ability of the firm is related with its unique historical conditions, (b) the relation between firm's carried resources and firm's sustained competitive advantage is causally ambiguous, or (c) the resource bringing out a firm's advantage is socially complex (Barney, 1991). *Non-Substitutability* is the source of competitive advantage that firms have discrete resources. Some scholars extended the scope of RBV to the dynamic market to determine how some firms can survive and sustain the competitiveness and organizational growth in a rapidly changing and unpredictable market. The concept of dynamic Capabilities (DCs) emerged (Eisenhardt & Martin, 2000; Wu, Lin & Hsu, 2007; Chien & Tsai, 2012). DC is defined as a firm's responses to constantly changing environment through integrating, reconfiguring and renewing its resources and capabilities and, above all upgrading and reconstructing its core capabilities to acquire and sustain competitive advantage. Zahra et al. (2006) argue that dynamic capabilities might be framed through the eyes of entrepreneurs as reconfiguring resources and routines of organizational capabilities by vision of decision makers. For instance, entrepreneurs deal quickly with conflict in decision making process or response timely to customer complaint.

Entrepreneurs might empower their core competencies through making investment in intellectual capital and philanthropic responsibilities. Findings showed that dynamic capabilities have positive contribution on intellectual capital as the output of dynamic capabilities (Wendra, Sule, Joeliaty & Azis, 2019; Ambrosini & Bowman, 2009; Koryak et al., 2015). The findings of the studies imply that dynamic capabilities might renew the knowledge assets in the organization.

The purpose of this chapter is to develop a literature review on CSR and IC conceptualization and summarize previous research findings of the relationship between CSR and IC for social entrepreneurs so that they can acquire necessary information based on what intellectual capital is and how it can be enhanced to internalize corporate social responsibility. The topics are strengthened by current examples.

Intellectual Capital

From the ancient times, information and its importance have been taken a place as human need. Intellectual capital that is in every aspect of life, but might be unforeseen has been become the main topic from the 1960s through researches known as ''*shop fame*'' *and includes all the intangible assets of the organization and appears in its budget* (Sullivan, 2001, p. 23). In 1990s, management of organizations focused on intellectual or intangible capital as true assets to have competitive and successful organization rather than material resource that creates wealth for organizations. In addition to all these, tangible assets such as; plant, equipment or property are crucial and form important functions for stimulating and enhancing competitive advantage. However, in recent years, organizations have focused on more intangible assets rather than material assets and those companies with sufficient intellectual capital have better chance of survival (Bontis, 2002). Since, these resources are hard to imitate, replicate or develop by competitors (Barney, 1991). *It is a unique ability that the organization excels over its competitors to achieve integration in different skills that individuals possess and which contribute to increasing the value offered to buyers; it is a source of a competitive advantage* (Hamel & Heene, 1994, p. 19).

Organization's competitive advantage can be explained by its DCs. DCs are defined as *the firm's ability to integrate, build, and reconfigure internal and external competences to address rapidly changing environments* (Teece, Pisano, & Suhen, 1997, p. 516). This integration can be achieved by *purposefully creating and extending or modifying its resource base* (Helfat, 2007, p. 1). The concept of dynamic capabilities is an extension of the RBV approach that has seen as crucial to acquire and sustain competitive advantage (Wernerfelt, 1984). RBV suggests that organizations should pay attention to their internal resources than external one. Since the organizations take place in a high level of dynamic environment and turbulence, RBV was evaluated as too static (Priem & Butler, 2001).

In order to produce higher valued set, intellectual capital/material is formalized, captured and leveraged that lead to create wealth (Stewart, 1997). In contemporary IC research, value creation was defined in four ways: *monetary*, *utility*, *social*, and *sustainable value* (Dumay, 2016). While value creation was traditionally shaped based on a shareholder or customer (utility) view (Bourguignon, 2005), the concept of value is extended to involve social and environmental value (Dumay, 2016).

According to Ulrich (1998), intellectual capital makes global entrepreneur while responding to customer's needs and create opportunities to be produced by technology through the set of skills available in the organization. The framework of Teece (2007) highlights three capacities of enterprises: sensing and shaping opportunities, seizing opportunities, managing threats and reconfiguring company assets (Hodgkinson & Healey, 2011). From competitive advantage point of view, there are three rooted capabilities (Prahalad & Hamel, 1990). *Innovation capability* that is acquiring abilities to develop new product and services to catch superior technology. *Production and service capability* is the ability to deliver differentiated product and services to the customer that are affordable, timely, and quality. *Market management capability* involves the marketing and selling abilities of products and services efficiently and effectively (Rangone, 1999).

From this point of view, it was underlined that competitive edge in the market can be achieved by the everything and everyone knows and achieves in the organization (Bontis, 2001). Organizations for Economic Cooperation and Development (OECD) defined two types of intangible assets of the organization: *structural capital, consisting regulatory processes, procedures, technology, intellectual property; human capital within the organization, and clients and suppliers of the organization, including expertise, knowledge and innovation* (Malhotra, 2003, p. 3).

Human capital reflects the capital of human resources including competencies, value of practices, creativity, relationship capacity and values. Human capital also consists of organizational culture and value of the organizations that are roots of innovation and renovation. On the other hand, structural capital reflects the infrastructure of the organization consisting of values and beliefs that enables human capital to function. It generates competitive edge and distinctive identity to an organization (Barney & Stewart, 2000). As Dumay (2016, p. 175) pointed out *when you take away physical capitals of financial, manufactured, and natural capital, the remaining three intangible capitals broadly align with IC's three capitals: human capital with human capital; social and relational capital with relational capital; and IC with structural capital.*

The common points of these definitions consist the notion that intellectual capital is intangible assets of the organizations that include competence, ability, skills, know-how, expertise of the employees and organizations where the external environment, customers and structure of the organization are emphasized. All of them contribute to the organization to increase its market share, enhance its competitive power in the market by perceiving intellectual capital as a holistic approach not at a particular managerial level.

According to Phillips and Phillips (2002) intellectual capital is different from physical capital with respect to its feature, location, sample, returns, wealth pattern, individual workers, the value and strengths and weaknesses-, as seen in Table 1.

Table 1. Differences between physical and intellectual capital

Data	Physical Capital	Intellectual Capital
The core feature	Physical-concrete and perspective	Intangible-ethereal-and invisible
Location	Within company	In the minds of individuals
Sample	Machine	The individual
Returns	Declining	Increasing
Wealth pattern	In resources	Inattention and concentration
Individual workers	Manual workers	Knowledge workers and professionals
The value	Value of use and exchange value	Exchange value when used
Strength and weakness	Aging cycle (weakness)	Self-generating and strengthening cycle (strength)

(Adapted from: Phillips & Phillips, 2002)

The Models of Intellectual Capital

Intellectual capital models have been developing since late 1980's. Firstly, researches have concentrated on managing intangible resources and then the models were expanded by including intellectual capital. The purposes of the models are differentiated that some of them measure intellectual capital for external reporting while others measure intellectual capital to manage intangible and intellectual resources (Alwert, Bornemann, & Will, 2009).

Skandia Navigator

This model has been one of the earliest Skandia model that Assurance and Financial Services (AFS) shared its corporate annual report. The Skandia model showed the value of intellectual capital in Skandia. The measurement of model underlines where human capital impacts the shareholders' structural capital and measures intellectual capital usage by comparing the preceding year. In Skandia model, measurement and comparison of the yearly relative value of intellectual capital is more crucial for organizations than focusing on the bottom-line value of human and intellectual capitals (White, Lee, Yuningsih, Nielsen, & Bukh, 2010).

The Skandia Navigator model gives information about the financial and intellectual perspectives within the organization. The model includes four dimensions of intellectual capital (i.e., human, customer, process and renewal/development dimensions) and then groups intellectual capital with respect to its dimensions in order to convert intellectual capital into financial capital (Skandia, 1999). While human capital includes knowledge, skills and competencies of employees to offer solutions, structural capital consists of reasons to stay in the organization when other employees leave the office. Structural capital embraces the process capital and renewal/development capital that provide opportunities the organization to operate (Skandia, 1999).

Intangible Assets Monitor

The Intangible Assets Monitor (IAM) measures the intangibles assets with the related indicators, and it was developed by Sveiby (2007). The indicators are not specified but identified by organization that applies the model. The aim of IAM is to give detail information about the intangible assets in the organization through monitoring growth, renewal, efficiency and stability. The indicators determine the external and internal structure and competency of the organization (Sveiby, 2007). External, internal structure and competency apply different indicators to concentrate on growth, renewal, efficiency and stability. For instance, growth and renewal in external structure can create customer profit whereas in internal structure can create investment information technology. Growth and renewal in competence can create increase in level of learning organization, training, education. Efficiency in external structure can result in rising of customer satisfaction index whereas in internal structure can result in rising of support staff proportion. Efficiency in competence can create proportion rising of professionals in organization. Additionally, stability in external structure can lead to frequentative customer demands whereas in internal structure can lead to turnover of the staff. Stability in competence can also result in professional turnover (Sveiby, 2007).

Balanced Scorecard

Balance Scorecard (BSC) was developed by Kaplan and Norton (1992) for the purpose of including new intangible assets based measurement for knowledge-based organizations. In other words, BSC measures strategic performance of the organization through focusing on intangible assets. BSC compares the customer processes and human resource management with the strategies of organization. By this way, BSC helps organizations to notice their implementations of strategic goals and objectives (Bose & Thomas, 2007).

BSC model focuses on performance evaluation in organizations. Therefore, *learning and growth* (i.e., creating value through people, systems and organization), *internal processes* (i.e., obligations of the organization to increase in outcome) are two views of BSC model. The current position, vision and mission and necessary actions to achieve the goals are the dimensions of measurement model. According to Kaplan and Norton (1992) BSC model can also be used for innovation processes that create value for business operations. They also added that customer satisfaction, success of retention, acquiring new customers, profitability, competitive market share and success in maintaining profitable relationships are important dimensions to create competitive segments in market. As it can be referred from the above mentioned, BSC model is not only limited for measurement of intellectual capital but also for measurement of overall performance of the organization.

Value Added Intellectual Coefficient

Value Added Intellectual Coefficient (VAIC) method was developed by Pulic (1997) to measure intellectual capital in organizations. VAIC model has similarity with Skandia Navigator on the basis of examination of efficiency in value creation. The indicators of efficiency are taken as human capital efficiency, capital employed efficiency, and structural capital efficiency (Pulic, 2000). Organization's financial report is used for measurement of intellectual capital in the organization. VAIC model concentrates on the volume and effectiveness of IC rather than traditional physical volumes and prices (Pulic, 1997). Kamath (2008) supported the validation of VAIC measurement for intellectual capital. The relationships between dimensions of intellectual capital (i.e., human, structural, physical) and dimensions of company performance (i.e., market value, productivity and profitability) showed that human capital has the greatest impact on productivity and profitability of the companies with respect to VAIC ranking. Another study also confirmed the VAIC measurement in terms of influences of government deregulation and reforms on developing and exploiting IC in banking sector (Deol, 2009).

The Management of Intellectual Capital

Intellectual capital studies have taken attention widely by scholars over decades. Intellectual capital has been treated as intangible asset and strategic asset. Management of intellectual capital offers organizations superior return on investment. Numerous scholars (Bontis, Keow & Richardson, 2000; Edvinsson & Malone, 1997; Martín-de Castro et. al., 2006; Martín-de Castro, 2014) have concentrated on management of intellectual capital and its benefits for organizations. They described intellectual capital as intangible asset that allows the organizational grow and occurrence of competitive advantage. Regarding to this point of view, organizations embraced new perspective that managing and recording their intangible assets in order to enhance its core competencies and organizational knowledge management (Wiig, 1997). Focusing on core competency and core products or services are the sources of maintaining sustainable competitive advantage (Prahalad & Hamel, 1990). Studies have confirmed that management of intangible assets in organizations contribute positively on organization's competitive advantage (Edvinsson & Malone, 1997; Hormiga, Batista-Canino & Sanchez-Medina, 2011). Urban and Joubert (2017) asserted that management of intangible assets underlines the organization's strategies through measurement of human capital, structural capital and relationship capital. Human capital is concerned with employee's intrinsic knowledge that is related with capabilities, skills, experience, creativity and innovation of employees (Edvinsson & Malone, 1998). Knowledge of individuals and skills are crucial elements for innovation (Subramaniam & Youndt, 2005). Therefore, human capital in the organization is valuable assets that turns into organization's property. Structural capital is characterized as organizational assets that are created by employees' knowledge through experience and creativity sharing. So, information technology and databases are structured with the aim of retaining human capital in the organization (Schmidt & Santos, 2002). Relational capital, on the other hand, is considered customer-focused relationship, thus, customer is the most important component of relational capital. Since, the global environment in which competitiveness are dominant force organizations' perspective from product-orientation to customer-orientation. Stewart and Ruckdeschel (1998) highlighted that relational capital is the most valuable intangible assets for organizations since it offers permanent relationship between customers and organizations. It can be inferenced that relational capital aims to develop long-lasting relationship with the stakeholders and organization through using exchange of knowledge between them. An organization in which intellectual capital is valued can gather inimitable competitive advantages in turn can keep stable its current condition in the market longer. Additionally, individuals who work in there will be able to know how to use their intellectual capital that can create value for the organization. Thus, it is clear that management of intellectual capital effectively will create wealth and strategic advantage for the organization.

Intellectual capital, intangible asset, is formed through the structure and cause-effect relationships of the organization. In other words, analyzing the complex structure of the organization or exporting the whole intellectual capital to another organization is not possible. That's why intellectual capital ranks as one of the most important resources within the sustainable competitive advantage of the organizations.

However, the existence of intangible assets does not guarantee that a firm can sustain its core competency. Most of the time, an organization can sustain its core competency when intellectual capital (e.g., intangible assets) are joining with other capabilities and assets (Rumelt, 2011). Hall (1992) classified intellectual capital as ''assets'' (e.g., brand, trademark, contracts, databases) or ''skills'' (e.g., know-how of employees, organizational culture).

Entrepreneurship

Entrepreneurs are considered as the important part of the integral system of sustainability and social responsibility. They *incorporate a triple bottom line approach and consider a wide range of stakeholder interests, including environment and society* (Bocken et al., 2014, p. 42). Entrepreneurs achieve multiple value creation to provide benefit to the larger part of the society. Godelnik and van der Meer (2019) suggested four-category for sustainability-oriented entrepreneurship: ecopreneurship (environmental entrepreneurship), institutional entrepreneurship, sustainable entrepreneurship and social entrepreneurship.

Ecopreneurship emerged from the sustainable business value of 1980s that focuses on environmental problems. The activities of ecopreneurship are listed by Schaper (2010) as (a) entrepreneurial activities, (b) net positive environmental activities (c) intentional activities that their impact is not accidental but deliberate. For instance, in Germany the government has increased the requirements for standards in 1990s. The ''zero energy house'' where the houses produce their own energy as they need. In 2015, the ''plus energy house'' was completed where the house generates more energy than the residents require (See Figure 1).

Figure 1. An Example of the plus energy house
Source: https://www.baufritz.com/en-ch/energy-and-safety/eco-energy-plus-house/plus-energy-house-wriedt/#site

Institutional entrepreneurship embraces the entrepreneurs who are seeking for changing setting of institutions, transformation of society, regulatory and market institutions (Schaltegger & Wagner, 2011). For example, second-hand market (Ebay), e-commerce (Amazon), accommodation (Booking.com), cleaning (Helpling.com) are online platforms that include new digital applications/website in which actors use to develop, provide and use products or services (Gawer & Cusumano, 2014).

Sustainable entrepreneurship focuses on the harmless ecological and social environment entrepreneurial activities (Muñoz & Cohen, 2018) that the benefits from the profits of agriculture, ecotourism or biodiversity products are shared. For example, People Tree is a website that creates eco-friendly fashion and environmental-friendly business idea for customers. People Tree focuses on collections that include organic cotton, wool and is made by hand weaving, hand knitting and hand block painting (See Figure 2).

Figure 2. An example of organic cotton of people tree
Source: https://www.peopletree.co.uk

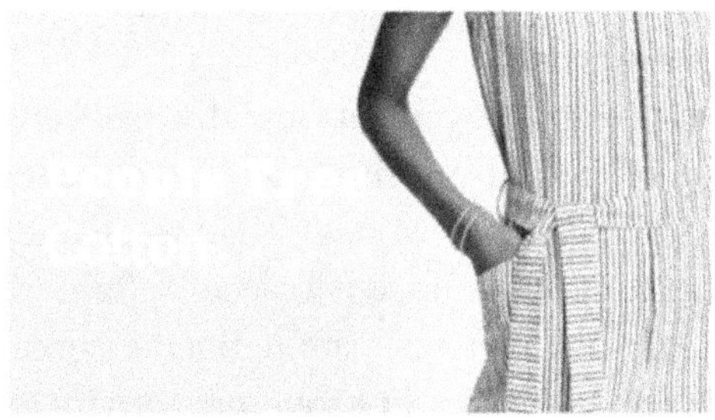

Social entrepreneurship creates systems for social change, develops sustainable solutions to the social problems. Of the four-category, this category is one the most interested type of entrepreneurship that social enterprises' management and performance are investigated (Doherty et al., 2014). Social entrepreneurs look for innovative and valuable solutions for poverty, education, healthcare, global warming and water shortages. For example, Edgar and Joe's Café is a gathering space and food operation in London, Ontario that focuses on increase in employee skills for underemployed groups. It provides a platform to

Figure 3. An example of community coffee program in edgar and Joe's Café
Source: https://edgarandjoes.ca

dialogue, showcase stories and learn/understand mental illness and social disadvantage with a view to breaking down stigma and eliminating attitudinal barriers (See Figure 3).

As it can be seen from the example above, social entrepreneurs develop venture to solve the social problems and to benefit the society. Robinson (2006) highlighted that the process of social entrepreneurship *includes the identification of a specific social problem and a specific solution (or set of solutions) to address it; the evaluation of the social impact, the business model and the sustainability of the venture; and the creation of a social mission-oriented for-profit or a business oriented non-profit entity that pursues the double (or triple) bottom line* (p. 95).

The intended mission creates the difference among traditional entrepreneurship and social entrepreneurship. Social purpose ventures exist with a mission to solve a social problem, but the venture is for-profit and economic effect on market can be seen. Another type of social enterprising non-profits that embrace the principles of social entrepreneurship to earn revenue and sustain their organizations with a mission-oriented approach. This type of entrepreneurship appears in the shape of philanthropy to increase the organization's social impact (Spinelli & Adams, 2012).

In fact, the hybrid arrangements fit more within the domain of social entrepreneurship than social ventures and non-profit social enterprising.

Today, social enterprises are more heterogeneous and diverse, serve various sectors and therefore managed in different ways. Non-profit and for-profit organizations are seen as their sustainable networks. Social enterprises act as hybrids (Mamabolo & Myres, 2019) where they embrace new business models between non-profit and for-profit sectors (Quelin, Kivleniece, & Lazzarini, 2017). Hybrid arrangements with the purpose of economic and social interests are defined as organizational arrangements within the scope of public, social and private spheres of economic activity (Mahoney et al., 2009). Lee and Jay (2015) posited that ''the recent success of hybrid social ventures builds on a generational shift in how business stakeholders perceive and respond to business' relationships with society and the natural environment. This shift allows hybrid social ventures to create economic value through favorable interactions with those stakeholders whose behaviors are guided by sustainability-oriented values'' (p. 128).

Corporate Social Responsibility

Emergence of civilization and the religions have started the evolution of the social responsibility. It can be evidence that the responsibilities of business parties and rights of workers were referred in the Sumerian tablets. Additionally, charity, trade, profit and working conditions were mentioned in religious texts (Yamak, 2007). Before the Industrial Revolution, religion had been taken into consideration in trade and economic activities. Accordingly, responsibilities of businessman and traders to the society were shaped by conscience and religion (Öcal, 2007). With the Industrial Revolution, process of manufacturing relocated to factories, modern business administration and management practices were existed.

In literature, the term of social responsibility is used instead of corporate social responsibility (CSR). The lack of prominence and dominance of corporations in those years might be the reason of the term usage (Carroll, 1999). Bowen's (1953) book of ''Social Responsibility of the Businessman'' drew attention as an early work that mentioned particularly about social responsibility. The book has been regarded as an origin of the modern literature of social responsibility (Carroll, 1979). In his book, social responsibility was defined as businessman obligations for pursuing policies, making decisions, following lines of action that are desirable in terms of the objectives and values of our society (Bowen, 1953). After the shifting of the social responsibilities of businessman to the corporate, the CSR concept was emerged. In this respect, expectations of societies, economic and legal responsibilities were put in the center in corporations.

Social responsibility of businessmen underlines the overseeing of the economic system operation that fulfills the public expectations (Frederick, 1960). In the mid of 1980s, Stakeholder Theory was developed (Freeman, 1984) which argues that all the stakeholders in the business should be satisfied by the managers through developing and implementing processes. Stakeholder theory suggests that the interests of employees, customers, shareholders, suppliers must be managed and integrated. In other words, interests of shareholders and stakeholders must be taken into consideration by managers in case of implementing new strategies (Harrison & Freeman, 1999). Stakeholder theory also focused the stakeholders' power on shaping organization's responsibility behavior (Barnett & Salomon, 2012; Delmas & Toffel, 2008). Lucchini and Moisello (2019) pointed out that media and social activist groups are two factors that shape an organization's engagement in CSR activities. Kassinis and Vafeas (2006) showed a positive relationship among pressures from community and environmental performance at the plant level. For example; Microsoft's YouthSpark Initiative and Office 365 for Nonprofits programs are shaped by the feedbacks from local communities in order to create best way to serve economic and social needs in their area.

Regarding the range of social obligations of corporates; economic, legal, ethical and discretionary expectations of society should be met (Carroll, 1979). Carroll (1991) developed a CSR pyramid that making a profit, obeying the law, being ethical and being good corporate citizen are responsibilities of the CSR firms. This pyramid shows organizations' CSR toward society (See Figure 4).

The dimensions are labelled as; *economic*, *legal*, *ethical* and *philanthropic responsibilities*. Economic responsibilities of the organization start with making profit and being able to create job opportunities for the candidates. Producing useful products and services are also economic responsibilities of the organization. Legal responsibilities of the organization involve the legal business practices and obeyed regulations to protect the needs of customers. Ethical responsibilities of the organization embrace minimizing waste, managing recycle and balancing consumption that lead to sustainability for future generations. Philanthropic responsibilities include promoting welfare of human and spreading good corporate citizen.

Figure 4. CSR Pyramid of Carroll's Development
(Carroll, 1991)

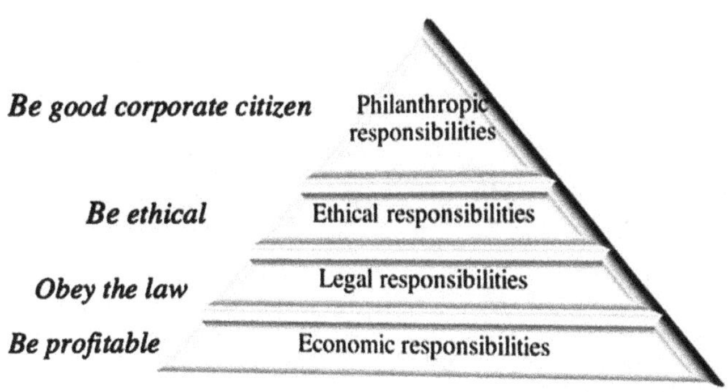

Figure 5. An example of a Starbucks' workplace
Source: https://www.starbucks.com

For economic responsibilities Starbucks creates pathways to opportunity through bringing people together, helping provide education and employment opportunities (See Figure 5). Balancing profitability and social conscience are common beliefs of Starbucks as a sustainable company.

For legal responsibilities, Turkish Airlines adopts business practices such as just-in-time-inventory management that relies on quick and reliable delivery of essential supplies. Turkish Airlines is also committed to complying all national regulations and those with related to the aviation industry (See Figure 6).

Figure 6. Visual examples of Turkish Airlines legal responsibilities
Source: https://investor.turkishairlines.com

For ethical responsibilities IKEA -the adventure of relaxing- takes initiatives to improve its business operation. It minimizes waste in manufacturing by creating collection points for customers to return waste such as; electrical and electronic equipment, discarded packaging, spent batteries for recycling (See Figure 7).

Figure 7. An example of ethical responsibility of IKEA
Source: https://www.ikea.com

For philanthropic responsibilities, Disney offers matching gifts up to $15,000 to educational institutions, health and human services, arts and cultural organizations, civic and community organizations, environmental organizations, and most other non-profits. Disney also offers a program called Disney's VoluntEARS of the year to provide grant awards $2,500 to the non-profit of the winner's choice (See Figure 8).

Figure 8. Disney's voluntears company logo
Source: https://publicaffairs.disneyland.com/voluntears/

Quazi and O'Brian (2000) have broaden the CSR model and have proposed the benefits of CSR actions and costs of CSR in the vertical line whereas responsibility of organization (i.e., wide and narrow) in the horizontal line (See Figure 9). The overall model is described in four quadrants combining the benefits of CSR action and wide responsibility with *modern view*, costs of CSR action and wide responsibility with *philanthropic view* whereas benefits of CSR action and narrow responsibility with *socio-economic view*, cost of CSR action and narrow responsibility with *classical view*.

The *modern view* highlights the responsibility of CSR on a large scale that offers high benefit. The *philanthropic view* underlines the engagement of CSR even it requires high costs. Charitable and ethical activities might create high costs when conducting CSR (Filgueiras et al., 2012). The *socio-economic view* points out creating balance between costs and benefits of CSR activities. Obtaining organizational benefit or strengthening customer relationship can be accepted as gains hence CSR activities should proceed (Filgueiras et al., 2012). The *classical view* embraces high costs of CSR activities and therefore it is only required in case of law and regulations (Quazi & O'Brien, 2000). Consequently, CSR activities are referred to the costs of organization (Filgueiras et al., 2012), not obligated by law.

When the CSR definitions are evaluated, the transition from legal obligations to being good corporate citizen can be realized. The reasons of this transition are environmental changings and sustainability (Tokgöz, 2012). Sustainability is a buzz topic that it has a significant influence on economy, society and nature. Szekely and Knirsch (2005) defined sustainability as *sustaining and expanding growth, shareholder*

Figure 9. Two-Dimensional model of CSR
(Quazi & O'Brien, 2000)

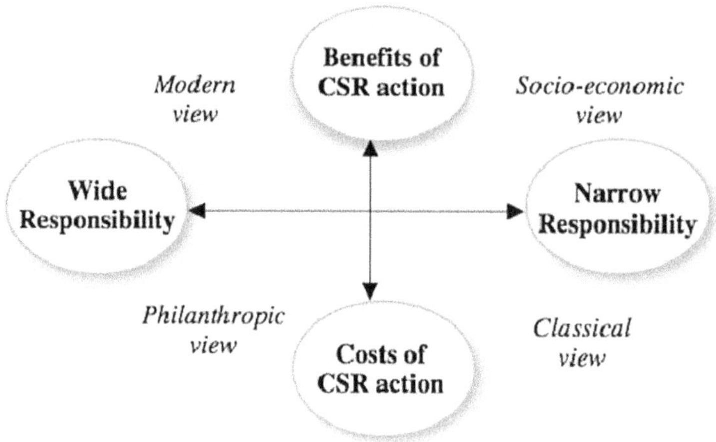

value, prestige, corporate reputation, customer relationships, and the quality of products and services as well as adopting and pursuing ethical business practices, creating sustainable jobs, building value for all the stakeholder and attending the needs of the underserved (p. 628). In particular, Elkington (1997) developed a ''triple bottom line'' approach underlines the combinations of ''people, profit and planet'' are the determinants of the success of organizations. He asserted the ideas that organizations are not only profit maker but also have social and environmental responsibilities for contributing to the sustainability. Montiel (2008) points out that *both CSR and corporate sustainability aim to balance economic prosperity, social integrity, and environmental responsibility, regardless of whether they conceptualize environmental issues as a subset of social issues or as the third element of sustainability* (p. 260). Montiel and Delgado-Ceballos (2014) propose new tridimensional construct ''corporate sustainability'' to minimize the ambiguity between triple bottom line and ''3Ps''.

To understand and show the convergence in corporate responsibility and corporate sustainability Bansal and Song (2017) reviewed the development and convergence in the two fields (See Figure 10). Their searching illustrated that corporate responsibility emerged in the 1950s whereas business sustainability did not appear until 1980s. They expressed that effect of markets on society was harmed through the bias of responsibility, whereas sustainability was directed in line with the harms of economic development on natural systems. In the later parts of the 20th century and the beginning part of the 21st century, the convergence between responsibility and sustainability emerged with a new strategic orientation regarding ''good'' social and environmental practices.

The socio-economic view which is based on social accountability asserts that organizations are social entities and they have legal, ethical and social obligations as a part of the community. When obligations are debated two perspectives come into sight. First one suggests that CSR is a duty of the organizations (i.e., normative), another one debates that CSR is optional and for the interest of the organizations (i.e., instrumental) (Dierkes & Antal, 1986). Most of the time, CSR is seen as a business strategy and benefit provider to the organization.

Financial benefits (Luo & Bhattarcharya, 2004), increasing market share (Linchestein, Drumrigt, Braig, 2004) are the benefits of CSR. Engaging in socially responsible behavior can create benefit for

Figure 10. The evolution of corporate responsibility and sustainability
(Bansal & Song, 2017: 108)

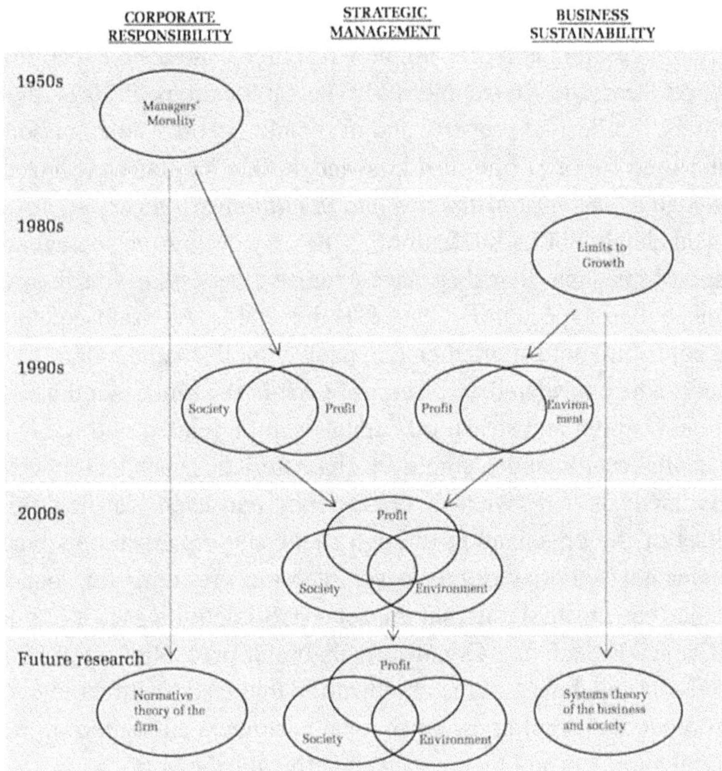

the organizations if only in circumstances as organizations involve CSR into their business strategy that shapes their core business choices (Porter & Kramer, 2006).

The Relationship Between IC, CSR and Social Entrepreneurship on the Basis of Dynamic Capabilities

Ideas of the individuals within the organization such as experience, creativity, managerial or entrepreneurial skills indicate efficiency in organizations.

Innovativeness, creating wealth, taking risks and combining resources without the fear of failure are skills of entrepreneurs (Crane & Crane, 2007). Entrepreneur's intangible skills or intellectual capital are determinants of the survival of start-ups (Peña, 2002). Concerning the entrepreneurs' characteristics and their relationship with other stakeholders to create long-term value maximization organizations create new standards. In order to reach success in the market, creating value for customers and also workers are seen as responsibilities for the organizations. These kinds of values are new corporate responsibilities for the society and external environment. Some of the responsibilities are seen as fulfillments of basic and economical needs of the legal entities. The fulfillments of needs generate both external and internal benefits (Sirsly & Lamertz, 2007). Both enhanced relationship between stakeholder and company and improvement in company reputation are external benefits whereas intangible resources such as novel and capabilities that are related with the know-how and company culture are internal benefits.

CSR activities create trust between company and its stakeholders. Primarily, socially responsible company is competent on creating and drawing new resources and even capabilities while generating relationship network. As Dean and Krestchmer (2007) posit locations of ideas might be in individuals, organizational structures, intellectual property and in social networks. Johannisson (2016) explain that networks are crucial source for acquiring new knowledge. In a similar way, Nieves and Haller (2014, p. 225) define knowledge as *the most distinctive and inimitable strategic asset available to firms*, and is evaluated as the main element of DCs (Denford, 2013). By definition, social entrepreneurs establish multifunctional relationships show that they have extensive access to vital knowledge about market developments and stakeholder expectations (Ince & Hahn, 2018). As a consequence, it can be said that CSR activities make contribution to strengthen company's intellectual capital.

Intellectual capital can be considered as a factor of CSR in the sense that the components of IC (i.e., human capital, relational capital and structural capital) can be related with CSR through the impacts they create. Human capital that includes employee characteristics such as knowledge, skills, abilities, motivation, creativity, analysis and synthesis competency and even learning skills effectuate social responsibility activities of the organization through rising the organization's tendency to participate in social and environmental activities or create volunteering programs for social and environmental causes. Relational capital can create significant impact on CSR activities via its components (e.g., brand, customer, supplier, financial relations). Organization's brand perception might contribute to advance in financial, social or economic image of the organization that lead to attract investors' attention. Deep relationship with customer and supplier establish loyal customers and empower cooperative relations, enhance performance of suppliers and their social and ethical behaviors.

Financial relation impacts the attractiveness level of the organization for investors. Structural capital can also have significant effect on CSR activities. The culture of organization, the process of management and strategy, R&D within the company are projected in CSR activities. Developing organizational commitment, revising strategies and informing stakeholders to become more familiar, boosting market position, strengthening relations with the stakeholders can lead to increase in CSR activities in organization. In other words, loyalty and commitment are two vital elements in maintaining relationships that social entrepreneurs develop close relationship with producers and markets (Kolk & Lenfant, 2016) consumers (Albert, Dean & Baron, 2016) and other hybrid organizations (Jenner & Oprescu, 2016) in order to accomplish social aims. Hybrid organizations goals are supporting and consulting each other in the process of strategic decision making (Jenner & Oprescu, 2016). Additionally, applying the corporate governance code of conduct will positive impact on social, environmental, health and safety issues and principle of transparency in decision making process.

It the last decade, intellectual capital and CSR have taken attention though they are independent concepts. However, there are convergences between intellectual capital and CSR based on the same theoretical approaches: stakeholder theory and legitimacy theory of enterprise. The performance of organizations can be understood by revealing intellectual capital information to the stakeholders (Oliveira, Rodrigues & Craig, 2010). Disclosure of intellectual capital information fulfills stakeholder's expectations and organization can generate valuable reputation-related IC through creating and maintaining good relationship with the stakeholders (Branco & Rodrigues, 2006). This kind of information sharing with the stakeholders helps organizations to develop their legitimacy and survive (Woodward, Edwards & Birkin, 2001). Legitimacy theory asserts that reporting of intangible information is perceived as legitimate; and that companies legitimize their position have corporate success (Guthrie, Petty & Ricceri, 2004). It can be noticed that the triggers (motivators) that disclose intellectual capital and CSR activities are parallel with respect to their theoretical point of views (i.e., economic approaches).

According to Tuzzolini & Armandi (1981) conducting CSR is related to motivation of the company that is the degree of CSR activities reflects the company's fulfilled internal and external ''self-actualization'' needs in which CSR activities are placed at the top of the hierarchical needs of organization. From this point of view, companies should fulfill their needs to perform CSR activities. Intellectual capital is one of the assets that is hidden value of the companies (Tseng & Goo, 2005). Since intellectual capital is ''combined intangible assets which enable the company to function'' (Brooking, 1996, p. 12). Pulic (2000), the founder of the VAIC method created equation that defines enterprise, as follows:

Enterprise = Tangible Assets + Intellectual Capital

This coefficient model is based on two dimensions such as human and structural capital. Chan, Cheng, and Hwang (2005) indicated that intellectual capital has impact on enterprise performance where the amount of intellectual capital, research and development activities, and advertising expenditures have positive contribution on return on assets. It can be concluded that intellectual capital is the main source of core competencies and therefore competitive advantages and innovations are crucial outcomes at the enterprise level.

FUTURE RESEARCH DIRECTIONS

Intellectual capital and CSR are important competitive advantage sources and main factors that make contribution on organizational performance. Therefore, future studies should focus on sharing of know-how and application of knowledge in individuals' minds. Human capital (i.e., individual's know-how), structural capital (i.e., implementation of gathered knowledge for organizational development) and relation capital (i.e., upward and downward communication in organization) should be taken into consideration to use intellectual capital effectively. Wry and Work (2017) clarify that communication and knowledge acquisition are meaningful for social entrepreneurs because the opportunity recognition is shaped by entrepreneur's previous knowledge and relationships.

Additionally, socially responsible activities (e.g., reduction in carbon footprints, donations of clothes to children in need or providing safe drinking water) can create impact on sharing of know-how or citizenship behaviors in organization. Since, a socially responsible organization influences the perceptions of employees about its prestige that create trustworthy environment.

CONCLUSION

Organizations need to achieve their strategic goals to actualize their existence by creating competitive advantage. One of the keys is intellectual capital that creates learning culture in organization. In this context, entrepreneurs are the main figures to raise potential of intellectual capital awareness. Since, entrepreneur has to create a culture that support intellectual capital activities (Soler & Celestino, 2007) in which intellectual capital can also affect the development of an entrepreneur. Learning organizations embraces knowledge sharing and enforces training and development activities (Cortini & Benevene, 2010). Therefore, entrepreneurs should motivate the teams to keep on learning, applying, and managing acquired knowledge to strengthen intellectual capital in the organization. Because intellectual capital is using knowledge and skills. Though the management of intellectual capital can create challenges, sustainable competitive advantage can be accomplished through the leadership style of entrepreneur in the organization. Findings of Yao and Koga (2017) showed that IC that contributes to the organizations involve unique management philosophy, CEO's strong leadership style, organizational culture and structure, gathering and matching information rapidly, and long-term relationships with various business partners.

Internalization of the creativity or innovations are the main indicators of the competitive advantage. IC has been defined as a source of innovation (Benner & Tushman, 2003). However, the expected positive relationship between IC and innovation is difficult because the process of innovation is unpredictable, input and output measurements are challenging. Besides, European Commission (2006) include a report that promote innovation through IC: *Intellectual Capital is a key element in an organization's future earning potential. Theoretical and empirical studies show that it is the unique combination of the different elements of Intellectual Capital and tangible investments that determines an enterprise's competitive advantage. R&D and innovation can be regarded as one element of Intellectual Capital. However, research intensive enterprises invest not only in R&D and innovation, but also in other forms of Intellectual Capital. Empirical studies provide evidence for the tight link and contingency between investments in R&D, Innovation, Human Resources and Relational Capital* (p. 10).

Changing firm's current state into innovative or transformative one requires three crucial dimensions to actualize the transformation. They are named as people, process and technology especially in customer relationship management (Chen & Popovich, 2003). Since people are in the center of organization and intellectual capital, the relationship between people dimension such as employee relations, training, top management role and intellectual capital dimension, human capital take attention. Hiring talented and competent employees leads to achieving higher level of intellectual capital. Haskel and Westlake (2017) confirmed that increased autonomy, reduced targets and access to supervisors are determinants of intellectual capital actualization from theory to practice.

Although maxim of ''the business of a business is business'' (Friedman, 1970) hold true in most of the context, relationship building with stakeholders and being responsible to the community are crucial values in today's business life. Social entrepreneurs balance CSR activities that they do not create a conflict between the economic and moral objectives of the organization. In other words, they know their role in stakeholders' welfare and take greater responsibility toward change and development. It can be claimed that social and sustainability-oriented values can be achieved by stakeholders' definition and implementation of business model modification, product design, operations of models, brands and technologies that create shared economic value. This might be taken into account as social innovation and has drawn attention of multinational companies to embrace successful hybrid business entity, such as Ben &Jerry's and Unilever. They focus on ''doing well'' and ''doing good'' through learning to integrate their social values into their missions, organizational culture, relationship with their stakeholders, production process and product characteristics (Austin & Leonard, 2008; Lee & Jay, 2015). Cavazos-Arroyo and Puente-Diaz (2019) confirmed that social innovation (i.e., being first to market with new social products or services, trying out new ideas, seeking out new ways to do things, being creative in methods of operations) contributes positively on social value creation (i.e., serving more beneficiaries in the community, providing more social products or services, expanding social products or services to different locations) that the main goal of social entrepreneurs is to create social value for their stakeholders.

Multinational companies that rely on strategies and innovation can achieve it business-to-nonbusiness (B2N) hybrid organization partnering in order to reach social impact. For multinational companies CSR is an international strategy (Clarke & Gibson-Sweet, 1999), especially as they operate in developing countries to create corporate reputation (Martín de Castro, Amores Salvadó, Navas López, & Balarezo Nuñez, 2019).

Socially responsible firms have better chance to keep valuable workers in the company as well as facilitate the utilization of intangible assets (Shen, Au, & Li, 2019). Organizational culture in which socially responsible actions are taken might be perceived as secure work environment by employees and strengthen employee satisfaction (Flammer & Kacperczyk, 2016). This kind of work environment increases the brainstorming actions and creation of intellectual capital. Intellectual capital which is a form of intangible assets supports the development of organization (Kaplan & Norton, 2006). From this point of view, entrepreneurs or leaders of the firms might concentrate on keeping intangible assets alive to accomplish CSR activities. As the saying goes: what you plant now you will harvest later.

REFERENCES

Albert, L. S., Dean, T. J., & Baron, R. A. (2016). From Social Value to Social Cognition. How Social Ventures Obtain the Resources They need for Social Transformation. *Journal of Social Entrepreneurship*, *7*(3), 289–311. doi:10.1080/19420676.2016.1188323

Alwert, K., Bornemann, M., & Will, M. (2009). Does intellectual capital reporting matter to financial analysts? *Journal of Intellectual Capital*, *10*(3), 354–368. doi:10.1108/14691930910977789

Ambrosini, V., & Bowman, C. (2009). What are dynamic capabilities and are they useful construct in strategic management? *International Journal of Management Reviews*, *11*(1), 29–49. doi:10.1111/j.1468-2370.2008.00251.x

Austin, J. E., & Leonard, H. B. D. (2008). Can the virtuous mouse and the wealthy elephant live happily ever after? *California Management Review*, *51*(1), 77–102. doi:10.2307/41166469

Bansal, P., & Song, H. (2017). Similar But Not the Same: Differentiating Corporate Sustainability from Corporate Responsibility. *The Academy of Management Annals*, *11*(1), 105–149. doi:10.5465/annals.2015.0095

Barnett, M., & Salomon, R. (2012). Does it pay to be really good? Addressing the shape of the relationship between social and financial performance. *Strategic Management Journal*, *33*(11), 1304–1320. doi:10.1002mj.1980

Barney, J. B. (1991). Firm resources and sustained competitive advantage. *Journal of Management Studies*, *17*(1), 99–120.

Barney, J. B., & Stewart, A. C. (2000). *Organizational identity as a moral philosophy: competitive implications for diversified operations*. Oxford University Press.

Benner, M. J., & Tushman, M. L. (2003). Exploitation, exploration, and process management: The productivity dilemma revisited. *Academy of Management Review*, *28*(2), 238–256. doi:10.5465/amr.2003.9416096

Bocken, N. M. P., Short, S. W., Rana, P., & Evans, S. (2014). A Literature and Practice Review to Develop Sustainable Business Model Archetypes. *Journal of Cleaner Production*, *65*(15), 42–56. doi:10.1016/j.jclepro.2013.11.039

Bontis, N. (2001). Assessing Knowledge Assets: A Review of the Models Used to Measure Intellectual Capital. *International Journal of Management Reviews*, *3*(1), 41–60. doi:10.1111/1468-2370.00053

Bontis, N. (2002). *World Congress on Intellectual Capital Readings*. Boston, MA: KMCI Butterworth-Heinemann Press.

Bontis, N., Keow, W. C. C., & Richardson, S. (2000). Intellectual capital and business performance in Malaysian industries. *Journal of Intellectual Capital*, *1*(1), 85–100. doi:10.1108/14691930010324188

Bose, S., & Thomas, K. (2007). Applying the balanced scorecard for better performance of intellectual capital. *Journal of Intellectual Capital*, *8*(4), 653–665. doi:10.1108/14691930710830819

Bourguignon, A. (2005). Management accounting and value creation: The profit and loss of reification. *Critical Perspectives on Accounting*, *16*(4), 353–389. doi:10.1016/j.cpa.2003.03.001

Bowen, H. R. (1953). *Social responsibilities of the businessman*. Harper & Row.

Branco-Castelo, M., & Rodriguez-Lima, L. (2006). Corporate social responsibility and resource- based perspectives. *Journal of Business Ethics*, *69*(2), 111–132. doi:10.100710551-006-9071-z

Brooking, A. (1996). *Intellectual Capital, Core Asset for the Third Millennium Enterprise*. International Thomson Business Press.

Cabrita, M. D. R., & Bontis, N. (2008). Intellectual capital and business performance in the Portuguese banking industry. *International Journal of Technology Management*, *43*(1-3), 212–237. doi:10.1504/IJTM.2008.019416

Carroll, A. B. (1979). A three-dimensional conceptual model of corporate social performance. *Academy of Management Review*, *4*(4), 497–505. doi:10.5465/amr.1979.4498296

Carroll, A. B. (1999). Corporate social responsibility. *Business & Society*, *38*(3), 268–295. doi:10.1177/000765039903800303

Cavazos-Arroyo, J., & Puente-Díaz, R. (2019). The Innuence of Marketing Capability in Mexican Social Enterprises. *Sustainability*, *11*(17), 1–15. doi:10.3390u11174668

Chan, M., Cheng, S., & Hwang, Y. (2005). An empirical investigation of the relationship between intellectual capital and firms market value and financial performance. *Journal of Intellectual Capital*, *2*(2), 159–176. doi:10.1108/14691930510592771

Chen, I. J., & Popovich, K. (2003). Understanding customer relationship management (CRM) People, process and technology. *Business Process Management Journal*, *9*(5), 672–688. doi:10.1108/14637150310496758

Cortini, M., & Benevene, P. (2010). Interaction between structural capital and human capital in Italian NPOs: Leadership, organizational culture and human resource management. *Journal of Intellectual Capital*, *11*(2), 123–139. doi:10.1108/14691931011039642

Crane, F., & Crane, E. (2007). Dispositional optimism and entrepreneurial success. *The Psychologist Manager Journal*, *10*(1), 13–25. doi:10.1080/10887150709336610

Delmas, M., & Toffel, M. W. (2008). Organizational responses to environmental demands: Opening the black box. *Strategic Management Journal*, *29*(10), 1027–1055. doi:10.1002mj.701

Denford, J. S. (2013). Building Knowledge: Developing a Knowledge-Based Dynamic Capabilities Typology. *Journal of Knowledge Management*, *17*(2), 175–194. doi:10.1108/13673271311315150

Deol, H. S. (2009). Strategic environment and intellectual capital of Indian banks. *Journal of Intellectual Capital*, *10*(1), 109–120. doi:10.1108/14691930910922932

Dierkes, M., & Antal, A. B. (1985). The Usefulness and Use of Social Reporting Information. *Accounting, Organizations and Society*, *10*(1), 29–34. doi:10.1016/0361-3682(85)90029-7

Doherty, B., Haugh, H., & Lyon, F. (2014). Social Enterprises as Hybrid Organizations: A Review and Research Agenda. *International Journal of Management Reviews*, *16*(4), 417–436. doi:10.1111/ijmr.12028

Dumay, J. (2016). A critical reflection on the future of intellectual capital: From reporting to disclosure. *Journal of Intellectual Capital*, *17*(1), 168–184. doi:10.1108/JIC-08-2015-0072

Edvinsson, L., & Malone, M. (1997). *Intellectual Capital*. Harper Business.

Eisenhardt, K. M., & Martin, J. A. (2000). Dynamic capabilities: What are they? *Strategic Management Journal*, *21*(10-11), 1105–1121. doi:10.1002/1097-0266(200010/11)21:10/11<1105::AID-SMJ133>3.0.CO;2-E

Elkington, J. (1998). Partnerships from cannibals with forks: The triple bottom line of 21st- century business. *Environmental Quality Management*, *8*(1), 37–51. doi:10.1002/tqem.3310080106

European Commission (EC). (2006). RICARDIS: Reporting Intellectual Capital to Augment Research, Development and Innovation in SMEs. European Commission, Directorate-General for Research, Brussels.

Filgueiras, J. L. M., de Oliveira, M. G., de Castro Neto, F. C., & da Silva Filho, J. C. L. (2012). Analysis of CSR in Midsize Retail: Application of the QuaziA and O'brien Model. *Journal of Operations and Supply Chain Management*, *5*(2), 54–68. doi:10.12660/joscmv5n2p54-68

Flammer, C., & Kacperczyk, A. (2019). Corporate social responsibility as a defense against knowledge spillovers: Evidence from the inevitable disclosure doctrine. *Strategic Management Journal*, *40*(8), 1243–1267. doi:10.1002mj.3025

Frederick, W. C. (1960). The growing concern over social responsibility. *California Management Review*, *2*(4), 54–61. doi:10.2307/41165405

Freeman, R. E. (1984). *Strategic management: A stakeholder approach*. Pitman.

Friedman, M. (1970, September 13). The social responsibility of business is to increase its profits. *The New York Times Magazine*, 122-126.

Gawer, A., & Cusumano, M. A. (2014). Industry Platforms and Ecosystem Innovation. *Journal of Product Development & Management Association*, *31*(3), 417–433.

Godelnik, R., & van der Meer, J. (2019). Sustainable Business Models in an Entrepreneurial Environment. In A. Aagaard (Ed.), *Sustainable Business Models* (pp. 239–276). Germany, Palgrave Macmillan. doi:10.1007/978-3-319-93275-0_9

Guthrie, J., Petty, R., Yongvanich, K., & Ricceri, F. (2004). Using content analysis as a research method to inquire into intellectual capital reporting. *Journal of Intellectual Capital*, *5*(2), 282–293. doi:10.1108/14691930410533704

Hall, R. (1992). The Strategic analysis of intangible resources. *Strategic Management Journal*, *13*(2), 135–144. doi:10.1002mj.4250130205

Hamel, G., & Heene, A. (1994). *Competence-Based Competition. The Strategic management series*. Wiley.

Harrison, J. S., & Freeman, R. E. (1999). Stakeholders, social responsibility and performance: Empirical evidence and theoretical perspectives. *Academy of Management Journal*, *42*, 479–487.

Haskel, J., & Westlake, S. (2017). *Capitalism without capital*. Princeton University Press. doi:10.2307/j.ctvc77hhj

Hormiga, E., Batista-Canino, R. M., & Sánchez-Medina, A. (2011). O papel do capital intelectual no sucesso de novos empreendimentos. *Revista Internacional de Empreendedorismo e Gestão*, *7*(1), 71–92.

Ince, I., & Hahn, R. (2018). How Dynamic Capabilities Facilitate the Survivability of Social Enterprises: A Qualitative Analysis of Sensing and Seizing Capacities. *Journal of Small Business Management*, 1–29.

Jenner, P., & Oprescu, F. (2016). The Sectorial Trust of Social Enterprise. Friend or Foe? *Journal of Social Entrepreneurship*, *7*(2), 236–261. doi:10.1080/19420676.2016.1158732

Johannisson, B. (2016). Economies of Overview—Guiding the External Growth of Small Firms. *International Small Business Journal: Researching Entrepreneurship*, *9*(1), 32–44. doi:10.1177/026624269000900104

Kamath, G. B. (2008). Intellectual capital and corporate performance in Indian pharmaceutical industry. *Journal of Intellectual Capital*, *9*(4), 684–704. doi:10.1108/14691930810913221

Kaplan, R. S., & Norton, D. P. (1992). The Balanced Scorecard—Measures that drive performance. *Harvard Business Review*, *70*(1), 71–79. PMID:10119714

Kaplan, R. S., & Norton, D. P. (2006). *Alignment: Using the balanced scorecard to create corporate synergies*. Harvard Business Review Press.

Kassinis, G., & Vafeas, N. (2006). Stakeholder pressures and environmental performance. *Academy of Management Journal*, *49*(1), 145–159. doi:10.5465/amj.2006.20785799

Kolk, A., & Lenfant, F. (2016). Hybrid Business Models for Peace and Reconciliation. *Business Horizons*, *59*(5), 503–524. doi:10.1016/j.bushor.2016.03.014

Koryak, O., Mole, K. F., Lockett, A., Hayton, J. C., Ucbasaran, D., & Hodgkinson, G. P. (2015). Entrepreneurial leadership, capabilities and firm growth. *International Small Business Journal*, *33*(1), 89–105. doi:10.1177/0266242614558315

Lee, M., & Jay, J. (2015). Strategic responses to hybrid social ventures. *California Management Review*, *57*(3), 126–147. doi:10.1525/cmr.2015.57.3.126

Lichtenstein, D. R., Drumwright, M. E., & Braig, B. M. (2004). The effect of corporate social responsibility on customer donations to corporate-supported nonprofits. *Journal of Marketing*, *68*(4), 16–32. doi:10.1509/jmkg.68.4.16.42726

Lucchini, A., & Moisello, A. (2019). Stakeholders' Pressure and CSR Engagement. A Case in the Apparel Sector. *American Journal of Industrial and Business Management*, *9*(01), 169–190. doi:10.4236/ajibm.2019.91012

Luke, B., & Chu, V. (2013). Social Enterprise versus Social Entrepreneurship: An Examination of the 'Why' and 'How' in Pursuing Social Change. *International Small Business Journal: Researching Entrepreneurship*, *31*(7), 764–784. doi:10.1177/0266242612462598

Luo, X., & Bhattacharya, C. B. (2006). Corporate social responsibility, customer satisfaction, and market value. *Journal of Marketing*, *70*(4), 1–18. doi:10.1509/jmkg.70.4.001

Mahoney, J. T., McGahan, A. M., & Pitelis, C. N. (2009). 'The interdependence of private and public interests'. *Organization Science*, *20*(6), 1034–1052. doi:10.1287/orsc.1090.0472

Malhotra, Y. (2003). *Measuring Knowledge Assets of a Nation Knowledge System for development*. Invited Research Paper Sponsored by the United Nations Department of Economic and Social Affairs. Keynote Presentation at the Ad Hoc Group of Experts Meeting at the United Nations Headquarters, New York, NY.

Martín-de Castro, G. (2014). Intellectual capital and the firm: Some remaining questions and prospects. *Knowledge Management Research and Practice*, *12*(3), 239–245. doi:10.1057/kmrp.2014.13

Martín-de Castro, G., Amores Salvadó, J., Navas-López, J. E., & Balarezo-Núñez, R. M. (2020). Corporate Environmental Reputation: Exploring its Definitional Landscape. *Business Ethics (Oxford, England)*, *29*(1), 130–142. doi:10.1111/beer.12250

Martín-de-Castro, G., Navas-Lopez, J. E., Lopez-Saez, P., & Alama-Salazar, E. (2006). Organizational capital as competitive advantage of the organization. *Journal of Intellectual Capital*, *7*(3), 324–337. doi:10.1108/14691930610681438

Montiel, I. (2008). Corporate social responsibility and corporate sustainability: Separate pasts, common futures. *Organization & Environment*, *21*(3), 245–269. doi:10.1177/1086026608321329

Montiel, I., & Delgado-Ceballos, J. (2014). Defining and measuring corporate sustainability are we there yet? *Organization & Environment*, *27*(2), 113–139. doi:10.1177/1086026614526413

Muñoz, P., & Cohen, B. (2018). Sustainable Entrepreneurship Research: Taking Stock and Looking Ahead. *Business Strategy and the Environment*, *27*(3), 300–322. doi:10.1002/bse.2000

Nieves, J., & Haller, S. (2014). Building Dynamic Capabilities Through Knowledge Resources. *Tourism Management*, *40*, 224–232. doi:10.1016/j.tourman.2013.06.010

Öcal, A. T. (2007). *İşletmelerin sosyal sorumluluğu*. Beta.

Oliveira, L., Lima Rodrigues, L., & Craig, R. (2010). Intellectual capital reporting in sustainability reports. *Journal of Intellectual Capital, 11*(4), 575–594. doi:10.1108/14691931011085696

Pache, A. C., & Santos, F. (2012). Inside the Hybrid Organization: Selective Coupling as a Response to Competing Institutional Logics. *Academy of Management Journal, 56*(4), 972–1001. doi:10.5465/amj.2011.0405

Peloza, J., & Shang, J. (2011). How can corporate social responsibility activities create value for stakeholders? A systematic review. *Journal of the Academy of Marketing Science, 39*(1), 117–135. doi:10.100711747-010-0213-6

Peña, I. (2002). Intellectual capital and business start-up success. *Journal of Intellectual Capital, 3*(2), 180–198. doi:10.1108/14691930210424761

Phillips, P., & Phillips, J. (2002). *Measuring Intellectual Capital: Twelve Case Studies from the Real World of Training*. American Society for Training and Development.

Porter, M. E., & Kramer, M. R. (2006). Strategy and society: The link between competitive advantage and corporate social responsibility. *Harvard Business Review, 84*(12), 78–92. PMID:17183795

Pulic, A. (1997). *The physical and intellectual capital of Austrian banks*. Retrieved from http://www.vaic-on.net

Pulic, A. (2000). An accounting tool for IC management. *International Journal of Technology Management, 20*(5), 702–714. doi:10.1504/IJTM.2000.002891

Quazi, A. M., & O'Brien, D. (2000). An empirical test of a cross-national model of corporate social responsibility. *Journal of Business Ethics, 25*(1), 33–51. doi:10.1023/A:1006305111122

Robinson, J. (2006). Navigating Social and Institutional Barriers to Markets: How Social Entrepreneurs Identify and Evaluate Opportunities. In J. Mair, J. Robinson, & K. Hockerts (Eds.), *Social Entrepreneurship* (pp. 95–120). Palgrave Macmillan UK. doi:10.1057/9780230625655_7

Rumelt, R. (2011). *Good strategy bad strategy: The difference and why it matters*. Crown Business.

Rumelt, R. (2011). *Good strategy bad strategy: The difference and why it matters*. Crown Business.

Schaltegger, S., & Wagner, M. (2011). Sustainable Entrepreneurship and Sustainability Innovation: Categories and Interactions. *Business Strategy and the Environment, 20*(4), 222–237. doi:10.1002/bse.682

Schaper, M. (2010). *Making Ecopreneurs: Developing Sustainable Entrepreneurship*. Gower/Ashgate Pub.

Schmidt, P., & Santos, J. L. (2002). *Avaliação de ativos intangíveis*. Atlas.

Schmidt, P., & Santos, J. L. (2002). *Avaliação de ativos intangíveis*. Atlas.

Shen, N., Au, K., & Li, W. (2019). Strategic alignment of intangible assets: The role of corporate social responsibility. *Asia Pacific Journal of Management*. Advance online publication. doi:10.100710490-019-09681-1

Sirsly, C. A., & Lamertz, K. (2007). When Does a Corporate Social Responsibility Initiative Provide a First-mover Advantage. *Business & Society, 47*(3), 343–369. doi:10.1177/0007650307299221

Skandia. (1999). *Skandia annual report 1998*. Retrieved from http://www.skandia.com/financials/pdfs/e9712Human.pdf

Soler, L. E. V., & Celestino, D. J. C. O. (2007). Evaluating the scope of IC in firms' value. *Journal of Intellectual Capital*, *8*(3), 470–493. doi:10.1108/14691930710774876

Spinelli, S. Jr, & Adams, R. (2012). *New venture creation: entrepreneurship for the 21st century*. The McGraw-Hill Companies.

Stewart, T., & Ruckdeschel, C. (1998). Intellectual capital: The new wealth of organizations. *Performance Improvement*, *37*(7), 56–59. doi:10.1002/pfi.4140370713

Stewart, T. A. (1997). *Intellectual Capital: The New Wealth of Organizations*. Doubleday.

Stewart, T. A. (1998). *Capital intelectual: A nova vantagem competitiva das empresas*. Campus.

Subramaniam, M., & Youndt, M. A. (2005). The influence of intellectual capital on the types of innovative capabilities. *Academy of Management Journal*, *48*(3), 450–463. doi:10.5465/amj.2005.17407911

Sullivan, P. (2001). *Value-driven Intellectual Capital: How to convert intangible corporate Assets into market value*. Wiley.

Sullivan, P. (2001). *Value-driven Intellectual capital: How to convert intangible corporate Assets into market value*. Wiley.

Sveiby, K. E. (2007). *Methods for measuring intangible assets*. Retrieved from https://www.sveiby.com/articles/IntangAss/CompanyMonitor.html

Szekely, F., & Knirsch, M. (2005). Responsible leadership and corporate social responsibility: Metrics for sustainable performance. *European Management Journal*, *23*(6), 628–647. doi:10.1016/j.emj.2005.10.009

Teece, D. J., Pisano, G., & Shuen, A. (1997). Dynamic capabilities and strategic management. *Strategic Management Journal*, *18*(7), 509–533. doi:10.1002/(SICI)1097-0266(199708)18:7<509::AID-SMJ882>3.0.CO;2-Z

Tokgöz, N. (2012). *Genel İşletme*. Anadolu Üniversitesi Yayınları.

Tseng, C. Y., & James Goo, Y. J. (2005). Intellectual capital and corporate value in an emerging economy: Empirical study of Taiwanese manufacturers. *R & D Management*, *35*(2), 187–201. doi:10.1111/j.1467-9310.2005.00382.x

Tuzzolino, F., & Armandi, B. R. (1981). A need-hierarchy framework for assessing corporate social responsibility. *Academy of Management Review*, *6*(1), 21–28. doi:10.5465/amr.1981.4287982

Ulrich, D. (1998). *Delivering results: A new mandate for human resource professionals*. Harward Business School Press.

Urban, B., & Joubert, G. C. D. S. (2017). Multidimensional and comparative study on intellectual capital and organisational performance. *Journal of Business Economics and Management*, *18*(1), 84–99. doi:10.3846/16111699.2016.1255990

Wendra, W., Sule, E. T., Joeliaty, J., & Azis, Y. (2019). Exploring dynamic capabilities, intellectual capital and innovation performance relationship: Evidence from the garment manufacturing. *Business: Theory and Practice*, *20*, 123–136. doi:10.3846/btp.2019.12

White, G., Lee, A., Yuningsih, Y., Nielsen, C., & Bukh, P. N. (2010). The nature and extent of voluntary intellectual capital disclosures by Australian and UK biotechnology companies. *Journal of Intellectual Capital*, *11*(4), 519–536. doi:10.1108/14691931011085669

Wiig, K. M. (1997). Integrating intellectual capital and knowledge management. *Long Range Planning*, *30*(3), 399–405. doi:10.1016/S0024-6301(97)90256-9

Woodward, D., Edwards, P., & Birkin, F. (2001). Some Evidence on Executives Views of Corporate Social Responsibility. *The British Accounting Review*, *33*(3), 357–397. doi:10.1006/bare.2001.0165

Wry, T., & York, J. G. (2017). An Identity- Based Approach to Social Enterprise. *Academy of Management Review*, *42*(3), 437–460. doi:10.5465/amr.2013.0506

Wu, S. H., Lin, L. Y., & Hsu, M. Y. (2007). Intellectual capital, dynamic capabilities and innovative performance of organisations. *International Journal of Technology Management*, *39*(3/4), 279. doi:10.1504/IJTM.2007.013496

Yamak, S. (2007). *Kurumsal sosyal sorumluluk kavramının gelişimi*. Beta Yayınları.

Yao, J., & Koga, C. (2017). Sustained competitive advantage and strategic intellectual capital management: Evidence from Japanese high performance small to medium sized enterprises. In J. Guthrie, J. Dumay, F. Ricceri, & C. Nielsen (Eds.), *The Routledge Companion to Intellectual Capital* (pp. 236–251). Routledge. doi:10.4324/9781315393100-15

Zahra, S. A., Sapienza, H. J., & Davidsson, P. (2006). Entrepreneurship and Dynamic Capabilities: A Review, Model and Research Agenda. *Journal of Management Studies*, *43*(3), 917–955. doi:10.1111/j.1467-6486.2006.00616.x

ADDITIONAL READING

Becker, G. S. (1964). *Human Capital*. Columbia University Press.

Bowen, H. R. (1953). *Social responsibilities of the businessman*. Harper & Row.

Brainbridge, D. I. (2012). *Intellectual Property*. Pearson.

Carroll, A. B. (1979). A three-dimensional conceptual model of corporate social performance. *Academy of Management Review*, *4*(4), 497–505. doi:10.5465/amr.1979.4498296

Carroll, A. B. (1991). The pyramid of corporate social responsibility: Toward the moral management of organizational stakeholders. *Business Horizons*, *34*(4), 39–48. doi:10.1016/0007-6813(91)90005-G

Drucker, P. F. (1969). *The age of discontinuity: guidelines to our changing society*. Heinemann.

Friedmann, M. (1962). *Capitalism and freedom*. University of Chicago Press.

Montiel, I., Gallo, P. J., & Antolin-Lopez, R. (2020). What on Earth Should Managers Learn About Corporate Sustainability? A Threshold Concept Approach. *Journal of Business Ethics*, *162*(4), 857–880. doi:10.100710551-019-04361-y

KEY TERMS AND DEFINITIONS

Competitive Advantage: A firm's having strong competition power in the market through using its skills and valuable resources.

Core Competence: A firm's core abilities and capabilities such as managerial expertise or innovation capabilities that lead to value generating activities.

Corporate Social Responsibility: A firm's voluntary activities that benefit the society without economic or technical interest by using social values and firm power.

Dynamic Capabilities: A firm's abilities to achieve and sustain its competitive advantage with the dynamic change in the market.

Entrepreneur: Someone who takes initiative and risk to make things happen.

Hybrid Organization: A firm's affective commitment to achieve positive social or environmental impacts through the non-profit and for-profit enterprises.

Intellectual Capital: A firm's intangible and non-monetary assets (e.g., knowledge, intellectual property) that contribute to achieve its value creation and competitive advantage in market.

Return on Investment: The financial ratio that measures the generated gain or loss of an investor relative to investment cost.

Social Entrepreneur: Someone who creates and grows a venture either for-profit or non-profit organization to deal with social challenges.

Strategic Performance Management: A comprehensive approach that includes understanding the strategic context through internal and external analysis in order to achieve firms' goals.

Sustainability: An approach which integrates environmental, social, and economic aspects that all of them should be taken into consideration to create lasting welfare.

Chapter 5
Effects of Social Entrepreneurship on Organizational Performance:
The Mediating Role of Corporate Social Responsibility

Ledian Valle Mestre
University of Murcia, Spain

Matilde García Pérez.
University of Murcia, Spain

Daniel Jiménez-Jiménez
University of Murcia, Spain

ABSTRACT

Social entrepreneurship (SE) is a crucial way to deal with the social problems produced by the last economic crisis. However, social entrepreneurship most creates economic results that contribute to supporting the activity of the organization. This study analyzes empirically the effects of social entrepreneurship on organizational performance, as well as the indirect effect through corporate social responsibility (CSR). Based on data collected from 213 social economy companies, structural equations models have been used to verify the research hypotheses. The results obtained confirm the positive effect of social entrepreneurship on economic performance and announce the existence of the mediatory effect of the practices of corporate social responsibility.

DOI: 10.4018/978-1-7998-4833-2.ch005

INTRODUCTION

In recent years, an important number of studies have focussed on the features and importance of social entrepreneurship (Durkin & Gunn, 2016; H. M. Haugh & Talwar, 2016; Hlady-Rispal & Servantie, 2018).

SE is understood as the ability to recognise opportunities to create social value, whereas the process of SE implies the construction, evaluation and pursuit of opportunities to achieve social change (Roberts & Woods, 2005). SE can be considered a competitive advantage generator where the income produced by this advantage leads to greater organisational performance (Liñán & Santos, 2007).

A key aspect in the success of SE is its capacity to generate social and economic value (Rawhouser, Cummings, & Newbert, 2017). This is the main difference between entrepreneurship in the traditional sector and social entrepreneurship.

Additionally, the literature has suggested that certain SE characteristics, such as the ability to detect opportunities, an innovative spirit and social commitment, have a positive impact on organisational performance (OP) (Sullivan, Carraher, Baker, Cochrane, & Robinson, 2009; Weerawardena & Sullivan-Mort, 2001). OP is a multidimensional concept with an indiscriminate combination of different indicators (Camisón & Villar-López, 2014). Some authors suggest that one way to improve these indicators is to incorporate organisational practices related to CSR (Paulík, Majková, Tykva, & Cervinka, 2015).

In general terms, CSR refers to a firm fulfilling its legal, economic, ethical and philanthropic responsibilities to society (Cho, Chung, & Young, 2019). However, different definitions have been suggested. The definition of CSR used in this study is based on the criteria of the European Commission (EEC) (2001). They define CSR as "the voluntary integration of social and environmental interests into an organisation's commercial operations and relations with interest groups". (EEC) (2001).

The literature recognises that CSR practices are important, insofar as they contribute to the improvement of an organisation's perceived reputation, access to new opportunities and the cohesion of the organisation's stakeholders (Luo & Bhattacharya, 2006).

Despite its relevance, empirical studies that analyse the relationship and effects of CSR on organisational performance remain scarce (Cho et al., 2019; Luo & Bhattacharya, 2006). Therefore, the purpose of this study is to empirically analyse the effect of SE on FP, as well as the role of CSR in this relationship. The study was conducted in the context of firms from the social economy sector.

In the Spanish context, social-economic firms are those organisations defined by the Law on Social Economy as "the set of economic and business activities carried out in the private sphere by those entities that pursue the collective interest of its members, either economic, social or both" (B.O.E, 2011). This law includes cooperatives and other entities that are part of the social economy (Monzon & Chaves, 2008).

This study tries to fill the gap outlined above by analysing the effect of SE on OP, as well as the mediating role of CSR in this relationship. Based on its relevance, this section supplies an empirical analysis related to the topic.

BACKGROUND

Social Entrepreneurship

Social entrepreneurship as an organisational practice is a crucial way to deal with the economic and social problems produced by the previous economic crisis. According to most studies, the main goal of any project of social entrepreneurship should be to find, address and solve the social, economic and environmental problems of a society in an innovative way (Tepthong, 2014; Zebryte & Jorquera, 2017).

According to Mair and Marti (2006), social entrepreneurship can be understood as:

"A process of creating value through new ways of combining resources which are destined to the exploration and exploitation of opportunities, creating social value and stimulating social change through the satisfaction of social needs" (Mair & Marti, 2006).

In this definition, the authors suggest that social entrepreneurship: a) does not restrict the implementation of social entrepreneurial projects to any specific sector; b) implies the offering of services and products by an organisation established or created for such purposes; c) recognises that social problems are potential opportunities to leverage entrepreneurial skills and provide (elaborating and applying) sustainable innovative responses to social problems; d) allows positive changes to be generated that will benefit both the organisation and society as well as create wealth. Therefore, the application of this type of entrepreneurship to solving social problems requires special motivation that must be reflected in the mission of the organisation.

Social Entrepreneurship and Financial Performance

Social entrepreneurship must contribute to building competitive advantages for society and the organisation (Curto, 2012; Dacin, Dacin, & Tracey, 2011; H. Haugh, 2005; Mair & Marti, 2006; Martin & Osberg, 2007; Nicholls, 2006; Styles, Gray, Sullivan Mort, & Weerawardena, 2006). It is understood that social entrepreneurship enhances the economic efficiency of an organisation, as it generates innovation, fills niche markets and strengthens the organisation confronting competition (Boettke, Coyne, & Leeson, 2007).

According to Kulfas (2003), when acts of entrepreneurship are put into practice, economic growth is boosted, contributing to the development and evolution of new and current markets. In addition, Boisot and MacMillan (2004) pointed out that social entrepreneurship is a determining factor in the improvement of production processes which are based on social innovation, proactivity and risk management as key components of the social entrepreneurial initiative (Styles et al., 2006).

Oeij, Kraan, and Vaas (2010) confirmed that the implementation of social entrepreneurship improves organisational performance by exploiting the opportunities for and maintenance of competitive advantages (Mozas, 2013; Vázquez-Maguirre & Portales, 2014).

Based on all the evidence above, the first hypothesis of this study is:

H_1: Social entrepreneurship is positively related to financial performance.

Social Entrepreneurship and Corporate Social Responsibility

Social entrepreneurship implies the responsibility to produce social value with great impact on the economy of the organisation, the environment and society (Palacios-Marqués, García, Sánchez, & Mari, 2019). To achieve this, firms must develop a special relationship with their stakeholders. For this reason, incorporating practices associated with corporate social responsibility is a choice often considered by researchers and practitioners.

In general terms, the stakeholder theory is used to interpret what will happen in a company based on a firm's behaviour (Waheed, Zhang, Rashid, & Zaman Khan, 2020). CSR is interpreted as a concept related to the responsibility and commitment that members of an organisation have both to themselves and society (Austin, Gutierrez, Ogliastri, & Reficco, 2006). According to the Commission of the European Communities (EEC) (2001), CSR can be understood as:

"The voluntary integration, by the organization, of the social and environmental concerns in their commercial operations and the relations with their groups of interest" (EEC) (2001).

This definition declares the responsibility of companies for their impact on society and explicitly refers to the need for collaboration with stakeholders to integrate social, environmental, and ethical concerns. Moreover, CSR policies contribute to the decision-making process (Tsoutsoura, 2004) and the fulfilment of economic and social responsibilities by ensuring the social welfare of all the members of the organisation (Lozano et al., 2018).

As has been previously pointed out, CSR has often been used as a reference in the integration of social and environmental dimensions into both business and community development. During the past few decades, its practices have been considered agents capable of driving the growth of organisations, especially in competitive and dynamic contexts where the maintenance and achievement of competitive advantages are becoming increasingly expensive. This reveals the importance and contribution of CSR to the maintenance of sustainable entrepreneurial activities, starting with economic results (Caraiani, Lungu, Dascalu, Cimpoeru, & Dinu, 2012).

Using this model, organisations can achieve goals related to social welfare, human rights, labour rights, consumer protection or fair trade (Camargo, Silva Velez, & Patiño Moncada, 2015). Thus, there seems to be a consensus about the importance CSR practices have for organisations. Based on all these arguments, the second hypothesis is proposed:

H_2: Social entrepreneurship is positively related to corporate social responsibility.

The Mediating Effect of Corporate Social Responsibility

While it is known that CSR helps in networking and resource and information mobilisation, evidence points to a mediating role in the relationship between SE and FP. Therefore, organisations that undertake new projects with social objectives tend to implement more responsible practices towards their clients, employees, society or the environment (Oeyono, Samy, & Bampton, 2011).

Despite the fact that there is no agreement on the strength of the connection between CSR and financial performance as this association has not been conclusively established, some authors, such as Pablo, Benito and Juan (2019) found a global link between CSR and the economic results of organisations based on the interest group theory. Oeyono et al. (2011) suggest that a firm can enhance its financial performance by adopting socially responsible practices based on ethical relationships. In the same line, Alafi and Hasoneh (2012) have pointed out that CSR potentiated the relation between SE and FP by affecting monetary performance, staff commitment and corporate integrity. All these results improve competitiveness and ensure the survival of the company in the future.

Additionally, Crişan-Mitra and Borza (2015) argued that those organisations that balance their decision-making from a financial and social perspective foster business success.

On the other hand, there is evidence that points out how CSR helps SE to achieve other types of organisational performance. Westhues and Einwiller (2006) suggest that CSR facilitates the adoption of ethical behaviours to respond to customer demands, affecting the culture of the organisation in a positive way. They also confirmed that CSR behaviour provides reputational benefit for the company (Guo, Sun, & Li, 2009), making it an effective way to improve organisational results.

Other authors have suggested that CSR allows firms to improve customer satisfaction. The study carried out by Loureiro, Sardinha and Reijnders (2012) concluded that CSR has a direct effect on customer satisfaction.

Another key area affected by CSR practices is communication. According to Malhotra and Mukherjee (2004), CSR practices connect the firm with its public, reinforcing brand loyalty.

Considering the evidence above exploring the role of CSR in the relationship between SE and FP, the authors propose the third hypothesis:

H_3: Corporate social responsibility is positively related to financial performance.

After the review of the literature and the formulation of the hypotheses, a model that graphically represents the relationships and fluxes of interaction among the components of this study is presented in Figure 1.

Figure 1.

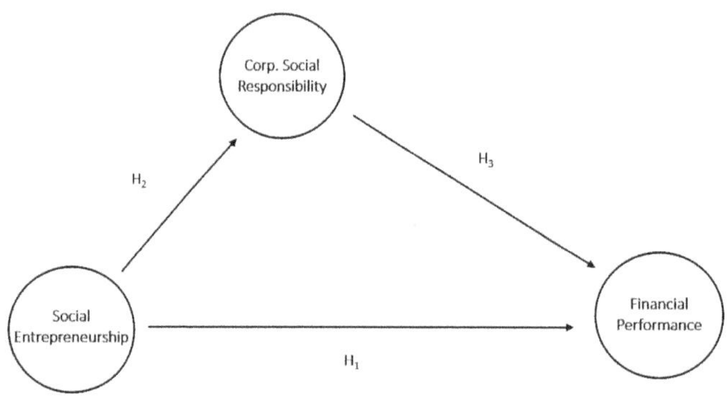

METHODS

Sample and Procedures

To find companies that carry out social entrepreneurial projects, the population of this study was composed of 1,053 companies from the social economy sector. In the case of Spain, the companies that make up this sector are regulated by the Social Economy Law 5/2011 of March 29, which, unlike in other regions of the world, includes organisations that operate in different economic areas and are not limited to non-profit organisations.

Table 1. Sample characteristics

Features	% of companies	%
Legal form	Partner cooperatives	38.24
	Agricultural cooperatives	2.9
	Public limited working companies	7.84
	Limited Labour Societies	47.06
	Other.	3.92
Activity sector	Agrarian	1.83
	Industrial	18.90
	Construction	7.93
	Services	71.34
Size	Fewer than 50 employees	89.65
	Between 51 and 100 employees	56.55
	More than 100 employees	5.52
Antique	Under 7 years old	20%
	Between 8 -15 years	33.85%
	Between 15-27 years old	13,85%
	Over 27 years	32.30%

The information-gathering process was supported by a self-administered survey. An online version of the questionnaire was developed which offered technical and security guarantees for the collection of information.

To contrast the proposed model, it was considered necessary to arrive at a sample of at least two hundred questionnaires. After collecting the data, a preliminary analysis was carried out to check whether they were complete, obtaining 213 valid questionnaires, which represented a response rate of 20.23% of the companies in the initial population. To verify that the sample values corresponded to those of the study population, the Pearson correlation coefficient was applied for the variables of size (0.999, $p < 0.01$), antiquity (0.993, $p < 0.01$) and sector of activity (0.991, $p < 0.01$). The characteristics of the sample are summarised in Table 1.

Measures

For the measurement of the model variables, a five-point Likert scale was used, which ranges from 'totally disagree' (1) to 'totally agree' (5). The literature suggests that this type of scale reduces respondent frustration, increases response rates and improves response quality (Sachdev & Verma, 2004).

The constructs of the questionnaire were configured in the following way:

Social entrepreneurship was measured using a scale developed and validated by Carraher, Welsh and Svilokos (2016). This scale is aimed at investigating the role of companies in influencing social change, the management of social problem-solving projects and the implementation of new solutions for their resolution, among other things, and has been used and validated in studies such as that developed by Sullivan et al. (2009). After the scale adjustment process, we have measured this construct with ten items.

Corporate social responsibility was measured with the same scale that was used in the study by Martinez-Conesa, Soto-Acosta and Palacios-Manzano (2017), which introduces five dimensions with twenty-two final items, to measure the creation of social value for employees, customers, suppliers, the community and, finally, the environment. With these constructs, we created a second-order construct. In this case, the five first-order constructs respond to reflective scales, while the second-order construct is formed from the previously mentioned dimensions.

Finally, *financial performance* was measured using the scale developed by Wang, Dou, Zhu and Zhou (2015), whose four items are oriented towards sales, profits, profitability and returns on investments.

Using post – hoc approaches, the impact of common method bias was assessed. The problem was verified using a Harman factor test (Podsakoff & Organ, 1986). As a result of the unrotated principal component analysis, factors with an eigenvalue greater than 1 were found. Thus, the absence of problems was confirmed.

Analysis

The hypotheses of this study were contrasted at the same time with the method of structural equation models. Partial least squares (PLS) has been used. This is a variance-based structural equation modelling technique (Carrión, Henseler, Ringle, & Roldán, 2016; Martínez Ávila & Fierro Moreno, 2018) that uses a principal component-based estimation approach suitable for modelling with structural equations (SEM).

Table 2. Psychometric properties and matrix of correlations of constructs

	*Statistical**			*Correlation matrix*						
	CA	*CR*	*AVE*	*1*	*2*	*3*	*4*	*5*	*6*	*7*
1. Social entrepreneurship	0.945	0.954	0.675	**0.822**	0.731	0.702	0.515	0.778	0.529	0.376
2 Corporate social responsibility 1	0.923	0.946	0.776	0.684	**0.881**	0.823	0.540	0.799	0.623	0.400
3 Corporate social responsibility 2	0.936	0.963	0.866	0.654	0.851	**0.930**	0.613	0.737	0.700	0.484
4 Corporate social responsibility 3	0.932	0.974	0.926	0.468	0.499	0.566	**0.962**	0.587	0.557	0.523
5 Corporate social responsibility 4	0.917	0.943	0.767	0.717	0.738	0.679	0.536	**0.876**	0.593	0.494
6 Corporate social responsibility 5	0.913	0.955	0.811	0.486	0.563	0.632	0.495	0.533	**0.901**	0.518
8 Financial performance	0.907	0.975	0.928	0.329	0.358	0.433	0.465	0.434	0.454	**0.963**

Note: AVE = average extracted variance; CR = composite reliability; α = Cronbach Alpha; Diagonal elements (bold figures) are the square root of the variance shared between the constructs and their measures. Below diagonal elements are the correlations between constructs. Above diagonal elements are the Heterotrait-Monotrait Ratio (HTMT) values.

To carry out the analysis through the partial least squares approach, 3.2.6 Smart PLS software has been used (Ringle, Wende, & Becker, 2015). SmartPLS 3 is one of the most powerful software programmes for modelling latent variables using PLS-SEM. This programme is frequently used in management, and the current versions of the model include many analyses that allow the desired results to be obtained (Sarstedt, Hair, Ringle, Thiele, & Gudergan, 2016).

Using PLS-SEM involves following a two-stage approach (Barclay, Higgins, & Thompson, 1995). The first step requires the assessment of the measurement model. This allows the relationships between the observable variables and theoretical concepts to be specified. This analysis is performed considering the reliability of individual items, the reliability of the constructs, the average variance extracted (AVE), and the discriminant validity of the indicators of the latent variables. In the second step, the structural model is evaluated.

To ensure adequate quality in the measures used in the study, different criteria were evaluated. In the first place, the reliability of the measurement scales was verified with the Cronbach alpha coefficient, obtaining a value higher than 0.7 in all the cases, which is considered adequate by the literature. The composite reliability ranged from 0.94 to 0.97, above the threshold of 0.7 (Nunnally, 1978). An examination of the average variance extracted (AVE) revealed that all the constructs exceeded the 0.50 cut-off set by the literature (Fornell & Larcker, 1981). On the other hand, the R^2 value for the endogenous constructs exceeded the recommended minimum value of 0.1, which shows that the model developed is suitable for hypothesis testing (Figure 2). The discriminant validity of the measures was then evaluated. As Fornell and Larcker (1981) suggested, the AVE for each construct should be greater than the correlations of the squared latent factors between pairs of constructs. Also, Table 2 shows that the Heterotrait-Monotrait Ratio (HTMT) values (elements above the diagonal) are below 0.85.

Consequently, it was determined that all the variables showed satisfactory discriminant validity. In short, our model has good convergent validity, reliability and discriminant validity. Consequently, the confirmatory factor analysis demonstrates the quality of the scales and dimension of this paper, and it is adequate to test our hypotheses.

Figure 2.

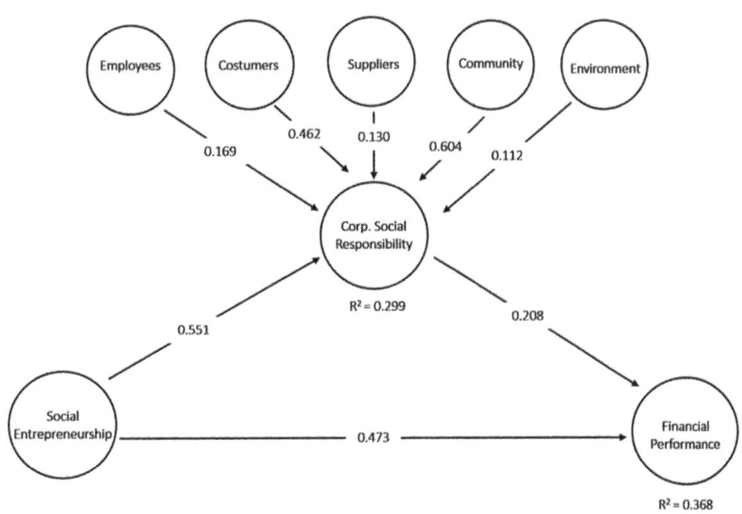

RESULTS

The model derived from the PLS-SEM analysis is shown in Figure 2. The standardised path coefficients (β) and the explained variance for endogenous variables (R^2), effect size (f^2) and predictive relevance (Q^2) are also included. R^2 shows moderate effects for each endogenous construct, f^2 suggests a great effect on CSR but medium and slight effects on FP, and Q^2 shows that the model has predictive capacity.

Table 3 shows the estimated model results with the standardised path coefficients and t values. Using the t- statistic obtained from the bootstrap test with 5,000 resamples, the stability of the estimates was examined (Chin, 1998).

Table 3. Results of the structural model for the contrast of the hypotheses

Model relationships	*Path value*	*St-Dev*	*T-Value*	*P values*	f^2
Social entrepreneurship → Financial Performance	0.473	0.085	5.537	0.000	0.250
Social entrepreneurship → Corporate Social Responsibility	0.551	0.062	8.941	0.000	0.435
Corporate Social Responsibility → Financial Performance	0.208	0.078	2.688	0.004	0.049
Note: Corporate Social Responsibility: R^2=0.299; Q^2=0.095; Financial Performance: R^2=0.368; Q^2=0.277; Fit model: SRMR=0.062; NFI=0.827; $\chi 2$=379.771					
Indirect effects					
Social entrepreneurship → Financial performance	0.115	0.042	2.729	0.003	

As shown in the values contained in Table 3, all the hypotheses proposed in this research were accepted, demonstrating the importance of the effects of interaction (Chin, 1998). In consequence, our theoretical model has found support in the empirical study, which confirms the implicit theory of their relationships.

The first hypothesis refers to the effect of social entrepreneurship on financial performance. In this case, we found positive evidence supporting H_1 ($\beta = 0.473$, $p < 0.001$). This result reinforces the arguments offered by the literature on social entrepreneurship and its effect on organisational performance.

Secondly, the relationship between social entrepreneurship and corporate social responsibility was studied, and evidence was also found to support this relationship (H_2) ($\beta = 0.551$, $p < 0.001$). In this case, social enterprises are companies that act responsibly with the diverse groups close to them; that is, employees, clients, suppliers, community, and the environment. The results show that the social concern of these entrepreneurs will make it easier for companies to develop business practices oriented towards acting responsibly with these groups.

The third hypothesis deals with the effect of CSR on FP. In this case, we find positive evidence that supports H_3 ($\beta = 0.208$, $p<0.01$). This implies that a company's responsible behaviours in each of the groups makes it easier to achieve greater results. This is achieved through more committed employees, customers and suppliers satisfied with the company's business practices or the improvement of the corporate image as a result of socially responsible practices in the community and the environment. All of this will certainly improve the organisation's results.

The indirect effect of social entrepreneurship on organisational performance through corporate social responsibility is reflected in Table 3. This analysis corresponds to the mediating effect of CSR on the relationship between SE and FP. The results ($\beta = 0.115$, $p < 0.01$) suggest that part of the effect of SE on FP is due to the promotion of CSR practices. This result is in line with the arguments found in the literature that suggest that part of the improvement in a company's results is because the company promotes responsible behaviours that affect various areas of the business, such as its clients and employees, resulting in an improvement in its corporate image and competitiveness. In consequence, a partial mediation of CSR is found.

The analysis of the contrast of the hypotheses and the most relevant aspects derived from this analysis are shown in Figure 2.

DISCUSSION AND CONCLUSION

Social entrepreneurship affects financial performance, and this research contributes to its development by showing the mediating role corporate social responsibility plays. Management of these variables reinforces firms confronting current challenges by articulating a system which integrates stakeholders into the organisational strategy. Specifically, the results support all the hypotheses, showing that a social entrepreneurial project can simultaneously influence financial performance by incorporating practices associated with corporate social responsibility.

The positive effect of SE on FP suggests that social entrepreneurship is committed to and propels organisational performance (Curto, 2012; Dacin et al., 2011; H. Haugh, 2005; Mair & Marti, 2006), building competitive advantages for both organisations and society. This study ratifies the idea that this type of entrepreneurship is a key factor in achieving better results through more committed and satisfied employees, customers, and suppliers as well as improving a company's corporate image through socially responsible practices with the community and the environment.

The results also support the importance of corporate social responsibility for the success of social entrepreneurship (Caraiani et al., 2012). Practices associated with corporate social responsibility reinforce collaboration with stakeholders in integrating social, environmental and ethical concerns.

Also, as a result of the analysis of the relationship between corporate social responsibility and financial performance, the evidence confirms that this relationship is in line with the arguments found in the literature (Alafi & Hasoneh, 2012; Oeyono et al., 2011). However, at the same time, it points out that this effect goes beyond the financial indicators most often justified in the literature and affects other non-economic indicators. According to the data obtained, the endogenous factors that most influence this relationship are employees and customers. This finding is in line with previous literature (Loureiro et al., 2012).

Finally, the evidence shows that part of the effect of social entrepreneurship on financial performance depends on practices associated with corporate social responsibility (Westhues & Einwiller, 2006). This confirms the generalisation that the incorporation of practices associated with corporate social responsibility is one of the most effective ways to promote results in the context of social entrepreneurship (Paulík et al., 2015).

This investigation has implications for this field of study. The results reveal the importance of social entrepreneurship as a strategy to achieve competitive advantages and complements the traditional vision of entrepreneurship. Second, it shows how CSR contributes to improving the competitiveness of companies. Also, it suggests that small businesses, such as firms in the social economy sector, can promote CSR.

In terms of managerial implications, our findings suggest the need for socially-oriented entrepreneurial projects to transform the social reality in which organisations operate and for the role these projects play in generating economic results. Second, companies should promote the adoption and implementation of organisational practices oriented towards corporate social responsibility that strengthen their human resource policies, increase transparency in the management and treatment of information, improve relationships with clients (internal and external), demonstrate their real commitment to solving the problems of the community where they operate and improve their commitment to and involvement in environmental care.

On the other hand, this study does not escape the restrictions derived from a cross-sectional study, which makes it impossible to analyse delayed effects in the variables studied or the determination of relationship causality. The information was collected from managers, who, although they have an informed view of the issues studied in this work, are no longer single informants. Finally, the information collected is based on the subjective opinion of the respondent, without the input of other objective information from external sources.

Therefore, the authors believe that it is necessary to extend the investigation through a longitudinal study that includes delayed effects over time. In this way, the study could be enriched with new moderating-mediating variables that affect the main structural model proposed, such as social capital.

REFERENCES

Alafi, K., & Hasoneh, A. (2012). Corporate social responsibility associated with customer satisfaction and financial performance a case study with Housing Banks in Jordan. *International Journal of Humanities and Social Science*, *2*(15), 102–115.

Austin, J. E., Gutierrez, R., Ogliastri, E., & Reficco, E. (2006). *Gestión efectiva de emprendimientos sociales: Lecciones extraídas de empresas y organizaciones de la sociedad civil en Iberoamérica*. Banco Interamericano de Desarrollo.

Barclay, D., Higgins, C., & Thompson, R. (1995). *The partial least squares (PLS) approach to causal modelling: personal computer adoption and use as an Illustration*. Academic Press.

B.O.E. (2011). *Ley 5/2011 (2011). de 29 de Marzo de Economía Social*. Cortes Generales.

Boettke, P. J., Coyne, C. J., & Leeson, P. T. (2007). Saving government failure theory from itself: Recasting political economy from an Austrian perspective. *Constitutional Political Economy*, *18*(2), 127–143. doi:10.100710602-007-9017-1

Boisot, M., & MacMillan, I. C. (2004). Crossing epistemological boundaries: Managerial and entrepreneurial approaches to knowledge management. *Long Range Planning*, *37*(6), 505–524. doi:10.1016/j.lrp.2004.09.002

Camargo, M. P., Silva Velez, E., & Patiño Moncada, J. D. A. (2015). *Análisis del comportamiento de los egresados del Programa Administración de Empresas de la Universidad de Cartagena en el período 2009-2012 frente al emprendimiento empresarial*. Universidad de Cartagena.

Camisón, C., & Villar-López, A. (2014). Organizational innovation as an enabler of technological innovation capabilities and firm performance. *Journal of Business Research, 67*(1), 2891–2902.

Caraiani, C., Lungu, C. I., Dascalu, C., Cimpoeru, M. V., & Dinu, M. (2012). Social and environmental performance indicators: Dimensions of integrated reporting and benefits for responsible management and sustainability. *African Journal of Business Management, 6*(14), 4990.

Carraher, S. M., Welsh, D. H., & Svilokos, A. (2016). Validation of a measure of social entrepreneurship. *European Journal of International Management, 10*(4), 386–402. doi:10.1504/EJIM.2016.077421

Carrión, G. C., Henseler, J., Ringle, C. M., & Roldán, J. L. (2016). Prediction-oriented modelling in business research by means of PLS path modelling: Introduction to a JBR special section. *Journal of Business Research, 69*(10), 4545–4551. doi:10.1016/j.jbusres.2016.03.048

Chin, W. (1998). The partial least squares approach to structural equation modelling. *Modern Methods for Business Research, 295*(2), 295-336.

Cho, S. J., Chung, C. Y., & Young, J. (2019). Study on the Relationship between CSR and Financial Performance. *Sustainability, 11*(2), 343. doi:10.3390u11020343

Crişan-Mitra, C., & Borza, A. (2015). Approaching CSR in Romania: An empirical analysis. *Procedia: Social and Behavioral Sciences, 207*, 546–552. doi:10.1016/j.sbspro.2015.10.125

Curto, M. (2012). Los emprendedores sociales: innovación al servicio del cambio. *Cuadernos de la Cátedra 'La Caixa' de Responsabilidad de la Empresa y Gobierno Corporativo, 13*, 1-23.

Dacin, M. T., Dacin, P. A., & Tracey, P. (2011). Social entrepreneurship: A critique and future directions. *Organization Science, 22*(5), 1203–1213. doi:10.1287/orsc.1100.0620

Durkin, C., & Gunn, R. (2016). *Social entrepreneurship: A skills approach.* Policy Press.

Europea, C. E. (2001). *Libro Verde: Fomentar un marco europeo para la responsabilidad social de las empresas*. CEE.

Fornell, C., & Larcker, D. F. (1981). Evaluating structural equation models with unobservable variables and measurement error. *JMR, Journal of Marketing Research, 18*(1), 39–50. doi:10.1177/002224378101800104

Guo, J., Sun, L., & Li, X. (2009). Corporate social responsibility assessment of Chinese corporation. *International Journal of Business and Management, 4*(4), 54–57. doi:10.5539/ijbm.v4n4p54

Haugh, H. (2005). A research agenda for social entrepreneurship. *Social Enterprise Journal, 1*(1), 1–12. doi:10.1108/17508610580000703

Haugh, H. M., & Talwar, A. (2016). Linking social entrepreneurship and social change: The mediating role of empowerment. *Journal of Business Ethics, 133*(4), 643–658. doi:10.100710551-014-2449-4

Hlady-Rispal, M., & Servantie, V. (2018). Deconstructing the way in which value is created in the context of social entrepreneurship. *International Journal of Management Reviews, 20*(1), 62–80. doi:10.1111/ijmr.12113

Kulfas, M. (2003). El contexto económico. Destrucción del aparato productivo y reestructuración regresiva. *Empresas Recuperadas. Ciudad de Buenos Aires, Secretaría de Desarrollo Económico. Gobierno de la Ciudad de Buenos Aires.*

Liñán, F., & Santos, F. J. (2007). Does social capital affect entrepreneurial intentions? *International Advances in Economic Research, 13*(4), 443–453. doi:10.100711294-007-9109-8

Loureiro, S. M., Sardinha, I. M. D., & Reijnders, L. (2012). The effect of corporate social responsibility on consumer satisfaction and perceived value: The case of the automobile industry sector in Portugal. *Journal of Cleaner Production, 37*, 172–178. doi:10.1016/j.jclepro.2012.07.003

Lozano, F. J., Lozano, R., Freire, P., Jiménez-Gonzalez, C., Sakao, T., Ortiz, M. G., Trianni, A., Carpenter, A., & Viveros, T. (2018). New perspectives for green and sustainable chemistry and engineering: Approaches from sustainable resource and energy use, management, and transformation. *Journal of Cleaner Production, 172*, 227–232. doi:10.1016/j.jclepro.2017.10.145

Luo, X., & Bhattacharya, C. B. (2006). Corporate social responsibility, customer satisfaction, and market value. *Journal of Marketing, 70*(4), 1–18. doi:10.1509/jmkg.70.4.001

Mair, J., & Marti, I. (2006). Social entrepreneurship research: A source of explanation, prediction, and delight. *Journal of World Business, 41*(1), 36–44. doi:10.1016/j.jwb.2005.09.002

Malhotra, N., & Mukherjee, A. (2004). The relative influence of organisational commitment and job satisfaction on service quality of customer-contact employees in banking call centres. *Journal of Services Marketing, 18*(3), 162–174. doi:10.1108/08876040410536477

Martin, R. L., & Osberg, S. (2007). Social entrepreneurship: The case for definition. *Stanford Social Innovation Review, 5*(2), 28–39.

Martínez Ávila, M., & Fierro Moreno, E. (2018). Aplicación de la técnica PLS-SEM en la gestión del conocimiento: Un enfoque técnico práctico. *RIDE Revista Iberoamericana para la Investigación y el Desarrollo Educativo, 8*(16), 130–164. doi:10.23913/ride.v8i16.336

Martinez-Conesa, I., Soto-Acosta, P., & Palacios-Manzano, M. (2017). Corporate social responsibility and its effect on innovation and firm performance: An empirical research in SMEs. *Journal of Cleaner Production, 142*(Part 4), 2374–2383. doi:10.1016/j.jclepro.2016.11.038

Monzon, J. L., & Chaves, R. (2008). The European Social Economy: Concept and dimensions of the third sector. *Annals of Public and Cooperative Economics, 79*(3-4), 549–577. doi:10.1111/j.1467-8292.2008.00370.x

Mozas, A. (2013). Emprendimiento y Economía Social. Presentación del número. *CIRIEC-España, Revista de Economía Pública. Social y Cooperativa., 78*, 7–9.

Nicholls, A. (2006). *Social entrepreneurship: New models of sustainable social change.* OUP Oxford.

Nunnally, J. C. (1978). *Psychometric Theory* (2nd ed.). McGraw-Hill.

Oeij, P. R., Kraan, K. O., & Vaas, F. (2010). *Impact of Social Innovation on Organisational Performance and Sickness Absence.* Paper presented at the XVII ISA World Congress of Sociology, Gothenburg, Sweden.

Oeyono, J., Samy, M., & Bampton, R. (2011). An examination of corporate social responsibility and financial performance: A study of the top 50 Indonesian listed corporations. *Journal of Global Responsibility*, *2*(1), 100–112. doi:10.1108/20412561111128555

Pablo, S.-I. H. J., Benito, Y.-A., & Juan, M.-G. (2019). Moderating effect of firm size on the influence of corporate social responsibility in the economic performance of micro-, small and medium-sized enterprises. *Technological Forecasting and Social Change*, 119774.

Palacios-Marqués, D., García, M. G., Sánchez, M. M., & Mari, M. P. A. (2019). Social entrepreneurship and organizational performance: A study of the mediating role of distinctive competencies in marketing. *Journal of Business Research*, *101*, 426–432. doi:10.1016/j.jbusres.2019.02.004

Paulík, J., Majková, M. S., Tykva, T., & Cervinka, M. (2015). Application of the CSR measuring model in a commercial bank in relation to their financial performance. *Economia e Sociologia*, *8*(4), 65–81. doi:10.14254/2071-789X.2015/8-4/5

Podsakoff, P. M., & Organ, D. W. (1986). Self-reports in organizational research: Problems and prospects. *Journal of Management*, *12*(4), 531–544. doi:10.1177/014920638601200408

Rawhouser, H., Cummings, M., & Newbert, S. L. (2017). Social impact measurement: Current approaches and future directions for social entrepreneurship research. *Entrepreneurship Theory and Practice.*

Ringle, C. M., Wende, S., & Becker, J. M. (2015). *SmartPLS 3.* Boenningstedt: SmartPLS GmbH.

Roberts, D., & Woods, C. (2005). Changing the world on a shoestring: The concept of social entrepreneurship. *University of Auckland Business Review, 7*(1), 45-51.

Sachdev, S. B., & Verma, H. V. (2004). Relative importance of service quality dimensions: A multisectoral study. *Journal of Services Research*, *4*(1).

Sarstedt, M., Hair, J. F., Ringle, C. M., Thiele, K. O., & Gudergan, S. P. (2016). Estimation Issues with PLS and CBSEM: Where the bias lies! *Journal of Business Research*, *69*(10), 3998–4010. doi:10.1016/j.jbusres.2016.06.007

Styles, C. (2006). Networking capability and international entrepreneurship: How networks function in Australian born global firms. *International Marketing Review*, *23*(5), 549–572. doi:10.1108/02651330610703445

Sullivan, S. E., Carraher, S. M., Baker, L., Cochrane, D., & Robinson, F. (2009). The Entrepreneurial Dilemma: Grow or Status Quo? A Real Case. *The Journal of Applied Management and Entrepreneurship*, *14*(4), 37.

Tepthong, S. (2014). *Social entrepreneurship and organizational performance: combining the resource dependence and resource-based views.* National Institute of Development Administration.

Tsoutsoura, M. (2004). *Corporate social responsibility and financial performance.* Academic Press.

Vázquez-Maguirre, M., & Portales, L. (2014). La empresa social como detonadora de calidad de vida y desarrollo sustentable en comunidades rurales [Social enterprise as a generator of quality of life and sustainable development in rural communities]. *Pensamiento & Gestión,* (37), 255-284.

Waheed, A., Zhang, Q., Rashid, Y., & Zaman Khan, S. (2020). The impact of corporate social responsibility on buying tendencies from the perspective of stakeholder theory and practices. *Corporate Social Responsibility and Environmental Management*, *27*(3), 1307–1315. doi:10.1002/csr.1885

Wang, G., Dou, W., Zhu, W., & Zhou, N. (2015). The effects of firm capabilities on external collaboration and performance: The moderating role of market turbulence. *Journal of Business Research*, *68*(9), 1928–1936. doi:10.1016/j.jbusres.2015.01.002

Weerawardena, J., & Sullivan-Mort, G. (2001). Learning, innovation and competitive advantage in not-for-profit aged care marketing: A conceptual model and research propositions. *Journal of Nonprofit & Public Sector Marketing*, *9*(3), 53–73. doi:10.1300/J054v09n03_04

Westhues, M., & Einwiller, S. (2006). Corporate foundations: Their role for corporate social responsibility. *Corporate Reputation Review*, *9*(2), 144–153. doi:10.1057/palgrave.crr.1550019

Zebryte, I., & Jorquera, H. (2017). Chilean tourism sector "B Corporations": evidence of social entrepreneurship and innovation. *International Journal of Entrepreneurial Behavior & Research*.

Chapter 6
The Impact of Triple Bottom Line on Sustainable Product Innovation:
Human, Social, and Economic Antecedents for Sustainable Development

Lucía Muñoz Pascual
IME, Department of Business Administration and Management, University of Salamanca, Spain

Jesús Galende
IME, Department of Business Administration and Management, University of Salamanca, Spain

ABSTRACT

Developing the pathways that lead to sustainable innovation in SMEs represents an important aspect of the business world and society. The aim of this chapter is to verify the relations and pathways that lead to sustainable product innovation performance while considering all three pillars of the triple bottom line approach. This study proposed a mixed methods approach to identify the antecedents of sustainable product innovation performance. The model was used to measure the effects of the three pillars of the triple bottom line: economic, social, and environmental developments. The model was also designed to account for the firm's type (public limited companies vs. general partnerships). The authors determined whether a firm's type moderates the effects of the three pillars. They identified alternative configurations of conditions and determined those that are likely to lead to sustainable product innovation performance. The findings show that social and environmental developments are two important antecedents for product innovation performance, and they contribute to different pathways.

DOI: 10.4018/978-1-7998-4833-2.ch006

INTRODUCTION

The aim of this chapter is to answer three questions and gaps: How are economic, social, and environmental antecedents balanced in innovation activities? What is needed to make the triple bottom line approach more effective (e.g., new communications, new human resources practices, and knowledge sharing management methods)? Does a firm's legal form (e.g., public limited companies versus general partnerships) affect its commitment toward sustainable innovation?

These questions are very interesting to the business world because their answers can facilitate an understanding of the key processes and pathways that allow companies to manage and integrate the three development goals with the most common innovation dynamics, e.g., knowledge search strategies and human resource management. Such a shift often calls for organizational restructuring and more diverse knowledge components or new routines, thus leading to novel pathways toward innovation. Furthermore, sustainable development requires a "society pool" approach to innovation whereby different stakeholders (e.g., trade partners, employees, governments for innovation's projects) are involved. In addition, our questions examine differences in innovation performance between Small and Medium Enterprises (SMEs) with different legal forms. SMEs with different legal forms can have different sustainability goals. In addition, this chapter is interesting to shed light on the relationships between knowledge management and corporate social responsibility in firms.

In this chapter, we identify the antecedents of the adoption of environmental practices (PRAC) and sustainable product innovation performance (PIP) in the context of the triple bottom line approach (TBL). TBL is evaluation system of corporate social responsibility. Corporate social responsibility is defined as the active and voluntary contribution to social, economic and environmental improvement by firms, generally with the objective to improve their competitive and value situation and their added value.

The adoption of environmental practices by a firm requires it to respond satisfactorily to the concerns of its various stakeholders (such as employees, customers, and suppliers) and address issues specific to its location (Dahlsrud, 2008). In our model, it is interesting to attend to the concerns of stakeholders because all its variables depend largely on the relationship with them (exports, shared knowledge, among others). Most firms' innovation efforts focus on only one development goal at a time, whereas the approach used here accounts for the economic, social, and environmental developments that lead to sustainable innovation, which benefits society. This chapter adopted a TBL to address a major gap in the literature on small- and medium-sized enterprises (SMEs). While previous research has focused primarily on the PRAC of large companies, interest in the sustainability of SMEs has grown for at least two reasons. SMEs are the backbone of the economy and represent more than 95% of enterprises across the world (Ayyagari et al., 2011). The PRAC of SMEs is significantly different from that of large companies as a result of several peculiarities: owners directly manage most SMEs; they are tightly linked to business partners and the local community; and they have financial, human, and time resource limitations that can hinder the implementation of PRAC commensurate to larger firms (Testa et al., 2016). This chapter also addressed sustainable paths for two SME types: Public Limited Companies (PLC) and General Partnerships (GP).

The literature recognizes that innovative activity, especially that of SMEs, is beneficial to society: increased employment, economic prosperity, and more competitive economies are among the advantages (Schramm, 2010). A company demonstrates innovative behavior by its desire to earn profits and acquire power and prestige, even at the expense of society. However, PIP often produces socially beneficial outcomes. Thus, we endeavored to expand our understanding of the specific antecedents that lead to sustainable PIP.

This chapter study the TBL to the sustainable PIP of SMEs. Specifically, we examined how the following antecedents lead to PRAC and sustainable PIP: the effects of the degree of internationalization, the costs of human resources, organizational learning capability at the firm level, and knowledge sharing at the interorganizational level.

This chapter can makes several contributions. First, the extend the sparse literature on antecedents of sustainable PIP in SMEs. Second, the chapter shows SME types that can enhance the effects of the antecedents. This chapter uses a double methodology to explain the effects of TBL on PIP. Therefore, the chapter aims to contribute to the fields of sustainability, technology, and human resource management (HRM) within SMEs. In addition, this study therefore makes a relevant theoretical contribution, as it proposes an integrative theoretical framework for analyzing sustainable development and innovation, the triple bottom line approach. We identify the main antecedents of economic and social development for the environmental development and PIP. This study is a detailed comparative analysis of the results obtained. These have been measured through the knowledge and objective perceptions that the CEO. The information and tools that the CEO has regarding information is relevant for managing their knowledge. Therefore, we present a new model for sustainable development and innovation.

BACKGROUND

Triple Bottom Line Approach

Since the 2005 world summit on social development, societies have been expected to design their growth strategies according to the three main sustainable development goals, i.e., economic development, social inclusion, and environmental protection, which reflect the three pillars of the triple bottom line approach characterizing sustainable business development (Cohen et al., 2008; Glavas and Mish, 2015). In recent years, one of the key topics tackled by the sustainable development discourse concerns the interrelated relationship between firms' innovation dynamics and sustainability. Indeed, the development and diffusion of sustainable innovations by companies have been deemed necessary conditions for the successful application of the triple bottom line approach, thus favoring social and environmental responsiveness while boosting economic growth (Dibrell et al., 2015). Accordingly, sustainable innovations represent a means through which organizations can actually foster sustainable development (Kennedy and Marting, 2016). At the same time, current sustainability challenges can become a source of inspiration for novel innovative trajectories, which may enhance firms' competitiveness and contribute to the construction of a better society (Wagner, 2009). However, academics have noticed that more than 20 years after sustainable development was first conceptualized, the triple bottom line approach is far from being the dominant business model for companies (Hall and Wagner, 2012). Furthermore, most firms' innovation efforts focus on only one development goal at a time, and research has yet to provide an in-depth discussion on how to reconcile the three sustainability pillars in innovation dynamics (Hart and Milstein, 2003; Longoni and Cagliano, 2018).

The Triple result, also called Triple Income Statement or Triple Balance, is a term related to sustainable business that refers to the impact that the activity of a firm has in the three dimensions: social, economic and environmental. The concept was developed by John Elkington in his book "*The Triple*

Bottom Line: Does it All Add Up?", published in 2004. Evidence of performance in relation to the triple bottom line is manifested in sustainability reports or corporate social responsibility.

The previous arguments emphasize that more research is needed to fully comprehend the interrelated nature of firms' innovation dynamics and sustainability. Furthermore, sustainable development requires a 'society pool' approach to innovation whereby different stakeholders (e.g., employees, customers, suppliers, and governments) are involved (Gasbarro et al. 2017; Vollenbroek, 2002; Wu, 2017). On the one hand, stakeholders' involvement helps to clarify the criteria for sustainable outcomes and then operationalize new strategic practices for innovation according to these criteria. In addition, there remains considerable uncertainty as to whether sustainable innovations actually lead to a more sustainable society (Hall and Wagner, 2012).

Therefore, we propose the following research questions and gaps:

- How are economic, social, and environmental aspects balanced in innovation activities?
- What is needed to make the triple bottom line approach more effective (e.g., new communications, new human resources practices, and knowledge sharing management methods)?
- Does a firm's legal form (e.g., public limited companies versus general partnerships) affect its commitment toward sustainable innovation?

In this line, the corporate social responsibility is the responsibility that each organization has with the environment in which it operates and with the society of which it is part, it is defined as the active and voluntary contribution to social, economic and environmental improvement by companies, generally with the objective to improve their competitive and value situation and their added value. The organization's joint performance evaluation system in these areas is known as the triple bottom line.

MAIN FOCUS OF THE CHAPTER

Issues, Controversies, Problems

Economic Development

Economic development ought to be a dimension that deals with the bottom line and the flow of money. It may involve looking at income or expenditures, business climate factors, employment, and business diversity factors. Specific examples include Personal income, Human Resource Cost, Establishment churn, Job growth, Percentage of firms in each sector, internationalization, and so forth. In this chapter, we propose two important dimensions of economic development. First, one external dimension of a firm: Internationalization. Second, one internal dimension of a firm: Human Resource Cost.

Internationalization

Internationalization is the process through which a firm expands its sales of goods or services around the world (Hitt et al., 2007). Internationalization is a strategy that is intended to increase a firm's competitive advantage and thus its value through enhanced economies of scale, growth opportunities, and diversification benefits while gaining access to new resources and knowledge (Attig and Boubakri,

2016). Therefore, some authors have considered international experience to be a relevant knowledge-based resource that can improve firms' PRAC (Ayuso et al., 2016). International firms are exposed to new and different ideas from diverse national contexts and various social, cultural, and environmental challenges. Thus, they can leverage the diverse knowledge acquired (Bansal, 2005). Companies that operate in foreign markets also gain experience in communicating, negotiating, and building relationships with stakeholders. This experience is conducive to developing a greater sensitivity to successful approaches to adapting their PRAC to the local context (Strike et al., 2006). Different empirical studies have shown the positive effect of internationalization on firms' environmental and social activities. Recently, Attig (2016) provided evidence of the link between internationalization and PRAC by using a large sample of firms from 44 countries. Therefore, foreign operations should lead to greater engagement in PRAC and sustainable PIP. In addition, exports can lead to the development of PIP for several reasons. First, international competition stimulates efforts to reduce costs, increase quality, and become more flexible, all of which force the company to continuously invest in technology and update and adapt their products. Further, with exports, the company increases the size of its market and thus increases its return and economies of scale. This is especially important given the significant fixed costs involved in PIP (Hoppmann, 2018).

Human Resource Cost

Investments in human resources should be oriented toward improving a firm's performance by instilling a culture of values in its employees (Celma et al., 2014). Human resources include three dimensions (intellectual, emotional, and social) that interact with each other to generate synergies that improve organizational capabilities (Gratton and Goshal, 2003). The continuous improvement of employees through new investments can lead to new PRAC and ideas for sustainable PIP (Muñoz-Pascual and Galende, 2017). Within each dimension of human resources, companies can invest in the development of a type of resource (knowledge, motivation, relationships). These resources are the source of new PRAC and sustainable PIP because they are unique and valuable (Gratton and Goshal, 2003).

Social Development

Social development refers to the social dimensions of a firm, community, or region and can include measurements of education, equity, and access to social resources, health and well-being, quality of life, and social capital (Muñoz-Pascual and Galende, 2020). The examples listed below are a small snippet of potential variables: Female labor force participation rate, Median income, Relative poverty, Percentage of employees with a post-secondary degree or certificate, Organizational learning capability, Interorganizational knowledge sharing, and so forth. In this chapter, we propose two important dimensions of social development. First, one internal dimension of firms: Organizational Learning Capability. Organizational Learning Capability is a relevant tool for SMEs because it grants access to social resources. In this way, SMEs with a high level of Organizational Learning Capability can collect and report information about what is going on inside and outside the company. Second, one external dimension of firms: Interorganizational Knowledge Sharing. Knowledge Sharing is another key tool to improve the social capital that is exchanged between companies. For instance, knowledge sharing may help to improve business partner relations, co-create new ideas and projects, share new viewpoints, and, consequently, have a greater knowledge of the social and business reality.

Organizational Learning Capability

Organizational learning capability (OLC) refers to the importance that facilitators place on organizational learning (Barney, 1995). Organizational learning represents the refinement and renewal of dynamic knowledge. The renewal of knowledge assets provides the ability to learn and explore new knowledge while exploiting existing knowledge (Jérez-Gómez et al., 2005). Organizational learning occurs in a context that consists of "both the organization and its external environment" (Jaw and Liu, 2003). Lichtenthaler (2009) classified organizational learning into three processes: explorative, exploitative, and transformative. All three processes have positive effects on PRAC and sustainable PIP. Organizational learning requires organizations to plan, envision, and transact. According to Chiva et al. (2007), OLC comes from experimentation, risk-taking, interaction with the external environment, dialogue, and participative decision-making. Experimentation is the extent to which firms try out new ideas, are curious about how things work, or carry out changes in work processes. Risk taking reflects the tolerance of ambiguity, uncertainty, and errors that facilitate organizational learning. Interaction with the external environment is the extent of the relationships that a firm has with its immediate environment. Dialogue is defined as a sustained collective inquiry into the processes, assumptions, and certainties that compose everyday experience. Finally, participative decision-making refers to the level of influence that employees have in the process. A degree of ambiguity and inconsistency still surrounds the question of how OLC affects PRAC and sustainable PIP (Valaei et al., 2017; Muñoz-Pascual and Galende, 2020).

Knowledge Sharing

Knowledge sharing (KS) refers to a firm's ability to exploit information from business partners or to identify market opportunities (Shih et al., 2012). Interorganizational KS enables firms to achieve a competitive advantage in rapidly changing business environments (Bhatti et al., 2016). Interorganizational KS is a complex issue with strategic importance for PRAC and sustainable PIP (Boer et al., 2011). Firms determine the level of KS by the perceived benefits, such as information exchange, social satisfaction, and dependence among the partners (Cheng, 2011). The ability to share knowledge influences an SME's sustainable innovation. The current knowledge on whether and how firms can leverage relational capital and KS for sustainable innovation is equivocal. The existing research has conceptualized few of the underlying processes responsible for mobilizing relational capital; thus, it has yielded mostly contradictory empirical results. We consider KS to be a resource of intellectual capital exchange between firms (Liu et al., 2017). Following Kianto et al. (2017), knowledge is the most important resource for PIP in firms. Xie et al. (2016) reported the positive effect of interorganizational links on PIP. Participation in interfirm KS appears to be an effective approach to obtaining new mechanisms and information to develop PRAC and sustainable PIP (Bhatti et al., 2016; Muñoz-Pascual et al., 2019; Muñoz-Pascual and Galende, 2020). In this paper, we analyze how KS at the interorganizational level contributes to the development of PRAC and sustainable PIP in SMEs. Since knowledge is the core factor that supports effective and efficient decision-making, KS contributes to the creation of a competitive advantage.

Environment Development

Environmental dimensions should represent the adoption of natural resources and reflect potential influences on its viability. It could incorporate air and water quality, energy consumption, natural resources, solid and toxic waste, and land use/land cover. Ideally, organizations should track long-range trends for each of the environmental dimensions to help identify the impacts that a project, policy, or product will have on an area, market, or community. In this context, we focus on a complete concept: Adoption of Environmental Practices in SMEs.

Adoption of Environmental Practices

The reinforcement of environmental regulations worldwide in recent years has motivated firms to pursue environmental management practices (Gavronski et al., 2008). Similarly, researchers have found that the main economic or social factors leading to the adoption of environmental practices are exports (internationalization), new investments in human resources, organizational learning capability, and knowledge sharing. In the case of SMEs, the main stakeholders in PRAC are customers, the government, local society, employees, and suppliers; other stakeholders include competitors, insurers, banks, and firms in the area (Fernández-Viñé et al., 2010). In addition, PRAC may directly affect sustainable PIP since it might require the application of more efficient methods of consumption and waste recycling, and a consequence of such methods is a reduction in the total amount of the company's operational costs (Ramanathan et al., 2010). Aragón-Correa et al. (2008) showed that a proactive environmental strategy requires changes in routines and operational methods. Chan and Hawkins (2010) added that the adoption of environmental practices helps to achieve better safety standards and healthier working conditions. Moreover, companies that are proactive in environmental practices can take advantage of public support or governmental subsidies (Mohamed, 2001). Fresner and Engelhardt (2004) asserted that the adoption of environmental practices is very beneficial to SMEs and produces an immediate and visible improvement in organizational efficiency and PIP.

Product Innovation Performance for Sustainable Development

PIP is the result of successfully exploiting new knowledge and sustainability (Amabile et al., 1996). This process comprises technical design, research and development, manufacturing, management, and the commercial activities that constitute the marketing of a new (or improved) product. Innovation involves two dimensions: technical and nontechnical; however, studies have mainly addressed the former (Ngo and O'Cass, 2013). On the basis of the relevant literature, we analyzed both dimensions while considering certain configurations of nontechnical innovations (OLC, KS, and PRAC) that stimulate the development of sustainable PIP (Chang, 2016). Product innovation performance involves two dimensions: efficiency (PIP_EFFICI) and efficacy (PIP_EFFICA) (Alegre et al., 2006). Innovation efficiency reflects the effort spent to achieve a certain degree of success, while innovation efficacy reflects an innovation's degree of success. The innovation process includes several stages from discovery to implementation (Kyffin and Gardien, 2009) that make success dependent on a firm's efforts. This process plays an important role in the success of innovation (Gupta and Malhotra, 2013). SMEs can achieve sustainable development through innovation if they take care of the process of innovation development. Thus, our study offers a complete analysis of PIP on the basis of different indicators ranging from the preparation to the implementation of the activities necessary for the development of PIP. Authors such as Curado et al. (2018) have indicated that PIP_EFFICI has a positive effect on PIP_EFFICA. Therefore, if we introduce PRAC as a set of activities that help in the preparation, implementation, and start-up of innovation, we can achieve PIP and, as a result, sustainable development.

In addition, the difference between environmental development and sustainable development is relevance. Environmental development is just a part of sustainable development as a whole. Sustainable development must be implemented by a set of business results that take into account economic, social and environmental development. Therefore, environmental development is one of the three central parts to achieve sustainable development.

Firm Type

The firm's organizational structure and its type can affect the adoption of environmental practices and sustainable PIP. Therefore, the adoption depends on whether a firm is a PLC or GP.

Public Limited Companies

A PLC is an organization type that is widely used among medium and large companies in which all capital is divided into shares. One of the characteristics of a PLC is that the responsibility of each partner is proportional to their share of the capital. Therefore, participating in a PLC has a fairly high level of financial security. In addition, a PLC is a personal organic structure. This means that you can act as a legal person. The founding of a PLC requires very high initial capital. In practically all legislation around the world, a PLC requires two or three obligatory events: The general shareholders' meeting (or assembly) is the venue in which all shareholders meet. One of its charges is the election of the company's administrators. The administrators are the managers that make up the executive team and, at the same time, are the representative body. The supervisory board has the task of supervising the administrators.

General Partnerships

In contrast to a PLC, a GP contracts debts. The partner or partners will only respond to them in relation to the amount of money contributed to the firm. The GP is an organization type widely used by SMEs. GPs have rules for the transmission of capital contributions, accounting, and internal bodies, and these rules differentiate them from PLCs. The required bodies of the general meeting make important decisions and are responsible for the election of the administrators. In addition, last year's accounts are approved during the general meeting. The administrators are in charge of the management of the firm. There can be one, two, or more administrators. The size, the organizational structure, and the legal form of the company are important aspects that can influence behavior, strategy, adoption of environmental practices, and, consequently, innovation. For instance, depending on its legal form, a company may have access to different amounts of funding under different conditions for the development of new innovation projects. In addition, the legal form of the company may influence the adoption of environmental practices. In light of these differences, we argue that the firm type moderates the main effects of the TBL on sustainable PIP.

Alternative Configurations

The configuration theory asserts that more than one configuration of conditions may lead to the same result — equifinality. The conditions that lead to the outcome differ from those that lead to its absence. A configuration is a specific combination of conditions that produces an outcome of interest. Configurations of conditions enable us to model complexity, even for a limited number of conditions. Configurational approaches admit that conditions can be causally related in one configuration, yet they can be unrelated or even inversely related in others. Such configurations expose asymmetric characteristics and synergetic effects that replace the traditional bivariate interaction effects. The consideration of complexity and ambiguity leads to nonlinear relations. We should explore the sets of alternative configurations that lead to both the outcome and its absence (Curado et al., 2018).

Research Model

Figure 1 summarizes the model research model.

Figure 1.

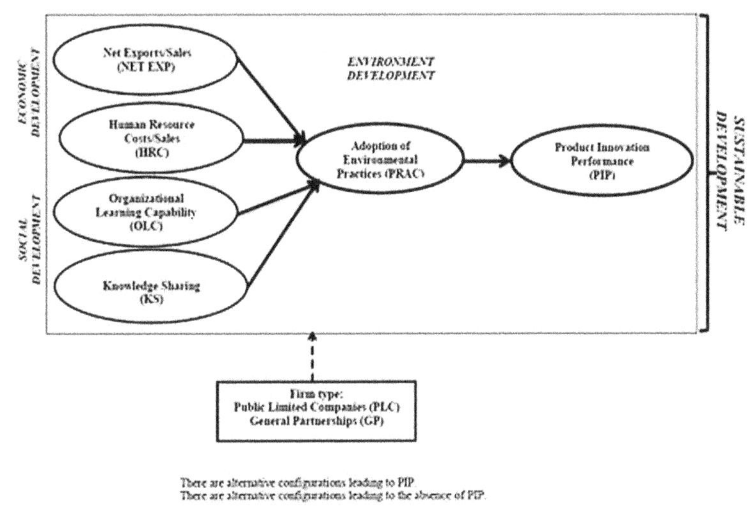

METHODOLOGICAL PROPOSAL

Mixed Methods Approach

Research as a way of knowing, interpreting, and transforming reality cannot ignore the constant demands of an increasingly unstable, complex, and diverse business world; hence, for some researchers (Valaei et al., 2017; Curado et al., 2018; Oyemomi et al., 2016), the two traditional research approaches (qualitative and quantitative) fall short in the resolution of problems and situations that require new perspectives. In this context, the application of mixed methods approaches is important, and it allows us to exploit the strengths of both approaches to achieve more complete understandings of economic, social, and environmental problems (Berkovich, 2018).

This chapter proposes to the study of sustainable development and PIP with a mixed methods approach. First, and from a quantitative perspective, SEM. SEM is a complex statistical technique for studying causal relationships between variables with direct and indirect effects. In addition, a multigroup analysis for testing one moderating variable in the model. Secondly, and from a qualitative perspective, fsQCA, which is a relevant statistical technique for studying alternative configurations that lead to PIP. Our study therefore provides a unique, complete, and coherent understanding of sustainable development and PIP.

The mixed methods approach can be defined as a kind of research that combines quantitative and qualitative techniques, methods, approximations, concepts, and language in a holistic study (Creswell and Plano, 2007).

This methodology leads to a complete and joint interpretation of the results. In accordance with Creswell and Plano (2007), this is a triangulation design for the application of the mixed methods approach. In short, the mixed methods approach

1. Combines the strengths provided by the two approaches.
2. Attenuates the weaknesses of their separate application.
3. Allows for a better understanding of PRAC and PIP.

This means that quantitative and qualitative methods are not incompatible. Moreover, their combination is relevant when looking for the causes and conditions that lead companies to sustainable PIP (Kraus et al., 2018).

DISCUSSION AND CONCLUSION

In this line, the importance of sustainability in business and society has been emphasized by many scholars (Muñoz-Pascual et al., 2019). The development of sustainable innovations represents a driving force for the creation of new job opportunities, regional/national/international competitiveness, and sustainable and social growth. Three pillars (economic, social, and environment development) play a significant role in the decision to develop new sustainable innovations.

However, few studies about SMEs have examined the three pillars together to increase sustainable innovations (Muñoz-Pascual et al., 2019). The previous arguments emphasize that more research is needed to fully comprehend the interrelated nature of firms' innovation dynamics and sustainability (Hart and Milstein, 2003; Longoni and Cagliano, 2018). In addition, this chapter offers the opportunity to understand whether SMEs with different legal forms behave differently in terms of sustainable innovations.

Drawing on the TBL, this chapter shows the impact of two economic factors (internationalization and human resources cost) and two social factors (organizational learning capability and knowledge sharing) on PRAC and sustainable PIP (González-Masip et al., 2019)

Our proposal indicates that internationalization is indeed positively associated with PRAC. Hence, the SMEs with positive outcomes from internationalization are better prepared to develop sustainable PIP (PLC or GP). Our proposal also indicates that human resource cost of GP SMEs exerts a positive influence on PRAC. Therefore, investments in HR are very important within GP SMEs. Thus, the managers engage in PRAC, and they use financial resources to foster an employee's knowledge, creativity, and motivation (Song and Yu, 2018). HR is a valuable resource, it is also a strategic for the adoption of PRAC (Glavas and Mish, 2015).

Following the TBL, this chapter show that the second pillar, social factors (organizational learning capability and knowledge sharing), has a positive impact on the third pillar (environment development). New meetings and knowledge exchanges lead to new practices, new environments, new products, and, consequently, sustainable societies. Finally, our chapter shows that the adoption of PRAC is the third pillar for sustainable PIP.

There are several theoretical and practical implications arising from our results. We provide support for the TBL within the context of sustainable PIP and confirm the importance of several resources and capabilities within the three pillars for SMEs' sustainable PIP. SMEs can contribute to sustainable development and thus respond to the great global challenges of sustainable development such as; a) climate change, b) greater investment for human development, and c) cooperation and creation of networks to share knowledge about ecological practices and policies among companies. Therefore, our chapter presents a real solution, available to academics and managers, showing how SMEs can develop new products that contribute to the quality and conservation of the environment, the social and human development and sustainable economic growth (Kraus et al., 2017; Musa and Mohamad, 2018).

Specifically, our chapter indicate that international activities are always relevant to the implementation of PRAC. The exploitation of new opportunities can help SMEs achieve sustainable development. Our findings show that HR investments are important for GPs. Here, SME managers focus on HR practices because they may more easily get to know their employees. Currently, firms are already beginning to show their concern in this regard. Max De Pree—founder and CEO of Herman Miller, a Fortune 500 company—completely restructured and invested in the organization on the basis of human values. De Pree believes that employees are the source of transformation that every company needs to face changes and generate new sustainable innovations. De Pree also believes that employees can more easily achieve the mission, vision, and sustainability values of the company. Sustainable innovative success is much more likely to be achieved by placing more focus on human and social values than other material resources. Along these lines, the Great Place to Work Institute (GPTW) indicates that the best companies to work for are those that foster relationships to improve the trust between leaders and employees or among the employees themselves, and they invest a great deal in HRM. Furthermore, the second pillar of social development indicates that organizational learning capability at the firm level and knowledge sharing at the interorganizational level can generate new resources for implementing sustainable PRAC in SMEs.

For SME managers, our chapter highlight the need to focus on aligning the pillars of the TBL for sustainable PIP. We propose the integration of external activities, such as internationalization and knowledge sharing, with internal activities, such as HR, organizational learning capability, and PRAC, for sustainable PIP development. Thus, the overall results of the study point to the importance of adopting the TBL as a way to better measure firms' strategic resources and capabilities by emphasizing ethical business behavior for sustainable PIP (Martín-de Castro, et al. 2016). Therefore, TBL is evaluation system of corporate social responsibility.

From a global perspective, governments should focus on promoting and formulating new regulations and cutting taxes to generate sustainable innovations. From an internal perspective of SMEs, managers may choose to implement the Eco-Management and Audit Scheme (EMAS) or other software for environmental regulation. This can be done by providing adequate financing, training, and networking between firms and countries.

FUTURE RESEARCH DIRECTIONS

Our proposal should be interpreted within the possible limitations of the study. The self-reported measures certainly have their weaknesses, since they measure the level of OLC, KS, PRAC, and PIP on the basis of managers' perceptions. However, other previous paper uses objective data with economic variables such as NET EXP and HRC (Muñoz-Pascual et al., 2019).

In addition, future researchers could implement additional measures to evaluate economic development such as ROA, ROE, sales, and economic growth.

The extent to which they can be generalized to other geographical contexts, large companies, and institutional settings remains questionable. To follow up on our findings and help us better understand our results, future studies could analyze the effects of other variables within the three dimensions of the TBL for sustainable development (creativity, technology, etc.). We argue that addressing such dimensions of sustainable development is a challenge worth pursuing by using the triple bottom line approach. Such influences should be explored at the individual, organizational, and interorganizational level. Longitudinal studies that incorporate several levels of analysis could provide evidence of the causal relations and interactions among the dimensions of the TBL. In addition, future studies could focus on examining sectorial effects, since firms from certain industries are exposed to more opportunities for PRAC than are firms from other industries.

Our chapter can serve as a useful guide for the design of future research on the development of sustainable innovations on the basis of the TBL. Our study analyzed SMEs because they represent 95% of the businesses in the world. In this sense, we propose that they are the best agents of change, transformation, development of sustainable innovations, and, therefore, global sustainable growth. Therefore, among SMEs, we analyzed whether there may be differences in the development of sustainable innovations due to their legal form. However, it would be very interesting to determine whether our results differ from the results of studying sustainable innovation in large companies. The application of our research model in the context of large companies may help to answer different research questions: Is it easier for large companies to access financing for sustainable innovations? Do large companies have more access to business partners for the development of sustainable innovations? Do large companies have more environmental advantages in national and international policies for the development of sustainable innovations? The results of investigating these three research questions will be very interesting for future research because they can be compared with our results obtained for SMEs.

It would also be interesting to analyze the influence of context-dependent institutional pressures, such as government regulation or consumer sensitivity for sustainable development. Finally, future research could undertake an international comparison to test for the consistency of our findings across countries and/or cultures and also uncover new sources of environmental development for sustainable PIP in SMEs.

RECOMMENDATIONS AND PRACTICAL IMPLICATIONS

The authors offer five relevant practical recommendations and implementation guidelines for SMEs:

1. International business for sustainable innovation:
    a. The willingness of experts to help with new international activities. For example: managers can develop new activities to implement new projects and products in firms.
    b. Presence in congresses and international fairs. The active participation of employees in this type of event can open their minds and make them become more proactive in implementing new tools and methodologies within the firm.
    c. Continuous vigilance to detect new investment and export opportunities.

   d. Joint innovation projects with foreign partners.

2. Investment in and development of new human resource practices for sustainable innovation:
   a. Courses and training in sustainable development. Continuous training of employees within the firm is the greatest symbol of good human resource management and, therefore, of innovation. A firm that innovates must give continuous training to its workers and recollect itself if it wants to obtain a sustainable competitive advantage.
   b. Encouragement of employee trust and motivation. Engaging employees' trust and motivation for developing new ideas. It is very important to create a climate of trust and motivation with employees so that they can feel comfortable learning, translate their knowledge into new ideas or share them with their colleagues.
   c. Creation of a culture that encourages sustainable development. It is possible that if there is a climate of trust and motivation within the firm, it is easier to implement a culture of creativity and innovation, that is, where it is allowed to make mistakes that allow us to grow and advance as people and as an organization.
   d. The build-up of norms that encourage sustainable development. In addition, if the firm implements standards and guidelines of conduct that require compliance, it will be easier to achieve innovative success and sustainable development.
3. Fast Organizational Learning Capability for sustainable innovation:
   a. Climate for learning and experimentation. Firms that foster a climate of learning and experimentation will guide the training of their employees as an investment or a long-term process. This favors the culture of continuous innovation and sustainability.
   b. Encouragement to take risks in the design of new sustainable products. In addition, firms that encourage their employees to take risks and new challenges will be achieving continuous learning in which they will gain knowledge whether they are successful or not in innovation results and sustainability.
   c. Implementation of environmental information collection systems to determine the needs of consumers.
   d. Teamwork and effective communication. For the exchange, interaction and effective implementation of employee knowledge, it is very important that the firm encourages teamwork and communication. Communication is an effective tool to improve and develop new projects and sustainable products.
   e. Involvement of employees in important decisions. In addition, if the firm offers security, autonomy and responsibility to its employees so that they can be part of decision-making, this will make the application of training and knowledge faster, more effective and voluntary. "If we are part of the decision we will also be part of the solution".
   f. Knowledge Sharing for sustainable innovation:
   g. Reinforcement of information sharing with new alliances and business partners. Generating a work environment where employees share information. For example: meeting rooms, breaks...
   h. Creation of a culture that encourages knowledge sharing.
   i. Encouragement of employees to share their knowledge and ideas with those outside partners. Firms can design compensation mechanisms for those employees who train, help and share their knowledge.

   j. Support for business networking (e.g., LinkedIn). Firms can design physical and electronic networks where their employees can have a space within their working day to exchange options, information, learning, knowledge, experiences, ideas...
   k. Use of performance management systems to promote voice and knowledge sharing.
   l. Creation of incentives (e.g., promotion, bonus, higher salary) to facilitate knowledge sharing.
4. Adoption of Environmental practices for sustainable innovation:
   a. Design of a code of environmental ethics for all members of the company and its business partners.
   b. Implementation of energy saving practices.
   c. Implementation of reverse logistics practices.
   d. Development of productive activity with ecological products.
   e. Advanced training in eco-innovation and social and environmental needs.

In short, this study invites the business community to identify the effects that can be derived from economic, social and environmental development. It may lead to extraordinary innovation results within the organization. Therefore, this chapter is interesting to shed light on the relationships between knowledge management and corporate social responsibility in firms.

ACKNOWLEDGMENT

The authors are grateful for the support provided by the Spanish Ministry of Science and Innovation (project PID2019-107546GA-I00 –AEI/FEDER, UE).

REFERENCES

Alegre, J., Lapiedra, R., & Chiva, R. (2006). A Measurement Scale for Product Innovation Performance. *European Journal of Innovation Management*, *9*(4), 333–346. doi:10.1108/14601060610707812

Amabile, T. M., Conti, R., Coon, H., Lazenby, J., & Herron, M. (1996). Assessing the Work Environment for Creativity. *Academy of Management Journal*, *39*, 1154–1184.

Aragón-Correa, J. A., Hurtado-Torres, N., Sharma, S., & García-Morales, V. J. (2008). Environmental Strategy and Performance in Small Firms: A Resource-Based Perspective. *Journal of Environmental Management*, *86*(1), 88–103. doi:10.1016/j.jenvman.2006.11.022 PMID:17239519

Attig, N., Boubakri, N., El Ghoul, S., & Guedhami, O. (2016). Firm Internationalization and Corporate Social Responsibility. *Journal of Business Ethics*, *134*(2), 171–197. doi:10.100710551-014-2410-6

Ayuso, S., Roca, M., Arevalo, J. A., & Aravind, D. (2016). What Determines Principle-Based Standards Implementation? Reporting on Global Compact adoption in Spanish Firms. *Journal of Business Ethics*, *133*(3), 553–565. doi:10.100710551-014-2412-4

Ayyagari, M., Demirgü-Kunt, A., & Maksimovic, V. (2011). *Small vs. Young Firms across the World—Contribution to Employment, Job Creation, and Growth*. Policy Research Working Paper 5631, World Bank.

Bansal, P. (2005). Evolving Sustainability: A Longitudinal Study of Corporate Sustainable Development. *Strategic Management Journal*, *26*(3), 197–218. doi:10.1002mj.441

Barney, J. B. (1995). Looking Inside for Competitive Advantage. *The Academy of Management Executive*, *9*(4), 49–61. doi:10.5465/ame.1995.9512032192

Berkovich, I. (2018). Beyond Qualitative/Quantitative Structuralism: The Positivist Qualitative Research and the Paradigmatic Disclaimer. *Quality & Quantity*, *52*(5), 2063–2077. doi:10.100711135-017-0607-3

Bhatti, W. A., Larimo, J., & Carrasco, I. (2016). Strategy's Effect on Knowledge Sharing in Host Country Networks. *Journal of Business Research*, *69*(11), 4769–4774. doi:10.1016/j.jbusres.2016.04.028

Boer, N. I., Berends, H., & Van Baalen, P. (2011). Relational Models for Knowledge Sharing Behavior. *European Management Journal*, *29*(2), 85–97. doi:10.1016/j.emj.2010.10.009

Celma, D., Martínez-Garcia, E., & Coenders, G. (2014). Corporate Social Responsibility in Human Resource Management: An Analysis of Common Practices and their Determinants in Spain. *Corporate Social Responsibility and Environmental Management*, *21*(2), 82–99. doi:10.1002/csr.1301

Chan, E. S. W., & Hawkins, R. (2010). (2010). Attitude Towards EMSs in an International Hotel: An Exploratory Case Study. *International Journal of Hospitality Management*, *29*(4), 641–651. doi:10.1016/j.ijhm.2009.12.002

Chang, C. H. (2016). The Determinants of Green Product Innovation Performance. *Corporate Social Responsibility and Environmental Management*, *23*(2), 65–76. doi:10.1002/csr.1361

Cheng, J. H. (2011). Inter-Organizational Relationships and Information Sharing in Supply Chains. *International Journal of Information Management*, *31*(4), 374–384. doi:10.1016/j.ijinfomgt.2010.09.004

Chiva, R., Alegre, J., & Lapiedra, R. (2007). Measuring Organizational Learning Capability Among the Workforce. *International Journal of Manpower*, *28*(3/4), 224–242. doi:10.1108/01437720710755227

Cohen, B., Smith, B., & Mitchell, R. (2008). Toward a Sustainable Conceptualization of Dependent Variables in Entrepreneurship Research. *Business Strategy and the Environment*, *17*(2), 107–119. doi:10.1002/bse.505

Creswell, J., & Plano, V. (2007). *Designing and Conducting Mixed Methods Research*. Sage Publications, Inc.

Curado, C., Muñoz-Pascual, L., & Galende, J. (2018). Antecedent to Innovation Performance in SMEs: A Mixed Methods Approach. *Journal of Business Research*, *89*, 206–215. doi:10.1016/j.jbusres.2017.12.056

Dahlsrud, A. (2008). How Corporate Social Responsibility is defined: An Analysis of 37 definitions. *Corporate Social Responsibility and Environmental Management*, *15*(1), 1–13. doi:10.1002/csr.132

Dibrell, C., Craig, J. B., Kim, J., & Johnson, A. J. (2015). Establishing How Natural Environmental Competency, Organizational Social Consciousness, and Innovativeness Relate. *Journal of Business Ethics*, *127*, 591–605. doi:10.100710551-013-2043-1

Elkington, J. (2004). *The Triple Bottom Line: Does It All Add Up?* Routledge., doi:10.4324/9781849773348

Fernández-Viñé, M. B., Gómez-Navarro, T., & Capuz-Rizo, S. F. (2010). Eco-efficiency in the SMEs of Venezuela. Current Status and Future Perspectives. *Journal of Cleaner Production*, *18*(8), 736–746. doi:10.1016/j.jclepro.2009.12.005

Fresner, J., & Engelhardt, G. (2004). Experiences with Integrated Management Systems for Two Small Companies in Austria. *Journal of Cleaner Production*, *12*(6), 623–631. doi:10.1016/j.jclepro.2003.09.013

Gasbarro, F., Annunziata, E., Rizzi, F., & Frey, M. (2017). The Interplay between Sustainable Entrepreneurs and Public Authorities: Evidence from Sustainable Energy Transitions. *Organization & Environment*, *30*(3), 226–252. doi:10.1177/1086026616669211

Gavronski, I., Ferrer, G., & Paiva, E. L. (2008). ISO 14001 Certification in Brazil: Motivations and Benefits. *Journal of Cleaner Production*, *16*(1), 87–94. doi:10.1016/j.jclepro.2006.11.002

Glavas, A., & Mish, J. (2015). Resources and Capabilities of Triple Bottom Line Firms: Going over Old or Breaking New Ground? *Journal of Business Ethics*, *127*(3), 623–642. doi:10.100710551-014-2067-1

González-Masip, J., Martín-de Castro, G., & Hernández, A. (2019). Inter-organizational knowledge spillovers: Attracting talent in science and technology parks and corporate social responsibility practices. *Journal of Knowledge Management*, *23*(5), 975–999. doi:10.1108/JKM-06-2018-0367

Gratton, L., & Ghoshal, S. (2003). Managing Personal Human Capital: New Ethos for the 'Volunteer' employee. *European Management Journal*, *21*(1), 1–10. doi:10.1016/S0263-2373(02)00149-4

Gupta, S., & Malhotra, N. (2013). Marketing Innovation: A Resource-Based View of International and Local Firms. *Marketing Intelligence & Planning*, *31*(2), 111–126. doi:10.1108/02634501311312026

Hall, J., & Wagner, M. (2012). Integrating Sustainability into Firms' Processes: Performance Effects and the Moderating Role of Business Models and Innovation. *Business Strategy and the Environment*, *21*(3), 183–196. doi:10.1002/bse.728

Hart, S. L., & Milstein, M. B. (2003). Creating Sustainable Value. *The Academy of Management Executive*, *17*(2), 56–67. doi:10.5465/ame.2003.10025194

Hitt, M. A., Ireland, R. D., & Hoskisson, R. E. (2007). *Strategic Management: Competitiveness and Globalization* (7th ed.). Thomson South-Western.

Hoppmann, J. (2018). The Role of Interfirm Knowledge Spillovers for Innovation in Mass-Produced Environmental Technologies: Evidence from the Solar Photovoltaic Industry. *Organization & Environment*, *31*(1), 3–24. doi:10.1177/1086026616680683

Jaw, B. S., & Liu, W. (2003). Promoting Organizational Learning and Self-Renewal in Taiwanese Companies: The Role of HRM. *Human Resource Management*, *42*(3), 223–241. doi:10.1002/hrm.10082

Jérez-Gómez, P., Cespedes-Lorente, J., & Valle-Cabrera, R. (2005). Organizational Learning and Compensation Strategies: Evidence from the Spanish Chemical Industry. *Human Resource Management, 44*(3), 279–299. doi:10.1002/hrm.20071

Kennedy, E. B., & Marting, T. A. (2016). Biomimicry Streamlining the Front End of Innovation for Environmentally Sustainable Products. *Research Technology Management, 59*(4), 40–47. doi:10.1080/08956308.2016.1185342

Kianto, A., Sáenz, J., & Aramburu, N. (2017). Knowledge-Based Human Resource Management Practices, Intelectual Capital and Innovation. *Journal of Business Research, 81*, 11–20. doi:10.1016/j.jbusres.2017.07.018

Kraus, S., Burtscher, J., Niemand, T., Roig-Tierno, N., & Syrjä, P. (2017). Configurational Paths to Social Performance in SMEs: The Interplay of Innovation, Sustainability, Resources and Achievement Motivation. *Sustainability, 9*(10), 18–28. doi:10.3390u9101828

Kraus, S., Ribeiro-Soriano, D., & Schüssler, M. (2018). Fuzzy-set Qualitative Comparative Analysis (fsQCA) in Entrepreneurship and Innovation Research – the Rise of a Method. *The International Entrepreneurship and Management Journal, 14*(1), 15–33. doi:10.100711365-017-0461-8

Kyffin, S., & Gardien, P. (2009). Navigating the Innovation Matrix: An Approach to Designled Innovation. *International Journal of Design, 3*, 57–69.

Lichtenthaler, U. (2009). Absorptive Capacity, Environmental Turbulence, and the Complementarity of Organizational Learning Processes. *Academy of Management Journal, 52*(4), 822–846. doi:10.5465/amj.2009.43670902

Liu, Y., Li, Y., Shi, L. H., & Liu, T. (2017). Knowledge Transfer in Buyer-Supplier Relationships: The role of transactional and relational governance mechanisms. *Journal of Business Research, 78*, 285–293. doi:10.1016/j.jbusres.2016.12.024

Longoni, A., & Cagliano, R. (2018). Sustainable Innovativeness and the Triple Bottom Line: The Role of Organizational Time Perspective. *Journal of Business Ethics, 151*(4), 1097–1120. doi:10.100710551-016-3239-y

Martín-de Castro, G., Amores-Salvadó, J., & Navas-López, J. (2016). Environmental management systems and firm performance: Improving firm environmental policy through stakeholders engagement. *Corporate Social Responsibility and Environmental Management, 23*(4), 243–256. doi:10.1002/csr.1377

Mohamed, S. T. (2001). The Impact of ISO 14,000 on developing World Businesses. *Renewable Energy, 23*(3-4), 579–584. doi:10.1016/S0960-1481(00)00145-2

Muñoz-Pascual, L., Curado, C., & Galende, J. (2019). The triple bottom line on sustainable product innovation performance: A mixed methods approach. *Sustainability, 11*(6), 1689. doi:10.3390u11061689

Muñoz-Pascual, L., Curado, C., & Galende, J. (2019). How does the use of informartion technologies affect the adoption of environmental practices in SMEs? A mixed-methods approach. *Review of Managerial Science, 2019*, 1–28.

Muñoz-Pascual, L., & Galende, J. (2017). The Impact of Knowledge and Motivation Management on Creativity: Employees of Innovative Spanish Companies. *Employee Relations*, *39*(5), 732–752. doi:10.1108/ER-05-2016-0096

Muñoz-Pascual, L., & Galende, J. (2020). Ambidextrous Relationships and Social Capability as Employee Well-Being: The Secret Sauce for Research and Development and Sustainable Innovation Performance. *International Journal of Environmental Research and Public Health*, *17*(9), 3072. doi:10.3390/ijerph17093072 PMID:32354118

Muñoz-Pascual, L., & Galende, J. (2020). Ambidextrous Knowledge and Learning Capability: The Magic Potion for Employee Creativity and Sustainable Innovation Performance. *Sustainability*, *12*(10), 3966. doi:10.3390u12103966

Muñoz-Pascual, L., Galende, J., & Curado, C. (2019). Human Resource Management Contributions to Knowledge Sharing for a Sustainability-Oriented Performance: A Mixed Methods Approach. *Sustainability*, *12*(1), 161. doi:10.3390u12010161

Musa, M. H., & Mohamad, M. N. (2018). Importance of Green Innovation in Malaysian SMEs: Advantages and Future Research. *Int. Acad. J. Bus. Manag.*, *5*(01), 64–73. doi:10.9756/IAJBM/V5I1/1810010

Ngo, L. V., & O'Cass, A. (2013). Innovation and Business Success: The Mediating Role of Customer Participation. *Journal of Business Research*, *66*(8), 1134–1142. doi:10.1016/j.jbusres.2012.03.009

Oyemomi, O., Liu, S., Neaga, I., & Alkhuraiji, A. (2016). How Knowledge Sharing and Business Process Contribute to Organizational Performance: Using the fsQCA Approach. *Journal of Business Research*, *69*(11), 4725–5546. doi:10.1016/j.jbusres.2016.04.116

Ramanathan, R., Black, A., Nath, P., & Muyldermans, L. (2010). Impact of Environmental Regulations on Innovation and Performance in the UK Industrial Sector. *Management Decision*, *48*(10), 1493–1513. doi:10.1108/00251741011090298

Schaltegger, S., Hansen, E. G., & Lüdeke-Freund, F. (2016). Business Models for Sustainability: Origins, Present Research, and Future Avenues. *Organization & Environment*, *29*(1), 3–10. doi:10.1177/1086026615599806

Schramm, C. (2010). All Entrepreneurship is Social. *Stanford Social Innovation Review*, *7*, 20–22.

Shih, S. C., Hsu, S. H. Y., Zhu, Z., & Balasubramanian, S. K. (2012). Knowledge Sharing, a Key Role in the Downstream Supply Chain. *Information & Management*, *49*(2), 70–80. doi:10.1016/j.im.2012.01.001

Song, W., & Yu, H. (2018). Green Innovation Strategy and Green Innovation: The Roles of Green Creativity and Green Organizational Identity. *Corporate Social Responsibility and Environmental Management*, *25*(2), 135–150. doi:10.1002/csr.1445

Strike, V. M., Gao, J., & Bansal, P. (2006). Being Good while Being Bad: Social Responsibility and International Diversification of US Firms. *Journal of International Business Studies*, *37*(6), 850–862. doi:10.1057/palgrave.jibs.8400226

Testa, F., Gusmerottia, N. M., Corsini, F., Passetti, E., & Iraldo, F. (2016). Factors Affecting Environmental Management by Small and Micro Firms: The Importance of Entrepreneurs' Attitudes and Environmental Investment. *Corporate Social Responsibility and Environmental Management, 23*(6), 373–385. doi:10.1002/csr.1382

Valaei, N., Rezaei, S., & Wan-Ismail, W. K. (2017). Examining Learning Strategies, Creativity, and Innovation at SMEs using fuzzy set Qualitative Comparative Analysis and PLS Path Modeling. *Journal of Business Research, 70*, 224–233. doi:10.1016/j.jbusres.2016.08.016

Vollenbroek, F. A. (2002). Sustainable Development and the Challenge of Innovation. *Journal of Cleaner Production, 10*(3), 215–223. doi:10.1016/S0959-6526(01)00048-8

Wagner, M. (2009). Innovation and Competitive Advantages from the Integration of Strategic Aspects with Social and Environmental Management in European Firms. *Business Strategy and the Environment, 18*(5), 291–306. doi:10.1002/bse.585

Wu, G. C. (2017). Effects of Socially Responsible Supplier Development and Sustainability-Oriented Innovation on Sustainable Development: Empirical Evidence from SMEs. *Corporate Social Responsibility and Environmental Management, 24*(6), 661–675. doi:10.1002/csr.1435

Xie, X., Fang, L., Zeng, S., & Huo, J. (2016). How does knowledge inertia affect firms' product innovation? *Journal of Business Research, 69*(5), 1615–1620. doi:10.1016/j.jbusres.2015.10.027

ADDITIONAL READING

Curado, C., Muñoz-Pascual, L., & Galende, J. (2018). Antecedents of innovation performance in SMEs: A mixed methods approach. *Journal of Business Research, 89*, 206–215. doi:10.1016/j.jbusres.2017.12.056

González-Masip, J., Martín-de Castro, G., & Hernández, A. (2019). Inter-organizational knowledge spillovers: Attracting talent in science and technology parks and corporate social responsibility practices. *Journal of Knowledge Management, 23*(5), 975–999. doi:10.1108/JKM-06-2018-0367

Martín-de Castro, G., Amores-Salvadó, J., & Navas-López, J. (2016). Environmental management systems and firm performance: Improving firm environmental policy through stakeholders engagement. *Corporate Social Responsibility and Environmental Management, 23*(4), 243–256. doi:10.1002/csr.1377

Martín-de Castro, G., Delgado-Verde, M., López-Sáez, P., & Navas-López, J. (2011). Towards an 'Intellectual Capital-Based View of the firm': Origings and nature. *Journal of Business Ethics, 98*(4), 649–662. doi:10.100710551-010-0644-5

Muñoz-Pascual, L., Curado, C., & Galende, J. (2019). The triple bottom line on sustainable product innovation performance: A mixed methods approach. *Sustainability, 11*(6), 1689. doi:10.3390u11061689

Muñoz-Pascual, L., Curado, C., & Galende, J. (2019). How does the use of informartion technologies affect the adoption of environmental practices in SMEs? A mixed-methods approach. *Review of Managerial Science, 2019*, 1–28.

Muñoz-Pascual, L., & Galende, J. (2017). The impact of knowledge and motivation management on creativity: Employees of innovative Spanish companies. *Employee Relations*, *39*(5), 732–752. doi:10.1108/ER-05-2016-0096

Muñoz-Pascual, L., & Galende, J. (2020). Ambidextrous Relationships and Social Capability as Employee Well-Being: The Secret Sauce for Research and Development and Sustainable Innovation Performance. *International Journal of Environmental Research and Public Health*, *17*(9), 3072. doi:10.3390/ijerph17093072 PMID:32354118

Muñoz-Pascual, L., & Galende, J. (2020). Ambidextrous Knowledge and Learning Capability: The Magic Potion for Employee Creativity and Sustainable Innovation Performance. *Sustainability*, *12*(10), 3966. doi:10.3390u12103966

Muñoz-Pascual, L., Galende, J., & Curado, J. (2019). Human Resource Management Contributions to Knowledge Sharing for a Sustainability-Oriented Performance: A Mixed Methods Approach. *Sustainability*, *12*(1), 161. doi:10.3390u12010161

KEY TERMS AND DEFINITIONS

Adoption of Environmental Practices: Adoption of environmental mechanisms helps to achieve better safety standards and healthier working conditions. For example: Design of a code of environmental ethics for all members of the company and its business partners; implementation of energy saving practices; implementation of reverse logistics practices; development of productive activity with ecological products and advanced training in eco-innovation and social and environmental needs.

Human Resource Costs: All investments in human resources: intellectual, emotional, and social. These resoruces generate synergies that improve organizational capabilities.

Knowledge Sharing: A firm's ability to exploit information from business partners or to identify market opportunities.

Net Exports: An export in international trade is a good or service produced in one country that is bought by someone in another country. The seller of such goods and services is an exporter; the foreign buyer is an importer. Export of goods often requires involvement of customs authorities. An export's reverse counterpart is animport.

Organizational Learning Capability: The importance that facilitators place on organizational learning.

Sustainable Product Innovation Performance: The result of successfully exploiting new knowledge and sustainability.

Triple Bottom Line Approach: An accounting framework with three parts: social, environmental (or ecological) and financial. Some organizations have adopted the TBL framework to evaluate their performance in a broader perspective to create greater business value

Chapter 7
Exploring the Links Between CSR, Good Governance, and Corporate Reputation:
A Proposal of Indicators in SMEs

Mercedes Rubio-Andrés
https://orcid.org/0000-0002-9112-7669
CEU San Pablo University, Spain

Mª del Mar Ramos-González
CEU San Pablo University, Spain

Miguel Ángel Sastre-Castillo
Complutense University of Madrid, Spain

ABSTRACT

The chapter looks to contribute in a theoretical way to the measurement of the concepts of CSR (corporate social responsibility), good governance, and reputation in SMEs, since they are concepts of great importance in business management and are related. Social responsibility actions through the exercise of good governance means that SMEs can obtain a solid reputation. The purpose of the chapter is to develop how companies that incorporate social responsibility into their business model achieve a better image in the eyes of their stakeholders. Codes of ethics play an important role as an instrument of good governance. As a result, the chapter proposes measurement indicators to be used in future empirical research to verify the effects of causality. They can be a valuable tool for knowledge management as a source of innovation for SMEs.

DOI: 10.4018/978-1-7998-4833-2.ch007

INTRODUCTION

Corporate Social Responsibility (CSR) and good governance have been increasingly considered by academics and practitioners in recent decades (Carroll and Buchholtz, 2006; Schwartz and Carroll, 2008). Traditionally, academic management research has focused on analyzing corporate social responsibility and business ethics in large companies. However, in small and medium-sized enterprises (SMEs) it has received little attention in academic literature (Gallo, 2004; Murillo and Lozano 2006; Spence 1999).

In the European Union, SMEs account for 99% of all corporations, they are responsible for creating two thirds of all jobs in the private sector as well as over half the total added value produced by companies (Fact Sheets on the European Union, 2018), there by generating economic value, since they are both clients and suppliers for major companies.

Despite their importance, SMEs have received little attention in the literature, and only in recent years have they come to be the focus of inquiry, as a result of greater academic interest (Fuller & Tian, 2006; Melé et al. 2006; Tilley, 2000; Graafland, Van de Ven, Stoffele, 2003; Jenkins, 2006; Lepoutre & Heene, 2006; Vives, 2006; Besser & Miller, 2001; Sarbutts, 2003; Perrini, 2006; Raynard & Forstater, 2002; Vázquez-Carrasco & López-Pérez, 2013), with many works seeking to center their efforts on pinpointing how SMEs differ from large as well as multinational firms (Murillo & Lozano, 2006; Jamali, Zanhour, & Keshishian, 2009; Russo & Tencati, 2009; Lamberti & Noci, 2012; Jenkins, 2006). Authors such as Spence (2007) advocate carrying out specific research in the field and adopting a personalised perspective to explore the sustainability of SMEs. For its part, the European Commission has also highlighted the importance of adopting a different approach for SMEs that used for large firms (CEC, 2002, 2005, 2006).

The aim of this chapter is to analyse the importance of good governance in SMEs in order to be socially responsible and to improve their image and business reputation.

Our approach is focused on linking social responsibility actions by exercising good governance, which means obtaining a solid reputation. In this sense, when companies incorporate social responsibility in their business model, they achieve a better image for their stakeholders. In SMEs, workers and customers stand out as the main stakeholders.

Following the literature analysed, a set of indicators are finally proposed to measure the three variables that are explained throughout the chapter.

METHODOLOGY

The present study uses as methodology the review of the literature related to CSR, good governance, codes ethics and reputation, from the last decades and specifically related to SMEs, which needs further study due to the scarcity of specific research and its importance.

The bibliometric study by Bikefe et al. (2020) shows that most CSR publications have focused on identifying the various ways in which SMEs are implementing CSR. Furthermore, most adopted the survey as the dominant research method. These authors propose that future studies should combine a variety of methods to gain a better understanding of CSR issues.

The proposed indicators should be measured using an owner-manager assessment questionnaire with questions with dichotomous answers or Likert scales. As an additional source, sustainability reports that are increasingly used and codes of conduct can be consulted.

We understand that this proposal for indicators can be a valuable tool for knowledge management as a source of innovation for SMEs. Generating a structure that facilitates its effective use. Although, it is complicated to incorporate to the organizational routines the knowledge that is generated through innovation processes, by means of the acquisition of technology, the relations with suppliers, clients and with the competitors. (Nagles, 2007).

Through this indicator-based tool it would be possible to generate sustainable and profitable solutions for SMEs, ensuring an effective interaction with the environment of the organizations and their different interest groups, to identify and understand the difficulties and challenges of the organizations and society, so that this is the starting point for innovative actions, allowing the development of products and services as well as the design of new processes and management systems that optimize the use of resources and capabilities of the organizations and society in general. (Figure 1).

Figure 1. Links between CSR, good governance and solid reputation
Source: own

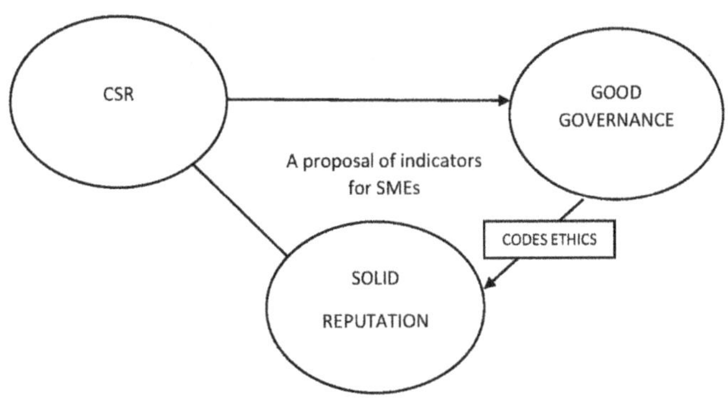

BACKGROUND

The nature of CSR for SMEs is different and the strategy cannot follow the same line as large companies, so they must develop their own methodology by integrating CSR into their objectives on a voluntary basis since they have fewer economic or knowledge resources (Williamson et al., 2006; Kechiche and Soparnot, 2012; Wickert, 2014; Moneva and Hernández, 2016).

The concept of CSR implies voluntary action by the company to commit itself to the development of its stakeholders and not just its shareholders and is therefore linked to the concept of Corporate Governance. For González Masip (2018), companies show a greater social commitment the greater the number of stakeholders considered and the lower the degree of dependence of the company on these groups for its survival and, therefore, the lower its performance for its own interest. In this case it is stated that social positioning tends to be ethical.

It highlights a research conducted by Jo and Harjoto (2011) that included information from more than 3,000 companies between 1993 and 2004, studied the relationship between Corporate Governance, corporate social responsibility and financial performance. The results show that the implementation of Corporate Governance practices has a positive effect on the execution of social responsibility practices;

in turn, it is evident that organizations that carry out social responsibility practices through stakeholder relations management perform better in terms of profitability and maximizing shareholder welfare.

The design of mechanisms to enable companies to create value for all stakeholders is a challenge for Corporate Governance. The power and decision-making structures within the governing bodies must incorporate corporate social responsibility concerns as a strategic imperative. (Jo and Harjoto: 2011)

It includes all the economic, legal, ethical and discretionary expectations that society has about companies at a given time (Carroll 1979). An integrative definition of CSR is provided by Marín and Ruiz, (2007) "the RSC is the involvement at strategic and operational level that the company has to adequately meet its economic, legal, social and discretionary responsibilities raised by its main interest groups".

In the model proposed by Fassin and Rossem (2011), differences are highlighted between the dimensions proposed, business ethics, CSR, sustainability, stakeholder management and corporate governance. However, the study considers that CSR and sustainability are very much in the minds of small and medium sized business owners. Both concepts have close similarities (business ethics, CSR, sustainability, stakeholder management and corporate governance).

In fact, the CSR can be seen as encompassing sustainability, confirming the approach of the European Commission, where the real objective of the CSR is sustainable development (Eberhard-Harribey, 2006).

Authors such as Jenkins (2006) or Habisch and Wegner (2005), have explained how small and medium-sized companies more difficulties have in assuming their social responsibility commitments, which is why the term CSR is often used for SMEs and CSR for big companies. Although, both terms, CSR and CSR are used interchangeably in the scientific literature (Rodríguez Piñero, 2005; Bigné et al., 2005; Lizcano and Nieto, 2006).

A question that we analyse is whether company size affects the development of CSR in companies. In this sense, we know that there are a series of advantages derived from the size of the company for the application of Corporate Social Responsibility (CSR).

On the one hand, the general impression seems to be that multinationals have implemented corporate social responsibility (CSR) to a greater extent than SMEs (Baumann-Pauly, Wickert, Spence, & Scherer, 2013; Campbell, 2007, McWilliams & Siegel, 2001), whilst other studies have failed to reach a consensus as to whether SMEs are better or worse prepared to organise CSR (Lepoutre & Heene, 2006).

But on the other hand, size can play a fundamental role for SMEs, in terms of their flexibility, their capacity for adaptation and innovation, they make it possible to carry out good practices designed for the closest interest groups, employees and customers, from a responsible management.

Recently, Bikefe et al., (2020) have conducted a study aims to systematically review the key characteristics and issues in Corporate Social Responsibility among Small and Medium Enterprises (CSRS) research.

They conclude that a significant majority of the papers reviewed were empirical in nature (89%, 55 out of 62). Empirical research is important as it validates existing theories and concepts. However, because of the limited number of conceptual CSRS articles in this review, more conceptual research needs to be done as this contributes to a better understanding of emerging norms and factors. Additionally, conceptual research will also provide direction and impetus for future empirical research enquiry into CSRS.

Small business managers must continue to advance in their overall awareness and improvement of social and environmental performance, with an interesting focus on implementing CSR and environmental management tools and systems (Friedman and Miles, 2002; Ammenberg and Hjelm, 2003; Lawrence et al., 2006; Halila, 2007; Zobel, 2007; Seiffert, 2008; Zorpas, 2010), which go beyond the pressures of environmental legislation and regulation (Rutherfoord et al., 2000). Johnson (2015) proposes social audits and sustainability reports adapted to SMEs.

We have to highlight the strategic role of social responsibility in SMEs. If we consider social responsibility as a fundamental part of the company's strategy, the vision and mission can be achieved (Burke and Logsdon, 1996).

In SMEs, because of their importance, we point out internal stakeholders, workers, and among external stakeholders, local suppliers, customers and the local community. This is not incompatible with the business management incorporating environmental concerns as a key element (De la Cuesta et al., 2002), being a complex concept that has become more important in the business decision-making process (Cochran, 2007). Figure 2.

Figure 2. Category of initiatives for fundamental stakeholderse in SMEs
Source: Own

Fundamental Stakeholders in SMEs	INITIATIVES
CUSTOMERS	➢ Transparent and adequate information on the products and services offered ➢ Good results in satisfaction surveys, minor claims ➢ Quality certificates and recognition awards
SUPPLIERS	➢ Priority for local and nearby suppliers ➢ Symbiotic relationships that imply advantages for different parties ➢ Relationship of transparency and loyalty with the commitments acquired ➢ Establishment of contracts that explicitly include social and environmental CSR dimensions ➢ Satisfaction surveys with supplier companies
EMPLOYEES	➢ Fluent dialogue with workers and their representatives ➢ Training for employees ➢ Stable and quality contracts ➢ Mixed remuneration systems with a fixed component of lower weight, and a variable component depending on the results ➢ Work-family balance ➢ Merit promotion processes (meritocracy) ➢ Establishment of career plans ➢ Additional social benefits to those strictly contemplated by law
ENVIRONMENT	➢ Reuse and recycling of raw materials ➢ Efficient use of energy resources and wáter ➢ Use of renewable energy ➢ Use of ecological and / or recycled containers and packaging ➢ Environmental Audits ➢ Specific environmental objectives (climate change)
LOCAL COMMUNITY	➢ Contribution to local growth ➢ Transparent and ethical relationship with local rulers ➢ Support of different social and recreational, cultural and sports activities in the nearby area ➢ Support of employment and local wealth

THE IMPORTANCE OF CORPORATE SOCIAL RESPONSIBILITY IN SMES

Academic studies are trying to explain and find the relationship between CSR and financial results. They emphasize that there are both positive relationships (Choi et al. 2010; Callan and Thomas 2009; Hammann et al. (2009) and Sweeney (2009), neutral or non-existent (Schuler and Cording 2006 in Rodriguez) and even negative associations (Griffin and Mahon, 1997; Roman, Hayibor, and Agle, 1999).

The reasons lie in problems of measuring CSR variables (which differ from one company to another), the omission of latent variables important in the formulation of the models, the absence of causality analysis, the lack of rigor in the methodology, (Margolis and Walsh, 2003), statistical errors (McWilliams and Siegel 2000)

The study by Margolis (2001) and Margolis and Walsh (2003) includes a significant number of studies on CSR and financial results, which highlights the positive relationship between CSR and financial results, although it warns that the studies do not consider the underlying factors that affect the CSR-financial results ratio. If we consider that CSR is a competitive advantage difficult to imitate by competitors, it can explain the positive relationship between both variables

Therefore, in those cases in which the company does not act with social responsibility, the resulting costs could be significant and represent a burden that reduces the benefits that would be obtained a priori. On the contrary, if companies that adopt socially responsible policies are more profitable, they will be an added incentive to increase investments in CSR programs (Pava and Kraus, 2008).

If we refer to the Spanish case, the investigation by Rodríguez-Fernández (2016), which raises the two-way relationship between both and Madueño et. al (2016) that study whether the development of CSR practices allows Spanish SMEs to improve their competitive performance.

On the other hand, Gallardo-Vázquez et. al (2013), analyzes the impact of Corporate Social Responsibility on the competitive success of microenterprises and the role of innovation, concluding that the CSR of small businesses, which depends on the willingness of their managers, increases their strength to Drive positive changes. The results show that CSR is not specific for large companies with resources, nor is it incompatible with innovation or business competitiveness, but quite the opposite.

There are opinions of authors who consider that CSR is used by companies as a marketing tool, to improve the image aesthetically, without a truly deep sense. According to some, it is a "fashion", something that companies currently need because it "sells" a good image of the company, (Garrigues, and Trullenque, 2008).

Faced with this idea, we consider the opposite. SMEs must be aware that the lack of social responsibility often entails a high cost for their image and market positioning.

Codes of Ethics as an Instrument of Good Governance

Corporate governance is substantially different from CSR in the dimensions linked to ethical content, theory, conviction, internal orientation and the degree of formalism (Fassin and Rossem, 2011).

Good governance in SMEs is essential, in Spain they are the main engine of the economy, in small and medium enterprises more than half of the employment is consolidated and the core of the business fabric meets. Good governance implies an ethical link of participation and dialogue with the stakeholders that surround and integrate the organization (Dopazo, 2012). In this sense, companies must provide information to their stakeholders about their responsible management. So that it also has a positive effect on the reputation of the company, it is necessary to prioritize and improve the information provided mainly through sustainability reports, which can be considered as the best dissemination instrument (De los Ríos, et. al. 2012).

There are still many SMEs that do not communicate their CSR efforts adequately, despite being in an advanced phase of good practices. They present more difficulties to access economic resources that allow a formal and periodic communication of their CSR activities (Knudsen 2011), hence their greatest effort to be able to carry out external and formal communication, such as the presentation of sustainability reports and dissemination of liability policies derived from good governance (Baumann-Pauly, 2013).

For Schwartz (2001), ethical codes represent a way of addressing misconduct in organizations. Even today, despite their popularity they still face resistance, scepticism within academic communities. In his study he finds the relationship between ethical codes and behavior in the company, which may be the first step towards the goal of encouraging ethical and legal behavior.

Ethical codes are a good start, but they cannot exist on their own. Codes are successful when employees know them and act on them. They must be part of the organizational culture and cannot be imposed, and it is up to managers to communicate the values of the organization. An important conclusion of Stevens' (1999) study is that codes seem to be useful for communicating ethical responsibility in organizations. Although little information is available about their effectiveness as vehicles of communication.

Johnson (2015) proposes a sustainability model for German SMEs, which includes codes of conduct as a management tool.

It is known that the issuance of sustainable information, and the elaboration of sustainability reports is a common practice in listed companies that need to provide the market with greater transparency (Vázquez-Otero, 2015), and in general a very typical work of the large companies, because they have in their boards of directors with greater presence of external directors (Ibrahim and Angelidis, 1991), more women (Cabeza, et. al. 2018), and are larger, these variables being directly related to the creation of sustainable reports (Rodríguez-Ariza 2014) We therefore consider that the size of the organization is a relevant variable in the dissemination of CSR (Waddock and Graves, 1997).

Large companies are the ones that use CSR reports to a greater extent as a means of communication and information (Archel and Lizarraga, 2001, Acero and Alcalde 2012), which positively influences the company's reputation (Orlizky, et. al. 2003), although it is not always accompanied by a significant advance in the contents, nor in the involvement of the interested parties in the process (Gray, 2000; O'Dwyer and Owen, 2005). Even this report can be criticized for lack of credibility (Adams and Evans, 2004; Dando and Swift, 2003).

Fassin and Rossem (2011) understand that the concepts of shareholder value, CSR and ethics are complementary and mutually reinforcing so that CSR requires wealth creation for shareholders, in turn shareholder value is essential for CSR, and CSR leads to increased shareholder value. In this way, it is possible for managers and owners of small and medium-sized enterprises to recognize profit as an important prerequisite for social responsibility.

In recent years, in countries of Europe, Australia and the USA there has been a large increase in companies choosing to adopt an ethical code of conduct (Adams et al., 2001; Potts and Maluszewski, 2004; Reynolds, 2000; Somers, 2001). This has occurred in part because it is good management practice (Paine, 1996) in relation to internal and external stakeholders (Treviño and Nelson, 1999).

Furthermore, there is little literature on the effectiveness of ethical codes of conduct (Stevens, 1994; Somers, 2001; Adam and Rachman-Moore; 2004). McKendall and others (2002) argue that even when companies adopt codes of ethical conduct and employ formal methods of enforcement (i.e., ethical compliance programmes), legal violations are sometimes not diminished.

The unethical practices of some business organizations have seriously damaged the trust required for national and global trade. Their direct and indirect negative effects on the wealth of society and their contribution to the feeling of distrust felt by individuals in the marketplace have led to a weakening of the market position of some organizations, even in some cases jeopardizing the existence of some prestigious companies. (Paine, 2003)

Adam and Rachman-Moore (2004) conducted a study in the USA to examine the level of perception of employees. The results of this study indicate that informal methods such as codes of conduct, social norms or good example of owner-managers achieve a greater commitment in employee attitudes than formal systems. Consequently, companies need to seek ways to improve ethical leadership qualities at the management level (Treviño and Nelson, 1999).

The ethical codes constitute an instrument of CSR management, a reflection of good governance, to which internal stakeholders adhere, mainly workers. Its origin was to be promulgated to guide individual behavior and to protect companies from illegal or unethical behavior by their employees. But this classic motivation based on building reputation and trust with clients (Cressey and Moore 1983), on managing risk (protecting organizations against criminal liability or damages as a result of inappropriate behavior, (Stevens 1994, Lefebvre and Singh, 1996) or corporate self-defense (Snell et al., 1996), have given way to motivations based on adherence to policies and procedures that promote company values, culture and philosophy (Svensson et al., 2006).

In this way, managers can use codes to shape change and to send messages to workers and managers about expectations that go beyond the behavior required by law. Thus, codes can be serious attempts to articulate the moral climate that is part of the culture of the organization (Stevens, 1994). In short, the codes express the culture of a company while developing it (Ruiz Lozano, et. al, 2016).

Responsibility related initiatives emerge as a result of good governance. Preuss and Perschke (2010) hold that responsibility in SMEs stems from the values and ethical behavior of owners-managers. It is also essential for the latter to possess a high level of training (Hsu & Chen, 2012), a personalized management style and for them to foster personal and interpersonal relations towards stakeholders (Jenkins, 2006; Murillo and Lozano, 2006; Fuller and Tian 2006). In fact, SMEs will become involved in sustainability activities depending on the will of their owners-managers (Cassell & Lewis, 2011; Johnson 2015).

With regard to the relation between good governance and responsible practices, one reference we highlight is the work of Jo and Harjoto (2012), who conduct an empirical analysis of the link between corporate governance and businesses' commitment to social responsibility, exploring their causal effects. Jamali et. al (2008) determine that corporate governance in a broad sense (good governance) implies responsibility, as well as the importance of taking into account the interests of all stakeholders, (Dunlop, 1998; Kendall, 1999). Bhimani and Soonawalla (2005) suggest that responsible practices and good governance are two sides of the same coin, although studies such as Ruangviset, Jiraporn and Kim (2014) do not support such a positive relation.

Corporate Reputation vs. CSR

The organization, essentially made up of people, can be affected by compliance or not with social rules or moral norms in a double way: as a subject of rights and obligations, it can increase the endowment of its intangible assets, such as reputation, if it is virtuous, or diminish it if its behavior is contrary to moral, and thus it is perceived by society. In addition, employees as direct actors within the company may feel responsible. (Durán Herrera, 2009).

Companies that promote human resources management based on a responsible direction inevitably require ethical values that guarantee their good image and prestige over time, becoming an intangible resource of incalculable value.

Ethical behavior is crucial and valuing people as a fundamental pillar to generate a good reputation, which in turn increases customer loyalty and helps retain talent (Ramos-González, et. al. 2017)

Cases of corruption, abuse of power, lack of transparency, embezzlement, etc., in influential entities, have led to the birth of a new body of doctrine around "values, business and economy", which includes voluntary actions Individual and Corporate Social Responsibility (Bénabou and Tirole, 2009), as well as the principles that can be applied by individuals and organizations (Jensen et al., 2010). In these cases, the image and reputation of the company is damaged.

From a strategic approach, CSR can be an intangible asset that generates value, directly related to a good reputation of the company, a higher level of satisfaction of the stakeholders and consequently an increase in the wealth generated in the medium and long term. Thus, it is recommended that the principles of CSR be integrated into the main activities of companies (core business), Cochran (2007).

This recent approach to measure the corporate image according to the stakeholders (Decker, 2004), considers that the actions of the CSR must be classified according to the different stakeholders of the companies most benefited by them, customers, shareholders, employees, among others.

Reputation as a multidisciplinary concept is considered as a resource that allows generating sustainable competitive advantages. Hall (1992) identifies reputation as the most important intangible for managers, and in Teece et al., (1997), the importance of this asset as a source of valuable information for customers, suppliers and competitors of the company was already considered. Martín de Castro et. al (2006), distinguishes as key components of corporate reputation, on the one hand the social reputation and on the other other hand, business reputation. Business reputation includes the different aspect of corporate reputation related to the stakeholders and social reputation is the result of the insights and perceptions of other stakeholders that are not so close today by day business.

In recent years, corporate reputation as an intangible asset has achieved major importance in the academic, business and professional sphere. There is no consensus in the academic literature about what it encompasses and what its main components are, because several disciplines study it, such as sociology referring to prestige or image marketing. Business management refers to the term reputation (Martín de Castro, 2008).

Reputation is the result of a process whose origin lies in the firm's behavior towards its stakeholders and in its ability to meet their expectations, both in terms of behavior as well as informational transparency (De Quevedo Puente, de la Fuente Sabaté, & García, 2005).

The analysis of reputation has adopted a multidisciplinary approach, prominent amongst which is Game Theory (Kreps & Wilson, 1982; Milgrom & Roberts, 1982), Information Theory (Milgrom & Roberts, 1986), Organizational (Fombrun & Shanley, 1990), the Agency Theory (Jensen, 1994), the Transaction Cost Theory (Fombrun, 1995), and the Resource-Based Theory (Hall, 1992; Barney, 1991). This latter theory to a great extent shaped the development of the theoretical fundamentals of corporate reputation in the 1990's and has continued to do so up to the present day. This view holds that corporate reputation is a source of competitive advantage since it is a strategic resource and dynamic capability which provides value that can be used strategically. In the opinion of Hall (1992), corporate reputation, together with product reputation and employee know-how, are considered the most important intangible resources that contribute to corporate success.

Companies with greater corporate reputation are an attraction for investors, who anticipate the company's future ability to access higher quality resources. There is ample empirical evidence that defends the positive relationship between corporate reputation and corporate financial performance (McGuire et al., 1990; Nanda et al., 1996; Roberts and Dowling, 1997; 2002; Fernández and Luna, 2007). SMEs have a specific capacity to positively manage their relationships with stakeholders and increase their competitiveness, optimizing their financial, social and environmental performance.

For Cochran (2007), responsibility evidences a direct relation with corporate reputation due to greater stakeholder satisfaction and enhanced performance in the medium and long term.

When firms include responsibility in their business model, they forge a better image for their main stakeholders. Internal reputation will thus depend on the information which the latter receive concerning the firm's social commitment through the actions they engage in related to social responsibility (Marín & Rubio, 2008, Greening & Turban, 2000; Luce, Barber, & Hillman, 2004).

When the management of employees in SMEs is carried out in accordance with criteria of responsibility, firms can retain talent more effectively, attract better applicants (Davies & Crane 2010), favour the selection of more qualified staff and provide better conditions for the organization. This encourages a good internal reputation for the firm (Stigler, 1962; Williamson, 1985), and strengthens prestige and image (Fombrun, 1995; Villafañe, 2004).

As regards customers, loyalty towards responsible firms is also bolstered, since there is a positive consumer reaction to responsible business behavior (Maignan, 2001), with customers being willing to pay a higher price for the products and services received (Klein & Leffler, 1981; Milgrom & Roberts, 1986). Results from the study by Alniacik et.al. (2011) show that positive information about social responsibility increases product purchase intention.

SMEs are thus able to appeal to a group of consumers who are concerned with firms' social responsibility (Baron, 2001), who value employees' working conditions, who reward firms that use fewer natural resources, who protect the environment and who show respect for human rights (Fernández &Merino, 2005). In SMEs, there is a closer-knit relation with consumers, who are more aware of bad social responsibility practices that cannot be atoned for through better prices (Mohr & Webb, 2005).

As a result, the good practices employed by socially responsible firms will have an impact on external reputation, even in small firms (Nejati, Quazi, Amran, & Ahmad, 2017) outperforming medium size firms in intensity (López-Pérez, Melero, & Sesé, 2017), exerting a positive influence on customer attitude towards the firm (Bhattacharya & Sen, 2003, 2004; Lichtenstein, Drumwright, & Braig, 2004; Fernández & Merino, 2005), unless this image is damaged through poor communication (Boulstrige & Carrigan, 2000; Bigné Alcañiz & Currás Pérez, 2008, Becker-Olsen, Cudmore, & Hill, 2006). Alniacik el. al. (2011) evidence the importance of providing enough information to stakeholders (consumers, employees, investors) regarding responsible activities when these perform well.

López-Pérez et. al. (2017) confirm the relations which link responsibility, corporate reputation and financial value for the SME domain, and conclude that the proposed causal relations intensify as the size of the firm increases.

CSR, Good Governance and Reputation: A Proposal of Indicators in SMEs

Once the relationships between CSR, Good Governance and Reputation have been identified, we propose the possible indicators that allow the measurement of each of the variables. CSR, is considered as a multidimensional construct, which includes employees dimension, environmental dimension and local community and society dimension.

Following Barrena-Martínez, et. al. (2017), Garay-Tamajón, et. al. (2013), Gallardo-Vázquez (2013), and other authors, below is a list of indicators of the three dimensions of the CSR, good governance and reputation. In subsequent studies, the indicators can be used to determine their measurement adequacy in each of the concepts.

In future research a detailed study of these indicators is recommended to verify their practical application (**Figure 3).**

Figure 3. CSR, Good Governance and Reputation Indicators
Source: Barrena-Martínez, et. al. (2017), Garay-Tamajón, et. al. (2013), Gallardo-Vázquez (2013)

CSR, Good Governance and Reputation Indicators	
EMPLOYEES DIMENSION	▪ Professional career for employees ▪ Strict staff selection procedures ▪ Investment in training ▪ Ongoing training programmes ▪ Improved employee satisfaction ▪ Performance assessment ▪ Equal pay ▪ Performance-related pay ▪ Attraction and retention of employees ▪ Training and continuous development ▪ Management of employment relations ▪ Communication, transparency and social dialogue ▪ Diversity and equal opportunities ▪ Fair remuneration and social benefits ▪ Prevention, occupational health and safety at work ▪ Work-Family Balance ▪ Promote gender equality in the employment practices ▪ Encourage people of all abilities to apply for jobs ▪ Occupational health and safety levels beyond legal minimums ▪ Committed to job creation ▪ We encourage employees to participate in volunteer activities or in collaboration with NGOs ▪ Mechanisms for dialogue with employees are dynamic
ENVIRONMENTAL DIMENSION	▪ Environmental practices ▪ Evaluates the environmental impact of the business ▪ Energy and water saving activities ▪ Renewable energy sources (solar, wind, biomass...) ▪ Waste recycling ▪ Use environmentally friendly products ▪ Choose environmentally friendly suppliers ▪ Encourage customers to save water and/or energy ▪ Encourage organic products consumption ▪ Encourage customers to participate in protection initiatives ▪ Encourage customers to be environmentally friendly in the property ▪ Encourage customers be environmentally friendly in nature ▪ Carries out actions that contribute to environmental conservation
LOCAL COMMUNITY AND SOCIETY	▪ Evaluates the social impact of the business ▪ Collaborate with social and charity projects ▪ Promotes local community development and heritage conservation ▪ Promotes local community development ▪ Choose local suppliers that demonstrate their social responsibility ▪ Encourage customers to contribute to social and charity initiatives ▪ Actively encourage respect for the culture and language of the area ▪ Facilities are adapted for disabled people ▪ Promotes civic attitudes among clients ▪ We participate in social projects for the community
GOOD GOVERNANCE	▪ Ethical codes ▪ Published reports ▪ Evaluate the workplace climate ▪ Decision-making opportunities ▪ Dissemination of good governance measures

SOLUTIONS AND RECOMMENDATIONS

When SMEs include responsibility in their business model, they achieve a better image for their main stakeholders, such as customers, workers, managers, local suppliers and society in general. Achieving CSR implies that management exercises responsible governance concerned with making responsible decisions considering the impact they have on stakeholders. An important instrument are the codes of conduct, which are used to a lesser extent in SMEs compared to large companies, but which are important despite the fact that they are not the only solution for exercising responsible management.

Responsible management in business administration, such as in human resource management, means achieving advantages such as retaining talent and attracting better candidates. Also SMEs concerned about social responsibility, find consumers who reward companies that use available resources better, consuming less energy, recycling and having other effective environmental management measures. Choosing local suppliers is also a social responsibility action that involves improving the SME's area of influence.

The recommendation for SMEs is to implement a good governance model based on responsible management and impact on all stakeholders, improving their internal and external reputation. It is important to consider the indicators that best define the variables studied, so that they are treated by the owners-managers of the SMEs.

FUTURE RESEARCH DIRECTIONS

The proposed subject is very current, with a significant increase in articles studying social responsibility and its impact on corporate reputation. Good corporate governance and ethical codes have also been studied. It is important to address these aspects in SMEs.

Small and medium-sized enterprises are commonly acknowledged to be a driver of economic growth, so these firms' CSR and the competitive advantages it generates are of great interest.

For these reasons, we propose that future empirical studies be carried out that, using the proposed model, study how good governance and corporate social responsibility influence corporate reputation in SMEs, using the indicators included in this chapter.

CONCLUSION

Good governance and social responsibility are concepts that perforce must be fostered in SMEs, yet which have traditionally been much more the focus of study in the case of large companies.

The size of the firm, which entails different organisational qualities, affects the way social responsibility is encouraged and has an impact on transparency and good governance.

There is also the problem that the social and environmental actions carried out by large corporations have eclipsed the actions undertaken by SMEs (Johnson, 2015). This might be because, unlike SMEs, large firms use sustainability reports to a greater extent as a means to communicate and convey information (Acero Fraile & Alcalde Fradejas, 2012; Dallo & Domench, 2001), which has a positive influence on the company's reputation (Orlitzky et al., 2003), although this does not always go hand in hand with significant progress either in terms of content or how the stakeholders involved in the process are considered (Gray, 2001; O'Dwyer & Owen, 2005). Indeed, reports may even be criticised for their lack of credibility (Adams & Evans, 2004; Dando & Swift, 2003); It is known that many SMEs, despite implementing them widely, fail to communicate their good practices externally and appropriately due to the lack of resources and management skills (Lee, Herold, & Yu, 2016). This might well be due to them having greater difficulties accessing the finance that would enable them to ensure they formally and regularly communicate said responsibility actions (Knudsen, 2011). Hence, they need to make a greater effort to provide external and formal communication, by presenting sustainability reports and by conveying the sustainable policies to come out of their good governance (Baumann-Pauly et al., 2013). To achieve this, it would be extremely advisable for SMEs to have a dynamic and flexible communication model, which would enable them to disseminate amongst stakeholders the good governance measures that reflect responsible management.

The codes of ethics stand out as a management tool for good governance (Arrigo, 2006), as well as the values of the organization and its responsible policies (Ruíz-Lozano et al., 2016). The elaboration of these codes may be more complex in the case of SMEs (Russo & Perrini, 2010), but this does not mean that they should give up having them, given the advantages they can bring.

With regard to the most advantageous organizational characteristics inherent in SMEs when applying a good governance model, Jenkins (2009) highlights flexibility, adaptation, creativity, less bureaucracy and more fluid internal communication, all of which are attributes that lead to greater development of social responsibility.

Governance must be reflected in good practices in order to generate reputation, which in turn will drive shared value. As a result, SMEs must be consistent in their visible commitments through their codes of conduct and sustainable reports and in their responsible action towards stakeholders if they are to achieve shared value. In this way, SMEs need to be responsible in a proactive manner, which will lead to forging a good reputation.

Reputation is founded based on responsible action which is, in turn, a reflection of good governance in firms. The relationship between these two variables has been borne out, as stated in the literature.

ACKNOWLEDGMENT

This research was funded by the UCM-Cofares Research Chair, INBOTS project H2020 (grant agreement 780073), Ministry of Economy and Competitiveness (Grant/Award Number: ECO2017-84209-P) and ISDI.

REFERENCES

Acero Fraile, I., & Alcalde Fradejas, N. (2012). Gobierno corporativo y rendición de cuentas: ¿existe algún efecto sobre la performance empresarial? *Revista de Contabilidad*, *15*(1), 143–178. doi:10.1016/S1138-4891(12)70041-9

Adam, A. M., & Rachman-Moore, D. (2004). The methods used to implement an ethical code of conduct and employee attitudes. *Journal of Business Ethics*, *54*(3), 225–244. doi:10.100710551-004-1774-4

Adams, C. A., & Evans, R. (2004). Accountability, completeness, credibility and the audit expectations gap. *Journal of Corporate Citizenship*, *14*(Summer), 97–115. doi:10.9774/GLEAF.4700.2004.su.00010

Adams, J. S., Tashchian, A., & Shore, T. H. (2001). Codes of ethics as signals for ethical behavior. *Journal of Business Ethics*, *29*(3), 199–211. doi:10.1023/A:1026576421399

Alniacik, U., Alniacik, E., & Genc, N. (2011). How corporate social responsibility information influences stakeholders' intentions. *Corporate Social Responsibility and Environmental Management*, *18*(4), 234–245. doi:10.1002/csr.245

Ammenberg, J., & Hjelm, O. (2003). Tracing business and environmental effects of environmental management systems—A study of networking small and medium-sized enterprises using a joint environmental management system. *Business Strategy and the Environment*, *12*(3), 163–174. doi:10.1002/bse.357

Archel, P., & Lizarraga, F. (2001). Algunos determinantes de la información medioambiental divulgada por las empresas españolas cotizadas. *Revista de Contabilidad*, *4*(7), 129–153.

Arrigo, E. (2006). Code of conduct and corporate governance. *Symphonya, Emerging Issues in Management*, (1), 93-109.

Arrow, K. J. (1974). Social Responsibility and Economic Efficiency. *Public Policy*, *21*, 303–317.

Barney, J. (1991). Firm resources and sustained competitive advantage. *Journal of Management*, *17*(1), 99–120. doi:10.1177/014920639101700108

Baron, D. P. (2001). Private politics, corporate social responsibility, and integrated strategy. *Journal of Economics & Management Strategy*, *10*(1), 7–45. doi:10.1162/105864001300122548

Barrena-Martínez, J., López-Fernández, M., & Romero-Fernández, P. M. (2017). Socially responsible human resource policies and practices: Academic and professional validation. *European Research on Management and Business Economics*, *23*(1), 55–61. doi:10.1016/j.iedeen.2016.05.001

Baumann-Pauly, D., Wickert, C., Spence, L. J., & Scherer, A. G. (2013). Organizing corporate social responsibility in small and large firms: Size matters. *Journal of Business Ethics*, *115*(4), 693–705. doi:10.100710551-013-1827-7

Becker-Olsen, K. L., Cudmore, B. A., & Hill, R. P. (2006). The impact of perceived corporate social responsibility on consumer behavior. *Journal of Business Research*, *59*(1), 46–53. doi:10.1016/j.jbusres.2005.01.001

Bénabou, R., & Tirole, J. (2010). Individual and corporate social responsibility. *Economica*, *77*(305), 1–19. doi:10.1111/j.1468-0335.2009.00843.x

Besser, T. L., & Miller, N. (2001). Is the good corporation dead? the community social responsibility of small business operators☆. *Journal of Socio-Economics*, *30*(3), 221–241. doi:10.1016/S1053-5357(01)00094-4

Bhattacharya, C. B., & Sen, S. (2003). Consumer-company identification: A framework for understanding consumers' relationships with companies. *Journal of Marketing*, *67*(2), 76–88. doi:10.1509/jmkg.67.2.76.18609

Bhattacharya, C. B., & Sen, S. (2004). Doing better at doing good: When, why, and how consumers respond to corporate social initiatives. *California Management Review*, *47*(1), 9–24. doi:10.2307/41166284

Bhimani, A., & Soonawalla, K. (2005). From conformance to performance: The corporate responsibilities continuum. *Journal of Accounting and Public Policy*, *24*(3), 165–174. doi:10.1016/j.jaccpubpol.2005.03.001

Bigné Alcañiz, J. E., & Currás Pérez, R. (2008). ¿Influye la imagen de responsabilidad social en la intención de compra? El papel de la identificación del consumidor con la empresa. *Universia Business Review*, *19*, 10–23.

Bikefe, G., Zubairu, U., Araga, S., Maitala, F., Ediuku, E., & Anyebe, D. (2020). *Corporate Social Responsibility (CSR) by small and medium enterprises (SMEs): a systematic review*. Academic Press.

Bondy, K., Matten, D., & Moon, J. (2006). *MNC codes of conduct: CSR or corporate governance?* International Centre for Corporate Social Responsibility.

Boulstridge, E., & Carrigan, M. (2000). Do consumers really care about corporate responsibility? Highlighting the attitude—Behaviour gap. *Journal of Communication Management (London)*, *4*(4), 355–368. doi:10.1108/eb023532

Burke, L., & Logsdon, J. M. (1996). How corporate social responsibility pays off. *Long Range Planning*, *29*(4), 495–502. doi:10.1016/0024-6301(96)00041-6

Cabeza-García, L., Fernández-Gago, R., & Nieto, M. (2018). Do board gender diversity and director typology impact CSR reporting? *European Management Review*, *15*(4), 559–575. doi:10.1111/emre.12143

Callan, S. J., & Thomas, J. M. (2009). Corporate financial performance and corporate social performance: An update and reinvestigation. *Corporate Social Responsibility and Environmental Management*, *16*(2), 61–78. doi:10.1002/csr.182

Campbell, J. L. (2007). Why would corporations behave in socially responsible ways? An institutional theory of corporate social responsibility. *Academy of Management Review*, *32*(3), 946–967. doi:10.5465/amr.2007.25275684

Carroll, A., & Buchholtz, A. (2006). *Business and Society: Ethics and Stakeholder Management*. Thompson Learning.

Carroll, A. B. (1979). A three-dimensional conceptual model of corporate performance. *Academy of Management Review*, *4*(4), 497–505. doi:10.5465/amr.1979.4498296

Cassells, S., & Lewis, K. (2011). SMEs and environmental responsibility: Do actions reflect attitudes? *Corporate Social Responsibility and Environmental Management*, *18*(3), 186–199. doi:10.1002/csr.269

CEC (Commission of the European Communities). (2002). *Communication from the commission concerning corporate social responsibility: A business contribution to sustainable development, 347*. Author.

CEC (Commission of the European Communities). (2005). Implementing the Community Lisbon Programme Modern SME Policy for Growth and Employment. *Communication from the Commission to the Council, the European Parliament, the European Economic and Social Committee and the Committee of the Regions*, 551.

CEC (Commission of the European Communities). (2006). Implementing the partnership for growth and jobs: Making Europe a pole of excellence of corporate social responsibility. *Communication from the Commission to the European Parliament, the Council and the European Economic and Social Committee*, 136.

Choi, J. S., Kwak, Y. M., & Choe, C. (2010). Corporate social responsibility and corporate financial performance: Evidence from Korea. *Australian Journal of Management*, *35*(3), 291–311. doi:10.1177/0312896210384681

Cochran, P. L. (2007). The evolution of corporate social responsibility. *Business Horizons*, *50*(6), 449–454. doi:10.1016/j.bushor.2007.06.004

Cressey, D. R., & Moore, C. A. (1983). Managerial values and corporate codes of ethics. *California Management Review*, *25*(4), 53–77.

Dallo, F. L., & Domench, P. A. (2001). Algunos determinantes de la información medioambiental divulgada por las empresas españolas cotizadas. *Revista de Contabilidad*, *4*(7), 129–154.

Dando, N., & Swift, T. (2003). Transparency and assurance minding the credibility gap. *Journal of Business Ethics*, *44*(2-3), 195–200. doi:10.1023/A:1023351816790

Davies, I. A., & Crane, A. (2010). Corporate social responsibility in small-and medium-size enterprises: Investigating employee engagement in fair trade companies. *Business Ethics (Oxford, England)*, *19*(2), 126–139. doi:10.1111/j.1467-8608.2010.01586.x

De la Cuesta González, M., Valor Martínez, C., Sanmartín Serrano, S., & Botija Buiza, M. (2002). *La Responsabilidad Social Corporativa: Una Aplicación a España* [CSR: An Application to Spain]. UNED.

De la Fuente Sabaté, J. M., & de Quevedo Puente, E. (2003). Empirical analysis of the relationship between corporate reputation and financial performance: A survey of the literature. *Corporate Reputation Review*, *6*(2), 161–177. doi:10.1057/palgrave.crr.1540197

De los Ríos Berjillos, A., Lozano, M. R., Valencia, P. T., & Ruz, M. C. (2012). Una aproximación a la relación entre información sobre la responsabilidad social orientada al cliente y la reputación corporativa de las entidades financieras españolas. *Cuadernos de Economía y Dirección de la Empresa*, *15*(3), 130–140. doi:10.1016/j.cede.2012.01.004

De Quevedo Puente, E., de la Fuente Sabaté, J. M., & García, J. B. D. (2005). Reputación corporativa y creación de valor. Marco teórico de una relación circular. *Investigaciones Europeas de Dirección y Economía de la Empresa*, *11*(2), 81–97.

Dopazo, M. P. (2012). Informes de responsabilidad social corporativa (RSC): fuentes de información y documentación. *Revista general de información y documentación, 22*, 279-305.

Dunlop, A. (1998). *Corporate governance and control*. Kogan Page Publishers.

Durán Herrera, J. J. (2009). Gobernanza, responsabilidad social y medioambiental de la empresa multinacional. Proceso estratégico. *Responsabilidad Social de la Empresa*, 15.

Eberhard-Harribey, L. (2006). Corporate social responsibility as a new paradigm in the European policy: How CSR comes to legitimate the European regulation process. *Corporate Governance*, *6*(4), 358–368. doi:10.1108/14720700610689487

Falk, R. F., & Miller, N. B. (1992). *A primer for soft modeling*. University of Akron Press.

Fassin, Y., Van Rossem, A., & Buelens, M. (2011). Small-business owner-managers' perceptions of business ethics and CSR-related concepts. *Journal of Business Ethics*, *98*(3), 425–453. doi:10.100710551-010-0586-y

Fernández Kranz, D., & Merino Castelló, A. (2005). ¿Existe disponibilidad a pagar por responsabilidad social corporativa? Percepción de los consumidores. *Universia Business Review*, *7*(3), 38–53.

Fernández Sánchez, J. L., & Luna Sotorrío, L. (2007). The creation of value through corporate reputation. *Journal of Business Ethics*, *76*(3), 335–346. doi:10.100710551-006-9285-0

Fombrun, C., & Shanley, M. (1990). What's in a name? Reputation building and corporate strategy. *Academy of Management Journal*, *33*(2), 233–258.

Fombrun, C. J. (1995). *Reputation: Realizing value from the corporate image*. Harvard Business School Press.

Friedman, A. L., & Miles, S. (2002). Developing stakeholder theory. *Journal of Management Studies*, *39*(1), 1–21. doi:10.1111/1467-6486.00280

Fuller, T., & Tian, Y. (2006). Social and symbolic capital and responsible entrepreneurship: An empirical investigation of SME narratives. *Journal of Business Ethics*, *67*(3), 287–304. doi:10.100710551-006-9185-3

Gallardo-Vázquez, D., Sánchez-Hernández, M. I., & Corchuelo-Martinez-Azua, M. B. (2013). Validación de un instrumento de medida para la relación entre la orientación a la responsabilidad social corporativa y otras variables estratégicas de la empresa. *Revista de Contabilidad*, *16*(1), 11–23. doi:10.1016/S1138-4891(13)70002-5

Gallo, M. A. (2004). The family business and its social responsibilities. *Family Business Review*, *17*(2), 135–148. doi:10.1111/j.1741-6248.2004.00009.x

Garay-Tamajón, L., & Font, X. (2013). Corporate social responsibility in tourism small and medium enterprises evidence from Europe and Latin America. *Tourism Management Perspectives*, *7*, 38–46. doi:10.1016/j.tmp.2013.03.002

Garrigues, A. & Trullenque, F. (2008) Responsabilidad social corporativa: ¿papel mojado o necesidad estratégica? *Harvard Deusto Business Review*, 19-36.

González Masip, J. (2018). Los grupos de interés y su importancia en la propuesta de valor de las empresas. *Boletín Económico de ICE*, (3096), 47-57.

Graafland, J., Van de Ven, B., & Stoffele, N. (2003). Strategies and instruments for organising CSR by small and large businesses in the Netherlands. *Journal of Business Ethics*, *47*(1), 45–60. doi:10.1023/A:1026240912016

Gray, R. (2001). Thirty years of social accounting, reporting and auditing: What (if anything) have we learnt? *Business Ethics (Oxford, England)*, *10*(1), 9–15. doi:10.1111/1467-8608.00207

Greening, D. W., & Turban, D. B. (2000). Corporate social performance as a competitive advantage in attracting a quality workforce. *Business & Society*, *39*(3), 254–280. doi:10.1177/000765030003900302

Griffin, J. J., & Mahon, J. F. (1997). The corporate social performance and corporate financial performance debate: Twenty-five years of incomparable research. *Business & Society*, *36*(1), 5–31. doi:10.1177/000765039703600102

Halila, F. (2007). Networks as a means of supporting the adoption of organizational innovations in SMEs: The case of Environmental Management Systems (EMSs) based on ISO 14001. *Corporate Social Responsibility and Environmental Management*, *14*(3), 167–181. doi:10.1002/csr.127

Hall, R. (1992). The strategic analysis of intangible resources. *Strategic Management Journal*, *13*(2), 135–144. doi:10.1002mj.4250130205

Hammann, E. M., Habisch, A., & Pechlaner, H. (2009). Values that create value: Socially responsible business practices in SMEs–empirical evidence from German companies. *Business Ethics (Oxford, England)*, *18*(1), 37–51. doi:10.1111/j.1467-8608.2009.01547.x

Hsu, J. L., & Cheng, M. C. (2012). What prompts small and medium enterprises to engage in corporate social responsibility? A study from Taiwan. *Corporate Social Responsibility and Environmental Management*, *19*(5), 288–305. doi:10.1002/csr.276

Ibrahim, N., & Angelidis, J. P. (1991). Effects of board members' gender on level of involvement in strategic management and corporate social responsiveness orientation. *Proceedings of the Northeast Decision Sciences Institute*, *208*, 210.

Jamali, D., Safieddine, A. M., & Rabbath, M. (2008). Corporate governance and corporate social responsibility synergies and interrelationships. *Corporate Governance*, *16*(5), 443–459. doi:10.1111/j.1467-8683.2008.00702.x

Jamali, D., Zanhour, M., & Keshishian, T. (2009). Peculiar strengths and relational attributes of SMEs in the context of CSR. *Journal of Business Ethics*, *87*(3), 355–377. doi:10.100710551-008-9925-7

Jenkins, H. (2006). Small business champions for corporate social responsibility. *Journal of Business Ethics*, *67*(3), 241 256. doi:10.100710551 006 9182-6

Jenkins, H. (2009). A 'business opportunity' model of corporate social responsibility for small- and medium-sized enterprises. *Business Ethics (Oxford, England)*, *18*(1), 21–36. doi:10.1111/j.1467-8608.2009.01546.x

Jensen, M. C. (1994). Self-interest, altruism, incentives, and agency theory. *Journal of Applied Corporate Finance*, *7*(2), 40–45. doi:10.1111/j.1745-6622.1994.tb00404.x

Jensen, N. M., Li, Q., & Rahman, A. (2010). Understanding corruption and firm responses in cross-national firm-level surveys. *Journal of International Business Studies*, *41*(9), 1481–1504. doi:10.1057/jibs.2010.8

Jo, H., & Harjoto, M. A. (2011). Corporate governance and firm value: The impact of corporate social responsibility. *Journal of Business Ethics*, *103*(3), 351–383. doi:10.100710551-011-0869-y

Jo, H., & Harjoto, M. A. (2012). The causal effect of corporate governance on corporate social responsibility. *Journal of Business Ethics*, *106*(1), 53–72. doi:10.100710551-011-1052-1

Johnson, M. P. (2015). Sustainability management and small and medium-sized enterprises: Managers' awareness and implementation of innovative tools. *Corporate Social Responsibility and Environmental Management*, *22*(5), 271–285. doi:10.1002/csr.1343

Kechiche, A., & Soparnot, R. (2012). CSR within SMEs: Literature review. *International Business Research*, *5*(7), 97. doi:10.5539/ibr.v5n7p97

Kendall, N. (1999). *Good corporate governance. Accountants' Digest, 40.* The ICA in England and Wales.

Klein, B., & Leffler, K. (1981). The role of price in guaranteeing quality. *Journal of Political Economy*, *89*(4), 615–641. doi:10.1086/260996

Knudsen, J. S. (2011). Company delistings from the UN Global Compact: Limited business demand or domestic governance failure? *Journal of Business Ethics*, *103*(3), 331–349. doi:10.100710551-011-0875-0

Kreps, D. M., & Wilson, R. (1982). Reputation and imperfect information. *Journal of Economic Theory*, *27*(2), 253–279. doi:10.1016/0022-0531(82)90030-8

Lamberti, L., & Noci, G. (2012). The relationship between CSR and corporate strategy in medium-sized companies: Evidence from Italy. *Business Ethics (Oxford, England)*, *21*(4), 402–416. doi:10.1111/beer.12002

Lawrence, S. R., Collins, E., Pavlovich, K., & Arunachalam, M. (2006). Sustainability practices of SMEs: The case of NZ. *Business Strategy and the Environment*, *15*(4), 242–257. doi:10.1002/bse.533

Lee, K. H., Herold, D. M., & Yu, A. L. (2016). Small and medium enterprises and corporate social responsibility practice: A Swedish perspective. *Corporate Social Responsibility and Environmental Management*, *23*(2), 88–99. doi:10.1002/csr.1366

Lefebvre, M., & Singh, J. B. (1992). The content and focus of Canadian corporate codes of ethics. *Journal of Business Ethics*, *11*(10), 799–808. doi:10.1007/BF00872312

Lepoutre, J., & Heene, A. (2006). Investigating the impact of firm size on small business social responsibility: A critical review. *Journal of Business Ethics*, *67*(3), 257–273. doi:10.100710551-006-9183-5

Lichtenstein, D. R., Drumwright, M. E., & Braig, B. M. (2004). The effect of corporate social responsibility on customer donations to corporate-supported nonprofits. *Journal of Marketing*, *68*(4), 16–32. doi:10.1509/jmkg.68.4.16.42726

Lizcano, J. L., & Nieto, P. (2006). *La semántica de la responsabilidad social corporativa.* AECA.

López-Pérez, M. E., Melero, I., & Javier Sese, F. (2017). Management for sustainable development and its impact on firm value in the SME context: Does size matter? *Business Strategy and the Environment*, *26*(7), 985–999. doi:10.1002/bse.1961

Luce, R. A., Barber, A. E., & Hillman, A. J. (2001). Good deeds and misdeeds: A mediated model of the effect of corporate social performance on organizational attractiveness. *Business & Society*, *40*(4), 397–415. doi:10.1177/000765030104000403

Madueño, J. H., Jorge, M. L., Sancho, M. P. L., & Martínez-Martínez, D. (2016). Responsabilidad social en las pymes: Análisis exploratorio de factores explicativos. *Revista de Contabilidad*, *19*(1), 31–44. doi:10.1016/j.rcsar.2014.10.003

Maignan, I. (2001). Consumers' perceptions of corporate social responsibilities: A cross-cultural comparison. *Journal of Business Ethics*, *30*(1), 57–72. doi:10.1023/A:1006433928640

Margolis, J. D., & Walsh, J. P. (2001). *People and profits? The search for a link between a company's social and financial performance*. Lawrence Erlbaum Associates. doi:10.4324/9781410600622

Margolis, J. D., & Walsh, J. P. (2003). Misery loves companies: Rethinking social initiatives by business. *Administrative Science Quarterly*, *48*(2), 268–305. doi:10.2307/3556659

Marin, L., & Ruiz, S. (2007). "I need you too!" Corporate identity attractiveness for consumers and the role of social responsibility. *Journal of Business Ethics*, *71*(3), 245–260. doi:10.100710551-006-9137-y

Marín, L. J., & Rubio, A. (2008). La responsabilidad social corporativa como determinante del éxito competitivo: Un análisis empírico. *Revista Europea de Dirección y Economía de la Empresa*, *17*(3), 27–42.

Martín de Castro, G. (2008). *Reputación empresarial y ventaja competitiva*. ESIC Editorial.

Martín De Castro, G., López, J. E. N., & Sáez, P. L. (2006). Business and social reputation: Exploring the concept and main dimensions of corporate reputation. *Journal of Business Ethics*, *63*(4), 361–370. doi:10.100710551-005-3244-z

McGuire, J. B., Schneeweis, T., & Branch, B. (1990). Perceptions of firm quality: A cause or result of firm performance. *Journal of Management*, *16*(1), 167–180. doi:10.1177/014920639001600112

McKendall, M., DeMarr, B., & Jones-Rikkers, C. (2002). Ethical compliance programs and corporate illegality: Testing the assumptions of the corporate sentencing guidelines. *Journal of Business Ethics*, *37*(4), 367–383. doi:10.1023/A:1015287823807

McWilliams, A., & Siegel, D. (2001). Corporate social responsibility: A theory of the firm perspective. *Academy of Management Review*, *26*(1), 117–127. doi:10.5465/amr.2001.4011987

Melé, D., Debeljuh, P., & Arruda, M. C. (2006). Corporate ethical policies in large corporations in Argentina, Brazil and Spain. *Journal of Business Ethics*, *63*(1), 21–38. doi:10.100710551-005-7100-y

Milgrom, P., & Roberts, J. (1982). Predation, reputation, and entry deterrence. *Journal of Economic Theory*, *27*(2), 280–312. doi:10.1016/0022-0531(82)90031-X

Milgrom, P., & Roberts, J. (1986). Price and advertising signals of product quality. *Journal of Political Economy*, *94*(4), 796–821. doi:10.1086/261408

Mohr, L. A., & Webb, D. J. (2005). The effects of corporate social responsibility and price on consumer responses. *The Journal of Consumer Affairs*, *39*(1), 121–147. doi:10.1111/j.1745-6606.2005.00006.x

Moneva, J. M., & Hernández-Pajares, J. (2018). Corporate social responsibility performance and sustainability reporting in SMEs: An analysis of owner-managers' perceptions. *International Journal of Sustainable Economy*, *10*(4), 405–420. doi:10.1504/IJSE.2018.095268

Murillo, D., & Lozano, J. M. (2006). SMEs and CSR: An approach to CSR in their own words. *Journal of Business Ethics*, *67*(3), 227–240. doi:10.100710551-006-9181-7

Murillo, D., & Lozano, J. M. (2006). SMEs and CSR: An approach to CSR in their own words. *Journal of Business Ethics*, *67*(3), 227–240. doi:10.100710551-006-9181-7

Nagles, N. (2007). La gestión del conocimiento como fuente de innovación. *Revista Escuela de Administración de Negocios*, (61), 97-102.

Nanda, V., & Yun, Y. (1997). Reputation and financial intermediation: An empirical investigation of the impact of IPO mispricing on underwriter market value. *Journal of Financial Intermediation*, *6*(1), 39–63. doi:10.1006/jfin.1996.0208

Nejati, M., Quazi, A., Amran, A., & Ahmad, N. H. (2017). Social responsibility and performance: Does strategic orientation matter for small businesses? *Journal of Small Business Management*, *55*, 43–59. doi:10.1111/jsbm.12305

O'Dwyer, B., & Owen, D. L. (2005). Assurance statement practice in environmental, social and sustainability reporting: A critical evaluation. *The British Accounting Review*, *37*(2), 205–229. doi:10.1016/j.bar.2005.01.005

Orlitzky, M., Schmidt, F. L., & Rynes, S. L. (2003). Corporate social and financial performance: A meta-analysis. *Organization Studies*, *24*(3), 403–441. doi:10.1177/0170840603024003910

Paine, L. S. (1996). Moral thinking in management: An essential capability. *Business Ethics Quarterly*, *6*(4), 477–492. doi:10.2307/3857500

Paine, L. S. (2003). *Value Shift: Why Companies Must Merge Social and Financial Imperatives to Achieve Superior Performance*. McGraw-Hill.

Pava, M. L., & Krausz, J. (1997). Criteria for evaluating the legitimacy of corporate social responsibility. *Journal of Business Ethics*, *16*(3), 337–347. doi:10.1023/A:1017920217290

Perrini, F. (2006). SMEs and CSR theory: Evidence and implications from an Italian perspective. *Journal of Business Ethics*, *67*(3), 305–316. doi:10.100710551-006-9186-2

Potts, S., & Maluszewski, I. (2004). Ethics and Corporate Governance. *Corporate Governance*, *12*(2), 177–179. doi:10.1111/j.1467-8683.2004.00357.x

Preuss, L., & Perschke, J. (2010). Slipstreaming the larger boats: Social responsibility in medium-sized businesses. *Journal of Business Ethics*, *92*(4), 531–551. doi:10.100710551-009-0171-4

Ramos-González, M., Rubio-Andrés, M., & Sastre-Castillo, M. (2017). Building Corporate Reputation through Sustainable Entrepreneurship: The Mediating Effect of Ethical Behavior. *Sustainability*, *9*(9), 1663. doi:10.3390u9091663

Raynard, P., & Forstater, M. (2002). *Corporate social responsibility: Implications for small and medium enterprises in developing countries*. United Nations Industrial Development Organization.

Reynolds, M. A. (2000). Professionalism, ethical codes and the internal auditor: A moral argument. *Journal of Business Ethics*, *24*(2), 115–124. doi:10.1023/A:1006179723979

Roberts, P. W., & Dowling, G. R. (1997). The value of a firm's corporate reputation: How reputation helps attain and sustain superior profitability. *Corporate Reputation Review*, *1*(1), 72–76. doi:10.1057/palgrave.crr.1540020

Roberts, P. W., & Dowling, G. R. (2002). Corporate reputation and sustained superior financial performance. *Strategic Management Journal*, *23*(12), 1077–1093. doi:10.1002mj.274

Rodríguez-Ariza, L., Aceituno, J. V. F., & Rubio, R. G. (2014). El consejo de administración y las memorias de sostenibilidad. *Revista de Contabilidad*, *17*(1), 5–16. doi:10.1016/j.rcsar.2013.02.002

Rodriguez-Fernandez, M. (2016). Social responsibility and financial performance: The role of good corporate governance. *BRQ Business Research Quarterly*, *19*(2), 137–151. doi:10.1016/j.brq.2015.08.001

Rodríguez-Piñero Royo, M. C. (2005). La responsabilidad social de la corporativa: una oportunidad y un desafío para todos. *Observatorio sobre la RSE y las Relaciones Laborales, Consejo Andaluz de Relaciones Laborales*. www.juntadeandalucía. es/empleo/carl/observatorio

Roman, R. M., Hayibor, S., & Agle, B. R. (1999). The relationship between social and financial performance: Repainting a portrait. *Business & Society*, *38*(1), 109–125. doi:10.1177/000765039903800105

Ruangviset, J., Jiraporn, P., & Kim, J. C. (2014). How does corporate governance influence corporate social responsibility? *Procedia: Social and Behavioral Sciences*, *143*, 1055–1057. doi:10.1016/j.sbspro.2014.07.554

Ruíz-Lozano, M., de los Ríos Berjillos, A., & Lara, S. M. (2016). ¿Son los códigos éticos un instrumento de gestión de la responsabilidad social? Un estudio exploratorio en Andalucía. *Intangible Capital*, *12*(2), 462–486. doi:10.3926/ic.702

Russo, A., & Perrini, F. (2010). Investigating stakeholder theory and social capital: CSR in large firms and SMEs. *Journal of Business Ethics*, *91*(2), 207–221. doi:10.100710551-009-0079-z

Russo, A., & Tencati, A. (2009). Formal vs. informal CSR strategies: Evidence from Italian micro, small, medium-sized, and large firms. *Journal of Business Ethics*, *85*(2), 339–353. doi:10.100710551-008-9736-x

Rutherfoord, R., Blackburn, R. A., & Spence, L. J. (2000). Environmental management and the small firm. *International Journal of Entrepreneurial Behavior & Research*.

Schuler, D. A., & Cording, M. (2006). A corporate social performance–corporate financial performance behavioral model for consumers. *Academy of Management Review*, *31*(3), 540–558. doi:10.5465/amr.2006.21318916

Schwartz, M. (2001). The nature of the relationship between corporate codes of ethics and behaviour. *Journal of Business Ethics*, *32*(3), 247–262. doi:10.1023/A:1010787607771

Schwartz, M. S., & Carroll, A. B. (2008). Integrating and unifying competing and complementary frameworks: The search for a common core in the business and society field. *Business & Society*, *47*(2), 148–186. doi:10.1177/0007650306297942

Seiffert, M. E. B. (2008). Environmental impact evaluation using a cooperative model for implementing EMS (ISO 14001) in small and medium-sized enterprises. *Journal of Cleaner Production*, *16*(14), 1447–1461. doi:10.1016/j.jclepro.2007.10.001

Shaw, W. H., & Barry, V. (2015). *Moral issues in business* (6th ed.). Wadsworth.

Snell, R. S., Chak, A. M. K., & Chu, J. W. H. (1996). Codes of ethics in Hong Kong: espousal, evidence and impact. *Proceedings of the ANZAM*, 96.

Somers, M. J. (2001). Ethical codes of conduct and organizational context: A study of the relationship between codes of conduct, employee behavior and organizational values. *Journal of Business Ethics*, *30*(2), 185–195. doi:10.1023/A:1006457810654

Spence, L. J. (1999). Does size matter? The state of the art in small business ethics. *Business Ethics (Oxford, England)*, *8*(3), 163–174. doi:10.1111/1467-8608.00144

Spence, L. J. (2007). CSR and small business in a European policy context: The five "C" s of CSR and small business research agenda 2007. *Business and Society Review*, *112*(4), 533–552. doi:10.1111/j.1467-8594.2007.00308.x

Stevens, B. (1994). An analysis of corporate ethical code studies: Where do we go from here? *Journal of Business Ethics*, *13*(1), 63–69. doi:10.1007/BF00877156

Stevens, B. (1999). Communicating ethical values: A study of employee perceptions. *Journal of Business Ethics*, *20*(2), 113–120. doi:10.1023/A:1005869431079

Stigler, G. J. (1962). Information in the labor market. *Journal of Political Economy*, *70*(5), 94–105. doi:10.1086/258727

Svensson, G., Wood, G., & Callaghan, M. (2006). Codes of ethics in corporate Sweden. *Corporate Governance: The International Journal of Business in Society*, *6*(5), 547-566.

Sweeney, L. (2009). *A Study of Current Practice of Corporate Social Responsibility (CSR) and an Examination of the Relationship between CSR and Financial Performance Using Structural Equation Modelling (SEM)* (PhD thesis). Dublin Institute of Technology.

Teece, D. J., Pisano, G., & Shuen, A. (1997). Dynamic capabilities and strategic management. *Strategic Management Journal*, *18*(7), 509–533.

Tilley, F. (2000). Small firm environmental ethics: How deep do they go? *Business Ethics (Oxford, England)*, *9*(1), 31–41. doi:10.1111/1467-8608.00167

Trevino, L. K., & Nelson, K. A. (1999). Managing Business Ethics. John Wiley & Sons.

Vázquez-Carrasco, R., & López-Pérez, M. E. (2013). Small & medium-sized enterprises and Corporate Social Responsibility: A systematic review of the literature. *Quality & Quantity*, *47*(6), 3205–3218. doi:10.100711135-012-9713-4

Villafañe, J. (2004). *La buena reputación*. Pirámide.

Vives, A. (2006). Social and Environmental Responsibility in Small and Medium Enterprises in Latin America. *Journal of Corporate Citizenship*, *21*(21), 39–50. doi:10.9774/GLEAF.4700.2006.sp.00006

Waddock, S., & Graves, S. (1997). The corporate social performance - financial performance link. *Strategic Management Journal*, *18*(4), 303–319. doi:10.1002/(SICI)1097-0266(199704)18:4<303::AID-SMJ869>3.0.CO;2-G

Weiss, J. W. (1994). Business ethics: A managerial, stakeholder approach (No. s 287). Belmont, CA: Wadsworth Publishing Company.

Wickert, C. (2016). "Political" corporate social responsibility in small-and medium-sized enterprises: A conceptual framework. *Business & Society*, *55*(6), 792–824. doi:10.1177/0007650314537021

Williamson, D., Lynch-Wood, G., & Ramsay, J. (2006). Drivers of environmental behaviour in manufacturing SMEs and the implications for CSR. *Journal of Business Ethics*, *67*(3), 317–330. doi:10.100710551-006-9187-1

Williamson, O. E. (1985). *The Economic Institutions of Capitalism: Firms, markets, relational Contracting*. Free Press.

Wu, M. L. (2006). Corporate social performance, corporate financial performance, and firm size: A meta-analysis. *The Journal of American Academy of Business, Cambridge*, *8*(1), 163–171.

Zahra, S. A., & Pearce, J. A. II. (1989). Boards of directors and corporate financial performance: A review and integrative model. *Journal of Management*, *15*(2), 291–334. doi:10.1177/014920638901500208

Zobel, T. (2007). The 'pros' and 'cons' of joint EMS and group certification: A Swedish case study. *Corporate Social Responsibility and Environmental Management*, *14*(3), 152–166. doi:10.1002/csr.125

Zorpas, A. (2010). Environmental management systems as sustainable tools in the way of life for the SMEs and VSMEs. *Bioresource Technology*, *101*(6), 1544–1557. doi:10.1016/j.biortech.2009.10.022 PMID:19906527

ADDITIONAL READING

Porter, M., & Kramer, M. (2006). Strategy and Society. The link between competitive advantage and corporate social responsibility. *Harvard Business Review*, *80*(12), 78–92. PMID:17183795

Shrivastava, R.K., (et al.,). (1997). The value of corporate reputation: Evidence from the equity markets. *Corporate Reputation Review*, *1*, 62–68.

Sommer, A. (2012): Managing green business model transformations. Ed. Springer, New York doi:10.1007/978-3-642-28848-7

Swift, T. (2001). Trust, Reputation and Corporate Accountability to Stakeholders. *Business Ethics (Oxford, England)*, *10*(1), 16–26. doi:10.1111/1467-8608.00208

KEY TERMS AND DEFINITIONS

Corporate Image: The corporate image or brand image, is the set of beliefs, attitudes, and perceptions that the public have about a company or brand. That is to say, it is the way in which that public interprets the set of signals coming from the products, services and communications, emitted by the brand.

Environment Management: It refers to environmental practices, such as energy and water saving activities, renewable energy sources (solar, wind, biomass), waste recycling, use environmentally friendly products.

Ethical Codes: Codes of Conduct are rules dictated, in most cases, unilaterally by companies whose application is generally not subject to external verification processes. A code is a formal statement of the principles that define the standards of a company's specific behaviour.

SR-HRM: Socially responsible human resource management. Human resources management initiatives that improve employee welfare such as, good working conditions, employees with stable contracts.

Stakeholders: In every organization, in addition to its owners, various key actors and social groups that are made up of people or entities that have direct or indirect interest in the performance of the company participate. In these groups we can count employees, customers, suppliers, shareholders, investors, public entities, non-governmental organizations, unions, civil organizations, the community, and society in general.

Transparency: Business transparency seeks to increase trust among those who have a relationship with the company, be it employees, customers, shareholders, or suppliers. Through transparency, the company lets society know how it acts, opening the way to possible criticism or value judgments. The way of transparency is communication, so we must strengthen the company's communication system both internally and externally.

Waste Recycling: It is a good practice of CSR, related to environmental management. Recyclable materials include glass, paper, metal, plastic, tires, textiles, batteries, and electronics.

Work-Family Balance: It is the balance between the professional, family, and personal life of the employees. Includes flexible work, remote work, short time.

Chapter 8
Challenges in Green Intellectual Capital and Knowledge Management in Sustainability and Industry 4.0

Irene Martín-Rubio
Universidad Politécnica de Madrid, Spain

ABSTRACT

The conceptual model proposed in this study is used to serve a guide for Industry 4.0 to understand the effect of GIC (green intellectual capital) and GKM (green knowledge management) on sustainability. Green challenge in Industry 4.0 has increasingly become a hot topic in both academia and practice. Among the Industry 4.0 topics, digital chain monitoring has a great impact on the performance of the company. The study of the industrial digital chain is a great green challenge in the 21st century in order to understand and manage the flows of green information. Knowledge of the human, relational, and structural (including technological aspects) will help to better understand and management the effects of traceability on sustainability. Several of the concepts and variables in the suggested model can easily be managed by organizations if they carefully measure their green intangible nature with smart sensors.

INTRODUCTION

As companies entered into the 1990s, knowledge has become one of the most important strategic resources and one of the key economic resource and the dominant and perhaps even the only source of competitive advantage. Researchers have paid a great attention to the topic of intangible assets, often referred to as intellectual capital in the early 1990s. Intellectual Capital operates as the most important contributor to justify the value difference between market value and book value of many organizations. Intellectual capital has become critical to sustaining competitive advantage, organizational success, innovation, superior organizational performance, core differentiator operator, improve new product

DOI: 10.4018/978-1-7998-4833-2.ch008

development performance, enhance shareholder value, create a framework that allows for describing all resources at the firm's disposal and how they interact to create value, organizational performance, etc.

Green challenge in industry has increasingly become a hot topic in both academia and practice. Green challenge refers to the development or improvement of products and processes about saving energy, controlling pollution, recycling waste, and implementing environmental management. Green innovation is related to products, processes, and services to protect environments, which is a process that firms continuously launch and implement green activities involved in energy saving, pollution prevention, and environmental quality improvement to eventually achieve economic benefits (Chen, 2008). The shift from pollution control to prevention is a good first step, but companies must go further and there is more synergy than conflict between the conventional and environmental paradigms (Porter and van der Linde, 1995, Pujari et al. 2003, Eiadat,Kelly et al. 2008).

The industry 4.0 paradigm is currently one of the domains that presents high challenges for research and manufacturing experts. Among the industry 4.0 topics, digital chain monitoring has a great impact on the performance of the company. Currently, Meski et al. (2019), Dev et al. (2020 a, b), Jabbour et al. (2020) are interested in the study of the industrial digital chain in order to understand and manage the flows of green information generated and exchanged. The principles and technologies of Industry 4.0 can influence how products are manufactured, as well as customer's perceptions of the value of products and green innovation. The use of knowledge-based frameworks is very trendy in the industrial field and represents one aspect in industry 4.0. The effectiveness, reliability and efficiency of this type of system depend heavily on how the knowledge base is structured and managed.

Sustainability has become a topic of interest for both academics and practitioners. A wide discussion and debates about the concept of sustainability, its important and the way to achieve it are pervasive. The economics profits of business activities have increased prosperity and living conditions globally: however it leads to environmental destruction and social inequality directly and indirectly.

Although the aim of sustainability is to keep balance of multidimensional performances, its meaning are inconsistent. In general, sustainability refers to the organizational aim to achieve profit and improve social development while accounting for environmental aspects.

Green Intellectual Capital is defined as sum of tangible resources or knowledge associated to the environmental protection or innovation (Chen, 2008, Liu, 2010, Huang and Kung, 2011). Three main components of GIC namely green human capital (GHC), green structural capital (GSC) and green relational capital (GRC). Few papers have focused on the green aspects of intellectual capital (GIC) and knowledge management (GKM) (Delgado et al. 2014, Yusoff et al. 2019, Yong, 2019, Wang et al. 2020). Nowadays, due to increasing concerns regarding environmental issues, it is essential to integrate the management of green intellectual capital and green knowledge management on Industry 4.0.

The conceptual model proposed in this study is used to serve as a guide for manufacturing firms to understand the management of GIC and GKM on Sustainability. The model (see Figure 1) suggests that without direct attention to green intellectual capital and green knowledge management, the development of Industry 4.0 and sustainability may not ultimately be defined as successful. Figure 1 shows how the model suggested draws from the need of enhancing the disclosure and management of data, information, knowledge and key green intangible performance indicators across the industry value chain. This is the traceability challenge in green innovation agenda.

In developing this argument, first, it is reviewed the Industry 4.0 and Business Sustainability' challenges, namely on traceability and interoperability of different sensors from different points of the Supply Chain. Then, it is described the impact of green intellectual capital, and green knowledge management

Figure 1. Model of management industry 4.0 and green intellectual capital

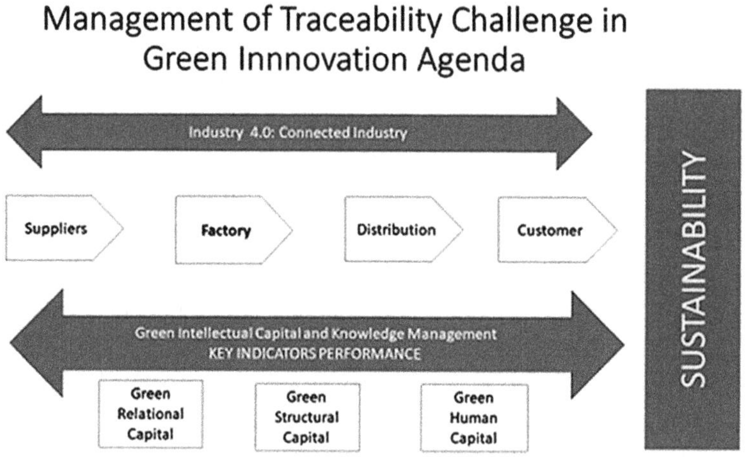

on industrial digital chains. This study provides several contributions to the Intellectual capital-based view and Knowledge Management on natural environment. First, a better understanding of the specificities of the industrial information flow guarantees a good traceability of the implementation conditions, resources and the processes used, the standards that control their use. Second, sustainability information disclosure can improve knowledge sharing and learning. Third, in this way, green intellectual capital can contribute to understand and promote green innovation among all stakeholders in the industry value chain.

This theoretical model stimulates longitudinal empirical research into the effects of green innovation and sustainability in XXI century.

BUSINESS SUSTAINABILITY: ECONOMIC, SOCIAL AND ENVIRONMENTAL PERFORMANCE

There is no one definition for sustainability. Many scholars offers more than seventy various definitions of the term reviewing sustainability as an organization's connection with planet earth, the mother of all stakeholders. The term 'sustainability development' was first introduced in a report entitled the limits of growth published in 1972 . The study was later reproduced in the Brundtland Report in 1987, and then further published in the World Commission on Environment and Development (WCED) in 1989. The report defined the sustainability of present development without ignoring the needs of future generations. According to the report, the term 'sustainability' is based on two concepts; the poor's necessary needs and the environmental limitation to meet future needs. Another contributor to the field is the introduction of the triple bottom line (TBL),which is a sustainability-related framework comprising three lines, namely profit, people, and planet or also known as the 3Ps . The concept not only introduced the report formatting for business report accounting but also the requirement to include the evaluation of the business in decisions of risks, accountability, and all financial aspects of social and environmental opportunities. The terms 'TBL' and 'sustainability' are usually used interchangeably (Yusoff et al. 2019).

Since 2000, the European Union has supported the development of CSR (Corporate Social Responsibility). Later, on 2011, the Comission launched a new document, which stresses CSR as "the responsibility of enterprises for their impacts on society" (Bona et al. 2017)n

The three dimensions of sustainability are closely related, in other words, sustainability aims to achieve three performance goals: economic, social, and environmental. Sustainability generates benefits for their stakeholders, improves the lives of the people whom it interacts with, and protects the environment. Sustainability it is linked to corporate social responsibility and moral issues. Although the aim of sustainability is to keep balance of multidimensional performances, its meaning are inconsistent. Consequently, the misconceptions of the term abound, with many different abstract and theoretical concepts being associated with it.

But, if organizations are aimed for profitability, they would increase their initiatives to minimize wastage while increasing profits, as well as recycle and reuse limited resources to enhance economic performance, which is one of the environmental aims of sustainability.

Following the above position, business sustainability in this study refers to the business purpose to achieve not only profit and social development but also environmental performance indicator (Bona-Sánchez, et al. 2011, Dev et al. 2020, Villers and Sharma, 2020)

Industry 4.0

Last decade, developed countries had proposed a Fourth Industrial Revolution: Industry 4.0 or Smart Manufacturing. One of the key points of Industry 4.0 is the construction of cyber-physical systems (CPSs) (Qian et al. 2017). Computers, communications and controls in CPS can define new business values and new supply chain configurations. Supply chain network involves several strategic decisions about the number, location and capacity of facilities in forms of production plans and distribution centers, and decisions about supplier selection. These decisions are extremely important for companies to manage and design products efficiently and responsively.

In changing business environment, organizations that have the competency to leverage information about their customers, marketplace and business operations can achieve competitive advantages. Challenges exist in terms of identifying appropriate business intelligence and performance measurements for the analysis of the supply chain and the configuration of new Smart Products. New emerging engineering approaches are needed.

It is recognized that since SCM has firm-level consequences, it is necessary to measure the effects of SCM practices on an organization's performance measures (Li et al, 2006).

The convergence between machine-gathered data and human intelligence across several organizations will advance, not only plant-wide optimization and enterprise-wide management objectives, but also supply chain economic performance and environmental sustainability. It will facilitate the use of Smart grids to Schedule energy-intensive activities during low-demand periods and slow production during peak energy demands.

Transformations around Smart Manufacturing follows three phases (SMLC, 2010):

1. Integration of Manufacturing Data. Integration of manufacturing data throughout individual plants and across enterprises will facilitate significant, immediate improvements in costs, safety and environmental impacts.

2. From Plant-Wide Optimization to Manufacturing Intelligence and Nanotechnology. This data, paired with advanced computer simulation and modelling, will create robust “manufacturing intelligence” that will enable variable-speed, flexible manufacturing, optimal production rates, and faster product customization. The second phase of Smart manufacturing connect factory-specific information to data throughout the supply chain –from raw material availability, energy efficiency and customer demand through the delivery of finished goods. It will enable greater product customization, new products simulations, and new, more efficient processes. It will support the production of safer products and precisely defined, faster product tracking.
3. Smart Products, New Business Models and Market Disruption. Smart manufacturing’s third phase will transform industry in a similar way to how the strategic use of information technology transformed the business model and customers shopping behavior. Manufacturing intelligence can inspire innovations in processes and products that comprises a major market disruption.

Flexible factories and IT-optimized supply chains will change manufacturing processes to allow manufacturers to customize products to individual need, such as medications with specific dosages and formulations.

New technologies related to information-based network architecture are providing self-sensing, self-computing, self-organizing, and self-maintaining methods for the decision-making optimization of production and management. New modern Knowledge Management Techniques that impacts intelligent sensing, information integration, knowledge-based automation, and optimal operations can develop Green Industry 4.0.

Industry 4.0 and Digital Chain Monitoring: Traceability and Interoperability in Industry Digital Chain

Industrial digital chains generates an enormous amount of data (big data), and considers not only the digital chain of the production system, but also all the other services: administrative, commercial, strategic, distribution, etc. While the use of gauges and sensors in industry has a long history, the combination of multiple sensors and internet-connected devices envisioned in Industry 4.0 represents a fundamental change in how data can be used to improve processes. The ability to quickly gather, coordinate, communicate and, crucially, analyze vast amounts of data has significant potential to expand the impact that sensors have on industry by maximizing the value of the data that sensors can collect.

Within this unlimited and disconnected information flow, one of the main challenges of the digital chain in most industries is the management of traceability. Another important challenge, is the analysis of these data to improve green innovation with green intellectual capital key indicators.

In the context of the industrial field, we can define **traceability** as the identification of the product (the mechanical part in our case), as well as the analysis of its situation and the generation of reports, at each step of the manufacturing process, as soon as the raw material is acquired until the delivery of a finished product. Therefore, a better understanding of the specificities of the industrial information flow guarantees a good traceability of the implementation conditions, resources and the processes used, the standards that control their use, etc (Meski et al. 2019). Traceability is crucial for production monitoring, and automatically ensures product quality, customer satisfaction and competitiveness of the industry.

In an extended company there is a wide diversification of hardware and software technologies used computer networks, etc. This multiplicity of production methods generates a diversity of formats in the generated information flow, and especially a difference on the delay of these data due to the variation in sampling, acquisition, and processing frequencies. This is therefore an incompatibility at the time of interoperability and/or collaboration.

ISO 25010:2011, which replaces ISO 9126:2001 about software quality, defines the notions of compatibility and interoperability.

Compatibility is the degree to which a product, system or component can exchange information with other products, systems or components, and/or execute its required functions, while sharing the same hardware or software environment. This feature include the following attributes: coexistence and interoperatibility.

-Coexistence: The degree to which a product can perform its required functions effectively while sharing a common environment and their resources with other products, without negatively impacting any other product.

-Interoperability: The degree to which two or more systems, products or components can exchange information and use the information that has been exchanged. The need of collaboration between the different actors of the company imposes the necessity of sharing a set of data which are shared by several resources and can be managed by several information systems.

There are many meanings and types of interoperability, and the large number of definitions that we can find with a literature review is the proof. Facing these varieties of definition, the four main ones are:

1. Technical interoperability that concerns the software and hardware communication, data formats, standards and telecommunications protocols. This first type deals with the technical problems of linking systems.
2. Semantic interoperability allows to define a common semantic reference. Here, it is more the semantic level and the meaning of the information exchanged that is treated. The objective is to provide the exact meaning of the information exchanged so that it can be understood by any other application.
3. Syntactic interoperability concerns the way in which data is coded and formatted, defining in particular the nature, type and format of the messages exchanged. It offers an open system allowing the heterogeneity of components.
4. The interoperability of organizations and processes facilitates communication between organizations, components of the same company, and between several companies. The principle of this type of interoperability is to define rules and principles to facilitate synchronization and connections between processes.

In the context of industry 4.0, interoperability is essential to ensure the capitalization, reintegration, and reuse of heterogeneous information and knowledge in the digital production chain. The development of new knowledge management frameworks around data extraction through sensors, analysis with new business intelligence tools and indicator, and also knowledge sharing, and its capitalization. Through the monitoring of key social, environmental and economic performance indicators (KPIs) decisions in Industry 4.0 can run easily to foster the re-evolution of Business Sustainability (Martín Rubio & Andina, 2018; Fombellida et al. 2018).

GREEN INTELLECTUAL CAPITAL AND GREEN KNOWLEDGE MANAGEMENT

In the era Industry 4.0 and Sustainability economies, intangible resources, knowledge, and competencies are crucial for firms to survive and monitor key performance indicators. However, Knowledge Management is a current challenge due to many barriers. Examples of these could be a firm's incentive system that is misunderstood and misaligned with the goals of Sustainability.

The intensification of sustainability concerns around the globe has led companies to adopt environmental practices at an increasing rate. In the pursuit of this green agenda, green intellectual capital and knowledge management plays an important role. Hence, embedding green practices within managerial functions, performance and its indicators could enhance the likelihood of a firm's sustainability.

Despite the lack of a common definition for intellectual capital, many researchers accept that there are three major categories for intellectual capital: human capital, structural (or organizational) capital and relational (or customer) capital. Such categorization in intellectual capital can help in making decisions about the actions that the firm must perform and about the implementation of programs that allow maintenance, leverage and building of those more valuable intangible assets (or intellectual capital). Hence, in order to explore the relationships between any specific kind of intellectual capital and competitive advantage, a clear identification of the main components of intellectual capital is required.

Definitions of green IC and environmental IC are scarce in the management literature (Yong et al. 2019, Huang and Kung, 2011). Among them, Chen (2008) defined green IC as "the total stocks of all kinds of intangible assets, knowledge, capabilities, and relationships, etc. about environmental protection or green innovation in the individual level and the organization level within a company" (p. 277). Liu (2010) defined green IC as "the integration of green and environment knowledge sources and knowing capability of companies for improving competitive advantage" (p. 2). Lopez-Gamero et al. (2011) proposed green IC as "the sum of all knowledge that an organization is able to leverage in the process of conducting environmental management to gain competitive advantage" (p. 21). Intangible assets can be said to be rare and not easily imitated (Yong et al. 2019).

Generally, the literature has identified three dimensions that encompass the classification of green IC, namely,

1. Green human capital;
2. Green structural/ organizational capital; and
3. Green relational capital.

Green human capital is the summation of employees' knowledge, skills, capabilities, experience, attitude, wisdom, creativities, and commitments, etc. about environmental protection or green innovation, and was embedded in employees not in organizations (Chen, 2008). The attributes of employees that could comprise tacit or explicit knowledge are an invaluable asset as they are not owned by organizations and cannot be imitated. According to Bontis et al. (2007), Wang et al. (2014) Massaro et al. (2018), green human capital is related to a core strategic resource for sustainable competitive advantage as better performance can be achieved with a change in the way of learning, thinking and acting with good motivation. Organizations must, therefore, improve their human capital by training them about sustainability issues.

Green structural capital has been defined as the stocks of organizational capabilities, organizational commitments, knowledge management systems, reward systems, information technology systems, databases, managerial mechanisms, operation processes, managerial philosophies, organizational culture, company images, patents, copy rights, and trademarks, etc. about environmental protection or green innovation within a company (Chen, 2008). Furthermore, green structural capital is defined as the institutionalized knowledge about the form of organizational processes, structures, technologies, policies and culture (Wang et al., 2014). An organization's environmental culture can be referred to as the set of assumptions, values, symbols, and organizational artefacts in an organization. Currently green E-HRM is a part of information technology system of green structural capital, (Yusoff et al., 2018). Green structural capital is owned by the organizations and will not disappear when employees leave (Chang and Chen, 2012). Business managers need to properly invest in the establishment of good information systems to protect their GIC. The green knowledge that resides in the minds of employees will not belong to the organization unless the organization codifies and stores it for future use. Thus, organizations need to retain all knowledge in proper technological information systems.

Green relational capital has been defined as the stocks of a company's interactive relationships with customers, suppliers, network members, and partners about corporate environmental management and green innovation, which enables it to create fortunes and obtain competitive advantages (Chen, 2008). For this reason, it is paramount for organizations to align their interests with those of their stakeholders to survive and to remain competitive. Going "green" is a recent concern for major stakeholders, including customers, suppliers and the government.

Guerci et al. (2016) showed that customer pressure (Relational Capital) has a strong relationship with green HRM (Human Capital). Collaboration is an asset, as it motivates partners to come together to grab opportunities that they would not have been able to pursue alone. All collaborative partners can receive significant benefits in return. It is believed that rich network connections are required to accelerate and enhance sustainability.

In Delgado-Verde et al. (2014) study, the results indicated that green organizational capital had an indirect impact on environmental product innovation through green capital. These findings highlighted that green organizational capital (i.e., environmental communication structures, procedures, responsibilities, and policy) had no direct and positive relationship with environmental product innovation. Rather, the success of the environmental product innovation depended heavily on the cooperative relationships among employees (i.e., green human capital).

Green Knowledge Management

To meet environment challenges, firms should engage in exploitative and exploratory green innovations simultaneously. Exploitative green innovation is the application of existing environmental knowledge, abilities and processes to improve existing green products and green designs (Chen et al., 2014), and exploratory green innovation focuses on new environmental information, knowledge and skills to create new green markets and green products.

Knowledge Management (KM) is a term difficult to understand without knowing and understanding the meaning of the word "knowledge". Further, it is also important to clearly differentiate between knowledge, information or data (see Table 1). The term and expression seemingly used as "Knowledge" does have multiple meanings according to its everyday use within a language, specific field or even similar disciplines (Davenport & Prusak, 2000). At the lowest level is the data, which is unstructured grouping of facts and figures; information at the middle level meaning structured data; and lastly knowledge which may be defined as "information about information"

Table 1. Data, information and knowledge

Data	Information	Knowledge
Facts and figures which relay something specific, but which are not organized in any way	Contextualized, categorized, calculated and condensed data	Know how, understanding, experience, insight, intuition, and contextualized information **1- Explicit Knowledge** Codified knowledge found in documents, databases etc. It is formal and systematic. For this reason, it can be easily communicated and shared, in product specifications or a scientific formula or a computer program. **2- Tacit Knowledge** It is deeply rooted in action in an individual's commitment to a specific context –a craft or profession, a particular technology or product market, or the activities of a work group or team. Consists partly of technical skills: informal, hard-to-pin skills captured in the term "know how", but unable to articulate the scientific or technical principles behind what he knows. It has a cognitive dimension: Mental models, beliefs taked from granted, and therefore cannot easily articulate them. This implicit models profoundly shape how we perceive the world around us.

Knowledge is considered as a mixture of grounded perception, contextual information, expert intuition, standards, and framed understanding that postulates a specific environment and structure for assessing and integrating new innovations in experiences and information. Nowadays, knowledge is an integral part of organizations that is embedded in routines, practices, norms and repositories of organizations. An important and crucial step in KM is to understand different forms of knowledge that exist and ability to differentiate between different types of knowledge. For example, the organization and management of the knowledge acquired in a document is done entirely by a different method as compared to knowledge collected by an expert project manager during his work over the years.

The theory of organizational learning in relation to KM is originated and lies in correlation between Explicit and Tacit knowledge In KM with reference to business terms, knowledge is usually referred to as "Explicit knowledge" that exists in documents in form of codified knowledge and "Tacit knowledge", often mentioned as experience of individuals and is in non-codified form. Nonaka (1994), and Nonaka and Takeuchi (1995) developed and explained this concept in 90s as a key foundation of this field. Explicit and Tacit knowledge types should not be considered as absolute points rather they must be comprehended as a spectrum in order to understand knowledge as a blend or combination of explicit and tacit elements rather being separate from each other.

The relevance of Knowledge Management, at different levels, organizational, team, individual, or other factors such a trust, culture/climate, management support, incentives, social networks and so on. Wang et al. (2014) investigated the impact of Knowledge Management on firm performance and the mediating role of intellectual capital (IC). They suggest that managers can enhance firm performance by enhancing their knowledge sharing and Intellectual Capital.

Green innovation needs more environmental knowledge than traditional innovations due to its complexity and costs (Wang et al. 2020). In order to quickly put green innovation into practice, firms should keep on learning and take a green learning orientation. Green learning orientation is the tendency that firms value the creation and use of green knowledge. Influenced by green values, firms will consciously adopt green learning to facilitate green innovation behaviors. The antecedents of green innovation, includes environmental ethics, environmental regulation, green supplier, quality management, absorptive capacity, and time consciousness.

Drawing on resource-based theory, knowledge resource is one of the basic elements of the firm. It is essential for firms to acquire many kinds of knowledge include green knowledge about green technology and green needs (Chen et al., 2019). Green knowledge acquisition focuses on obtaining green knowledge and affects green innovation. Green learning orientation thus may influences green knowledge acquisition, which in turn facilitates exploitative and exploratory green innovations.

Ambidextrous organizations pursues both exploitative and exploratory innovations, and tends to achieve better performance (Lin and Ho, 2016).

Green Knowledge Acquisition: Learning Orientation and Smart Sensors

Green knowledge acquisition is the process that firms acquire knowledge related to environmental protection (Chen et al., 2014), which is essential for firms to utilize environmental knowledge and enrich environmental technology resources to facilitate ambidextrous green innovation. To survive and meet environmental regulations, firms should acquire and assimilate green knowledge to conduct. Thus, green knowledge acquisition may play a mediating role between green learning orientation and ambidextrous green innovation.

Knowledge acquisition is important and machine learning techniques can be used to achieve automated knowledge acquisition. Smart sensors are essential parts of smart factories, serving as the interface between the digital and physical worlds. This makes them the drivers of Industry 4.0. Beyond the implementation of specific tasks, sensors can allow for quicker responses to consumer feedback and order modifications, helping to make it more profitable for a company to produce smaller numbers of customized products. In addition, the combination of smart sensors with artificial intelligence that is a central aspect of Industry 4.0 means that sensors can be self-testing, monitoring and improving their own performance, and so reducing the instances of corrupted data. Optimal industrial processes will increasingly involve sensors that warn that they are becoming damaged before a failure occurs

Smart sensors are the drivers of Industry 4.0 and the Internet of Things (IoT) in factories and workplaces. Once implemented at scale, the combination of sophisticated sensors and increased computational power will enable new ways to analyze data and gain actionable insights to improve many areas of operations. The result will be responsive and agile production processes that ensure and enhance performance across a range of industrial sectors. Looking ahead to how the implementation of sensors can help companies, the fundamental aspect is the Knowledge Management (of data, information and knowledge). Who provides the data generated by sensors and who will be owning it . The provider of the sensor and data processing infrastructure or the users that are generating the data? If companies get access to, or even ownership of, user-generated data by providing the infrastructure, then they will certainly have a competitive advantage. They can develop additional services and gain early knowledge and insights into client demands (Ernst & Young, 2019). There will be significant entry barriers into such ecosystems, however. Clients and companies are reluctant to share "their" data, although this is already happening on the consumer side, for example in passenger vehicles or from most Apps that are given access to information on consumers' smart phones.

Only with green learning orientation can firms accurately find and identify environmental knowledge, choose the best way to acquire green knowledge according to the characteristics of knowledge, and further effectively integrate and orchestrate green knowledge. Green learning orientation includes the shared values that guide firms to learn green knowledge. It is embodied in firms' commitment and can facilitate ambidextrous (explorative and exploitative) green innovation in the following ways:

1. With shared values, as the core of green learning orientation, influence firms' direction of learning and employees' attitudes to acquire new skills (Huang et al 2011), and promote employees' initiative and enthusiasm to participate in green innovation (Chen et al., 2014).
2. Firms with green learning orientation have the propensity to scan environmental changes, and can encourage employees' proactive thinking. Thus, environmental ideas and thoughts to satisfy green innovation goals can be accumulated, further facilitating exploitative and exploratory green innovations.
3. Firms with green learning orientation have strong green organizational identity, which reinforce firms' environmental vision, and incentivize to carry out learning about environmental issues and solutions.

In summary, firms with green learning orientation actively search and assimilate existing environmental knowledge about data on process, customers' sensors and markets, which will facilitate exploitative green innovations, and, will identify new environmental knowledge that come up with novel thoughts to nurture exploratory green innovation.

From knowledge sharing point of view, organizations can take up environmental initiatives to improve profit margin, reduce production cost due to waste, increase labor productivity and foster circular economy. In addition, firms can actively participate in industry associations that provide guidelines for cultivating better understanding and knowledge of environmental and new infrastructures regulations that are now on the rise. Another initiative that can be taken for the organization to actively join industry associations related to environmental protection.

Without understanding insiders' incentives for disclosing environmental and corporate social responsibility information, data disclosures and knowledge sharing could be not reliable. According to previous literature, the need to adhere to social norms and expectations to obtain external stakeholders' approval constitutes an important motivation for sustainability disclosure (Hahn and Lülfs,2014). According to signalling theory, sustainability reporting is a way to manage the reputational risk of the firm. By demonstrating that companies operate with ethical and social criteria, they can build reputation, whereas failing to do so can be a source of reputational risk. Thus, sustainability disclosure might significantly and positively impact corporate reputation because attending to the concerns of the different stakeholders results in lasting relations based on trust, respect, and credibility (Bona-Sánchez et al. 2017).

CONCLUSION

Parallel to the development of Industry 4.0, organizational sustainability has flourished through the integration of economic and environmental issues into organizations' operations management decision-making processes.

Sensors are the drivers of Industry 4.0 and Sustainability. They provide information that can be analyzed with Green Intellectual Capital and processed with Green Knowledge Management, in order to foster green innovation. Green Knowledge acquisition, green learning orientation with sensors and through machine learning are key aspects to consider in Green Intellectual Capital.

The new green agenda should consider the management of the effects across the industry value chain. Knowledge of the human, relational and structural (including technological aspects) will help to better understand and management the effects of traceability on sustainability. Several of the concepts and variables in the suggested model can easily be manipulated by organizations if they are carefully measure their green "intangible" nature. And this challenge also holds promise for organizations in understanding how they can improve green innovation in the management of the dynamics of their relationships.

The conceptual model proposed in this study is used to serve as a guide for companies to understand the effect of GIC dimensions on Business Sustainability and Industry 4.0. Environmental knowledge management strategies can open up new business chances for organizations to attain sustainability. Using this model, the organizations can improve their capabilities to achieve cleaner production as well as use GIC as a strategy to sustain their business model.

This study provides several contributions to the Intellectual capital-based view and Knowledge Management on natural environment. First, a better understanding of the specificities of the industrial information flow guarantees a good traceability of the implementation conditions, resources and the processes used, the standards that control their use. Second, sustainability information disclosure can improve knowledge sharing and learning. Third, in this way, green intellectual capital can contribute to understand the risk of green innovation among all stake holders.

Finally, this model assumes that the division between interfirm and intrafirm decision makers (stakeholders) it is clear. One potential direction for future inquiry involves the roles and trade-offs of quasi-related decision makers, such as suppliers and customers. Deeper green inter-organizational learning may be gained by examining carefully green traceability issues that new technologies make possible.

REFERENCES

Arshad, A., Noordin, A. F., & Othman, R. (2016). A comprehensive Knowledge Management Process Framework for Healthcare Information Systems in Healtcare Industry of Pakistan. *2016 6th International Conference on Information and Communication Technology for The Muslim World (ICT4M).* DOI: 10.1109/ICT4M.2016.019

Bona-Sánchez, C., Pérez-Alemán, J., & Santana-Martín, D. J. (2017). Sustainability disclosure, dominant owners and earnings informativeness. *Research in International Business and Finance*, *39*, 625–639. doi:10.1016/j.ribaf.2016.07.020

Bontis, N., Seleim, A., & Ashour, A. (2007). Human capital and organizational performance: a study of Egyptian software companies. *Manag. Decis.*, *45*(4), 789-801.

Casilla Polo, F., & Gallardo Vázquez, D. (2008). Social information within the intellectual capital report. *Journal of International Management*, *14*(4), 353–363. doi:10.1016/j.intman.2007.09.007

Cavicchi, C., & Vagnoni, E. (2017). Does intelectual capital promote the shift of healthcare organizations towards sustainable development? Evidence from Italy. *Journal of Cleaner Production, 153.*

Chang, C., & Chen, Y. (2012). The determinants of green intellectual capital. *Management Decision*, *50*(1), 74–94. doi:10.1108/00251741211194886

Chen, C.-J., Hsiao, Y.-C., & Chu, M.-A. (2014). Transfer mechanisms and knowledge transfer: The cooperative competency perspective. *Journal of Business Research*, *67*(12), 2531–2541. doi:10.1016/j.jbusres.2014.03.011

Chen, Y. (2008). The Positive Effect of Green Intellectual Capital on Competitive Advantages of Firms. *Journal of Business Ethics*, *77*(3), 271–286. doi:10.100710551-006-9349-1

Davenport, T. H., & Prusak, L. (2000). *Working knowledge: How organizations manage what they know*. Harvard Business School Press.

De Villers, C., & Sharma, U. (2018). A critical reflection on the future of financial, intelectual capital, sustainability and integrated reporting. *Critical Perspectives on Accounting*.

Delgado-Verde, M., Amores-Salvado, J., Castro, G.M., & Navas-Lopez, J.E. (2014). Green intellectual capital and environmental product innovation: the mediating role of green social capital. *Knowl. Manag. Res. Pract., 12*(3), 1-15.

Dev, N. K., Shankar, R., & Qaiser, F. H. (2020). Industry 4.0 and circular economy: Operational excellence for sustainable reverse supply chain performance. *Resources, Conservation and Recycling*, *153*(104583), 1–15. doi:10.1016/j.resconrec.2019.104583

Dev, N.K., Shankar, R., & Swami, S. (2020). Diffussion of green products in industry 4.0: Reverse logistics issues during design of inventory and production planning system. *International Journal of Production Economics*. (in press)

Dosi, M., Pahi, M. H., Magsi, H. B., & Umrani, W. A. (2019). Influence of the best practices of environmental management on Green product development. *Journal of Environmental Management*, *241*, 219–225. doi:10.1016/j.jenvman.2019.04.006 PMID:31004999

Eiadat, Y., Kelly, A., Roche, F., & Eyatad, H. (2008). Green and competitive? An empirical test of the mediating role of environmental innovation strategy. *Journal of World Business*, *43*(2), 131–145. doi:10.1016/j.jwb.2007.11.012

Ernst & Young GMBH. (2019). *Sensors as drivers of Industry 4.0. A study on Germany, Switzerland, & Austria*. BMCEYGSA. https://www.ey.com/Publication/vwLUAssets/ey-at-studie-sensoren-treiber-industrie-40-2019/$FILE/EY%20Studie%20-%20Sensors%20as%20drivers%20of%20Industry%204.0.pdf

Fombellida, J., Martín-Rubio, I., & Torres-Alegre, S. (2018). *Tackling business intelligence with bioinspired deep learning*. Neural Comput & Applic. doi:10.100700521-018-3377-5

Guerci, M., Longoni, A., & Luzzini, D. (2016). Translating stakeholder pressures into environmental performance e the mediating role of green HRM practices. *International Journal of Human Resource Management*, *27*(2), 262–289. doi:10.1080/09585192.2015.1065431

Hahn, R., & Lülfs, R. (2014). Legitimizing negative aspects in GRI-oriented sustainability reporting: A qualitative analysis of corporate disclosure strategies. *Journal of Business Ethics*, *123*(3), 401–420. doi:10.100710551-013-1801-4

Harris, L. C., & Crane, A. (2002). The greening of organizational culture: Management views on the depth, degree and diffusion of change. *Journal of Organizational Change Management*, *15*(3), 214–234. doi:10.1108/09534810210429273

Huang, C.L., & Kung, F.H. (2011). Environmental consciousness and intellectual capital management: evidence from Taiwan's manufacturing industry. *Manag. Decis., 49*(9), 1405-1425.

ISO/IEC 25010:2011 Systems and software engineering — Systems and software Quality Requirements and Evaluation (SQuaRE) — System and software quality models. https://www.iso.org/standard/35733.html

ISO/IEC 9126-1:2001 Software engineering — Product quality — Part 1: Quality model. This THIS STANDARD HAS BEEN REVISED BY ISO/IEC 25010:2011 https://www.iso.org/standard/22749.html

Jabbour, A. B. L. (2018). When titans meet – Can industry 4.0 revolutionise the environmentally-sustainable manufacturing wave? The role of critical sucess factors. *Technological Forecasting and Social Change*, *132*, 18–25. doi:10.1016/j.techfore.2018.01.017

Kazemi, M., Nazemi, S., & Pooya, A. (2012). Intellectual capital: concepts, components and indicators: a literature review. *Management Science Letters, 2.*

Li, S., Ragu-Nathan, B., Ragu-Nathan, T., & Subba Rao, S. (2006). The impact of supply chain management practices on competitive advantage and organizational performance. *Omega Int. J. Mang. Sc.*, *34*(2), 107–124. doi:10.1016/j.omega.2004.08.002

Liu, C. (2010). Developing green intellectual capital in companies by AHP. *2010 8th International Conference on Supply Chain Management and Information*, 1-5.

London, K., & Siva, J. P. S. (2011). The role of reflexive capability in relation to intellectual capital in multi-international partnerships. *International Journal of Project Management*, *29*(7), 846–855. doi:10.1016/j.ijproman.2011.05.007

Lopez-Gamero, M. D., Zaragoza-Saez, P., Claver-Cortés, E., & Molina-Azorín, J. F. (2011). Sustainable development and intangibles: Building sustainable intellectual capital2. *Business Strategy and the Environment*, *20*(1), 18–37. doi:10.1002/bse.666

MacGillivray, B. H. (2018). Beyond social capital: The norms, belief systems, and agency embedded in social networks shape resilience to climatic and geophysical hazards. *Environmental Science & Policy*, *60*, 116–125. doi:10.1016/j.envsci.2018.07.014

Martín Rubio, I., & Andina, D. (2018). Smart Manufacturing in a SoSE Perspective. In Advances in Renewable Energies and Power Technologies. Vol 2 Biomass, Fuel Cess, Geothermal Energies and Smart Grids. Elsevier.

Massaro, M., Dumay, J., Garlatti, A., & Dal Mas, F. (2018). Practitioners' views on intellectual capital and sustainability: From a performance-based to a worth-based perspective. *Journal of Intellectual Capital*, *19*(2), 367–386. doi:10.1108/JIC-02-2017-0033

McDowell, W. C., Peake, W. O., Coder, L., & Harris, M. L. (2018). Building small firm performance through intellectual capital development: Exploring innovation as the "black box". *Journal of Business Research*, *88*, 321–327. doi:10.1016/j.jbusres.2018.01.025

Meski, O., Belkadi, F., Laroche, F., & Furet, B. (2019). Towards a knowledge-based framework for digital chain monitoring within the industry 4.0 paradigm. *29th CIRP 84 Design 2019*, 118-123.

Michelon, G. (2011). Sustainability disclosure and reputation: A comparative study. *Corporate Reput. Rev., 14*(2), 79–96. doi:10.1057/crr.2011.10

Morgan, T., Anokhin, S., & Wincent, J. (2018). When the fog dissipates: The choice between value creation and value appropriation in a partner as a function of information asymmetry. *Journal of Business Research, 88*, 498–504. doi:10.1016/j.jbusres.2017.11.032

Moser, D. V., & Martin, P. R. (2012). A broader perspective on corporate social responsibility research in accounting. *The Accounting Review, 87*(3), 797–806. doi:10.2308/accr-10257

Nonaka, I. (1994). A dynamic theory of organizational knowledge creation. *Organization Science, 5*(1), 14–37. doi:10.1287/orsc.5.1.14

Nonaka, I., & Takeuchi, K. (1995). *The Knowledge Creating Company*. Oxford University Press.

Ogbeibu, S., Emelifeonwu, J., Senadki, A., Gaskin, J., & Kaivo-oja, J. (2020). Technological turbulence and greening of team creativity, product innovation, and human resource management: Implications for sustainaiblity. *Journal of Cleaner Production, 244*(118703), 1–15. doi:10.1016/j.jclepro.2019.118703

Porter, M. E., & van der Linde, C. (1995). Green and Competitive: Ending the Stalemate. *Harvard Business Review*.

Pujari, D., Wright, G., & Peattie, K. (2003). Green and competitive: Influences on environmental new product development performance. *Journal of Business Research, 56*(8), 657–671. doi:10.1016/S0148-2963(01)00310-1

Qian, F., Zhong, W., & Du, W. (2017). Fundamental Theories and Key Technologies for Smart and Optimal Manufacturing in the Process Industry. *Engineering, 3*(2), 154–160. doi:10.1016/J.ENG.2017.02.011

Rossi, C., Cricelli, L., Grimaldi, M., & Greco, M. (2016). The strategic assessment of intelectual capital assets: An application within Terradure Srl. *Journal of Business Research, 69*(5), 1598–1603. doi:10.1016/j.jbusres.2015.10.024

SMLC (Smart Manufacturing Leadership Coalition). (2011). *SMLC. Implementing 21st century smart manufacturing*. https://smartmanufacturingcoalition.org/sites/default/files/implementing_21st_century_smart_manufacturing_report_2011_0.pdf

Villers, Ch., & Sharma, U. (2020). A critical reflection on the future of financial, intellectual capital, sustainability and integrated reporting. *Critical Perspectives on Accounting, 79*(July), 101999. Advance online publication. doi:10.1016/j.cpa.2017.05.003

Wang, C.N., Chang, Y.L., Huang, Q.H., & Wang, C.H. (2011). Assessment on intelectual capital management for Taiwanese pharmaceutical industry: using GRA and MPI. *Afr. J. Bus. Manag., 5*(7), 2950-2958.

Wang, J., Xue, Y., Sun, X., & Yang, J. (2020). Green Learning orientation, Green knowledge acquisition and ambidextrous Green innovation. *Journal of Cleaner Production, 250*, 119475. doi:10.1016/j.jclepro.2019.119475

Wang, Z., & Huigang, L. (2014). Knowledge sharing, intellectual capital and firm performance. *Management Decision*, *52*(2), 230–258. doi:10.1108/MD-02-2013-0064

Yong, J. Y., Yusliza, M.-Y., Ramayah, T., & Fawehinmi, O. (2019). Nexus between Green intelectual capital and Green human resource management. *Journal of Cleaner Production*, *215*, 363–374. doi:10.1016/j.jclepro.2018.12.306

Younis, H., Sundarakani, B., & O'Mahony, B. (2019). Green suppluy chain and corporate performance: Developing a roadmap for future research using a mixed method approach. *IIMB Management Review*. Advance online publication. doi:10.1016/j.iimb.2019.10.011

Yusoff, Y. M., Nejati, M., Kee, D. M. H., & Amran, A. (2018). Linking green human resource management practices to environmental performance in hotel industry. *Global Business Review*, *21*(3), 1–18.

Yusoff, Y. M., Omar, M. K., Zaman, M. D. K., & Samand, S. (2019). Do all elements of Green intelectual capital contribute toward business sustainability? Evidence from the Malaysian context using the Partial Least Squares method. *Journal of Cleaner Production*, *234*, 626–637. doi:10.1016/j.jclepro.2019.06.153

KEY TERMS AND DEFINITIONS

Business Sustainability: Sustainability is a comprehensive approach to management of organizations which is focused on creating and maximizing long-term economic, social and environmental value. It is a response to the challenges of the modern world facing organizations from the public and private sectors (e.g., https://www2.deloitte.com/ru/en/pages/risk/solutions/sustainability-and-csr.html).

CPS: A CPS is a multi-dimensional, complicated system in a computing, networking, and physical environment that realizes real-time sensing, dynamic control, and the information service of large engineering systems. It is based on the inherent natural integration and cooperation of the "3C" technologies: computers, communication, and control. CPS realization can achieve the integration of computing, communication, and physical systems, thus enhancing the reliability, efficiency, and timeliness of large engineering systems. Therefore, the CPS presents a wide-ranging and significant prospect for practical applications. Specifically, a CPS includes ubiquitous environmental awareness and embedded computing, communication, and networked control; these factors grant physical systems the capabilities of computing, communication, precise control, remote cooperation, and autonomy. In addition, a CPS focuses on the close integration and coordination of computing and physical resources; such integration and coordination have been widely applied to various intelligent systems, such as device interconnection, smart homes, robots, intelligent navigation, and so forth (Qian et al., 2017).

Green Intellectual Capital: Lopez-Gamero et al. (2011) proposed green IC as "the sum of all knowledge that an organization is able to leverage in the process of conducting environmental management to gain competitive advantage" (p. 21). Intangible assets can be said to be rare and not easily imitated (Yong et al., 2019). Generally, the literature has identified three dimensions that encompass the classification of green IC, namely: green human capital; green structural/ organizational capital; and green relational capital.

SCM (Supply Chain Management): SCM is defined as identifying the strategic nature of coordination within a specific organization and across trading partners within the supply chain for the purpose of improving an individual organization's performance and the performance of the whole supply chain (Li et al., 2006).

Traceability: It is the identification of the product (the mechanical part in our case), as well as the analysis of its situation and the generation of reports, at each step of the manufacturing process, as soon as the raw material is acquired until the delivery of a finished product. Therefore, a better understanding of the specificities of the industrial information flow guarantees a good traceability of the implementation conditions, resources and the processes used, the standards that control their use, etc. (Meski et al., 2019). Traceability is crucial for production monitoring, and automatically ensures product quality, customer satisfaction, and competitiveness of the industry.

Chapter 9
Corporate Social Responsibility and the Local Community Effect:
Insights From the Spanish Footwear Cluster

Isabel Diez-Vial
Faculty of Economics and Business, Complutense University of Madrid, Spain

Jose Antonio Belso-Martínez
Department of Economic and Financial Studies, Miguel Hernandez University, Spain

MªJosé López-Sanchez
Department of Economic and Financial Studies, Miguel Hernandez University, Spain

ABSTRACT

The objective of the chapter is to take a multilevel perspective to better understand how CSR practices are developed inside a cluster. The authors aim to describe how CSR practices are developed comparing both firm's characteristics (e.g., innovative capacity, marketing innovation, international activities) and local interactions inside the cluster. In particular, they evaluate how internal dynamics of the cluster, defined by the networks of relationships that are developed with supporting organizations, along with leading firms in the cluster, shape a new institutional framework that locally legitimates CSR practices.

INTRODUCTION

The agglomeration of firms, providers, clients and supporting organization in specific locations has attracted the attention of scholars late in the 19th century. The concept of clusters of economic activity dates back to Marshall (1890, 1920), who was the first scholar to investigate the concentration of specialized activities in certain localities. He explained such cluster of firms in related activities by the existence

DOI: 10.4018/978-1-7998-4833-2.ch009

of external economies: specialized labour, specialized related trades, and specialized firms in different stages of the production cycle. Since them, abundant research has evaluated these benefits in terms of higher economic performance for firms localized in those spaces (Díez-Vial, 2011; Hervás-Oliver and Albors-Garrigos, 2009; Kukalis, 2010; Molina-Morales and Martínez-Fernández, 2009).

In general, it has been broadly considered that much of the agglomeration benefits are a consequence of knowledge exchange and knowledge creation between collocated agents in the cluster (Owen-Smith and Powell, 2004). Physical proximity facilitates the transfer of knowledge through formal means, such as technology partnership, strategic alliances, or supply contracts with other firms or institutions in the same location (Belso-Martinez et al., 2018). Also, proximity foster face-to-face contact and informal interactions, which has turned to be even more relevant than formal interactions in explaining firm performance (Belso-Martinez et al., 2015; Zaheer and Bell, 2005). Moreover, these clusters are considered local communities where shared standings, norms, and rules favour mutual understanding and learning (Inkpen and Tsang, 2005). Knowledge tends to be tacit and it requires certain cognitive proximity in order to communicate, understand and process knowledge successfully (Boschma, 2005). A firm's capacity to learn is conditioned by the specific investment and complementary assets it possesses, or has possessed in the past, its social context and culture, and the portfolio of activities, technologies and markets in which it has been involved. All of these conditions propel firms towards a specific learning path determined by the prior and historical knowledge of the firm and reflected in their specific routines and procedures (Teece et al., 1997; Zahra and George, 2002).

In recent research, the benefits of clusters for improving the economic performance of firms have been extended to explain social performance (Husted et al., 2016; van Wijk et al., 2019). In particular, Corporate Social Responsibility (CSR) has been tightly related to the internal dynamics of concentrated spaces (González-Masip et al., 2019). The central idea is that CSR is not an individual action that firms undertake, but it also depends on the local community that they are embedded on (Hoffman, 1999; Marquis et al., 2007). Local geographic environments, that is, communities, are especially important influences on corporate social action because they facilitate the diffusion of social and ecological practices throughout the cluster. In this sense, CSR practices are based on knowledge and learning abilities that need to be transmitted, combined and absorbed between firms; being it easier among co-located firms with similar values and norms. As well as other kinds of knowledge, CSR practices are sticky, in the sense that they need of proximity to be better transmitted and assimilated among firms(Husted et al., 2016). In particular, firms located in clusters tend to develop local interactions with their stakeholders that make communication and discussion of new practices easier as it is in proximity (Dorado, 2005). Along with the individual capacity of the firms to develop, assimilate and implement CSR practices, it is necessary to consider the interactions among diverse actors and their engagement in understanding each other's perspectives and interests and negotiating shared perspectives in "interactive spaces". It is at this meso level, where interactions between different actors, such as clients, providers, employees, frame new kind of CSR practices (van Wijk et al., 2019). In a complementary way, these local communities are embedded in an institutional context where firms can legitimize their corporate social action by either adapting to it or trying to change existing institutional framework and incorporate social and ecological practices (Lund-Thomsen and Nadvi, 2010). The establishment of local social standings, norms and rules that configure each institutional context vary from a community to another, so do what is accepted and valued in terms CSR practices by their firms (Marquis et al., 2007).

The objective of the chapter is to take this multilevel perspective -the community and the firm- to better understand how CSR practices are developed inside a cluster. We aim to describe how CSR practices are developed comparing both firm characteristics and local interactions inside the cluster. We combine previous studies of CSR practices focused on the firm-level characteristics that determine their CSR practices -e.g. innovative capacity, international activities- (McWilliams and Siegel, 2001) with this recent meso-level of analysis that is the cluster (Hoffman, 1999; Husted et al., 2016; van Wijk et al., 2019). In particular, we evaluate how internal dynamics of the cluster, defined by the networks of relationships that are internally developed, along with firm characteristics affect the implementation of CSR practices.

Empirical evidence has been gathered in the Spanish footwear industry, with detailed data of 175 footwear manufacturers and suppliers surveyed. Spain has been traditionally one of the top footwear manufacturing countries in Europe. Although firms spread across the country, several industrial clusters mostly agglomerate productive and international operations. Despite the relevance of other locations (Balearic Islands, La Rioja, etc), the Vinalopo cluster in the Valencia region comprises almost 60% of the shoes manufacturers and suppliers (leather, heels, insoles, last, textile, among others).

CLUSTERS AS LOCAL COMMUNITIES OF CSR PRACTICES

By concentrating on CSR practices firms as well as scholars embark in a research journey in which social and environmental issues increasingly become involved in their activities and objectives (Matten and Crane, 2005), engendering a greater legitimacy and strategic value for advanced responsibility strategies (Porter and Kramer, 2011). In management literature, corporate Social Responsibility (CSR) is a phenomenon of growing interest in recent decades (González-Masip et al., 2019) related to a company's pursuit and promotion of results of social interest and stakeholders' interests that go beyond the company's economic benefits and the requirements of existing regulations (McWilliams and Siegel, 2001). By undertaking CSR initiatives, firms voluntarily integrate social and environmental issues into their business operations and their interactions with their stakeholders (European Commission, 2001, p. 6). which holds that voluntary CSR actions positively affect primary stakeholders' interests and the firm's legitimacy.

While most research has focused on the characteristics of the firm in explaining CSR practices, the community in which these practices are identified and introduced is an increasingly relevant factor (van Wijk et al., 2019). Following Moulaert and Nussbaumer (2005), the term community in this context refers to "the nature of human interactions within groups that can be defined according to geographic, sociological, political or economic considerations [..] being a way of integrating market relations as historically situated in the wider world of human organization, in which these market relations are embedded as well as constrained". From an institutional perspective, the cluster would be an "organizational field" (Scott, 1985), that is, "those organizations that, in the aggregate, constitute a recognized area of institutional life: key suppliers, resource and product consumers, regulatory agencies and other organizations that produce similar services and products" (DiMaggio and Powell, 1983).

Incorporating the local community as a unit of analysis for evaluating CSR practices extends the interests from individual firms toward the establishment of a community-based pattern. By different norms, rules, values, expectations and ideal references shared by its members, the local community established the level expected level and characteristics of social and ecological practices undertaken (Hoffman, 1999; Scott, 1995). Moreover, it is in this local community where most of the stakeholders to be considered are: most employees, clients, community and institutions tend to reside in the same location as the firms that have relationships with them (Marquis et al., 2007).

This understanding of clusters as local communities is clearly coherent with previous studies undertaken from a network perspective for explaining the governance of the cluster (Jones et al., 1997; Powell et al., 1996). From this approach, relationships between firms and other members of the cluster are coordinated by social coordination and control such as collective sanctions -excluding those firms that do not fulfil the expectative-, creating a shared culture between their members or developing a strong local reputation by spreading information about behaviour among parties, among others (Jones et al., 1997). This form of collective governance of relationships works as long as there are multiple connections between one another, so firms do not only have relationships with each other but with the same parties as well, being indirectly connected to many others of the cluster -structural embeddedness (Granovetter, 1985).

It is at this meso-level where we can understand how this web of relationships informally governed foster the diffusion and incorporation of new CSR practices in the community -e.g. development of sustainable products, new relationships with investors, employees, etc. Since they are locally established and share common understanding and beliefs, it is expected that they would find it easier the diffusion of CSR between their members. Also, it is at this level that we can identify new internal dynamics in the relationships between firms and their stakeholders that imply a change in the governance of the community. That is, we can observe how new beliefs, rules, norms and patter of relationships can be translated into new social and ecological practices incorporated by their members (van Wijk et al., 2019).

THE DIFFUSION OF CSR PRACTICES IN PROXIMITY

It has been generally accepted that the main sources of demand for social practices are related to stakeholders, such as consumers, investors, employees, and the community (McWilliams and Siegel, 2001). While requirements from these stakeholders may be present in any context, local cluster favours the identification and application of these requirements more easily (Husted et al., 2016; Lund-Thomsen et al., 2016). New CSR practices are faster spread because most of these stakeholders are in the cluster, which increases face-to-face interactions, direct observation, along with informal meetings. This context foster "the capacity to identify opportunities, supply leaders, recruit participants, craft mobilizing action frames, and fashion new identities, tasks essential to sustained mobilization" (Polletta, 1999:8). Moreover, this interactive proximity between stakeholders allows them to create new agreements often through intense struggles, negotiations and bargaining, or through collaborative efforts to solve problems (van Wijk et al., 2019). It is at this cluster level that the main agents involved interact and frame the new opportunities derived from incorporating CSR practices (Lund-Thomsen and Nadvi, 2010).

In many cases, behind this positive effect of proximity on developing new CSR practices lies the necessity of exchange tacit knowledge between those different agents involved (Vachon and Klassen, 2006). If most of the relevant knowledge is tacit, then the transfer of knowledge between organizations and stakeholders is difficult: they have to embark on a long, costly process of persuading, coordinating and learning from other firms (Podolny and Page, 1998). This costly process is attenuated when agents are in the same cluster because knowledge tends to be highly contextual or "sticky," so its transmission often requires formal meetings, negotiation processes and on-site discussion between stakeholders (Zaheer and Bell, 2005). It was clearly exemplified by Saxenian and Hsu (2001) in Silicon Valley, where the transmission of technological knowledge but also new managerial practices was clearly diffused in the community by the eight founders of the Shockley Semiconductor company.

This knowledge exchange is accentuated by the interest of local firms in their local competitors. As Porter (1998) has pointed out, inside firms tend to have stronger competition as they tend to focus more o those rivals that are that are at distance. The presence in the cluster of firms that are undertaking CSR practices is an stimuli to imitate these practices as long as they need to preserve relationships with existing customers, suppliers and other stakeholders (Campbell, 2007).

Also, inside clusters employees have higher mobility between companies, favouring the diffusion of CSR practices between companies (González-Masip et al., 2019). Clusters tend to attract high qualified and specialized employees because there are multiple alternative companies to work on in a related field (Mccann and Folta, 2008). Based on the same reason, once they are installed in the community they find it easier to move from one firm to another taking their knowledge and experiences to other firms (Husted et al., 2016).

Finally, the cluster understood as a community of practice also tend to develop trust-based relationships, enabling knowledge exchange among different local agents. Trust reflects the belief that a partner's word or promise is reliable and that a partner will fulfil its obligations in the relationship (Inkpen and Tsang, 2005). Trust plays a key role in the willingness of network actors to share knowledge by reducing the opportunism risk (Mu et al., 2008). Trust makes people more willing to give useful knowledge (Levin and Cross, 2004; Tsai and Ghoshal, 1998) and are also more willing to listen to and absorb others' knowledge (Wijk et al., 2008). That is, the strength of a relationship leads to more effective communication through the development of non-transferable common knowledge among parties (Grant, 1996). In this sense, it has been observed that trust-based relationships between stakeholders and firms (Castaldo et al., 2009; Hansen et al., 2011) or between firms in different stages of social and ecological involvement (Husted et al., 2016) tend to favour the development of CSR practices.

THE RELEVANCE OF INSTITUTIONAL SUPPORT AND LOCAL LEGITIMACY

Incorporating CSR in the cluster involves not only the diffusion of CSR practices through the community but also institutional changes (Moulaert and Nussbaumer, 2005). New social and ecological practices imply new configurations of local relationships between stakeholders, which often involves re-negotiations of settled institutions with conflicting logics or even developing new routines, procedures, communications flows and historical beliefs (van Wijk et al., 2019; Westley and Antadze, 2010). As long as CSR practices become extended and accepted in the community, they would be more institutionalized and locally legitimated (Frynas and Yamahaki, 2016; Husted et al., 2016). Previous studies have pointed out the difficulties in introducing institutional changes for incorporating CSR practices in geographically concentrated spaces (Dorado, 2005; Hoffman, 1999).

Following Scott (1995), social behaviour becomes institutionalized by three main aspects which he called pillars: the regulative, the normative, and the cognitive. The regulative pillar deals with explicit regulative processes, such as rule-setting, monitoring and sanctioning activities. The primary mechanism of control would be coercion (DiMaggio and Powell, 1983), and it can be thee results of formal or informal rules and laws. Although members of the community can comply with these rules, it does not imply that they would be accepted are proper, not being locally legitimated. The normative pillar includes values and norms into social life that would legitimate not only the objectives but also the way to pursue them. They define the normative expectations of the community: what actors are supposed to do and can take multiple forms such as rules-of-thumb, standard operating procedures, occupational standards, and educational curricula (Hoffman, 1999). The cognitive pillar embodies symbols-words, signs, and gestures as well as cultural rules and frameworks that shape the understanding of the nature of reality and the frames through which that meaning is developed. Organizations will often abide by them without conscious thought. Each of these three aspects affects legitimacy in different ways: the regulative emphasis in the conformity to rules, the normative one is related to the interiorization of moral obligations, and the cognitive view focuses on the legitimacy that comes from adopting a common frame of reference.

Supporting organizations, such as trade associations, universities or professional training institutions, play a key role in shaping new institutional context (Hoffman, 1999). These institutions have a primary role in industrial clusters, with reference to the integration of local and social values (Battaglia et al., 2010; Martínez-del-Río and Céspedes-Lorente, 2014). In many contexts, these supporting organizations play the role of peer pressures to conform new CSR standards established by regulation, trying to ensure that their members act in socially responsible ways (Campbell, 2007). But also, supporting institutions can change existing routines, norms, authority flows, or beliefs of the social system in which the local community is established (van Wijk et al., 2019). Supporting organizations can enhance the possibility of defining common effective policies and strategies, and it can improve relations with the local stakeholders. (Battaglia et al., 2010). These supporting organizations serve as go-betweens for firms with complementary interests in the cluster; they interact with a large number of firms, all undertaking similar activities and facing similar problems, so they compile and develop extensive practices, routines and ways of understanding reality through the cluster (Molina-Morales et al., 2016). As long as supporting organizations have an extensive network of ties in the cluster, they can introduce new norms, values, rules and interpretations of reality coherent with new social requirements. As Amin and Thrift (1995) point out, supporting organizations increase the influence of local cultural and historical factors by establishing habits, norms, and routines that underpin the social structure of a region, and this is referred to as "institutional thickness". While pressure to conform to these common understandings may exist throughout the entire cluster, when firms establish direct relationships with the institutions they signal their adherence to certain institutional views (Baum and Oliver, 1992).

Firms play also an important role in changing the institutional context of the local community, especially by the cognitive pillar (Scott, 1995). Firms tend to imitate competitors that are in proximity that arises from moral bases, -"what is right to do around here?" (Marquis et al., 2007:934). As competitors incorporate news CSR practices, more firms would resemble them doing the same (Husted et al., 2016). Managers are more likely to regard the CRS practices undertaken by proximate firms operating in the same environment as more appropriate and legitimate than others' undertaken by distant firms with which they are not related (Marquis et al., 2007). Even if there are regulative forces in the cluster that, by norms and laws tries to foment the development of CSR practices, leading firms with the capacity to incorporate these new practices into their internal process are necessary. As a consequence, firms can lead the incorporation of new CSR practices in the cluster, initiating changes in the institutional settling of the cluster, being necessary to identify which the characteristics of these firms are.

THE SPANISH FOOTWEAR INDUSTRY AND CLUSTERS

During the end of the last century, the Spanish footwear industry experienced an impressive growth driven by a deep restructuring of the manufacturing and commercial bases inspired in the Italian model. Production processes became fragmented and decentralized, while traditional informal practices were displaced by an emphasis on value creation strategies. After peaking in 1997 with about 150 million pairs, the fierce competition in the global arena has progressively eroded the leading position of the industry. Even though offshoring and the implementation of innovative strategies based on the geographical agglomeration of activities in clusters spread across the country, have counterbalanced this negative trend.

Today, the industry has morphed to become a more complex and variegated reality where a fragmented entrepreneurial structure articulates around a fragmented value chain. The need for adaptation to the economic context has forced the coexistence of different business models in which geo-location, cooperation and knowledge-based strategies play a crucial role. Industry 4.0 technological developments, branding and design have partly attenuated the negative post-crisis scenario, raising exports up to 100 million pairs. As the national business association (Federación de Industrias del Calzado-FICE) highlights, the main figures of sector evolved positively almost uninterruptedly since 2011. In 2018, production rose about 1% in pairs and by 5% in value.

Table 1. The Spanish footwear industry

Region	Clusters	Number of Firms (% Medium-Large)	Average Price	Footwear Exports	Input Exports
Andalusia	Valverde	144 (8.33)	15.32 €	1.06%	2.83%
Aragon	Brea Illueca	119 (0.00)	12.98 €	3.19%	1.58%
Balearic Islands	Inca Ciutadela	105 (3.81)	41.28 €	4.78%	0.23%
Castilla-La Mancha	Almansa Fuensalida	349 (3.15)	22.31 €	5.57%	1.27%
Valencia	Vinalopó Vega Baja	2,335 (2.23)	16.74 €	55.46%	71.22%
Murcia	Caravaca Alama	163 (3.07)	6.70 €	3.17%	0.66%
La Rioja	Arnedo Calahorra	246 (4.88)	16.97 €	6.23%	9.74%
Spain		3,530 (2.41)	16.19 €	100%	100%

Source: Own elaboration based on data from the Spanish Statistical Institute, FICE and AEC.

The industry comprises a myriad of small and medium enterprises (SMEs) with limited endogenous potential for carrying out technological developments, over 73% of the 3530 firms account for less than 10 employees. From the spatial perspective, the concentration of productive and international operations in certain regions and clusters is noticeable. As Table 1 reveals, the Vinalopó cluster in the Valencia region comprises the vast majority of the shoe manufacturers, suppliers (leather, heels, insoles, last, machinery or textiles). Also, it can be observed that the Valencia cluster is clearly oriented toward international business, exporting 55.46% of the products and 71.22% of the inputs.

Additionally, price differences highlight marked asymmetries in terms of value creation and competitive strategies. Balearic Islands manufacture and commercialize top products through highly recognized brands (Camper, Lotusse, Mascaró, among others), the Vinalopó cluster combines subcontracting for rather diverse global players (Coach, Zara, H&M, Geox, Gucci, LVMH, among others) with indigenous footwear brands (Pikolonos, Panama Jack, Unisa or Hispanitas), and Murcia mostly focus in rustic shoes made with textile and jute.

The Spanish footwear industry represents a unique opportunity for the analysis of CSR practices. During decades, specific sectorial, historic and territorial aspects have favoured the generalization of informal practices which run against sustainable practices (Ybarra, 2000). Despite institutional and social controls, informalization is still considered as a rooted and widespread phenomenon by over 82.4% of the population living at the heart of the Vinalopo cluster (Aparicio-Baeza et al., 2017). Although a growing interest on CSR exists among business owners and managers, Bermejo-Sales (2018) points out the long way that footwear firms should walk on CSR due to the entrenchment of improvable behaviours in aspects like recycling, waste, working days, patronage, diversity or gender.

Population and Sample

The research context is the Spanish footwear industry. Despite several challenges that continue to exist, there has been a noticeable effort in the last decade by national and regional governments and private entities to promote CSR practices. This has resulted in an increasing number of firms formally or informally implementing social responsibility practices. In order to evaluate the stage of development of these practices in the footwear industry and how cluster dynamics affect them, a survey has been undertaken. Three different sources were used to generate our population and sample: the Spanish Association of Footwear Manufacturers (FICE), Spanish Association of Footwear Components (AEC) and the SABI database provided Bureau Van Dijk.[1] After a detailed examination with business association representatives and the removal of non-active companies, an initial population of 3,252 firms was obtained.

Data gathering method was a web-based survey approach because the population of interest is businesses, and coverage issues are not present due to high rates of computer use and the large sample size (Dillman, 2000). An online tool was used to design a website on which the questionnaire appeared. All questionnaire items were marked as mandatory to ensure completeness of collected data. The online survey was disseminated via email containing the main objectives of our research and a link to the electronic survey during October 2018. Particularly, the benefits of the project were explained, confidentiality guaranteed and an executive summary of the results offered as an incentive (Miller et al., 1997).

As our database originally did not contain the top manager's email addresses, web searches and phone calls were conducted to compile their contacts. This process generated significant attrition and reduced our roaster to 2,013 firms.

After the initial email, over a period of two months, several reminders and a phone call tried to persuade firms to participate. Both invitation email and subsequent reminders were constructed to provide the same verbal and visual presentation to avoid confusions. Finally, a total of 175 companies replied, representing an overall response rate of 9%. Non-response bias was checked following Mentzer and Flint (1997). A total of 25 randomly selected non-respondents were contacted and asked to respond two items from each of the CSR constructs. The T-test analysis between these answers and those given by respondents revealed no statistical differences, rejecting the risk of bias. In addition, we employed Harman's single factor test to evaluate for common method bias (Podsakoff et al., 2003). The single factor explained about 25% of the variance, so concerns were discarded.

On average, the firms that answer the questionnaire have been in business for 22.7 years, employed 25.72 people and presented a turnover of 4.3 million euros.[2] The two prevalent forms of the legal structure were private and public limited liability, 86.9% and 9.1% respectively. 76% of the firms manufactured shoes, while the remainder focused on inputs or machinery. From the technological or marketing innovation perspective, 10.7% of firms have registered patents and 28.6% trademarks. The majority of the firms were located in clusters and export-orientated, 91.4%, and 53.7%. The descriptive analysis also revealed that 32,6% were members of the footwear business association and 21.5% of the technological institute.

Measurement of the Variables

Before starting the data collection process, we distributed a pilot questionnaire to 5 industry experts. The survey covered a broad range of CSR topics including multiple environmental, stakeholders, barriers and performance measures obtained from our literature review. Once this preliminary tool was polished with their feedback about item wording and structure, we submitted it to 10 top-level managers or business owners of footwear firms to ensure clarity and comprehension. According to Moyano Fuentes *et al.* (2019), this profile of informants is the most reliable information sources about social corporate responsibility related activities. This procedure dissipated doubts about content validity.

CSR and its main dimensions were the variables of interest in this study. Based on previous literature, our structured the questionnaire was designed to identify the most frequent CSR practices conducted inside and outside the firm (Agudo-Valiente et al., 2015; Chow, W.S. and Chen, 2012). Using 5 points Likert scale (1= strongly disagree; 5=strongly agree), top-level managers and business owners were asked to indicate to what extent they agreed with 31 statements related to different aspects such as Considering previous studies, we have grouped CSR practices into two main categories: Eco-responsibility dimensions and socio-responsibility dimensions. Dealing with eco-responsibility dimensions we included several items to evaluate to what extent companies develop sustainable products, recycle, and try to reduce energy and water consumption. Within the social dimension, four different stakeholders' groups were included: customers, suppliers, employees and the local community. Table 2 has incorporated all the items included in the survey.

Scores on this large number of social responsibility actions were factor analyzed using maximum-likelihood estimation method to synthesize information in a more structured and operational way (KMO>.500; Bartlett sphericity test with p-value<.01). The 7 factors obtained yielded sufficient internal consistency with Cronbach's alpha ranging from .67 to .90, see Table 2. In a second step, using the same methodological procedure, these different factors were combined in a unique global CSR showing a satisfactory Cronbach's alpha .75 (KMO>.500; Bartlett sphericity test with p-value<.01).

Also, we have incorporated specific measures of the firm's characteristics in order to understand to which profile of firms can lead the institutional change inside the cluster and incorporate CSR practices in the community. To explore the influence of certain firm's characteristics and strategic behaviours on the different CSR dimensions, we defined the following binary variables: International operations (1: firm exports and imports; 0: otherwise), Technical innovation (1: firm has 1 or more patents; 0: otherwise), Marketing innovation (1: firm has 1 or more trademarks; 0: otherwise). We have focused on these aspects following previous studies that have tested how firms with international activities (Attig et

Table 2. Exploratory factor analysis for main CSR constructs

Dimension	Variable	Factor Loading	Cronbach's Alpha	Variance Explained
Eco-responsibility Dimensions		.		
Sustainable products			.76	59.2%
	Environmental impact is considered when developing a product	.774		
	Environmentally friendly products are used	.815		
	Sustainable packaging is used	674		
	Environmentally friendly products are developed	.807		
Recycling			.78	81.5%
	Actions are taken to reduce waste and residues	.903		
	Waste is recycled	.903		
Efficiency			.67	75.4%
	Measures are taken to reduce energy consumption	.868		
	Measures are taken to reduce water consumption	.868		
Socio-responsibility Dimensions				
Investors			.80	62.6%
	Easily obtains funds from banks and/or investors	.509		
	Social and/or environmental responsibility activities make it easier for us to obtain financing from banks and financial institutions.	.788		
	The social and/or environmental responsibility policies of its banks and financial institutions are valued.	.874		
	Social and/or environmental responsibility activities make it easier for us to attract investors	.857		
	In your company, the social and/or environmental responsibility policies of your investors are valued.	.868		
Employees			.85	56.3%
	The wages set by your employees	.640		
	Occupational health and safety levels	.727		
	Facilities for the conciliation of professional and working life of your employees	.833		
	The relevance of social and labour responsibility in hiring	.805		
	Actions to improve the well-being of your employees (e.g. internal events, facilities, ...)	.817		
	Permanence of the employee in the company	.658		
Suppliers			.90	77.2%
	Controls compliance with environmental regulations by its suppliers	.896		
	Establishes or maintain an effective grievance process with suppliers	.762		
	Promotes the social and environmental responsibility of its suppliers	.939		
	Follows the same social and/or environmental responsibility guidelines as their suppliers.	.874		
	Transmits its guidelines of social responsibility and/or environment to its suppliers	.913		
Customers			.80	45.5%
	The quality criteria for production and/or service are met in your company	.600		
	Your company registers and responds to customer complaints effectively	.591		
	Your company's catalog and labeling provides clear and accurate information, including after-sales service	.721		
	Your company tries to sensitize its customers on aspects of social and environmental responsibility.	.760		
	Measures are taken to reduce energy consumption	.642		
	Your company takes into account the accessibility of customers with disabilities	.670		
	Social and environmental responsibility policies are relevant for attracting and/or retaining customers.	.708		
Local Community			.75	63.3%
	Makes donations and/or sponsorships	.825		
	Carries out projects and policies that favor the local environment (purchasing, contracting,...)	.778		
	Integrates or collaborates in local movements (neighborhoods, associations, ...)	.859		
	Encourage employees participation in activities for the benefit of the community during working hours or with remuneration.	.714		
Global CSR Index			.75	80.2%

al., 2016), highly innovative firms (Gallego-Álvarez et al., 2011) and with relevant marketing activities (McWilliams and Siegel, 2001).

We have also measured the influence of having relationships with supporting organizations inside the cluster. Knowledge spillovers are not homogeneously distributed among all the agents in a cluster, but there can be certain asymmetries that depend on the links created between firms and supporting organizations (Morrison and Rabellotti, 2009). Also, the establishment of relationships with supporting organizations plays a key role in the diffusion and institutionalization of CSR practices in the cluster. As a consequence, we have measured links with two main kinds of supporting organizations: technical institutions and business associations. We have measured them with a dummy variable that takes value 1 if there is this relationship and 0 otherwise (Deeds et al., 1999; May et al., 2001; McEvily and Zaheer, 1999)

Statistical Analysis and Results

In order to evaluate our theoretical framework, T-Tests were performed. Once checked the homogeneity of the variance between the groups selected for the analysis, the corresponding T-statistic and significance level is observed. This technique has frequently been applied in the field of business research to compare factors and variables between two business groups: firms that present a specific characteristic, and those which do not. In our case, the above-explained binary variables (international operations, technical innovations, marketing innovations, technical networks and social networks) allowed us to generate sub-samples to examine whether a significant difference exists in the implementation of CSR.

Table·3 shows the results obtained from different T-test. Model 1 and Model 2 compare the average for firms engaged in innovation with the average for those that do not. According to the analysis of the

Table 3. T-test on Technical innovation, Market innovation and International operations

	Model 1: Technical Innovation			Model 2: Market Innovation			Model 3: International Operations		
	Value=0 Mean	Value=1 Mean	T-Statistic (p-Value)	Value=0 Mean	Value=1 Mean	T-Statistic (p-Value)	Value=0 Mean	Value=1 Mean	T-Statistic (p-Value)
Eco-responsibility Dimensions									
Sustainable products	-.056	.398	*-1.741	-.132	.285	**-2.359	-.110	.208	*-1.796
Recycling	-.041	.458	**-2.196	-.047	.129	-1.103	-.034	.087	-.706
Efficiency	.032	.018	0.55	.169	-.312	***2.655	-.007	.128	-.835
Socio-responsibility Dimensions									
Investors	-.009	-.021	047	-.082	.205	*-1.729	-.055	.131	1.1277
Employees	-.010	.249	-.728	-.063	.157	**-.2017	-.097	.227	**-2.055
Suppliers	-.009	.249	-.516	-.098	.247	**-2.085	-.094	.222	**-2.122
Customers	.037	-.260	1.187	-.013	.033	-.282	-.030	.071	-.607
Local Community	-.036	.234	-1.084	-.028	.069	.704	-.033	.079	-.649
Global CSR Index	-.012	.183	-.195	-.096	.236	**-1.997	-.095	.221	**-1.968

*** p-value>.01; ** p-value<.05; *p-value<.1

eco-responsibility dimensions, the implementation of sustainable product development by technological or marketing innovators is significantly better than those of non-innovators at 10% and 5% significance level. Recycling is just higher for technological innovators at 5%, while efficiency is significantly lower for marketing innovators at 1%.

Table 4. T-test on supporting organizations

	Technical Institutions			Business Associations		
	Value=0 Mean	**Value=1 Mean**	**T-Statistic (p-Value)**	**Value=0 Mean**	**Value=1 Mean**	**T-Statistic (p-Value)**
Eco-responsibility Dimensions						
Sustainable products	-.050	.096	-.147	-.102	.0226	-.702
Recycling	-.014	.053	-.388	.104	-.179	*1.673
Efficiency	.052	-.024	.411	-.023	.209	-1.409
Socio-responsibility Dimensions						
Investors	-.089	.265	***-2.785	.087	-.090	.177
Employees	-.076	.230	-1.374	.057	-.025	.378
Suppliers	-.007	.020	-.164	-.035	.057	-.549
Customers	-.008	.025	-.033	-.006	.008	-.082
Local Community	-.023	.070	-.524	-.003	.072	-.450
Global CSR Index	-.037	.118	-.155	.023	-.035	.338

*** p-value>.01; ** p-value<.05; *p-value<.1

Table 4 represents the results dealing with the relationships with supporting organizations. As it can be observed, there are no significant differences in CSR practices related to having relationships with technical institutions or business associations. Moreover, in only two cases that there are significant differences -social responsibility with investors and recycling- the results seem to contradict the theoretical expectations.

CONCLUSION AND IMPLICATIONS

Empirical evidence gathered in Spanish clusters specialized in the footwear industry have provided interesting insights for better understanding the role that clusters play in fostering CSR practices. First, clusters can be understood as local communities of practices, that is, group of firms, providers, clients, employees and supporting organizations that shape CSR practices by institutional factors. That is, each cluster is configured by specific formal and informal constraint of actions -regulative aspects-, certain standards of appropriateness and evaluation of social actions -normative aspects- and they tend to develop shared frameworks of interpretation under a common cognitive framework -cognitive aspects- (Scott, 1995; van Wijk et al., 2019). As long as incorporating stakeholders demands on their practices become institutionalized by any of these three aspects in the cluster, firms that undertake CSR practices would become more legitimate. Moreover, as long as more and more firms and supporting organizations undertake CSR practices in the cluster, the diffusion of these practices would be easily spread in proximity, through the community, increasing the overall local involvement in ecological and social responsibility actions (Husted et al., 2016).

Secondly, we could not confirm the key role in diffusing social and ecological practices and promoting institutional change traditionally associated to supporting organizations -mainly technical institutions and trade associations (Battaglia et al., 2010; Marquis et al., 2007). Since they are connected to many different organizations, they can more easily transmit tacit knowledge-based practices. Also, they would find it easier to establish both new local expectations about what actors are expected to do in CSR practices and up-to-date beliefs, shared logic of actions, they are taken from granted in dealing with CSR. Empirical evidence does not seem to confirm this point, not being able to find significant differences between firms that have relationships with them and those that do not have these relationships. In this sense, it could be that just belonging to trade associations or other supporting organizations is not enough to introduce social and ecological changes when there is a high diversity of positions between their members to introduce changes (Lund-Thomsen et al., 2016).

Finally, what we have observed is that in these clusters CSR practises seem to be led by firms. Our findings signal that firms traditionally engaged in innovation-related practices or in international activities has the necessary internal routines and structures to absorb the specific local knowledge that facilitates the implantation of novel social responsibility strategies. As firms in the community incorporate news CSR practices, more firms would resemble them doing the same (Husted et al., 2016; Lund-Thomsen and Nadvi, 2010). Managers are more likely to regard the CRS practices undertaken by proximate firms operating in the same environment as more appropriate and legitimate than others' undertaken by distant firms with which they are not related (Marquis et al., 2007). Even if there are regulative forces in the cluster that, by norms and laws tries to foment the development of CSR practices, leading firms with the capacity to incorporate these new practices into their internal process are necessary.

The results that we obtain have important implications for academics and practitioners. Despite the exponential growth of cluster literature, aspects related to social and responsibility dimension has been traditionally relegated or circumscribed to environmental aspects and empirical evidence from developing countries. In this paper, we deal with this gap using insights from cluster and management literature. Our research represents an attempt to enlarge the conventional innovation-cluster research tradition, highlighting the need for the development of robust theoretical constructs and suggesting the partial transferability of the paradigms derived from the microeconomics of innovation grounded in solid corpus like the network approach or the resource-based view.

REFERENCES

Agudo-Valiente, J. M., Garcés-Ayerbe, C., & Salvador-Figueras, M. (2015). Corporate social performance and stakeholder dialogue management. *Corporate Social Responsibility and Environmental Management*, *22*(1), 13–31. doi:10.1002/csr.1324

Amin, A., & Thrift, N. (1995). Globalisation, institutional 'thickness' and the local economy. In *Managing Cities* (pp. 91–108). The New Urban Context.

Aparicio-Baeza, J., Martiinez-Mayoral, A., Morales-Socuuellamos, J., & Ortiz-Henarejos, L. (2017). Percepción de la ciudadanía de Elche sobre la economía sumergida. Academic Press.

Attig, N., Boubakri, N., El Ghoul, S., & Guedhami, O. (2016). Firm Internationalization and Corporate Social Responsibility. *Journal of Business Ethics*, *134*(2), 171–197. doi:10.100710551-014-2410-6

Battaglia, M., Bianchi, L., Frey, M., & Iraldo, F. (2010). An innovative model to promote CSR among SMEs operating in industrial clusters: Evidence from an EU project. *Corporate Social Responsibility and Environmental Management*, *17*(3), 133–141. doi:10.1002/csr.224

Baum, J. A. C., & Oliver, C. (1992). Institutional embeddedness and the dynamics of organizational populations. *American Sociological Review*, *57*(4), 540–559. doi:10.2307/2096100

Belso-Martinez, J. A., Díez-Vial, I., Lopez-Sanchez, M. J., & Mateu-Garcia, R. (2018). The brokerage role of supporting organizations inside clusters: How does it work? *European Planning Studies*, *26*(4), 706–725. doi:10.1080/09654313.2017.1422482

Belso-Martinez, J. A., Molina-Morales, F. X., & Martínez-Cháfer, L. (2015). Contributions of brokerage roles to firms' innovation in a confectionery cluster. *Technology Analysis and Strategic Management*, *27*(9), 1014–1030. doi:10.1080/09537325.2015.1045858

Bermejo-Sales, E. (2018). *Análisis de la responsabilidad social corporativa como estrategia de comunicación en el sector del calzado ilicitano*. Universidad Miguel Hernández.

Boschma, R. A. (2005). Proximity and innovation: A critical assessment. *Regional Studies*, *39*(1), 61–74. doi:10.1080/0034340052000320887

Campbell, J. L. (2007). Why would corporations behave in socially responsible ways? An institutional theory of corporate social responsibility. *Academy of Management Review*, *32*(3), 946–967. doi:10.5465/amr.2007.25275684

Castaldo, S., Perrini, F., Misani, N., & Tencati, A. (2009). The missing link between corporate social responsibility and consumer trust: The case of fair trade products. *Journal of Business Ethics*, *84*(1), 1–15. doi:10.100710551-008-9669-4

Chow, W. S., & Chen, Y. (2012). Corporate sustainable development: Testing a new scale based on the mainland chinese context. *Journal of Business Ethics*, *105*(4), 519–533. doi:10.100710551-011-0983-x

Deeds, D. L., Decarolis, D. M., & Coombs, J. (1999). Dynamic capabilities and new product development in high technology ventures: An empirical analysis of new biotechnology firms. *Journal of Business Venturing*, *15*(3), 211–229. doi:10.1016/S0883-9026(98)00013-5

Díez-Vial, I. (2011). Geographical cluster and performance: The case of Iberian ham. *Food Policy*, *36*(4), 517–525. doi:10.1016/j.foodpol.2011.04.002

DiMaggio, P. J., & Powell, W. W. (1983). The iron cage revisited: Institutional isomorphism and collective rationality in organizational fields. *American Sociological Review*, *48*(2), 147–160. doi:10.2307/2095101

Dorado, S. (2005). Institutional entrepreneurship, partaking, and convening. *Organization Studies*, *26*(3), 385–414. doi:10.1177/0170840605050873

Frynas, J. G., & Yamahaki, C. (2016). Corporate social responsibility: Review and roadmap of theoretical perspectives. *Business Ethics (Oxford, England)*, *25*(3), 258–285. doi:10.1111/beer.12115

Gallego-Álvarez, I., Prado-Lorenzo, J. M., & García-Sánchez, I. M. (2011). Corporate social responsibility and innovation: A resource-based theory. *Management Decision*, *49*(10), 1709–1727. doi:10.1108/00251741111183843

González-Masip, J., Martín-de Castro, G., & Hernández, A. (2019). Inter-organisational knowledge spillovers: Attracting talent in science and technology parks and corporate social responsibility practices. *Journal of Knowledge Management*, *23*(5), 975–997. doi:10.1108/JKM-06-2018-0367

Granovetter, M. S. (1985). Economic action and social structure: The problem of embeddedness. *American Journal of Sociology*, *91*(3), 481–510. doi:10.1086/228311

Grant, R. M. (1996). Toward a knowledge-based theory of the firm. *Strategic Management Journal*, *17*(S2), 109–122. doi:10.1002mj.4250171110

Hansen, S. D., Dunford, B. B., Boss, A. D., Boss, R. W., & Angermeier, I. (2011). Corporate social responsibility and the benefits of employee trust: A cross-disciplinary perspective. *Journal of Business Ethics*, *102*(1), 29–45. doi:10.100710551-011-0903-0

Hervás-Oliver, J.-L., & Albors-Garrigos, J. (2009). The role of the firm's internal and relational capabilities in clusters: When distance and embeddedness are not enough to explain innovation. *Journal of Economic Geography*, *9*(2), 263–283. doi:10.1093/jeg/lbn033

Hoffman, A. J. (1999). Institutional Evolution and Change : Environmentalism and the U. S. *Chemistry & Industry*, *42*, 351–371.

Husted, B. W., Jamali, D., & Saffard, W. (2016). Near and dear? The role of location in CSR engagement. *Strategic Management Journal*, *37*(10), 2050–2070. doi:10.1002mj.2437

Inkpen, A. C., & Tsang, E. W. K. (2005). Social capital, networks, and knowledge transfer. *Academy of Management Review*, *30*(1), 146–165. doi:10.5465/amr.2005.15281445

Jones, C., Hesterly, W. S., & Borgatti, S. P. (1997). A General Theory of Network Governance: Exchange conditions and social mechanisms. *Academy of Management Review*, *22*(4), 911–945. doi:10.5465/amr.1997.9711022109

Kukalis, S. (2010). Agglomeration economies and firm performance: The case of industry clusters. *Journal of Management*, *36*(2), 453–481. doi:10.1177/0149206308329964

Levin, D. Z., & Cross, R. (2004). The strength of weak ties you can trust: The mediating role of trust in effective knowledge transfer. *Management Science*, *50*(11), 1477–1490. doi:10.1287/mnsc.1030.0136

Lund-Thomsen, P., Lindgreen, A., & Vanhamme, J. (2016). Industrial Clusters and Corporate Social Responsibility in Developing Countries: What We Know, What We do not Know, and What We Need to Know. *Journal of Business Ethics*, *133*(1), 9–24. doi:10.100710551-014-2372-8

Lund-Thomsen, P., & Nadvi, K. (2010). Clusters, Chains and Compliance: Corporate Social Responsibility and Governance in Football Manufacturing in South Asia. *Journal of Business Ethics*, *93*(S2), 201–222. doi:10.100710551-010-0561-7

Marquis, C., Glynn, M. A., & Davis, G. F. (2007). Community Isomorphism and Corporate Social Action. *Academy of Management Review, 32*(3), 925–945. doi:10.5465/amr.2007.25275683

Marshall, A. (1920). *Principles of economics.* MacMillan, Londo.

Martínez-del-Río, J., & Céspedes-Lorente, J. (2014). Competitiveness and Legitimation: The Logic of Companies going Green in Geographical Clusters. *Journal of Business Ethics, 120*(1), 131–146. doi:10.100710551-013-1636-z

Matten, D., & Crane, A. (2005). Corporate citizenship: Toward an extended theoretical conceptualization. *Academy of Management Review, 30*(1), 166–179. Advance online publication. doi:10.5465/amr.2005.15281448

May, W., Mason, C., & Pinch, S. (2001). Explaining industrial agglomeration : The case of the British high- fidelity industry. *Geoforum, 32*(3), 363–376. doi:10.1016/S0016-7185(01)00004-5

Mccann, B. T., & Folta, T. B. (2008). Location Matters: Where We Have Been and Where We Might Go in Agglomeration Research. *Journal of Management, 34*(3), 532–565. doi:10.1177/0149206308316057

McEvily, B., & Zaheer, A. (1999). Bridging ties: A source of firm heterogeneity in competitive capabilities. *Strategic Management Journal, 20*(12), 1133–1156. doi:10.1002/(SICI)1097-0266(199912)20:12<1133::AID-SMJ74>3.0.CO;2-7

McWilliams, A., & Siegel, D. (2001). Corporate Social Responsibility: A Theory of the Firm Perspective. *Corp. Soc. Responsib. A Theory Firm Perspect., 26*, 117–127.

Miller, C. C., Cardinal, L. B., & Glick, W. H. (1997). Retrospective reports in organizational research: A reexamination of recent evidence. *Academy of Management Journal, 40*, 189–204. doi:10.2307/257026

Molina-Morales, F. X., Belso-Martinez, J. A., & Mas-Verdú, F. (2016). Interactive effects of internal brokerage activities in clusters: The case of the Spanish Toy Valley. *Journal of Business Research, 69*(5), 1785–1790. doi:10.1016/j.jbusres.2015.10.056

Molina-Morales, F. X., & Martínez-Fernández, M. T. (2009). Too much love in the neighborhood can hurt: How an excess of intensity and trust in relationships may produce negative effects on firms. *Strategic Management Journal, 30*(9), 1013–1023. doi:10.1002mj.766

Morrison, A., & Rabellotti, R. (2009). Knowledge and information networks in an Italian wine cluster. *European Planning Studies, 17*(7), 983–1006. doi:10.1080/09654310902949265

Moulaert, F., & Nussbaumer, J. (2005). Defining the social economy and its governance at the neighbourhood level: A methodological reflection. *Urban Studies (Edinburgh, Scotland), 42*(11), 2071–2088. doi:10.1080/420980500279752

Moyano Fuentes, J., Jiménez Delgado, J. J., & Rodríguez Martínez, A. (2019). Territorial agglomerations and corporate social responsibility: The role of science and technology parks. *International Journal of Entrepreneurship and Innovation Management, 23*(2), 180. Advance online publication. doi:10.1504/IJEIM.2019.10018520

Mu, J., Peng, G., & Love, E. (2008). Interfirm networks, social capital, and knowledge flow. *Journal of Knowledge Management*, *12*(4), 86–100. doi:10.1108/13673270810884273

Owen-Smith, J., & Powell, W. W. (2004). Knowledge networks as channels and conduits: The effects of spillovers in the Boston Biotechnology community. *Organization Science*, *15*(1), 5–21. doi:10.1287/orsc.1030.0054

Podolny, J. M., & Page, K. L. (1998). Networks forms of organization. *Annual Review of Sociology*, *24*(1), 57–76. doi:10.1146/annurev.soc.24.1.57

Podsakoff, P. M., MacKenzie, S. B., Lee, J.-Y., & Podsakoff, N. P. (2003). Common method biases in behavioral research: A critical review of the literature and recommended remedies. *The Journal of Applied Psychology*, *88*(5), 879–903. doi:10.1037/0021-9010.88.5.879 PMID:14516251

Polletta, F. (1999). "Free spaces" in collective action. *Theory and Society*, *28*(1), 1–38. doi:10.1023/A:1006941408302

Porter, M. E. (1998). Clusters and the new economics of competition. *Harvard Business Review*, •••, 77–90. PMID:10187248

Porter, M. E., & Kramer, M. R. (2011). Creating Shared Value. *Harvard Business Review*, *89*, 62–77. doi:10.1108/09600039410055963

Powell, W. W., Koput, K. W., & Smith-Doerr, L. (1996). Interorganizational and the collaboration locus of innovation: Networks of learning in Biotechnology. *Administrative Science Quarterly*, *41*(1), 116–145. doi:10.2307/2393988

Saxenian, A., & Hsu, J. Y. (2001). The Silicon Valley–Hsinchu connection: Technical communities and industrial upgrading. *Industrial and Corporate Change*, *10*(4), 893–920. doi:10.1093/icc/10.4.893

Scott, R. W. (1995). *Institutions and Organizations.* SAGE Publications.

Teece, D., Pisano, G., & Shuen, A. (1997). Dynamic capabilities and strategic management. *Strategic Management Journal*, *18*(7), 509–533. doi:10.1002/(SICI)1097-0266(199708)18:7<509::AID-SMJ882>3.0.CO;2-Z

Tsai, W., & Ghoshal, S. (1998). Social Capital and value creation: The role of intrafirm networks. *Academy of Management Journal*, *41*, 464–476.

Vachon, S., & Klassen, R. D. (2006). Extending green practices across the supply chain: The impact of upstream and downstream integration. *International Journal of Operations & Production Management*, *26*(7), 795–821. doi:10.1108/01443570610672248

van Wijk, J., Zietsma, C., Dorado, S., de Bakker, F. G. A., & Martí, I. (2019). Social Innovation: Integrating Micro, Meso, and Macro Level Insights From Institutional Theory. *Business & Society*, *58*(5), 887–918. doi:10.1177/0007650318789104

Van Wijk, R., Jansen, J. J. P., & Lyles, M. A. (2008). Inter- and intra-organizational knowledge transfer : A Meta-analytic review and assessment of its antecedents and consequences. *Journal of Management Studies*, *45*(4), 830–853. doi:10.1111/j.1467-6486.2008.00771.x

Westley, F., & Antadze, N. (2010). Making a Difference: Strategies for Scaling Social Innovation for Greater Impact Frances Westley and Nino Antadze A. *Innov. J. Public Sect. Innov. J.*, *15*, 2–20.

Ybarra, J. A. (2000). La infomalización como estrategia productiva. Un análisis del calzado valenciano. *Rev. Estud. Reg.*, *57*, 199–217.

Zaheer, A., & Bell, G. G. (2005). Benefiting from network position: Firm capabilities, structural holes, and performance. *Strategic Management Journal*, *26*(9), 809–825. doi:10.1002mj.482

Zaheer, A., & George, G. (2002). Absorptive capacity: A review, reconceptualization, and extension. *Academy of Management Review*, *27*(2), 185–203. doi:10.5465/amr.2002.6587995

ENDNOTES

1 SABI is a directory of Spanish and Portuguese companies provided by Bureau Van Dijk that collects both general information and financial data. We used the corresponding code of the *National Classification of Economic Activities* CNAE *2009* (152 Footwear industry). CNAE-2009 is the National Classification of Economic Activities, and has been compiled according to the conditions set out in the Regulation approving NACE Rev.2.

2 Due to the empirical strategy, larger firms are overrepresented in the sample. This must be kept in mind when results are interpreted. Despite this circumstance, the sample is representative for the total population and sufficiently valid for the purpose of this research. Additionally, lager firms are considered more relevant in terms of value creation and RSC practices.

Chapter 10
CSR in the Spotlight:
Location and Gender as Drivers of Its Development

Enrique Claver-Cortés
University of Alicante, Spain

Bartolomé Marco-Lajara
University of Alicante, Spain

Esther Poveda-Pareja
University of Alicante, Spain

ABSTRACT

This study has as its aim to analyze the existence of a possible theoretical relationship between corporate social responsibility (CSR) development and two factors, namely business location and managers' gender. The industrial district (ID) theory serves as the basis to demonstrate the possible influence of location on this type of environment with an improved implementation of social practices. At the same time, the authors will also consider the possible influence of internationalization within the cluster on CSR development since globalization itself can further favor the implementation of CSR practices. The study additionally examines the role that the variable 'directors' gender', and more precisely, women directors, can play as a key factor in the development of such practices. The implications that the concurrence of these factors might have, along with the future lines of research that would derive therefrom, will finally be considered.

INTRODUCTION

The current business environment is facing what could be referred to as *the age of social demand*, where the concern for CSR has gone from simply being an option to becoming a must for business survival. In fact, some authors consider that CSR has become a modern corporate mantra (Sarkar and Searcy, 2016). The emergence of present-day historical landmarks such as *the Climate Emergency Statement* by

DOI: 10.4018/978-1-7998-4833-2.ch010

the European Parliament on November 28, 2019, whereby the European commitment to neutralize all of its greenhouse gas emissions by 2050 was expressed, casts serious doubts on many of the practices implemented by companies over the last few decades. Despite their great relevance, environmental problems are not the only ones that need to be solved within the scope of CSR. Thus, authors such as Husted (2015) referred to the paradoxical fact that although the infrastructure available in the current economic reality is sufficiently developed to carry out CSR practices, companies make fewer efforts.

It is evident that in the period from the first references to caring for social issues to the most current visions, in addition to not bearing fruit, this concept is not being efficiently implemented. This can be seen in the Taylorist practices which are still implemented in different types of businesses and in the unsuccessful efforts of various national and supranational organizations to achieve what they began to promote centuries ago. Thus, from the elaboration of the well-known *UN Global Compact* (1999) to the most current global plans such as the *Sustainable Development Goals* approved in 2015 by the United Nations, efforts continue to be made not only to achieve stable fundamental human rights principles but also to foster initiatives aimed at developing environmental and social responsibility through a wide range of objectives. In spite of these efforts and although some progress has already been made, quite a few of these principles remain unfulfilled, both in developing countries (which is one of the main goals that should be addressed) and in many of the countries considered to be developed. For this reason, numerous researchers have focused their lines of research on analyzing factors that can reduce the difficulties faced by companies in the development and effective implementation of CSR practices.

In this regard there are 2 issues that still need a more in-depth examination. Firstly, the role played by location in CSR (Lund-Thomsen and Pillay, 2012; Husted et al., 2016). More specifically, this chapter looks at how Industrial Districts (IDs), as concrete environments in which companies can choose to locate, can stimulate the development of CSR practices through the well-known *district effect*, amongst many other factors that will be analyzed. This line of research is of great contemporary interest (Battaglia et al., 2010; Von Weltzien Høivik and Shankar, 2011; Testa at al., 2012; Santos, 2014; Horzela, 2019). We will also consider the possible influence of internationalization within the cluster on CSR development since, according to many current researchers (Lund-Thomsen and Pillay 2012; Attig et al., 2016; Zyglidopoulos et al., 2016), globalization itself can further favor the implementation of CSR practices and this information, along with the benefits gained from an ID, could be of great importance to managers and business studies students as it can guide them towards the best locations in which to develop their CSR strategies.

Secondly, the influence of gender on CSR practices is another interesting line of research. Thus, diversity in the boardroom can be considered a key variable, because it will impact on board decisions (Cabeza-García, 2018). One could say that a company's board of directors, as an important component of corporate governance, is expected to play a fundamental role in CSR decisions (Kruger 2009). Concretely, the analysis of factors that lead boards with more women members to adopt more CSR practices than male dominated boards (Landry et al., 2016; Alonso-Almedia et al., 2017; Rajasekar and Deepa, 2017; Cabeza-García et al., 2018; Pucheta-Martínez et al., 2018; Cullinan et al., 2019) is an emerging line of research and thus constitutes the second element analyzed in this chapter.

Therefore, a combined model is proposed which allows us to harness two types of benefits. Firstly, the advantages that an ID can bring to CSR development, while simultaneously understanding that IDs can operate globally, and that an international presence would make it easier to implement CSR. Secondly, an understanding of the factors that show how women can facilitate the development of CSR practices.

The chapter is structured as follows: an initial theoretical background section which presents the foundations of CSR so that its origin and evolution can be properly understood gives way to the analysis of the two central points: the relationship between CSR and location (studying the ID as an optimal area for CSR development, also favored by the inclusion of globalization); and the gender variable —added as a management characteristic that would help improve the outcome of CSR practices. Through the analysis of the two central points, the theoretical model will be developed, what would lead to the main conclusions as well as the future lines of research derived from it.

Consequently, this chapter carries out a theoretical analysis of two topics which have hitherto been largely neglected in the CSR literature, namely: (a) the combined consideration of the industrial district and globalization perspectives with the development of CSR; and (b) the study of management gender in order to improve CSR practices.

BACKGROUND

Although it is argued that the beginning of academic debates on CSR dates back to the 1950s or 1960s, it is actually a much older concept which, despite the countless definitions and explanations associated with it, first started to be discussed in the nineteenth-century business environment. Indeed, several researchers (Drucker, 1984; Martín, 2010; Husted, 2015; García, 2012) confirm that the true antecedents of CSR were the actions of certain businessmen who, due to their condition as executives and thanks to their principles and values which were ahead of their time, included social actions in their business environment, thus setting an example for both coeval and subsequent generations. Good examples would be the industrialist Robert Owen (1825) with his reduction of working hours, Jamsetji Tata (1877) through the introduction of different worker welfare initiatives such as medical services or the tips system, among many other figures. The outstanding initiatives described above somehow meant a starting point for both businessmen and academics to begin considering the need to include social practices as an effective way to ensure the strategic success of organizations. One of the first to deal with the notion of CSR was Bowen (1953), who pioneered the adoption of a definition close to what is currently known as CSR through the expression *Social Responsibilities*, which he conceived as *the obligations of businessmen to pursue those policies, to make those decisions, or to follow those lines of action which are desirable in terms of our society's objectives and values.* Other studies were later developed to identify the actions that could be covered by CSR. Thus, Carroll (1974;1979;1991) in various studies, brought together the four major aspects of the concept of CSR. He listed the four basic pillars of CSR that allowed him to define it as *the social responsibility of business that encompasses the economic, legal, ethical, and discretionary expectations that society has of organizations at a given point in time.* All these theories promoted the emergence of numerous visions according to which CSR was, and continues to be, positively related to an improvement in business results (Chrisman and Carroll, 1984; Galbreath, 2008; Rettab et al., 2009; Gómez-Bezares et al., 2017; Cook et al., 2019), as well as to the achievement of advantages associated with reputation and consumer satisfaction, amongst others (Alafi and Hasoneh, 2012; Rothenhoefer, 2019; Zhang et al., 2019; Bianchi et al., 2019). Despite the above, the debate over whether businesses have a responsibility to society is a continuing one and the literature is replete with arguments both for and against the assumption of such an obligation (Ackerman, 1973). Thus, despite its importance, there have been several skeptical positions towards the concept (Friedman; 1970; Davis, 1973; Halme et al.,

2018; Brulhart et al., 2019; Doane, 2005). Consequently, further study is worthwhile, even though the establishment of a single and universally accepted definition seems unfeasible (Okoye, 2009).

The evolution of the concept continued in this way until the arrival of authors who considered it necessary to include CSR in the company's core business, thus leaving behind its conception as a mere tool to improve individual company performance. A special mention must be made in this regard for the contribution of Porter and Kramer (2002). On the basis of the existing dichotomy between shareholders' requests on the one hand, and society's growing demands on the other, these authors suggested abandoning the traditionally studied concept of corporate philanthropy to begin embracing strategic philanthropy, which could help the company direct its investments towards certain social aspects. They proposed the philanthropy strategy as a way to improve the competitive context which surrounds companies, understanding that a link between social and economic objectives might arise in the long run; and it is precisely in this convergence point that the objective of strategic philanthropy would be achieved. In order to integrate this new way of understanding philanthropy within business decision processes, Porter and Kramer (2002) put forward a number of steps: (1) *examine the competitive context in each of the company's important geographic locations*; (2) *review the existing philanthropic portfolio to see how it fits this new paradigm*; (3) *assess existing and potential corporative giving initiatives against the four forms of value creation*; (4) *seek opportunities for collective action within a cluster and with other partners*; and (5) *rigorously track and evaluate results*.

The analysis of CSR from a strategic perspective leads to the idea that managers should focus on factors that may strengthen the development of CSR. Accordingly, and following the proposal of Porter and Kramer (2002), as well as other authors who will be discussed in the next section (Battaglia et al., 2010; Von Weltzien Høivik and Shankar, 2011; Testa at al., 2012; Santos, 2014; Horzela, 2019), we consider that certain aspects associated with location, specifically inside Industrial Districts, could play a key role in the achievement and implementation of CSR practices. Additionally, from the strategic perspective, the influence of other factors such as management characteristics should be considered as they can drive or slow down the development of CSR. We will analyze management gender as one of the factors that may influence CSR (Ibrahim and Angelidis, 1994; Burgess and Tharenou (2002); Williams, 2003; Wirth, 2015; Setó-Pamies, 2015; Landry et al., 2016; Alonso-Almedia et al., 2017; Rajasekar y Deepa, 2017; Cabeza-García et al., 2018 Pucheta-Martínez et al., 2018; Cullinan et al., 2019)

RELATIONSHIP BETWEEN LOCATION AND CSR

Industrial Districts as a CSR Development Tool

In the field of management, location is one of the most important strategic decisions to be made. In recent decades, location decisions have been studied from an economic perspective, considering its cost and income implications (Dixit, 2019).

In this line of research, geographical concentration is one of the most studied aspects and it is understood to mean the concentration of a number of firms in a certain location in order to obtain some kind of benefit over and above their respective internal capacities (Marco-Lajara et al., 2015). The antecedents of this concept are found in the work of Marshall (1890) and his Industrial District Theory, which highlighted 3 main benefits: (1) the possibility of sharing common resources; (2) the creation of a specialized labor market (3) the possibility of sharing knowledge among agents in the ID (knowledge spillovers). Becattini (1979) further developed the ID concept, understanding it as *a socio-territorial entity which is characterized by the active presence of both a community of people and a population of firms in one naturally and historically bounded area*, to which he adds the need for a permanent network of relationships between the elements that make it up. Becattini (1979) considered that the firms in an ID would obtain benefits derived from the district effect, which allows firms to achieve improved aggregate performances. These studies informed the work of other authors such as Porter (1990), whose work *The Competitive Advantage of Nations* provided evidence that belonging to a given country, as well as to a very characteristic environment inside it, is decisive for the achievement of competitive advantages. From this approach he developed the concept of the cluster, which he defined as *geographic concentrations of interconnected companies, specialized suppliers, service providers, firms in related industries, and associated institutions (e.g., universities, standards agencies, trade associations) in a particular field that compete but also cooperate*.

From the three above mentioned classical definitions of business concentration, in this chapter the concepts of ID and cluster will be treated as synonymous as, despite their subtle differences, there is a certain substitutability between them (Sforzi, 2008). Another common element in location studies is that traditionally they have all taken an economic perspective with the aim of improving the competitive positions of a firm through location. One of the issues that still needs a more in-depth examination is the role played by location in CSR (Lund-Thomsen and Pillay, 2012; Husted et al., 2016; Ding et al., 2019).

A study worthy of consideration is that of Husted et al. (2016), which puts forward an empirical model to show the existence of two factors that impact on CSR commitment level. On the one hand, they propose that a dense geographic environment in CSR increases the commitment to such practices assumed by the companies belonging to it —due to the spillover effect (especially referring to tacit knowledge for its ability to reduce the costs related to CSR) as well as to the institutional pressure which take place in such contexts. Seeking to verify this statement, they based their study on the concept of *local density* proposed by Sorenson and Audia (2000), who define it as the spatial distribution of CSR commitment by companies, taking as a reference point the head office of one of them. In this type of environment, Husted et al. (2016), add to the aforementioned spillover effect the rise of CSR legitimacy. The three aspects mentioned above (spillover, institutional pressure and legitimacy) make up the first factor presented by the authors to improve CSR practices. On the other hand, they provided evidence of a relationship between locations close to large cities and financial centers and a stronger commitment to CSR. This relationship constitutes the second factor that impacts on CSR defended by the authors and was demonstrated on grounds such as: (a) The tendency to locate CSR decisions in head offices, which are usually based in large cities (Marquis et al., 2007); (b) The possibility to establish personal contact between the actors involved (i.e. NGOs, trade unions and media, amongst others, which, according to Taylor (2005), are usually located near or within this type of environment) and the business organizations; (c) Its ability to reduce the costs associated with CSR due to a greater ease of access to them as well as to the generation of the well-known spillover effect between the company and its stakeholders; (d) Existence of an enhanced legitimization.

In line with Husted et al. (2016), Ding et al. (2019) find a link between the socioeconomic conditions of a company's location and its CSR profile. To reach this conclusion the authors base their work on the KLD database (Kinder, Lydenberg, and Domini) and the CRPS database (Center for Research in Securities Prices) in the period between 1991 and 2009, analyzing firms located in different US metropolitan statistical areas (MSA). Their study underlines the importance of knowledge spillovers as a key element of CSR. They also highlight socioeconomic conditions as impulse elements for the relationships among actors in the areas that lead to CSR. Ding et al. (2019) reach the conclusion that societies characterized by high education levels, with a tendency towards the common good and which do not tolerate illegal practices have firms with a greater commitment to social responsibility and consequently, lower levels of irresponsible behavior.

After demonstrating the existence of a relationship between location and CSR practices the rest of this chapter focuses on demonstrating that business concentration can be the most desirable location type for the optimal development of CSR practices. Insofar as the above mentioned studies hold that knowledge transfer is a key element of CSR we can stress that the intellectual antecedents of the cluster concept alluded to possible social benefits (as opposed to the traditionally studied economic benefits) derived from these economic agglomerations. Marshall and Paley (1920) underlined the capacity of *manufacturing districts* to bring numerous social advantages while simultaneously being characterized by their high levels of specialization or division of labor. This last characteristic was especially highlighted because they found that the growth of cities and the promotion of the division of labor resulted in the creation of more organized structures where citizens worked together to ensure their common welfare. Thus, they spoke about the emergence of trade associations, called craft guilds, whose actions prioritized the worker's moral conduct or his safety and that of his family, to quote but two aspects.

Turning to more recent research, Becattini (2004) under the title of *The Marshallian Industrial District as a Socio-Economic Notion*, summarizes the essential elements underlying his deep analysis of the concept of ID. Chief amongst the factors listed by the author are those which could enhance the development of social practices. Thus, attention is initially paid to the influence exerted by the local community, characterized by the shaping of a homogeneous system of values and perceptions, which develops into an ethical expression of work and family activity, reciprocity and change. This system of values is complemented by the institutions and rules that serve as a support system, facilitating the exchange of values throughout the district and passing them on to later generations, thus becoming the main driving factor for CSR in local companies belonging.

Other characteristics highlighted by the author are: The existence of personal relationships within the ID, such as the kinship between businessmen and other directors of companies operating in different production phases, which can favor the dissemination of CSR practices due to the deep interactions between the community and the different production processes; the performance of the market to which IDs are directed. Price information in such markets would not be enough to make purchase decisions so there is a need to produce and supply a large amount of additional information, including that related to the CSR practices implemented during the manufacture of the product.

The last characteristic of IDs highlighted by Becattini (2004) which could favor CSR is the juxtaposition of competitive behavior between companies and semi-conscious cooperation between them, resulting from the special way in which the sociocultural system permeates and structures the market inside the district. This has a two-fold effect on CSR actions. On the one hand, the existence of a competitive environment where companies apply these kinds of practices would force the others to put them into practice to maintain their competitive advantage. On the other hand, the cooperation between agents belonging to an ID would favor the flow of information required for all ID companies (both those with the greatest CSR knowledge and the least advanced ones) to be able to implement the CSR practices in question.

In line with the above conclusions around how the theory of Becattini (2004) could affect CSR, other authors have studied the relationship between CSR and clusters (Battaglia et al., 2010; Von Weltzien Høivik and Shankar, 2011; Testa at al., 2012; Santos, 2014; Horzela, 2019). Battigla et al. (2010) analyze the opportunities gained by SMEs in clusters by CSR practices, from a perspective of CSR of the system, which means that CSR is developed by the cluster as a whole rather than at the individual company level. They analyze three IDs in Tuscany, Italy, and find local relationship systems that could favor social practices. The same authors also distinguish three activity levels in the cluster that could influence the above relationship. First, a macro-level in which policies and actions are developed at the cluster or group level thus obtaining benefits from the cluster brand. Second, cooperation and shared use of resources at the meso-level. Finally, at the micro-level they show how clusters can be a key element for the sample firms to overcome the difficulties around costs and complexity when implementing CSR.

Along similar lines, Von Weltzien Høivik and Shankar (2011) propose that firms can implement CSR in clusters through the network model, which entails strengthening collaboration between firms that share the same location and have similar results. In this way they achieve a two-fold objective. First, they minimize the challenges faced by SMEs in terms of individual CSR (lack of human and financial resources, not knowing the real problems related with CSR, lack of understanding of the local and foreign situation, difficulty in obtaining credit, low negotiation power, lack of tools to implement CSR). Second, they highlight the innovation improvements derived from both the competitive and the cooperative attitudes of the cluster members. Finally, and as with Battiglia et al. (2010), Von Weltzien Høivik and Shankar (2011) allude to Campi (2008) to differentiate between three CSR activity levels (macro, meso and micro) and make similar conclusions to those mentioned above.

Another very useful study is that of Testa et al. (2012) who, similar to the other authors analyzed, study the determinant factors of the adoption and diffusion of social initiatives. They firstly highlight the role of secondary stakeholders such as public and local institutions as key players for clusters that produce non-financial products. Second, they show the important role of primary stakeholders (specifically customers, suppliers and employees) for businesses that sell direct to the final consumer. They also point to the role of public institutions and commercial associations as key elements to support CSR and its diffusion among SMEs in IDs.

Other authors have taken a step further in analyzing the paths that should be taken in clusters, assuming the existence of benefits from CSR activities.

Firstly, the Social Responsibilities Territories approach proposed by Santos (2014) is an appropriate approach to the way in which all the above benefits can be put into practice and have real effects and a greater impact on firms in an ID/cluster, combining individual firm CSR actions with a coordinated strategy for the whole ID. The authors propose the creation of CSR networks within clusters which will establish group objectives and reach a wider concept of CSR to encourage collective action.

A similar coordinated action is found in Horzela (2019) who also details the requirements for a cluster to qualify as socially responsible. These include naming a coordinator to oversee the compliance of CSR principles in the ID. This person will have to be able to judge compliance and have the leadership skills necessary to convince cluster members to operate under CSR principles. It would also be advisable to mount publicity campaigns to inform the members of the ID (Horzela, 2019).

Based on all of the above, the first part of the theoretical model is presented as the following proposal:

P1: IDs/clusters are key locations for the development of CSR by companies as they avoid the problems associated with individual CSR development.

Internationalization as an Enhancer of the Relationship Between IDs and CSR Development

The assumption of the ID/Cluster-CSR relationship thus serves as the basis to delve deeper into the subject, adding the internationalization variable to the aforementioned relationship. The analysis of the resources associated with locating a company to improve performance should not be limited to the national panorama (Marco-Lajara et al., 2015), and the same applies to those associated with CSR. Along these lines, it is worth considering the way in which Sforzi (2002) understands the characteristics of an ID, which he conceives as a model that combines local roots with global openness and prioritizes attention to social matters (taking it as a system where production processes would be subordinated to the demands of its host society), as opposed to the Taylorist models of large companies (where production processes would depend on the company itself, without the need for any additional considerations). In this respect, Sforzi (2002) draws one of his most relevant conclusions for the subject of this chapter, namely: the conception of globalization as a challenge for IDs in commercial terms, and not from a productive point of view, as had traditionally been suggested. What this author refers to is the hitherto prevailing intention within globalization processes of expanding homogeneous consumption cultures worldwide and leaving local cultures relegated to oblivion, which would ultimately generate a loss of cultural diversity and local development. To cope with this situation, Sforzi (2002) proposes IDs as favorable environments to fight such homogenization mechanisms. Amongst his proposals stand out: (1) the creation of a commercial network (thanks to the use of new technologies) which allows IDs to benefit from the advantages of globalization while maintaining their respective local idiosyncrasies; (2) the demand for a higher level of commitment from local governments of the places where IDs are located in terms of regulations aimed at safeguarding their cultural tradition. They would represent key aspects to maintain cultural diversity worldwide and, consequently, to increase the chances for developing countries to become part of this global network —IDs could benefit and develop a capacity to exchange useful information on CSR, which in turn makes it easier for the small member businesses to overcome their usual shortcomings when trying to implement such practices.

In tune with this line of reasoning, numerous research works have provided evidence of the pressures exerted by global markets on companies which lead them to try and meet the ever-changing social expectations, or expressed differently, they focus on analyzing how internationalization influences the way

Figure 1. Relationship between location in ID's/Cluster environments and CSR development (first part of the model)
Source: Own work

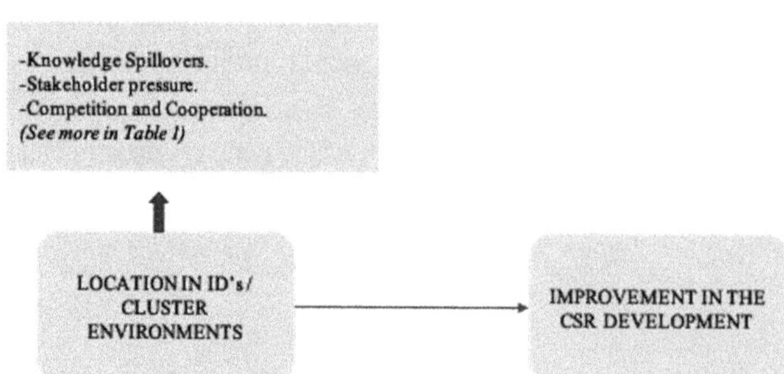

in which companies develop their respective CSR strategies (Moon et al., 2011; Von Weltzien Hoivik, 2011; Lund-Thomsen and Pillay 2012; Attig et al., 2016; Zyglidopoulos et al., 2016).

Firstly, the work of Moon et al. (2011), who take a more strategic view of CSR with the aim of improving the Creating Shared Value (CSV) model of Porter and Kramer, propose internationalization as a future research line of great interest to improve the model. Moon et al. (2011) propose that the conditions required to achieve CSV improve through internationalization thanks to collaboration between local and foreign firms. Von Weltzein Hoivik (2011) analyze two Norwegian firms that decided to begin CSR practices at the same time as they began to internationalize. One of their main findings was that the adoption of CSR practices was linked to the firms' ability to respond to the demands of their international stakeholders. Both factors (collaboration and the demands of international stakeholders) could further strengthen the development of CSR in firms located in IDs.

Lund-Thomsen and Pillay (2012) studied the relationship between globalization and IDs, focusing on developing countries. In their work *CSR in Industrial Clusters: An Overview of the Literature*, Lund-Thomsen and Pillay (2012) focus on analyzing the earliest theories about IDs in developing countries, examining not only their effects on poverty reduction in those areas but also the relationship between IDs and CSR practices. Emphasis must be placed on the critical evaluation of the way in which developing countries would have managed to communicate with developed ones, the former concentrating on low-cost-labor tasks while the latter remained in charge of greater added value tasks. Lund-Thomsen and Pillay (2012) highlighted yet another risk related to this type of production model, the uncertainty that developing countries had before the possibility of multinationals deciding to move their production elsewhere. Finally, it is worth highlighting the last contribution made by the authors with regard to internationalization in clusters. Important aspects include the request made by multinationals to cluster companies for the latter to apply their social and environmental codes of conduct, the actions undertaken by specific international agencies to help develop such practices, as well as the claiming role assumed by certain local actors. More importantly, Lund-Thomsen and Pillay (2012) add the need to connect these international CSR claims with the cluster's economic, social, and cultural reality, thus supporting what Sforzi (2002) had already put forward. To that end, they insist on the need to map out the perceptions of the different actors (institutions, associations, multinationals, local companies…) as a way to ensure an accepted standard which can balance all their perceptions.

Additionally, subsequent studies show that the positive significant relationship between the level of internationalization and CSR could be based on: (1) demands by more diverse interest groups to operate internationally (social, political, institutional, among others); (2) a reduction in managerial employment risk because multinationals depend on management experience, which allows them to take CSR decisions; (3) higher risks derived from internationalization (legitimacy, regulation differences and increased management risk aversion) which lead firms to opt for CSR to reduce them (Attig et al., 2016).

Along these same lines, and in the context of developing countries, Zyglidopoulos (2016) demonstrates that internationalized firms have better Corporate Social Performance (CSP) than firms that only operate nationally. The author identifies two factors that produce this relationship. First, internationalized firms from developing nations face legitimacy problems because the destination countries associate them with lax legislation systems and will have concerns over how the firm will adapt to the rules and values of their country. To cope with this risk, these firms improve their CSP to obtain license to operate in their target destinations. Second, reputation can also be damaged, which means that CSP improvement will allow them to demonstrate to the destination country that they meet their expectations and can be as good as local firms.

Through all these perspectives we have shown the different factors that lead internationalization to further strengthen CSR practices within the already demonstrated ID-social practices relationship. However, before we finish this section, we should point out that an inverse relationship is also possible. Internationalization can be influenced by IDs, which would cause an effect on the CSR of the member firms.

To demonstrate this, we can refer to Marco-Lajara et al. (2015), who follow Boix and Galletto (2009) in the tourism sector and hold that the more firms there are in an ID, the more chances of acquiring new knowledge and of internationalizing. They demonstrate that there are more internationalized hotels in tourism IDs with higher degrees of agglomeration. Following the approach of this chapter, if we transpose the results of Marco-Lajara et al. (2015) to CSR, we can consider that location in an ID increases the possibilities of internationalization and once internationalized the firms concerned will be under greater pressure (as mentioned above) to enhance their CSR strategies.

Both in terms of the direct influence proposed in the first part of this chapter – in which internationalization has a direct effect on CSR in ID firms- and of the indirect influence through which internationalization is derived from the benefits of IDs, which will subsequently impact on CSR, we can present the second proposal of this chapter:

P2: The level of internationalization of firms in IDs/clusters will influence the relationship between location in an ID and the development of CSR practices.

Figure 2. Internationalization as an enhacer of the relationship between IDs and CSR development (second part of the model)
Source: Own work

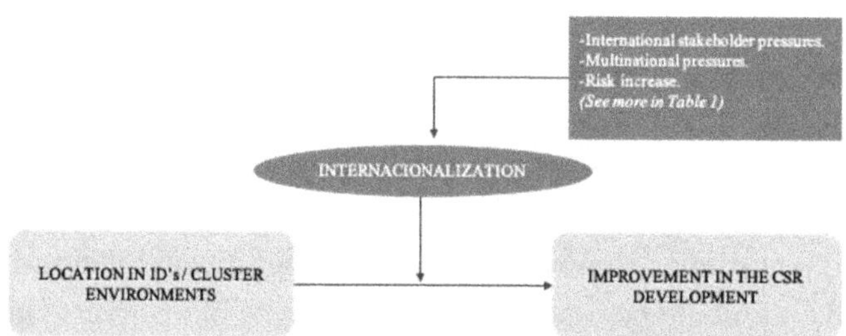

INFLUENCE OF THE GENDER CHARACTERISTIC ON CSR DEVELOPMENT

In addition to the influence aspects associated with company location, several authors have concentrated on examining the effect that certain characteristics of management members may have on the extent to which organizations develop CSR (Kang et al., 2019; Peña-Miranda et al., 2019). Porter and Kramer (2011) in their search for shared value creation refer to the need for company leaders and managers to develop new skills and knowledge. By way of example, they discuss the ability of managers to identify society's needs, as well as to collaborate across profit/nonprofit boundaries. The authors also stress the need to combine social and economic objectives, due to the traditionally distinct educational models used to train the social leader (more linked to the public sector and lacking in management knowledge, but knowledgeable in social aspects) and the business manager (belonging to the private sector and highly knowledgeable in management matter, but lacking in social knowledge). In order to reach the joint shared value creation goals, both types of leaders should possess management as well as social knowledge and accordingly have the characteristics required to achieve the common objective.

Following this premise, gender is one of the most important management characteristics due to its positive influence on CSR (Ibrahim and Angelidis, 1994; Burgess and Tharenou 2002; Williams, 2003; Wirth, 2015; Setó-Pamies, 2015; Landry et al., 2016; Alonso-Almedia et al., 2017; Rajasekar y Deepa, 2017; Cabeza-García et al., 2018 Puchcta-Martínez et al., 2018; Cullinan et al., 2019).

Before we analyze gender differences and their effect on CSR we should point out that equality between men and women in management has not yet been reached (Albiol and López, 2019; ILO, 2019). The data provided by the International Labor Office in its report *Women in business management, gaining momentum,* elaborated by Wirth (2015), showed inequality despite noting the beginnings of an increase in the number of women with management experience. Furthermore, it is worth noting the concept of *glass walls* described in this report to highlight the fact that, despite the higher number of women in management positions, there is a series of invisible barriers which inevitably relegates them to certain types of management, including corporate social responsibility, and often prevents them from rising to higher positions.

To this should be added the study of the International Labor Office (ILO, 2019), which finds that at the global level there is still a large gap between the percentage of men in management positions and that of women.

These figures are surprising when we consider the work over recent decades by national and international institutions to achieve equality between men and women. As an example, one of the goals established for SDG 5 (gender equality) is to *Assure the full and effective participation of women and*

Figure 3. Total percentage of men and women in management positions
Source: Own elaboration through the data extracted from ILO (2019)

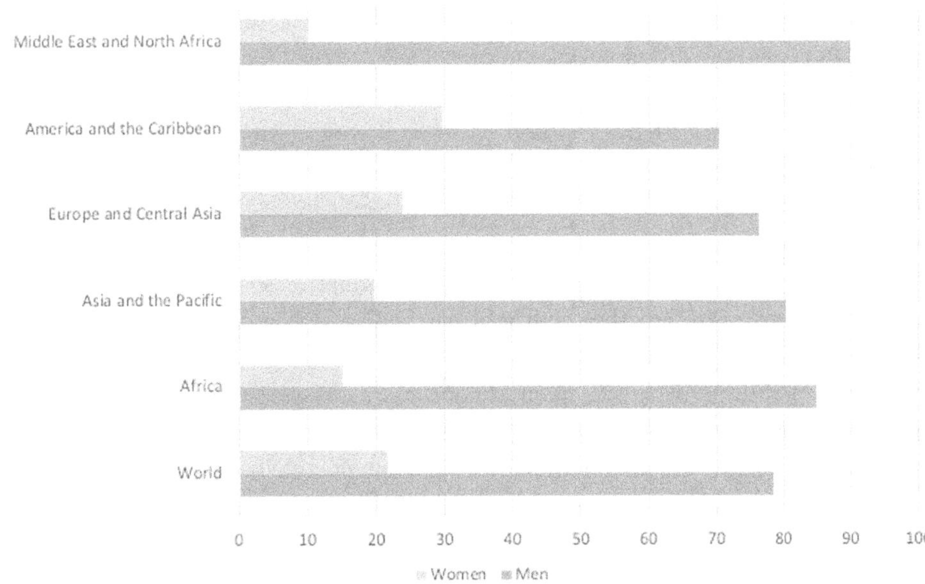

equal leadership opportunities at all decision-making levels in political, economic and public life (Ortega and Román, 2018).

In light of this situation, and in order to find factors that lead managers to reduce the gender gap, we will analyze women in management as a key factor in the development of CSR. The contribution of Ibrahim and Angelidis (1994) stands out in this context as they demonstrated that women who held managerial positions showed a higher level of discretion in relation to CSR than their male counterparts. They also defended women's philanthropic orientation as opposed to men's economic concerns. Ibrahim and Angelidis (1994) also examined the typology of female directors and found that the status of many women managers was external to the organization, which would increase their responsibility towards such practices.

Other recent studies analyze the proposed relationship through the examination of the link between the number of women on boards of directors and the volume of charitable donations —as one of the activities inherent to CSR— made by the companies that they ran (Williams, 2003). The authors found that firms with a larger number of women in managerial positions showed a higher degree of involvement in charitable donations than those with a lower female presence. One of the most surprising conclusions reached by this author was the absence of donations for educational purposes or public policies by these women managers.

In line with the above, the study *Women and Business Power* by Castaño et al. (2009) for the Spanish Women's Institute questioned the supposedly different management styles or ways of exercising leadership between men and women, placing the emphasis on the role of women as executives. The study refers to Burgess and Tharenou (2002), according to whom these differences in management style influence the way in which the strategies are developed, the style of female managers being more closely linked to philanthropic aspects due to their higher level of social awareness. These authors argue that women have a more collaborative way of conceiving power, show greater concern for people's well-being, and leave objectives of an economic nature in the hands of male figures.

Along these same lines, Setó-Pamies (2015) provided evidence of the strategic role that women managers could play in the proper performance and management of social responsibility practices. More specifically, she demonstrated that an increase in the number of female board members resulted in a higher level of CSR practice development. In this case, the main justifications for her statement was the improved relationships with the different stakeholders thanks to the presence of women, as well as their greater concern for the environment.

Alternatively, Landry et al. (2016) proposed a different way of studying the relationship between managers' gender and CSR. In this case, the authors chose to operationalize CSR through the recognition of companies on the best lists of actions concerning these issues, more specifically on the *Most Admired Companies*, the *Most Ethical Companies*, the *Best Companies to Work For*, and the *Best Corporate Citizens*, and found that companies with a higher number of female directors were more likely to appear on them. In tune with the other contributions analyzed, Landry et al. (2016) concluded that a greater female presence in managerial positions should be encouraged in order to create more ethical companies that could additionally be perceived as good places to work.

The importance of the characteristics held to be uniquely female is such that authors that consider that in cultures classified as female (e.g., Scandinavia), management style is characterized as: "Considering an effective manager as the one who is supportive to his/her people, and decision making is achieved through involvement. Managers in these cultures strive for consensus and people value equality, solidarity and quality in their working lives" which differs from male cultures (e.g., USA or Japan) (The Hofstede Center, 2016 in Freeman et al., 2017, 117).

Although cultures can be classified as female or male according to the preponderant management style, there seems to be a general consensus at the global level on the relationship between female culture and improved CSR. Examples of this are found in in studies of similar characteristics in different countries. An analysis of women on management boards in India concluded that the presence of women has a positive impact on CSR as, among other reasons, women in management are more concerned about conciliation of working life, thc crcation of work places free of harassment of women and measures to guarantee gender diversity (Rajasekar and Deepa, 2017). Similar positions were adopted by Alonso-Almeida et al. (2017), who analyzed a sample of 391 top managers in Spain, concluding that female leaders are more aware of the importance of CSR than their male counterparts and affirming that transformational and dual leadership styles (implemented by women in top management) lead to better CSR development. The authors differentiate between the transformational style and other more dominant styles in that the former follows the principles of empathy (Kotter, 1999) and is more closely linked to social capacities, thus justifying its link with the female gender (Alimo-Metcalfe, 2010). Alonso-Almeida et al. (2017) also highlight that the dual style of management, characterized by the ability to adapt to the context (according to the conditions of the company, management will adopt different management styles), and emphasize that women are more likely to opt for a transformational style than men.

Along similar lines, the outstanding work of Cabeza-García et al. (2018) constitutes a rigorous attempt to relate managers' gender as well as their typology to the influence that both factors would exert simultaneously on CSR dissemination. To this end they first carried out a literature review to identify the characteristics of women in management that favor CSR. Apart from agreeing with the previously mentioned authors in that women are more orientated towards social issues and the needs of the different stakeholders, they highlight three characteristics of great interest: (1) psychological features that tend towards sympathy, affection and helpfulness (Zhang et al., 2013); (2) an educational background that allows them to broaden their perspective; (3) the identification of studies that call for the inclusion of women in management to increase informational transparency. Secondly, they analyze the differences between outside directors (who have more social sensitivity to attend to the demands of interest groups), independents (independent of the CEO and representatives of the owners) and inside directors (affected by more competitive pressure to maximize profits). For these authors, it would be important to take into account not only the number but also the typology of female directors, with the conviction that the existence of more external and independent directives would help improve CSR dissemination.

Similar to the aforementioned works, Cullinan et al. (2019) have recently performed a study focused on examining the possible association between the role played by the female director, drawing a distinction between executive and outsider (independent of management or grey-outsiders, who have a different relationship with management) female directors and the CSR performance that her company can achieve; in other words, the potential impact of different management styles on the organization's CSR strategy. From the premise that there is a positive relationship between women in management and CSR, the authors analyze whether the relationship is influenced by management style. Amongst their main conclusions they find that different management styles do influence the relationship between CSR and management gender. Thus, they demonstrate that the presence of independent directors is bound to improve a company's performance in CSR matters, to which they added that grey and executive directors will also influence CSR performance, albeit to a lesser extent than independent directors; findings that are similar to those of other studies.

To conclude, through the above review, we have demonstrated the relationship between women in management and CSR, as well as the characteristics that produce it (see Graph 2). The same characteristics were underlined by Pucheta-Martínez et al., (2018) who performed a literature review that found key characteristics in female managers, such as their greater focus on education, regulations and non-profit activities; and their commitment to stakeholders at all levels of the organization. A similar conclusion was drawn by Galbreath (2019) when he related the availability of certain capital resources (women in leadership positions) to a strengthened relationship between exports and what he refers to as *green practices*. All of the above allows the presentation of the third theoretical proposal, which will definitively formulate the model:

P3: Women in management improve the development of CSR practices.

Figure 4. Relationship between female gender in management positions and CSR development (complete model)
Source: Own work

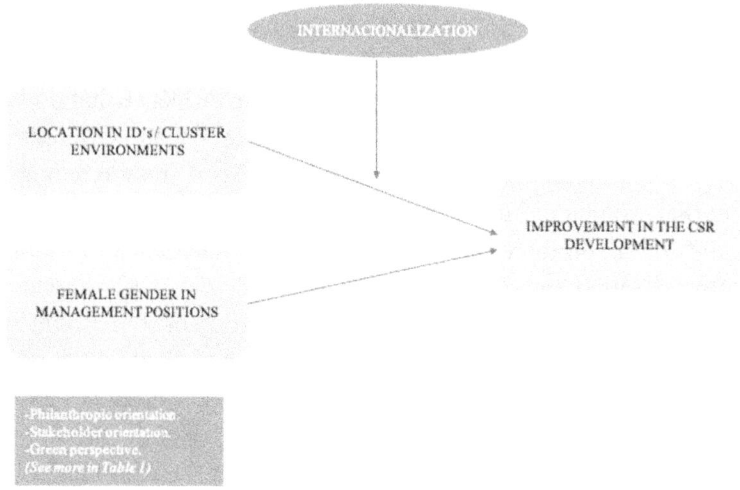

CONCLUSION

The aim of research is to make a contribution to the existing literature on CSR and, particularly, to analyze two factors which could prove essential in favoring its development and implementation by every company, namely: location and management gender. In terms of location, bringing the industrial district perspective and that of globalization together provides a more holistic vision that takes advantage of both approaches when implementing CSR. Based on the idea of preserving the local cultural roots of each area (Sforzi, 2002) and considering the great extent to which globalization influences CSR, a new theoretical approach is proposed which essentially seeks to take advantage of IDs when developing CSR.

The need to include the internationalization variable in the relationship between IDs and the development of CSR practices has accordingly been demonstrated. Pressure from international interest groups, increased risk and collaboration between local and global firms, among others, are key factors in the

Table 1. Summary of the driving factors of CSR development analyzed in the chapter

Impulse Factors of CSR	Authors
1) LOCATION 1.1) LOCATED IN AN ID -Influence of the local community (homogenous value system)	Becattini (2004)
-Support system (Institutions and rules)	Becattini (2004); Testa et al. (2012)
-Personal relationships within the ID	Becattini (2004)
-Knowledge Spillovers	Marshall (1890); Becattini (2004); Porter (1990)
-Stakeholder pressure	Becattini (2004); Testa et al. (2012)
-Competition and cooperation	Becattini (2004); Von Weltzien Høivik and Shakar (2011)
-Idea of local relational system	Battigla et al. (2010); Von Weltzien Høivik and Shakar (2011); Santos (2014); Horzela (2019)
1.2) GLOBALIZATION AS AN ENHACER OF RELATIONSHIP: ID AND CSR -Protection of local culture	Sforzi (2002)
-Collaboration between local and global companies	Moon et al. (2011)
-More pressure from stakeholders	Von Weltzien Høivik (2011); Lund-Thomsen and Pillay (2012); Attig et al. (2016)
-Pressure from multinationals located in the cluster	Lund-Thomsen and Pillay (2012)
-Increased risk from operating abroad	Attig et al. (2016); Zyglidopoulos (2016)
2) MANAGEMENT GENDER - Philanthropic orientation	Ibrahim and Angelidis (1994); Burgess and Tharenou (2002); Landry et al. (2016); Zhang et al. (2013)
-External female directors	Ibrahim and Angelidis (1994); Alonso-Almeida et al. (2017); Cabeza-García et al. (2018); Zhang et al. (2013)
-Higher charitable donations	Williams (2003)
-More focus on the needs of stakeholders	Setó-Pamies (2015); Cabeza-García et al. (2018); Pucheta-Martínez et al. (2018)
-Conciliation of working life and orientation towards gender diversity	Rajasekar y Deepa (2017)
-Focus towards Green Practices	Galbreath (2019)

Source: Own work

influence of internationalization on CSR. In this context, IDs —individually and benefiting from joint actions undertaken by their respective research institutes and associations, knowledge spillovers as well as stakeholder pressure— will develop much more rooted CSR practices able not only to meet global demands but also to incorporate local ones that will take advantage of the network to sell their CSR models worldwide.

As for the second objective, related to the gender variable as a driver of CSR practices, different investigations have provided the necessary evidence to demonstrate that certain characteristics of women associated with their leadership style and orientation when making decisions favor CSR implementation. Among the characteristics discussed in the chapter we can highlight their philanthropic orientation, a focus on the needs of stakeholders and green practices, among others. These characteristics will also be strengthened in the case of external management. Consequently, organizations which fulfil the requirements examined, i.e. being ran by a female director and being simultaneously located in an ID open to foreign markets, would stand better chances to implement CSR practices far more homogeneously, quickly and acceptably, in accordance with the growing demands of present-day society. This chapter can be of great help to academics, researchers and business students as it is centered on revealing two lines of research of great current interest which could solve the problems faced by firms around the effective development and implementation of CSR practices.

FUTURE RESEARCH LINES

As for future lines of research, they are diverse, since this work only constitutes an initial theoretical analysis meant to lay the foundations of more in-depth research undertakings over the next few years. Thus, the first possible extension would be to conduct an empirical study (through the use of structural equation modelling) that can allow us to confirm the relationship which both location and gender have with CSR development —shown here in a theoretical approach. Consideration should additionally be given to the possibility of including other variables in the model associated with management characteristics (such as leadership capacity, religion or managerial education) which could complement the role of gender in CSR implementation. A final proposal is the need to study the feasibility of applying global CSR information and connection network according to company size, insofar as it is intended for both large and small companies.

REFERENCES

Ackerman, R. W. (1973). How companies respond to social demands. *Harvard Business Review*, *51*(4), 88–98.

Alafi, K., & Hasoneh, A. B. (2012). Corporate social responsibility associated with customer satisfaction and financial performance a case study with Housing Banks in Jordan. *International Journal of Humanities and Social Science*, *2*(15), 102–115.

Albiol, N. C., & López, E. J. (2019). Mujeres en Consejos de Administración. *Economistas*, (161), 22-33.

Alimo-Metcalfe, B. (2010). An investigation of female and male constructs of leadership and empowerment. *Women in Management Review*, *10*(2), 3–8. doi:10.1108/09649429510146901

Alonso-Almeida, M. D. M., Perramon, J., & Bagur-Femenias, L. (2017). Leadership styles and corporate social responsibility management: Analysis from a gender perspective. *Business Ethics (Oxford, England)*, *26*(2), 147–161. doi:10.1111/beer.12139

Attig, N., Boubakri, N., El Ghoul, S., & Guedhami, O. (2016). Firm internationalization and corporate social responsibility. *Journal of Business Ethics*, *134*(2), 171–197. doi:10.100710551-014-2410-6

Battaglia, M., Bianchi, L., Frey, M., & Iraldo, F. (2010). An innovative model to promote CSR among SMEs operating in industrial clusters: Evidence from an EU project. *Corporate Social Responsibility and Environmental Management*, *17*(3), 133–141. doi:10.1002/csr.224

Becattini, G. (1979). Dal settore industrial al distretto industrial. Alcune considerazioni sull'unità di indagine in economia industriale. *Revista di Economía e Politica Industriale*, (1), 7-14.

Becattini, G. (2014). The Marshallian industrial district as a socio-economic notion. *Revue d'Économie Industrielle, 1*, 13-32.

Bianchi, E., Bruno, J. M., & Sarabia-Sanchez, F. J. (2019). The impact of perceived CSR on corporate reputation and purchase intention. *European Journal of Management and Business Economics, 28*(3), 206–221. doi:10.1108/EJMBE-12-2017-0068

Boix, R., & Galleto, V. (2009). Innovation and Industrial Districts: A First Approach to the Measurement and Determinants of the I-District Effect. *Regional Studies, 43*(9), 1117–1133. doi:10.1080/00343400801932342

Bowen, H. R. (1953). *Social Responsibilities of the Businessman*. Harper & Row.

Brulhart, F., Gherra, S., & Quelin, B. V. (2019). Do stakeholder orientation and environmental proactivity impact on firm profitability? *Journal of Business Ethics, 158*(1), 25–46. doi:10.100710551-017-3732-y

Burgess, Z., & Tharenou, P. (2002). Women board directors: Characteristics of the few. *Journal of Business Ethics, 37*(1), 39–49. doi:10.1023/A:1014726001155

Cabeza-García, L., Fernández-Gago, R., & Nieto, M. (2018). Do board gender diversity and director typology impact CSR reporting? *European Management Review, 15*(4), 559–575. doi:10.1111/emre.12143

Campi, S. (2008). A Cluster Approach for the Promotion of CSR Among SMEs. Scuola Superiore Sant'Anna, Italy.

Carroll, A. B. (1974). Corporate social responsibility: Its managerial impact and implications. *Journal of Business Research, 2*(1), 75–88. doi:10.1016/S0148-2963(74)80008-1

Carroll, A. B. (1979). A three-dimensional conceptual model of corporate performance. *Academy of Management Review, 4*(4), 497–505. doi:10.5465/amr.1979.4498296

Carroll, A. B. (1991). The pyramid of corporate social responsibility: Toward the moral management of organizational stakeholders. *Business Horizons, 34*(4), 39–48. doi:10.1016/0007-6813(91)90005-G

Castaño Collado, C., Laffarga Briones, J., Iglesias Fernández, C., Fuentes Ruiz, P. D., Martín Fernández, J., Llorente Heras, R., & Martínez Cantos, J. L. (2009). *Mujeres y Poder Empresarial en España*. Instituto de la Mujer, Ministerio de Igualdad.

Chrisman, J. J., & Carroll, A. B. (1984). SMR forum: Corporate responsibility—reconciling economic and social goals. *Sloan Management Review, 25*(2), 59–65.

Cook, K. A., Romi, A. M., Sánchez, D., & Sánchez, J. M. (2019). The influence of corporate social responsibility on investment efficiency and innovation. *Journal of Business Finance & Accounting, 46*(3-4), 494–537. doi:10.1111/jbfa.12360

Cullinan, C. P., Mahoney, L., & Roush, P. B. (2019). Directors & Corporate Social Responsibility: Joint Consideration of Director Gender and the Director's Role. *Social and Environmental Accountability Journal, 39*(2), 100–123. doi:10.1080/0969160X.2019.1586556

Davis, K. (1973). The case for and against business assumption of social responsibilities. *Academy of Management Journal, 16*(2), 312–322.

Dhavala, S. (2017). *The philanthropic legacy of JRD Tata*. Retrieved on 06 December 2019 from: https://www.asiatimes.com/2017/11/opinion/philanthropic-legacy-jrd-tata/

Ding, D. K., Ferreira, C., & Wongchoti, U. (2019). The geography of CSR. *International Review of Economics & Finance, 59*, 265–288. doi:10.1016/j.iref.2018.09.003

Dixit, A., Clouse, C., & Turken, N. (2019). Strategic business location decisions: Importance of economic factors and place image. *Rutgers Business Review, 4*(1), 73–91.

Doane, D. (2005). The myth of CSR. *Stanford Social Innovation Review, 3*(3), 22–29.

Drucker, P. F. (1984). Converting social problems into business opportunities: The new meaning of corporate social responsibility. *California Management Review, 26*(2), 53.

European Parliament. (2019). *National Geographic website*. Retrieved on 11 December 2019 from https://www.nationalgeographic.com.es/naturaleza/parlamento-europeo-declara-emergencia-climatica_14997

Freeman, E. R., Dmytriyev, S., & Strand, R. G. (2017). Managing for Stakeholders in the Digital Age. In Corporate Social Responsibility: Strategy, Communication, Governance (pp. 110-135). Cambridge University Press.

Friedman, M. (1970). A Friedman doctrine: The social responsibility of business is to increase its profits. *The New York Times Magazine, 13*(1970), 32-33.

Galbreath, J. (2008). The benefits of corporate social responsibility: An empirical study. *ANZAM Conference Proceedings (22nd Annual Conference. Auckland).*

Galbreath, J. (2019). Drivers of green innovations: The impact of export intensity, women leaders, and absorptive capacity. *Journal of Business Ethics, 158*(1), 47–61. doi:10.100710551-017-3715-z

García, F. N. (2012). *Responsabilidad social corporativa: teoría y práctica.* ESIC editorial.

Gómez-Bezares, F., Przychodzen, W., & Przychodzen, J. (2017). Bridging the gap: How sustainable development can help companies create shareholder value and improve financial performance. *Business Ethics (Oxford, England), 26*(1), 1–17. doi:10.1111/beer.12135

Halme, M., Rintamäki, J., Knudsen, J. S., Lankoski, L., & Kuisma, M. (2018). When is there a sustainability case for CSR? Pathways to environmental and social performance improvements. *Business & Society*. Advance online publication. doi:10.1177/0007650318755648

Horzela, A. (2019). The Cluster as a Socially Responsible Entity. *Zeszyty Naukowe. Organizacja i Zarządzanie/Politechnika Śląska*, (140), 99-108. DOI: 10.29119/1641-3466.2019.140.9

Husted, B. W. (2015). Corporate social responsibility practice from 1800–1914: Past initiatives and current debates. *Business Ethics Quarterly, 25*(1), 125–141. doi:10.1017/beq.2014.1

Husted, B. W., Jamali, D., & Saffar, W. (2016). Near and dear? The role of location in CSR engagement. *Strategic Management Journal, 37*(10), 2050–2070. doi:10.1002mj.2437

Ibrahim, N. A., & Angelidis, J. P. (1994). Effect of board members' gender on corporate social responsiveness orientation. *Journal of Applied Business Research*, *10*(1), 35. doi:10.19030/jabr.v10i1.5961

Jia, M., & Zhang, Z. (2013). Critical mass of women on BODs, multiple identities, and corporate philanthropic disaster response: Evidence from privately owned Chinese firms. *Journal of Business Ethics*, *118*(2), 303–317. doi:10.100710551-012-1589-7

Kang, Y. S., Huh, E., & Lim, M. H. (2019). Effects of Foreign Directors' Nationalities and Director Types on Corporate Philanthropic Behavior: Evidence from Korean Firms. *Sustainability*, *11*(11), 1–18. doi:10.3390u11113132

Kotter, J. P. (1999). *John Kotter on What Leaders Really Do*. Harvard Business School Press.

Krüger, P. (2009). *Corporate social responsibility and the board of directors. Job Market Paper*. Toulouse School of Economics.

Landry, E. E., Bernardi, R. A., & Bosco, S. M. (2016). Recognition for sustained corporate social responsibility: Female directors make a difference. *Corporate Social Responsibility and Environmental Management*, *23*(1), 27–36. doi:10.1002/csr.1358

Lund-Thomsen, P., & Pillay, R. G. (2012). CSR in industrial clusters: An overview of the literature. *Corporate Governance: The International Journal of Business and Society*, *12*(4), 568–578.

Marco-Lajara, B., Claver-Cortés, E., Zaragoza Sáez, P. D. C., & Úbeda García, M. (2015). Grado de aglomeración de los distritos turísticos españoles y procesos de internacionalización de empresas hoteleras. *Economía Industrial,* (397), 21-35.

Marquis, C., Glynn, M. A., & Davis, G. F. (2007). Community isomorphism and corporate social action. *Academy of Management Review*, *32*(3), 925–945. doi:10.5465/amr.2007.25275683

Marshall, A. (1890/1920). *Principles of Economics*. MacMillan.

Marshall, A., & Marshall, M. P. (1920). *The economics of industry*. Macmillan and Company.

Martín, R. D. (2010). Tomando en serio al sector privado empresarial como actor de la ayuda: la responsabilidad social corporativa para el desarrollo. In A. Guerra, J. F. Tezanos, & S. Tezanos (Eds.), *La lucha contra el hambre y la pobreza* (pp. 265–297). Fundación Sistema.

Moon, H. C., Parc, J., Yim, S. H., & Park, N. (2011). An extension of Porter and Kramer's creating shared value (CSV): Reorienting strategies and seeking international cooperation. *Journal of International and Area Studies*, *28*(2), 49–64.

Oficina Internacional del Trabajo. (2019). *Las mujeres en la gestión empresarial: argumentos para un cambio*. Ginebra.

Okoye, A. (2009). Theorising corporate social responsibility as an essentially contested concept: Is a definition necessary? *Journal of Business Ethics*, *89*(4), 613–627. doi:10.100710551-008-0021-9

Ortega Carpio, M. L., & Román, A. (2018). *Anexo estadístico para el seguimiento de la agenda 2030 en españa*. Academic Press.

Peña-Miranda, D. D., Arteaga-Ortiz, J., & Ramón-Cardona, J. (2019). Determinants of CSR application in the hotel industry of the Colombian Caribbean. *Sustainability*, *11*(18), 5045. doi:10.3390u11185045

Porter, M., & Kramer, M. (2002). The Competitive Advantage of Corporate Philanthropy. *Harvard Business Review. Collection Redefining Corporate Social*, *80*(12), 56–68. PMID:12510538

Porter, M., & Kramer, M. R. (2011). Creating shared value. *Harvard Business Review*, *89*(1/2), 62–77.

Porter, M. E. (1990). The Competitive Advantage of Nations. *Harvard Business Review*, *68*(2), 73–93.

Pucheta-Martínez, M. C., Bel-Oms, I., & Olcina-Sempere, G. (2018). The association between board gender diversity and financial reporting quality, corporate performance and corporate social responsibility disclosure. *Academia (Caracas)*, *31*(1), 177–194. doi:10.1108/ARLA-04-2017-0110

Rajasekar, D., & Deepa, S. R. (2017). Mandatory Corporate Social Responsibility in India and the Impact on Women Board of Directors: A Review. *International Journal of Civil Engineering and Technology*, *8*(12), 400–409.

Rettab, B., Brik, A. B., & Mellahi, K. (2009). A study of management perceptions of the impact of corporate social responsibility on organisational performance in emerging economies: The case of Dubai. *Journal of Business Ethics*, *89*(3), 371–390. doi:10.100710551-008-0005-9

Rothenhoefer, L. M. (2019). The impact of CSR on corporate reputation perceptions of the public—A configurational multi-time, multi-source perspective. *Business Ethics (Oxford, England)*, *28*(2), 141–155. doi:10.1111/beer.12207

Santos, M. J. (2014). Theoretical contributions towards rethinking corporate social responsibility. *Management Research*, *12*(3), 288–307. doi:10.1108/MRJIAM-12-2013-0533

Sarkar, S., & Searcy, C. (2016). Zeitgeist or chameleon? A quantitative analysis of CSR definitions. *Journal of Cleaner Production*, *135*, 1423–1435. doi:10.1016/j.jclepro.2016.06.157

Setó-Pamies, D. (2015). The relationship between women directors and corporate social responsibility. *Corporate Social Responsibility and Environmental Management*, *22*(6), 334–345. doi:10.1002/csr.1349

Sforzi, F. (2002). Los distritos industriales ante el reto de la globalización. *Geographicalia*, (41), 5–18. doi:10.26754/ojs_geoph/geoph.2002411364

Sforzi, F. (2008). Unas realidades ignoradas: de Marshall a Becattini. *Mediterráneo Económico,* (13), 43-54.

Sorenson, O., & Audia, P. G. (2000). The social structure of entrepreneurial activity: Geographic concentration of footwear production in the United States, 1940–1989. *American Journal of Sociology*, *106*(2), 424–462. doi:10.1086/316962

Tata. (n.d.). Retrieved on 06 December 2019 from https://www.tata.com/about-us/tata-group-our-heritage/tata-titans/jamsetji-tata

Taylor, P. J. (2005). Leading world cities: Empirical evaluations of urban nodes in multiple networks. *Urban Studies (Edinburgh, Scotland)*, *42*(9), 1593–1608. doi:10.1080/00420980500185504

Testa, F., Battaglia, M., & Bianchi, L. (2012). The diffusion of CSR initiatives among SMEs in industrial clusters: Some findings from Italian experiences. *International Journal of Technology Management, 58*(1/2), 152–170. doi:10.1504/IJTM.2012.045793

The Hofstede Centre. (2016). *The Hofstede Centre website*. Retrieved on 1 March 2016 from http://geert-hofstede.com/sweden.html

United Nations. (1999, February 1). *Secretary-General address to the World Economic Forum in Davos* [Press Release SG/SM/6881]. New York: UN.

United Nations. (2020). *The United Nations website*. Retrieved on 22 May 2020 from https://www.un.org/sustainabledevelopment/es/development-agenda/

Von Weltzien Hoivik, H. (2011). Embedding CSR as a learning and knowledge creating process: The case for SMEs in Norway. *Journal of Management Development, 30*(10), 1067–1084. doi:10.1108/02621711111182547

Von Weltzien Høivik, H., & Shankar, D. (2011). How can SMEs in a cluster respond to global demands for corporate responsibility? *Journal of Business Ethics, 101*(2), 175–195. doi:10.100710551-010-0708-6

Williams, R. J. (2003). Women on corporate boards of directors and their influence on corporate philanthropy. *Journal of Business Ethics, 42*(1), 1–10. doi:10.1023/A:1021626024014

Wirth, L. (2015). *La mujer en la gestión empresarial: Cobrando impulso*. Organización Mundial del Trabajo. Ginebra.

Zhang, Q., Cao, M., Zhang, F., Liu, J., & Li, X. (2019). Effects of corporate social responsibility on customer satisfaction and organizational attractiveness: A signaling perspective. *Business Ethics (Oxford, England), 29*(1), 20–34. doi:10.1111/beer.12243

Zyglidopoulos, S., Williamson, P., & Symeou, P. (2016). The corporate social performance of developing country multinationals. *Business Ethics Quarterly, 26*(3), 379–406. doi:10.1017/beq.2016.41

ADDITIONAL READING

Alberti, F. G., & Belfanti, F. (2019). Creating shared value and clusters: The case of an Italian cluster initiative in food waste prevention. *Competitiveness Review, 29*(1), 39–60. doi:10.1108/CR-01-2017-0008

Bocquet, R., Le Bas, C., Mothe, C., & Poussing, N. (2019). Strategic CSR for innovation in SMEs: Does diversity matter? *Long Range Planning, 52*(6), 101913. doi:10.1016/j.lrp.2019.101913

Collazzo Yelpo, P., & Kubelka, L. (2019). Shared value clusters in Austria. *Competitiveness Review, 29*(1), 61–76. doi:10.1108/CR-08-2016-0050

Colovic, A., Henneron, S., Huettinger, M., & Kazlauskaite, R. (2019). Corporate social responsibility and SMEs: Evidence from a transition and a developed economy. *European Business Review, 31*(5), 785–810. doi:10.1108/EBR-01-2017-0022

Furlotti, K., Mazza, T., Tibiletti, V., & Triani, S. (2019). Women in top positions on boards of directors: Gender policies disclosed in Italian sustainability reporting. *Corporate Social Responsibility and Environmental Management*, *26*(1), 57–70. doi:10.1002/csr.1657

Gulzar, M. A., Cherian, J., Hwang, J., Jiang, Y., & Sial, M. S. (2019). The Impact of Board Gender Diversity and Foreign Institutional Investors on the Corporate Social Responsibility (CSR) Engagement of Chinese Listed Companies. *Sustainability*, *11*(2), 307. doi:10.3390u11020307

Mefford, R. N. (2019). Sustainable CSR in Global Supply Chains. *Journal of Management and Sustainability*, *9*(1), 82. doi:10.5539/jms.v9n1p82

Peña-Miranda, D. D., Arteaga-Ortiz, J., & Ramón-Cardona, J. (2019). Determinants of CSR application in the hotel industry of the Colombian Caribbean. *Sustainability*, *11*(18), 5045. doi:10.3390u11185045

Ye, M., Lu, W., Flanagan, R., & Chau, K. W. (2019). Corporate social responsibility "glocalisation": Evidence from the international construction business. *Corporate Social Responsibility and Environmental Management*. Advance online publication. doi:10.1002/csr.1831

KEY TERMS AND DEFINITIONS

Corporate Social Responsibility: Attitude of a company focused on meeting the needs of all the interest groups within its organization, going beyond the traditional economic objective. This is an approach which should integrate economic, social, philanthropic, and environmental aspects into corporate level decisions.

CSR Location: Physical location of an organization that will have the capacity to increase or decrease its potential to generate CSR practices.

Gender With CSR: Characteristic inherent to the manager that will have the capacity to enhance or disadvantage CSR practice development.

Global CSR Networks: Global communication tool by means of which the different Research Institutes located in their respective Industrial Districts may share useful information about CSR to overcome the potential deficiencies of other IDs.

Industrial District: Group of small businesses located in the same geographical area and dedicated to the same activity whose location provides them with certain advantages derived from the characteristics of the society that surrounds them or the specific district composition, amongst other factors.

Internationalization: Corporate strategy carried out by companies which decide to operate abroad using different methods to enter and develop in the country of destination.

Shared Value Creation: Competitive actions performed by a company to jointly improve the economic and social conditions of its environment.

Chapter 11
CSR and Stakeholders' Engagement:
A Relational Perspective – Suppliers' Social Responsibility: Auditing vs. Engagement in a Relational Capital Reference

Ignacio Tobaruela Delgado
Universidad Complutense de Madrid, Spain

ABSTRACT

Companies implement corporate social responsibility (CSR) practices along their supply chains to fulfil stakeholder requirements. Failures and no-compliances also emerge, caused by supply chain members. This chapter aims to analyse CSR from relational perspective, exploring supplier engagement to compliance with CSR framework and the relationship firm/stakeholder. On the basis of general research question of how to enhance CSR practices in vertical relationships, the main aim of this chapter is to identify the corporate practices that better support compliance with CSR standards or CSR codes of conduct. Relational perspective emphasizes relationships, which become the nucleus of the studies that consider relationships between the corporation and society as first and most important issue. Consequently, relational perspective contributes towards understanding of compliance of stakeholders in CSR implementation. The chapter introduces an exploratory study about practices, attitudes of stakeholders, and knowledge sharing in a collaborative environment of relational capital.

INTRODUCTION

Consumers and governments are focusing their attention on corporate social responsibility (CSR) practices (Prentice, 2002). CSR continues to evolve and it reaches now to supply chain partners, suppliers, logistic providers and customers. (Emmelhainz and Adams, 1999). Consumer opinion of perceived CSR deficiencies can be extremely negative to corporate performance and market share (Devinney, Auger, and Eckhardt, (2010).Thus, firms should anticipate future CSR issues in their supply chains and imple-

DOI: 10.4018/978-1-7998-4833-2.ch011

ment supply chain CSR standards, since lessons learned in one area might very well apply to other CSR activities (Carter, 2004)

Although many scholars have argued for that any manufacturing firm should develop that satisfy the needs of stakeholders in sustainable ways, creating value through environmental and social performance (Ciliberti, Pontrandolfo and Scozzi, 2008; Vachon and Klassen, 2008), manufacturers are affected by misbehaviors in production processes and supply chains (DeLaurentis, 2009).

CSR implementation has induced an important attention on organizational relationships with stakeholders (Burchell and Cook, 2006) during which those expectations are identified. Therefore, stakeholder engagement would be framed through a corporate CSR framework (Crane and Livesey, 2003) and because organizations need to engage with their stakeholders to determine what stakeholder expectations are according to socially responsible behaviors (Johansen and Nielsen, 2011; Pedersen, 2006).

Scandals spread into a global concern since recalls, bans, or warnings of contaminated food, for example, has been reported from all the World (DeLaurentis, 2009). Investigations revealed that suppliers were the cause of those problems. Consequently, large number companies, especially multinational corporations, have introduced Codes of Conducts what are intended to improve the firm's social and environmental performance. Companies are increasingly being held responsible for the production conditions, because they realize that CSR issues arise throughout the supply chain. Codes often go well beyond the boundaries of the company and include social and environmental requirements for suppliers (Roberts, 2003; Jenkins, 2005).

There is an extensive literature dealing with the analysis of the reliability and effectiveness of corporate responsibility initiatives in relation to different social actors of interest, but much less has been researched about how companies safeguard CSR in supply chains: Question is how a company can be convinced that suppliers accomplish obligations according with their code of conduct.

The aim of this study is to explore the supplier engagement to compliance with CSR framework and the relationship firm/stakeholder. On the basis of general research question of How to enhance CSR practices in vertical relationships, the main aim of this chapter is to identify, in the realm of supplier/buyer relationships, the corporate practices or safeguard mechanisms that better support compliance with CSR standards or CSR Codes of conduct. Moreover, this can introduce clear concepts about the need for companies to change from a transactional to a collaborative strategy in stakeholder relationships (Vos and Achterkamp, 2015). Considering the extant literature on stakeholder management and stakeholder relationship quality, the aim of this exploration is to expand scholarly and management awareness, knowledgement and understanding beyond the usual managers instrumental perceptions about CSR.

BACKGROUND

Since philanthropic definition of Corporate Social Responsability (Bowen, 1953), to firm contribution provides solving social challenges (Wood and Logsdon, 2002), numerous studies have been focused on managing buyer-supplier relationships to obtain better performance (Jap, 2001; Ulaga and Eggert, 2006). Thus, three issues are noted: Performance, Management, and Relationship.

Garriga and Melé (2004) identify four perspectives, or theory groups, paying attention to wealth creation (instrumental), acceptation of social duties and rights in socio-political environment of firm (political), integration of social demands as strategic objectives (integrative) and ethical values of society (ethical). However, overlapping and absence of multidisciplinarity are no solved aspects in this proposal

(Secchi, 2007). Other researchers face CSR categorization from deontological/philosophical perspective (Boatright, 2003); beginning the analysis in the essence of the business.

Breaking normative basis of analysis, Secchi (2007) goes deeply into CSR theories to define how relations between corporations and society are and where responsibility is allocated, analyzing CSR from a multidisciplinary perspective, noting three perspectives: Utilitarian, Managerial and Relational. The first one affirms the firm's behavior is a profit maximizing function, very close to Liberals and Keynesians thoughts (Velo, 2003). Managerial considers social responsibility from inside the firm and everything from outside is addressed to management decisions, including social environment factors (Carroll and Buchholtz, 1996). The third one emphasizes relationships, which become the nucleus of the studies that consider relationships between the corporation and society as first and most important issue: Enterprise is no longer the main object and happens to be an interactive part of the economic system. Managerial and relational differences are relating to the differences between closed and open systems paradigms (Scott, 2003).

Secchi (2007) finds four subgroups of relational theories: 1) companies and society; 2) stakeholder approach; 3) corporate citizenship; and 4) social contract theory. Relational perspective is very sensitive to stakeholder approach. Freeman (1984) develops stakeholder approach model, suggesting that a more useful unit of analysis for thinking about strategy was the stakeholder relationship and, therefore, for improving the management of the firm. Now, it is a way to foster social responsibility issues (Freeman and Liedtka 1991) and to be conscious of the effects of business on the stakeholders (Freeman and Moutchnik, 2013). Separating it from corporate practices, it remains a model for studying relationships, and this is the way it is taken here (Secchi, 2007).

Stakeholder approach may be enriching with concepts that help in analyzing the complex contractual and political relationships, for instance, the boycott phenomenon, what emerges as a typical reaction to suspected corporate misbehavior (Hirschman, 1970)[1]. Many models, theories and concepts may be connected with socially responsible behavior: Since surge of alternative 'voices' in a market dominated by 'exits' to "lack of cooperation" (Axelrod, 1984), or to "docility", as Simon (1993)[2] says.

However, the aim of welcomed scholars to stakeholder approach of the relational perspective varies according to the intention of the research objective: Freeman (1984) notes complementarity of ethical aspects and stakeholder approach. Spence, Coles and Harris (2001) seek to broaden the stakeholder definition, including competition actors in business ethics analysis. Carrol (2006) points to it also recommends attitudes, structures, and practices of the stakeholder management. To improve CSR practices and doctrine (Freeman and Liedtka 1991) because stakeholder theory is one about how to run business and business is about how you create value for stakeholders (Freeman and Moutchnik, 2013). Moreover, Missonier and Loufrani-Fedida (2014) propose a different conceptual approach by moving from a stakeholder relational perspective, anchored in Social Network Theory, to a stakeholder relational ontology, anchored in Actor–Network Theory (ANT)[3].

The idea of corporate social responsibility has its roots[4] in two principles: The charity principle requires that fortunate members of society to assist its less fortunate members. Institutions as churches, settlement houses, and other community groups would assist them directly or indirectly. On the other hand, the stewardship principle is Judeo-Christian doctrine that requires businesses and wealthy individuals to view themselves as stewards, or caretakers (Leviticus 25:23), holding their property in trust for the benefit of the whole society (Avila, 1983). Principle of social responsibility is a modern joint redaction of these two principles. It assumes that business has an obligation to act in the profit of society. Thus, it have been invoked to justify many different business actions, from patronage, donations or contributions to political figures: Firm must see itself as a citizen in the community and do what it can to make the community a better place. (Eades, Laseter, Skurnik, Rodriguez, Isabella, and Simko, 2010).

Along these lines, Freeman and Liedtka (1991) state that the CSR as defined above should be abandoned for seven reason, mainly because it promotes manager incompetence, it implies that the corporation and society are two distinct domains, connected by responsibility, and "rights" and "responsibility" have no relevance in terms of everyday management.

Lack of dynamism and without any connection with corporate management practice, it implies a new theory is needed: Freeman introduce the 'new conversation' perspective by three propositions: (1) The stakeholder proposition considers the firm as an interconnected net of different stakeholder interests, expanding "conversation" and including suppliers, employees, and customers, among others, as legitimate partners in the dialogue. (2) Since corporations are places where individual and communities are engaged in mutual support activities, unprecedented performances can be achieved, because individuals behave selflessly. (3) Lastly, the enterprise is the vehicle of human creativity, individual and community, (Freeman and Liedtka 1991). Therefore, 'self-creation' and 'community creation' are 'two sides of the same coin', which open up to many institutions the possibility of jointly achieving the common objectives of the individual and collective good.

Pedersen (2006) argues Network theory and the institutional economics maintain an intense controversy about the importance of trust and opportunism in socio-economic relations (Granovetter, 1985; Ring and Ven, 1992; Podolny and Page, 1998). Both Agency theory and Transaction costs theory are in favour of considering opportunism as main behavioral assumption, whereas Network theory favors the concept of trust (Williamson and Ouchi, 1981; Petersen, 1993), although both agree that trust/opportunism are not specific characteristics of all economic agents (Williamson and Ouchi, 1981).

Many of the concepts collected above appear in literature dedicated to relational capital and collaborative relationships between supplier and buyer. Nelson and Winter (1982) point that if interaction between partners grows, organizational routinization is strengthened, and the investments and mutual dependence also increases in co-specilization environment (Teece, 1986; Levinthal and Fichman, 1988). Doz (1996) describes collaborative relationships evolution and Reuer, Zollo y Singh (2002) argued that previous collaborative experience improves future monitoring mechanisms, since familiarity and inter-organizational routines development.

Moreover, trust increases in long-term relationships (Helper, 1991a; Sako and Helper, 1998), and there is stronger effect on knowledge by repeating partner in equity based alliances (Gulati, 1995; Reuer et al., 2002). Previous transactions reduce expectations of opportunism (Parkhe, 1993) and perceptions of hazards (Deeds and Hill, 1998), decreasing the expected cost of dealing with suppliers (Ring and Van de Ven, 1994; Gulati, 1995). Thus, relational practices of prior exchanges may substitute explicit contracts or vertical integration rules (Dyer and Singh, 1998; Zaheer and Venkatraman, 1995).

Hoetker (2005) notes that communication and coordination routines develop over time improving communication between buyers and suppliers (Mitchell and Singh, 1996), because the best knower of the skills of his interlocutors will assign the tasks to the one most capable (Levinthal and Fichman, 1991). Multiple buyers and suppliers interactions are useful for developing common linguistics routines for discussing technical issues (Buckley and Casson, 2002). Hoetker (2005) argues that knowledge of past behaviors provides information and that opportunistic conducts are therefore less likely (Granovetter, 1995). Villena, Revilla and Choi (2011) point out relational capital issues, focusing on personal relationships that develop trust, respect, friendship, and reciprocity over time and that reduce monitoring cost and reinforce cooperation environment. Social interactions of decision makers of partner firms can mark their behaviors beyond the contractual setting (Granovetter, 1992; Bendoly, and Swink, 2010). Moreover, repeated interactions developed trust becomes institutionalized, enduring independently of the specific people who led these inter-organizational relationships (Zaheer, McEvily, and Perrone, 1998) and increasing relationships contacts (Heide and Miner, 1992). Thus, confidence increases as long as relationship lasts (Helper, 1991a) and cost reductions and new capabilities are the main benefits (Stuart, Deckert, McCutcheon, and Kunst, 1998). Thus, buyer–supplier relationship time and dependency relationship of buyer and supplier represent the relational capital, what is related to buyer performance improvement positively (Krause, 2007).

SUPPLY CHAIN AND CSR: THE ROLE OF RELATIONAL CAPITAL

To prevent opportunism is necessary to promote the supplier (Petersen, 1993), by supervising the conduct or satisfying payoff (Eisenhardt, 1989; Petersen, 1993; O'Donnell, 2000)[5]. Therefore, planning and implementation of Codes of Conduct in global supply chains is very significant (see e.g. O'Donnell, 2000; Das and Rahmann, 2000) and CSR standards, in relation to opportunism, are expensive initiatives, in term of costs and time (Walley and Whitehead, 1994; Kolk, Van Tulder, and Welters, 1999; Utting, 2000; Kapstein, 2001). The risk of opportunistic actions increases by conflict of interest between supply chain members who bear unevenly the economic effort from introducing a Code of Conduct or implementing CSR initiatives.

Contracting relationship would be easy solution to deal with this opportunism if it were possible to formulate an enforceable contract or to adhere to a comprehensive code of conduct, including all contingencies (Milgrom and Roberts, 1992). However, most contracts and codes of conduct are usually incomplete or ambiguous (Utting, 2000).

Buyer company size has effect in CSR practices: When a large purchaser extends CSR for its supply chain, it must design an audit program of monitoring suppliers. However, Jamison and Murdoch (2004) note that only shows an instantaneous state of the supplier's behavior, but it does not explore nor causes neither solutions to mitigate or improve the no-compliance situations. Therefore, audits alone or spot audits are questionable to be effective without follow-up and assessment (Fabian and Hill, 2005): Conventional audit or assessment mechanisms will not work for small suppliers if control practices are not tailored to suit the supplier dimension because small providers are difficult for having the same levels of procedures in place as large one.

Moreover, codes can not be conventional audit or assessment enforced in the same way and consequences as legal or contract requirements, and they are not drafted according with each supplier that they are directed towards (Klein, 2000)[6]. Sethi (2002) criticizes Codes of Conduct for being a lofty intent and purpose without a specific content, which makes compliance verification of supplier more difficult. Codes of conduct are often blamed for the lack of effective control systems and few companies include in their drafting tools to monitor practices associated with proper supplier behavior (Kolk et al., 1999; Kolk and van Tulder, 2001; OECD, 2000).

Trust feeding relationship between buyer and supplier can reduce costs from control and auditing practices but buyer does not know which will be trusted suppliers. Although Agency theory prefers control, since to separate one agent from another is difficult, but both perspectives admits that some kind of confidence may come to exist (Eisenhardt, 1989; Petersen, 1993; Podolny and Page 1998). New buyer–supplier relationships are expected to be no trust based, but all relationship is evolved over time and trust emerges, relaxing the governance (Ring and Ven, 1992; Child, 2000).

Conflict of interest between supply chains partners and Codes of Conduct deficiencies make it relevant to look for 'safeguard' mechanism. Safeguards are means to ensure that a supplier fulfils his obligations according to the agreement. The safeguards/protective mechanisms are direct sanctions, goal congruence, third-party intervention, trust and reputation effects (Koch, 1997), and additionally procedural justice process as basic context for a fruitful relationship (Boyd, Spekman, Kamauff, and Werhane, 2007)[7].

Direct Sanctions and Relational Capital

Neither monitoring practices nor the consequences of non-compliance are often included in Codes of Conduct (Kolk et al., 1999). Obviously, the most ultimate sanction is to break off the relationship with the supplier in case of non-compliance but this practice has limits: Exit is applicable as a protection mechanism if it is a credible threat. But this isn't an option if supplier is strategic to the buyer (buyer-dependence). On the other hand, if the future of the supplier firm depends on relationship the buyer (supplier-dependence), supplier will be inclined to fulfil code of conduct terms on its own. (Helper, 1991b; Hill and Jones, 1992).

Goal Congruence and Relational Capital

Buyer-supplier early "conversation" can be an important element in the implementation of Codes of Conduct when some kind of motivation or commitment strategy is used. Buyer must draw the attention of supplier to act socially responsible. Supplier no interest in CSR or limited bargaining power buyer are the huge difficulties to overcome (Hartmann, 2011).

If there is a conflict of interest, higher levels of goal congruence in relation to Codes of Conduct can be acquired in numerous ways, some of them need "contractual[8] relationship" to be assumed by the parties (Milgrom and Roberts, 1992):

(1) Buyer compensates the supplier for associated code compliance costs, for example, investing jointly in "green" machinery; (2) rewarding for complying with the code, for instance, with exclusive delivering rights; (3) undertaking joint investments in transaction specific assets which will commit both of them to the relationship[9 10].

Collaborative relationship can deep in trust (4) when because buyer convinces the supplier that they will be better if they implement CSR practices. (5) Moreover, the buyer can even involve the supplier in the planning and implementation of the Codes of Conduct, stimulating commitment and goal congruence.

If it is possible to create Codes of Conduct engagement, the more likely compliance will be reached. If the Codes of Conduct are imposed from top to down and bargaining power suppliers is little, commitment will be little too. A bottom-up voice approach, involving buyer and supplier in whole process, could be important for a successful implementation CSR practices (Helper, 1991b). If buyer provides its suppliers with technical as well as financial support and does efforts to change the mind-sets of suppliers, and hence improve their knowledge, creating goal congruence, it will prevent against non-compliance, establishing efficient safeguards. However, social demands and responsible practices are evolving over time. It requires continuous interrelation between the buyer and supplier (Koch, 1997).

Third-Party Intervention and Relational Capital

When buyer detects contract breach, courts and arbitrators say last word to resolve the conflict. The normative legal system is the most important protective mechanism, but also there are limitations to ensure compliance with Codes of Conduct, more especially in global supply chains: Legal system has to know about it in the regulation in force to impose sanctions. However, many Codes of Conduct are beyond the legal requirements, and non-compliances with codes are not necessarily breach of the laws, even more in countries with a weak institutional structure. As mentioned above, Codes of Conduct are incomplete contracts. No foreseen contingencies, imprecise language, etc., result in ambiguity, therefore buyer and arbitrators can't prove that the supplier has failed to comply with the agreement obligations (Milgrom and Roberts, 1992).

NGOs and other agencies or legal authorities (Diller, 1999; Kolk et al., 1999). Internal or external auditors could be indifferent in contractual relationship, but third parties usually have special evaluating competences they could introduce improvements in the codes. Even more, customers and other stakeholders might perceive third party monitoring as being more reliable and credible, although it may not be so (Kapstein (2001). Pedersen (2006) notes that third-party intervention might serve two purposes: Most importantly, third parties' monitoring is a protective mechanism, preventing fail of the codes. On the other hand, third parties improve the credibility of the codes and signal commitment to the company's stakeholders.

Trust Relational Capital

Trust can be an efficient safeguard in collaborative and long-term relationships (Diller, 1999). A high degree of trust between the buyer and supplier can be an efficient safeguard since it can reduce the costs from monitoring and results assessment. Cooperation has to be a continuous evaluating process. Buyers must get a 'historical record' of supplier experiences. Then, buyer will know better about level monitoring of each provider.

Pedersen (2006) identifies trust question: How the buyer knows which suppliers should be trustworthy. New buyer–supplier relationships tend to show low levels of confidence. However, relationship evolves over time and partners may feel a moral obligation to cooperate. Thus, trust emerges, and the governance can be less strict (Ring and Ven, 1992,; Child, 2000). In this way, a supplier that enjoyed of confidence in the past, he will also be trustworthy in the future.

However, supplier control systems variability that buyers uses to monitor supplier CSR behavior has drawn criticism from researchers. Critics have also stated that this monitoring variance has led to suppliers questioning buyers' commitment toward CSR (Emmelhainz and Adams, 1999). The argument in favour of efforts towards supplier monitoring with respect to the implementation of CSR initiatives within supply chains is based on the assumption that higher levels of monitoring reduce lacks of information between buyers and suppliers. Yet the literature suggests higher levels of monitoring may not be the best strategy for increasing supplier compliance (Murry and Heide, 1998). Therefore, high levels of strict monitoring can signal lack of trust, and they note that a common reaction by the distrusted party is reprisals against buyer, such as noncompliance: Obtrusive control systems can induce opportunistic acts or noncompliance with previous agreements in force (John, 1984).

Companies, previously engaged in short-term relationships with many smaller suppliers, are now increasingly engaging in long-term collaborative relationships with fewer suppliers. Moreover, they demanded a certain level of quality, service, price and environmental and social responsibility of its suppliers, but now they are developing capacities together with suppliers (Andersen, 2005). This way implies that buyer and suppliers are engaged in a common effort to make the relationship work. Supplier exit is less likely today, since all parties have invested money and time in the collaborative relationship. On the other hand, a stronger control would probably induce suppliers believe that buyer does not trust in them.

Reputation Effects

To adopt Codes of Conduct is a Reputation issue, which objective is to convince[11] customers that firm activities are carried out in a socially responsible way. When not all actors in the supply chain are interested in keeping the reputation, compliance with codes will be affected. There are reputation costs associated with establishing and maintaining it y the supplier's choice will depend on costs and benefits from being a reliable partner, and reputation depends, at the same time, on the supplier's interest to preserve good relationship with the buyer (Pedersen, 2006).

Reputation is a significant safeguard, when the supplier and buyer can benefit from future collaborations, or supplier reputation may be affected if buyer has access to business network where supplier non-compliances may be very harm. Hegemony in the relationship, transactions characteristics, and environment are relevant variables in evaluating reputation as protective mechanism (Pedersen, 2006).

Procedural Justice

Procedural justice considers the fairness with which decisions between individuals are made and implemented, focusing on the means by which outcomes surge from the interaction between exchange partners. Considering procedural justice from a group perspective, Tyler (1989) pays attention on individual member's attachment to the group involved in the exchange and if this attachment is strengthen or weaken. Procedural justice perceptions (in group-value model) will depend on the decision-making process neutrality, the actors' motivation and the respect of individual and their status (Boyd et alt., 2007).

Leventhal (1980) suggests six principles to be used in determining how fair suppliers will consider a buyer's CSR implementation from an instrumental and procedural perspective, but also focusing buyer supplier relationship: Those principles include consistently applying criteria; suppressing bias; using accurate information; affording opportunity for correcting errors; providing adequate representation in the decision-making process; and ensuring ethical treatment. So, procedural justice should help to ensure the supplier that their concerns are represented in the buyer's decision-making process and their interests are being protected. Suppliers will often sacrifice short-term financial profits if buyer shows intention to establish a longer-term relationship. Investment in procedural justice or fairness conveys a deeper engagement in exchange relationship, implying that previous interactions influence in future behaviors and relationships between parties. Reinforced engagement means the supplier is more inclined to be responsive to the buyer needs, and more flexible in its interpretation of contractual clauses when environmental conditions change. At last, supplier CSR compliance is strengthen communicating to each supplier that is valued by buyer as an exchange partner in front of other low cost suppliers.

Tyler and Lind (1993) suggest implementing of initiatives in a fair manner, where buyer is communicating relational information regarding their status and value as member of supply chain member to its suppliers. This relational information, in turn, serves as a socialization mechanism through which suppliers will increase their identification with the buying firm and its supply chain, raising the probability that suppliers will adhere to the buying firm's management initiatives.

As seen above, fairness is a relevant issue in CSR researches since long time ago. Focusing implementation on the objective of greater reliance on procedural justice than strict and rigorous monitoring levels may improve the performance of buyer/supplier relationship. High levels of monitoring can decrease supply chain performance by new conflicts that reduce previous state of trust and engagement (Ring and Van de Ven, 1994; Kwon and Suh, 2004).

From a resource based theory, a shared vision of the future; open and frequent information and knowledge sharing and constant feedback result by facilitating mutual interdependence; more flexible control mechanisms to improve performance and firm competitive position (Hipkin and Naudé, 2006). Similarly, factors that contribute to better competitive advantage, performance, and apprenticeship are the same antecedent relational variables of the procedural justice (Hoffmann and Schlosser, 2001). Collaboration allows a common understanding of the CSR level of the supplier. Collaborative advantage builds a common bond, a shared framework that guides the implementation of a code of conduct. (Huxham and Vangen, 2013), and recognizing the importance of the interacting actors to assess reciprocal understanding and knowledge that are obtained from information sharing (Tashman and Raelin, 2013).

INFORMATION AND COMMUNICATION, MONITORING AND TRUSTING

Before propose a way to answer core question, "state of the art" should be described in companies with CSR awareness with respect dissertation matters. Thus, Ciliberti, et al. (2008) note some interesting aspects[12]:

Regarding to communication issues, and differently from what is stated in the literature (Jenkins, 2006; Murillo and Lozano, 2006), companies become aware of the importance of communicating of CSR objectives and practices to external stakeholders to show their engagement and to involve external stakeholders in CSR initiatives. Strategic areas are the target of the external communication activities (Murillo and Lozano, 2006). As result, a high number of suppliers are signing buyer codes of conduct. Supplier selection usually is according to CSR criteria standards, which can include Fair Trade Principles, although such criteria are often considered as subordinate to economic issues and/or product quality evaluations.

Moreover, firms try to build knowledge and abilities by participating jointly in innovation activities and providing them with special tools or process. Availability to share information with stakeholders can be considered a manifestation of company willingness to build collaborative relationships with stakeholders (Jiang, 2009).

Spiller (2000) collects non-exhaustively supplier key business practices as stakeholder: Developing and maintaining long-term purchasing relationships, clear expectations, paying fair prices and bills according to terms agreed upon, fair and competent handling of conflicts and disputes, reliable anticipated purchasing requirements, encouragement to provide innovative suggestions, assisting suppliers to improve their environmental/social performance, local suppliers, sourcing from minority-owned suppliers, and inclusion of environmental/social criteria in the supplier selection. Leppelt, Foerstl, and Hartmann (2013) point different management tools can be adopted to get suppliers more involved in CSR: written requirements by adopting a CSR management system, implement information and communication activities as well as training initiatives, and monitor supplier performance. They should preferably have long-term and close relationships with suppliers and adopt a continuous improvement philosophy. Also, joining fair trade consortiums can also be useful to retrieve as well as to provide more information on CSR. If a permissive regulation exists wherein suppliers are located, to transfer behavior practices to suppliers, promoting visits of suppliers to the buyer plants or showing suppliers environmental or social best practices implemented by other companies.

Regarding monitoring suppliers, Ciliberti et al. (2006) notes all companies follow techniques and control of supplier performance, according to procedures defined in CSR standards and most of suppliers signed CSR principles. So, companies conduct direct or third party audits. Direct inspections are preferred but not always conducted due to time shortage and nor do they have the established frequency. Therefore, it is difficult to check CSR supplier compliance. When a non-compliance is detected, buyers react in different ways: Explaining to suppliers the relevance of the matter, breaking up the relationship with a noncompliant supplier, but also discussing with suppliers and finding solutions together with them, in a collaborative atmosphere.

This finding is consistent with previous contributions regarding the strategic relevance of communication in defining long-term relationships between companies and stakeholders (Cornelissen, 2014). Firm size is relevant: Grayson (2006) notes the identification of stakeholders and relationships becomes much more personal in SMEs, from supervisor/subordinate relation to care relation with suppliers into a long-term practices, moreover, with the local community into a strong integration.

Not only trust may be the answer of how a company can be convinced that suppliers accomplish obligations according with their code of conduct, but also the perception of the value held by buyers when they do business with their suppliers of goods or services. In this way, the supplier needs to be recognized as "trustworthy" by the buyer: the buyer seeks to rely on the supplier, and this seeks to gain the confidence of the buyer. Therefore, they are both sides of the same "supply chain management" coin. Petrash (1996) defines this value perception of the customer as relational capital.

Based on firms depend on relations with groups of interest, relational capital considers the value generated by all these relations, not only with customers, suppliers, or shareholders. Bontis (1998) points out even more: it is the knowledge associated to relationships with its groups of reference. Relational capital refers to network of associates and their satisfaction with and loyalty to the company. However, relational capital, as value, only can be measured from customer perspective. Because it is a perceived and subjective value some indicators are useful: market share (knowledge of market channels), the number of related companies (customer and supplier relationships and industry associations) or the times the buyer repeats orders to same provider (loyalty). Also, longevity of relationships and satisfaction are measurable elements of relational capital.

However, according to Kim (2011), CSR practices[13] increase purchase intention and improve purchaser's attitudes, and improve relationship performances. Thus, it is clear that corporations should effort on CSR activities and that B2B relationship performances should be considered as a performance measurement evaluating benefits against the implementation cost of CSR activities. In sum, relational capital reduces opportunistic conduct and promotes collaborative behavior. On the contrary, a low level of relational capital reduces the confidence and means rationing events of relevant resources (Uzzi, 1997; Dyer and Chu, 2003; Perrone, Zaheer and McEvily, 2003). Leppelt et al. (2013) explore how strategic suppliers effectively organize a supply chain-oriented CSR management capability in B2B markets and how expected reputational effects for top-tier suppliers define their behavior. In particular, top-tier suppliers assure upstream CSR standards and they simultaneously market upstream practices as a service to their direct industrial customers. Moreover, that suppliers too can benefit from being perceived as a

CSR leader, without forget that in many cases CSR awareness implies to be an order qualifier but not an order winner.

Risks in Relational Capital Managing

Accumulating high relational capital does not imply the disappearance of opportunistic behaviors neither the disappearance of unfairness in the supplier-buyer relationship. Granovetter (1985) notes relational capital increases may facilitate the emergence of enabling environments to opportunistic behavior. Overconfidence induces the buyer to relax in control tasks, which allows the supplier to abuse his privileged position or simply reduce the level of demand for a safe business (Wuyts and Geyskens, 2005). Meanwhile, the buyer is less and less aware of it, and the situation lengthens with the consequent loss of performance. It might develop "unnecessary" routines that generates lock-in and path dependence, compromising resources and restricting the implementation of new, more effective strategies (Uzzi, 1997; Gargiulo and Benassi, 1999; Bendoly and Swink, 2007). Supplier can take advantage of such buyer conducts: Attend to supplier exorbitant demands, fears of break off the relationship with the supplier (Anderson and Jap, 2005; Poppo, Zhou, and Ryu, 2008), buyer emotional attachment (Mayer, Davis, and Schoorman, 1995), or strong vinculation (Kim, Oh, and Swaminathan, 2006), avoiding personal conflicts (Jeffries and Reed, 2000; Selnes and Sallis, 2003), negative reputation as a reliable partner (Gulati, 1995), or simply preference (Gargiulo and Benassi, 1999).

In short, buyer will be more vulnerable if he is reluctant to switch suppliers. Feedback and information sharing could be lost in high relational capital, limiting inter-firm learning and threatens buyer results. Finally, since investments in relationship-specific socialization mechanisms are costly and time consuming (Cousins, Handfield, Lawson, and Petersen, 2006), buyer may inadvertently lose opportunities for finding new, more suppliers (Bendoly et al., 2010). Thus, while an initially positive relationship between relational capital and performance would be expected, high level of relational capital might lead to declining performance: The relational capital has a higher marginal effect on performance than the frequency and diversity of contacts (structural capital) and that a shared vision (cognitive capital) has a positive linear relationship with performance… But buyers should expect that when they are working in a collaborative environment they will reach the point of diminishing performance (Villena et al., 2011). Not only performance, but also knowledge: Preston, Chen, Swink, and Meade (2017) suggest that knowledge accumulation of collaborative supplier diminishes over time. If levels of buyer–supplier dependence, switching costs, and "lock-in" grow, buyer feels less of a need for knowledge compensation regardless of the duration of the relationship, but suppliers will benefit more from earlier efforts at building relational capital. Thus, supplier knowledge dependence, in case, will diminish too. In this way, buyers wishing to build relational capital should investment in cognitive capital, and combining with unilateral adaptations, to achieve the higher return, trust and supplier understanding (Roden, and Lawson, 2014). So, buyers' investments in supplier development build relational capital, resulting in mutual benefits (Blonska, Storey, Rozemeijer, Wetzels, and de Ruyter, 2013), at least, while diminishing point isn't overcome.

However, high relational capital may cause reactive emotions as anxiety in supplier under buyer development program by feeling indebted, which negatively may affect economic results of the relationship. On the other hand, we must not forget that relational capital is affective in nature and interpersonal interaction is key: Groups of buyer and supplier employees with similar responsibilities can align opinions, views, feelings, and behaviors and build cohesiveness and trust between organizations (McGrath and Sparks, 2005; Blonska, et al., 2013).

SOLUTIONS AND RECOMMENDATIONS: AUDITING AND ENGAGEMENT

Engagement between buyer and supplier is an important condition to achieve performance goals, and provides value to buying firms that seek to increase relational capital with suppliers. Relational capital explains buyer performance achievements in cost and total cost (Krause, 2007).

Recalling the exploratory question about how a company can be convinced that suppliers accomplish obligations according with their code of conduct or *how the buyer knows which suppliers should be trusted* (Pedersen, 2006), we are able to propose different answers from relational perspective (see Table 1).

First one, according with kind of relationship confidence:

- **Standard Trust:** Related to standard or Code of Conduct, the purchaser has confidence in the control, auditing, monitoring, direct or indirect, or in the existence of a recognized certificate attesting the good behavior practices of the supplier. It´s a coercitive protection mechanism based on sanction procediment.
- **Economic Trust:** Supplier's choice will depend on costs and benefits from being a reliable partner. Compensation, rewards or joint investment, or cost and reputational benefits will be valued.
- **Corporative Trust or Simply Trust:** Based on collaborative relationship, fairness and transparency between parties.

Second one. Regarding to hegemony in stakeholder relationship characteristics:

- **Supplier Dependence:** When the future of the supplier firm depends on relationship the buyer, provider must fulfil code of conduct prescriptions if he wants to keep the business. Buyer company is hegemonic and can impose behavior conditions.
- **Indifferent:** Hegemonic position is no important. Contractual or agreement clauses are enough.
- **Indifferent but Willingness of Fairness:** Procedural justice ensures the supplier that their concerns are represented in the buyer decision-making process and their interests are protected.
- **Resource Management:** There isn't hegemonic position, only reputation performances.

While some level of supplier monitoring is seen as necessary, literature suggests that high levels of supplier control can reduce supplier CSR compliance, affecting negatively the supply chain relationships efficiency. Recommended CSR system will be one which combines low levels of control with high trust rates, gaining a high level of supplier compliance, too. This approach respects the importance of relationships in the effective management of supply chains. Moreover, implementing procedural justice can increase supplier compliance and to improve supply chain performance. CSR implementation regime characterized by procedural justice offers an alternative and potentially more effective means of increasing supplier CSR compliance than that offered by high levels of supplier monitoring. (Boyd, et al., 2007).

Liu, Luo and Liu (2009) show that relational investments reduce opportunism and improve relational performance. Williamson defined such investments as a part of ''mutual hostage'', which in turn escalates members' incentive to cooperate (1983).

On the other hand, opportunism (lack of trust) and trust (lack of opportunism) are interrelated and all collaborative activities will include aspects of both. Thus, cooperation must be seen as continuous evaluating process between buyer and supplier. In this way, buyers should record experiences to have enough information about which supplies should be monitored most carefully (Pedersen, 2006). Obviously not all implantations of CSR practices are successful. Also, Cheung, Myers and Mentzer (2011) indicate that although relational learning participation fails, suppliers results can increase. In case, buyers must to determine which activities are necessary for the future of the relationship and whether resources dedicated are justified. If firms believe relational benefits are lacking compared to their partner's, it is questionable whether this would result in improved relationship.

In spite of the relational capital has a high marginal effect on performance, buyers should expect that when they are working in a collaborative environment they will reach the point of diminishing performance (Villena et al., 2011). So, they should strive to monitor relationships with their trusted suppliers to avoid such a reduction in results. In other words, the relational capital that gives value to collaborative relationships in the supply chain should be reviewed and updated, audited and monitored as if it were any other asset of the company. In this way, safeguard mechanisms should be applied, combining collaborative, economic and coercive attributes in order to keep CSR compliance upstream and downstream, along the entire supply chain.

Table 1. Supply chain relationships, safeguard mechanisms, supplier/buyer relationship characteristics

<table>
<tr><th>Relationship</th><th colspan="2">Safeguard Mechanisms</th><th>Stakeholder relationship Characteristics</th><th>Mechanism Characteristics</th></tr>
<tr><td rowspan="4">Contractual</td><td colspan="2">Auditing/monitoring</td><td rowspan="2">Supplier dependence or indifferent</td><td rowspan="2">Coercive:
Correction/Sanction process</td></tr>
<tr><td>• Direct</td><td>• Third part</td></tr>
<tr><td colspan="2">Goal congruence</td><td rowspan="2">Indifferent</td><td rowspan="2">Economic</td></tr>
<tr><td colspan="2">• Compliance cost compensation.
• Rewarding compliance.
• Joint investment.</td></tr>
<tr><td rowspan="2">Collaborative in targets</td><td colspan="2">Goal congruence</td><td rowspan="3">Fairness, Procedural justice</td><td rowspan="2">Collaboration</td></tr>
<tr><td colspan="2">• Goal convincement
• Common CSR implementation</td></tr>
<tr><td>Collaborative</td><td colspan="2">Trust</td><td>Long-term collaboration</td></tr>
<tr><td>Collaborative</td><td colspan="2">Reputation effects</td><td>Resource management</td><td>Economic</td></tr>
</table>

Source: Author's own creation

FUTURE RESEARCH DIRECTIONS

Since this is an exploratory approach to stakeholder engagement phenomena, future researches must deep in the generalization of proposed relationship categories and contrast it in an extent sample of firms. Also, we recommend to explore other engagement relationship in CSR issues which could be more appropriate as mechanism for promoting collaborative and good practices of the small firm in the supply chain, for example, Supply Chain Responsability (Spence and Bourlakis, 2009). As definitively Trust is attributed to relationships between people, the perception of engagement in CSR and consequences could be refined and enhanced through application to more cases what empower human emotions.

CONCLUSION

This exploratory study contributes to the theorizing of stakeholder engagement by examining the connection between the concepts of CSR, stakeholder and engagement from a relational perspective of the Supply Chain. Thus, it provides more understanding CSR-related engagement. Findings of this article also provide a stimulating contribution to the theorizing of engagement on the wider stage of communication and public relations, especially in B2B markets. Relationship categorizations allow to state ways to perform better CSR practices between supplier and purchaser firm in relational capital environment.

However, the information obtained from the literature lacks of the wide and depth what author wishes. Most of sources of information are studies of case or about short number of buyer companies, which identify misalignments between elements of the process and CSR targets.

ACKNOWLEDGMENT

The author acknowledges the insightful comments of the editors and anonymous reviewers, whose input resulted in a significantly improved paper. Also, he I would like to express my thanks to members of the UCM consolidated research group ECI: Strategic Management, Knowledge, Innovation and the Natural Environment and Department of Business Organization and Marketing for their confidence and help.

REFERENCES

Anderson, E., & Jap, S. D. (2005). The dark side of close relationships. *MIT Sloan Management Review*, *46*(3), 75.

Avila, C. (1983). Ownership: Early Christian Teaching. Orbis.

Axelrod, R. (1984). *The Evolution of Cooperation*. Basic Books.

Bendoly, E., & Swink, M. (2007). Moderating effects of information access on project management behavior, performance and perceptions. *Journal of Operations Management*, *25*(3), 604–622. doi:10.1016/j.jom.2006.02.009

Blonska, A., Storey, C., Rozemeijer, F. A., Wetzels, M. G. M., & de Ruyter, J. C. (2013). Decomposing the effect of supplier development on relationship benefits: The role of relational capital. *Industrial Marketing Management*, *42*(8), 1295–1306. doi:10.1016/j.indmarman.2013.06.007

Boatright, J. R. (2003). *Ethics and the Conduct of Business* (4th ed.). Prentice Hall.

Bontis, N. (1998). Intellectual Capital: An Exploratory Study that Develops Measures and Models. *Management Decision*, *36*(2), 63–76. doi:10.1108/00251749810204142

Bowen, H. R. (1953). *Social Responsibilities of Businessman*. Harper and Row.

Boyd, D. E., Spekman, R. E., Kamauff, J. W., & Werhane, P. (2007). Corporate social responsibility in global supply chains: A procedural justice perspective. *Long Range Planning*, *40*(3), 341–356. doi:10.1016/j.lrp.2006.12.007

Buckley, P. J., & Casson, M. (2002). The future of the multinational enterprise (25th anniversary). Palgrave MacMillan.

Burchell, J., & Cook, J. (2006). It's good to talk? Examining attitudes towards corporate social responsibility dialogue and engagement processes. *Business Ethics (Oxford, England)*, *15*(2), 154–170. doi:10.1111/j.1467-8608.2006.00439.x

Carroll, A. B. (1991). The Pyramid of Corporate Social Responsibility: Toward the Moral Management of Organizational Stakeholders. *Business Horizons*, *34*(4), 39–48. doi:10.1016/0007-6813(91)90005-G

Carroll, A. B., & Buchholtz, A. K. (1996). *Ethics and stakeholder management*. South-Western.

Carter, C. R. (2004). Purchasing and social responsibility: A replication and extension. *The Journal of Supply Chain Management*, *40*(3), 4–16. doi:10.1111/j.1745-493X.2004.tb00175.x

Carter, C. R., & Jennings, M. M. (2004). The role of purchasing in corporate social responsibility: A structural equation analysis. *Journal of Business Logistics*, *25*(1), 145–186. doi:10.1002/j.2158-1592.2004.tb00173.x

Cheung, M. S., Myers, M. B., & Mentzer, J. T. (2011). The value of relational learning in global buyer-supplier exchanges: A dyadic perspective and test of the pie-sharing premise. *Strategic Management Journal*, *32*(10), 1061–1082. doi:10.1002mj.926

Child, J. (2000). Trust and international strategic alliances: the case of Sino-foreign joint ventures. In C. Lane & R. Bachmann (Eds.), *Trust Within and Between Organisations* (pp. 241–272). Oxford University Press.

Ciliberti, F., Pontrandolfo, P., & Scozzi, B. (2008). Investigating corporate social responsibility in supply chains: A SME perspective. *Journal of Cleaner Production*, *16*(15), 1579–1588. doi:10.1016/j.jclepro.2008.04.016

Cornelissen, J. (2014). *Corporate communication: A guide to theory and practice*. Sage.

Cousins, P. D., Handfield, R. B., Lawson, B., & Petersen, K. J. (2006). Creating supply chain relational capital: The impact of formal and informal socialization processes. *Journal of Operations Management*, *24*(6), 851–863. doi:10.1016/j.jom.2005.08.007

Crane, A., & Livesey, S. (2003). Are you talking to me? Stakeholder communication and the risks and rewards of dialogue. In J. Andriof, S. Waddock, S. Rahman, and B. Husted (Eds.), Unfolding Stakeholder Thinking vol II: Relationships, communication, reporting and performance (pp. 39–52). Sheffield, UK: Greenleaf. doi:10.9774/GLEAF.978-1-909493-32-2_4

DeLaurentis, T. (2009). Ethical supply chain management. *The China Business Review*, *36*(3), 38–41.

Devinney, T. M., Auger, P., & Eckhardt, G. M. (2010). *The Myth of the Ethical Consumer*. Cambridge University Press.

Diller, J. (1999). A Social Conscience in the Global Marketplace-Labour Dimensions of Codes of COnduct, Social Labelling and Investor Initiatives. *Int'l Lab. Rev.*, *138*(2), 99–129. doi:10.1111/j.1564-913X.1999.tb00062.x

Doz, Y. L. (1996). The evolution of cooperation in strategic alliances: Initial conditions or learning processes? *Strategic Management Journal*, *17*(S1), 55–83. doi:10.1002mj.4250171006

Dyer, J. H. (1996). How Chrysler created an American keiretsu. *Harvard Business Review*, *74*(4), 42–52.

Dyer, J. H., & Chu, W. (2003). The role of trustworthiness in reducing transaction costs and improving performance: Empirical evidence from the United States, Japan, and Korea. *Organization Science*, *14*(1), 57–68. doi:10.1287/orsc.14.1.57.12806

Dyer, J. H., & Singh, H. (1998). The relational view: Cooperative strategy and sources of interorganizational competitive advantage. *Academy of Management Review*, *23*(4), 660–679. doi:10.5465/amr.1998.1255632

Eades, K. M., Laseter, T. M., Skurnik, I., Rodriguez, P. L., Isabella, L. A., & Simko, P. J. (2010). *The portable MBA* (Vol. 34). John Wiley and Sons. doi:10.1002/9781118256213

Elkington, J. (1998). *Cannibals with Forks: The Triple Bottom Line of 21st Century Business*. New Society Pbublishers.

Emmelhainz, M. A., & Adams, R. J. (1999). The apparel industry response to "sweatshop" concerns: A review and analysis of codes of conduct. *The Journal of Supply Chain Management*, *35*(2), 51–57. doi:10.1111/j.1745-493X.1999.tb00062.x

Fabian, T., & Hill, C. (2005). *Sourcing Overseas for the Retail Sector: CSR and the Ethical Supply Chain*. Price Waterhouse Coopers.

Freeman, E., & Moutchnik, A. (2013). Stakeholder management and CSR: questions and answers. *UmweltWirtschaftsForum*, *21*(1-2), 5-9.

Freeman, R. E. (1984). *Strategic Management: A Stakeholder Approach*. Pittman.

Freeman, R. E., & Liedtka, J. (1991). Corporate social responsibility: A critical approach. *Business Horizons*, *34*(July–August), 92–98. doi:10.1016/0007-6813(91)90012-K

Gargiulo, M., & Benassi, M. (1999). The dark side of social capital. In *Corporate social capital and liability* (pp. 298–322). Springer. doi:10.1007/978-1-4615-5027-3_17

Garriga, E., & Melé, D. (2004). Corporate social responsibility theories: Mapping the territory. *Journal of Business Ethics*.

Granovetter, M. (1995). Coase revisited: Business groups in the modern economy. *Industrial and Corporate Change*, *4*(1), 93–130.

Grayson, D. (2006). Inspiring smaller firms with the responsible business mindset. In M. Epstein & K. Hansen (Eds.), *The accountable corporation: Corporate social responsibility* (pp. 279–298). Praeger.

Gulati, R. (1995). Social structure and alliance formation patterns: A longitudinal analysis. *Administrative Science Quarterly*, *40*(4), 619–652. doi:10.2307/2393756

Gulati, R. (1999). Network location and learning: The influence of network resources and firm capabilities on alliance formation. *Strategic Management Journal*, *20*(5), 397–420. doi:10.1002/(SICI)1097-0266(199905)20:5<397::AID-SMJ35>3.0.CO;2-K

Hartmann, M. (2011). Corporate social responsibility in the food sector. *European Review of Agriculture Economics*, *38*(3), 297–324. doi:10.1093/erae/jbr031

Heide, J. B., & Miner, A. S. (1992). The shadow of the future: Effects of anticipated interaction and frequency of contact on buyer-seller cooperation. *Academy of Management Journal*, *35*(2), 265–291. doi:10.5465/256374

Helper, S. (1991a). *An exit-voice analysis of supplier relations. In Morality, rationality, and efficiency: new perspectives on socio-economics*. Sharp.

Helper, S. (1991b). How much has really changed between US automakers and their suppliers? *MIT Sloan Management Review*, *32*(4), 15.

Hill, C. W., & Jones, T. M. (1992). Stakeholder-agency theory. *Journal of Management Studies*, *29*(2), 131–154. doi:10.1111/j.1467-6486.1992.tb00657.x

Hipkin, I., & Naudé, P. (2006). Developing effective alliance partnerships: Lessons from a case study. *Long Range Planning*, *39*(1), 51–69. doi:10.1016/j.lrp.2005.09.003

Hirschman, A. O. (1970). *Exit, Voice, and Loyalty. Responses to Decline in Firms, Organizations, and States*. Cambridge University Press.

Hoetker, G. (2005). How much you know versus how well I know you: Selecting a supplier for a technically innovative component. *Strategic Management Journal*, *26*(1), 75–96. doi:10.1002mj.453

Hoffmann, W. H., & Schlosser, R. (2001). Success factors of strategic alliances in small and medium-sized enterprises—An empirical survey. *Long Range Planning*, *34*(3), 357–381. doi:10.1016/S0024-6301(01)00041-3

Huxham, C., & Vangen, S. (2013). *Managing to collaborate: The theory and practice of collaborative advantage*. Routledge. doi:10.4324/9780203010167

Jamison, L., & Murdoch, H. (2004). *Taking the Temperature: Ethical Issues in the Supply Chain*. Institute of Business Ethics.

Jap, S. D. (2001). "Pie sharing" in complex collaboration contexts. *JMR, Journal of Marketing Research*, *38*(1), 86–99. doi:10.1509/jmkr.38.1.86.18827

Jeffries, F. L., & Reed, R. (2000). Trust and adaptation in relational contracting. *Academy of Management Review*, *25*(4), 873–882. doi:10.5465/amr.2000.3707747

Jenkins, H. (2006). Small business champions for corporate social responsibility. *Journal of Business Ethics*, *67*(3), 241–256. doi:10.100710551-006-9182-6

Jenkins, R. (2005). Globalization, corporate social responsibility and poverty. *International Affairs*, *81*(3), 525–540. doi:10.1111/j.1468-2346.2005.00467.x

Jiang, B. (2009). Implementing supplier codes of conduct in global supply chains: Process explanations from theoretic and empirical perspectives. *Journal of Business Ethics*, *85*(1), 77–92. doi:10.100710551-008-9750-z

Johansen, T. S., & Nielsen, A. E. (2012). CSR in corporate self-storying—Legitimacy as a question of differentiation and conformity. *Corporate Communication: An International Journal*, *17*(4), 434–448. doi:10.1108/13563281211274130

John, G. (1984). An empirical investigation of some antecedents of opportunism in a marketing channel. *JMR, Journal of Marketing Research*, *21*(3), 278–289. doi:10.1177/002224378402100305

Kapstein, E. B. (2001). The corporate ethics crusade. *Foreign Affairs*, *80*(5), 105–119. doi:10.2307/20050254

Kim, J. K. (2011). Effects of corporate social responsibility on BtoB relational performance. *International Journal of Business and Management*, *6*(2), 24. doi:10.5539/ijbm.v6n2p24

Kim, T. Y., Oh, H., & Swaminathan, A. (2006). Framing interorganizational network change: A network inertia perspective. *Academy of Management Review*, *31*(3), 704–720. doi:10.5465/amr.2006.21318926

Klein, N. (2000). *No Logo. Taking Aim at the Brand Bullies*. Flamingo.

Kolk, A., & Van Tulder, R. (2001). Multinationality and corporate ethics: Codes of conduct in the sporting goods industry. *Journal of International Business Studies*, *32*(2), 267–283. doi:10.1057/palgrave.jibs.8490952

Kolk, A., Van Tulder, R., & Welters, C. (1999). International codes of conduct and corporate social responsibility: can transnational corporations regulate themselves? *Transnational Corporations, 8*(1), 143-180.

Krause, D. R., Handfield, R. B., & Tyler, B. B. (2007). The relationships between supplier development, commitment, social capital accumulation and performance improvement. *Journal of Operations Management*, *25*(2), 528–545. doi:10.1016/j.jom.2006.05.007

Kwon, I. W. G., & Suh, T. (2004). Factors affecting the level of trust and commitment in supply chain relationships. *The Journal of Supply Chain Management*, *40*(1), 4–14. doi:10.1111/j.1745-493X.2004.tb00165.x

Leppelt, T., Foerstl, K., & Hartmann, E. (2013). Corporate social responsibility in buyer-supplier relationships: Is it beneficial for top-tier suppliers to market their capability to ensure a responsible supply chain? *Business Research*, *6*(2), 126–152. doi:10.1007/BF03342746

Leventhal, G. S. (1980). What should be done with equity theory? In *Social exchange* (pp. 27–55). Springer. doi:10.1007/978-1-4613-3087-5_2

Levinthal, D. A., & Fichman, M. (1988). Dynamics of interorganizational attachments: Auditor-client relationships. *Administrative Science Quarterly*, *33*(3), 345–369. doi:10.2307/2392713

Levinthal, D. A., & Fichman, M. (1991). History dependence in professional relationships: Ties that bind (No. 1991-33). Carnegie Mellon University, Tepper School of Business.

Lindgreen, A., Swaen, V., Maon, F., Andersen, M., & Skjoett-Larsen, T. (2009). Corporate social responsibility in global supply chains. *Supply Chain Management*.

Liu, Y., Luo, Y., & Liu, T. (2009). Governing buyer–supplier relationships through transactional and relational mechanisms: Evidence from China. *Journal of Operations Management*, *27*(4), 294–309. doi:10.1016/j.jom.2008.09.004

Maloni, M. J., & Brown, M. E. (2006). Corporate social responsibility in the supply chain: An application in the food industry. *Journal of Business Ethics*, *68*(1), 35–52. doi:10.100710551-006-9038-0

Mayer, R. C., Davis, J. H., & Schoorman, F. D. (1995). An integrative model of organizational trust. *Academy of Management Review*, *20*(3), 709–734. doi:10.5465/amr.1995.9508080335

Milgrom, P., & Roberts, J. (1992). *Economics, organization and management*. Prentice Hall Inc.

Missonier, S., & Loufrani-Fedida, S. (2014). Stakeholder analysis and engagement in projects: From stakeholder relational perspective to stakeholder relational ontology. *International Journal of Project Management*, *32*(7), 1108–1122. doi:10.1016/j.ijproman.2014.02.010

Mohr, J., & Spekman, R. (1994). Characteristics of partnership success: Partnership attributes, communication behavior, and conflict resolution techniques. *Strategic Management Journal*, *15*(2), 135–152. doi:10.1002mj.4250150205

Murillo, D., & Lozano, J. M. (2006). SMEs and CSR: An approach to CSR in their own words. *Journal of Business Ethics*, *67*(3), 227–240. doi:10.100710551-006-9181-7

Murry, J. P. Jr, & Heide, J. B. (1998). Managing promotion program participation within manufacturer–retailer relationships. *Journal of Marketing*, *62*(1), 58–68.

Nelson, R. R., & Winter, S. G. (1982). *An evolutionary theory of economic change*. Belknap Press.

Parkhe, A. (1993). Strategic alliance structuring: A game theoretic and transaction cost examination of interfirm cooperation. *Academy of Management Journal*, *36*(4), 794–829.

Pedersen, E. R. (2006). Making corporate social responsibility (CSR) operable: How companies translate stakeholder dialogue into practice. *Business and Society Review*, *111*(2), 137–163. doi:10.1111/j.1467-8594.2006.00265.x

Pedersen, E. R., & Andersen, M. (2006). Safeguarding corporate social responsibility (CSR) in global supply chains: How codes of conduct are managed in buyer-supplier relationships. *Journal of Public Affairs: An International Journal*, *6*(3-4), 228–240. doi:10.1002/pa.232

Perrone, V., Zaheer, A., & McEvily, B. (2003). Free to be trusted? Organizational constraints on trust in boundary spanners. *Organization Science*, *14*(4), 422–439. doi:10.1287/orsc.14.4.422.17487

Petersen, T. (1993). The economics of organization: The principal-agent relationship. *Acta Sociologica*, *36*(3), 277–293. doi:10.1177/000169939303600309

Petrash, G. (1996). Dow's journey to a knowledge value management culture. *European Management Journal, 14*(4), 365–373. doi:10.1016/0263-2373(96)00023-0

Podolny, J. M., & Page, K. L. (1998). Network forms of organization. *Annual Review of Sociology, 24*(1), 57–76. doi:10.1146/annurev.soc.24.1.57

Poppo, L., Zhou, K. Z., & Ryu, S. (2008). Alternative origins to interorganizational trust: An interdependence perspective on the shadow of the past and the shadow of the future. *Organization Science, 19*(1), 39–55. doi:10.1287/orsc.1070.0281

Porter, M. E., & Kramer, M. R. (2006). The link between competitive advantage and corporate social responsibility. *Harvard Business Review, 84*(12), 78–92. PMID:17183795

Prentice, R. (2002). Enron: A brief behavioral autopsy. *American Business Law Journal, 40*(2), 417–444. doi:10.1111/j.1744-1714.2002.tb00851.x

Preston, D. S., Chen, D. Q., Swink, M., & Meade, L. (2017). Generating supplier benefits through buyer-enabled knowledge enrichment: A social capital perspective. *Decision Sciences, 48*(2), 248–287. doi:10.1111/deci.12220

Preston, L. E. (1988). *Social Issues and Public Policy in Business and Management: Retrospect and Prospect*. University of Maryland.

Reuer, J. J., Zollo, M., & Singh, H. (2002). Post-formation dynamics in strategic alliances. *Strategic Management Journal, 23*(2), 135–151. doi:10.1002mj.214

Ring, P. S., & Van de Ven, A. H. (1994). Developmental processes of cooperative interorganizational relationships. *Academy of Management Review, 19*(1), 90–118. doi:10.5465/amr.1994.9410122009

Roberts, S. (2003). Supply chain specific? Understanding the patchy success of ethical sourcing initiatives. *Journal of Business Ethics, 44*(2-3), 159–170. doi:10.1023/A:1023395631811

Sako, M., & Helper, S. (1998). Determinants of trust in supplier relations: Evidence from the automotive industry in Japan and the United States. *Journal of Economic Behavior & Organization, 34*(3), 387–417. doi:10.1016/S0167-2681(97)00082-6

Scott, W. R. (2003). *Organizations. Rational, Natural, and Open Systems* (5th ed.). Prentice-Hall.

Scott, W. R., & Davis, G. F. (2015). *Organizations and organizing: Rational, natural and open systems perspectives*. Routledge.

Secchi, D. (2007). Utilitarian, managerial and relational theories of corporate social responsibility. *International Journal of Management Reviews, 9*(4), 347–373. doi:10.1111/j.1468-2370.2007.00215.x

Selnes, F., & Sallis, J. (2003). Promoting relationship learning. *Journal of Marketing, 67*(3), 80–95. doi:10.1509/jmkg.67.3.80.18656

Simon, H. A. (1993). Altruism and economics. *The American Economic Review, 83*(2), 156–161.

Sinéad, R. (2014). Developing social capital in buyer-supplier relationships: The contingent effect of relationship-specific adaptations. *International Journal of Production Economics, 151*, 89–89. doi:10.1016/j.ijpe.2014.01.008

Singh, K., & Mitchell, W. (1996). Precarious collaboration: Business survival after partners shut down or form new partnerships. *Strategic Management Journal, 17*(S1), 99–115. doi:10.1002mj.4250171008

Spence, L., & Bourlakis, M. (2009). The evolution from corporate social responsibility to supply chain responsibility: The case of Waitrose. *Supply Chain Management, 14*(4), 291–302. doi:10.1108/13598540910970126

Spence, L. J., Coles, A.-M., & Harris, L. (2001). The forgotten stakeholder? Ethics and social responsibility in relation to competitors. *Business and Society Review, 106*(4), 331–352. doi:10.1111/0045-3609.00119

Spiller, R. (2000). Ethical Business and Investment: A Model for Business and Society. *Journal of Business Ethics, 27*(1/2), 149–160. doi:10.1023/A:1006445915026

Stuart, I., Deckert, P., McCutcheon, D., & Kunst, R. (1998). Case study: A leveraged learning network. *MIT Sloan Management Review, 39*(4), 81.

Tashman, P., & Raelin, J. (2013). Who and what really matters to the firm: Moving stakeholder salience beyond managerial perceptions. *Business Ethics Quarterly, 23*(4), 591–616. doi:10.5840/beq201323441

Teece, D. J. (1986). *Profiting from technological innovation: Implications for integration, collaboration, licensing and public policy*. Academic Press.

Tom, R. (n.d.). The Psychology of Procedural Justice: A Test of the Group-value Model. *Journal of Personality and Social Psychology, 57*, 830–838.

Tyler, T. R. (1989). The psychology of procedural justice: A test of the group-value model. *Journal of Personality and Social Psychology, 57*(5), 830–838. doi:10.1037/0022-3514.57.5.830

Tyler, T. R., & Lind, E. A. (1992). A Relational Model of Authority in Groups. *Advances in Experimental Social Psychology*, 24.

Ulaga, W., & Eggert, A. (2006). Value-based differentiation in business relationships: Gaining and sustaining key supplier status. *Journal of Marketing, 70*(1), 119–136. doi:10.1509/jmkg.2006.70.1.119

Utting, P. (2000). *Business responsibility for sustainable development* (No. 2). Geneva 2000 Occasional Paper.

Uzzi, B. (1997). Social structure and competition in interfirm networks: The paradox of embeddedness. *Administrative Science Quarterly, 42*(1), 35–67. doi:10.2307/2393808

Vachon, S., & Klassen, R. D. (2008). Environmental management and manufacturing performance: The role of collaboration in the supply chain. *International Journal of Production Economics, 111*(2), 299–315. doi:10.1016/j.ijpe.2006.11.030

Velo, D. (2003). Corporate social responsibility in the global market. *European Union Review, 8*(1–2), 29–42.

Villena, V. H., Revilla, E., & Choi, T. Y. (2011). The dark side of buyer–supplier relationships: A social capital perspective. *Journal of Operations Management, 29*(6), 561–576. doi:10.1016/j.jom.2010.09.001

Vos, J., & Achterkamp, M. C. (2015). Bridging the transactional and relational view on management-stakeholder cooperation. *The International Journal of Organizational Analysis, 23*(4), 652–663. doi:10.1108/IJOA-07-2013-0692

Walley, N., & Whitehead, B. (1994). It's not easy being green. *Reader in Business and the Environment, 36*(81), 4.

Williamson, O. E. (1983). Credible commitments: Using hostages to support exchange. *The American Economic Review, 73*(4), 519–540.

Williamson, O. E., & Ouchi, W. G. (1981). The markets and hierarchies and visible hand perspectives. *Perspectives on organization design and behavior*, 347-370.

Wood, D. J., & Logsdon, J. M. (2002). Corporate citizenship: From individuals to organizations. *The Ruffin Series, 3*, 59–94.

Wuyts, S., & Geyskens, I. (2005). The formation of buyer–supplier relationships: Detailed contract drafting and close partner selection. *Journal of Marketing, 69*(4), 103–117. doi:10.1509/jmkg.2005.69.4.103

Zaheer, A., McEvily, B., & Perrone, V. (1998). Does trust matter? Exploring the effects of interorganizational and interpersonal trust on performance. *Organization Science, 9*(2), 141–159. doi:10.1287/orsc.9.2.141

Zaheer, A., & Venkatraman, N. (1995). Relational governance as an interorganizational strategy: An empirical test of the role of trust in economic exchange. *Strategic Management Journal, 16*(5), 373–392. doi:10.1002mj.4250160504

KEY TERMS AND DEFINITIONS

Collaboration: Here, a synonym of cooperation.

Procedural Justice or Fairness: Means that the procedures and criteria used for making and executing decisions are unbiased, ethical, transparent, and correctable. Procedural justice focuses on the means by which outcomes arise from the interaction between exchange partners.

ENDNOTES

1. Albert O. Hirschman (1970) makes distinction between alternative reacting ways to degradation business and consequently dissatisfaction with organizations: one, "exit", is for the member to quit the organization or for the customer to choose competing products, and the other, "voice", is for members or customers to agitate for change *ab intra*.
2. Docility, here, means a tendency to accept knowledge and advice that is through social channels.

3 To observe the stakeholder network with a stakeholder relational ontology implies focusing on the relationships to identify the stakeholders.

4 For a complete discussion of the history of the concept of corporate social responsibility, see Preston (1988).

5 Agency Theory affirms these alternatives are associated with costs, depending on activity characteristics (complexity of the assignment, monitoring ability, correspondence between outcome and suppliers behaviour etc.).

6 Klein (2000, p. 430) says literally 'codes of conduct are awfully slippery'.

7 In a general sense, procedural justice or procedural fairness means that the procedures and criteria used for making and executing decisions are unbiased, ethical, transparent and correctable. procedural justice focuses on the means by which outcomes arise from the interaction between exchange partners.

8 Here, contractual refers to the fact that the terms of the supplier-buyer agreement include conditions more extant than mere adherence to the code of conduct or other CSR practices.

9 Another approach is for companies to engage in *consortia*, independent groups of companies, such as suppliers, customers and even competitors, who come together to share skills, resources, costs and access to each other's markets, as the *keiretsu* corporations in Japan or Korean *chaebol* (Ring and Van de Ven, 1994; Dyer,1996).

10 Supplier development may not be sufficient to guarantee preferential access to scarce supply resources; to become a customer of choice, buyers need to build relational capital. Without this supporting mechanism, the returns on their supplier development investments likely are negligible, or even negative. (Bloksma, et al., 2013, p. 1303)

11 OECD (2000) made an investigation of 246 voluntary Codes of Conduct, it was concluded that enhancement of the company's reputation and stronger customer loyalty was a strong motivation for implementing codes.

12 Referred to the examined cases and to be no-generalized to all SMEs.

13 Leppelt et al. (2013) collect customer oriented CSR practices that serve to inform to customer about supplier CSR practices: CSR information at top of corporate website, promotion of CSR-related product features or product lines, target group-specific communication of CSR topics, sustainability report covering the triple bottom line (Elkington 1998), CSR communication strategy in place, active positioning as CSR innovator, CSR-related info material for external and internal use, joint CSR initiatives with NGOs driven by marketing.

Chapter 12
University Social Responsibility:
A Framework That Places It as a Strategic Partner to a European Digital Single Market – The Role of Technology-Based Universities

Doina Stratu-Strelet
Universitat Politècnica de València, Spain

Anna Karina López-Hernández
Universitat Politècnica de València, Spain

Vicente Guerola-Navarro
Universitat Politècnica de València, Spain

Hermenegildo Gil-Gómez
Universitat Politècnica de València, Spain

Raul Oltra-Badenes
Universitat Politècnica de València, Spain

ABSTRACT

This chapter highlights the role of technology-based universities in public-private partnerships (PPP) to strengthen and deploy the digital single market strategy. Moreover, it analyzes how these collaboration channels have link knowledge management as a tool for sustainable collaboration. Given the need to establish collaboration channels with the private sector, according to Lee, it is critical to establish the impact of sharing sophisticated knowledge and partnering at the same time. This chapter wants to highlights two relevant aspects of PPP: on the one hand, the importance of integrating the participation of a technology-based university with three objectives: (1) the coordination, (2) the funding management, and (3) the dissemination of results; and the other hand, the participation private sector that is represented by agile agents capable to execute high-value actions for society. With the recognition of these values, the investment and interest of the projects under way are justified by public-private partnership.

DOI: 10.4018/978-1-7998-4833-2.ch012

INTRODUCTION

The presence of universities information and communication technologies are incrementing the global needs to pursue new knowledge and new value creation through cooperation instead competitiveness (Hagen, 2002). The understanding of the interorganizational collaboration relationship between Public-Private Partnership (PPP) is considered knowledge-based add high value to the network involved and breed new knowledge (Boland et al., 2012). The role of PPP applied in the development of digital infrastructure contributes to the European Market transition processes to a standardized Digital Single Market (DSM). The present chapter is based on the analysis of the role of universities as strategic knowledge management partners in European Consortiums to DSM initiative funded by Connecting Europe Facility Telecom- European Commission.

The relevance of knowledge management in collaborative environments is an essential tool that add value and strength the sustainable advantage between the partners involved (Pérez et al., 2004). Collaboration between government, universities and business starts to be a common condition to effective results, where the role of government is to ensure the economic growth on a national, regional level and beyond. Meanwhile the universities provide knowledge and ensure the dissemination of the results and the private sector is on charge provide practical solutions and contribute to the increment of competitiveness (Kesting et al. 2018).

The current European PPP conditions create a symbiotic environment that enhance the university involvement. However, to what extend the government-university-industry alliance meet success regarding technology-based projects? On the one hand, the PPP application and effectiveness in the creation of a sustainable DSM pursues the application of knowledge shared and corporate social responsibility under collaborative conditions. On the other hand, the DSM partnerships funding require adequate guidelines to accomplishing the goals and its sustainability in the long term where the digital innovation is centered on knowledge sharing.

BACKGROUND

Collaboration between entities and knowledge management in network contexts is considered as a key success factor in the development of shared information management units. Recently the attention has been focused on how organizations learn from their partners and develop new capabilities through knowledge sharing throughout collaborative endeavors (Tesavrita et al.2017). Due to knowledge management in collaborative environments is considered as an enabler that facilitate trusts, learning, formalization of new skills and capabilities to develop new processes and to improve the organizational performance (Dixon et al. 2014; Lee & Choi, 2003; Lopez Hernandez et al. 2019).

Knowledge management processes are established, as well as the incentives and barriers that arise when public and private entities come together in extensive agreements for the management and governance of joint action and work segments (Emerson et al. 2012). Sharing knowledge basis are used to developing and launching technological based projects, driven through European Consortiums. These consortiums focus on integrating regions and removing cross-border barriers (Boland et al., 2012).

The European Consortiums that works toward the DSM development is integrated by private-public organization that sometimes are leaded by other public entities such as –universities and government, and private sector, that most of them are Electronic Data Interchange Providers (EDI Providers). The

PPP trending pursues transparency, interaction and continuity in infrastructure development projects and where the university presence gets a strategical relevance to make the knowledge management more accountable (Ng et al. 2013).

PUBLIC-PRIVATE PARTNERSHIP (PPP)

The study of public-private partnership (PPP) pursues to develop know-how from the stakeholders in collaboration and produce relevant impacts (Kassen, 2018). The PPP refers to the procurement approach where the project is executed with a broader span of contractual relationships between public and private sectors to provide and asset or a service (Guarnieri and Gomes, 2019). It is a procurement model to deliver public infrastructure and service crossing various sectors.

The European technology-based consortiums lead the improvement of digital sectors (Ettlie et al., 2006), where the developed product is an advanced and critical technology in the deployment of key cross-border solutions of commonly used services. The collaboration through PPP consortium in cross-border digital services such as, eDelivery, eIdentification and eInvoicing are key elements that strengthen the DSM. Moreover, these collaboration channels have link knowledge management as a tool (Schmitz et al., 2017).

The transitions of the PPP as subject of study since the 1970s, as can be seen in the Web of Science (WoS), one of the most recognized repositories of scientific information in all fields of research. However, it is from the year 2000 when interest in his study rebounds and becomes a matter of preferential interest with exponential growth until today, going from 112 citations in 2000 to 14,317 appointments in 2019 (year still I live on the date of this study and live ahead). Likewise, the growing interest in the exponential growth of publications from the 60s of the year 2000 to the 884s of the year 2018 and the 776s of the year 2019 is observed (even this last year open to more publications).

Nonetheless, Hodge and Greve (2007) debate on the effectiveness of PPPs in terms of performance ranks and indicators. It states that, despite the growing popularity of PPPs as a tool agreement for the development of powerful national and international draft infrastructure, it is necessary to review the history of results before promoting this type of consortium for the development of large technical infrastructures and functional. Similarly, Zhang (2005) lists and studies the differences between known PPPs, together with the results obtained, virtues and problems encountered, and with all of this the critical success factors (CSFs) for PPP in infrastructure development.

DIGITAL SINGLE MARKET (DSM)

The Digital Single Market structure is currently regulated mainly by the European Parliament and of the Council of 23 July 2014 Regulation on electronic identification and trust services for electronic transactions in the internal market. The Connecting Europe Facility Telecom (CEF Telecom) is a European financial mechanism to support the development of high performing, sustainable and efficiently interconnected trans-European networks in the field of digital services. The main goal of this key funding instrument is to fill the current gap in the European investments to fill the missing links in Europe's digital backbone (European Commission, 2019).

The European Commission established the Innovation and Networks Executive Agency (INEA) who control and run the Connecting Europe Facility and parts of Horizon 2020, creating the conditions to incentive the new capabilities building to the cross-border digital service integration (Antonioli et al. 2013). There is a clear interest and recognition of the benefits of integrating services in a DSM, however among the projects associated with the European initiative of CEF Telecom. However, there persist certain barriers in the PPP implementation in telecommunication sector (Guerola-Navarro et al., 2019).

The DSM is topic that despite having an exponential development also since 2000, has not yet reached levels of interest similar to those of PPP, probably because it is a subject of study much more specific than PPP, but probably with the same future travel potential for both. Reviewing the number of publications and citations collected in WoS, we can see the growing interest of DSM that has gone from the 97 citations that it had in 2000, to 952 in 2019 (not yet finished). In terms of publications, it has gone from 17 in 2000 to 120 in 2018 and 65 (still with many live publications) in 2019.

Much has been studied on the digitization of services in countries and in territorial integrations such as the European Union. However, there are cases of studies undertaken in other region, such as the case of Ivanova et al., (2019) who exposed a case study on the development of the digital economy and e-government of the Russian Federation. Regarding the European cases, Cascón (2019) considers its application to adapt the intellectual property legislation to the new problems and demands that arise in the Digital Single Market, about the interest of new business models introduction on the mass exploitation of content protected by copyright and related rights. It includes other cases related to access information for academic, research and cultural stakeholders.

Recent studies on the special characteristics of emerging businesses based on the digital market led the need to evaluate the existing regulatory framework and propose potential alternative solutions. The dynamics of the European DSM is associated to define a strategy and digital indicators that contribute the PPP impacts assessment. (Lutz 2019). Also, Bodiroga and Martinovic (2019) state that Online platform services in the sharing economy represent an important segment of the digital market. which might not hinder innovation and development of digital technology and services.

RESEARCH DESIGN AND HYPOTHESIS

This research focused on case studies of Public-Private Partnerships which are boosting innovation on the DSM in Europe. Moreover, there is a strong presence of the university where processes explicitly demand knowledge management as requirement. The main objective of these PPP projects is to implement interoperable generic services (eDelivery, eIdentification and eInvoicing) connected to the Core Services Platforms of the CEF building blocks of as part of a trans-European digital infrastructure. Their aim to support exchanges and collaboration between citizens, business and public authorities. The first hypothesis is:

Hypothesis One: The European Union is committing to financing public-private partnerships within the implementation (deployment, uptake and update) of its Digital Single Market.

The collaboration among government-university-business pursue a common goal: more digital opportunities based on interoperability and standardization of cross border digital services implemented by PPP model. The selected projects aim to reduce transaction costs across the different Member States, allowing all the consortium to participate and contribute on intense know-how production, and where knowledge management is fully valuable in cross-border activities. The role of universities is to promote a standardized a singular digital network created and maintained by a public authority because one of their main roles is the dissemination of the results of the management of technical knowledge produced by the interaction of the partners. The second hypothesis is:

Hypothesis Two: The European Union is supporting Universities with a technological profile in the Digital Single Market implementation.

DATABASE ANALYSYS OF PPP

The research design involves a literature review complemented with a database analysis of the PPP regarding eDelivery, eIdentification and eInvoicing consortiums, in the period 2014-2019. The procedure consisted to identify the calls and identified their requirements where specificity consist on public-private collaboration. Then analyze the CEF Telecom proposals selected for funding searching for the presence of technology-based university. From them we identified 110 projects, where just the 42% were participated by technology-based university, and other 58% is divided between government institutions actions (33 projects) and government-private (31 Projects) collaboration. The following table introduces the number of CEF Actions projects where technology-based universities participated as beneficiaries.

Additionally, three case studies regarding to eDelivery, eIdentification and eInvoicing respectively, where a technology-based university act as coordinator, were selected. These case studies were selected due to the implication of the Polytechnic University of Valencia in the and the authors in the coordination of the three actions, having first-hand management and research experience in the Digital Single Market and CEF Telecom. The main goal is to capture the current practices of the implementation of the Digital Single Market through partnerships among public and private actors and to analyze the potential of integrating a universities with a technological profile as strategic partner because one of their main roles is the dissemination of the results of the management of technical knowledge produced by the interaction of the partners.

CASE STUDIES: THREE EUROPEAN PROJECTS

Action Entitled 'Promoting the AS4 Between PEPPOL Access Points Around EU (AS4EU)'

The main objective of AS4EU Action it to promote the use of the eDelivery DSI (Digital Service Infrastructure) amongst public and private public entities by implementing four PEPPOL Access Points. The private entities of the AS4EU consortium developed their eDelivery solution according to the EU Core Service platform, improving their electronic registered delivery services in compliance with European requirements and having access to the cross-border exchange of electronic documents according to the technical European technical framework. The main data of the European project composed by public and private actors is shown in Table 1.

Figure 1. CEF Actions with technology-based universities' participation
Source: European Commission, 2020

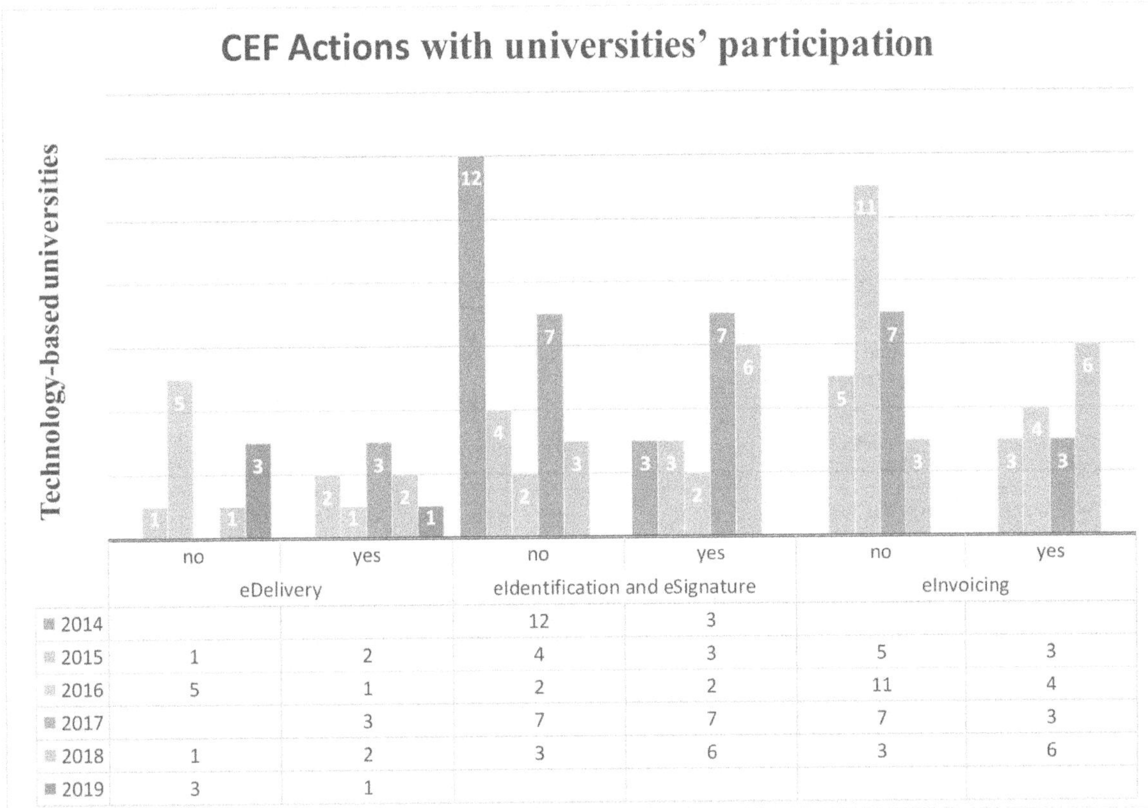

The knowledge produced throughout the entire duration of the project regarding the technical implementation was organized and stored under the leadership of the university with the collaboration of the partners due to their responsibility for communicating knowledge produced for the specific tasks they

Table 1. AS4EU Action characteristics

Action Characteristics	Data
CEF Telecom Call	eDelivery (CEF-TC-2017-2)
Location of the Action	Belgium, Ireland, Italy, Spain, United Kingdom
Action Number	2017-EU-IA-0104
Agreement Number	INEA/CEF/ICT/A2017/1527217
Number of partners	6
Public University	1
EDI Providers	4
Other	1

Source: (Grant Agreement of the Project)

have been assigned. To better identify the specific strategic role of each partner in the deployment of the Digital Single Market the data shown in Table 2 is analyzed by project's activities and its specific tasks.

Table 2. Project's Roles

Activity Title	Tasks	Leadership Role	Implementing Role
Project Management	Administrative and Funding Management, Knowledge Management, Quality Assurance	University	University
Technical Requirements	Consortium Support to the Technicians, Technical Requirements, Implementation Strategy	University	Private technical consultant
AS4 and SMP Implementation and Integration	AS4 Server Configuration, Protocol Implementation and Connection to the SMP, Interoperability Tests and Conformance Tests.	University	EDI Providers
Project Communication, Dissemination and Exploitation	Communication Plan and Project website implementation, Dissemination and Exploitation actions.	University	University and Private technical consultant

Source: (Grant Agreement of the Project)

Action Entitled 'Cross-border Authentication in European Cloud Platforms According to the eIDAS Regulation-Eurologin'

This action integrated the eID DSI (Digital Service Infrastructure) into the system of 4 EDI Providers. The 4 EDI providers will be connected to 4 different eIDAS nodes making the eID services available for cross-border authentication in a production environment. The main objective of this Action is promoting the uptake and the use of the eID DSI, facilitating access to the services provided by the 4 EDI Providers to all european citizens and business using the national eID, and the ensure the cross-border mobility and support the Digital Single Market. The main data of this project are shown in Table 3.

As well as, the previous action, the knowledge produced throughout the entire duration of the action regarding the Digital Single Market, was organized, stored and disseminated in order to facilitate new connections to the eIDAS node in the future. In this action, the University could reuse the knowledge

Table 3. EUROLOGIN Action characteristics

Action Characteristics	Data
CEF Telecom Call	eIdentification (CEF-TC-2018-1)
Location of the Action	Belgium, Cyprus, Italy, Spain, United Kingdom
Action Number	2018-EU-IA-0026
Agreement Number	INEA/CEF/ICT/A2018/1633379
Number of partners	6
Public Universities	1
EDI Providers	4
Others	1

Source: (Grant Agreement of the Project)

gained in its previous action. Table 4 will summarize the activities, identifying the role of each actor of the Public-Private Consortium financed by the European Commission to implement the eIDentification service as part of the DSM.

Table 4. EUROLOGIN project's Roles

Activity Title	Tasks	Leadership Role	Execution Role
Project Management	Administrative and Financial Management, Knowledge Management, Quality Assurance	University	University
Communication and Dissemination	Action Website and Social Media, Communication and Dissemination Plan, Consortium Sustainability Plan.	University	University and Private technical consultant
Requirement Analysis and Software Design	Technical Coordination, Implementation Strategy and eIDAS node assistance, Technical Analysis and Software Design.	University	EDI Providers and a Private technical consultant
Connection of cloud platform and the eIDAS nodes for cross-border authentication	EDI Provider's platforms connected to 4 different eIDAS Node (Belgian, Italian, Cypriot and British eIDAS Node)	EDI Providers	EDI Providers

Source: (Grant Agreement of the Project)

Action Entitled 'Implementing the European Standard in Consolidated eInvoicing Cloud'

In this action, the main goal is to support the EDI Providers and their clients to meet the European eInvoicing Standard (EN) for cross-border transactions according to the Directive 2014/55/EU, achieving advanced eInvoicing functionalities: Send/receive invoices compliant with the European Norm, translate invoices into different formats for the data integration in Enterprise Resource Planning (ERP) systems, real time reporting of invoices and cross-border transactions guarantying the interoperability with ERP systems. The main data of the Action is presented as shown in Table 5.

Table 5. EURINV Action characteristics

Action Characteristics	Data
Location of the Action	Belgium, Finland, France, Germany, Ireland, Italy, Netherlands, Slovakia, Spain
Action Number	2018-EU-IA-0073
Agreement Number	INEA/CEF/ICT/A2018/1760846
Number of partners	12
Public Universities	2
EDI Providers	8
Others	2

Source: (Grant Agreement of the Project)

As in the other actions, the University has the responsibility, among others, to manage the knowledge of this action regarding the eInvoicing Building Block and the outcomes produced by the interactions of the different actors, disseminating the results to a broad audience. As well as, disseminating the potential impact of the adoption of the eInvoicing solution in terms of efficiency for business and public institutions as part of the European Digital Single Markets. The importance of integrating a University in a Public-Private partnership as a strategic actor can be analyzed in Table 6.

Table 6. EURINV Project's Roles

Activity Title	Tasks	Leadership Role	Execution Role
Coordination and Management	Action Coordination, Technical requirements and solution design	University	University
Technical requirements and solution design	Consortium support to the technicians, Analysis of national context and Solution Design, Test Plan, Review of Access points of the EDI Providers.	Private technical consultant	EDI Providers
Dissemination of the Action	Definition and preparation of the Dissemination Plan, Action website implementation, Dissemination of the Action by each beneficiary.	University	University, EDI Providers and Private technical consultant.
EDI Providers eInvoicing Solutions adapted to European Norm	Implementation Planning, Software Implementation, Quality tests, Use case demonstration.	EDI Providers	EDI Providers and a Private technical consultant
Consortium interoperability tests and validation for cross-border transactions	Interoperability tests, Conformance tests and Internal Quality Assurance	Private technical consultant and University	EDI Providers

Source: (Grant Agreement of the Project)

SOLUTIONS AND RECOMMENDATIONS

The results of these case studies lead to several observations that have been identified as critical success factors for deploying the Digital Single Market as a high technology project based on a common knowledge (in this case, the Digital Services Infrastructures) shared among public and private actors.

Firstly, the main objective of empowering the uptake of the DSI by financing projects composed by public and private actors is to ensure alignment between policy implementation and between the operational practices. CEF Telecom is dedicated to deploying common infrastructures across the European Union, providing functioning services which will be maintained over time by the European Commission, making the market more interconnected and effective based on collaboration between citizens, business and public authorities.

Secondly, during the creation of the consortium it is needed a common vision and goals within the actors involved for participating in a Public-Private Partnership with the aim of deploying the Digital Single Market. The main benefits for using common Digital Services Infrastructures for the services provider (public or private actor) reduce costs, cut the time-to-market processes and facilitate interoperability by creating an efficient flow between private and public investment. To digital companies as partners ensures a successful collaboration translate in more opportunities based on interoperable and secure cross-border services, for instance in transactions with public sector in short time and cut the costs. Finally, to public administrations, the benefits are to enable and spread digital infrastructure focus on efficiency, easy operability and instant transactions among different States Members.

Thirdly, the contractual public-private arrangements in high technological projects avoid risks of the complexity operations through signing legal contract among the partners. The partnership relationship among the consortium participants ensure to share the risks and the benefits among the partners. The contract or Consortium Agreement includes mechanisms of control the execution of all the operations.

In conclusion, the public and private actors integrating the partnership should have the ability to learn and acquire the need of knowledge from other organizations in a collaboration environment. For that reason, a strategic partner as a technology-based University is fundamental to guarantee a successful knowledge management.

CONCLUSION

In consideration of the previous analysis based on the CEF Telecom Actions (eIdentification, eDelivery y eInvoicing) and the three case studies selected in each of the three areas these are the following conclusion:

1. The relevance to developing a common digital strategy involving all Member States is essential to create and deploy generic services. These efforts enable a faster interoperability to the market and encouraging economic transactions in the European region.
2. It is confirmed that the European Commission financial priority is given to projects based on Public-Private Partnerships.
3. The model of Public-Private Partnerships is positive for know-how transfer regarding technical knowledge among different organization.
4. The university role in a Public-Private Partnership is considered a strategical condition that guarantee and ensure the adequate project results responsibility according to the European Commission's policy and the operation of the services purposes.
5. The highlight of technology-based universities participation ensures the knowledge management and dissemination the results to the public and private organizations. Additionally, the public-private relationship improves the corporate social responsibility of the Consortium because very clear rules the it.

ACKNOWLEDGMENT

This research was supported by the Innovation and Networks Executive Agency (INEA) [grant number: INEA/CEF/ICT/A2018/1633379]; [grant number INEA/CEF/ICT/A2018/1760846].

REFERENCES

Antonioli, D., Mancinelli, S., & Mazzanti, M. (2013). Is environmental innovation embedded within high-performance organisational changes? the role of human resource management and complementarity in green business strategies. *Research Policy*, *42*(4), 975–988. doi:10.1016/j.respol.2012.12.005

Bodiroga-Vukobrat, N., & Martinovic, A. (2019). Challenges of Providing Services on the EU Digital Market. *Zbornik Pravnog Fakulteta Sveucilista u Rijeci*, *40*(1), 37–58. doi:10.30925/zpfsr.40.1.2

Boland, W. P., Phillips, P. W. B., Ryan, C. D., & McPhee-Knowles, S. (2012). Collaboration and the Generation of New Knowledge in Networked Innovation Systems: A Bibliometric Analysis. *Procedia: Social and Behavioral Sciences*, *52*, 15–24. doi:10.1016/j.sbspro.2012.09.437

Carlsson, S. A. (2001). Knowledge management in network contexts. *ECIS 2001 Proceedings*, 9.

Cascón, F. C. (2019). Hacia un nuevo marco normativo de los derechos de autor y derechos conexos en el mercado único digital. *Revista Electrónica de Direito*, *19*(2), 1–10. doi:10.24840/2182-9845_2019-0002_0001_

Dixon, S., Meyer, K., & Day, M. (2014). Building dynamic capabilities of adaptation and innovation: A study of micro-foundations in a transition economy. *Long Range Planning*, *47*(4), 186–205. doi:10.1016/j.lrp.2013.08.011

Emerson, K., Nabatchi, T., & Balogh, S. (2012). An integrative framework for collaborative governance. *Journal of Public Administration: Research and Theory*, *22*(1), 1–29. doi:10.1093/jopart/mur011

Ettlie, J. E., & Pavlou, P. A. (2006). Technology-based new product development partnerships. *Decision Sciences*, *37*(2), 117–147. doi:10.1111/j.1540-5915.2006.00119.x

European Commission. (2019). *Innovation and Networks Executive Agency*. https://ec.europa.eu/inea/en

Guarnieri, P., & Gomes, R. C. (2019). Can public procurement be strategic? A future agenda proposition. *Journal of Public Procurement*.

Guerola-Navarro, V., Oltra-Badenes, R., Gil-Gómez, H., & Stratu-Strelet, D. (2019). Eid@ Cloud: Integración De La Identificación Electrónica En Plataformas Europeas En La Nube De Acuerdo Con El Reglamento Eidas. *3C Empresa, 8*(3).

Hagen, R. (2002). Globalization, university transformation and economic regeneration: A UK case study of public/private sector partnership. *International Journal of Public Sector Management*, *15*(3), 204–218. doi:10.1108/09513550210423370

Hodge, G. A., & Greve, C. (2007). Public–private partnerships: An international performance review. *Public Administration Review*, *67*(3), 545–558. doi:10.1111/j.1540-6210.2007.00736.x

Ivanova, V., Poltarykhin, A., Szromnik, A., & Anichkina, O. (2019). Economic policy for country's digitalization: A case study. *Entrepreneurship and Sustainability Issues*, *7*(1), 649–661. doi:10.9770/jesi.2019.7.1(46)

Kassen, M. (2018). E-participation actors: Understanding roles, connections, partnerships. *Knowledge Management Research and Practice*, *00*(00), 1–22. doi:10.1080/14778238.2018.1547252

Kesting, T., Muros, V. G., & Vogt, H. (2018). Reflecting on the status quo of university business collaboration in Europe: An overview of current trends and challenges. *International Journal of Technology Management*, *76*(1–2), 1–9.

Lee, H., & Choi, B. (2003). Knowledge Management Enablers, Processes, and Organizational Performance: An Integrative Wiew and Empirical Examination. *Journal of Management Information Systems*, *20*(1), 179–228. doi:10.1080/07421222.2003.11045756

Lopez Hernandez, A. K., Fernandez-Mesa, A., & Edwards-Schachter, M. (2019). Team collaboration capabilities as a factor in startup success. *Journal of Technology Management & Innovation*, *13*(4), 13–23. doi:10.4067/S0718-27242018000400013

Lutz, S. U. (2019). The European digital single market strategy: Local indicators of spatial association 2011–2016. *Telecommunications Policy*, *43*(5), 393–410. doi:10.1016/j.telpol.2018.10.003

Ng, S. T., Wong, J. M. W., & Wong, K. K. W. (2013). A public private people partnerships (P4) process framework for infrastructure development in Hong Kong. *Cities (London, England)*, *31*, 370–381. doi:10.1016/j.cities.2012.12.002

Pérez López, S., Manuel Montes Peón, J., & José Vázquez Ordás, C. (2004). Managing knowledge: The link between culture and organizational learning. *Journal of Knowledge Management*, *8*(6), 93–104. doi:10.1108/13673270410567657

Schmitz, P., Francesconi, E., Hajlaoui, N., & Batouche, B. (2017, June). Towards a Public Multilingual Knowledge Management Infrastructure for the European Digital Single Market. In LDK Workshops (pp. 33-42). Academic Press.

Tesavrita, C., Suryadi, K., Wiratmadja, I. I., & Govindaraju, R. (2017). Intra-organizational and inter-organizational knowledge sharing in collaborative learning process: A conceptual framework for SME. *2017 4th International Conference on Industrial Engineering and Applications, ICIEA 2017*, 187–191. 10.1109/IEA.2017.7939204

Zhang, X. (2005). Critical success factors for public–private partnerships in infrastructure development. *Journal of Construction Engineering and Management*, *131*(1), 3–14. doi:10.1061/(ASCE)0733-9364(2005)131:1(3)

Chapter 13
Understanding Relationships Between Corporate Social Responsibility, Organizational Identification, and Ethical Organizational Behavior:
USVI Retail Employees' Perceptions

Kenny Hendrickson
University of the Virgin Islands, USA

Aletha Baumann
University of the Virgin Islands, USA

Robert H. Thompson
University of the Virgin Islands, USA

ABSTRACT

This chapter presents elements of a student-faculty collaborative research that quantitatively examined the predictive relationships of retail employees' perceptions of corporate social responsibility (PCSR) and organizational identification (POI) on their perceptions of ethical organizational behavior (PEOB). One hundred and eighteen retail employees from 20 companies in the United States Virgin Islands (USVI) participated in an online survey. While no predictive relationship was found, the findings of this study identified significant relationships between retail employees PCSR, POI, and perceived ethical organizational behavior PEOB. The strongest association was discovered between PCSR and POI. Thus, this chapter spotlights a need for retail organizations to focus on the potential of employees' PSCR and POI in creating more authentic and responsible organizational environment.

DOI: 10.4018/978-1-7998-4833-2.ch013

INTRODUCTION

Over the past decade, corporate social responsibility (CSR) has generated mainstream attention in both the private- and public-sectors. Although there is no singular or agreed upon definition of the concept, as recognized by Dahlsrud (2008), CSR can be defined as a private-sector organizations' integration of societal concerns, and social accountability and obligations within its operations. Additionally, CSR can be considered as positive and socially responsible interactions with organization's stakeholders (e.g., customers, society, managers, suppliers, creditors, shareholders) that go beyond its economic interest (Turker, 2009, p. 413). Like other parts of the world, many companies in the Caribbean have also sought to increase their CSR presence due to public encouragement, pressuring, and incentivization from customers, suppliers, investors, activist organizations, the media and government.

Unfortunately, there is limited research to support these important and necessary social movements within the Caribbean Region. Additionally, most CSR research has generally centered on macro-level/external organizational initiatives (i.e., community-directed philanthropy, eco-efficiency, charities, humanitarian concerns) and profitable marketability (i.e., brand image). There is a definite contextual space and need for more micro-level/internal CSR research in the Caribbean. Specifically, more attention must be given to employees and their perceptions. Lindsey Hall, Baker, Andrews, Hunt and Rapp (2016) confirmed that employees are undoubtedly integral to any service or product delivery, especially regarding sales or retail (p. 25). Thus, more investigations should be performed to gain empirical evidence-based knowledge on the associations between employee perceptions of CSR and their organizational identity and performance.

This chapter provides an account of a student-faculty collaborative exploratory research study on employee-centered CSR. A successful student-faculty collaborative research is rooted in evenly co-operative efforts that offer an enriching learning experience and produces useful and usable scientific knowledge on a specific subject matter. As the retail industry is the largest industry in the United States Virgin Islands (USVI, a Caribbean territory of the United States), this research study quantitatively investigated the hypothetical possibilities of a predictive relationships between USVI retail employees' perceived corporate social responsibility (PCSR) and perceived organizational identification (POI) towards their perceived ethical organizational behavior (PEOB). This chapter presents the key segments of the study: background/literature review, methodology, empirical findings, limitations, future directions, and conclusion.

BACKGROUND/LITERATURE REVIEW

There are global surges of research interests in corporate social responsibility (CSR), due to an increased demand for comprehensive knowledge by external organizational stakeholders (e.g., customers, society, government, managers, suppliers, creditors, shareholders). CSR knowledge is the awareness and understanding of an organization's CSR culture, initiatives, and engagement in positive contributions to society (Kim, 2019). CSR knowledge can also be defined as context-based information (internal and external) about organizational CSR acquired through experiences and observations (Kim, 2019). Lai, Yang and Wu (2015) affirmed that "increasing volume of research investigating CRS" is due to the "academic or practical values" of CRS knowledge (p. 554). As of 2018, there have been 2,386 publications in CSR from 100 countries (Low & Siegel, 2019, p. 8).

Relevantly, Kim and Scullion (2013) noticed a research gap resulting from the lack of attention to or absence of the "significance of employees" in CSR knowledge (pp. 7-8). Gangi, Mustilli and Varrone (2019) noted that the use of CSR knowledge based "employee-facing initiatives" offers private organizations a capacity to "enhance the design and implementation of CSR efforts that match the needs of stakeholder" (p. 125). Zaher (2014) considered that employee-centered knowledge is based on employees' experience interacting with each other along with management. Interestingly, Kim and Scullion (2013) observed motivation and human resources management (HRM) as the focal point to employee-centered CSR knowledge. From the perspectives of motivation and HRM, Aju and Beddewela (2019) asserted that employee-centered CSR knowledge is contingent on information obtained and used in providing for employees' social needs (e.g., participation, training, professional development and mentoring) (p. 1).

In their work, Slack, Corlett, and Morris (2015) found that employee-centered CSR knowledge offers essential information on employees' level of CSR organizational engagement (p. 538). They contended that the significance of employee-centered CSR knowledge languishes within "morale, recruitment and retentions" (2015, p. 537). Relevantly, Slack et al. (2015) spotlighted that not enough research has been done to examine the significance of employees' perceptions in regards "their engagement with CSR" (p. 537). To put things into clearer perspective, further literary examination of CSR knowledge based on employee perceptions is extended.

CSR Knowledge Based on Employee Perceptions

Öberseder, Schlegelmilch, and Murphy (2013), Sharma, Sharma and Devi (2009), and Stoian and Zaharia (2012) observed that employees' perceptions are often overlooked in understanding various CSR relational (related) organizational context and domains. Kim, Kim, Choi, and Phetvaroon (2019) drew attention to the opportunity that the higher employees' perception of organizational practices, "the higher the levels of their service behavior" (p. 85). Edinger-Schons, Lengler-Graiff, Scheidler, and Wieseke (2019) found that employees are "the primary communicators" of an organizations' CSR (p. 359).

Sharma et al. (2009) considered CSR as representing "a strong commitment to social obligations and internalization throughout the organizational culture which lays emphasis on the execution of the obligations towards the employees and involving them in responsible endeavors" (p. 207). Within the employee-domain, CSR offers organizations opportunities to develop and express socially conscious organizational cultures (Rupp et al., 2006). Singhapakdi, Lee, Sirgy, and Senasu (2015), in their research on the incongruity between organization's and employees' CSR orientation, viewed socially responsible employees as attracted to organizations that are socially responsible (p. 64).

Descriptive and cognitive in nature, employee's perceptions are invaluable to CSR knowledge. Based on the employee perception theory, an employee's assessment of the work environment, influences the effectiveness of their behavior (Chatzoglou, Chatzoude, Amarantou, & Aggelidis, 2017). Employee perception can be considered as diagnoses and individual self-assessment of organizational culture, beliefs, practices and procedures (Morrison, 1995; Schneider, Parkington, & Buxton, 1980). Prutina and Šehić (2016) noted that employee buy-in is what determines if CSR will develop within an organizational culture "or remain a PR gimmick" (p. 239).

In understanding how employees are affected by CSR, Glavas and Goodwin (2013) pointed to a need for studying employees' perceptions. Employee perception is the cognitive process by which organizational information, experiences, and events are interpreted (Dy & Caballero, 2015, p. 33). In their view of employee perception, Dy and Caballero (2015) considered perceptions to be different from organizational reality. Manning (1982) provided an interesting perspective to organizational reality. He also stated that organizational reality is "conceptual fiction" (1982, p. 130). From this outlook, organizational reality is a reference point for employee perceptions (Manning, 1982p. 130).

Agarwal and Dewan (2016) shared that employee perception offers individual views of situations inclusive of sensory impressions. Glavas and Goodwin (2013) advanced that perception is a stronger driving force of employees' organizational behavior than actual or dominant organization reality. Glavas and Kelley (2014) deliberated that employee perceptions are primarily centered around "what the organization is doing to others" as well as how they are directly treated by the organizations (p. 167). López-Fernández, Romero-Fernández, and Aust (2018) advanced that perceptions are crucial in determining the level (and degree) of impact that organizational policies and practices have on employee behavior.

Lastly, Shin, Hur and Kang (2016) offered a simple and helpful truth, that people generally behave according to their perceptions of reality, and not reality itself (p. 2). This truth recognizes perception as a central "driving force" of an employee's individual behavior (2016, p. 2). In tandem, Farouq, Rupp and Farouq (2017) offered a vital theoretical contribution, that internal CSR (i.e., practices of stewardship with employees) and organizational identification are predictive to several behavioral outcomes (i.e., ethical) (p. 978). They noted that employees' perceptions of "CSR influence identification via more focused judgements, which serve to catalyze behaviors" (2017, p.961). Consequently, the need for further discussions, on employee- perceived corporate social responsibility (PCSR), perceived organizational identification (POI) and perceived ethical organizational behavior (PEOB), is required to support this study's hypothesis:

PCSR

Perceived corporate social responsibility (PSCR) of an organization can be described as the perceptions of "a company's strategies and operating practices on the well-being of all its key stakeholders and the natural environment" (Glavas & Goodwin, 2013, p. 17). Jeon, Lee and Jeon (2020) depicted PSCR as more of "perceived societal or stakeholder obligations" (p. 2). From this standpoint, private-sector organizations are not only obligated to protect its best interests and sustainability, but also the welfare and sustainability of society (p. 3). Jeon et al. (2020) also offered three dimensions to PSCR (as a stakeholder obligation), "economy (socially required), ethics (socially expected), and environment (socially desired)" (p. 3).

Interestingly, Othman and Hafez (2019) favored considering PSCR to be a stake holder obligation (p. 1179). A classical view of CSR depicts it as an unnecessary added expense that cannot create economic value or profit (Chaudary et al., 2016, p. 264). Thus, the conceptualizing of PSCR as a stakeholder obligation reduces responsibility of private-sector organizations, to only consider a portion of the community that were identified as capitalist stakeholders (i.e., shareholders, customers, government and media; entities and individuals, who will ensure strong market position, reputation and/or accessibility to crucial resources) (Huang and Gardner, 2007; Othman and Hafez, 2019, p. 1179). Succinctly, Rupp and Mallory (2015) defined stakeholder obligation, in terms of PSCR, as an organization's course of action compelled by "moral, ethical and humanitarian ideals" (p. 214).

While organizational PCSR can be recognized through stakeholder obligations (macrofoundations), there is a need to understand the microfoundations of PSCR. Microfoundational PSCR can be considered as the utilization of employees' cognition and learning in shaping their views of organizational-level CSR (Gavetti, 2005). Ng, Yam and Aguinis (2019) posed that microfoundational or employee PSCR is formed through employees' "emotions, attitudes, and behavior targeted at the organization", in tandem with "summed CSR activities in which their organizations have participated" (p. 108).

Similarly, De Roeck, El Akremi, and Swaen (2016) asserted that employee PCSR suggests reflections or assessments of employees' influence on their "organization's discretionary actions intended to improve the well-being of their stakeholders" (p. 1142). Azim (2016) confirmed that employee PCSR is "personal evaluations and interpretations of an organization's CSR activities, which may differ from the actual CSR practices of the organization" (p. 211). Attention can be directed to the subjectivity of employee PCSR strong influences on an employee's attitudes and behaviors (Azim, 2016). Glavas and Goodwin (2013) believed that employee PSCR offers a more altruistic and authentic position for cognizing "what CSR behaviors their organization is—or is not—engaged in" (p. 17). As a practice, employee PCSR is an affirmation to which employees perceive an organizational support of their CSR-related activities (Choi & Yu, 2014, p. 350). Lee, Park, and Newman (2012) staked that effective activities of PCSR centers on supporting organizational initiatives associated with their employees' social causes.

An employee PCSR can be better appreciated and realized as an element of an employee's identity and self-description built on the organizations' good social reputation and CSR initiatives (Shuli & Suwandee, 2017). Additionally, PCSR can be regarded as employees' usage of their organization's CSR (i.e., image and initiatives) as positive benchmarks for their organizational performance and commitment. Wang, Xu and Wang (2020) found that employee PCSR "promoted positive behaviors" (e.g. commitment, identity, creativity) and "reduces employee's negative attitudes and behaviors" (e.g. cynicism, turnover intention, deviation) (p. 1).

POI

The findings of Farooq, Farooq, and Jasimuddin (2014) suggested that CSR investments in employees are strong predictors of "employees' attitudes in terms of organizational identification and knowledge sharing behavior" (p. 923). Glavas and Goodwin (2013) argued that the nature of PCSR is a stronger determinant of organization identification (OI) than reality (p. 17). Zaman and Nadeem (2019) and Lythreatis, Mustafa and Wang (2019) contended that OI is the sharing of similar goals and value by organizations and their employees. Tian and Robertson (2019) and John, Qadeer, Shahzadi, and Jia (2019) also found that organizational identification (OI) creates a serial mediation between employees' PCSR and workplace behaviors.

Mael and Ashforth (1992) clearly defined organizational identification "as a perceived oneness with an organization and the experience of the organization's successes and failures as one's own" (p. 103). Additionally, Su and Swanson (2019) offered that organizational identification is a form of social identification for employees, in which they are given a degree of freedom to find attributional similarities between themselves and their organization of employment as well as fulfill their need to belong (pp. 439-440). Employees' actual or perceived organizational identification (POI) generates a sense of organizational loyalty, devotion, and virtuousness that influences their actions, behaviors, and levels of commitment (Foster & Hyatt, 2007, p. 197).

Tolukan, Sahin, and Koç (2016) found that the levels of employee POI are based on employees' internalization of contributions to their organization "performance and efficiency" (p. 380). Additionally, Cha, Chang and Kim (2014) found that "the fit and misfit between organizational and personal prosocial identities significantly affect the employees' perceived organizational identification" (p. 67). Prosocial identities revolve around a self-perception of caring and giving. Cha et al. emphasized that employees'

POI strengthens as their organizational prosocial identities increase towards personal prosocial identities. Conversely, Cha et al. also noted that POI weakens as employees perceive their organizational and personal prosocial identities to be separate.

Kirpik and Akdemir (2019) considered the dimensionality of POI. They categorized POI as comprising of primarily cognitive and affective dimensions. The affective dimension of POI is associated with an employee's feelings about group membership (e.g., pride and belongingness) (p. 6). The affective dimension is also related an employee's irrational feelings of meaningful organizational connectedness (Tanis & Beukeboom, 2011, p. 6). Carmeli, Gilat, and Weisberg (2006) described the cognitive dimension of POI as perceptions of oneness based on shared experiences (e.g., organizational success and failures) and the self-reflection entrenched with organizational standing (p. 95). Johnson and Morgeson (2005) defined cognitive dimensions of POI as thoughts or beliefs regarding self-definition based on a social reference (p. 2). Kirpik and Akdemir (2019) found that cognitive identification increases as affective identification increases. Tanis and Beukeboom (2011) also considered the need for adding other dimensions to POI. They noted that POI could inclusive of dimensions of belongingness that is triggered by situational cues.

Su and Swanson (2019) also extended that PCSR can increase an employee's desire for stronger organizational identification. They believed that the connection between CSR and OI fulfills an employee's desire for positive recognition as well as obtaining opportunities for "ingroup uniqueness" and greater societal reputation (p. 440). Tian and Roberston (2019) found that PCSR not only stimulates employee's empathy (sharing of feelings towards the well-being of others), but also increases their likelihood of identifying with their organizations. Explicitly, Glavas and Godwin (2013) posited that "employees are affected by CSR through organizational identification" (p. 16). They posited that employees' perceptions have a greater impact on CSR and organizational identification than actual reality. Glavas and Godwin (2013) clearly referred to organizational identification as cognitive linking of employees with the organization. This relational connection creates for employees a symbiotic relationship of shared experiences with their organizations. Thus, the more employees positively perceive corporate social responsibility (PCSR), the stronger their POI will be and vice versa (Glavas & Godwin, pp. 18-19).

PEOB

Additional to their views on the relationship between PCSR and POI, Galvas and Godwin (2013) also suggested that an employee's PCSR affects their organizational behaviors (p. 17). Glavas and Kelley (2014) discerned a lack of clarity regarding specific "mechanisms through which employee perceptions of CSR impact their work behaviors and attitudes" (p. 175). An employee's organizational behavior can be considered as patterns of behaviors that encompass organizational performance, effectiveness, and achievements. It can also be viewed as rational decisions in achieving outcomes through the allocation of personal and organization resources (e.g., time and energy) (Slocombe, & Dougherty, 1998, p. 471). Succinctly, Miron, Erez, and Naveh (2004) emphasized employees' organizational behavior can also be considered as contingent on personal characteristics (e.g., traits, trust, satisfaction, loyalty, intentions, commitment, innovation and creativity) in conjunction with their interpretation or perceptions of organization characteristics and requirements.

Understanding the role of ethics in employee organizational behavior can be challenging. Ethical behavior can be described as a "format of activity in accordance with social norms such as fairness and honesty" (Demirgüneş, 2015, p. 27). Rubel, Kee, Quah, and Rimi (2017) considered ethical organizational behavior to require an adherence to organizational procedures protocols and most importantly formal codes and guidelines of conduct (pp. 62-63). Rubel et al. also recognized that an organizational ethical climate (e.g., organizational policies, practices, and procedures) directly and indirectly influence "employee's perception of how things are done in the organization" (p. 63). Sukmadi (2019) affirmed that ethics in organizational behavior is contingent on behaviors in accordance with institutional norms of morality. Singhapakdi and Vitell (2007) defined institutional ethics as "the degree to which an organization explicitly and implicitly incorporate ethics into its decision-making processes" (p. 284).

However, Cleek and Leonard (1998) offered that institutional ethics is not a primary determinant or influence of employees' ethical behavior. Whitaker and Godwin (2013) proclaimed in their work, that "the current research agenda for exploring ethical behavior in organizations" is driven by "studies that can help derive organizational-level prescriptions for positively influencing individual-level morality and moral motivation" (p. 61). Thus, ethical behavior can be viewed as a function of individual characteristics and various environments (e.g., work, social, legal, professional, personal) as mediated through an individual decision-making process that filters and processes information. Ethical behavior as a socio-cognitive construct is directed by employees' perceptions. Askew, Beisler, and Keel (2015) deliberated that perceptions of ethical organizational behavior or perceived ethical organizational behavior (PEOB) is influenced by employees' perceived treatment, organizational culture and environment, the organizational behavior itself (pp. 109 & 110).

Low and Siegel (2019) reported that ethics and social responsibility have become the main source of employee-centered CSR publications. Their justification for this opinion is based on their study, in which they descriptively analyzed bibliometric data (from 2000-2018) obtained from Scopus using a social network analysis and visualization tool. Their findings noted "the main domain of employee-centered CSR arises from business ethics and corporate social responsibility" (p. 16). Potocan, Mulej, and Nedelko (2013) believed ethical behavior can define an organization's CSR (p. 498). They identified that, as overlying practical concepts, CSR and ethics are "socially negotiated, contextual with different meanings and relationships" (p. 491). Singhapakdi et al. (2015) also asserted that CSR is equivalent to institutionalized ethics (p. 61).

Strikingly, Ferrell, Harrison, Ferrell and Hair (2019) asserted that CSR research has "conflicting and incomplete" views on the relationship between organizational ethics and CSR (p. 491). Glavas (2016) found that although CSR and ethics are related concepts, the research on ethics and CSR has been developed mostly separately from one another. Ferrell et al. proposed that the interrelationship of business ethics and CSR is generally found in matters related to marketing, branding and organizational identification. However, Bowen, Freidank, Wannow, and Cavallone (2018) offered a plausible definition of perceived ethical organizational behavior (PEOB) that is contextualized by PCSR and POI. Bowen et al. (2018) defined PEOB as a "diagnostic belief that consequently influences attitudes toward the organization" (p. 89). PEOB is "a degree to which individuals perceive the company as behaving responsibly both socially and ethically" (p. 91). Bowen et al. (2018) believed PEOB to be a means of organizational identification based on personal knowledge, what "individual perceives to be true" (87). Finally, Bowen et al. mentioned that PEOB is inclusive of individually formed ethical beliefs based on a discernment on the degree of situational and behavioral controllability.

METHODOLOGY

At the time of this study, few research has examined the impact of retail employees' perceived corporate social responsibility (CSR) and perceived organizational identification (POI), on their organizational behavior. Furthermore, no research on this topic exists in the retail industry within the US Virgin Islands. Thus, the research discussed in this chapter hypothesized that USVI retail employees' PSCR and POI are predictively related to their PEOB. The null hypothesis considered employees' PSCR and POI as not having predictive relationships with PEOB. As seen Figure 1, the study's conceptual model spotlights a belief of definite interrelationship between PCSR, OI, and PEOB. The model also offers the possibility that employees' PCSR and OI have a predictive relationship with PEOB. Accordingly, this study utilized a correlational research design. The correlational research design can be used to investigate (e.g. describe, measure and verify) associations between two or more variables or score sets (Creswell, 2014). The correlational research design employed in this study incorporated descriptive, multiple regression and correlational analysis.

Figure 1. Employees' PCSR, POI, and PEOB model

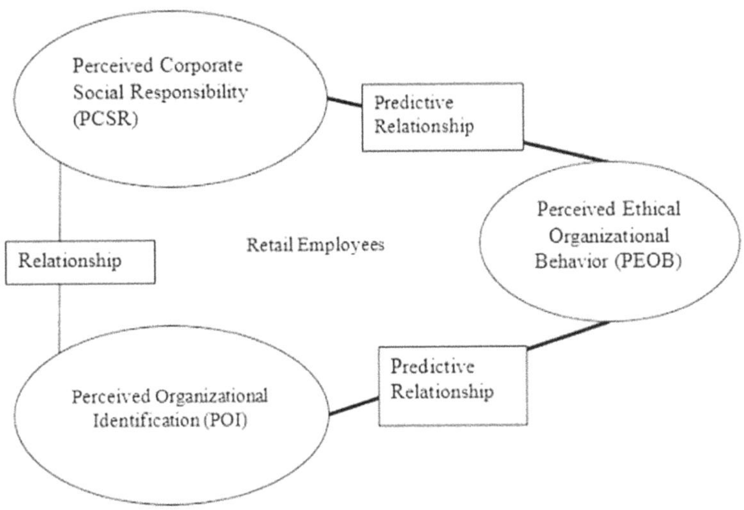

A modified cross-sectional survey method was used to obtain the perceptions of employees at one particular point in time. A modified cross-sectional survey method has several benefits. The modified cross-sectional survey method provides a more reflective picture of variations within a population of participants. It also affords opportunities to determine the relationships between variables and their effect on each other at the same time (Awobamise, 2018). Anatory (2015) also noted that a modified cross-sectional survey method offers openings "to see the reality more closely," based on practical approach of collecting data within social situations (e.g., attitudes, perceptions, experiences) and facilitates openings to draw generalizations (p. 18). For this reason, a modified cross-sectional design was used to gather and analyze the data collected based upon an online distributed survey. The following sections (i.e., selection of participants, instrument and data collection) provides detailed discussion of the research techniques employed in this current study:

Selection of Participants

The unit of analysis for this study was retail employees. Retail accounts for a high percentage of total establishments and employment in the USVI. Data were collected using a three-scale questionnaire (30 item) from 118 full and part-time adult employees working within 20 randomly selected retail organizations with at least 5 and not more than 50 employees. The sample size used in this study was considered enough and having adequate power. Van Voorhis and Morgan (2007) confirmed that a better power to detect a small effect size is 30 participants per variable (p. 48). The retail organizations selected for examination was taken from USVI Department of Licensing and Consumer Affairs website organizational database of licensed businesses on St. Croix (DCLA, 2017). As seen in Table 1, most of the 118 participants worked in small companies (under 10 employees). On average, 54.3% of employees in each organization were surveyed.

Table 1. Selection of participants

Company	Number of Employees	Number Surveyed	Number Surveyed
1	12	5	41.7%
2	50	18	36.0%
3	5	4	80.0%
4	15	13	86.7%
5	8	8	100%
6	6	5	83.3%
7	6	3	50.0%
8	9	5	55.6%
9	10	2	20.0%
10	10	3	30.0%
11	10	1	10.0%
12	48	9	18.75%
13	5	3	60.0%
14	5	4	80.0%
15	5	2	40.0%
16	25	10	40.0%
17	5	5	100.0%
18	7	3	42.9%
19	12	7	58.3%
20	15	8	53.3%

Instrument

The survey for this research consisted of three scales that provided participants' views on PCSR, POI, and PEOB. To begin with, a modified CSR scale developed by Turker (2009) was used to measure employee PCSR. The scale consists of 18 items (as seen in Table 2) divided into four-dimensional structure of corporate social responsibility, including CSR to social and nonsocial stakeholders, employees, customers, and government. The grouping items were as follow:

- First dimension- including CSR to society (6th item and 8th items), natural environment (1stand 3rd items), future generations (2nd and 4th items) and nongovernmental organizations (NGO) (5th and items);
- Second dimension-CSR to employees (9th, 10th, 11th, 12th, and 13th, items);
- Third dimension- CSR to customers (14th, 15th, and 16th items);
- Fourth dimension- CSR to government (17th and 18th items).

The CSR was shown to be reliable, α =.090. It also has a collective significance of the 0.0001. Turker's analysis of the scale found that employees "ignored their self-interest and perceived that the CSR to society, natural environment, future generations, and NGOs are more important than CSR related to themselves" (2009, p. 424) In this study, the CSR scale used a Likert scale from 1 to 7, with 1 (*strongly agree*) to 7 (*strongly disagree*). Each item, rated on a 7-point Likert scale, is summed to yield a total

Table 2. Corporate Social Responsibility Scale

1. Our company participates in activities which aim to protect and improve the quality of the natural environment.
2. Our company makes investment to create a better life for future generations.
3. Our company implements special programs to minimize its negative impact on the natural environment.
4. Our company targets sustainable growth which considers future generations.
5. Our company supports nongovernmental organizations working in problematic areas.
6. Our company contributes to campaigns and projects that promote the well-being of the society.
7. Our company encourages its employees to participate in voluntarily activities.
8. Our company emphasizes the importance of its social responsibilities to the society.
9. Our company policies encourage the employees to develop their skills and careers.
10. The management of our company is primarily concerned with employees' needs and wants.
11. Our company implements flexible policies to provide a good work & life balance for its employees.
12. The managerial decisions related to the employees are usually fair.
13. Our company supports employees who want to acquire additional education.
14. Our company respects consumer rights beyond the legal requirements.
15. Our company provides full and accurate information about its products to its customers.
16. Customer satisfaction is highly important for our company.
17. Our company always pays its taxes on a regular and continuing basis.
18. Our company complies with legal regulations completely and promptly.

Source: Turker (2009)

score to yield a total summed score within a range from 18 (strongly disagreeing with all items) to 126 (strongly agreeing with all items).

Secondly, the Organizational Identification Scale, developed by Mael and Ashforth (1992), was used to measure POI. The scale consists of 6 items. The purpose of the scale was to evaluate the extent to which participants feel oneness or a belongingness to an organization and perceives themselves as a member or stakeholder (Mael & Ashforth). Based on previous usage, the organizational identification scale has had a range of reliability scores between .81 to .85 (Demirgüneş, 2015; Mael & Ashforth, 1992). The OI scale used a Likert scale from 1 to 7, with 1 (*strongly disagree*) to 7 (*strongly agree*). Each item, rated on a 7-point Likert scale, is summed to yield a total score to yield a total score within a range from 6 (strongly disagreeing with all items) to 42 (strongly agreeing with all items).

Table 3. Organizational Identification Scale

1. When someone criticizes the organization/company where I work, it feels like a personal insult. 2. I am very interested in what others think about the organization/company where I work. 3. When I talk about this organization/company, I usually say 'we' rather than 'they'. 4. This organization/company's successes are my successes. 5. When someone praises this organization/company, it feels like a personal compliment. 6. If a story in the media criticized the organization/company, I would feel embarrassed.

Source: Mael and Ashforth (1992)

Lastly, the ethical behavioral scale, developed by Fraedrich (1993), was utilized to examine PEOB. This ethical behavioral scale is a modified version of a scale by Ferrell and Skinner (1988). The scale was designed specifically for assessing retail managers' unethical behavior. The scale was also written with items applicable to the general population of retail employees. The scale exhibits internal validity by way of confirmatory factor analysis, with standardized loading scores of each item .46 and greater, surpassing the minimum threshold of .30. Normally, ethical behavioral scale is scored from 1 to 7, with 1 (*strongly agree*) to 7 (*strongly disagree*). In this study, the ethical behavioral scale was reverse scored to measure retail employees' ethical behavior rather than unethical behavior. Thus, a Likert scale from 1 to 7, with 1 (*strongly agree*) and 7 (*strongly disagree*). The participants selections is summed to yield a total score ranging from 6 (strongly disagreeing with all items) to 56 (strongly agreeing with all items).

Data Collection

Google Forms was used to host the survey instrument for this research study. Google Forms guaranteed trouble-free accessibility of the instrument, by its delivery as an electronic survey or e-survey (e.g., available online). Google Forms allowed participants' responses to be collected from the e-survey and automatically appended as data into a spreadsheet. Google Forms also created a uniform resource locator (URL), so that the e-survey could be shared via email. The collected data, within the spreadsheet,

Table 4. Ethical Behavior Scale

1. In my job I sometimes compromise my beliefs to do my job the way the company wants me to do it. 2. Sometimes I report only part of the truth to my boss. 3. Sometimes I have to alter things (documents, time cards, etc.) in order to please the company. 4. Sometimes I have to break company policy to do what's necessary. 5. Sometimes I say one thing even though I know I must do something else. 6. Sometimes I claim to have done something when I have not.

Source: Fraedrich (1993)

was displayed as anonymized entries. By using Google Forms as the host, the collected data were only accessible via a Google account.

Upon obtaining university permission (i.e., Institutional Review Board) and organizational access (i.e., receipt of permission from the owner or manager of the company), the e-survey was disseminated using electronic tablet-based and email-based data collection methods. Electronic tablet-based data entailed the completion of an e-survey utilizing an electronic tablet. Electronic tablet-based data collection provided participants an opportunity to complete the survey individually and confidentially, upon reviewing the consent notice which was the first section in the online survey and consenting. Electronic tablet-based data collection also eliminates "additional data entry step that can result in delays, costs, and errors" (Crane et al., 2007, p. 115). Thus, the participants were asked to review the consent notice, which was part of the survey, and checked that they consented to participate. The student-researcher remained available to answer any questions prior to and after the e-survey was completed. Email-based data collection method was also used in this study. Email invitations were sent to the retail employees. The invitation included the survey's URL.

EMPIRICAL FINDINGS

As the collected data was quasi-interval, variables were created by summing participants responses to the items within the various scales (e.g. Corporate Social Responsibility, Organizational Identification and Ethical Behavioral). Descriptive statistics observed were the median and mean as measures of central tendency and standard deviation as a measure of variance. Multiple regression analysis was used to examine the relationships between the independent variables and dependent variables. Asatryan & Asamoah (2014) noted that multiple regression aids researchers in "determining the value of the dependent variables as it is influenced by the alterations in the value of the independent variable as other extraneous variables are controlled" (p. 11). The multiple regression analysis was appropriate because all variables were continuous and there was only one outcome variable. Inferential statistics observed were a t-test to compare means, Pearson's r, r^2, $y = b_0 + b_1x_1 + b_2x_2 + \text{error}$ (of a forced entry multiple linear regression equation), F and the correlation. The adjusted R^2 will observed as it can be used to identify the explanatory power of the regression model with multiple predictors. The Cronbach's alpha was set at .05 to reduce the chances of Type I error.

Table 5 presents descriptive statistics of the total summed scores for each variable, based on the retail employees' responses. The mean of total summed score for PEOB is 32.83. The highest total summed

Table 5. Descriptive Statistics

Variables	Mean	Median	Minimum	Maximum	Standard Deviation	Reliability
PEOB	32.83	36	11	42	8.040	.75
POI	21.78	22	6	30	6.030	.83
PCSR	81.81	83.50	18	126	28.95	.96

PEOB = Perceived Ethical Organizational Behavior; POI = Organizational Identification; PCSR = Perceived Corporate Social Responsibility

score for PEOB was 42 and the lowest total summed score was 11 with a standard deviation of 8.040. Secondly, the mean of total summed score fore OI is 21.78. The highest total summed score for OI was 30 and the lowest total summed score was 6 with a standard deviation of 6.030. Thirdly, the mean of the total summed score fore PCSR is 81.81. The highest total summed score for PSCR was 126 and the lowest total summed score was 18 with a standard deviation of 6.030. As seen in Table 5, each scales' results were shown to be reliable, with POI $\alpha = .83$, PCSR $\alpha = .96$, and PEOB $\alpha = .75$. Mallery and George (2003) provided a more expansive rules of thumb for Cronbach's Alpha: > 0.9 = excellent, > 0.8 = good, > 0.7 acceptable, > 0.6 questionable, > 0.5 poor, < 0.5 unacceptable (p. 231). Thus, PSCR's reliability is excellent. POI's reliability is good. PEOB's reliability is acceptable.

Table 6 offers the results of association PCSR, POI and PEOB. The coefficient of determination R^2, F ratio, beta coefficients and t-statistics for the regression model and summarized results of the dependent variable on the explanatory variables, as seen in Table 6. The results indicate an R^2 of .70, Adjusted R^2 of. 50 and an F value of 4.327, which is significant at the 0.015. This means that the linear regression explains 70% of the variance in the data. The model accounts for 54% of the variation. The F-test is significant. Thus, it can be assumed that the model could explain a significant amount of the variance in PEOB. Furthermore, the analysis showed a significant intercept. However, none of the coefficients

Table 6. Regression Analysis Results

Variable	Beta Coefficient	Standard Error	Beta t values	Significance
Constant	24.749	2.958		.000
POI	.176	.129	1.372	.173
PCSR	.052	.027	1.936	.055

R Square = 0.70
Adjusted R Square = .54
F Value = 4.327
F significance = .015
PEOB = Perceived Ethical Organizational Behavior; OI = Organizational Identification; PCSR = Perceived Corporate Social Responsibility

were found to be significant. The intercept within a multiple regression model provides a mean for the response, if all explanatory variables yield a value 0.

Significant predictive relationships between PSCR, POI and PEOB could not be identified from the analysis results. The predictive relationship between PSCR and PEOB was just beyond acceptable limits (e.g. a level significance of .055). Nevertheless, the results of the correlation (as seen in table 7) showed that PSCR was observed to be significantly associated with POI (medium at .359) and PEOB (small at .234). OI was also observed to be significantly associated to PEOB (small at .199). Figure 2 shows a model of the relationships between of the USVI retail employees PCSR, POI and PEOB.

LIMITATIONS/FUTURE DIRECTIONS

Despite this study's implications and potential contributions to CSR research, there were several limitations. All data was self-reported and collected within multiple sites with different workplace conditions and cultures, as well as during a time period that the US Virgin Islands faced great cultural and economic disruptions, due to Hurricanes Irma and Maria. It is possible that the diverse workplace cultures, hurricane disasters as well as other factors had great impact on the retail employees' PCSR, POI and PEOB. Moreover, there might have also been research limitations, as a result of social desirability bias. Social desirability bias occurs, "whereby the respondents may respond to what they perceive as desirable because employees may fear to expose too much information about the company" (Jie & Hasn, 2018, p. 5). All attempts were made to minimize limitations, using anonymous instruments and the giving of respondents' assurance about their confidentiality within the consent notice. Additionally, the sample size and its convenient nature of participants is not be reflective of all retail employees. Thus, the study's results might not be generalizable. Nonetheless, this study's outcomes provide insight into PCSR, POI and PEOB, even considering the inherent limitations pertaining to the used sampling frame.

Lastly, due to PCSR's significance-level (.055) and its stronger relationship between POI as well, multi-collinearity was suspected. Multicollinearity is a problem, which the independent variables (e.g. PCSR and POI) would be highly correlated with another. Multicollinearity could have undermined the statistical significance of the PCSR (Field, 2013). However, multicollinearity was not an issue based on a face-value review of correlations showing no correlations between variables nearing a concerning

Table 7. Pearson Correlation Analysis Results (N=118)

Variables	PEOB	OI	PSCR
PEOB	1.000	.199****	.234**
POI	.199****	1.000	. 359*
PSCR	.234**	.359*	1.00

* Correlation is significant at the .000 level (2-tailed).
** Correlation is significant at the 0.005 level (2-tailed).
*** Correlation is significant at the .01 level (2-tailed).
**** Correlation is significant at the 0.05 level (2-tailed).
PEOB = Perceived Ethical Organizational Behavior; POI = Organizational Identification; PCSR = Perceived Corporate Social Responsibility

Figure 2. USVI retail employee PCSR, POI, and PEOB model

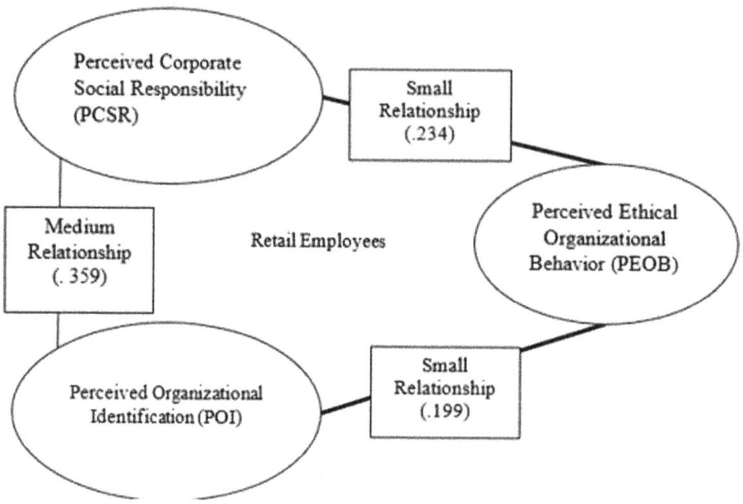

.80 or .90, as well as acceptable variance inflation factor (1.148) and tolerance levels (.871). VIF scores should be less than ten and on average not much greater than 1, and tolerance levels should be above 0.2 (Field, 2013, pp. 342-343). Score distributions for each variable were non-normally distributed. For POI, the skewness was -0.741 (*SE* = .223) and kurtosis was .101 (*SE* = .442). For PCSR, the skewness was -0.356 (*SE* = .223) and kurtosis was -0.885 (*SE* = .442). For EB, the skewness was -0.996 (*SE* = .223) and kurtosis was 0.217 (*SE* = .442).

A study, done by Raut and Pawar (2016), identified that demographics of the retail employees influences their performance and could also be a potential identifier of skills. Elias (2004) found that demographic factors play a major role in perceptions of corporates social responsibility. This study did not differentiate between full-time and part-time employees. Full-time employees may be more motivated to identify with their organization in order to justify their time investment in an organization. These two variables will be considered regarding PCSR, POI and PEOB in future studies. Future research on PCSR, POI and PEOB will also include other demographic predictors such as duration of employment, organization size, age, gender, education, retail-position, employee satisfaction and income level. Inclusion of demographic data allows for a more complete examination of PCSR, POI and PEOB within various parameters and patterns.

CONCLUSION

This chapter showcased a successful student-faculty collaborative CSR research effort within the social sciences. This research study provided an opportunity for student-learning within applied research, as well as academic, scholarly and professional development. It also gave the student researcher a practical and "hands-on" experience in implementing an actual organizational research and employee assessment. Dotterer (2002) acknowledged student-faculty collaborative research initiatives as "the pedagogy for the twenty-first century" (p. 81). Gregerman, Lerner, Von Hippel, Jonides and Nagda (1998) believed that student-faculty collaborations provide opportunities to increase student retention and success in higher education. Equally, student-faculty collaborative research efforts provide opportunities for the faculty to pass on research skills and techniques. Low and Siegel (2019) found that not enough collaborative research is found amongst CSR scholars. Consequently, the success of this present research can be found, not just in terms of the findings, but in the completed collaborative multi-disciplinary effort.

Regarding the research findings, this study intended to determine if USVI retail employee's PSCR and POI have a predictive relationship with their PEOB. No significant predictive relationship could be determined. Nonetheless, this study provided further insight into the relationship between PCSR, OI and PEOB. Although some relationships were found between the variables in this study. The strongest association with this study was found between the USVI retail employees' PSCR and POI. The findings of this chapter suggest that USVI retail organization should focus on retail organizations CSR initiatives (i.e. workshops, written policies as well as promotional and participative activities) to support employees' development of their PSCR and OI. Considerations of employee's PSCR and OI have the potential of building authentic organizational cultures of acceptable, ethical, empathetic, and socially responsible organizational behavior. Further studies on the relationship between PSCR and POI within the Caribbean may prove to be a fertile area of future CSR research.

REFERENCES

Agarwal, R. N., & Dewan, P. (2016). A study on the relationship of employee satisfaction VIZ-A-VIZ attitude and perception of the employees towards the organization. *International Journal of Information, Business and Management, 8*(1), 67-87.

Aju, O., & Beddewela, E. (2019). Afrocentric attitudinal reciprocity and social expectations of employees: The role of employee-centred CSR in Africa. *Journal of Business Ethics*, 1–19. doi:10.100710551-019-04346-x

Anatory, J. (2015). Consumer preferences for mobile carriers in Tanzania: A case of group, family, age and gender. *International Journal of Computer Applications, 115*(16), 16-23. doi: 10.1.1.695.5880

Asatryan, R., & Asamoah, E. S. (2014). Perceived corporate social responsibility (CSR) activities and the antecedents of customer loyalty in the airline industry. *Scientific Papers of the University of Pardubice. Series D, Faculty of Economics and Administration, 32*(3).

Askew, O. A., Beisler, J. M., & Keel, J. (2015). Current trends of unethical behavior within organizations. *International Journal of Management & Information Systems (Online), 19*(3), 107. doi:10.19030/ijmis.v19i3.9374

Astaryan, R., & SelaseAsamoah, E. (2014). Perceived Corporate Social Responsibility (CSR) Activities and the Antecedents of Customer Loyalty in the Airline Industry. *Scientific Papers of the University of Pardubice. Series D, Faculty of Economics & Administration, 21*(32), 5–17. https://www.upce.cz/sites/default/binary_www_old/fes/veda-vyzkum/fakultni-casopisy/scipap/archiv/e-verze-sborniku/2014/scipap-32-9-2014.pdf#page=6

Awobamise, A. O. (2018). Increased consumerism in a Networked-Nigeria: A Study on the effect of e-malls and social media on youth spending. *Editors-in-Chief, 1*(2), 40–55. doi:10.34624/jdmi.v1i2.949

Azim, M. T. (2016). Corporate social responsibility and employee behavior: Mediating role of organizational commitment. *Review of Business Management, 18*(60), 207–205. doi:10.7819/rbgn.v18i60.2319

Bowen, M., Freidank, J., Wannow, S., & Cavallone, M. (2018). Effects of severity and knowledge of a scandal on the perceived ethical behavior and attitude towards a company: An intercultural perspective on CSR management. In *Excellence in Services: 21th International Conference* (pp. 83-103). EISIC-LeCnam.

Carmeli, A., Gilat, G., & Weisberg, J. (2006). Perceived external prestige, organizational identification and affective commitment: A stakeholder approach. *Corporate Reputation Review, 9*(2), 92–104. doi:10.1057/palgrave.crr.1550014

Cha, J., Chang, Y. K., & Kim, T. Y. (2014). Person–organization fit on prosocial identity: Implications on employee outcomes. *Journal of Business Ethics, 123*(1), 57–69. doi:10.100710551-013-1799-7

Chatzoglou, P., Chatzoudes, D., Amarantou, V., & Aggelidis, V. (2017). Examining the antecedents and the effects of CSR implementation: An explanatory study. *EuroMed Journal of Business, 12*(2), 189–206. doi:10.1108/EMJB-12-2016-0035

Chaudary, S., Zahid, Z., Shahid, S., Khan, S. N., & Azar, S. (2016). Customer perception of CSR initiatives: Its antecedents and consequences. *Social Responsibility Journal, 12*(2), 263–279. doi:10.1108/SRJ-04-2015-0056

Choi, Y., & Yu, Y. (2014). The influence of perceived corporate sustainability practices on employees and organizational performance. *Sustainability, 6*(1), 348–364. doi:10.3390u6010348

Cleek, M. A., & Leonard, S. L. (1998). Can corporate codes of ethics influence behavior? *Journal of Business Ethics, 17*(6), 619–630. doi:10.1023/A:1017969921581

Crane, H. M., Lober, W., Webster, E., Harrington, R. D., Crane, P. K., Davis, T. E., & Kitahata, M. M. (2007). Routine collection of patient-reported outcomes in an HIV clinic setting: The first 100 patients. *Current HIV Research, 5*(1), 109–118. doi:10.2174/157016207779316369 PMID:17266562

Creswell, J. W. (2014). *Research design: Qualitative, quantitative, and mixed methods approaches* (4th ed.). Sage.

Dahlsrud, A. (2008). How corporate social responsibility is defined: An analysis of 37 definitions. *Corporate Social Responsibility and Environmental Management, 15*(1), 1–13. doi:10.1002/csr.132

DCLA. (2017). *Government of United States Virgin Islands Department of Licensing and Consumer Affairs (DCLA)*. Retrieved from https://dlca.vi.gov/

De Roeck, K., El Akremi, A., & Swaen, V. (2016). Consistency matters! How and when does corporate social responsibility affect employees' organizational identification? *Journal of Management Studies, 53*(7), 1141–1168. doi:10.1111/joms.12216

Demirgüneş, B. K. (2015). Ethical behavior of salesperson: The impact of consumer's perception on trust, satisfaction and repeat purchasing behavior. *Turkish Journal of Business Ethics, 8*(1), 26–46. doi:10.12711/tjbe.2015.8.1.0009

Dotterer, R. L. (2002). Student-faculty collaborations, undergraduate research, and collaboration as an administrative model. *New Directions for Teaching and Learning*, *2002*(90), 81–90. doi:10.1002/tl.58

Dy, R. C., & Caballero, R. T. (2015). A Strategic Employee Retention Model Based on Employee Perception. *European Journal of Business and Management*, *2*(5), 25–35.

Edinger-Schons, L. M., Lengler-Graiff, L., Scheidler, S., & Wieseke, J. (2019). Frontline employees as corporate social responsibility (CSR) ambassadors: A quasi-field experiment. *Journal of Business Ethics*, *157*(2), 359–373. doi:10.100710551-018-3790-9

Elias, R. Z. (2004). An examination of business students' perception of corporate social responsibilities before and after bankruptcies. *Journal of Business Ethics*, *52*(3), 267–281. doi:10.1023/B:BUSI.0000037558.74693.d5

Farooq, M., Farooq, O., & Jasimuddin, S. M. (2014). Employees response to corporate social responsibility: Exploring the role of employees' collectivist orientation. *European Management Journal*, *32*(6), 916–927. doi:10.1016/j.emj.2014.03.002

Farooq, O., Rupp, D. E., & Farooq, M. (2017). The multiple pathways through which internal and external corporate social responsibility influence organizational identification and multifoci outcomes: The moderating role of cultural and social orientations. *Academy of Management Journal*, *60*(3), 954–985. doi:10.5465/amj.2014.0849

Ferrell, O. C., Harrison, D. E., Ferrell, L., & Hair, J. F. (2019). Business ethics, corporate social responsibility, and brand attitudes: An exploratory study. *Journal of Business Research*, *95*, 491–501. doi:10.1016/j.jbusres.2018.07.039

Ferrell, O. C., & Skinner, S. J. (1988). Ethical behavior and bureaucratic structure in marketing research organizations. *JMR, Journal of Marketing Research*, *25*(1), 103–109. doi:10.1177/002224378802500111

Field, A. (2013). *Correlational research methods. Discovering statistics using IBM SPSS Statistics* (4th ed.). Sage.

Foster, W. M., & Hyatt, C. (2007). I despise them! I detest them! Franchise relocation and the expanded model of organizational identification. *Journal of Sport Management*, *21*(2), 194–212. doi:10.1123/jsm.21.2.194

Fraedrich, J. P. (1993). The ethical behavior of retail managers. *Journal of Business Ethics*, *12*(3), 207–218. doi:10.1007/BF01686448

Gangi, F., Mustilli, M., & Varrone, N. (2019). The impact of corporate social responsibility (CSR) knowledge on corporate financial performance: Evidence from the European banking industry. *Journal of Knowledge Management*, *23*(1), 110–134. doi:10.1108/JKM-04-2018-0267

Gavetti, G. (2005). Cognition and hierarchy: Rethinking the microfoundations of capabilities' development. *Organization Science*, *16*(6), 599–617. doi:10.1287/orsc.1050.0140

Glavas, A. (2016). Corporate social responsibility and organizational psychology: An integrative review. *Frontiers in Psychology*, *7*, 1–13. doi:10.3389/fpsyg.2016.00144 PMID:26909055

Glavas, A., & Godwin, L. N. (2013). Is the perception of 'goodness' good enough? Exploring the relationship between perceived corporate social responsibility and employee organizational identification. *Journal of Business Ethics*, *114*(1), 15–27. doi:10.100710551-012-1323-5

Glavas, A., & Kelley, K. (2014). The effects of perceived corporate social responsibility on employee attitudes. *Business Ethics Quarterly*, *24*(2), 165–202. doi:10.5840/beq20143206

Gregerman, S. R., Lerner, J. S., Von Hippel, W., Jonides, J., & Nagda, B. A. (1998). Undergraduate student-faculty research partnerships affect student retention. *The Review of Higher Education*, *22*(1), 55–72. doi:10.1353/rhe.1998.0016

Huang, X., & Gardner, S. (2007). A stakeholder view of strategic management in Chinese firms. International Journal of Business Studies: A Publication of the Faculty of Business Administration. *Edith Cowan University*, *15*(1), 1–13.

Jeon, M. M., Lee, S., & Jeong, M. (2020). Perceived corporate social responsibility and customers' behaviors in the ridesharing service industry. *International Journal of Hospitality Management*, *84*, 1–10. doi:10.1016/j.ijhm.2019.102341

Jie, C. T., & Hasan, N. A. M. (2018). Predictors of employees' job satisfaction through corporate social responsibility (CSR) practices in Malaysian banking company. *Advanced Science Letters*, *24*(5), 3072–3078. doi:10.1166/asl.2018.11320

John, A., Qadeer, F., Shahzadi, G., & Jia, F. (2019). Getting paid to be good: How and when employees respond to corporate social responsibility? *Journal of Cleaner Production*, *215*, 784–795. doi:10.1016/j.jclepro.2019.01.074

Johnson, D., & Morgeson, F. (2005). Cognitive and Affective Identification in Organizational Settings. *Proceedings of the 65th Academy of Management Conference*. 10.5465/ambpp.2005.18780944

Kim, C. H., & Scullion, H. (2013). The effect of Corporate Social Responsibility (CSR) on employee motivation: A cross-national study. *Poznan University of Economics Review, 13*(2), 5-30.

Kim, S. (2019). The process model of corporate social responsibility (CSR) communication: CSR communication and its relationship with consumers' CSR knowledge, trust, and corporate reputation perception. *Journal of Business Ethics*, *154*(4), 1143–1159. doi:10.100710551-017-3433-6

Kim, Y. J., Kim, W. G., Choi, H. M., & Phetvaroon, K. (2019). The effect of green human resource management on hotel employees' eco-friendly behavior and environmental performance. *International Journal of Hospitality Management*, *76*, 83–93. doi:10.1016/j.ijhm.2018.04.007

Kirpik, G., & Akdemir, B. (2019). Investigation of perceived organizational identification from different generations: TRC1 (Gaziantep, Adiyaman, Kilis) zone example of organized industrial enterprises. *Journal of Education and Practice*, *10*(22), 74–85. doi:10.7176/JEP

Lai, C. S., Yang, C. F., & Wu, H. C. (2015). The influence of product-harm crises on consumer attribution and identification: The moderating effect of corporate social responsibility. *Procedia: Social and Behavioral Sciences*, *207*, 553–559. doi:10.1016/j.sbspro.2015.10.126

Lee, E. M., Park, S. Y., Rapert, M. I., & Newman, C. L. (2012). Does perceived consumer fit matter in corporate social responsibility issues? *Journal of Business Research*, *65*(11), 1558–1564. doi:10.1016/j.jbusres.2011.02.040

Lindsey Hall, K. K., Baker, T. L., Andrews, M. C., Hunt, T. G., & Rapp, A. A. (2016). The importance of product/service quality for frontline marketing employee outcomes: The moderating effect of leader-member exchange (LMX). *Journal of Marketing Theory and Practice*, *24*(1), 23–41. doi:10.1080/10696679.2016.1089762

López-Fernández, M., Romero-Fernández, P. M., & Aust, I. (2018). Socially responsible human resource management and employee perception: The influence of manager and line managers. *Sustainability*, *10*(12), 4614–4623. doi:10.3390u10124614

Low, M. &Siegel, D. (2019). A bibliometric analysis of employee-centred corporate social responsibility research in the 2000s. *Social Responsibility Journal*. ahead-of-print. doi:10.1108/SRJ-09-2018-0243

Lythreatis, S., Mostafa, A. M. S., & Wang, X. (2019). Participative leadership and organizational identification in SMEs in the MENA Region: Testing the roles of CSR perceptions and pride in membership. *Journal of Business Ethics*, *156*(3), 635–650. doi:10.100710551-017-3557-8

Mael, F., & Ashforth, B. E. (1992). Alumni and their alma matter: A partial test of the reformulated model of organizational identification. *Journal of Organizational Behavior*, *13*(2), 103–123. doi:10.1002/job.4030130202

Mallery, P., & George, D. (2003). *SPSS for Windows step by step: a simple guide and reference*. Allyn & Bacon.

Manning, P. (1982). Organizational work: Structuration of environments. *The British Journal of Sociology*, *33*(1), 118–134. doi:10.2307/589339

Miron, E., Erez, M., & Naveh, E. (2004). Do personal characteristics and cultural values that promote innovation, quality, and efficiency compete or complement each other? *Journal of Organizational Behavior*, *25*(2), 175–199. doi:10.1002/job.237

Morrison, R. S. (1995). Validation of nursing management diagnoses. *Image—the Journal of Nursing Scholarship*, *27*(4), 267–271. doi:10.1111/j.1547-5069.1995.tb00886.x PMID:8530113

Ng, T. W., Yam, K. C., & Aguinis, H. (2019). Employee perceptions of corporate social responsibility: Effects on pride, embeddedness, and turnover. *Personnel Psychology*, *72*(1), 107–137. doi:10.1111/peps.12294

Öberseder, M., Schlegelmilch, B. B., & Murphy, P. E. (2013). CSR practices and consumer perceptions. *Journal of Business Research*, *66*(10), 1839–1851. doi:10.1016/j.jbusres.2013.02.005

Othman, A. A. E., & Hafez, M. G. (2019). A framework integrating corporate social responsibility for marketing architectural design firms in developing countries. Journal of Engineering. *Design and Technology*, *17*(6), 1174–1191. doi:10.1108/JEDT-11-2018-0202

Potocan, V., Mulej, M., & Nedelko, Z. (2013). The influence of employees' ethical behavior on enterprises' social responsibility. *Systemic Practice and Action Research*, *26*(6), 497–511. doi:10.100711213-013-9299-3

Prutina, Ž., & Šehić, D. (2016). Employee's perceptions of corporate social responsibility: A case study of award recipients. *Ekonomska Misao i Praksa*, (1), 239–260.

Raut, U. R., & Pawar, P. A. (2016). Analysis of the relationship between young retail frontline employees and their demographic profile: Skill development perspective. *International Journal of Commerce and Management Research, 2*(3), 124-128.

Rubel, M. R. B., Kee, D. M. H., Quah, C. H., & Rimi, N. N. (2017). Ethical climate and employee turnover intention in the ready-made garment industry of Bangladesh. *Global Business and Organizational Excellence*, *36*(2), 61–73. doi:10.1002/joe.21770

Rupp, D. E., Ganapathi, J., Aguilera, R. V., & Williams, C. A. (2006). Employee reactions to corporate social responsibility: An organizational justice framework. Journal of Organizational Behavior: The International Journal of Industrial. *Occupational and Organizational Psychology and Behavior*, *27*(4), 537–543. doi:10.1002/job.380

Rupp, D. E., & Mallory, D. B. (2015). Corporate social responsibility: Psychological, person-centric, and progressing. *Annual Review of Organizational Psychology and Organizational Behavior*, *2*(1), 211–236. doi:10.1146/annurev-orgpsych-032414-111505

Schneider, B., Parkington, J. J., & Buxton, V. M. (1980). Employee and customer perceptions of service in banks. *Administrative Science Quarterly*, *25*(2), 252–267. doi:10.2307/2392454

Sharma, S., Sharma, J., & Devi, A. (2009). Corporate social responsibility: the key role of human resource management. *Business Intelligence Journal, 2*(1), 205-213. doi: 10.1.1.514.7758

Shin, I., Hur, W. M., & Kang, S. (2016). Employees' perceptions of corporate social responsibility and job performance: A sequential mediation model. *Sustainability*, *8*(5), 1–12. doi:10.3390u8050493

Shuli, G., & Suwandee, S. (2017). Effect of corporate social responsibility on employee job performance: A case study of household products manufacturers in southern China. *Journal of Thai Interdisciplinary Research*, *12*(5), 57–63. doi:10.14456/jtir.2017.43

Singhapakdi, A., Lee, D. J., Sirgy, M. J., & Senasu, K. (2015). The impact of incongruity between an organization's CSR orientation and its employees' CSR orientation on employees' quality of work life. *Journal of Business Research*, *68*(1), 60–66. doi:10.1016/j.jbusres.2014.05.007

Singhapakdi, A., & Vitell, S. (2007). Institutionalization of ethics and its consequences: A survey of marketing professionals. *Journal of the Academy of Marketing Science*, *35*(June), 284–294. doi:10.100711747-007-0030-8

Slack, R. E., Corlett, S., & Morris, R. (2015). Exploring employee engagement with (corporate) social responsibility: A social exchange perspective on organisational participation. *Journal of Business Ethics*, *127*(3), 537–548. doi:10.100710551-014-2057-3

Slocombe, T. E., & Dougherty, T. W. (1998). Dissecting organizational commitment and its relationship with employee behavior. *Journal of Business and Psychology*, *12*(4), 469–491. doi:10.1023/A:1025055122988

Stoian, C., & Zaharia, R. M. (2012). CSR development in post-communist economies: Employees' expectations regarding corporate socially responsible behaviour–the case of Romania. *Business Ethics (Oxford, England)*, *21*(4), 380–401. doi:10.1111/beer.12000

Su, L., & Swanson, S. R. (2019). Perceived corporate social responsibility's impact on the well-being and supportive green behaviors of hotel employees: The mediating role of the employee-corporate relationship. *Tourism Management*, *72*, 437–450. doi:10.1016/j.tourman.2019.01.009

Sukmadi, B. H. (2019). The Effect of Leadership and Ethics on Motivation in The Military. *International Humanities and Applied Sciences Journal.*, *2*(3), 49–57. doi:10.22441/ihasj.2019.v2i3.05

Tanis, M., & Beukeboom, C. J. (2011). Organizational identification and the communication of identity: Effects of message characteristics on cognitive and affective identification. *British Journal of Social Psychology*, *50*(4), 784–791. doi:10.1111/j.2044-8309.2011.02036.x PMID:21749414

Tian, Q., & Robertson, J. L. (2019). How and when does perceived CSR affect employees' engagement in voluntary pro-environmental behavior? *Journal of Business Ethics*, *155*(2), 399–412. doi:10.100710551-017-3497-3

Tolukan, E., Şahin, M. Y., & Koç, M. (2016). The relationship of organizational identification levels of gymnastic trainers and the intention to leave the job. *Electronic Turkish Studies*, *11*(8), 377–398. doi:10.7827/TurkishStudies.9558

Turker, D. (2009). Measuring corporate social responsibility: A scale development study. *Journal of Business Ethics*, *85*(4), 411–427. doi:10.100710551-008-9780-6

VanVoorhis, C. W., & Morgan, B. L. (2007). Understanding power and rules of thumb for determining sample sizes. *Tutorials in Quantitative Methods for Psychology*, *3*(2), 43–50. doi:10.20982/tqmp.03.2.p043

Wang, Y., Xu, S., & Wang, Y. (2020). The consequences of employees' perceived corporate social responsibility: A meta-analysis. *Business Ethics (Oxford, England)*, *29*(3), 1–26. doi:10.1111/beer.12273

Whitaker, B. G., & Godwin, L. N. (2013). The antecedents of moral imagination in the workplace: A social cognitive theory perspective. *Journal of Business Ethics*, *114*(1), 61–73. doi:10.100710551-012-1327-1

Zaher, D. (2014). How to create a knowledge based organizational culture. *The JF Oberlin Journal of Business Management Studies*, *4*, 63–73.

Zaman, U., & Nadeem, R. D. (2019). Linking Corporate Social Responsibility (CSR) and affective organizational commitment: Role of CSR strategic importance and organizational identification. *Pakistan Journal of Commerce and Social Sciences, 13*(3), 704-726.

ADDITIONAL READING

Aguinis, H., & Glavas, A. (2012). What we know and don't know about corporate social responsibility: A review and research agenda. *Journal of Management*, *38*(4), 932–968. doi:10.1177/0149206311436079

Arslanb, A. A. A. A., & Demirtaşc, Ö. (2016). A strategic influence of corporate social responsibility on meaningful work and organizational identification, via perceptions of ethical leadership. *Procedia: Social and Behavioral Sciences*, *235*, 259–268. doi:10.1016/j.sbspro.2016.11.029

Barney, J. A. Y., & Felin, T. (2013). What are microfoundations? *The Academy of Management Perspectives*, *27*(2), 138–155. doi:10.5465/amp.2012.0107

González-Masip, J., Martín-de Castro, G., & Hernández, A. (2019). Inter-organisational knowledge spillovers: Attracting talent in science and technology parks and corporate social responsibility practices. *Journal of Knowledge Management*, *23*(5), 975–997. doi:10.1108/JKM-06-2018-0367

Hsieh, Y. H., & Chan, J. Y. (2012). Corporate social responsibility: A concern among employees. *Human Systems Management*, *31*(3-4), 219–230. doi:10.3233/HSM-2012-0770

Jia, Y., Yan, J., Liu, T., & Huang, J. (2019). How does internal and external CSR affect employees' work engagement? Exploring multiple mediation mechanisms and boundary conditions. International Journal of Environmental Research and Public health, 16(14), 2476.67, 1-17. doi:10.3390/ijerph16142476

Jones, D. A., Willness, C. R., & Glavas, A. (2017). When corporate social responsibility (CSR) meets organizational psychology: New frontiers in micro-CSR research, and fulfilling a quid pro quo through multilevel insights. *Frontiers in Psychology*, *8*(520), 1–14. doi:10.3389/fpsyg.2017.00520 PMID:28439247

Smith, K. V., & Bartunek, J. M. (2013). Embedded versus peripheral CSR from the perspective of CSR professionals. *Industrial and Organizational Psychology: Perspectives on Science and Practice*, *6*(4), 338–341. doi:10.1111/iops.12062

Turker, D. (2009). Measuring corporate social responsibility: A scale development study. *Journal of Business Ethics*, *85*(4), 411–427. doi:10.100710551-008-9780-6

Tziner, A. (2013). Corporative social responsibility (CSR) activities in the workplace: A comment on Aguinis and Glavas (2013). *Revista de Psicología del Trabajo y de las Organizaciones*, *29*(2), 91–93. doi:10.5093/tr2013a13

KEY TERMS AND DEFINITIONS

Corporate Social Responsibility (CSR): An organization's integration of social accountability and obligations within its operations.

Corporate Social Responsibility Knowledge: Context-based information about organizational CSR activities, experiences, and events.

Organizational Ethical Behavior (OEB): Application (activities) of ethics based on organizational standards, values, strategies, and protocols.

Organizational Ethics (OE): The values, standards, ideologies, and principles by which businesses operate.

Organizational Identification (OI): The sharing of goals and values between an organization and its shareholders.

Perceived Corporate Social Responsibility (PCSR): The stakeholders' perceptions of a business' social responsibility perceptions.

Perceived Ethical Organizational Behavior (PEOB): Application (activities) of ethics based on stakeholders' perceptions of organizational standards, values, strategies, and protocols.

Perceived Organizational Identification (POI): Stakeholders sharing goals and values with an organization, based on their perceptions.

Perceptions: the cognitive process of interpreting information, experiences, and events.

Retail: The process of selling of goods to consumers.

Stakeholders: Are persons or institutions that have an interest or concern in an organization (e.g., employees, customers, society, government, managers, suppliers, creditors, and shareholders).

Chapter 14
Environmentally Proactive Strategies and Absorptive Capacity:
The Role of the Directors Interlocks

Cristian González-Zubieta
Universidad Complutense de Madrid, Spain

Javier Amores-Salvadó
Universidad Complutense de Madrid, Spain

ABSTRACT

The objective of this chapter is to deepen into the association between corporate governance and the adoption of environmentally proactive strategies. The theoretical approach used is the knowledge-based view. This chapter explains how the environmentally proactive strategies could be enhanced by the director interlocks, who help the company to acquire environmental knowledge. The concept of the environmental absorptive capacity is used to inquire how the knowledge from the director interlocks is utilized to improve the company's environmental responsiveness. The results of the analysis conducted indicates that the main contribution of the director interlocks is to help companies to acquire resources and environmental knowledge, useful to deploy environmentally proactive strategies. This study is of particular importance for firms, establishing environmentally proactive strategies. The study invites investors, CEOs, and managers to consider the director interlocks to renew the environmental capacities and comply the most stringent requirement of stakeholders.

DOI: 10.4018/978-1-7998-4833-2.ch014

INTRODUCTION

The concern about the impact of human action on the environment has received considerable attention for more than twenty-five years, due to the consequences that affect the availability and preservation of resources. For this reason, companies carry out environmental strategies aimed to reduce the environmental impact (Buysse and Verbeke, 2003). However, these strategies are not uniform, not all have the same scope, nor do they serve to all the stakeholders. The environmental strategy evolves as environmental awareness also evolves in companies (González-Benito and González-Benito, 2006).

Environmental strategies require intangible resources for their renewal and maturity, therefore, it is intended to explore the means that the company can exploit to bring useful knowledge and improve business environmental practices (González-Benito y González-Benito, 2006).

For this purpose, the absorptive capacity of Board of director is taken into consideration, on the one hand (Cohen and Levinthal, 1990), since, through its mechanisms, it provides the basis for a successful proactive environmental strategy, allowing the company to anticipate future regulations and social trends and design or alter operations, processes and products to prevent negative environmental impacts. And, on the other hand, specifically the director interlocks (Ortiz-de-Mandojana and Aragón-Correa, 2015) are considered, because they are a valuable source of inter-business connections and knowledge. Furthermore, given their characteristics, they can participate in all the dimensions of absorptive capacity, so it is interesting to analyse these two elements together. Thus, this chapter is directed to recognize the director interlocks as an expression of the environmental absorptive capacity.

Hereunder, the fundamental aspects of the Natural-Resource-Based View and of the Knowledge based view will be exposed, later on, characteristics of environmentally proactive strategies, corporate governance will be disclosed, to then deepen into the environmental absorptive capacity, and director interlocks.

This chapter is organized as follows; in section two, the introduction of topic and their aspects and generals characteristic are exposed. In section three, the framework and the development of the main arguments are explained. Consecutively, in section four, the recommendations and implications are argued. Subsequently, the future research directions are suggested; and finally, the main contributions of this chapter are framed in the conclusions.

ENVIRONMENTALLY PROACTIVE STRATEGIES AND CORPORATE GOVERNANCE: AN APPROACH FROM KNOWLEDGE MANAGEMENT

The Natural-Resource-Based View of the Firm was born as a response to the growing concern for environmental problems, their limitations and the challenges that companies face in this matter (Hart, 1995).

Hart (1995) carries the principles of the resource-based view[1], to a new scenario, that of the progressive environmental concern, both for the company and for society. Consequently, it develops the Natural-Resource-Based View, where it affirms that there is an opportunity for competitive advantage, to the extent that companies identify, develop, and accumulate resources and capacities oriented to the environment.

The Natural-Resource-Based View and its three interconnected strategies (pollution prevention, product stewardships and sustainable development) offer the theoretical support necessary for the analysis of companies' environmental strategies and their evolution, understanding by environmental strategy those patterns of corporate practices aimed to managing the interaction between companies and the natural environment over the time (Sharma, 2000).

The Natural-Resource-Based View is based on the accumulation of resources and capacities that are mostly intangible, which allow progressively improving the environmental performance. The evolution of the environmentally proactive strategy begins with the prevention of pollution, focusing on productive efficiency and reducing costs (Christmann, 2000) until reaching more complete approaches, oriented to the product life cycle related to differentiation (Reinhardt, 1998), or even with the redefinition of the business models (Prahalad and Hart, 2002).

With regard to the above, the Natural-Resource-Based View and the Knowledge-Based View are connected. Among other things, owing to knowledge management is used to understand how it is possible to counteract the degradation of the natural environment through the efficient use of finite natural resources (Hart, 1995). Hejduk (2005) state that the knowledge developed by human minds grow as it accumulates, develops and strengthens the current knowledge base; however, natural resources, even when recycled, decrease in quality with time and use.

The Natural-Resource-Based View and the Knowledge-Based View are blended to achieve competitive advantage through resources and organizational specific capacities of the company (Sharma and Vredenburg, 1998). And based on the knowledge of the management of limited natural resources (Hart, 1995). The prior presence of particular knowledge and capabilities facilitate the implementation of certain environmental approaches, for instance, Bowen, Cousins, Lamming and Farukt (2001), emphasizes in the efficient use of the resources on value chains. Besides, Christmann (2000) highlights the influence of knowledge-based organizational capabilities on environmental outcomes. In the same vain, Huang and Shih (2009) remarked that environmental knowledge management is becoming a popular tool for companies and decision makers.

Thus, to maintain competitive advantages through environmentally proactive strategies, it will be necessary a constant reconfiguration and coordination of the resource and capacity's base (Russo and Fouts, 1997) mostly intangible, such as the sustainable corporate image, legitimacy (Bhupendra and Sangle, 2018), reputation (Andersen and Skjoett-Larsen, 2009), capacity for stakeholder's integration (Aragon-Correa and Sharma, 2003), capacity for continuous innovation, capacity for learning (Mårtensson and Westerberg, 2016) and communication skills (Bhupendra and Sangle, 2017).

Hence, if the environmental strategy evolves and is enhanced reaching states of proactivity, largely due to the intangible resources and capacities, it will be necessary to explore in depth how knowledge management can be considered a key facilitator (Albort-Morant, Leal-Rodríguez and De Marchi, 2018). The competitive advantage of an environmentally responsible company lies in its ability to compile, accumulate and use environmental knowledge (Zahra, Neubaum and Naldi, 2007).

Nowadays, organizations must build, integrate, transfer and safeguard the environmental knowledge from either product, processes or their stakeholders. Companies must have the capacity to face a rapidly changing environment; because of this, they must create new resources, renew or modify their combination of resources (Teece, 2000).

To this purpose, the corporate governance helps in its monitoring role; it recognizes the company's environmental responsibilities as a fundamental part of its long-term financial and environmental performance (Berrone and Gomez-Mejia, 2009). Consequently, the corporate governance deal with the principles constitution and the guideline standards that regulate the design, integration and operation of the company, maintaining a suitable and environmentally responsible competitive position (Walls, Berrone and Phan, 2012).

Regarding the approach used to study the corporate governance, it should be noted that the agency theory (Eisenhardt, 1989) is the most widely used, in an attempt to define which the most appropriate alternatives to pursue long-term objectives are. Overall, agency theory predicts that shareholder's wealth and organizational performance will be maximized when a board of directors oversees the CEO's propensity to behave in his own interest. The agency theory perspective emphasizes the importance of separating property from control (Miller, 2002).

The principal function of the corporate governance is to protect the wealth of the owners; as well as, monitor and serve the demands of different stakeholders (Cohen, Krishnamoorthy and Wright, 2008). In order to keep its competitive advantage and positives business results; within their responsibilities, they must observe the environmental procedure of the top managers. An ecological mismanagement, bring negative consequences, such as a bad corporate image, lost legitimacy and business reputation, productive inefficiencies and regulatory sanctions, consequently, loss of value (Christmann, 2000).

Therefore, the corporate governance seeks to generate and recombine knowledge-based resources that allow it to drive the organization to high levels of environmental proactivity. For this, it has the board of directors, which is characterized by being the main driver in the process of creating environmental knowledge (Walls et al, 2012).

The board of directors should be sensitive to the environmental issues and improve the company's environmental practices. The board members are an important source of knowledge, characterized by providing external information and contributing to the transformation of knowledge for corporate environmental management. (Schønning, Walther, Machold and Huse, 2019).

In addition, the corporate environmental management is embodied in organizational policies by the corporate government and the members of the board of directors. As they recognize that, the environmentally proactive strategy requires a particular accumulation of resources and capabilities, which requires interconnectivity and a dependent trajectory for be developed and perfected through socially complex, knowledge-based organizational processes (Darnall, Henriques and Sadorsky, 2010).

From this perspective, this accumulation of knowledge-based resources and capacities (Van Den Bosch, Volberda and De Boer, 1999) will take the company to more advanced states of environmental proactivity.

PROACTIVE ENVIRONMENTAL STRATEGIES: DEFINITION AND SCOPE

Definition

Environmentally proactive strategies are a response to the greening of the corporate strategy, due to the competitive scenario around environmental problems, which is continually changing because of new regulations and standards, pressure from stakeholders and the updating of the technology (Sharma and Vredenburg, 1998).

There is a consensus in considering that proactive environmental strategies are associated with a corporate environmental orientation that goes beyond current legislation (Hart, 1995; Buysse and Verbeke, 2003; González-Benito And González-Benito, 2006).

Along with the goal of going beyond environmental regulation, some authors emphasize in the technological aspects of proactivity, others highlights the implementation of more advanced environmental practices, such as redesign, pollution prevention, clean production or waste minimization (Russo and Fouts, 1997; Klassen and McLaughlin, 1996).

However, the definition of environmentally proactive strategies that is taken as reference in this chapter, is the proposal by Sharma and Vredenburg (1998) whose main virtue is to cover a wide range of situations beyond specific environmental practices. Therefore, according to these authors, an environmentally proactive strategy is "a consistent pattern of environmental voluntary practices, must be characterized by involve all the dimensions of the company's activities, it does not need to be undertaken in the fulfilment of environmental regulations or in response to the pressures within the industry as standard business practices (Sharma and Vredenburg, 1998).

Scope

González-Benito and González-Benito (2006) argues that environmentally proactive strategies can be articulated through environmental practices of different type. The scope refers to the magnitude and to what extent the company is interested in environmental management. Three dimensions that involve the entire company are distinguished, which will be explained below (Potrich, Cortimiglia and de Medeiros, 2019).

1. **Planning and Organization Practices**: Indicates the extent to which the company has defined an environmental policy, it is specified what the strategic objectives are, the allocation of resources and environmental responsibilities, it is defined the type of environmental policy. The mechanisms, by which environmental knowledge will flow and be extracted, are established.

To this category, it is also established the amount of resources that will be destined for environmental purposes, the greater the commitment; the more resources are involved (Klassen and Whybark, 1999). In addition, the mechanisms for evaluation and continuous improvement are determined, which are of great relevance for the assimilation and management of environmental knowledge (Gluch, Gustafsson and Thuvander, 2009). Additionally to the purpose of knowing the strengths and weaknesses of the company's environmental practices (Gavronski, Klassen, Vachon and Nascimento, 2011)

2. **Operational Practices**: This is other of the relevant categories for environmentally proactive strategies according to Gupta (1994) cited in González-Benito and González-Benito (2006), these play a fundamental role in environmental issues, since they generate changes in the production and operations system.

Potrich et al., (2019) describes seven practices aimed to change processes, some highlighted activities are; emissions control and remediation, recycling, reuse of material, minimization of waste, minimization of use of resources (Daugherty, Autry and Ellinger, 2001).

Regarding product operating practices, Potrich et al., (2019) highlight the Analysis of the Life Cycle, which is defined as "is an examination of consecutive and inter-linked stages of a product system, from raw material acquisition or generation of natural resources to final disposal (end-of-life) (Pujari, 2006: 79). Another practice in this category is design for the environment; its objective is to allow the design team to create eco-efficient products without compromising their cost, quality and programming limitations (Guang et al., 2012). These environmental practices are carried out through the formalization of processes, interdisciplinary work, connectivity and routinization, among others; these activities promote the accumulation of environmental knowledge (Jansen, Van Den Bosch and Volberda, 2005).

3. **Communicational Practices**: In this respect, González-Benito and González-Benito (2006), point out that there is a growing demand to know the social and environmental impact of the company, therefore, communicational practices are intended to disclose to various stakeholders the actions related to the natural environment of the company. According to this, Yusoff, Lehman and Mohd (2006) affirm that communicational practices seek the support of the stakeholders. Finally, Eco-labelling is other of the practices highlighted in this chapter, its objective is to provide information to the stakeholders about the effects on the environment of the production, consumption and waste phases of the consumed products or services (Galarraga, 2002). It is expected to obtain a compensation for those products and processes with reduced environmental impacts (Erskine and Collins, 1997).

In the same vein, and in line with Sharma and Vredenburg (1998), environmentally proactive strategies will follow a consistent pattern of environmental practices in the organizational, operational and communicational dimensions of the company.

The environmentally proactive strategy is usually built over time, and depends on the route followed by the company and on the progressive way of linking a series of socially complex capacities that are difficult to imitate (Aragón-Correa and Sharma, 2003).

This leads us to think that the environmentally proactive strategy evolves, that means, it may vary depending on the type of response that the company decides to give through its strategic planning to environmental pressures of the stakeholders (Aragon-Correa and Sharma, 2003). In regards to this, the breadth and depth of environmental practices will be determined by their orientation and environmental sensitivity (Rhee and Lee, 2003), the accumulation, combination, coordination, and reconfiguration of causally ambiguous resources and capacities at a given moment (Russo and Fouts, 1997).

Therefore, the role in this environmental orientation and sensitivity of the corporate governance will be exposed below, which are the mechanisms that this body has to materialize its orientation and environmental sensitivity in proactive environmental practices and strategies.

Corporate Governance and Absorptive Capacity in Environmentally Proactive Strategies

The board of directors as part of the corporate governance brings together the members with greater decision-making power, due to its knowledge, and to the information, they have. Because of this, they are able to assign organizational priorities (Barka and Dardour, 2015). This body operates as structures and processes that serve as a means to monitor the assets and activities of an organization (Hambrick, Werder and Zajac, 2008). It leads organizations in the way they act, manage and control their operations, taking as a reference the objectives of these and managing fiduciary on behalf of the shareholders, in their condition of essential or prior stakeholders (Jensen and Meckling, 1976). Besides, this attends to the requirements of the multiple stakeholders, which generate reputation and value in the company (Cohen et al., 2008).

Cohen et al (2008) consider the corporate governance as an organ and vehicle, which includes owners, board of directors and top management. Its mission is to help the company to achieve or promote its strategic objective, including the environmental ones. Walls et al., (2012) highlight that the greatest contribution to environmental management comes from the board of directors, particularly from the independent directors, although the active position of the shareholders in this matter is also remarkable.

The characteristics of the corporate governance systems help to add the sustainable development thinking into your organizations. To maintain a sustainable corporate governance model, the company must have a board member with solid training and experience in environmental practices, the environmental objectives must be defined at the corporate level, the sustainability must be an integral part of corporate governance and be infused into the corporate system (Ortiz-de-Mandojana, et al., 2012).

The connections of the members of the board of directors confer the access to the necessary strategic resources, networking and information (Dalton and Daily, 1999). From a strategic environmental perspective, the valuable attributes of a board member include industry experience, knowledge, and the discretion to establish a corporate environmental strategy and provide access to necessary external resources (Pfeffer and Salancik, 2003).

The link between the corporate governance, through the board of directors, is relevant to the success of the corporate sustainability. The development of proactive environmental strategies is linked to an important set of financial, material and intangible resources, these requires the availability of specific technologies, an innovative long-term orientation of environmental business routines and practices (Ortiz-de-Mandojana et al., 2012). It involves the entire company; therefore, it requires the support of the corporate governance and top management, and especially from experienced directors.

Cowden, Alhorr and Bendickson (2015) highlight two aspects, first, the director's environmental human capital, which builds the path to environmental proactivity, and helps to generate an ecological vision that influence in the identity and values of companies. This leads to organizational changes in environmental matters. In addition, it identifies ecological technologies that can guide the development of the environmental innovation from a high level and, secondly, the environmental relational capital of the director member of the board. This intangible resource is created through networks of social ties that allow the members of a group to trust each other and cooperate. This capital creates credit and legitimacy, provides access to other groups that may have considerable and extensive knowledge about environmental sustainability and green technology, including the knowledge of the ethics of other boards of directors.

Thus, considering the corporate governance, it stands out above all the members of the board of directors as a source of tacit and explicit environmental knowledge (Ortiz-de-Mandojana and Aragón-Correa, 2015).

One of the keys to obtain and assimilate the tacit knowledge is the interaction between individuals and the training. The key to acquire tacit knowledge is to share experiences, while explicit knowledge presents fewer barriers to its transfer due to its encodable nature (Grant and Baden-Fuller, 1995). Liebeskind, Oliver, Zuckery and Brewer (1995) express the importance of maintaining inter-organizational networks in the same industry in order to mainly integrate explicit knowledge. Subsequently, Liebeskind (1996) warns that companies must protect their knowledge from the expropriation or imitation more effectively than other companies. In this regard, Nonaka (1994) highlights the importance of converting explicit knowledge into tacit knowledge, which has some similarity with the notion of organizational learning and is called "internalization" here. In short, it refers to the company's ability to bring external knowledge, deepen in it, and incorporate it into the company's processes.

Therefore, it shall be considered the absorptive capacity of the board of director, particularly from the director interlocks, as a boost for the knowledge that allows the company to renew its skills and develop innovative capacities, with the purpose of continually evolving and improving the management of proactive environmental practices. As previously exposed and regarding this Ortiz-de-Mandojana states that, the company also requires the incorporation of knowledge and resources from multiple external sources. For this, the director interlocks, who is the person that affiliated with one organization sits on the board of directors of another organization, are taken into consideration. For having a significant presence in the company worldwide, besides their functionality, quality of human and relational capital (Ortiz-de-Mandojana and Aragón-Correa, 2015), and as drivers and source of external knowledge (Zahra, Filatotchev and Wright, 2009; Pacheco et al., 2018).

The absorptive capacity corresponds to the ability of companies to identify, assimilate and exploit the knowledge of their dynamic environment (Cohen and Levinthal, 1990), and facilitate organizational learning. The Absorptive capacity prepares the board of directors to understand the heterogeneous environmental demands of their stakeholders, by improving knowledge (Pacheco, Alves and Liboni, 2018).

The absorptive capacity concept enables an organization to develop its internal capabilities, which can help the organization to respond to the requirements of other stakeholder groups more effectively. This ability allows board of directors, to address the claims of external stakeholders on environmental issues, that is, the absorption of environmental knowledge represents a way of leverage for companies to improve the design and implementation of their environmental policies (Gangi, Mustilli and Varrone, 2019).

The Absorptive capacity denotes a board of directors' ability to accumulate, process, and use the new knowledge obtained from external sources. The view based on knowledge, states that having this capability can significantly improve the ability to recognize and explore new opportunities, developing new skills and reduces cognitive rigidity. This reconfiguration of external knowledge can lead the company to explore different options of environmental response (Zahra et al., 2009).

The deployment of a proactive environmental policy requires specific knowledge because the environmental problem is highly complex (Gluch et al., 2009). Pacheco et al., (2018) suggest that absorptive capacity is a promising construction to understand the mechanisms and variables related to environmental practices and performances, such as ecological inertia and how to overcome it.

Environmental Absorptive Capacity

The importance of absorptive capacity lies in the need for specific knowledge-based capacities to drive the organization's green practices because they connect internal and external drivers (Hashim, Bock and Cooper, 2015).

Based on Zahra and George (2002), Pacheco et al., (2018), they proposed a framework applied to the environment context. Some authors highlights the importance of how knowledge is used to improve the company's environmental practices (Gluch et al., 2009). Sustainability is a complex phenomenon that involves complex processes and mechanisms, so that various authors suggest referring to the capacity of environmental absorptive as the ability to understand, communicate, combine, identify and commercialize environmental knowledge (Chen, Lin, Lin, and Chang, 2015).

Based on the absorptive capacity (Cohen and Levinthal 1990; Zahra and George, 2002), the concept of "environmental absorptive capacity" is considered a proper term to understand the mechanisms and variables related to innovation and environmental strategies (Pacheco et al, 2018). Therefore, the environmental absorptive capacity is an expression that allows to convert the knowledge into new environmentally responsible products, services or processes.

According to Zahra and George (2002), Albort-Morant, Henseler, Cepeda-Carrión and Leal-Rodríguez (2018) describe characteristics of the environmental absorptive capacity, establishing two subsets, the potential and realized environmental absorptive capacity. The potential capacity includes the acquisition assimilation capacities of the knowledge.

The potential absorptive capacity represents the incorporation of external knowledge within the repository knowledge of a company, while the realized absorptive capacity represents its combination, use and application (Albort-Morant et al., 2018).

The arguments of the four dimensions are presented, here below.

Dimensions of the Environmental Absorptive Capacity

Potential Absorptive Capacity

- **Acquisition:** Obtaining skills to manage the natural environment is a complicated process, since socially constructed elements are involved, which often must be modified (Marcus and Geffen, 1998). Acquisition, that lies on absorptive capacity, improving the ability to recognize the value of new information. The acquisition of knowledge refers to a company's ability to identify and acquire knowledge from abroad, which is key to operations; it also implies the ability to recognize the value of new environmental information (Aliasghar, Rose and Chetty, 2019).

The acquisition routines must have three fundamental attributes: intensity, speed, and direction. The intensity and speed are necessary to identify and collect knowledge, the greater the overlap, the faster the acquisition. In this stage, the initial reviews of environmental routines are carried out. They adopt routines to comply with environmental demands and legislation, the routine tasks establish automatic patterns of behaviour and increase the understanding of environmental practices, (Jansen, et al., 2005), with what it generates the accumulation of environmental knowledge. The routines lead to internalize knowledge; this allows identifying inefficiencies and new environmental demands of stakeholders and putting them in an important place within the company (Gluch et al., 2009).

- **Assimilation:** It concerns the routines and processes of the company that allow to analyse, process, interpret and understand the environmental information obtained from an external source (Aliasghar et al., 2019). It describes the ability to understand new external knowledge and link them to the previous knowledge base, deals with the interpretation and understanding of the knowledge of individuals (Leal-Rodríguez, Roldán, Ariza-Montes and Leal-Millán, 2014).

The ideas and discoveries that are beyond the limits of the company are often difficult to understand, due to their tacit and heuristic development, which often prevents the knowledge acquired from being understood or replicated. Therefore, it is necessary the development of comprehension capacity since it encourages the assimilation of knowledge that allows the company to process and internalize externally generated knowledge (Gluch et al., 2009).

Environmental assimilation mechanisms that work effectively in an organization aim to develop analytical routines and evaluations, such as life cycle analysis of the product or environmental training programs, action plans that have set measurable goals, and implemented analytical tools, to identify the environmental impact (Aliasghar et al., 2019).

Well-designed environmental plans and procedures capture previous experiences that can allow employees to seek and assimilate new external knowledge. The ability to socialize is also relevant, as it helps to create broad and tacitly understood rules for appropriate action and allows sharing of experience (Jansen et al., 2005).

This ability is deeply rooted in the understanding of the individual and the interpretation of environmental knowledge. In this way, the assimilation of knowledge is based on the ability of a company to capture new external knowledge and make sense of it (Albort-Morant et al., 2018).

Well-designed environmental plans and procedures capture previous experiences that can allow employees to seek and assimilate new external knowledge. The ability to socialize is also relevant, as it helps to create broad and tacitly understood rules for appropriate.

The Absorptive capacity helps the companies align between external sources of knowledge and internal knowledge base and improves the company's environmental responsiveness to external changes (Kim, Lee and Kang, 2018).

The potential of organizations to generate environmentally proactive strategies depends on the prior accumulation of knowledge they have absorbed (Fiol, 1996), hence the importance of this category. Both acquisition and assimilation delve into the underlying generative mechanisms that help explain why events observed in a particular sequence occur (Gluch et al., 2009). Both can be seen as a door of environmental knowledge, through which external influences travel (Gluch et al., 2009).

Furthermore, the potential capacity allows companies to recognize the nature of their own knowledge assets through an evaluation of them; companies can identify knowledge gaps that prevent them from improving their environmental performance (Kim et al., 2018).

The potential absorptive capacity prevents companies from being locked into a specific area of expertise and taking the risk of not seeking new alternatives for environmental practices, potential capacity makes companies more flexible, helping companies quickly to adapt to new environmental requirements (Enkel and Heil, 2014).

However, if companies focus only on potential absorptive capacity, they could continually renew their stock of knowledge, but may suffer from acquisition costs without exploitation profit (Jansen et al., 2005). For this reason, the development of transformation and exploitation capacities are equally important and necessary.

Realized Absorptive Capacity

- **Transformation:** Points to the company's ability to develop routines that allow the conjunction between the existing knowledge and the acquired and assimilated knowledge, this is done by eliminating, adding or simply interpreting knowledge differently. Therefore, the capacity for transformation involves recognizing two apparently inconsistent sets of information, then combining them and reaching a new state of knowledge. This facilitates the recognition of opportunity, the vision of the competitive landscape and the generation of new competencies, which can be incorporated into environmental operations and practices. The flow of knowledge must be effectively harnessed and transformed into products or services that satisfy the most demanding environmental requirements (Albort-Morant et al., 2018; 8). In addition, the ability to eliminate obsolete environmental knowledge and practices and stimulate the search for innovative environmental management alternatives is required (Camisón and Forés, 2010).
- **Exploitation:** Considering the seminal articles on absorptive capacity by Cohen and Levinthal (1989, 1990), the application and exploitation of the acquired knowledge have been emphasized. The exploitation reflects a company's ability to collect and incorporate technical knowledge into

> the company's environmental practices. The results of the exploitation routines will be the persistent creation of new goods, process systems, and new forms of organization or improve existing environmental practices. The unfold thresholds of the exploitation requires the support of the top management for its proper functioning, they should influence in the strategic and practical decisions on how environmental procedures will be carried out (Gluch et al., 2009).

Thus, the realized absorptive capacity influences on environmental performance. Through new products and processes by adapting externally acquired knowledge to organizational routines, and by transforming external knowledge and successfully integrating it with internal knowledge, creating new systems, processes and competencies that can be used to more effectively relate a company to the environmental requirements of its stakeholders (Schønning et al., 2019).

The realized absorptive capacity promote transformative learning that allows companies to develop new perceptual schemes, by dealing with strategic decisions and being better able to change their cognitive repertoire to absorb new knowledge and develop environmental skills over time (Schønning et al., 2019).

The potential absorptive capacity and the realized absorptive capacity have different functions, both coexist at the same time and each one are necessary conditions but insufficient, individually, for the improvement of the environmental performance of the firm (Zahra and George, 2002).

The subdivision allows to easily identifying the degree of efficiency of the environmental absorptive capacity, assuming that a high degree of efficiency of the realized absorptive capacity will be highly correlated with the potential absorptive capacity. Therefore, this theoretical distinction helps to explain why some firms are more efficient than others using absorptive capacity. In this way, the division into subsets can help to detect gaps in the organization's absorptive capacity more easily.

The organizations require incorporating knowledge from different domains (Pacheco et al., 2018). Thus, to this the director interlocks may be considered as a source of external knowledge, consequently, these directors can enhance the existing skills in the company or mitigate the limitations of the firm's environmental knowledge. Companies need expert knowledge to carry out their proactive environmental policies; this knowledge can often be found outside the company (Zahra and Filatotchev, 2004).

Thus, the director interlocks are considered as an expression that improves the environmental absorptive capacity to gain access to multiple and current knowledge, which can enrich and push companies to improve their environmental strategies (Zahra et al., 2009).

The Director Interlocks as an Expression of the Environmental Absorptive Capacity

Considering the main idea of the contributions of Zahra and George (2002), it deduces that the concepts of potential and realized environmental absorptive capacity are complementary, both are necessary for the effective absorptive of external environmental knowledge. A company may have the ability to acquire external knowledge, but this does not guarantee the exploitation of this knowledge. On the other hand, a company may have the ability to influence and exploit knowledge, but is unable to effectively acquire it. Both subsets of absorptive capacity coexist and jointly participate in improving environmental performance (Albort-Morant et al., 2018; 8).

The literature argues that the efforts to gather environmental knowledge probably depend on the information that flows within and through the boards of directors, it is established that the connections and ties of the board members facilitate the flows of information from outside the company. The learning, assimilation, transformation and exploitation of environmental knowledge can be better understood as a continuous process of interrelated activities (Van Den Bosch et al., 1999; Schønning et al., 2019). In consequence, the director interlock will be considerate as an important part of the environmental absorptive capacity.

Thus, the corporate governance, specifically the director interlocks, are perceived as a source of competitive advantage. These director interlocks can provide important channels for the exchange of information and strategic knowledge between companies, in addition, they can play an important role of resources from external sources, and add knowledge in strategic decision-making (Zahra and Filatotchev, 2004).

The director interlocks, who sit on more than one board of directors, will be a valuable source of knowledge. Since they can increase the organization's capacity to process a greater volume and variety of information, they have the ability to propose innovative strategic, they provide complementary capacities to make the best decision, given the alternatives and the information available (Ortiz-de-Mandojana et al., 2012).

The director interlocks can be an internal or external director. Internal directors are those whose main affiliation is with the organization and who generally include the CEO of the company and other top positions. External directors are individuals whose main affiliation is with organizations different from the firm where they apply their functions as director, they may be top executives of different types of financial institutions, companies from different sectors, or representatives of civil groups (Mizruchi, 1996).

A prominent feature of the director interlocks is that they have a greater monitoring capacity; companies can take advantage of their monitoring capabilities to avoid misappropriation of resources and improve the exploitation of resources within the organization (Chen, Lin, Lin and Hsiao, 2016).

The director interlocks provides direct strategic experience and indirect access to relevant information through social ties with other directors, which is used to monitor strategic decisions and make recommendations to the board of directors (Carpenter and Westphal, 2001).

The presence of the director interlocks is expected to affect the behaviour of a company in terms of environmental management, since he must provide the company with renewed and necessary knowledge for the adoption of an environmentally proactive strategy, in addition, of technological equipment, and financial resources (Ortiz-de-Mandojana et al., 2012).

The director interlocks is considered a privileged channel for the transfer of knowledge in environmental matters, the directors interlock can play an important role in the adoption and modification of organizational practices, which can be observed and carried out in other Boards of Directors where they occupy a place (Barka and Dardour, 2015).

The board of directors together with the director interlocks, according to Mizruchi (1996), operates as an inter-organizational network, where knowledge and information flows. Companies that develop strategies or belong to the same industry tend to adopt the same practices; therefore, the director interlocks could guide the company to incorporate certain prevailing environmental practices in the industry (DiMaggio and Powell, 1983).

Likewise, Ortiz-de-Mandojana et al., (2012) argue that having director interlocks with knowledge of environmental technology, could help companies to acquire resources and incorporate knowledge about internal processes that improve environmental quality and provide ecological equipment to increase the knowledge about new technologies.

Besides, Ortiz-de-Mandojana et al., (2012) found that the effect of director interlocks is contingent on the type of firms to which board members are connected with. Particularly, their results disclosed that director interlocks with firms providing fossil fuel are negatively related to the assumption of environmental strategies, due to their activities would be involved with environmental established course of action. The same to, director interlocks with firms providing financial resources reject the adoption of proactive environmental strategies, because they think this activities increase their level of risk of investments.

Mizruchi (1996) established that the presence of financial institutions in the board of directors increases inasmuch as the level of debt increase, these institutions look for control and to decide on the companies' investments, meanwhile, the companies look for financing, although they have to give their control of decision.

On the other hand, Galbreath (2012) argues that Boards who have director interlocks with firms in high impact industries and members of major sustainability indexes companies have quite credibility that is important to obtain sustainability. This generates valuable and timely resources that have a positive influence on the future sustainability.

Similarly, Dalziel, Gentry and Bowerman (2011) find that the technical experience of director interlocks influences positively on the level of spending for research and development and also agree on a positive relationship between the director interlocks linked to high-tech companies, with an improvement in the technological efficiency of the company where he works as a director. Likewise, Galbreath (2012) indicates that the director interlocks are interlocutors of responsible environmental practices when they are linked to companies with desirable sustainability indices, therefore, both in technological and environmental matters, the presence of the director interlocks is a useful way to acquire knowledge and skills (Del Vecchio, 2010).

Han, Bose, Hu, Qi and Tian (2015) expose a substitute effect between absorptive capacity and director interlocks. Consequently, they add that director interlocks are especially important when the performance of the absorptive capacity is limited. The monitoring capabilities and the management of resources and knowledge accumulated by director interlocks can improve the abilities of these companies to absorb and apply their resources effectively, while when the company has high levels of absorptive capacity, the value of the director interlocks as an elemental instrument to implement proactive environmental policies is reduced.

From another perspective, the director interlocks is a manifestation of the absorptive capacity, energizes and drives both the potential and the realized absorptive capacity (Kim, 2018). Regarding the potential absorptive capacity, the director interlocks in his monitoring function has the ability to identify routines and practices required by various stakeholders, assimilate them and claim them to put them in an important place within the company in order that these generate value (Zahra et al., 2009).

In addition, the director interlocks can provide environmental information from governments, competitors or third parties, helping to establish new proactive environmental policies, practices and processes. Thus, it is remarkable that the director interlock has a great importance and presence in the potential absorption capacity, specifically as a means of acquiring knowledge (Kim, 2018).

In addition, the director interlocks can provide environmental information from governments, competitors or third parties, in this way the difficulties of director interlocks must be noted by ethical reason (Hamilton and Stiegert, 2000). In spite of that, they help to establish new proactive environmental policies, practices and processes (Kim, 2018).

The proactive environmental knowledge management depends on the accumulation of internal competencies and learning over a period of time (Darnall and Edwards, 2006). However, in many cases environmental knowledge is outside the organization, so the director interlocks can help to acquire and assimilate changes in the operating systems (Kim, 2018).

Regarding the realized absorptive capacity carried out, the director interlocks may contribute criteria in the exploitation decision-making (Gluch et al., 2009). For example, the director interlocks based on their experience can influence in the formalization of proactive environmental rules and procedures, making it easier for employees to identify opportunities for transformation of new external knowledge. Through this, the best practices are codified; this generates greater efficiency in exploration, facilitates the application and makes its implementation faster (Jansen et al., 2005).

IMPLICATIONS FOR ENVIRONMENTAL MANAGEMENT

The introduction of the concept of environmental absorptive capacity into the research on board of directors, specifically in the director interlocks is a novel contribution in the academic research. In this respect, we discussed how the external knowledge and dimensions of the environmental absorptive capacity facilitates the environmental decision-making and the deployment of environmentally proactive strategies (Gluch et al., 2009; Albort-Morant et al, 2018).

Considering the importance of the environmental absorptive capacity, its functions is remarked as a key element to the identification of new knowledge and its utilization for financial ends, the environmental absorptive capacity allow the environmental strategies to comply the most stringent requirement of stakeholders. This capacity enable the company to extract the external knowledge and adapt it for enhance the environmental responds. Besides, the environmental absorptive capacity, also supply other importance capabilities to the company, such as green innovation capacity, facilitating a competitive advantage environmentally responsible.

The environmental absorptive capacity reinforce the argument that explain how important the director interlocks is to provide a deeper understanding about environmental practices and to get to know new environmental information of inaccessible source to the company (Ortiz-de-Mandojana y Aragon-Correa, 2015).

The importance of the environmental absorptive capacity for the environmentally proactive strategies lies on the identification of their dimensions, each one necessaries to yield successful practices and environmental performance. According to this, the director interlocks strengthen the environmentally proactive strategies, when they place emphasis on recognizing and understanding external knowledge and when they are able to maintaining and developing knowledge over time.

Therefore, the experiences of the director interlocks from highly rated companies could also influence significantly in the acquisition and assimilation of the environmental management processes, therefore, external and internal links are crucial to improve the environmental absorptive capacity (Albort-Morant et al., 2018).

Thus, it is noticed that the director interlock plays an important role as an expression of the potential absorptive capacity helping firms to align between external knowledge sources and the internal knowledge base and enhances the firm's responsiveness to external changes (Kim, 2018).

Besides, this chapter brings out that the director interlocks have a minor participation regarding the realized absorptive capacity. In spite of this, the director interlocks can offer a criteria and influence on the decision-making concerning some activities, routines and organizational procedures that generate the application of new environmental practices (Albort-Morant et al, 2018).

Finally, it is undoubtedly that the director interlocks as an expression of absorptive capacity provides environmental experience, relevant information and environmental knowledge about products and processes (Hoskisson, Hitt, Johnson and Grossman, 2002). This will be useful for managers and employees to transform and explore assimilated external knowledge (Kotlar, Massis, Frattini and Kammerlander, 2020), which can improve the materialization of environmentally proactive strategies

Accordingly, as a recommendation, companies are encouraged to stimulate and conduct their efforts in the development of the absorptive capacity. In the same way, the environmental experts should be considered for the board of directors, who can bring innovative knowledge for the purpose to incorporate resources, adjusting the demands of stakeholders, carrying out proactive environmental practices that allow maintaining a responsible competitive advantage with the environment.

FUTURE RESEARCH DIRECTIONS

The reflections outlined in this chapter could be the beginning of future research. The analysis of other variables could further enhance the understanding of the development and evolution of the environmentally proactive strategies.

It would be interesting that future research could delve into the intellectual capital of the company's top managers, how their knowledge can influence in the proactive environmental policies. Another aspect that has rarely been handled by knowledge and environmental management researchers (Keenan and Aggestam, 2001), is the role of the shareholder, what characteristics do owners have that encourage managers to manage knowledge with environmental purposes, and how does the concentration of the ownership influence or the temporary orientation of the ownership.

Another subject of interest would be to look into the compensation to the top managers for environmental objectives as an effective mechanism to attract environmental knowledge in order to improve their performance.

Finally, it is interesting to know how the corporate governance influences in the evolution of the environmentally proactive strategies stages. Besides, it is recommending enquiring about how the evolution and change of the corporate governance' s confirmation could accelerate or slow down the evolution of the environmentally proactive strategies stages (Calza, Profumo and Tutore, 2016).

CONCLUSION

The current chapter has pretend to step forward the discussion about the environmentally proactive strategies of the companies. It is exposed and argued the importance of the intangible resource to enhance the environmentally proactive strategies.

We explore and blend the concepts that have been rarely expose before in the academic literature. In this respect, it is determined a theoretical link between the environmentally proactive strategies of the companies, environmental absorptive capacity and corporate governance, in particular, the analysis highlight the salience of director interlocks as a source of the environmental knowledge.

The lens of the knowledge based view is used, because, it allows an adequate recognition on how director interlocks could bring external knowledge to enhances the environmental strategies in the companies.

The concept of environmental absorptive capacity has been developed in the chapter, this is recognized as a quite appropriate mechanism to evaluate and manage the environmental knowledge, which comes from an external source that is brought to companies by director interlocks.

Furthermore, the director interlock has been identified as a relevant channel for the exchange of information and as a strategic knowledge between companies, useful to achieve higher levels of environmental proactivity.

In sum, this chapter tries to bright to light the relevance of the environmental absorptive capacity to implement the environmental policies and underlines the importance of director interlocks as a manifestation of the environmental absorptive capacity that energizes and drives mainly the potential absorptive capacity, enhancing the environmentally proactive strategies.

In addition, the importance of encouraging the decision-makers to cultivate environmental knowledge management in the field of the proactive environmental strategies is also highlighted.

REFERENCES

Albort-Morant, G., Henseler, J., Cepeda-Carrión, G., & Leal-Rodríguez, A. L. (2018). Potential and realized absorptive capacity as complementary drivers of green product and process innovation performance. *Sustainability*, *10*(2), 381. doi:10.3390u10020381

Albort-Morant, G., Leal-Rodríguez, A. L., & De Marchi, V. (2018). Absorptive capacity and relationship learning mechanisms as complementary drivers of green innovation performance. *Journal of Knowledge Management*, *22*(2), 432–452. doi:10.1108/JKM-07-2017-0310

Aliasghar, O., Rose, L., & Chetty, S. (2019). Building absorptive capacity through firm openness in the context of a less-open country. *Industrial Marketing Management*, *83*, 81–93. doi:10.1016/j.indmarman.2018.11.007

Andersen, M., & Skjoett-Larsen, T. (2009). Corporate Social Responsibility in Global Supply Chains'. *Supply Chain Management*, *14*(2), 75–86. doi:10.1108/13598540910941948

Barka, H., & Dardour, A. (2015). Investigating the relationship between director's profile, board interlocks and corporate social responsibility. *Management Decision*, *53*(3), 553–570. doi:10.1108/MD-12-2013-0655

Barney, J. B., Ketchen, D. J. Jr, & Wright, M. (2011). The future of resource-based theory: Revitalization or decline? *Journal of Management*, *37*(5), 1299–1315. doi:10.1177/0149206310391805

Berrone, P., & Gomez-Mejia, L. R. (2009). Environmental performance and executive compensation: An integrated agency-institutional perspective. *Academy of Management Journal*, *52*(1), 103–126. doi:10.5465/amj.2009.36461950

Bhupendra, K. V., & Sangle, S. (2018). Product Stewardship Strategy: A Study of Indian Firms. *Corporate Social Responsibility and Environmental Management*, *25*(2), 124–134. doi:10.1002/csr.1444

Bowen, E., Cousins, D., Lamming, C., & Farukt, C. (2001). The role of supply management capabilities in green supply. *Production and Operations Management*, *10*(2), 174–189. doi:10.1111/j.1937-5956.2001.tb00077.x

Buysse, K., & Verbeke, A. (2003). Proactive environmental strategies: A stakeholder management perspective. *Strategic Management Journal*, *24*(5), 453–470. doi:10.1002mj.299

Calza, F., Profumo, G., & Tutore, I. (2016). Corporate ownership and environmental proactivity. *Business Strategy and the Environment, 25*(6), 369–389. doi:10.1002/bse.1873

Camisón, C., & Forés, B. (2010). Knowledge absorptive capacity: New insights for its conceptualization and measurement. *Journal of Business Research, 63*(7), 707–715. doi:10.1016/j.jbusres.2009.04.022

Carpenter, M. A., & Westphal, J. D. (2001). The strategic context of external network ties: Examining the impact of director appointments on board involvement in strategic decision-making. *Academy of Management Journal, 44*(4), 639–660.

Chen, Y. S., Lin, H., Lin, Y., & Chang, C. (2015). Enhancing green absorptive capacity, green dynamic capacities and green service innovation to improve firm performance: An analysis of structural equation modeling (SEM). *Sustainability, 7*(11), 15674–15692. doi:10.3390u71115674

Christmann, P. (2000). Effects of "best practices" of environmental management on cost advantage: The role of complementary assets. *Academy of Management Journal, 43*(4), 663–680.

Cohen, J. R., Krishnamoorthy, G., & Wright, A. M. (2008). Form versus substance: The implications for auditing practice and research of alternative perspectives on corporate governance. *Auditing, 27*(2), 181–198. doi:10.2308/aud.2008.27.2.181

Cohen, W. M., & Levinthal, D. A. (1990). Absorptive capacity: A new perspective on learning and innovation. *Administrative Science Quarterly, 35*(1), 128–152. doi:10.2307/2393553

Collis, D.J., & Montgomery, C.A. (1995). Competing on Resources: Strategy in the 1990s. *Knowledge and Strategy, 73*(4), 25-40.

Cowden, B., Alhorr, H. S., & Bendickson, J. (2015). Experience-Based Green Board Capital: Linking Board of Directors and Firm Environmental Performance. *Journal of Leadership, Accountability and Ethics, 12*(3).

Dalton, D. R., & Daily, C. M. (1999). What's wrong with having friends on the board? *Across the Board, 36*(3), 28–32.

Dalziel, T., Gentry, R. J., & Bowerman, M. (2011). An integrated agency – resource dependence view of the influence of directors 'human and relational capital on firms' R&D spending. *Journal of Management Studies, 48*(6), 1217–1242. doi:10.1111/j.1467-6486.2010.01003.x

Darnall, N., & Edwards, D. (2006). Predicting the cost of environmental management system adoption: The role of capabilities, resources and ownership structure. *Strategic Management Journal, 27*(4), 301–320. doi:10.1002mj.518

Darnall, N., Henriques, I., & Sadorsky, P. (2010). Adopting proactive environmental strategy: The influence of stakeholders and firm size. *Journal of Management Studies, 47*(6), 1072–1094. doi:10.1111/j.1467-6486.2009.00873.x

Daugherty, P. J., Autry, C. W., & Ellinger, A. E. (2001). Reverse logistics: The relationship between resource commitment and program performance. *Journal of Business Logistics, 22*(1), 107–123. doi:10.1002/j.2158-1592.2001.tb00162.x

DiMaggio, P. J., & Powell, W. W. (1983). The iron cage revisited: Institutional isomorphism and collective rationality in organizational fields. *American Sociological Review*, *48*(2), 147–160. doi:10.2307/2095101

Eisenhardt, K. M. (1989). Agency theory: An assessment and review. *Academy of Management Review*, *14*(1), 57–74. doi:10.5465/amr.1989.4279003

Enkel, E., & Heil, S. (2014). Preparing for distant collaboration: Antecedents to potential absorptive capacity in cross-industry innovation. *Technovation*, *34*(4), 242–260. doi:10.1016/j.technovation.2014.01.010

Erskine, C. C., & Collins, L. (1997). Eco-labeling: Success or failure? *The Environmentalist*, *17*(2), 125–133. doi:10.1023/A:1018552000651

Fiol, C. M. (1996). Squeezing harder doesn't always work: Continuing the search for consistency in innovation research. *Academy of Management Review*, *21*(4), 1012–1021. doi:10.5465/amr.1996.15868543

Galarraga, I. (2002). The use of eco-labels: A review of the literature. *European Environment*, *12*(6), 316–331. doi:10.1002/eet.304

Galbreath, J. (2012). Are boards on board? A model of corporate board influence on sustainability performance. *Journal of Management & Organization*, *18*(4), 445–460. doi:10.5172/jmo.2012.18.4.445

Gangi, F., Mustilli, M., & Varrone, N. (2019). The impact of corporate social responsibility (CSR) knowledge on corporate financial performance: Evidence from the European banking industry. *Journal of Knowledge Management*, *23*(1), 110–134. doi:10.1108/JKM-04-2018-0267

Gavronski, I., Klassen, R. D., Vachon, S., & Nascimento, L. F. M. (2011). A resource-based view of green supply management. *Transportation Research Part E, Logistics and Transportation Review*, *47*(6), 872–885. doi:10.1016/j.tre.2011.05.018

Gluch, P., Gustafsson, M., & Thuvander, L. (2009). An absorptive capacity model for green innovation and performance in the construction industry. *Construction Management and Economics*, *27*(5), 451–464. doi:10.1080/01446190902896645

González-Benito, J., & González-Benito, Ó. (2006). A review of determinant factors of environmental proactivity. *Business Strategy and the Environment*, *15*(2), 87–102. doi:10.1002/bse.450

Grant, R. M., & Baden-Fuller, C. (1995). A knowledge-based theory of inter-firm collaboration. *Academy of Management Journal*, (1), 17–21.

Guang, L. (2012). Natural resource based green supply chain management. *Supply Chain Management*, *17*(1), 54–67. doi:10.1108/13598541211212203

Gupta, M. C. (1994). Environmental management and its impact on the operations function. *International Journal of Operations & Production Management*, *15*(8), 34–51. doi:10.1108/01443579510094071

Hambrick, D. C., Werder, A. V., & Zajac, E. J. (2008). New directions in corporate governance research. *Organization Science*, *19*(3), 381–385. doi:10.1287/orsc.1080.0361

Hamilton, F., & Stiegert, K. (2000). Vertical coordination, antitrust law, and international trade. *The Journal of Law & Economics*, *43*(1), 143–156. doi:10.1086/467450

Hart, S. (1995). A natural-resource-based view of the firm. *Academy of Management Review*, *20*(4), 986–1014. doi:10.5465/amr.1995.9512280033

Hashim, R., Bock, A. J., & Cooper, S. (2015). The relationship between Absorptive Capacity and Green Innovation. *World Academy of Science, Engineering and Technology*, *9*(4), 1049–1056.

Hejduk, I. K. (2005). On the way to the future: The knowledge-based enterprise. *Human Factors and Ergonomics in Manufacturing & Service Industries*, *15*(1), 5–14. doi:10.1002/hfm.20010

Hoskisson, R., Hitt, M., Johnson, R., & Grossman, W. (2002). Conflicting voices: The effects of institutional ownership heterogeneity and internal governance on corporate innovation strategies. *Academy of Management Journal*, *45*(4), 697–716.

Huang, P. S., & Shih, L. H. (2009). Effective environmental management through environmental knowledge management. *International Journal of Environmental Science and Technology*, *6*(1), 35–50. doi:10.1007/BF03326058

Jansen, J. J., Van Den Bosch, F. A., & Volberda, H. W. (2005). Managing potential and realized absorptive capacity: How do organizational antecedents matter? *Academy of Management Journal*, *48*(6), 999–1015. doi:10.5465/amj.2005.19573106

Jensen, M. C., & Meckling, W. (1976). Theory of the firm: Managerial behaviour, agency costs, and ownership structure. *Journal of Financial Economics*, *3*(4), 305–360. doi:10.1016/0304-405X(76)90026-X

Keenan, J., & Aggestam, M. (2001). Corporate governance and intellectual capital: Some conceptualizations. *Corporate Governance*, *9*(4), 259–275. doi:10.1111/1467-8683.00254

Kim, C., Lee, C., & Kang, J. (2018). Determinants of firm's innovation-related external knowledge search strategy: The role of potential absorptive capacity and appropriability regime. *International Journal of Innovation Management*, *22*(6). doi:10.1142/S1363919618500445

Kim, J. (2018). *A Multi-Step Model of Boundary Spanning and Absorptive Capacity: The Differential Impact of Board and Top Management Team Experience on the Development of Sustainability-Related Capabilities*. Arizona State University.

Klassen, R. D., & McLaughlin, C. P. (1996). The impact of environmental management on firm performance. *Management Science*, *42*(8), 1199–1214. doi:10.1287/mnsc.42.8.1199

Klassen, R. D., & Whybark, D. C. (1999). The impact of environmental technologies on manufacturing performance. *Academy of Management Journal*, *42*(6), 599–615.

Kotlar, J., De Massis, A., Frattini, F., & Kammerlander, N. (2020). Motivation gaps and implementation traps: The paradoxical and time-varying effects of family ownership on firm absorptive capacity. *Journal of Product Innovation Management*, *37*(1), 2–25. doi:10.1111/jpim.12503

Leal-Rodríguez, A. L., Roldán, J. L., Ariza-Montes, J. A., & Leal-Millán, A. (2014). From potential absorptive capacity to innovation outcomes in project teams: The conditional mediating role of the realized absorptive capacity in a relational learning context. *International Journal of Project Management*, *32*(6), 894–907. doi:10.1016/j.ijproman.2014.01.005

Liebeskind, J. (1996). Knowledge, strategy, and the theory of the firm. *Strategic Management Journal*, *17*(2), 93–107. doi:10.1002mj.4250171109

Liebeskind, J., Oliver, A., Zucker, L., & Brewer, M. (1996). Social networks, learning, and flexibility: Sourcing scientific knowledge in new biotechnology firms. *Organization Science*, *7*(4), 428–443. doi:10.1287/orsc.7.4.428

Lim, K., Tseng, L., Tan, H., & Bui, D. (2017). Knowledge management in sustainable supply chain management: Improving performance through an interpretive structural modeling approach. *Journal of Cleaner Production*, *162*, 806–816. doi:10.1016/j.jclepro.2017.06.056

Marcus, A., & Geffen, D. (1998). The dialectics of competency acquisition: Pollution prevention in electric generation. *Strategic Management Journal*, *19*(12), 1145–1168. doi:10.1002/(SICI)1097-0266(1998120)19:12<1145::AID-SMJ6>3.0.CO;2-B

Mårtensson, K., & Westerberg, K. (2016). Corporate environmental strategies towards sustainable development. *Business Strategy and the Environment*, *25*(1), 1–9. doi:10.1002/bse.1852

Miller, J. (2002). The board as a monitor of organizational activity: The applicability of agency theory to non-profit boards. *Nonprofit Management & Leadership*, *12*(4), 429–450. doi:10.1002/nml.12407

Mizruchi, M. S. (1996). What do interlocks do? An analysis, critique, and assessment of research on interlocking directorates. *Annual Review of Sociology*, *22*(1), 271–298. doi:10.1146/annurev.soc.22.1.271

Nonaka, I. (1994). A dynamic theory of organizational knowledge creation. *Organization Science*, *5*(1), 14–37. doi:10.1287/orsc.5.1.14

Ortiz-de-Mandojana, N., & Aragon-Correa, J. A. (2015). Boards and sustainability: The contingent influence of director interlocks on corporate environmental performance. *Business Strategy and the Environment*, *24*(6), 499–517. doi:10.1002/bse.1833

Ortiz-de-Mandojana, N., Aragón-Correa, J. A., Delgado-Ceballos, J., & Ferrón-Vílchez, V. (2012). The effect of director interlocks on firms' adoption of proactive environmental strategies. *Corporate Governance*, *20*(2), 164–178. doi:10.1111/j.1467-8683.2011.00893.x

Pacheco, L. M., Alves, M. F. R., & Liboni, L. B. (2018). Green absorptive capacity: A mediation-moderation model of knowledge for innovation. *Business Strategy and the Environment*, *27*(8), 1502–1513. doi:10.1002/bse.2208

Porter, M., & van der Linde, C. (1995). *Green and competitive*. Harvard Business Review.

Potrich, L., Cortimiglia, M. N., & de Medeiros, J. F. (2019). A systematic literature review on firm-level proactive environmental management. *Journal of Environmental Management*, *243*, 273–286. doi:10.1016/j.jenvman.2019.04.110 PMID:31102895

Prahalad, & Hart, S. (2002). The fortune at the bottom of the pyramid. *Strategy and Business*, 54-54.

Pujari, D. (2006). Eco-innovation and new product development: Understanding the influences on market performance. *Technovation*, *26*(1), 76–85. doi:10.1016/j.technovation.2004.07.006

Reed, R., & De Fillippi, R. J. (1990). Causal ambiguity, barriers to imitation, and sustainable competitive advantage. *Academy of Management Review*, *15*(1), 88–102. doi:10.5465/amr.1990.4308277

Reinhardt, F. L. (1998). Environmental product differentiation: Implications for corporate strategy. *California Management Review*, *40*(4), 43–73. doi:10.2307/41165964

Rhee, S. K., & Lee, S. Y. (2003). Dynamic change of corporate environmental strategy: Rhetoric and reality. *Business Strategy and the Environment*, *12*(3), 175–190. doi:10.1002/bse.356

Russo, M. V., & Fouts, P. A. (1997). A resource-based perspective on corporate environmental performance and profitability. *Academy of Management Journal*, *40*, 534–559.

Salancik, G. R., & Pfeffer, J. (1978). A social information processing approach to job attitudes and task design. *Administrative Science Quarterly*, *23*(2), 224–253. doi:10.2307/2392563 PMID:10307892

Sangle, S. (2010). Empirical analysis of determinants of adoption of proactive environmental strategies in India. *Business Strategy and the Environment*, *19*(1), 51–63.

Schønning, A., Walther, A., Machold, S., & Huse, M. (2019). The Effects of Directors 'Exploratory, Transformative and Exploitative Learning on Boards' Strategic Involvement: An Absorptive Capacity Perspective. *European Management Review*, *16*(3), 683–698. doi:10.1111/emre.12186

Sharma, S. (2000). Managerial interpretations and organizational context as predictors of corporate choice of environmental strategy. *Academy of Management Journal*, *43*(4), 681–697.

Sharma, S., & Vredenburg, H. (1998). Proactive corporate environmental strategy and the development of competitively valuable organizational capabilities. *Strategic Management Journal*, *19*(8), 729–753. doi:10.1002/(SICI)1097-0266(199808)19:8<729::AID-SMJ967>3.0.CO;2-4

Spender, J. C. (1996). Making knowledge the basis of a dynamic theory of the firm. *Strategic Management Journal*, *17*(S2), 45–62. doi:10.1002mj.4250171106

Srikantaiah, T. K., & Koenig, E. D. (2000). *Knowledge management: For the information professional*. Information Today, Inc.

Teece, D. J. (2000). Strategies for managing knowledge assets: The role of firm structure and industrial context. *Long Range Planning*, *33*(1), 35–54. doi:10.1016/S0024-6301(99)00117-X

Van Den Bosch, F. A., Volberda, H. W., & De Boer, M. (1999). Coevolution of firm absorptive capacity and knowledge environment: Organizational forms and combinative capabilities. *Organization Science*, *10*(5), 551–568. doi:10.1287/orsc.10.5.551

Vecchio, N. (2010). Réseaux de conseils d'administration et adoption de pratiques de gouvernance d'entreprise. *Revue Française de Gestion*, *202*(3), 145–161. doi:10.3166/rfg.202.145-161

Veleva, V. (2008). Product stewardship in the United States: the changing policy landscape and the role of business. *Sustainability: Science. Practice and Policy*, *4*(2), 29–35.

Walls, L., Berrone, P., & Phan, H. (2012). Corporate governance and environmental performance: Is there really a link? *Strategic Management Journal*, *33*(8), 885–913. doi:10.1002mj.1952

Yusoff, H., Lehman, G., & Mohd, N. (2006). Environmental engagements through the lens of disclosure practices: A Malaysian story. *Asian Review of Accounting*, *14*(1/2), 122–148. doi:10.1108/13217340610729509

Zahra, S., & George, G. (2002). Absorptive Capacity: A Review, Reconceptualization, and Extension. *Academy of Management Review*, *27*(2), 185–203. doi:10.5465/amr.2002.6587995

Zahra, S. A., & Filatotchev, I. (2004). Governance of the entrepreneurial threshold firm: A knowledge-based perspective. *Journal of Management Studies*, *41*(5), 885–897. doi:10.1111/j.1467-6486.2004.00458.x

Zahra, S. A., Filatotchev, I., & Wright, M. (2009). How do threshold firms sustain corporate entrepreneurship? The role of boards and absorptive capacity. *Journal of Business Venturing*, *24*(3), 248–260. doi:10.1016/j.jbusvent.2008.09.001

Zahra, S. A., Neubaum, D. O., & Naldi, L. (2007). The effects of ownership and governance on SMEs' international knowledge-based resources. *Small Business Economics*, *29*(3), 309–327. doi:10.100711187-006-9025-y

KEY TERMS AND DEFINITIONS

Board of Directors: The link between the shareholders and the management, that runs the company; it is a decision-making group facing complex tasks pertaining to strategic-issue processing. Furthermore, boards are responsible for the standing of their firm in the community.

Corporate Governance: It is an organ, which includes owners, board of directors, and top management. Its main mission is to help the company to achieve or promote its strategic objective.

Director Interlocks: Director, who affiliated with one organization, sits on the board of directors of another organization.

Environmental Absorptive Capacity: Expression that allows converting the knowledge into new environmentally responsible products, services, or processes.

Knowledge Management: Dynamic process that guide the activities for acquiring, organizing, and communicating tacit and explicit knowledge with the purpose of increase innovativeness, responsiveness, and competitive advantage.

Proactive Environmental Strategy: Response to the greening of the corporate strategy, associating with a corporate environmental orientation that goes beyond current legislation.

Stakeholders: Individual or collective, market, network, public, or society who can affect positive or negative by the performance of a corporation.

ENDNOTE

1 The resource-based view: explain and predict organizational relationships and for understanding the sources of companies' competitive advantage (Barney et al., 2011). It is characterized by attaching great importance to the resources and capacities developed within the company and to their consideration as key factors to face the competitive environment in which it is immersed (Collis and Montgomery, 1995).

Chapter 15
Micro-Foundations of Corporate Sustainability

Remy Balarezo
Universidad de Piura (UDEP), Peru

Paul Corcuera
Universidad de Piura (UDEP), Peru

ABSTRACT

This chapter introduces readers to the micro-foundation framework in corporate sustainability. Traditionally, strategic management and corporate sustainability research have explained why firms become more sustainable from a macro-level perspective. In recent years, new research has focused on the micro-level mechanism at the individual or group level. This research stream is known as the micro-foundations movement and tries to highlight individual characteristics, knowledge, background, etc. when firms decide to become more sustainable. Through the literature review, the authors tried to identify the studies published in top journals about the micro-foundation framework. Therefore, the aim of this chapter is to give a primary introduction and an overview of the micro-foundations framework in corporate sustainability and identify what mechanisms have been found at the micro-level that explain why firms become more sustainable.

INTRODUCTION

The economic system has relied on capitalism since the second half of the last century (Barney & Rangan, 2019). Market competition has stimulated innovation (Adler, 2016), and the capitalist system has brought many benefits and outputs. For example, since the 90s, more than one billion people left abject poverty (Barney & Rangan, 2019). In addition, the average individual material well-being has improved markedly; "for the first time in history, there is the potential to achieve material comfort for all" (Adler, 2016, p. 124). Nevertheless, these benefits have brought important costs. The market competition characteristics do not give incentives for firms to incorporate their impact on the social and natural environment (Adler, 2016). Therefore, the results have not always produced expected outcomes

DOI: 10.4018/978-1-7998-4833-2.ch015

(Barney & Rangan, 2019). Some negative outcomes include climate change, income inequality, and job destruction (Howard-Grenville et al., 2014; Tsui et al., 2018; Zink, 2019).

The capitalism system is multifaceted. On the one hand, awards efficiency, which normally destroys jobs (Davis, 2016; Zink, 2019); and on the other, the reinvestment incentives create new jobs and industries by creating wealth and promising to capture the profits to investors (Zink, 2019). In the latter, the system destroys jobs while in the former, it creates new ones to replace the ones that were destroyed. In this context, the capitalism system is stable only under growth (Zink, 2019). Economies require increased resource consumption, which produces waste while also creating new jobs that efficiently eliminate or cannibalize others. Nowadays, it seems that the economies are not fulfilling both conditions since new technology eliminate more jobs than they create, and produces environmental problems (Zink, 2019). Therefore, the capitalist system has created two current crises: technological job destruction and global ecological destruction (Zink, 2019).

This chapter focuses on environmental degradation and social problems using the micro-foundations framework to explain how firms can tackle these issues. It is oriented toward firms because they explain the economic system and society. Thus, understanding the firms will help to recognize the great strengths and limitations of market capitalism (Barney & Rangan, 2019). Environmental and social issues are gaining momentum in the business and management community. From an academic point of view, different authors have used firms to tackle grand challenges (George et al., 2016), and define alternative objective functions (Lankoski & Smith, 2018), reinvent themselves (Mayer, 2016), redefine its business model (Laasch, 2018) and discover its purpose (Hollensbe et al., 2014).

The practitioner world has not stayed behind, and the importance of the social and natural environment is also gaining momentum. For example, the study carried out by BCG-MIT Sloan Review showed that 90% of firm executives considered sustainability very important; 50% of companies changed their business models to more sustainable ones, and 60% developed a clear sustainability strategy (Kiron et al., 2017). These issues are also important for investment firms. Another study by BCG-MIT Sloan Review showed that 75% of investment firms considered sustainability performance when making an investment decision and 50% of them would not invest in a company with a record of poor sustainability performance (Unruh et al., 2016).

Every time there are hurricanes, wildfires, and storms around the world (cf. the coastal El Niño effect in northern Peru in 2017) the consequences are devastating, such as life and economic losses. Also, social nonconformity and inequality are raising (cf. Chile and Ecuador social protest in 2019 and the yellow vests in France 2018/2019). Therefore, firms can watch how the degradation of the natural and social environment continue to grow, or they can become part of the solution. Organizations, especially the executives and the workers, can be important players in tackling these grand challenges (George et al., 2016).

This chapter attempts to explain, from a theoretical point of view, how members inside the organization can drive firms to tackle the environmental and social problems and therefore be more sustainable. The authors made a literature review through the business source complete with the keywords micro-foundations of sustainability, social micro-foundations, environmental micro-foundations and strategy micro-foundations. The search was focused to top management journals and in specific academic journals, like Business Strategy and Environment, or Organization and Environment from 2010 until 2019. The objective was to identify micro-foundations of corporate sustainability studies in the last years and show the reader the importance of the micro mechanisms that explain why firms can become more sustainable. The chapter is divided as follows. There is an introduction to the micro-foundation lens to explain why some firms are more sustainable than others; and then, four main sections. The first one defines and explains sustainability from the management and business perspective. Section two explains the different theoretical views that have explained why firms become more sustainable. Section three introduces the micro-foundations view, and section four focuses on the micro-foundations of corporate sustainability

As the former UN Secretary General Ban Ki-Moon said[1], "There is no Plan B for action, as there is no Planet B". This chapter can help practitioners re-think their role in making more sustainable their businesses and how their actions can leave a better world and society for future generations.

CORPORATE SUSTAINABILITY

"Half a truth is often a great lie" Benjamin Franklin

Besides the significant increase of corporate sustainability research in the last years (Montiel & Delgado-Ceballos, 2014), there is a lack of concept clarity (Meuer et al., 2019). As Montiel and Delgado-Ceballos (2014) highlighted in their study, "a standardized definition of corporate sustainability does not exist" (p. 10). Therefore, when there is no precision in the construct or if it is ambiguous, it contributes to confusion and limits the growth of a field (Bansal & Song, 2017).

Early definitions of responsibility and sustainability were very distinct compared to the definitions offered today. The first responsibility studies focused on social issues, especially the harms of markets on society, while sustainability research focused more on environmental issues, mainly in how economic development harmed the natural systems (Bansal & Song, 2017). That is why the origin of corporate sustainability can be linked to the Brundtland report (Keeble, 1988) and its definition (Montiel & Delgado-Ceballos, 2014). This report defines sustainable development as "development that meets the need of the present without compromising the ability for future generations to meet their own needs" (WCED, 1987). The Brundtland definition highlighted two important components. One related to economic development and its impact on resource availability, and the other, related to a long-term perspective (Bansal & DesJardine, 2014; Montiel & Delgado-Ceballos, 2014).

The concept of sustainable development appeared in the management literature by the mid-90s with the pioneer studies of Gladwin, Kennelly, and Krause (1995) and Hart (1995). The special issues of the *Academy of Management Review* in 1995 and the *Academy of Management Journal* in 2000 gave legitimacy and acceptance of corporate sustainability as a research topic (Hahn et al., 2017). The 1995 publication highlighted the relevance and meaning of sustainability for managers and firms, while the 2000 publication showed the role of environmental issues in management. During this period of time, the concepts of responsibility and sustainability converged to fit the business case for such organizational practices (Bansal & Song, 2017; Hahn et al., 2017). Much of the research during that time increased the understanding of how and under which circumstances firms reacted in a strategic way to sustainability challenges, and if it was financially beneficial to the firm to follow such strategies (Hahn et al., 2017). In other words, research focused on discovering the business case for sustainability (Kaplan, 2020), but also on increased the risk of unethical executives acting in a sustainable way only when the business profited from it (Bansal & Song, 2017).

Bansal (2005) first attempted to operationalize corporate sustainability, originally labeled as corporate sustainable development, based on three principles: "economic prosperity, social equity, and environmental integrity" (p. 198). Since then, there have been different definitions, as shown in Table 1. Hart

Table 1. Corporate sustainability similar definitions in academic management journals

Author	Construct - Terminology	Definition
Gladwin et al., (1995)	Sustainability Concept - Sustain centrism	Process of achieving human development in an inclusive, connected, equitable, prudent, and secure manner.
Shrivastava, (1995)	Sustainability Concept – Ecological Sustainability	It can be achieved through four different mechanisms: total quality environmental management, ecological sustainable competitive strategies, technology for nature swaps and corporate population impact control.
Hart (1995)	Sustainability Concepts – Sustainable Development	It is a strategy that dictates that the effort must be made to sever the negative links between environment and economic activity in the developing countries of the south.
P. Bansal & Roth (2000)	Sustainability Concepts – Corporate Sustainability	A set of corporate initiatives aimed at mitigating a firm impact on the natural environment.
Dyllick & Hockerts (2002)	Sustainability Concepts – Corporate Sustainability	Meeting the needs of a firm´s direct and indirect stakeholders (shareholders, employees, clients, communities, etc.), without compromising its ability to meet the needs of future stakeholders as well.
Hart & Milstein (2003)	Sustainability Concepts – Corporate Sustainability	A firm contributes to sustainable development by delivering simultaneously economic, social and environmental benefits. Sustainable development is the process of achieving human development in an inclusive, connected, equitable, prudent and secure manner.
Van Marrewijk (2003)	Sustainability Concepts – Corporate Sustainability	Corporate sustainability and CSR refer to company activities demonstrating the inclusion of social and environmental concerns in business operations and interactions with stakeholders.
Figge & Hahn (2004)	Sustainability Concepts – Corporate Sustainability	Corporate sustainability is the efficiency with which a company uses resources relative to other companies together with the effectiveness with which it contributes to the three dimensions (environmental, social and economic) of sustainability.
Bansal (2005)	Sustainability Concepts – Corporate Sustainability	Three conditions are required to achieve sustainable development: environmental integrity, economic prosperity, and social equity.
Hart & Dowell (2011)	Sustainability Concepts – Sustainable Development	One of the three key strategic capabilities in the natural resource-based view (also: pollution prevention and product stewardship) has evolved in two distinct areas: clean technology and base of the pyramid (BoP) strategies.
Flammer (2013)	Sustainability Concepts – Environmental CSR	While the original focus on CSR was on social responsibility, a recent development is the inclusion of environmental responsibility
Bansal & DesJardine (2014)	Sustainability Concepts - Business Sustainability	The ability of firms to respond to their short-term financial needs without compromising their (or others) ability to meet their further needs.
Eccles, Ioannou, & Serafeim, (2014)	Sustainability Concepts – Corporate Sustainability	Integrating the social and environmental issues into a company strategy and business model through the adoption of corporate policies.
Dyllick & Muff, (2016)	Sustainability Concepts – Business Sustainability 3.0	Truly sustainable business shifts its perspective from seeking to minimize its negative impact on understanding how it can create a significant positive impact in critical and relevant areas for society and the planet.

Source: Adapted from Bansal & Song (2017), Meuer et al. (2019), Montiel & Delgado-Ceballos (2014)

and Dowell (2011) added that sustainable development was not restricted to environmental issues, but should also include economic and social impacts.

As seen in Table 1, there are different definitions of corporate sustainability, which makes it difficult to find a standardized meaning. For Montiel and Delgado-Ceballos (2014), the concept of corporate sustainability shows ambiguity in the number of dimensions to consider (tridimensional: economic, social and environmental; bidimensional: social and environmental) or if it is the same as environmental management because it accounts only the environmental dimension. This generates an overlap of the construct definition between corporate responsibility and business sustainability (Ashrafi et al., 2018; Bansal & Song, 2017).

Most of the these definitions agree that the concept encompasses the economic, social, and environmental dimensions, which have been labeled as the "triple-bottom-line", "3Ps", etc. (Montiel & Delgado-Ceballos, 2014). In trying to minimize the ambiguity, the proposed construct is based on Meuer et al. (2019) and Montiel and Delgado-Ceballos (2014). It is helpful to understand the different components in the corporate sustainability definition, as Meuer et al. (2019) labeled "different species in the same family of corporate sustainability" (p. 12). In fact, they have found a three-dimension cube of corporate sustainability. The first dimension, *level of ambitions*, specifies the amount of effort a firm must do to become sustainable. This ranges from high ambitions to low ambitions. For example, a high ambition firm could be an oil and gas company that connects its sustainability performance with the UN Sustainable Development Goals changing its business operations and process to achieve them. Basically, the firm must question: How ambitious are my sustainable objectives and how ambitiously we are trying to achieve them? (Meuer et al., 2019).

The second dimension, *level of integration,* refers to the extent to which sustainability issues are introduced to the core strategy of the firm, or to its business model and day-to-day operations (Meuer et al., 2019). Wunder (2019) calls this level of integration "sustainable strategizing 2.0", which refers to firms that change their mindset from the inside-out vision to the outside-in, extending the boundaries of the firm to include the social and natural environments, and seeing its strategy as system-based (Bansal et al., 2018; Schad & Bansal, 2018). So, the question is what the firm can do for sustainability: can they increase business, address the cause of the problem, or help reverse the damages? (Mintzberg, 2019) Some authors trying to introduce sustainability in firms have recommended different varieties of capitalism (VOC) as alternative types of organizations (Davis, 2016).

Finally, the third dimension, *specificity of sustainable development*, refers to the restrictiveness or roominess of the definitions of corporate sustainability; a level of broadness and deepness of the understanding of corporate sustainability (Meuer et al., 2019). Therefore, they define corporate sustainability as:

a bundle of activities fully integrated into a firm's overall strategy that contributes effectively to the welfare of current and future generations through protecting and enhancing the resilience of the biosphere, social equity and cohesion, and economic prosperity" or lenient definitions "a firm attempt to respond to environmental and social issues. (Meuer et al., 2019, p. 12)

It is important to reduce the ambiguity of the construct definition. The authors lean towards like Montiel and Delgado-Ceballos (2014) corporate sustainability definition. They propose using "corporate sustainability to refer to the tridimensional construct (economic, social, and environmental) and to use "corporate environmental sustainability" when focusing on just the environmental aspects. Likewise, "corporate economic sustainability" and "corporate social sustainability" refer to the economic or social dimensions. Therefore, to prevent ambiguity or confusion, this chapter uses the label "corporate sustainability" as proposed by Montiel and Delgado-Ceballos (2014).

THEORETICAL LENSES

It is worth considering some pioneering studies in the theoretical and conceptual contribution of the field. Especially Bowen (1953), recognized as the first comprehensive discussion of business ethics and social responsibility; and Carroll (1979), who tried to reconcile defenders with opponents of CSR in the management arena. These authors highlighted the moral responsibilities to society from managers and introduced frameworks to guide managers decisions related to sustainability, especially to social actions

The study of corporate sustainability has been conducted using different theoretical approaches (Montiel & Delgado-Ceballos, 2014). Montiel, Gallo, and Antolin-Lopez (2020) classify these theories in two categories: established organizational theories and new frameworks for corporate sustainability. The established organizational theories are institutional theory, stakeholder theory, and resource-based view theory.

Institutional Theory

This theory explains that firms respond to sustainability issues for gaining and maintaining legitimacy due to the pressure of its institutional environment (Hahn et al., 2017). It focusses on how institutional pressures shape the decisions made by the firm's managers and top executives (DiMaggio & Powell, 1983). Initially, firms' responses to social and environmental issues are because of government regulation. This type of response is known as "coercive isomorphism". As time passes and corporate sustainability gains momentum, the type of response has evolved to a more voluntary and strategic response (Montiel, Antolin-López, & Gallo, 2020). The types of isomorphic pressures (normative, coercive, and mimetic) help explain how firms respond to sustainability issues (DiMaggio & Powell, 1983).

The drivers of institutional theory explain why firms become more sustainable, and it helps firms' executives understand how external pressures affect and define their decision making (Montiel et al., 2020). This theoretical lens has been used to explain the emergence of new sustainable industries (Hiatt et al., 2009; J. Jones et al., 2019; York et al., 2018; York & Lenox, 2014), certifiable sustainable standards (Christmann & Taylor, 2001; Delmas & Montes-Sancho, 2009; Husted et al., 2016; Montiel et al., 2012, 2019), the emergence of "pollution havens" transfer by multinational enterprises to their foreign subsidiaries (Surroca et al., 2013), the gain of environmental legitimacy (Bansal & Clelland, 2004), differences practices between regions (Matten & Moon, 2008), and implementation of practices (Delmas & Toffel, 2004).

Montiel et al. (2020) found four threshold concepts in this theory that allow managers to make and integrate many previously unrelated ideas within corporate sustainability. The first one, *Moral Legitimizing,* highlights the importance of having managers interpret the foundations of their firm's legitimacy and how these may affect the susceptibility to commit to corporate sustainability behavior and responsible management practices. The second threshold concept, *Disruption-Linked Contagion*, goes beyond the isomorphism types defined by DiMaggio and Powell (1983). This concept introduces the idea that managers must consider the influence of activists on peers' adoption practices, and how the activist's tactics may lead them to ignore certain corporate sustainability initiatives despite the potential value or importance to the firm.

The third threshold concept, *Means-ends-Decoupling,* helps managers understand that achieving corporate sustainability is not easy. Implementing corporate sustainability practices in the firm is not following simple instructions. For a firm to adopt new corporate sustainability practices, it must understand the desired sustainability goals and allow firm executives to adjust practices to ensure the firm's goals are accomplished (Montiel et al., 2020). The final threshold concept, *Pollution Haven*, identifies how firms respond to institutional pressures for responsible management practices or corporate sustainability practices. Firms may respond by sending management abroad or transferring their irresponsible management to countries where the institutional environment is weaker and where institutions have less influence (Montiel et al., 2020).

The institutional theoretical lens has been important for researchers and practitioners for understanding why firms develop or introduce corporate sustainability practices. The new drivers and threshold concepts that emerge from new research on corporate sustainability are framed with institutional theory. The theory recommends pushing forward to understand how managers can respond to their firm's external pressures in a better way while becoming more sustainable (Montiel et al., 2020).

Stakeholder Theory

The main premise of this theory is that firms must consider all of the groups and individuals that can affect or are affected by the firm while addressing its purpose. These groups or individuals are called stakeholders (Freeman, 1984). Thus, firms should not be managed in isolation, and firms must consider the concerns of different groups, not just financial stakeholders or shareholders. A firm trying to implement a strategy and generate economic profit will require access to critical resources that stakeholders have that are within or outside the boundaries of the firm (Barney, 2018).

Firms trying to develop a sustainable corporate strategy must consider the multiple and conflicting objectives of different stakeholders (Montiel et al., 2020). Corporate sustainability literature has focused on how stakeholders influence a firm's sustainable strategy (Montiel & Delgado-Ceballos, 2014). For example, Buysse and Verbeke (2003) studied the connection between proactive environmental strategies and stakeholder management; while Sharma and Henriques (2005) showed how stakeholder pressure influenced the development of more proactive environmental strategies. Finally, Delmas and Toffel (2008) studied stakeholder (market and non-market) pressure for the adoption of environmental practices. Most of the studies have focused on the pressure from stakeholders to adopt corporate sustainability strategies. Hart and Sharma (2004) studied the impact of how more marginalized stakeholders influence such strategies.

As can be seen, this framework has given important insights to managers, scholars, and practitioners about why firms adopt different types of corporate sustainable strategies when considering stakeholder pressures. Montiel et al. (2020) have also found threshold concepts in this theoretical lens. The first concept is *Corporate social performance (CSP) Consistency*, which helps managers focus on their level of engagement and on their commitment over time.

The second concept is *Dynamic Stakeholder Salience*, which reveals the complexities that managers must understand if they want to have a consistent relationship with their stakeholders because it differs from the information the environment. For instance, a firm that is trying to have a consistent relationship with the local government but is in a local office that does not have a good relationship with the community, would have to manage the problem of the community talking about their problem.

Finally, the third concept is *CSR Enabled Corporate Social Irresponsibility (CSiR)*. It helps managers understand that prior CSR achievements may have potential traps. Thus, prior CSR achievements may drive managers or firms to decisions that result in irresponsible management (Luo et al., 2018; Montiel et al., 2020; Ormiston & Wong, 2013). The stakeholder theory has been an important framework for explaining why firms adopt corporate sustainability practices that are triggered by their stakeholders.

Resource-Based View (RBV)

The resource-based view (RBV) argues that firms can only obtain a competitive advantage if markets (resources and capabilities) are imperfect (Barney, 1986, 1991). Hart (1995) extended this theory by including the interaction of the firm with its natural environment. He argued that firms that considered their natural environment while strategizing would develop specific resources and capabilities that would let them achieve a competitive advantage. Thus, the *natural resource-based view* (NRBV) was developed. This framework has allowed researchers to examine how the conditions for tackling environmental and social issues can result in a sustained competitive advantage (Hahn et al., 2017).

This theoretical lens allows managers to understand how firms can gain competitive advantage by developing corporate sustainability strategies (Hahn et al., 2017). NRBV or RBV framework has tried to connect corporate sustainability performance with financial performance, and accordingly, is a relevant theory for studying corporate sustainability (Montiel and Delgado-Ceballos, 2014). Examples of studies that have used this theoretical framework include Russo and Fouts (1997), Klassen and Whybark (1999), Aragón-Correa and Sharma (2003), and McWilliams and Siegel (2011), among others.

Montiel et al. (2020) have also found important concepts in this theory. The first concept is *Time and Stock Dampening*. Stock dampening refers to rare resources that firms require for corporate sustainability implementation. Time dampening refers to the loss of value creation of the rare resources if too much time has passed since the market initially demanded such resources. The second concept is *CSR as Insurance*, which means that firms can communicate their sustainability initiatives to reduce the negative impact on the firm bonds and stocks if a negative issue arises. Both concepts were developed by Flammer's (2013) study.

The third concept is *Innovation in Resource Depleted Markets*, which can help firm executives realize that entering markets with high resource munificence may hinder innovation. Finally, the authors found two more concepts, *Bi-directional Environmental Capability Transfer* and *Context-Specific Micro-Foundations*. Both related to dynamic capabilities. The first explains how corporate sustainability capabilities may be transferred through complex corporate entities, and the second one refers to how changes in the environmental, social, and cultural environment determine different corporate sustainability practices (Montiel et al., 2020).

These new threshold concepts found by Montiel et al. (2020) identify new types of resources and capabilities that firms can develop to execute a better corporate sustainability strategy and maintain its competitive advantage. It is important to highlight that this theoretical lens shifts the focus of the study from corporate sustainability to inside the firm.

The three revised theories have advanced understanding in the corporate sustainability field. Stakeholder theory has been used by different studies to identify and analyze the diversity of corporate sustainability while the firm pursues the interests of its stakeholders. Institutional theory helps explain the adaptation, evolution, and diffusion of institutionalization of different corporate sustainability practices when firms search for legitimacy. Finally, RBV helps to understand how firms' resources and capabilities can be used to implement more advanced corporate sustainability practices while maintaining their competitive advantage (Montiel & Delgado-Ceballos, 2014). New theories and frameworks have evolved the field of corporate sustainability and help advance the understanding of how firms can implement corporate sustainability strategies. One of these is the new micro-foundations of corporate sustainability framework (Montiel et al., 2020).

In the next section, the micro-foundation framework is introduced to the corporate sustainability field to see how it is helpful for understanding why firms introduce corporate sustainability practices.

NEW THEORETICAL FRAMEWORKS

Most of the theoretical lenses review in this chapter has focused on external and internal factors of why firms develop corporate sustainability strategies. It is important to highlight that internal factors refer to resources, static or dynamic capabilities that lie at a macrolevel. Therefore, none of these theoretical lenses highlights the importance of micro-foundations mechanism that try to explain why firms become more social and environmental proactive.

Figure 1. Theoretical lenses that have been used to study corporate sustainability
Source: *Self-elaboration*

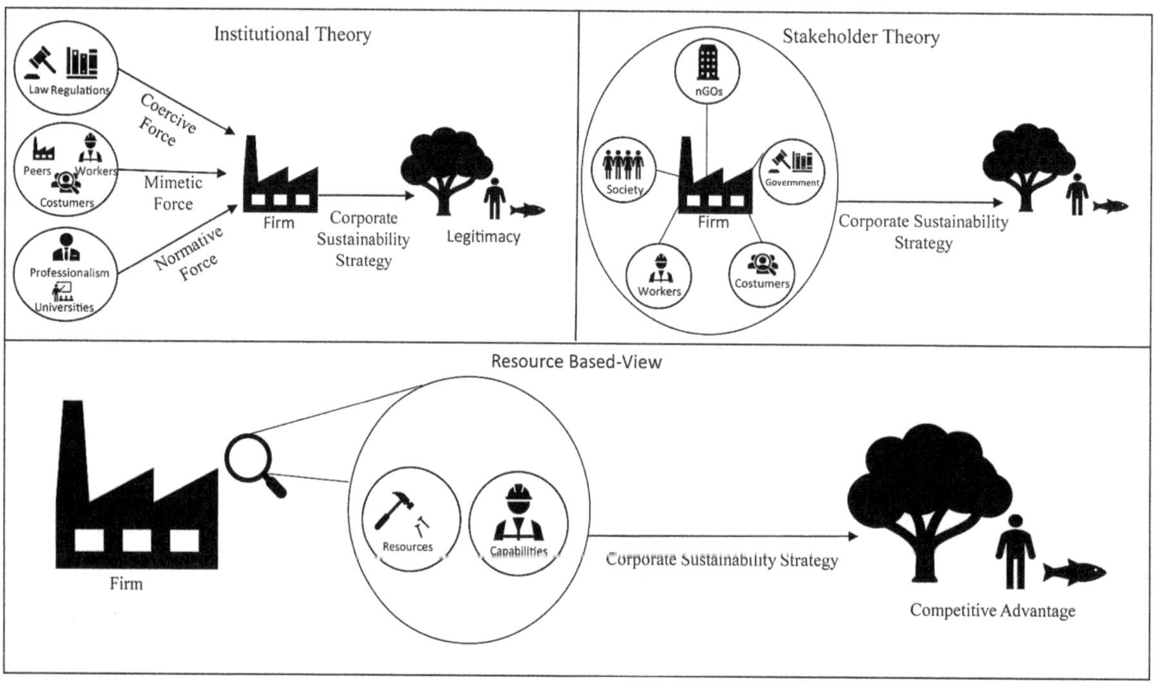

The theoretical lenses try to connect the importance for a firm to improve its relationship with its social and environmental environment, because the better performance with such environments would lead the firms to gain competitive advantage. In other words, trying to find the "business case" or connect the corporate sustainability strategies to the bottom line (Kaplan, 2020). Considering other stakeholders beside shareholders for rent creation (Barney, 2018), means that the way to measure performance must consider other dimensions, not only economic profit (Barney, 2020). In this line of reasoning, Barney

(2020) proposes that profits must be measured at three levels; at firm level (macro), at the level of "each of the individuals and organizations who make profit-generation resources available to a firm" (micro Level) (p. 6) and at the level of all the group that are involved to generate profit (micro and macro). Therefore, the limitations that theoretical lenses reviewed can be surpassed by the Micro-foundation framework.

Micro-foundations: Strategic Management View

Most of the strategic management research has been done at the macro level, and this prompted the emergence of the micro-foundations view. Firm-level studies have been important for explaining the origins of competitive advantage and firm's heterogeneity, especially when management research moved forward in trying to open the "black box" and conceptualize firms as a set of resources and capabilities. Now, research is trying to open the "black-box" of such aggregations (resources and capabilities) to understand how organizational factors and advantages emerge (Barney & Felin, 2013). This highlights the importance of understanding the micro-foundations of strategy and using this framework in research as well as in practice.

The main proposition of this view is that firms or organizations are made up of individuals and therefore, there is no firm or organization without individuals (Felin & Foss, 2006). Besides these elementary characteristics of organizations, strategy and management research has focused on structure, routines, capabilities, culture, institutions, and other collective constructs. This has negatively affected theory building, empirical research, and managerial practices in the field (Felin & Foss, 2006). Thus, this framework tries to highlight the importance of the individual level origins (micro-foundations) of collective constructs as they emerge from the individual action and interaction of the members of the organization (Felin & Foss, 2006).

One of the main objectives of strategic management research is to uncover or understand firm-level or industry-level heterogeneity (Hoskisson et al., 1999). At the firm-level, many strategy scholars have converged to highlight organizational capabilities as key mechanisms (Winter, 2003). Organizational capabilities are the most important level of analysis, and organizations must be seen as a central repository of them (Abell et al., 2008; Felin & Foss, 2006). Besides this, to understand such heterogeneity, it requires putting substantial attention to explanatory mechanisms located at the micro-level, which means focusing on the individual action and interaction (Abell et al., 2008). The neglect of the individual level can be seen in Zollo and Winter's (2002) definition of capabilities "learned and stable pattern of collective activity" (p. 340). This definition highlights the importance of collective constructs and misses potentially important individual-level information (Felin & Foss, 2006). Therefore, much of the research in strategy and management has been done in the links between organizational capabilities and firm outcomes, but research on the foundations or origins of those capabilities at the individual level is missing (Abell et al., 2008).

Micro-foundations literature proposes that macro-outputs, like firm-level capabilities, performance, strategies, etc. must be understood by studying their underlying actions, interactions, and characteristics of micro-level entities, for example, individuals and managers (Contractor et al., 2019). The focus on firm-level analysis supposes that the firms can think or decide on their own, and neglect the fact that there are the executives and managers who think or make decisions. Thus, the characteristics, motivations, and interactions of managers in companies have been missing in the explanation of the firm's strategy formulation (Contractor et al., 2019). The framework of micro-foundations asserts that the micro-level has explanatory primacy and the behaviors and characteristics of individual managers and actors must be studied for a more complete explanation of firm strategy (Felin & Foss, 2006; Teece, 2007).

Micro-foundations research breaks down the macro-level variables in terms of actions and interactions of lower-level organizational members, with the objective of understanding how firm-level performance emerges from the interactions of these members (Foss, 2011; Foss & Pedersen, 2016). That is opening the "black-box" of the mechanism and entities at lower-levels that explains macro constructs such as competitive advantage. Therefore, according to Foss and Pedersen (2016), micro-foundations are "an analytical level of argument and not necessarily an argument about individuals" (p. E24). The framework locates (theoretically and empirically) the proximate causes of a phenomenon (mechanism, explanations of outcomes, etc.) at a level of analysis lower than the phenomenon itself (Linder & Foss, 2018).

Any theoretical or empirical research that tries to explain an organizational phenomenon (the explanandum–dependent variables) has to choose the level of analysis at which the important mechanism or components of the explanans (independent variables) are located. In the case of micro-foundations, the competitive advantage (explanandum) of the firm is not explained by the firm's capabilities (macro-level); instead, it is explained by the characteristics of the CEO (explanans), such as their age or educational background (Abell et al., 2008; Felin & Foss, 2006). The authors use this framework to focus specifically on the origins of capabilities and competitive advantage (Barney & Felin, 2013).

When analyzing organizations and firms, a fundamental concern is how individual factors aggregate at a collective level (Barney & Felin, 2013). Barney (1986) explained that the origins of competitive advantage occurred due to unique information or expectations from firms' markets, or maybe by luck. This exclusive information or knowledge of the market by a specific firm does not make the market competitive; thus, the reference is underpriced. This proposal supposed that knowledge or information was held by the firm. But, because firms are collections of individuals, focusing only on the firm-level would be shorthanded. Information and knowledge are not possessed by firms *per se*, but rather by individuals within it or the shared knowledge or information between them, that can be aggregated up to the firm-level (Barney & Felin, 2013). One of the main ideas is that managers' decisions and actions enable firms to gain a competitive advantage (Molina-Azorín, 2014).

Managers' characteristics and interactions with other firm members influence the constructions of capabilities (Winter, 2012). They are key authors of big or more important decisions in the firm (Contractor et al., 2019) and define firm objectives or goals (Linder & Foss, 2018). These actions inevitably take place at the micro-level and not at the macro-level. So, for individuals, micro-foundations are really important and matter for explaining the collective strategic phenomena (Molina-Azorín, 2014). This reinforces the importance of deeply understanding the individuals within organizations or firms (Felin & Foss, 2006). The micro-foundation framework aims to "unpack or decompose aggregate firm-level concepts in terms of individual actions and interactions; to understand how individual-level factors impact organizations; and to understand the process that aggregate individual actions into resultant strategy outcomes" (Contractor et al., 2019, p. 6).

In the next section, there is an explanation of the micro-foundations of corporate sustainability, what mechanisms explain the corporate sustainability strategies firms develop, and how it has become an emerging framework in the corporate sustainability field (Montiel et al., 2020).

Micro-foundations in Corporate Sustainability

Relationship Between Macro and Micro Foundations

Research in corporate sustainability (CS) has been analyzed primarily at the macro level rather than at the micro-level (Aguinis & Glavas, 2012; Cooper et al., 2017; Hahn et al., 2017). Many researchers have proposed that the micro-foundations framework can help reach a more complete understanding of CS (Montiel et al., 2020) by highlighting the role of individuals in making the firm more sustainable (De Roeck and Maon, 2018; Wang, Tong, Takeuchi, & George, 2016). Studies in CS have tried to uncover the antecedents of why firms become more sustainable (Bansal & Roth, 2000; Darnall, Henriques, & Sadorsky, 2010), the outcomes of firms adopting CS practices, which have basically focus in the relationship between sustainability performance and financial performance (Kaplan, 2020; Barnett & Salomon, 2012; Grewatsch & Kleindienst, 2017), and finally, the process of implementation or decision making when firms become more sustainable (Bansal & Song, 2017; Montiel et al., 2020; Wang et al., 2016).

Shevchenko, Lévesque, & Pagell, (2016) state that for a firm to become truly sustainable depends on its own capabilities. This is because firms need to fundamentally change how they do business and not rely on non-renewable resources and unethical practices. The firms need to generate profit but that is not a sufficient condition for its long-term survival. Sustainability issues do not have simple solutions, and firms need to find novel ways to introduce sustainable practices. To achieve this, firms will have to develop breakthrough technologies and new business models, for example firms have developed fast responsible innovation during the COVID-19 pandemic in developed economies (Gutiérrez et al., 2020) and emerging economies (Balarezo & Montiel, 2020) to adapt to extreme changes and tackle grand challenges (George et al., 2016). This is why firms need to develop capabilities; to become truly sustainable, firms need to make radical innovations rather than incremental innovations.

Micro-foundations

Helfat and Peteraf (2003) define capability as "the ability of an organization to perform a coordinated set of tasks, utilizing organizational resources, for the purpose of achieving a particular end result" (p. 999). This definition considers capabilities at the firm-level. However, as in the micro-foundation framework, decisions are made at an individual level (Devinney, 2013). The development of firm capabilities depends on the cognitive frame dimension of managers (Grewatsch & Kleindienst, 2017) and the skills and knowledge of one or few managers to develop dynamic capabilities (Teece, 2012). Dynamic capabilities are a key issue when firms address rapidly changing business environments, such as environmental and social issues (Teece, 2007). Thus, it is important to understand how capabilities are built, the role of specific managers or workers in building them, and other explanations of aggregation (Barney & Felin, 2013). This highlights the importance that CEOs and top management teams in making the firm more sustainable (Bansal & Song, 2017).

In CS, it is important to understand what behaviors pops or predetermines as antecedents to actions and plans made by executives in firms to become more sustainable (Cooper et al., 2017). Similar to strategic management research, where managers are key for firms to gain and sustain competitive advantage through their decisions and actions (Molina-Azorín, 2014), the same is true for a firm to introduce corporate sustainability strategies. This action must take place at the micro-level and has been labeled in the micro-foundation of the corporate sustainability field as *managerial power* (Montiel et al., 2020).

Figure 2. Micro-foundations of corporate sustainability
Source*: Self-elaboration*

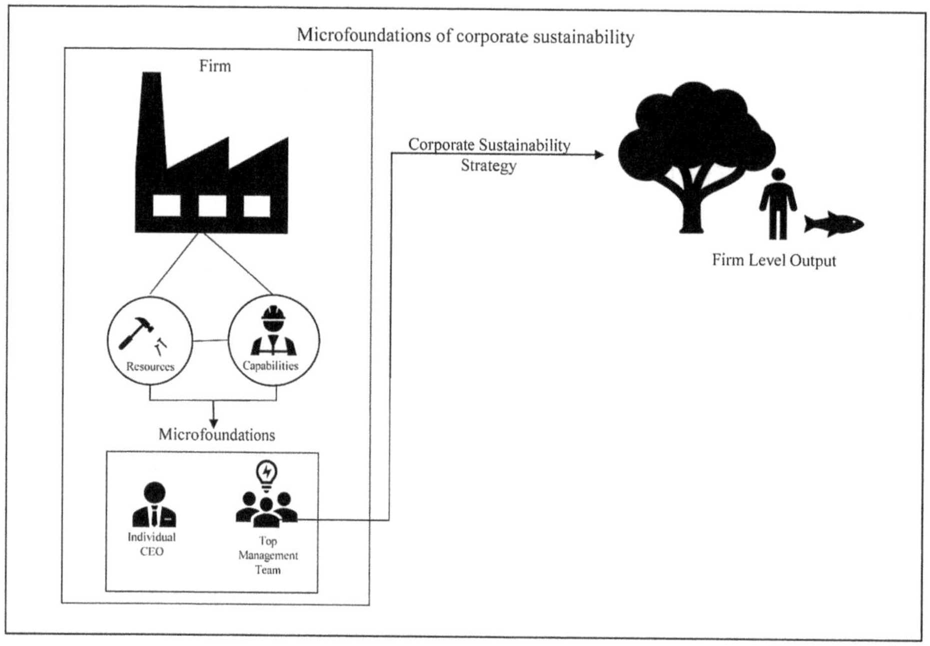

The idea of managerial power is to study the role that managers have in CS decision making and commitment (Montiel et al., 2020). Thus, to understand the collective CS phenomenon, it is important to study the micro-level (Molina-Azorín, 2014).

For firms to become truly sustainable, they need to develop capabilities and understand that the origins of the firm's capabilities are rooted at the micro or individual level. The role that abilities, propensities, purposes, expectations, heterogeneity, and motivations have in firms' managers need to be understood for them to develop corporate sustainability strategies and produce heterogeneity afterwards (Foss & Pedersen, 2016; Molina-Azorín, 2014). In other words, and using James Coleman's (1990) model, studies using the micro-foundations are trying to explain the independent variables (X) in corporate sustainability with dependent variables (Y) at the level of individuals (Abell et al., 2008; Felin & Foss, 2006).

Figure 3 shows that corporate sustainability studies may focus on macro variables or micro variables. Most of the studies have been focused on the macro-level (see line 4). The macro output (Y) represents the sustainability, environmental, social or economic performance of the firms, while the macro conditions represent the independent variables, such as firm-level capabilities, institutional environment, or social culture. When trying to understand why a firm becomes more sustainable or develop corporate sustainability strategies, mechanisms, drivers, or explanations can focus on the macro level. For example, firms may develop more advanced sustainable strategies because of the environmental and social legislation of the country or industry or because of stakeholders' pressures or economic opportunities (Bansal & DesJardine, 2014; Darnall et al., 2010).

Sometimes, firms may introduce corporate sustainability practices because there are bribery practices or corrupt culture in the country to show desire conduct (Montiel et al., 2012). In addition, research has focused on the effect of such practices in financial performance (Eccles et al., 2014; Grewatsch &

Figure 3. Relationship between Micro and Macro levels of Sustainability Studies
Source: *Self-elaboration modeled after Coleman's (1990) framework idea.*

Sustainability studies (From Coleman 1990; Felin and Foss, 2005)

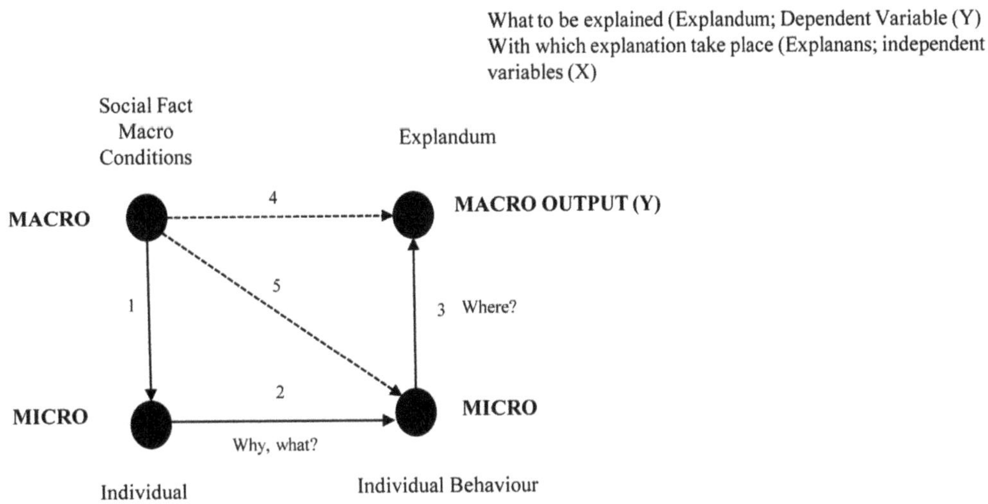

Line 4: X = Macro, Y = Macro. Examples, X (Capabilities, Culture, Environment, Institution, etc.); Y (Organizational outcome, competitive advantage, etc.)
Line 5; X = Macro, Y = Micro. Examples, X (Capabilities, Culture, Environment, etc.); Y (Individual behaviour)
Line 1: X = Macro, Y = Micro, Examples, Idem line 5
Line 2: X = Micro, Y = Micro
Line 3: X = Micro, Y = Macro

Line 1, 4 and 5 not give casual consideration to lower levels, completely discarding; lower levels inherently are determined by higher levels cause. What there contextual factors are and how they cause an individual behaviour?
Line 2 focus on individual interaction and associated outcomes

Kleindienst, 2017; Kaplan, 2020) and non-financial performance such as stock market risk (Bansal & Clelland, 2004). Nevertheless, usually, the explanation of why firms have adopted more advanced corporate sustainability practices and the impact of such practices of firm performance has focused on an aggregate level or macro-level.

Lines 1 and 5 in Figure 3 illustrate how macro-level independent variables (X) act as mechanisms or drivers of dependent variables at the micro-level or individual. For example, the institutional environment or culture of a country may affect the individual environmental and social values of managers or CEOs. Egri and Herman (2000) show how leadership values affect the introduction of corporate sustainability practices in firms while Bansal & Roth (2000) show the importance of ethical motives of managers for greening the firm.

In his research project the leading author realized that Peruvian CEOs who have lived during the terrorism years[2] were more sensitive to social values (i.e., they were more concerned with poor people, so they worked closely with the community) than CEOs that were too young to remember the terrorism years. Conversely, the young ones were more sensitive to environmental values (i.e., they were more concerned about climate change, overconsumption, etc.). Line 5 shows how stakeholder pressures, institutional environment, or the culture of a country can work as mechanisms to promote sustainable behavior of managers in a firm. For example, Jamali and Sidani (2008) studied show how the cultural and institutional realities affected the managerial perspectives of CSR in Lebanon.

Finally, lines 2 and 3 focus on the micro-level, where both dependent (Y) and independents variables (X) are located at the individual or micro level of analysis (line 2) or the X variables are located at the micro-level and the Y variable at the macro level. Therefore, in the case of line 2, some researchers have focused on trying to explain how demographics (genre, age, religion, etc.) explained sustainable managerial behaviors (Cheah et al., 2011). In line 3, studies have focused on how the behaviors of managers and workers, as individuals or teams, have improved the sustainable performance of the firm. For example, the study of Branzei, Ursacki-Bryant, Vertinsky, & Zhang (2004) showed how "champions" in Chinese firms develop and advance environmental strategies. Further, Shea and Hawn (2019) conclude that individual social perceptions (such as warmth and competence) lead to specific CSR outcomes.

Figure 4. Micro-foundations mechanisms and antecedents that trigger Corporate Sustainability output at macro and micro level

Source: *Self elaboration elaborate from: Akhtar et al., 2018, 2018; Antolin-Lopez & Montiel, 2018; Arena et al., 2018; Bansal et al., 2018; Bushee et al., 2019; Chin et al., 2013; Hafenbrädl & Waeger, 2017; Huang, 2013; Jansson et al., 2017; Lewis et al., 2014; Mazutis & Eckardt, 2017; Reimer et al., 2018; Shahab et al., 2018; Stahl & Sully de Luque, 2014; Tang et al., 2015; Walls & Berrone, 2017; Wijethilake & Lama, 2019*

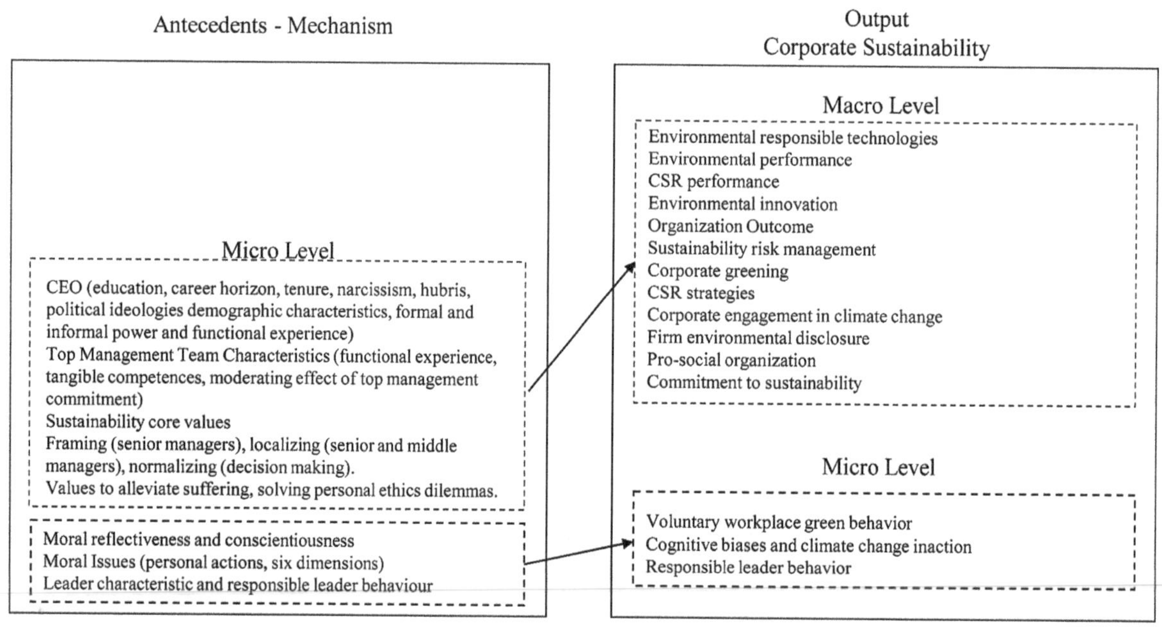

For a firm to become more sustainable, it needs to develop capabilities and redefine its purpose, which means going beyond operating the firm profitably (Hollensbe et al., 2014). Thus, the purpose is connected with the goals an organization wants to address. When referring to corporate sustainability, the goal is more long-term than short-term, and the purpose of the firm must include shareholders as well as other stakeholders (Bansal & DesJardine, 2014). To address that, firms must change their business models by "doing business as usual" practices (Shevchenko et al., 2016), making trade-offs between short-term benefits (profits) and long-term ones (Bansal & DesJardine, 2014). As seen early in this chapter, organizations or firms do not have goals; individual, managers, or management teams have goals (Linder & Foss, 2018). The micro-foundations framework helps understand the individual level of firms and how firms become more sustainable over time. Figure 4 shows the different drives at the micro level that explains sustainability outputs at the firm and micro level.

Usually, research has focused on trying to find or build a business case for sustainability (Kaplan, 2020). In doing so, much of the research has been oriented to the mechanisms or drivers at a macro level that explain why or how firms introduce or develop more advanced corporate sustainability strategies while obtaining positive financial performance. But it seems that researchers have forgotten that there are individual, micro-level factors that could determine the corporate sustainable posture a firm takes. Further, research has found support in how demographics characteristics of CEOS, CEOs' political characteristics, CEOs' psychological characteristics, managers' team characteristics, etc. (Cf. figure 4) act as mechanisms for firms to become more sustainable. Thus, advancing the research in the CS field using the micro-foundations framework helps extend the understanding of how and why firms become more sustainable and also helps managers and practitioners understand how they can make their business more sustainable.

To make a firm sustainable is not an easy job (Shevchenko et al., 2016). There is not also a unique receipt. Sometimes a firm can decide to address grand challenges (George et al., 2016), but as time passes, they can go back to do "business as usual" (Wright & Nyberg, 2017) or sometimes these grand challenges are displaced by lower challenges in society (Grodal & O'Mahony, 2017). This because as different researchers (e.g., Bansal, George, Grodal, & O´Mahony) have said, grand challenges are complex problems that lack a clear solution and must be studied not only at the macro-levels but also on the micro-levels.

For example, Wright and Nyberg (2017) studied why firms that decided to tackle grand challenges, such as climate change, later went back to their old non-sustainable practices. Interestingly, they discovered that firms decided to tackle climate change because it was a highly publicized negative environmental and social event in the corporate arena. For instance, a mining company that generates chemical pollution in a river in The Andes would be widely covered in the media and on social networks. Different stakeholders -both nationally and worldwide- would start complying and judging the mining firm and the whole mining industry. Thus, managers from the mining firms respond to the external critiques made by the government, NGOs, costumers, and other external stakeholders that care about climate change and decide to introduce sustainable practices that go beyond the law. In this first stage, Wright and Nyberg (2017) found that corporate sustainability actions were related to market discourse. In other words, the mining firm tries to manage its risk and gain new customer segments by improving its corporate sustainability reputation Basically, the managers frame this opportunity as a win-win situation.

It is important to highlight that besides the mechanism that triggers the implementation of a corporate sustainability strategy by the mining firm at the macro-level (pressure by stakeholders), it is at the micro-level that managers of a firm frame the opportunity and how to respond to pressures coming from stakeholders. In other words, the micro-foundations complement the explanation of the sustainability posture of the firm. So, as Wright and Nyberg (2017) highlight, framing of the managers is the first step in how organizations translate grand challenges not being a permanent fix. As time passes, the framing of managers may change and, therefore, the firm may drop off the grand challenge.

Suppose now that the firm introduces new environmental technology, makes huge investment in the community, and decides to use a pipeline to transport the mineral to the sea port instead of using trucks. These actions can be valuable for stakeholders such as environmental NGOs, local governments, and the community. However, they can be challenged by other stakeholders, such as financial firms, rating agencies, or the stock exchange market in how such initiatives contribute to the bottom line of the firm or how essential they are to the business. These tensions generate a second stage that Wright and Nyberg (2017) labeled as *localizing*. In this stage, the firm's corporate sustainability practices try to satisfy both the sustainability and profitability initiatives. For example, the mining firm can decide to use a mineral mix transportation system. Some kilometers by trucks and others (where there is population) with the pipeline, so the firm can save on investment and operational costs of the pipeline. This may satisfy the community, local government, and the financial stockholders by increasing the firm's margin. In this stage, firms have a big risk of greenwashing because they are not correctly introducing sustainable practices that maximize the sustainability performance of the firm (Wright & Nyberg, 2017). Again, the framing of managers affects the type of corporate sustainability practice the firm makes (micro-foundations).

In the end, there is a deterioration of the sustainable practices and the firm prefers to satisfy shareholders and drops out the many advanced practices they previously introduced. Now, top management teams and shareholders ask a threshold of profitability for the firm to introduce a corporate sustainability strategy. In other words, if the practice is not profitable it is not introduced, the mining firm will be more likely to go back to its business as usual, because the firm have not found the business case (Kaplan, 2020). Wright and Nyberg (2017) found that the CEOs or managers that championed the grand challenges issue left the firm once the firm went back to do business as usual. This highlights the importance of the individual, managers, and top management teams in making the firm more sustainable. Therefore, the micro-foundation framework is important for the corporate sustainability field.

Grodal and O´Mahony (2017) study also highlighted the importance of the micro-foundation framework. They tried to understand why so many field initiatives, where diverse communities-societies tried to address ambitious goals (like climate change, corruption, pandemic, etc.), fell short and ended up reverting back to lower or selfish objectives. They found that institutional research normally focused on field mobilization, not on how goals were pursued. Institutional theorists have assumed that individuals are stable and their goals are easily translated into practices; but, they found that this assumption was far from reality. Fields are dynamic and individuals' goals change, so a grand challenge can be displaced with a less ambitious goal. This highlights the importance of understanding the characteristics of individuals, their background, their thought, and their motivation; in order to understand how macro results could change over time.

The above study can be clarified using a hypothetical example. For instance, consider a country where the society decides to tackle climate change. Government, NGOs, consumers, firms, and universities work together to develop new laws, regulations, practices, and other initiatives to become a truly sustainable country. Moreover, they decide to reduce their carbon emission in the next 15–25 years, and the government and firms manage using sustainable development goals as indicators. So, as a country and society, all are in a sustainable car! But as time passes, each constituent starts searching for their own objective. For example, the metal industry realizes that they need to invest in new costly technologies to make their process more sustainable and reduce its CO_2 emissions. As such, they decide to start lobbying with the government or decide to introduce not to advanced sustainability practices, such as using natural gas engines that have lower emissions (but not zero) instead of using coal or oil engines. In the other hand, some costumers do not want to pay higher prices for organic food/products or more sustainable products, so they continue buying "brown" products. Sometimes, costumers continue paying for plastic bags in supermarkets. Thus, the grand challenge is displaced for a less ambitious goal, that would only be compliance with some international or national environmental regulations.

As has been demonstrated, the micro-foundation framework in corporate sustainability is gaining momentum and importance (Montiel et al., 2020). New concepts have arisen from it. Montiel et al.

(2020) found moral as driver for firms to engage in corporate sustainability initiatives. For example, the importance of personal values and managers' role in introducing sustainable practices in firms, the importance of the personal effects and how they mold managers' decisions on sustainability issues, and the importance of the beliefs and knowledge of managers and how they make the firm more sustainable. These have been labeled by Montiel et al. (2020) "Moral Outrage" and "Unactivated Positive Affect".

The other domain of the micro-foundation in corporate sustainability is the individuals' evaluations (Montiel et al., 2020). One threshold concept is *Managerial Judgment and Attributions of CSR*, which refers to how middle managers are influenced by their superiors and how their judgments and attributions promote or reduce sustainable practices in the firm (Montiel et al., 2020). Also, the "harmonious environmental passion" is a positive driver in how individuals engage in pro-sustainable behaviors. Finally, the micro-foundations in corporate sustainability have studied individual reactions to CSR, where a threshold was "task significance", meaning that an employee's work has a positive impact on other individuals (Montiel et al., 2020).

The micro-foundation framework in corporate sustainability is an important lens to study the mechanism, process, and results of sustainable strategies made by firms. It helps us understand why firms in the same institutional contexts introduce different sustainable actions, and therefore, they have heterogenous sustainability performance at the macro level. This fact makes researchers highlight the importance of agency inside the firm (Goodrick & Salancik, 1996). Thus, understanding and identifying these mechanisms (some examples are shown in figure 4) at the individual level helps managers make their businesses more sustainable.

Finally, Shea and Hawn (2019) pointed out that more cross-disciplinary research should be developed. Especially Psychology (D.A. Jones et al., 2017) will extend the boundaries and understanding of corporate sustainability, focusing on how attitudes and characteristics of managers and workers affect organizational outcomes. Therefore, deepening the understanding of psychology and demographic characteristic of teams, managers and workers can guide firms in developing more advance corporate sustainability strategies; and therefore, tackle grand challenges such as climate change and social inequality.

CONCLUSION

Firms are the best agents to address climate change and other grand challenges (Adler, 2016; Davis, 2016; George et al., 2016), but they have also been the most significant contributors to carbon emissions (Wright & Nyberg, 2017), unemployment (Davis, 2016) and social inequality (Adler, 2016; Tsui et al., 2018). Therefore, firms need to become truly sustainable, and they must change their "doing business as usual" mindset by acquiring and developing capabilities (Shevchenko et al., 2016). This is not an easy job. As the MIT-BCG (2017) study corroborates, 90% of the CEOs of the surveyed companies consider sustainability as an important issue, while only 60% have developed a sustainability strategy, and only 25% have a business case for sustainability.

The business case, mechanisms, and drivers need to be understood so that firms may become more sustainable in the future. Firms need capabilities to reach that objective, and capabilities are grounded in the individuals, managers, workers that are part of the firm. The macro foundation framework does not allow analysis at the individual level; therefore, it is important to study the micro-foundations of corporate sustainability. Doing so sheds light on how managers transform their business into a sustainable business. As there is no Planet B[3], firms must act on sustainability issues the micro-level factors and drivers that explain the social and greening of the company must be understood. The micro-foundations framework and future research using this framework will help managers and management scholars understand how firms can tackle grand challenges.

Hopefully, this chapter can help management scholars and managers understand the importance of the micro-foundations framework and allow them develop more advanced corporate sustainability strategies.

ACKNOWLEDGMENT

The authors are really grateful for the research assistance of Carolina Mendes de Barros.

REFERENCES

Abell, P., Felin, T., & Foss, N. (2008). Building micro-foundations for the routines, capabilities, and performance links. *Managerial and Decision Economics*, *29*(6), 489–502. doi:10.1002/mde.1413

Adler, P. S. (2016). Alternative Economic Futures: A Research Agenda for Progressive Management Scholarship. *The Academy of Management Perspectives*, *30*(2), 123–128. doi:10.5465/amp.2016.0054

Aguinis, H., & Glavas, A. (2012). What We Know and Don't Know About Corporate Social Responsibility: A Review and Research Agenda. *Journal of Management*, *38*(4), 932–968. doi:10.1177/0149206311436079

Akhtar, P., Khan, Z., Frynas, J. G., Tse, Y. K., & Rao-Nicholson, R. (2018). Essential Micro-foundations for Contemporary Business Operations: Top Management Tangible Competencies, Relationship-based Business Networks and Environmental Sustainability. *British Journal of Management*, *29*(1), 43–62. doi:10.1111/1467-8551.12233

Antolin-Lopez, R., & Montiel, I. (2018). Entrepreneurial Collective Responses to Sustainability-related Grand Challenges. *Academy of Management Proceedings*, *2018*(1), 11471. doi:10.5465/AMBPP.2018.83

Aragón-Correa, J. A., & Sharma, S. (2003). A Contingent Resource-Based View of Proactive Corporate Environmental Strategy. *Academy of Management Review*, *28*(1), 71–88. doi:10.5465/amr.2003.8925233

Arena, C., Michelon, G., & Trojanowski, G. (2018). Big Egos Can Be Green: A Study of CEO Hubris and Environmental Innovation: CEO Hubris and Environmental Innovation. *British Journal of Management*, *29*(2), 316–336. doi:10.1111/1467-8551.12250

Ashrafi, M., Adams, M., Walker, T. R., & Magnan, G. (2018). 'How corporate social responsibility can be integrated into corporate sustainability: A theoretical review of their relationships'. *International Journal of Sustainable Development and World Ecology*, *25*(8), 672–682. doi:10.1080/13504509.2018.1471628

Balarezo, R., & Montiel, I. (2020). *Covid-19: Un llamado a la acción a las empresas peruanas*. Academic Press.

Bansal, P. (2005). Evolving sustainably: A longitudinal study of corporate sustainable development. *Strategic Management Journal*, *26*(3), 197–218. doi:10.1002mj.441

Bansal, P., & Clelland, I. (2004). Talking Trash: Legitimacy, Impression Management, and Unsystematic Risk in the Context of the Natural Environment. *Academy of Management Journal*, *47*(1), 93–103.

Bansal, P., & DesJardine, M. R. (2014). Business sustainability: It is about time. *Strategic Organization*, *12*(1), 70–78. doi:10.1177/1476127013520265

Bansal, P., Kim, A., & Wood, M. O. (2018). Hidden in Plain Sight: The Importance of Scale in Organizations' Attention to Issues. *Academy of Management Review*, *43*(2), 217–241. doi:10.5465/amr.2014.0238

Bansal, P., & Roth, K. (2000). Why Companies Go Green: A Model of Ecological Responsiveness. *Academy of Management Journal*, *43*(4), 717–736.

Bansal, P., & Song, H.-C. (2017). Similar But Not the Same: Differentiating Corporate Sustainability from Corporate Responsibility. *The Academy of Management Annals*, *11*(1), 105–149. doi:10.5465/annals.2015.0095

Barnett, M. L., & Salomon, R. M. (2012). Does it pay to be really good? Addressing the shape of the relationship between social and financial performance. *Strategic Management Journal*, *33*(11), 1304–1320. doi:10.1002mj.1980

Barney, J. (1986). Strategic Factor Markets: Expectations, Luck, and Business Strategy. *Management Science*, *32*(10), 1231–1241. doi:10.1287/mnsc.32.10.1231

Barney, J. (1991). Firm Resources and Sustained Competitive Advantage. *Journal of Management*, *17*(1), 99–120. doi:10.1177/014920639101700108

Barney, J. (2018). Why resource-based theory's model of profit appropriation must incorporate a stakeholder perspective. *Strategic Management Journal*, *39*(13), 3305–3325. doi:10.1002mj.2949

Barney, J., & Felin, T. (2013). What Are Microfoundations? *The Academy of Management Perspectives*, *27*(2), 138–155. doi:10.5465/amp.2012.0107

Barney, J., & Rangan, S. (2019). Editors' Comments: Why Do We Need a Special Issue on New Theoretical Perspectives on Market-Based Economic Systems? *Academy of Management Review*, *44*(1), 1–5. doi:10.5465/amr.2018.0425

Barney. (2020). Measuring Firm Performance in a Way that Is Consistent with Strategic Management Theory. *Academy of Management Discoveries, 6*(1), 5-7.

Bowen, H. R. (1953). *Social responsibilities of the businessman*. Harper & Row.

Branzei, O., Ursacki-Bryant, T. J., Vertinsky, I., & Zhang, W. (2004). The formation of green strategies in Chinese firms: Matching corporate environmental responses and individual principles. *Strategic Management Journal*, *25*(11), 1075–1095. doi:10.1002mj.409

Bushee, B. J., Goodman, T. H., & Sunder, S. V. (2019). Financial Reporting Quality, Investment Horizon, and Institutional Investor Trading Strategies. *The Accounting Review*, *94*(3), 87–112. doi:10.2308/accr-52202

Buysse, K., & Verbeke, A. (2003). Proactive environmental strategies: A stakeholder management perspective. *Strategic Management Journal*, *24*(5), 453–470. doi:10.1002mj.299

Carroll, A. B. (1979). A Three-Dimensional Conceptual Model of Corporate Performance. *Academy of Management Review*, *4*(4), 497–505. doi:10.5465/amr.1979.4498296

Cheah, E.-T., Jamali, D., Johnson, J. E. V., & Sung, M. C. (2011). Drivers of Corporate Social Responsibility Attitudes: The Demography of Socially Responsible Investors: Drivers of Corporate Social Responsibility Attitudes. *British Journal of Management*, *22*(2), 305–323. doi:10.1111/j.1467-8551.2011.00744.x

Chin, M. K., Hambrick, D. C., & Treviño, L. K. (2013). Political Ideologies of CEOs: The Influence of Executives' Values on Corporate Social Responsibility. *Administrative Science Quarterly*, *58*(2), 197–232. doi:10.1177/0001839213486984

Christmann, P., & Taylor, G. (2001). Globalization and the Environment: Determinants of Firm Self-Regulation in China. *Journal of International Business Studies*, *32*(3), 439–458. doi:10.1057/palgrave.jibs.8490976

Coleman, J. S. (1990). Foundations of social theory (3rd ed.). Belknap Press of Harvard Univ. Press.

Contractor, F., Foss, N. J., Kundu, S., & Lahiri, S. (2019). Viewing global strategy through a microfoundations lens. *Global Strategy Journal*, *9*(1), 3–18. doi:10.1002/gsj.1329

Cooper, S. C. L., Stokes, P., Liu, Y., & Tarba, S. Y. (2017). Sustainability and organizational behavior: A micro-foundational perspective. *Journal of Organizational Behavior*, *38*(9), 1297–1301. doi:10.1002/job.2242

Darnall, N., Henriques, I., & Sadorsky, P. (2010). Adopting Proactive Environmental Strategy: The Influence of Stakeholders and Firm Size: Environmental Strategy, Stakeholders, and Size. *Journal of Management Studies*, *47*(6), 1072–1094. doi:10.1111/j.1467-6486.2009.00873.x

Davis, G. F. (2016). Can an Economy Survive Without Corporations? Technology and Robust Organizational Alternatives. *The Academy of Management Perspectives*, *30*(2), 129–140. doi:10.5465/amp.2015.0067

Delmas, M., & Montes-Sancho, M. J. (2009). Voluntary agreements to improve environmental quality: Symbolic and substantive cooperation. *Strategic Management Journal*.

Delmas, M., & Toffel, M. W. (2004). Stakeholders and environmental management practices: An institutional framework. *Business Strategy and the Environment*, *13*(4), 209–222. doi:10.1002/bse.409

Delmas, M., & Toffel, M. W. (2008). Organizational responses to environmental demands: Opening the black box. *Strategic Management Journal*, *29*(10), 1027–1055. doi:10.1002mj.701

Devinney, T. M. (2013). Is Microfoundational Thinking Critical to Management Thought and Practice? *The Academy of Management Perspectives*, *27*(2), 81–84. doi:10.5465/amp.2013.0053

DiMaggio, P. J., & Powell, W. W. (1983). The Iron Cage Revisited: Institutional Isomorphism and Collective Rationality in Organizational Fields. *American Sociological Review*, *48*(2), 147. doi:10.2307/2095101

Dyllick, T., & Hockerts, K. (2002). Beyond the business case for corporate sustainability. *Business Strategy and the Environment*, *11*(2), 130–141. doi:10.1002/bse.323

Dyllick, T., & Muff, K. (2016). Clarifying the Meaning of Sustainable Business: Introducing a Typology From Business-as-Usual to True Business Sustainability. *Organization & Environment*, *29*(2), 156–174. doi:10.1177/1086026615575176

Eccles, R. G., Ioannou, I., & Serafeim, G. (2014). The Impact of Corporate Sustainability on Organizational Processes and Performance. *Management Science*, *60*(11), 2835–2857. doi:10.1287/mnsc.2014.1984

Egri, C. P., & Herman, S. (2000). Leadership in the North American environmental sector: Values, leadership styles and contexts of environmental leaders and their organizations. *Academy of Management Journal*, *43*(4), 571–604.

Felin, & Foss, N. (2006). Individuals and organizations: Further thought on a microfoundations project for strategic management and organizational analysis. *Research Methodology in Strategy and Management, 1*. http://site.ebrary.com/id/10169693

Figge, F., & Hahn, T. (2004). Sustainable Value Added—Measuring corporate contributions to sustainability beyond eco-efficiency. *Ecological Economics*, *48*(2), 173–187. doi:10.1016/j.ecolecon.2003.08.005

Flammer, C. (2013). Corporate Social Responsibility and Shareholder Reaction: The Environmental Awareness of Investors. *Academy of Management Journal*, *56*(3), 758–781. doi:10.5465/amj.2011.0744

Foss, N. J. (2011). Invited Editorial: Why Micro-Foundations for Resource-Based Theory Are Needed and What They May Look Like. *Journal of Management*, *37*(5), 1413–1428. doi:10.1177/0149206310390218

Foss, N. J., & Pedersen, T. (2016). Microfoundations In Strategy Research. *Strategic Management Journal*, *37*(13), E22–E34. doi:10.1002mj.2362

Franklin, B. (2003). *Quotations of Benjamin Franklin*. Applewood Books.

Freeman, R. E. (1984). *Strategic Management: A Stakeholder Approach*. Cambridge University Press.

George, G., Howard-Grenville, J., Joshi, A., & Tihanyi, L. (2016). Understanding and Tackling Societal Grand Challenges through Management Research. *Academy of Management Journal*, *59*(6), 1880–1895. doi:10.5465/amj.2016.4007

Gladwin, T. N., Kennelly, J. J., & Krause, T. S. (1995). Shifting Paradigms for Sustainable Development: Implications for Management Theory and Research. *Academy of Management Review*, *20*(4), 874–907. doi:10.5465/amr.1995.9512280024

Goodrick, E., & Salancik, G. R. (1996). Organizational Discretion in Responding to Institutional Practices: Hospitals and Cesarean Births. *Administrative Science Quarterly*, *41*(1), 1. doi:10.2307/2393984

Grewatsch, S., & Kleindienst, I. (2017). When Does It Pay to be Good? Moderators and Mediators in the Corporate Sustainability–Corporate Financial Performance Relationship: A Critical Review. *Journal of Business Ethics*, *145*(2), 383–416. doi:10.100710551-015-2852-5

Grodal, S., & O'Mahony, S. (2017). How does a Grand Challenge Become Displaced? Explaining the Duality of Field Mobilization. *Academy of Management Journal*, *60*(5), 1801–1827. doi:10.5465/amj.2015.0890

Gutiérrez, L., Montiel, I., & Castillo, A. (2020). JBE virtual special issue: Responsible Innovation in Times of Crisis. *Journal of Business Ethics*.

Hafenbrädl, S., & Waeger, D. (2017). Ideology and the Micro-foundations of CSR: Why Executives Believe in the Business Case for CSR and how this Affects their CSR Engagements. *Academy of Management Journal, 60*(4), 1582–1606. doi:10.5465/amj.2014.0691

Hahn, T., Figge, F., Aragón-Correa, J. A., & Sharma, S. (2017). Advancing Research on Corporate Sustainability: Off to Pastures New or Back to the Roots? *Business & Society, 56*(2), 155–185. doi:10.1177/0007650315576152

Hart, S. L. (1995). A Natural-Resource-Based View of the Firm. *Academy of Management Review, 20*(4), 986–1014. doi:10.5465/amr.1995.9512280033

Hart, S. L., & Dowell, G. (2011). Invited Editorial: A Natural-Resource-Based View of the Firm: Fifteen Years After. *Journal of Management, 37*(5), 1464–1479. doi:10.1177/0149206310390219

Hart, S. L., & Milstein, M. B. (2003). Creating sustainable value. *The Academy of Management Perspectives, 17*(2), 56–67. doi:10.5465/ame.2003.10025194

Hart, S. L., & Sharma, S. (2004). Engaging fringe stakeholders for competitive imagination. *The Academy of Management Perspectives, 18*(1), 7–18. doi:10.5465/ame.2004.12691227

Helfat, C. E., & Peteraf, M. A. (2003). The dynamic resource-based view: Capability lifecycles. *Strategic Management Journal, 24*(10), 997–1010. doi:10.1002mj.332

Hiatt, S. R., Sine, W. D., & Tolbert, P. S. (2009). From Pabst to Pepsi: The Deinstitutionalization of Social Practices and the Creation of Entrepreneurial Opportunities. *Administrative Science Quarterly, 54*(4), 635–667. doi:10.2189/asqu.2009.54.4.635

Hollensbe, E., Wookey, C., Hickey, L., George, G., & Nichols, C. V. (2014). Organizations with Purpose. *Academy of Management Journal, 57*(5), 1227–1234. doi:10.5465/amj.2014.4005

Hoskisson, R. E., Hitt, M. A., Wan, W. P., & Yiu, D. (1999). Theory and research in strategic management: Swings of a pendulum. *Journal of Management, 25*(3), 417–456. doi:10.1177/014920639902500307

Howard-Grenville, J., Buckle, S. J., Hoskins, B. J., & George, G. (2014). Climate Change and Management. *Academy of Management Journal, 57*(3), 615–623. doi:10.5465/amj.2014.4003

Huang, S. K. (2013). The Impact of CEO Characteristics on Corporate Sustainable Development: CSR Drivers, CSR CEO Characteristics, Hypotheses, Method [Discussion]. *Corporate Social Responsibility and Environmental Management, 20*(4), 234–244. doi:10.1002/csr.1295

Husted, B. W., Montiel, I., & Christmann, P. (2016). Effects of local legitimacy on certification decisions to global and national CSR standards by multinational subsidiaries and domestic firms. *Journal of International Business Studies, 47*(3), 382–397. doi:10.1057/jibs.2016.3

Jamali, D., & Sidani, Y. (2008). Learning organizations: Diagnosis and measurement in a developing country context: The case of Lebanon. *The Learning Organization, 15*(1), 58–74. doi:10.1108/09696470810842466

Jansson, J., Nilsson, J., Modig, F., & Hed Vall, G. (2017). Commitment to Sustainability in Small and Medium-Sized Enterprises: The Influence of Strategic Orientations and Management Values: Commitment to Sustainability in SMEs. *Business Strategy and the Environment*, *26*(1), 69–83. doi:10.1002/bse.1901

Jones, D. A., Willness, C. R., & Glavas, A. (2017). When Corporate Social Responsibility (CSR) Meets Organizational Psychology: New Frontiers in Micro-CSR Research, and Fulfilling a Quid Pro Quo through Multilevel Insights. *Frontiers in Psychology*, *8*, 8. doi:10.3389/fpsyg.2017.00520 PMID:28439247

Jones, J., York, J. G., Vedula, S., Conger, M., & Lenox, M. (2019). The Collective Construction of Green Building: Industry Transition Toward Environmentally Beneficial Practices. *The Academy of Management Perspectives*, *33*(4), 425–449. doi:10.5465/amp.2017.0031

Kaplan, S. (2020). Beyond the Business Case for Social Responsibility. *Academy of Management Discoveries*, *6*(1), 1–4. doi:10.5465/amd.2018.0220

Keeble, B. R. (1988). The Brundtland report: 'Our common future'. *Medicine and War*, *4*(1), 17–25. doi:10.1080/07488008808408783

Kiron, D., Unruh, G., Kruschwitz, N., Reeves, M., Rubel, H., & Mayer Zum Felde, A. (2017). *Corporate Sustainability at a Crossroads: Progress Toward Our Common Future in Uncertain Times*. MIT Sloan Mgt. Rev.

Klassen, R. D., & Whybark, D. C. (1999). The Impact of Environmental Technologies on Manufacturing Performance. *Academy of Management Journal*, *42*(6), 599–615.

Laasch, O. (2018). Beyond the purely commercial business model: Organizational value logics and the heterogeneity of sustainability business models. *Long Range Planning*, *51*(1), 158–183. doi:10.1016/j.lrp.2017.09.002

Lankoski, L., & Smith, N. C. (2018). Alternative Objective Functions for Firms. *Organization & Environment*, *31*(3), 242–262. doi:10.1177/1086026617722883

Lewis, B. W., Walls, J. L., & Dowell, G. W. S. (2014). Difference in degrees: CEO characteristics and firm environmental disclosure: Research Notes and Commentaries. *Strategic Management Journal*, *35*(5), 712–722. doi:10.1002mj.2127

Linder, S., & Foss, N. J. (2018). Microfoundations of Organizational Goals: A Review and New Directions for Future Research. *International Journal of Management Reviews*, *20*, S39–S62. doi:10.1111/ijmr.12154

Luo, J., Kaul, A., & Seo, H. (2018). Winning us with trifles: Adverse selection in the use of philanthropy as insurance. *Strategic Management Journal*, *39*(10), 2591–2617. doi:10.1002mj.2935

Matten, D., & Moon, J. (2008). "Implicit" and "Explicit" CSR: A Conceptual Framework for a Comparative Understanding of Corporate Social Responsibility. *Academy of Management Review*, *33*(2), 404–424. doi:10.5465/amr.2008.31193458

Mayer, C. (2016). Reinventing the corporation. *Journal of the British Academy*, *4*, 53–72. doi:10.5871/jba/004.053

Mazutis, D., & Eckardt, A. (2017). Sleepwalking into Catastrophe: Cognitive Biases and Corporate Climate Change Inertia. *California Management Review*, *59*(3), 74–108. doi:10.1177/0008125617707974

McWilliams, A., & Siegel, D. S. (2011). Creating and Capturing Value: Strategic Corporate Social Responsibility, Resource-Based Theory, and Sustainable Competitive Advantage. *Journal of Management*, *37*(5), 1480–1495. doi:10.1177/0149206310385696

Meuer, J., Koelbel, J., & Hoffmann, V. H. (2019). On the Nature of Corporate Sustainability. *Organization & Environment*.

Mintzberg, H. (2019). Please Welcome CSR 2.0. In Rethinking strategic management: Sustainable strategizing for positive impact (1st edition). Springer Berlin Heidelberg.

Molina-Azorín, J. F. (2014). Microfoundations of strategic management: Toward micro–macro research in the resource-based theory. *BRQ Business Research Quarterly*, *17*(2), 102–114. doi:10.1016/j.brq.2014.01.001

Montiel, I., Antolin-López, R., & Gallo, P. J. (2020). What on Earth should managers learn about corporate sustainability? A threshold concept approach. *Journal of Business Ethics*, *162*(4), 857–880. doi:10.100710551-019-04361-y

Montiel, I., Christmann, P., & Zink, T. (2019). The Effect of Sustainability Standard Uncertainty on Certification Decisions of Firms in Emerging Economies. *Journal of Business Ethics*, *154*(3), 667–681. doi:10.100710551-016-3350-0

Montiel, I., & Delgado-Ceballos, J. (2014). Defining and Measuring Corporate Sustainability: Are We There Yet? *Organization & Environment*, *27*(2), 113–139. doi:10.1177/1086026614526413

Montiel, I., Husted, B. W., & Christmann, P. (2012). Using private management standard certification to reduce information asymmetries in corrupt environments. *Strategic Management Journal*, *33*(9), 1103–1113. doi:10.1002mj.1957

Ormiston, M. E., & Wong, E. M. (2013). License to Ill: The Effects of Corporate Social Responsibility and CEO Moral Identity on Corporate Social Irresponsibility. *Personnel Psychology*, *66*(4), 861–893. doi:10.1111/peps.12029

Reimer, M., Van Doorn, S., & Heyden, M. L. M. (2018). Unpacking Functional Experience Complementarities in Senior Leaders' Influences on CSR Strategy: A CEO–Top Management Team Approach. *Journal of Business Ethics*, *151*(4), 977–995. doi:10.100710551-017-3657-5

Russo, M. V., & Fouts, P. A. (1997). A resource-based perspective on corporate environmental performance and profitability. *Academy of Management Journal*, *40*(3), 534–559.

Schad, J., & Bansal, P. (2018). Seeing the Forest and the Trees: How a Systems Perspective Informs Paradox Research: How a Systems Perspective Informs Paradox Research. *Journal of Management Studies*, *55*(8), 1490–1506. doi:10.1111/joms.12398

Shahab, Y., Ntim, C. G., Chengang, Y., Ullah, F., & Fosu, S. (2018). Environmental policy, environmental performance, and financial distress in China: Do top management team characteristics matter? *Business Strategy and the Environment*, *27*(8), 1635–1652. doi:10.1002/bse.2229

Sharma, S., & Henriques, I. (2005). Stakeholder influences on sustainability practices in the Canadian forest products industry. *Strategic Management Journal*, *26*(2), 159–180. doi:10.1002mj.439

Shea, C. T., & Hawn, O. V. (2019). Microfoundations of Corporate Social Responsibility and Irresponsibility. *Academy of Management Journal*, *62*(5), 1609–1642. doi:10.5465/amj.2014.0795

Shevchenko, A., Lévesque, M., & Pagell, M. (2016). Why Firms Delay Reaching True Sustainability: Firms Delaying in Reaching True Sustainability. *Journal of Management Studies, 53*(5), 911-935.

Shrivastava, P. (1995). Environmental technologies and competitive advantage. *Strategic Management Journal*, *16*(S1), 183–200. doi:10.1002mj.4250160923

Stahl, G. K., & Sully de Luque, M. (2014). Antecedents of Responsible Leader Behavior: A Research Synthesis, Conceptual Framework, and Agenda for Future Research. *The Academy of Management Perspectives*, *28*(3), 235–254. doi:10.5465/amp.2013.0126

Surroca, J., Tribó, J. A., & Zahra, S. A. (2013). Stakeholder Pressure on MNEs and the Transfer of Socially Irresponsible Practices to Subsidiaries. *Academy of Management Journal*, *56*(2), 549–572. doi:10.5465/amj.2010.0962

Tang, Y., Qian, C., Chen, G., & Shen, R. (2015). How CEO hubris affects corporate social (ir)responsibility: CEO Hubris and CSR. *Strategic Management Journal*, *36*(9), 1338–1357. doi:10.1002mj.2286

Teece, D. J. (2007). Explicating dynamic capabilities: The nature and microfoundations of (sustainable) enterprise performance. *Strategic Management Journal*, *28*(13), 1319–1350. doi:10.1002mj.640

Teece, D. J. (2012). Dynamic Capabilities: Routines versus Entrepreneurial Action: Routines versus Entrepreneurial Action. *Journal of Management Studies*, *49*(8), 1395–1401. doi:10.1111/j.1467-6486.2012.01080.x

Tsui, A. S., Enderle, G., & Jiang, K. (2018). Income Inequality in the United States: Reflections on the Role of Corporations. *Academy of Management Review*, *43*(1), 156–168. doi:10.5465/amr.2016.0527

Unruh, G., Kiron, D., Kruschwitz, N., Reeves, M., Rubel, H., & zum Felde, A. M. (2016). Investing For a Sustainable Future. *MIT Sloan Management Review*.

van Marrewijk, M. (2003). Concepts and Definitions of CSR and Corporate Sustainability: Between Agency and Communion. *Journal of Business Ethics*, *44*(2), 95–105. doi:10.1023/A:1023331212247

Walls, J. L., & Berrone, P. (2017). The Power of One to Make a Difference: How Informal and Formal CEO Power Affect Environmental Sustainability. *Journal of Business Ethics*, *145*(2), 293–308. doi:10.100710551-015-2902-z

Wang, H., Tong, L., Takeuchi, R., & George, G. (2016). Corporate Social Responsibility: An Overview and New Research Directions: Thematic Issue on Corporate Social Responsibility. *Academy of Management Journal*, *59*(2), 534–544. doi:10.5465/amj.2016.5001

Wijethilake, C., & Lama, T. (2019). Sustainability core values and sustainability risk management: Moderating effects of top management commitment and stakeholder pressure. *Business Strategy and the Environment*, *28*(1), 143–154. doi:10.1002/bse.2245

Winter, S. G. (2003). Understanding dynamic capabilities. *Strategic Management Journal*, *24*(10), 991–995. doi:10.1002mj.318

Winter, S. G. (2012). Capabilities: Their Origins and Ancestry: Capabilities: Their Origins and Ancestry. *Journal of Management Studies*, *49*(8), 1402–1406. doi:10.1111/j.1467-6486.2012.01081.x

Wright, C., & Nyberg, D. (2017). An Inconvenient Truth: How Organizations Translate Climate Change into Business as Usual. *Academy of Management Journal*, *60*(5), 1633–1661. doi:10.5465/amj.2015.0718

Wunder, T. (2019). *Rethinking strategic management: Sustainable strategizing for positive impact* (1st ed.). Springer Berlin Heidelberg. doi:10.1007/978-3-030-06014-5

York, J. G., & Lenox, M. J. (2014). Exploring the sociocultural determinants of *de novo* versus *de alio* entry in emerging industries: Exploring Sociocultural Determinants. *Strategic Management Journal*, *35*(13), 1930–1951. doi:10.1002mj.2187

York, J. G., Vedula, S., & Lenox, M. J. (2018). It's Not Easy Building Green: The Impact of Public Policy, Private Actors, and Regional Logics on Voluntary Standards Adoption. *Academy of Management Journal*, *61*(4), 1492–1523. doi:10.5465/amj.2015.0769

Zink, T. (2019). The Inevitable Labor and Environmental Crises and the Need for a New Economic System. *Journal of Management Inquiry*, *28*(3), 311–315. doi:10.1177/1056492619827382

Zollo, M., & Winter, S. G. (2002). Deliberate Learning and the Evolution of Dynamic Capabilities. *Organization Science*, *13*(3), 339–351. doi:10.1287/orsc.13.3.339.2780

ENDNOTES

1. Peoples Climate March in New York City, September 2014. Extracted from George et al. (2016, p. 1893).
2. Peru passed through a tough time of terrorist attacks locally from 1980 to 1995. It cost the life of more than 25,000 people.
3. See Endnote 1.

Compilation of References

Abell, P., Felin, T., & Foss, N. (2008). Building micro-foundations for the routines, capabilities, and performance links. *Managerial and Decision Economics*, *29*(6), 489–502. doi:10.1002/mde.1413

Acero Fraile, I., & Alcalde Fradejas, N. (2012). Gobierno corporativo y rendición de cuentas: ¿existe algún efecto sobre la performance empresarial? *Revista de Contabilidad*, *15*(1), 143–178. doi:10.1016/S1138-4891(12)70041-9

Ackerman, R. W. (1973). How companies respond to social demands. *Harvard Business Review*, *51*(4), 88–98.

Acosta, C. (2016). *Son famosos y millonarios, pero ¿son responsables?* Retrieved from: https://www.expoknews.com/son-famosos-y-millonarios-pero-son-responsables/

Adam, A. M., & Rachman-Moore, D. (2004). The methods used to implement an ethical code of conduct and employee attitudes. *Journal of Business Ethics*, *54*(3), 225–244. doi:10.100710551-004-1774-4

Adams, C. A., & Evans, R. (2004). Accountability, completeness, credibility and the audit expectations gap. *Journal of Corporate Citizenship*, *14*(Summer), 97–115. doi:10.9774/GLEAF.4700.2004.su.00010

Adams, J. S., Tashchian, A., & Shore, T. H. (2001). Codes of ethics as signals for ethical behavior. *Journal of Business Ethics*, *29*(3), 199–211. doi:10.1023/A:1026576421399

Adler, P. S. (2016). Alternative Economic Futures: A Research Agenda for Progressive Management Scholarship. *The Academy of Management Perspectives*, *30*(2), 123–128. doi:10.5465/amp.2016.0054

Agarwal, R. N., & Dewan, P. (2016). A study on the relationship of employee satisfaction VIZ-A-VIZ attitude and perception of the employees towards the organization. *International Journal of Information, Business and Management*, *8*(1), 67-87.

Agudo-Valiente, J. M., Garcés-Ayerbe, C., & Salvador-Figueras, M. (2015). Corporate social performance and stakeholder dialogue management. *Corporate Social Responsibility and Environmental Management*, *22*(1), 13–31. doi:10.1002/csr.1324

Aguilera, R. V., Rupp, D. E., Williams, C. A., & Ganapathi, J. (2007). Putting the S back in corporate social responsibility: A multilevel theory of social change in organizations. *Academy of Management. Academy of Management Review*, *32*(3), 836–863. doi:10.5465/amr.2007.25275678

Aguinis, H. (2011). Organizational responsibility: Doing good and doing well. In S. Zedeck (Ed.), *APA handbook of industrial and organizational psychology* (pp. 855–879). American Psychological Association. doi:10.1037/12171-024

Aguinis, H., & Glavas, A. (2012). What we know and don't know about corporate social responsibility: A review and research agenda. *Journal of Management*, *38*(4), 932–968. doi:10.1177/0149206311436079

Aju, O., & Beddewela, E. (2019). Afrocentric attitudinal reciprocity and social expectations of employees: The role of employee-centred CSR in Africa. *Journal of Business Ethics*, 1–19. doi:10.100710551-019-04346-x

Akhtar, P., Khan, Z., Frynas, J. G., Tse, Y. K., & Rao-Nicholson, R. (2018). Essential Micro-foundations for Contemporary Business Operations: Top Management Tangible Competencies, Relationship-based Business Networks and Environmental Sustainability. *British Journal of Management*, *29*(1), 43–62. doi:10.1111/1467-8551.12233

Alafi, K., & Hasoneh, A. (2012). Corporate social responsibility associated with customer satisfaction and financial performance a case study with Housing Banks in Jordan. *International Journal of Humanities and Social Science*, *2*(15), 102–115.

Albert, L. S., Dean, T. J., & Baron, R. A. (2016). From Social Value to Social Cognition. How Social Ventures Obtain the Resources They need for Social Transformation. *Journal of Social Entrepreneurship*, *7*(3), 289–311. doi:10.1080/19420676.2016.1188323

Albiol, N. C., & López, E. J. (2019). Mujeres en Consejos de Administración. *Economistas*, (161), 22-33.

Albort-Morant, G., Henseler, J., Cepeda-Carrión, G., & Leal-Rodríguez, A. L. (2018). Potential and realized absorptive capacity as complementary drivers of green product and process innovation performance. *Sustainability*, *10*(2), 381. doi:10.3390u10020381

Albort-Morant, G., Leal-Rodríguez, A. L., & De Marchi, V. (2018). Absorptive capacity and relationship learning mechanisms as complementary drivers of green innovation performance. *Journal of Knowledge Management*, *22*(2), 432–452. doi:10.1108/JKM-07-2017-0310

Alegre, J., Lapiedra, R., & Chiva, R. (2006). A Measurement Scale for Product Innovation Performance. *European Journal of Innovation Management*, *9*(4), 333–346. doi:10.1108/14601060610707812

Aliasghar, O., Rose, L., & Chetty, S. (2019). Building absorptive capacity through firm openness in the context of a less-open country. *Industrial Marketing Management*, *83*, 81–93. doi:10.1016/j.indmarman.2018.11.007

Alimo-Metcalfe, B. (2010). An investigation of female and male constructs of leadership and empowerment. *Women in Management Review*, *10*(2), 3–8. doi:10.1108/09649429510146901

Alniacik, U., Alniacik, E., & Genc, N. (2011). How corporate social responsibility information influences stakeholders' intentions. *Corporate Social Responsibility and Environmental Management*, *18*(4), 234–245. doi:10.1002/csr.245

Alonso-Almeida, M. D. M., Perramon, J., & Bagur-Femenias, L. (2017). Leadership styles and corporate social responsibility management: Analysis from a gender perspective. *Business Ethics (Oxford, England)*, *26*(2), 147–161. doi:10.1111/beer.12139

Alwert, K., Bornemann, M., & Will, M. (2009). Does intellectual capital reporting matter to financial analysts? *Journal of Intellectual Capital*, *10*(3), 354–368. doi:10.1108/14691930910977789

Amabile, T. M., Conti, R., Coon, H., Lazenby, J., & Herron, M. (1996). Assessing the Work Environment for Creativity. *Academy of Management Journal*, *39*, 1154–1184.

Amaeshi, K., Adegbite, E., Ogbechie, C., Idemudia, U., Kan, K. A. S., Issa, M., & Anakwue, O. I. (2016). Corporate social responsibility in SMEs: A shift from philanthropy to institutional works? *Journal of Business Ethics*, *138*(2), 385–400. doi:10.100710551-015-2633-1

Ambrosini, V., & Bowman, C. (2009). What are dynamic capabilities and are they useful construct in strategic management? *International Journal of Management Reviews*, *11*(1), 29–49. doi:10.1111/j.1468-2370.2008.00251.x

Amin, A., & Thrift, N. (1995). Globalisation, institutional 'thickness' and the local economy. In *Managing Cities* (pp. 91–108). The New Urban Context.

Ammenberg, J., & Hjelm, O. (2003). Tracing business and environmental effects of environmental management systems—A study of networking small and medium-sized enterprises using a joint environmental management system. *Business Strategy and the Environment, 12*(3), 163–174. doi:10.1002/bse.357

Anatory, J. (2015). Consumer preferences for mobile carriers in Tanzania: A case of group, family, age and gender. *International Journal of Computer Applications, 115*(16), 16-23. doi: 10.1.1.695.5880

Andersen, M., & Skjoett-Larsen, T. (2009). Corporate Social Responsibility in Global Supply Chains'. *Supply Chain Management, 14*(2), 75–86. doi:10.1108/13598540910941948

Anderson, E., & Jap, S. D. (2005). The dark side of close relationships. *MIT Sloan Management Review, 46*(3), 75.

Antolin-Lopez, R., & Montiel, I. (2018). Entrepreneurial Collective Responses to Sustainability-related Grand Challenges. *Academy of Management Proceedings, 2018*(1), 11471. doi:10.5465/AMBPP.2018.83

Antonioli, D., Mancinelli, S., & Mazzanti, M. (2013). Is environmental innovation embedded within high-performance organisational changes? the role of human resource management and complementarity in green business strategies. *Research Policy, 42*(4), 975–988. doi:10.1016/j.respol.2012.12.005

Aparicio-Baeza, J., Martiinez-Mayoral, A., Morales-Socuuellamos, J., & Ortiz-Henarejos, L. (2017). Percepción de la ciudadanía de Elche sobre la economía sumergida. Academic Press.

Aragón-Correa, J. A., Hurtado-Torres, N., Sharma, S., & García-Morales, V. J. (2008). Environmental Strategy and Performance in Small Firms: A Resource-Based Perspective. *Journal of Environmental Management, 86*(1), 88–103. doi:10.1016/j.jenvman.2006.11.022 PMID:17239519

Aragón-Correa, J. A., & Sharma, S. (2003). A Contingent Resource-Based View of Proactive Corporate Environmental Strategy. *Academy of Management Review, 28*(1), 71–88. doi:10.5465/amr.2003.8925233

Archel, P., & Lizarraga, F. (2001). Algunos determinantes de la información medioambiental divulgada por las empresas españolas cotizadas. *Revista de Contabilidad, 4*(7), 129–153.

Arena, C., Michelon, G., & Trojanowski, G. (2018). Big Egos Can Be Green: A Study of CEO Hubris and Environmental Innovation: CEO Hubris and Environmental Innovation. *British Journal of Management, 29*(2), 316–336. doi:10.1111/1467-8551.12250

Arnold, M. F. (2010). Competitive Advantage from CSR Programmes. In C. Louche, S. O. Idowu, & W. L. Filho (Eds.), *Innovative CSR: From Risk Management to Value Creation*. Greenleaf Publishing Limited. doi:10.9774/GLEAF.978-1-907643-26-2_7

Arrigo, E. (2006). Code of conduct and corporate governance. *Symphonya, Emerging Issues in Management*, (1), 93-109.

Arrow, K. J. (1974). Social Responsibility and Economic Efficiency. *Public Policy, 21*, 303–317.

Arshad, A., Noordin, A. F., & Othman, R. (2016). A comprehensive Knowledge Management Process Framework for Healthcare Information Systems in Healtcare Industry of Pakistan. *2016 6th International Conference on Information and Communication Technology for The Muslim World (ICT4M)*. DOI: 10.1109/ICT4M.2016.019

Asatryan, R., & Asamoah, E. S. (2014). Perceived corporate social responsibility (CSR) activities and the antecedents of customer loyalty in the airline industry. *Scientific Papers of the University of Pardubice. Series D, Faculty of Economics and Administration, 32*(3).

Ashrafi, M., Adams, M., Walker, T. R., & Magnan, G. (2018). 'How corporate social responsibility can be integrated into corporate sustainability: A theoretical review of their relationships'. *International Journal of Sustainable Development and World Ecology*, *25*(8), 672–682. doi:10.1080/13504509.2018.1471628

Askew, O. A., Beisler, J. M., & Keel, J. (2015). Current trends of unethical behavior within organizations. *International Journal of Management & Information Systems (Online)*, *19*(3), 107. doi:10.19030/ijmis.v19i3.9374

Astaryan, R., & SelaseAsamoah, E. (2014). Perceived Corporate Social Responsibility (CSR) Activities and the Antecedents of Customer Loyalty in the Airline Industry. *Scientific Papers of the University of Pardubice. Series D, Faculty of Economics & Administration, 21*(32), 5–17. https://www.upce.cz/sites/default/binary_www_old/fes/veda-vyzkum/fakultni-casopisy/scipap/archiv/e-verze-sborniku/2014/scipap-32-9-2014.pdf#page=6

Atkinson, G. (2000). Measuring corporate sustainability. *Journal of Environmental Planning and Management*, *43*(2), 235–252. doi:10.1080/09640560010694

Attig, N., Boubakri, N., El Ghoul, S., & Guedhami, O. (2016). Firm Internationalization and Corporate Social Responsibility. *Journal of Business Ethics*, *134*(2), 171–197. doi:10.100710551-014-2410-6

Auld, G., Bernstein, S., & Cashore, B. (2008). The new corporate social responsibility. *Annual Review of Environment and Resources*, *33*(1), 413–435. doi:10.1146/annurev.environ.32.053006.141106

Austin, J. E., Gutierrez, R., Ogliastri, E., & Reficco, E. (2006). *Gestión efectiva de emprendimientos sociales: Lecciones extraídas de empresas y organizaciones de la sociedad civil en Iberoamérica.* Banco Interamericano de Desarrollo.

Austin, J. E., & Leonard, H. B. D. (2008). Can the virtuous mouse and the wealthy elephant live happily ever after? *California Management Review*, *51*(1), 77–102. doi:10.2307/41166469

Avila, C. (1983). Ownership: Early Christian Teaching. Orbis.

Awobamise, A. O. (2018). Increased consumerism in a Networked-Nigeria: A Study on the effect of e-malls and social media on youth spending. *Editors-in-Chief*, *1*(2), 40–55. doi:10.34624/jdmi.v1i2.949

Axelrod, R. (1984). *The Evolution of Cooperation.* Basic Books.

Ayuso, S., Roca, M., Arevalo, J. A., & Aravind, D. (2016). What Determines Principle-Based Standards Implementation? Reporting on Global Compact adoption in Spanish Firms. *Journal of Business Ethics*, *133*(3), 553–565. doi:10.100710551-014-2412-4

Ayyagari, M., Demirgü-Kunt, A., & Maksimovic, V. (2011). *Small vs. Young Firms across the World—Contribution to Employment, Job Creation, and Growth.* Policy Research Working Paper 5631, World Bank.

Azim, M. T. (2016). Corporate social responsibility and employee behavior: Mediating role of organizational commitment. *Review of Business Management*, *18*(60), 207–205. doi:10.7819/rbgn.v18i60.2319

B.O.E. (2011). *Ley 5/2011 (2011). de 29 de Marzo de Economía Social.* Cortes Generales.

Balaguer, M., Fernández, M., & Muñoz, M. (2007). *La responsabilidad social de la empresa. Relaciones entre la performance social, financiera y bursátil.* Conselleria de Empresa, Universidad y Ciencia. Generalitat Valenciana.

Balarezo, R., & Montiel, I. (2020). *Covid-19: Un llamado a la acción a las empresas peruanas.* Academic Press.

Bansal, P. (2005). Evolving Sustainability: A Longitudinal Study of Corporate Sustainable Development. *Strategic Management Journal*, *26*(3), 197–218. doi:10.1002mj.441

Bansal, P., & Clelland, I. (2004). Talking Trash: Legitimacy, Impression Management, and Unsystematic Risk in the Context of the Natural Environment. *Academy of Management Journal, 47*(1), 93–103.

Bansal, P., & DesJardine, M. R. (2014). Business sustainability: It is about time. *Strategic Organization, 12*(1), 70–78. doi:10.1177/1476127013520265

Bansal, P., Kim, A., & Wood, M. O. (2018). Hidden in Plain Sight: The Importance of Scale in Organizations' Attention to Issues. *Academy of Management Review, 43*(2), 217–241. doi:10.5465/amr.2014.0238

Bansal, P., & Roth, K. (2000). Why Companies Go Green: A Model of Ecological Responsiveness. *Academy of Management Journal, 43*(4), 717–736.

Bansal, P., & Song, H. (2017). Similar but not the same: Differentiating corporate sustainability from corporate responsibility. *The Academy of Management Annals, 11*(1), 105–149. doi:10.5465/annals.2015.0095

Barclay, D., Higgins, C., & Thompson, R. (1995). *The partial least squares (PLS) approach to causal modelling: personal computer adoption and use as an Illustration*. Academic Press.

Barka, H., & Dardour, A. (2015). Investigating the relationship between director's profile, board interlocks and corporate social responsibility. *Management Decision, 53*(3), 553–570. doi:10.1108/MD-12-2013-0655

Barnett, M. L. (2007). Stakeholder influence capacity and the variability of financial returns to corporate social responsibility. *Academy of Management Review, 32*(3), 794–816. doi:10.5465/amr.2007.25275520

Barnett, M., & Salomon, R. (2012). Does it pay to be really good? Addressing the shape of the relationship between social and financial performance. *Strategic Management Journal, 33*(11), 1304–1320. doi:10.1002mj.1980

Barney. (2020). Measuring Firm Performance in a Way that Is Consistent with Strategic Management Theory. *Academy of Management Discoveries, 6*(1), 5-7.

Barney, J. (1986). Strategic Factor Markets: Expectations, Luck, and Business Strategy. *Management Science, 32*(10), 1231–1241. doi:10.1287/mnsc.32.10.1231

Barney, J. (1991). Firm resources and sustained competitive advantage. *Journal of Management, 17*(1), 99–120. doi:10.1177/014920639101700108

Barney, J. (2018). Why resource-based theory's model of profit appropriation must incorporate a stakeholder perspective. *Strategic Management Journal, 39*(13), 3305–3325. doi:10.1002mj.2949

Barney, J. B. (1991). Firm resources and sustained competitive advantage. *Journal of Management Studies, 17*(1), 99–120.

Barney, J. B. (1995). Looking Inside for Competitive Advantage. *The Academy of Management Executive, 9*(4), 49–61. doi:10.5465/ame.1995.9512032192

Barney, J. B., Ketchen, D. J. Jr, & Wright, M. (2011). The future of resource-based theory: Revitalization or decline? *Journal of Management, 37*(5), 1299–1315. doi:10.1177/0149206310391805

Barney, J. B., & Stewart, A. C. (2000). *Organizational identity as a moral philosophy: competitive implications for diversified operations*. Oxford University Press.

Barney, J., & Felin, T. (2013). What Are Microfoundations? *The Academy of Management Perspectives, 27*(2), 138–155. doi:10.5465/amp.2012.0107

Barney, J., & Rangan, S. (2019). Editors' Comments: Why Do We Need a Special Issue on New Theoretical Perspectives on Market-Based Economic Systems? *Academy of Management Review, 44*(1), 1–5. doi:10.5465/amr.2018.0425

Baron, D. P. (2001). Private politics, corporate social responsibility, and integrated strategy. *Journal of Economics & Management Strategy*, *10*(1), 7–45. doi:10.1162/105864001300122548

Barragán. (2017). *Ventajas de la Responsabilidad Social*. Retrieved from: http://www.pymerang.com/direccion-de-negocios/1035-aplicando-el-design-thinking-para-resolver-problemas-de-negocio-cuando-su-mente-se-ha-bloqueado

Barrena-Martínez, J., López-Fernández, M., & Romero-Fernández, P. M. (2017). Socially responsible human resource policies and practices: Academic and professional validation. *European Research on Management and Business Economics*, *23*(1), 55–61. doi:10.1016/j.iedeen.2016.05.001

Basu, K., & Palazzo, G. (2008). Corporate social responsibility: A process model of sensemaking. *Academy of Management Review*, *33*(1), 122–136. doi:10.5465/amr.2008.27745504

Battaglia, M., Bianchi, L., Frey, M., & Iraldo, F. (2010). An innovative model to promote CSR among SMEs operating in industrial clusters: Evidence from an EU project. *Corporate Social Responsibility and Environmental Management*, *17*(3), 133–141. doi:10.1002/csr.224

Bauman, C. W., & Skitka, L. J. (2012). Corporate social responsibility as a source of employee satisfaction. *Research in Organizational Behavior*, *32*, 63–86. doi:10.1016/j.riob.2012.11.002

Baumann-Pauly, D., Wickert, C., Spence, L. J., & Scherer, A. G. (2013). Organizing corporate social responsibility in small and large firms: Size matters. *Journal of Business Ethics*, *115*(4), 693–705. doi:10.100710551-013-1827-7

Baum, J. A. C., & Oliver, C. (1992). Institutional embeddedness and the dynamics of organizational populations. *American Sociological Review*, *57*(4), 540–559. doi:10.2307/2096100

Becattini, G. (1979). Dal settore industrial al distretto industrial. Alcune considerazioni sull'unità di indagine in economia industriale. *Revista di Economía e Politica Industriale*, (1), 7-14.

Becattini, G. (2014). The Marshallian industrial district as a socio-economic notion. *Revue d'Économie Industrielle*, *1*, 13-32.

Becker-Olsen, K. L., Cudmore, B. A., & Hill, R. P. (2006). The impact of perceived corporate social responsibility on consumer behavior. *Journal of Business Research*, *59*(1), 46–53. doi:10.1016/j.jbusres.2005.01.001

Belso-Martinez, J. A., Díez-Vial, I., Lopez-Sanchez, M. J., & Mateu-Garcia, R. (2018). The brokerage role of supporting organizations inside clusters: How does it work? *European Planning Studies*, *26*(4), 706–725. doi:10.1080/09654313.2017.1422482

Belso-Martinez, J. A., Molina-Morales, F. X., & Martínez-Cháfer, L. (2015). Contributions of brokerage roles to firms' innovation in a confectionery cluster. *Technology Analysis and Strategic Management*, *27*(9), 1014–1030. doi:10.1080/09537325.2015.1045858

Bénabou, R., & Tirole, J. (2010). Individual and corporate social responsibility. *Economica*, *77*(305), 1–19. doi:10.1111/j.1468-0335.2009.00843.x

Bendoly, E., & Swink, M. (2007). Moderating effects of information access on project management behavior, performance and perceptions. *Journal of Operations Management*, *25*(3), 604–622. doi:10.1016/j.jom.2006.02.009

Benner, M. J., & Tushman, M. L. (2003). Exploitation, exploration, and process management: The productivity dilemma revisited. *Academy of Management Review*, *28*(2), 238–256. doi:10.5465/amr.2003.9416096

Berkovich, I. (2018). Beyond Qualitative/Quantitative Structuralism: The Positivist Qualitative Research and the Paradigmatic Disclaimer. *Quality & Quantity*, *52*(5), 2063–2077. doi:10.100711135-017-0607-3

Bermejo-Sales, E. (2018). *Análisis de la responsabilidad social corporativa como estrategia de comunicación en el sector del calzado ilicitano*. Universidad Miguel Hernández.

Berrone, P., & Gomez-Mejia, L. R. (2009). Environmental performance and executive compensation: An integrated agency-institutional perspective. *Academy of Management Journal*, *52*(1), 103–126. doi:10.5465/amj.2009.36461950

Besser, T. L., & Miller, N. (2001). Is the good corporation dead? the community social responsibility of small business operators☆. *Journal of Socio-Economics*, *30*(3), 221–241. doi:10.1016/S1053-5357(01)00094-4

Bhattacharya, C. B., & Sen, S. (2003). Consumer-company identification: A framework for understanding consumers' relationships with companies. *Journal of Marketing*, *67*(2), 76–88. doi:10.1509/jmkg.67.2.76.18609

Bhattacharya, C. B., & Sen, S. (2004). Doing better at doing good: When, why, and how consumers respond to corporate social initiatives. *California Management Review*, *47*(1), 9–24. doi:10.2307/41166284

Bhatti, W. A., Larimo, J., & Carrasco, I. (2016). Strategy's Effect on Knowledge Sharing in Host Country Networks. *Journal of Business Research*, *69*(11), 4769–4774. doi:10.1016/j.jbusres.2016.04.028

Bhimani, A., & Soonawalla, K. (2005). From conformance to performance: The corporate responsibilities continuum. *Journal of Accounting and Public Policy*, *24*(3), 165–174. doi:10.1016/j.jaccpubpol.2005.03.001

Bhupendra, K. V., & Sangle, S. (2018). Product Stewardship Strategy: A Study of Indian Firms. *Corporate Social Responsibility and Environmental Management*, *25*(2), 124–134. doi:10.1002/csr.1444

Bianchi, E., Bruno, J. M., & Sarabia-Sanchez, F. J. (2019). The impact of perceived CSR on corporate reputation and purchase intention. *European Journal of Management and Business Economics*, *28*(3), 206–221. doi:10.1108/EJMBE-12-2017-0068

Bigné Alcañiz, J. E., & Currás Pérez, R. (2008). ¿Influye la imagen de responsabilidad social en la intención de compra? El papel de la identificación del consumidor con la empresa. *Universia Business Review*, *19*, 10–23.

Bikefe, G., Zubairu, U., Araga, S., Maitala, F., Ediuku, E., & Anyebe, D. (2020). *Corporate Social Responsibility (CSR) by small and medium enterprises (SMEs): a systematic review*. Academic Press.

Blonska, A., Storey, C., Rozemeijer, F. A., Wetzels, M. G. M., & de Ruyter, J. C. (2013). Decomposing the effect of supplier development on relationship benefits: The role of relational capital. *Industrial Marketing Management*, *42*(8), 1295–1306. doi:10.1016/j.indmarman.2013.06.007

Boatright, J. R. (2003). *Ethics and the Conduct of Business* (4th ed.). Prentice Hall.

Bocken, N. M. P., Short, S. W., Rana, P., & Evans, S. (2014). A Literature and Practice Review to Develop Sustainable Business Model Archetypes. *Journal of Cleaner Production*, *65*(15), 42–56. doi:10.1016/j.jclepro.2013.11.039

Bodiroga-Vukobrat, N., & Martinovic, A. (2019). Challenges of Providing Services on the EU Digital Market. *Zbornik Pravnog Fakulteta Sveucilista u Rijeci*, *40*(1), 37–58. doi:10.30925/zpfsr.40.1.2

Boer, N. I., Berends, H., & Van Baalen, P. (2011). Relational Models for Knowledge Sharing Behavior. *European Management Journal*, *29*(2), 85–97. doi:10.1016/j.emj.2010.10.009

Boettke, P. J., Coyne, C. J., & Leeson, P. T. (2007). Saving government failure theory from itself: Recasting political economy from an Austrian perspective. *Constitutional Political Economy*, *18*(2), 127–143. doi:10.100710602-007-9017-1

Boisot, M., & MacMillan, I. C. (2004). Crossing epistemological boundaries: Managerial and entrepreneurial approaches to knowledge management. *Long Range Planning*, *37*(6), 505–524. doi:10.1016/j.lrp.2004.09.002

Boix, R., & Galleto, V. (2009). Innovation and Industrial Districts: A First Approach to the Measurement and Determinants of the I-District Effect. *Regional Studies, 43*(9), 1117–1133. doi:10.1080/00343400801932342

Boland, W. P., Phillips, P. W. B., Ryan, C. D., & McPhee-Knowles, S. (2012). Collaboration and the Generation of New Knowledge in Networked Innovation Systems: A Bibliometric Analysis. *Procedia: Social and Behavioral Sciences, 52*, 15–24. doi:10.1016/j.sbspro.2012.09.437

Bona-Sánchez, C., Pérez-Alemán, J., & Santana-Martín, D. J. (2017). Sustainability disclosure, dominant owners and earnings informativeness. *Research in International Business and Finance, 39*, 625–639. doi:10.1016/j.ribaf.2016.07.020

Bondy, K., Matten, D., & Moon, J. (2006). *MNC codes of conduct: CSR or corporate governance?* International Centre for Corporate Social Responsibility.

Bontis, N., Seleim, A., & Ashour, A. (2007). Human capital and organizational performance: a study of Egyptian software companies. *Manag. Decis., 45*(4), 789-801.

Bontis, N. (1998). Intellectual Capital: An Exploratory Study that Develops Measures and Models. *Management Decision, 36*(2), 63–76. doi:10.1108/00251749810204142

Bontis, N. (2001). Assessing Knowledge Assets: A Review of the Models Used to Measure Intellectual Capital. *International Journal of Management Reviews, 3*(1), 41–60. doi:10.1111/1468-2370.00053

Bontis, N. (2002). *World Congress on Intellectual Capital Readings*. Boston, MA: KMCI Butterworth-Heinemann Press.

Bontis, N., Keow, W. C. C., & Richardson, S. (2000). Intellectual capital and business performance in Malaysian industries. *Journal of Intellectual Capital, 1*(1), 85–100. doi:10.1108/14691930010324188

Boone, L. E., & Kurtz, D. L. (1994). *Business and society*. Harper Collins.

Boschma, R. A. (2005). Proximity and innovation: A critical assessment. *Regional Studies, 39*(1), 61–74. doi:10.1080/0034340052000320887

Bose, S., & Thomas, K. (2007). Applying the balanced scorecard for better performance of intellectual capital. *Journal of Intellectual Capital, 8*(4), 653–665. doi:10.1108/14691930710830819

Boulding, K. E. (1956). General systems theory—The skeleton of science. *Management Science, 2*(3), 197–208. doi:10.1287/mnsc.2.3.197

Boulstridge, E., & Carrigan, M. (2000). Do consumers really care about corporate responsibility? Highlighting the attitude—Behaviour gap. *Journal of Communication Management (London), 4*(4), 355–368. doi:10.1108/eb023532

Bourguignon, A. (2005). Management accounting and value creation: The profit and loss of reification. *Critical Perspectives on Accounting, 16*(4), 353–389. doi:10.1016/j.cpa.2003.03.001

Bowen, M., Freidank, J., Wannow, S., & Cavallone, M. (2018). Effects of severity and knowledge of a scandal on the perceived ethical behavior and attitude towards a company: An intercultural perspective on CSR management. In *Excellence in Services: 21th International Conference* (pp. 83-103). EISIC-LeCnam.

Bowen, E., Cousins, D., Lamming, C., & Farukt, C. (2001). The role of supply management capabilities in green supply. *Production and Operations Management, 10*(2), 174–189. doi:10.1111/j.1937-5956.2001.tb00077.x

Bowen, H. R. (1953). *Social Responsibilities of Businessman*. Harper and Row.

Bowen, H. R. (1953). *Social Responsibilities of the Businessman*. Harper & Row.

Bowen, H. R. (1953). *Social responsibilities of the businessman*. Harper.

Boyd, D. E., Spekman, R. E., Kamauff, J. W., & Werhane, P. (2007). Corporate social responsibility in global supply chains: A procedural justice perspective. *Long Range Planning*, *40*(3), 341–356. doi:10.1016/j.lrp.2006.12.007

Brammer, S. J., & Pavelin, S. (2006). Corporate reputation and social performance: The importance of fit. *Journal of Management Studies*, *43*(3), 435–455. doi:10.1111/j.1467-6486.2006.00597.x

Branco-Castelo, M., & Rodriguez-Lima, L. (2006). Corporate social responsibility and resource- based perspectives. *Journal of Business Ethics*, *69*(2), 111–132. doi:10.100710551-006-9071-z

Branzei, O., Ursacki-Bryant, T. J., Vertinsky, I., & Zhang, W. (2004). The formation of green strategies in Chinese firms: Matching corporate environmental responses and individual principles. *Strategic Management Journal*, *25*(11), 1075–1095. doi:10.1002mj.409

Brennan, N. M., & Solomon, J. (2008). Corporate governance, accountability and mechanisms of accountability: An overview. *Accounting, Auditing & Accountability Journal*, *21*(7), 885–906. doi:10.1108/09513570810907401

Brooking, A. (1996). *Intellectual Capital, Core Asset for the Third Millennium Enterprise*. International Thomson Business Press.

Brulhart, F., Gherra, S., & Quelin, B. V. (2019). Do stakeholder orientation and environmental proactivity impact on firm profitability? *Journal of Business Ethics*, *158*(1), 25–46. doi:10.100710551-017-3732-y

Buckley, P. J., & Casson, M. (2002). The future of the multinational enterprise (25th anniversary). Palgrave MacMillan.

Budsaratragoon, P., & Jitmaneeroj, B. (2019). Measuring causal relations and identifying critical drivers for corporate sustainability: The quadruple bottom line approach. *Measuring Business Excellence*.

Burchell, J., & Cook, J. (2006). It's good to talk? Examining attitudes towards corporate social responsibility dialogue and engagement processes. *Business Ethics (Oxford, England)*, *15*(2), 154–170. doi:10.1111/j.1467-8608.2006.00439.x

Burgess, Z., & Tharenou, P. (2002). Women board directors: Characteristics of the few. *Journal of Business Ethics*, *37*(1), 39–49. doi:10.1023/A:1014726001155

Burke, L., & Logsdon, J. M. (1996). How corporate social responsibility pays off. *Long Range Planning*, *29*(4), 495–502. doi:10.1016/0024-6301(96)00041-6

Bushee, B. J., Goodman, T. H., & Sunder, S. V. (2019). Financial Reporting Quality, Investment Horizon, and Institutional Investor Trading Strategies. *The Accounting Review*, *94*(3), 87–112. doi:10.2308/accr-52202

Buysse, K., & Verbeke, A. (2003). Proactive environmental strategies: A stakeholder management perspective. *Strategic Management Journal*, *24*(5), 453–470. doi:10.1002mj.299

Cabeza-García, L., Fernández-Gago, R., & Nieto, M. (2018). Do board gender diversity and director typology impact CSR reporting? *European Management Review*, *15*(4), 559–575. doi:10.1111/emre.12143

Cabrita, M. D. R., & Bontis, N. (2008). Intellectual capital and business performance in the Portuguese banking industry. *International Journal of Technology Management*, *43*(1-3), 212–237. doi:10.1504/IJTM.2008.019416

Cai, L., Cui, J., & Jo, H. (2016). Corporate environmental responsibility and firm risk. *Journal of Business Ethics*, *139*(3), 563–594. doi:10.100710551-015-2630-4

Callan, S. J., & Thomas, J. M. (2009). Corporate financial performance and corporate social performance: An update and reinvestigation. *Corporate Social Responsibility and Environmental Management*, *16*(2), 61–78. doi:10.1002/csr.182

Calza, F., Profumo, G., & Tutore, I. (2016). Corporate ownership and environmental proactivity. *Business Strategy and the Environment*, *25*(6), 369–389. doi:10.1002/bse.1873

Camargo, M. P., Silva Velez, E., & Patiño Moncada, J. D. A. (2015). *Análisis del comportamiento de los egresados del Programa Administración de Empresas de la Universidad de Cartagena en el período 2009-2012 frente al emprendimiento empresarial*. Universidad de Cartagena.

Camisón, C., & Forés, B. (2010). Knowledge absorptive capacity: New insights for its conceptualization and measurement. *Journal of Business Research*, *63*(7), 707–715. doi:10.1016/j.jbusres.2009.04.022

Camisón, C., & Villar-López, A. (2014). Organizational innovation as an enabler of technological innovation capabilities and firm performance. *Journal of Business Research*, *67*(1), 2891–2902.

Campbell, J. L. (2007). Why would corporations behave in socially responsible ways? An institutional theory of corporate social responsibility. *Academy of Management Review*, *32*(3), 946–967. doi:10.5465/amr.2007.25275684

Campi, S. (2008). A Cluster Approach for the Promotion of CSR Among SMEs. Scuola Superiore Sant'Anna, Italy.

Caraiani, C., Lungu, C. I., Dascalu, C., Cimpoeru, M. V., & Dinu, M. (2012). Social and environmental performance indicators: Dimensions of integrated reporting and benefits for responsible management and sustainability. *African Journal of Business Management*, *6*(14), 4990.

Carlsson, S. A. (2001). Knowledge management in network contexts. *ECIS 2001 Proceedings*, 9.

Carmeli, A., Gilat, G., & Weisberg, J. (2006). Perceived external prestige, organizational identification and affective commitment: A stakeholder approach. *Corporate Reputation Review*, *9*(2), 92–104. doi:10.1057/palgrave.crr.1550014

Carpenter, M. A., & Westphal, J. D. (2001). The strategic context of external network ties: Examining the impact of director appointments on board involvement in strategic decision-making. *Academy of Management Journal*, *44*(4), 639–660.

Carraher, S. M., Welsh, D. H., & Svilokos, A. (2016). Validation of a measure of social entrepreneurship. *European Journal of International Management*, *10*(4), 386–402. doi:10.1504/EJIM.2016.077421

Carrión, G. C., Henseler, J., Ringle, C. M., & Roldán, J. L. (2016). Prediction-oriented modelling in business research by means of PLS path modelling: Introduction to a JBR special section. *Journal of Business Research*, *69*(10), 4545–4551. doi:10.1016/j.jbusres.2016.03.048

Carroll, A., & Buchholtz, A. (2006). *Business and Society: Ethics and Stakeholder Management*. Thompson Learning.

Carroll, A. B. (1974). Corporate social responsibility: Its managerial impact and implications. *Journal of Business Research*, *2*(1), 75–88. doi:10.1016/S0148-2963(74)80008-1

Carroll, A. B. (1979). A three-dimensional conceptual model of corporate performance. *Academy of Management. Academy of Management Review*, *4*(4), 497–505. doi:10.5465/amr.1979.4498296

Carroll, A. B. (1983). Corporate social responsibility. *Vital Speeches of the Day*, *49*(19), 604.

Carroll, A. B. (1991). The pyramid of corporate social responsibility: Toward the moral management of organizational stakeholders. *Business Horizons*, *34*(4), 39–4. doi:10.1016/0007-6813(91)90005-G

Carroll, A. B. (1999). Corporate social responsibility. *Business & Society*, *38*(3), 268–295. doi:10.1177/000765039903800303

Carroll, A. B. (2008). A history of corporate social responsibility: concepts and practices. In A. M. Andrew Crane, D. Matten, J. Moon, & D. Siegel (Eds.), *The Oxford handbook of corporate social responsibility* (pp. 19–46). Oxford University Press.

Carroll, A. B., & Buchholtz, A. K. (1996). *Ethics and stakeholder management.* South-Western.

Carroll, A. B., & Buchholtz, A. K. (2008). *Business and Society: Ethics, Sustainability, and Stakeholder Management* (9th ed.). Cengage Learning.

Carter, C. R. (2004). Purchasing and social responsibility: A replication and extension. *The Journal of Supply Chain Management, 40*(3), 4–16. doi:10.1111/j.1745-493X.2004.tb00175.x

Carter, C. R., & Jennings, M. M. (2004). The role of purchasing in corporate social responsibility: A structural equation analysis. *Journal of Business Logistics, 25*(1), 145–186. doi:10.1002/j.2158-1592.2004.tb00173.x

Casa de Bolsa Monex. (2018). *Conoce los tres tipos de responsabilidad social: individual, empresarial y pública.* Retrieved from: https://blog.monex.com.mx/conoce-los-tres-tipos-responsabilidad-social-individual-empresarial-publica

Cascón, F. C. (2019). Hacia un nuevo marco normativo de los derechos de autor y derechos conexos en el mercado único digital. *Revista Electrónica de Direito, 19*(2), 1–10. doi:10.24840/2182-9845_2019-0002_0001_

Casilla Polo, F., & Gallardo Vázquez, D. (2008). Social information within the intellectual capital report. *Journal of International Management, 14*(4), 353–363. doi:10.1016/j.intman.2007.09.007

Cassells, S., & Lewis, K. (2011). SMEs and environmental responsibility: Do actions reflect attitudes? *Corporate Social Responsibility and Environmental Management, 18*(3), 186–199. doi:10.1002/csr.269

Castaldo, S., Perrini, F., Misani, N., & Tencati, A. (2009). The missing link between corporate social responsibility and consumer trust: The case of fair trade products. *Journal of Business Ethics, 84*(1), 1–15. doi:10.100710551-008-9669-4

Castaño Collado, C., Laffarga Briones, J., Iglesias Fernández, C., Fuentes Ruiz, P. D., Martín Fernández, J., Llorente Heras, R., & Martínez Cantos, J. L. (2009). *Mujeres y Poder Empresarial en España.* Instituto de la Mujer, Ministerio de Igualdad.

Castka, P., Balzarova, M. A., Bamber, C. J., & Sharp, J. M. (2004). How can SMEs effectively implement the CSR agenda? A UK case study perspective. *Corporate Social Responsibility and Environmental Management, 11*(3), 140–149. doi:10.1002/csr.62

Cavazos-Arroyo, J., & Puente-Diaz, R. (2019). The Inñuence of Marketing Capability in Mexican Social Enterprises. *Sustainability, 11*(17), 1–15. doi:10.3390u11174668

Cavicchi, C., & Vagnoni, E. (2017). Does intelectual capital promote the shift of healthcare organizations towards sustainable development? Evidence from Italy. *Journal of Cleaner Production, 153.*

CEC (Commission of the European Communities). (2002). *Communication from the commission concerning corporate social responsibility: A business contribution to sustainable development, 347.* Author.

CEC (Commission of the European Communities). (2005). Implementing the Community Lisbon Programme Modern SME Policy for Growth and Employment. *Communication from the Commission to the Council, the European Parliament, the European Economic and Social Committee and the Committee of the Regions*, 551.

CEC (Commission of the European Communities). (2006). Implementing the partnership for growth and jobs: Making Europe a pole of excellence of corporate social responsibility. *Communication from the Commission to the European Parliament, the Council and the European Economic and Social Committee*, 136.

Celma, D., Martínez-Garcia, E., & Coenders, G. (2014). Corporate Social Responsibility in Human Resource Management: An Analysis of Common Practices and their Determinants in Spain. *Corporate Social Responsibility and Environmental Management, 21*(2), 82–99. doi:10.1002/csr.1301

Chaffee, E. C. (2017). The origins of corporate social responsibility. *University of Cincinnati Law Review, 85*, 347–373.

Cha, J., Chang, Y. K., & Kim, T. Y. (2014). Person–organization fit on prosocial identity: Implications on employee outcomes. *Journal of Business Ethics, 123*(1), 57–69. doi:10.100710551-013-1799-7

Chan, E. S. W., & Hawkins, R. (2010). (2010). Attitude Towards EMSs in an International Hotel: An Exploratory Case Study. *International Journal of Hospitality Management, 29*(4), 641–651. doi:10.1016/j.ijhm.2009.12.002

Chang, C. H. (2016). The Determinants of Green Product Innovation Performance. *Corporate Social Responsibility and Environmental Management, 23*(2), 65–76. doi:10.1002/csr.1361

Chang, C., & Chen, Y. (2012). The determinants of green intellectual capital. *Management Decision, 50*(1), 74–94. doi:10.1108/00251741211194886

Chan, M., Cheng, S., & Hwang, Y. (2005). An empirical investigation of the relationship between intellectual capital and firms market value and financial performance. *Journal of Intellectual Capital, 2*(2), 159–176. doi:10.1108/14691930510592771

Chatzoglou, P., Chatzoudes, D., Amarantou, V., & Aggelidis, V. (2017). Examining the antecedents and the effects of CSR implementation: An explanatory study. *EuroMed Journal of Business, 12*(2), 189–206. doi:10.1108/EMJB-12-2016-0035

Chaudary, S., Zahid, Z., Shahid, S., Khan, S. N., & Azar, S. (2016). Customer perception of CSR initiatives: Its antecedents and consequences. *Social Responsibility Journal, 12*(2), 263–279. doi:10.1108/SRJ-04-2015-0056

Cheah, E.-T., Jamali, D., Johnson, J. E. V., & Sung, M. C. (2011). Drivers of Corporate Social Responsibility Attitudes: The Demography of Socially Responsible Investors: Drivers of Corporate Social Responsibility Attitudes. *British Journal of Management, 22*(2), 305–323. doi:10.1111/j.1467-8551.2011.00744.x

Chen, C.-J., Hsiao, Y.-C., & Chu, M.-A. (2014). Transfer mechanisms and knowledge transfer: The cooperative competency perspective. *Journal of Business Research, 67*(12), 2531–2541. doi:10.1016/j.jbusres.2014.03.011

Cheng, J. H. (2011). Inter-Organizational Relationships and Information Sharing in Supply Chains. *International Journal of Information Management, 31*(4), 374–384. doi:10.1016/j.ijinfomgt.2010.09.004

Chen, I. J., & Popovich, K. (2003). Understanding customer relationship management (CRM) People, process and technology. *Business Process Management Journal, 9*(5), 672–688. doi:10.1108/14637150310496758

Chen, Y. (2008). The Positive Effect of Green Intellectual Capital on Competitive Advantages of Firms. *Journal of Business Ethics, 77*(3), 271–286. doi:10.100710551-006-9349-1

Chen, Y. S., Lin, H., Lin, Y., & Chang, C. (2015). Enhancing green absorptive capacity, green dynamic capacities and green service innovation to improve firm performance: An analysis of structural equation modeling (SEM). *Sustainability, 7*(11), 15674–15692. doi:10.3390u71115674

Cheung, M. S., Myers, M. B., & Mentzer, J. T. (2011). The value of relational learning in global buyer-supplier exchanges: A dyadic perspective and test of the pie-sharing premise. *Strategic Management Journal, 32*(10), 1061–1082. doi:10.1002mj.926

Child, J. (2000). Trust and international strategic alliances: the case of Sino-foreign joint ventures. In C. Lane & R. Bachmann (Eds.), *Trust Within and Between Organisations* (pp. 241–272). Oxford University Press.

Chin, W. (1998). The partial least squares approach to structural equation modelling. *Modern Methods for Business Research, 295*(2), 295-336.

Chin, M. K., Hambrick, D. C., & Treviño, L. K. (2013). Political Ideologies of CEOs: The Influence of Executives' Values on Corporate Social Responsibility. *Administrative Science Quarterly, 58*(2), 197–232. doi:10.1177/0001839213486984

Chiva, R., Alegre, J., & Lapiedra, R. (2007). Measuring Organizational Learning Capability Among the Workforce. *International Journal of Manpower*, *28*(3/4), 224–242. doi:10.1108/01437720710755227

Choi, J. S., Kwak, Y. M., & Choe, C. (2010). Corporate social responsibility and corporate financial performance: Evidence from Korea. *Australian Journal of Management*, *35*(3), 291–311. doi:10.1177/0312896210384681

Choi, Y., & Yu, Y. (2014). The influence of perceived corporate sustainability practices on employees and organizational performance. *Sustainability*, *6*(1), 348–364. doi:10.3390u6010348

Cho, S. J., Chung, C. Y., & Young, J. (2019). Study on the Relationship between CSR and Financial Performance. *Sustainability*, *11*(2), 343. doi:10.3390u11020343

Chow, W. S., & Chen, Y. (2012). Corporate sustainable development: Testing a new scale based on the mainland chinese context. *Journal of Business Ethics*, *105*(4), 519–533. doi:10.100710551-011-0983-x

Chrisman, J. J., & Carroll, A. B. (1984). SMR forum: Corporate responsibility—reconciling economic and social goals. *Sloan Management Review*, *25*(2), 59–65.

Christmann, P. (2000). Effects of "best practices" of environmental management on cost advantage: The role of complementary assets. *Academy of Management Journal*, *43*(4), 663–680.

Christmann, P., & Taylor, G. (2001). Globalization and the Environment: Determinants of Firm Self-Regulation in China. *Journal of International Business Studies*, *32*(3), 439–458. doi:10.1057/palgrave.jibs.8490976

Christmann, P., & Taylor, G. (2006). Firm self-regulation through international certifiable standards: Determinants of symbolic versus substantive implementation. *Journal of International Business Studies*, *37*(6), 863–878. doi:10.1057/palgrave.jibs.8400231

Christofi, A., Christofi, P., & Sisaye, S. (2012). Corporate sustainability: Historical development and reporting practices. *Management Research Review*.

Ciliberti, F., Pontrandolfo, P., & Scozzi, B. (2008). Investigating corporate social responsibility in supply chains: A SME perspective. *Journal of Cleaner Production*, *16*(15), 1579–1588. doi:10.1016/j.jclepro.2008.04.016

Clarkson, M. (1994). A risk based model of stakeholder theory. *Proceedings of the Second Toronto Conference on Stakeholder Theory*, 18-19.

Clarkson, M. B. E. (1995). A stakeholder framework for analyzing and evaluating corporate social performance. *Academy of Management Review*, *20*(1), 92–117. doi:10.5465/amr.1995.9503271994

Cleek, M. A., & Leonard, S. L. (1998). Can corporate codes of ethics influence behavior? *Journal of Business Ethics*, *17*(6), 619–630. doi:10.1023/A:1017969921581

Cochran, P. L. (2007). The evolution of corporate social responsibility. *Business Horizons*, *50*(6), 449–454. doi:10.1016/j.bushor.2007.06.004

Cohen, B., Smith, B., & Mitchell, R. (2008). Toward a Sustainable Conceptualization of Dependent Variables in Entrepreneurship Research. *Business Strategy and the Environment*, *17*(2), 107–119. doi:10.1002/bse.505

Cohen, J. R., Krishnamoorthy, G., & Wright, A. M. (2008). Form versus substance: The implications for auditing practice and research of alternative perspectives on corporate governance. *Auditing*, *27*(2), 181–198. doi:10.2308/aud.2008.27.2.181

Cohen, W. M., & Levinthal, D. A. (1990). Absorptive capacity: A new perspective on learning and innovation. *Administrative Science Quarterly*, *35*(1), 128–152. doi:10.2307/2393553

Coldwell, D. A., Billsberry, J., Van Meurs, N., & Marsh, P. J. G. (2008). The effects of person-organization ethical fit on employee attraction and retention: Towards a testable explanatory model. *Journal of Business Ethics*, *78*(4), 611–622. doi:10.100710551-007-9371-y

Coleman, J. S. (1990). Foundations of social theory (3rd ed.). Belknap Press of Harvard Univ. Press.

Collis, D.J., & Montgomery, C.A. (1995). Competing on Resources: Strategy in the 1990s. *Knowledge and Strategy*, *73*(4), 25-40.

Contractor, F., Foss, N. J., Kundu, S., & Lahiri, S. (2019). Viewing global strategy through a microfoundations lens. *Global Strategy Journal*, *9*(1), 3–18. doi:10.1002/gsj.1329

Cook, K. A., Romi, A. M., Sánchez, D., & Sánchez, J. M. (2019). The influence of corporate social responsibility on investment efficiency and innovation. *Journal of Business Finance & Accounting*, *46*(3-4), 494–537. doi:10.1111/jbfa.12360

Cooper, S. C. L., Stokes, P., Liu, Y., & Tarba, S. Y. (2017). Sustainability and organizational behavior: A micro-foundational perspective. *Journal of Organizational Behavior*, *38*(9), 1297–1301. doi:10.1002/job.2242

Cornelissen, J. (2014). *Corporate communication: A guide to theory and practice*. Sage.

Cortini, M., & Benevene, P. (2010). Interaction between structural capital and human capital in Italian NPOs: Leadership, organizational culture and human resource management. *Journal of Intellectual Capital*, *11*(2), 123–139. doi:10.1108/14691931011039642

Cousins, P. D., Handfield, R. B., Lawson, B., & Petersen, K. J. (2006). Creating supply chain relational capital: The impact of formal and informal socialization processes. *Journal of Operations Management*, *24*(6), 851–863. doi:10.1016/j.jom.2005.08.007

Cowan, A., Welch, S., & Welch, O. (2011). *An empirical investigation of the link between performance and Corporate Social Responsibility in the oil and gas industry*. Midwest Finance Association, Annual Meetings Paper. 10.2139srn.1929113

Cowden, B., Alhorr, H. S., & Bendickson, J. (2015). Experience-Based Green Board Capital: Linking Board of Directors and Firm Environmental Performance. *Journal of Leadership, Accountability and Ethics*, *12*(3).

Crane, A., & Livesey, S. (2003). Are you talking to me? Stakeholder communication and the risks and rewards of dialogue. In J. Andriof, S. Waddock, S. Rahman, and B. Husted (Eds.), Unfolding Stakeholder Thinking vol II: Relationships, communication, reporting and performance (pp. 39–52). Sheffield, UK: Greenleaf. doi:10.9774/GLEAF.978-1-909493-32-2_4

Crane, F., & Crane, E. (2007). Dispositional optimism and entrepreneurial success. *The Psychologist Manager Journal*, *10*(1), 13–25. doi:10.1080/10887150709336610

Crane, H. M., Lober, W., Webster, E., Harrington, R. D., Crane, P. K., Davis, T. E., & Kitahata, M. M. (2007). Routine collection of patient-reported outcomes in an HIV clinic setting: The first 100 patients. *Current HIV Research*, *5*(1), 109–118. doi:10.2174/157016207779316369 PMID:17266562

Cressey, D. R., & Moore, C. A. (1983). Managerial values and corporate codes of ethics. *California Management Review*, *25*(4), 53–77.

Creswell, J. W. (2014). *Research design: Qualitative, quantitative, and mixed methods approaches* (4th ed.). Sage.

Creswell, J., & Plano, V. (2007). *Designing and Conducting Mixed Methods Research*. Sage Publications, Inc.

Crişan-Mitra, C., & Borza, A. (2015). Approaching CSR in Romania: An empirical analysis. *Procedia: Social and Behavioral Sciences*, *207*, 546–552. doi:10.1016/j.sbspro.2015.10.125

Cullinan, C. P., Mahoney, L., & Roush, P. B. (2019). Directors & Corporate Social Responsibility: Joint Consideration of Director Gender and the Director's Role. *Social and Environmental Accountability Journal, 39*(2), 100–123. doi:10.1080/0969160X.2019.1586556

Curado, C., Muñoz-Pascual, L., & Galende, J. (2018). Antecedent to Innovation Performance in SMEs: A Mixed Methods Approach. *Journal of Business Research, 89*, 206–215. doi:10.1016/j.jbusres.2017.12.056

Curran, M. A. (2009). Wrapping our brains around sustainability. *Sustainability, 1*(1), 5–13.

Curto, M. (2012). Los emprendedores sociales: innovación al servicio del cambio. *Cuadernos de la Cátedra 'La Caixa' de Responsabilidad de la Empresa y Gobierno Corporativo, 13*, 1-23.

Dacin, M. T., Dacin, P. A., & Tracey, P. (2011). Social entrepreneurship: A critique and future directions. *Organization Science, 22*(5), 1203–1213. doi:10.1287/orsc.1100.0620

Dahlsrud, A. (2008). How corporate social responsibility is defined: An analysis of 37 definitions. *Corporate Social Responsibility and Environmental Management, 15*(1), 1–13. doi:10.1002/csr.132

Dalton, D. R., & Daily, C. M. (1999). What's wrong with having friends on the board? *Across the Board, 36*(3), 28–32.

Dalziel, T., Gentry, R. J., & Bowerman, M. (2011). An integrated agency – resource dependence view of the influence of directors 'human and relational capital on firms' R&D spending. *Journal of Management Studies, 48*(6), 1217–1242. doi:10.1111/j.1467-6486.2010.01003.x

Dando, N., & Swift, T. (2003). Transparency and assurance minding the credibility gap. *Journal of Business Ethics, 44*(2-3), 195–200. doi:10.1023/A:1023351816790

Darnall, N., & Edwards, D. (2006). Predicting the cost of environmental management system adoption: The role of capabilities, resources and ownership structure. *Strategic Management Journal, 27*(4), 301–320. doi:10.1002mj.518

Darnall, N., Henriques, I., & Sadorsky, P. (2010). Adopting proactive environmental strategy: The influence of stakeholders and firm size. *Journal of Management Studies, 47*(6), 1072–1094. doi:10.1111/j.1467-6486.2009.00873.x

Daugherty, P. J., Autry, C. W., & Ellinger, A. E. (2001). Reverse logistics: The relationship between resource commitment and program performance. *Journal of Business Logistics, 22*(1), 107–123. doi:10.1002/j.2158-1592.2001.tb00162.x

Davenport, T. H., & Prusak, L. (2000). *Working knowledge: How organizations manage what they know*. Harvard Business School Press.

Davies, I. A., & Crane, A. (2010). Corporate social responsibility in small-and medium-size enterprises: Investigating employee engagement in fair trade companies. *Business Ethics (Oxford, England), 19*(2), 126–139. doi:10.1111/j.1467-8608.2010.01586.x

Davis, K. (1960). Can business afford to ignore social responsibilities? *California Management Review, 2*(3), 70.

Davis, K. (1973). The case for and against business assumption of social responsibilities. *Academy of Management Journal, 16*(2), 312.

Davis, G. F. (2016). Can an Economy Survive Without Corporations? Technology and Robust Organizational Alternatives. *The Academy of Management Perspectives, 30*(2), 129–140. doi:10.5465/amp.2015.0067

Davis, K. (1973). The case for and against business assumption of social responsibilities. *Academy of Management Journal, 16*(2), 312–322.

Davis, K., & Blomstrom, R. L. (1966). *Business and society: Environment and responsibility*. McGraw-Hill.

DCLA. (2017). *Government of United States Virgin Islands Department of Licensing and Consumer Affairs (DCLA)*. Retrieved from https://dlca.vi.gov/

De Bakker, F. G., Groenewegen, P., & Den Hond, F. (2005). A bibliometric analysis of 30 years of research and theory on corporate social responsibility and corporate social performance. *Business & Society*, *44*(3), 283–317. doi:10.1177/0007650305278086

De la Cuesta González, M., Valor Martínez, C., Sanmartín Serrano, S., & Botija Buiza, M. (2002). *La Responsabilidad Social Corporativa: Una Aplicación a España* [CSR: An Application to Spain]. UNED.

De la Fuente Sabaté, J. M., & de Quevedo Puente, E. (2003). Empirical analysis of the relationship between corporate reputation and financial performance: A survey of the literature. *Corporate Reputation Review*, *6*(2), 161–177. doi:10.1057/palgrave.crr.1540197

De los Ríos Berjillos, A., Lozano, M. R., Valencia, P. T., & Ruz, M. C. (2012). Una aproximación a la relación entre información sobre la responsabilidad social orientada al cliente y la reputación corporativa de las entidades financieras españolas. *Cuadernos de Economía y Dirección de la Empresa*, *15*(3), 130–140. doi:10.1016/j.cede.2012.01.004

De Quevedo Puente, E., de la Fuente Sabaté, J. M., & García, J. B. D. (2005). Reputación corporativa y creación de valor. Marco teórico de una relación circular. *Investigaciones Europeas de Dirección y Economía de la Empresa*, *11*(2), 81–97.

De Roeck, K., El Akremi, A., & Swaen, V. (2016). Consistency matters! How and when does corporate social responsibility affect employees' organizational identification? *Journal of Management Studies*, *53*(7), 1141–1168. doi:10.1111/joms.12216

De Villers, C., & Sharma, U. (2018). A critical reflection on the future of financial, intelectual capital, sustainability and integrated reporting. *Critical Perspectives on Accounting*.

Deeds, D. L., Decarolis, D. M., & Coombs, J. (1999). Dynamic capabilities and new product development in high technology ventures: An empirical analysis of new biotechnology firms. *Journal of Business Venturing*, *15*(3), 211–229. doi:10.1016/S0883-9026(98)00013-5

DeLaurentis, T. (2009). Ethical supply chain management. *The China Business Review*, *36*(3), 38–41.

Delgado-Verde, M., Amores-Salvado, J., Castro, G.M., & Navas-Lopez, J.E. (2014). Green intellectual capital and environmental product innovation: the mediating role of green social capital. *Knowl. Manag. Res. Pract.*, *12*(3), 1-15.

Delmas, M., & Montes-Sancho, M. J. (2009). Voluntary agreements to improve environmental quality: Symbolic and substantive cooperation. *Strategic Management Journal*.

Delmas, M., & Toffel, M. W. (2004). Stakeholders and environmental management practices: An institutional framework. *Business Strategy and the Environment*, *13*(4), 209–222. doi:10.1002/bse.409

Delmas, M., & Toffel, M. W. (2008). Organizational responses to environmental demands: Opening the black box. *Strategic Management Journal*, *29*(10), 1027–1055. doi:10.1002mj.701

Deloitte & Touche. (1992). Business strategy for sustainable development: Leadership and accountability for the 90s. IISD.

Deloitte. (2018). *Responsabilidad Social y Gobierno Corporativo*. Retrieved from: https://www2.deloitte.com/es/es/pages/governance-risk-and-compliance/articles/responsabilidad-social-y-gobierno-corporativo.html

Demirgüneş, B. K. (2015). Ethical behavior of salesperson: The impact of consumer's perception on trust, satisfaction and repeat purchasing behavior. *Turkish Journal of Business Ethics*, *8*(1), 26–46. doi:10.12711/tjbe.2015.8.1.0009

Denford, J. S. (2013). Building Knowledge: Developing a Knowledge-Based Dynamic Capabilities Typology. *Journal of Knowledge Management*, *17*(2), 175–194. doi:10.1108/13673271311315150

Deol, H. S. (2009). Strategic environment and intellectual capital of Indian banks. *Journal of Intellectual Capital*, *10*(1), 109–120. doi:10.1108/14691930910922932

Dev, N.K., Shankar, R., & Swami, S. (2020). Diffussion of green products in industry 4.0: Reverse logistics issues during design of inventory and production planning system. *International Journal of Production Economics*. (in press)

Devinney, T. M. (2013). Is Microfoundational Thinking Critical to Management Thought and Practice? *The Academy of Management Perspectives*, *27*(2), 81–84. doi:10.5465/amp.2013.0053

Devinney, T. M., Auger, P., & Eckhardt, G. M. (2010). *The Myth of the Ethical Consumer*. Cambridge University Press.

Dev, N. K., Shankar, R., & Qaiser, F. H. (2020). Industry 4.0 and circular economy: Operational excellence for sustainable reverse supply chain performance. *Resources, Conservation and Recycling*, *153*(104583), 1–15. doi:10.1016/j.resconrec.2019.104583

Dhanesh, G. S. (2012). The view from within: Internal publics and CSR. *Journal of Communication Management (London)*, *16*(1), 39–58. doi:10.1108/13632541211197987

Dhavala, S. (2017). *The philanthropic legacy of JRD Tata*. Retrieved on 06 December 2019 from: https://www.asiatimes.com/2017/11/opinion/philanthropic-legacy-jrd-tata/

Dibrell, C., Craig, J. B., Kim, J., & Johnson, A. J. (2015). Establishing How Natural Environmental Competency, Organizational Social Consciousness, and Innovativeness Relate. *Journal of Business Ethics*, *127*, 591–605. doi:10.100710551-013-2043-1

Dierkes, M., & Antal, A. B. (1985). The Usefulness and Use of Social Reporting Information. *Accounting, Organizations and Society*, *10*(1), 29–34. doi:10.1016/0361-3682(85)90029-7

Díez-Vial, I. (2011). Geographical cluster and performance: The case of Iberian ham. *Food Policy*, *36*(4), 517–525. doi:10.1016/j.foodpol.2011.04.002

Diller, J. (1999). A Social Conscience in the Global Marketplace-Labour Dimensions of Codes of COnduct, Social Labelling and Investor Initiatives. *Int'l Lab. Rev.*, *138*(2), 99–129. doi:10.1111/j.1564-913X.1999.tb00062.x

DiMaggio, P. J., & Powell, W. W. (1983). The iron cage revisited: Institutional isomorphism and collective rationality in organizational fields. *American Sociological Review*, *48*(2), 147–160. doi:10.2307/2095101

Dimson, E., Karakaş, O., Li, X., & Ownership, A. (2015). *Review of Financial Studies*. Available at SSRN: https://ssrn.com/abstract=2154724

Ding, D. K., Ferreira, C., & Wongchoti, U. (2019). The geography of CSR. *International Review of Economics & Finance*, *59*, 265–288. doi:10.1016/j.iref.2018.09.003

Dixit, A., Clouse, C., & Turken, N. (2019). Strategic business location decisions: Importance of economic factors and place image. *Rutgers Business Review*, *4*(1), 73–91.

Dixon, S., Meyer, K., & Day, M. (2014). Building dynamic capabilities of adaptation and innovation: A study of microfoundations in a transition economy. *Long Range Planning*, *47*(4), 186–205. doi:10.1016/j.lrp.2013.08.011

Doane, D. (2005). The myth of CSR. *Stanford Social Innovation Review*, *3*(3), 22–29.

Dodd, E. M. (1932). For whom are corporate managers trustees? *Harvard Law Review*, *45*(7), 1145–1163. doi:10.2307/1331697

Doherty, B., Haugh, H., & Lyon, F. (2014). Social Enterprises as Hybrid Organizations: A Review and Research Agenda. *International Journal of Management Reviews*, *16*(4), 417–436. doi:10.1111/ijmr.12028

Donaldson, T., & Preston, L. E. (1995). The stakeholder theory of the corporation: Concepts, evidence, and implications. *Academy of Management. Academy of Management Review*, *20*(1), 65–91. doi:10.5465/amr.1995.9503271992

Dopazo, M. P. (2012). Informes de responsabilidad social corporativa (RSC): fuentes de información y documentación. *Revista general de información y documentación, 22*, 279-305.

Dorado, S. (2005). Institutional entrepreneurship, partaking, and convening. *Organization Studies*, *26*(3), 385–414. doi:10.1177/0170840605050873

Dosi, M., Pahi, M. H., Magsi, H. B., & Umrani, W. A. (2019). Influence of the best practices of environmental management on Green product development. *Journal of Environmental Management*, *241*, 219–225. doi:10.1016/j.jenvman.2019.04.006 PMID:31004999

Dotterer, R. L. (2002). Student-faculty collaborations, undergraduate research, and collaboration as an administrative model. *New Directions for Teaching and Learning*, *2002*(90), 81–90. doi:10.1002/tl.58

Doz, Y. L. (1996). The evolution of cooperation in strategic alliances: Initial conditions or learning processes? *Strategic Management Journal*, *17*(S1), 55–83. doi:10.1002mj.4250171006

Drucker, P. F. (1984). Converting social problems into business opportunities: The new meaning of corporate social responsibility. *California Management Review, 26*(2), 53.

Drucker, P. F. (1996). *La gestión en tiempos de grandes cambios*. Ediciones Gestión 2000 S.A.

Dumay, J. (2016). A critical reflection on the future of intellectual capital: From reporting to disclosure. *Journal of Intellectual Capital*, *17*(1), 168–184. doi:10.1108/JIC-08-2015-0072

Dunlop, A. (1998). *Corporate governance and control*. Kogan Page Publishers.

Durán Herrera, J. J. (2009). Gobernanza, responsabilidad social y medioambiental de la empresa multinacional. Proceso estratégico. *Responsabilidad Social de la Empresa*, 15.

Durkin, C., & Gunn, R. (2016). *Social entrepreneurship: A skills approach*. Policy Press.

Dyer, J. H. (1996). How Chrysler created an American keiretsu. *Harvard Business Review*, *74*(4), 42–52.

Dyer, J. H., & Chu, W. (2003). The role of trustworthiness in reducing transaction costs and improving performance: Empirical evidence from the United States, Japan, and Korea. *Organization Science*, *14*(1), 57–68. doi:10.1287/orsc.14.1.57.12806

Dyer, J. H., & Singh, H. (1998). The relational view: Cooperative strategy and sources of interorganizational competitive advantage. *Academy of Management Review*, *23*(4), 660–679. doi:10.5465/amr.1998.1255632

Dyllick, T., & Hockerts, K. (2002). Beyond the business case for corporate sustainability. *Business Strategy and the Environment*, *11*(2), 130–141. doi:10.1002/bse.323

Dyllick, T., & Muff, K. (2016). Clarifying the Meaning of Sustainable Business: Introducing a Typology From Business-as-Usual to True Business Sustainability. *Organization & Environment*, *29*(2), 156–174. doi:10.1177/1086026615575176

Dy, R. C., & Caballero, R. T. (2015). A Strategic Employee Retention Model Based on Employee Perception. *European Journal of Business and Management, 2*(5), 25–35.

Eades, K. M., Laseter, T. M., Skurnik, I., Rodriguez, P. L., Isabella, L. A., & Simko, P. J. (2010). *The portable MBA* (Vol. 34). John Wiley and Sons. doi:10.1002/9781118256213

Eberhard-Harribey, L. (2006). Corporate social responsibility as a new paradigm in the European policy: How CSR comes to legitimate the European regulation process. *Corporate Governance, 6*(4), 358–368. doi:10.1108/14720700610689487

Eccles, R. G., Ioannou, I., & Serafeim, G. (2014). The Impact of Corporate Sustainability on Organizational Processes and Performance. *Management Science, 60*(11), 2835–2857. doi:10.1287/mnsc.2014.1984

Edinger-Schons, L. M., Lengler-Graiff, L., Scheidler, S., & Wieseke, J. (2019). Frontline employees as corporate social responsibility (CSR) ambassadors: A quasi-field experiment. *Journal of Business Ethics, 157*(2), 359–373. doi:10.100710551-018-3790-9

Edvinsson, L., & Malone, M. (1997). *Intellectual Capital.* Harper Business.

Egri, C. P., & Herman, S. (2000). Leadership in the North American environmental sector: Values, leadership styles and contexts of environmental leaders and their organizations. *Academy of Management Journal, 43*(4), 571–604.

Eiadat, Y., Kelly, A., Roche, F., & Eyatad, H. (2008). Green and competitive? An empirical test of the mediating role of environmental innovation strategy. *Journal of World Business, 43*(2), 131–145. doi:10.1016/j.jwb.2007.11.012

Eilbirt, H., & Parket, I. R. (1973). The practice of business: The current status of corporate social responsibility. *Business Horizons, 16*(4), 5–14. doi:10.1016/0007-6813(73)90043-8

Eisenhardt, K. M. (1989). Agency theory: An assessment and review. *Academy of Management Review, 14*(1), 57–74. doi:10.5465/amr.1989.4279003

Eisenhardt, K. M., & Martin, J. A. (2000). Dynamic capabilities: What are they? *Strategic Management Journal, 21*(10-11), 1105–1121. doi:10.1002/1097-0266(200010/11)21:10/11<1105::AID-SMJ133>3.0.CO;2-E

Elhauge, E. (2005). Sacrificing corporate profits in the public interest. *New York University Law Review, 80*(3), 733; 733.

Elias, R. Z. (2004). An examination of business students' perception of corporate social responsibilities before and after bankruptcies. *Journal of Business Ethics, 52*(3), 267–281. doi:10.1023/B:BUSI.0000037558.74693.d5

Elkington, J. (1997). *Cannibals with forks.* Capstone.

Elkington, J. (1998). *Cannibals with Forks: The Triple Bottom Line of 21st Century Business.* New Society Pbublishers.

Elkington, J. (1998). Partnerships from cannibals with forks: The triple bottom line of 21st- century business. *Environmental Quality Management, 8*(1), 37–51. doi:10.1002/tqem.3310080106

Elkington, J. (2004). *The Triple Bottom Line: Does It All Add Up?* Routledge., doi:10.4324/9781849773348

Emerson, K., Nabatchi, T., & Balogh, S. (2012). An integrative framework for collaborative governance. *Journal of Public Administration: Research and Theory, 22*(1), 1–29. doi:10.1093/jopart/mur011

Emmelhainz, M. A., & Adams, R. J. (1999). The apparel industry response to "sweatshop" concerns: A review and analysis of codes of conduct. *The Journal of Supply Chain Management, 35*(2), 51–57. doi:10.1111/j.1745-493X.1999.tb00062.x

Enkel, E., & Heil, S. (2014). Preparing for distant collaboration: Antecedents to potential absorptive capacity in cross-industry innovation. *Technovation, 34*(4), 242–260. doi:10.1016/j.technovation.2014.01.010

Epstein, E. M. (1987). The corporate social policy process: Beyond business ethics, corporate social responsibility, and corporate social responsiveness. *California Management Review*, *29*(3), 99–114. doi:10.2307/41165254

Ernst & Young GMBH. (2019). *Sensors as drivers of Industry 4.0. A study on Germany, Switzerland, & Austria.* BMC-EYGSA. https://www.ey.com/Publication/vwLUAssets/ey-at-studie-sensoren-treiber-industrie-40-2019/$FILE/EY%20Studie%20-%20Sensors%20as%20drivers%20of%20Industry%204.0.pdf

Erskine, C. C., & Collins, L. (1997). Eco-labeling: Success or failure? *The Environmentalist*, *17*(2), 125–133. doi:10.1023/A:1018552000651

Ettlie, J. E., & Pavlou, P. A. (2006). Technology-based new product development partnerships. *Decision Sciences*, *37*(2), 117–147. doi:10.1111/j.1540-5915.2006.00119.x

Europea, C. E. (2001). *Libro Verde: Fomentar un marco europeo para la responsabilidad social de las empresas*. CEE.

European Commission (EC). (2006). RICARDIS: Reporting Intellectual Capital to Augment Research, Development and Innovation in SMEs. European Commission, Directorate-General for Research, Brussels.

European Commission. (2001). *Green paper. promoting a european framework for corporate social responsibility.* European Commission.

European Commission. (2001). *Green paper. Promoting a European framework for corporate social responsibility.* European Commission.

European Commission. (2019). *Innovation and Networks Executive Agency*. https://ec.europa.eu/inea/en

European Parliament. (2019). *National Geographic website*. Retrieved on 11 December 2019 from https://www.nationalgeographic.com.es/naturaleza/parlamento-europeo-declara-emergencia-climatica_14997

Fabian, T., & Hill, C. (2005). *Sourcing Overseas for the Retail Sector: CSR and the Ethical Supply Chain.* Price Waterhouse Coopers.

Falk, R. F., & Miller, N. B. (1992). *A primer for soft modeling*. University of Akron Press.

Farooq, M., Farooq, O., & Jasimuddin, S. M. (2014). Employees response to corporate social responsibility: Exploring the role of employees' collectivist orientation. *European Management Journal*, *32*(6), 916–927. doi:10.1016/j.emj.2014.03.002

Farooq, O., Rupp, D. E., & Farooq, M. (2017). The multiple pathways through which internal and external corporate social responsibility influence organizational identification and multifoci outcomes: The moderating role of cultural and social orientations. *Academy of Management Journal*, *60*(3), 954–985. doi:10.5465/amj.2014.0849

Fassin, Y., Van Rossem, A., & Buelens, M. (2011). Small-business owner-managers' perceptions of business ethics and CSR-related concepts. *Journal of Business Ethics*, *98*(3), 425–453. doi:10.100710551-010-0586-y

Felin, & Foss, N. (2006). Individuals and organizations: Further thought on a microfoundations project for strategic management and organizational analysis. *Research Methodology in Strategy and Management, 1*. http://site.ebrary.com/id/10169693

Fernández Kranz, D., & Merino Castelló, A. (2005). ¿Existe disponibilidad a pagar por responsabilidad social corporativa? Percepción de los consumidores. *Universia Business Review*, *7*(3), 38–53.

Fernández Sánchez, J. L., & Luna Sotorrío, L. (2007). The creation of value through corporate reputation. *Journal of Business Ethics*, *76*(3), 335–346. doi:10.100710551-006-9285-0

Fernández-Viñé, M. B., Gómez-Navarro, T., & Capuz-Rizo, S. F. (2010). Eco-efficiency in the SMEs of Venezuela. Current Status and Future Perspectives. *Journal of Cleaner Production*, *18*(8), 736–746. doi:10.1016/j.jclepro.2009.12.005

Ferrell, O. C., Harrison, D. E., Ferrell, L., & Hair, J. F. (2019). Business ethics, corporate social responsibility, and brand attitudes: An exploratory study. *Journal of Business Research*, *95*, 491–501. doi:10.1016/j.jbusres.2018.07.039

Ferrell, O. C., & Skinner, S. J. (1988). Ethical behavior and bureaucratic structure in marketing research organizations. *JMR, Journal of Marketing Research*, *25*(1), 103–109. doi:10.1177/002224378802500111

Field, A. (2013). *Correlational research methods. Discovering statistics using IBM SPSS Statistics* (4th ed.). Sage.

Figge, F., & Hahn, T. (2004). Sustainable Value Added—Measuring corporate contributions to sustainability beyond eco-efficiency. *Ecological Economics*, *48*(2), 173–187. doi:10.1016/j.ecolecon.2003.08.005

Filgueiras, J. L. M., de Oliveira, M. G., de Castro Neto, F. C., & da Silva Filho, J. C. L. (2012). Analysis of CSR in Midsize Retail: Application of the QuaziA and O'brien Model. *Journal of Operations and Supply Chain Management*, *5*(2), 54–68. doi:10.12660/joscmv5n2p54-68

Fiol, C. M. (1996). Squeezing harder doesn't always work: Continuing the search for consistency in innovation research. *Academy of Management Review*, *21*(4), 1012–1021. doi:10.5465/amr.1996.15868543

Fitch, H. G. (1976). Achieving corporate social responsibility. *Academy of Management Review*, *1*(1), 38–46. doi:10.5465/amr.1976.4408754

Flammer, C. (2013). Corporate Social Responsibility and Shareholder Reaction: The Environmental Awareness of Investors. *Academy of Management Journal*, *56*(3), 758–781. doi:10.5465/amj.2011.0744

Flammer, C., & Kacperczyk, A. (2019). Corporate social responsibility as a defense against knowledge spillovers: Evidence from the inevitable disclosure doctrine. *Strategic Management Journal*, *40*(8), 1243–1267. doi:10.1002mj.3025

Fombellida, J., Martín-Rubio, I., & Torres-Alegre, S. (2018). *Tackling business intelligence with bioinspired deep learning*. Neural Comput & Applic. doi:10.100700521-018-3377-5

Fombrun, C. J. (1995). *Reputation: Realizing value from the corporate image*. Harvard Business School Press.

Fombrun, C., & Shanley, M. (1990). What's in a name? Reputation building and corporate strategy. *Academy of Management Journal*, *33*(2), 233–258.

Foran, T. (2001). *Corporate social responsibility at nine multinational electronics firms in Thailand: A preliminary analysis, report to the California global corporate accountability project*. Nautilus Institute for Security and Sustainable Development.

Forética. (2018). *INFORME FORÉTICA 2018 sobre la evolución de la RSE y Sostenibilidad. La recompensa del optimista*. Retrieved from: https://www.foretica.org/informe_foretica_2018.pdf

Fornell, C., & Larcker, D. F. (1981). Evaluating structural equation models with unobservable variables and measurement error. *JMR, Journal of Marketing Research*, *18*(1), 39–50. doi:10.1177/002224378101800104

Forrester. (2017). *The Power Of A Values-Based Strategy*. Retrieved from: https://go.forrester.com/what-it-means/ep15-values-based-strategy/

Foss, N. J. (2011). Invited Editorial: Why Micro-Foundations for Resource-Based Theory Are Needed and What They May Look Like. *Journal of Management*, *37*(5), 1413–1428. doi:10.1177/0149206310390218

Foss, N. J., & Pedersen, T. (2016). Microfoundations In Strategy Research. *Strategic Management Journal, 37*(13), E22–E34. doi:10.1002mj.2362

Foster, W. M., & Hyatt, C. (2007). I despise them! I detest them! Franchise relocation and the expanded model of organizational identification. *Journal of Sport Management, 21*(2), 194–212. doi:10.1123/jsm.21.2.194

Fraedrich, J. P. (1993). The ethical behavior of retail managers. *Journal of Business Ethics, 12*(3), 207–218. doi:10.1007/BF01686448

Franklin, B. (2003). *Quotations of Benjamin Franklin*. Applewood Books.

Frederick, W. C. (1960). The growing concern over business responsibility. *California Management Review, 2*(4), 54.

Frederick, W. C. (1960). The growing concern over social responsibility. *California Management Review, 2*(4), 54–61. doi:10.2307/41165405

Frederick, W. C. (1994). From CSR1 to CSR2 the maturing of business-and-society thought. *Business & Society, 33*(2), 150–164. doi:10.1177/000765039403300202

Freeman, E. R., Dmytriyev, S., & Strand, R. G. (2017). Managing for Stakeholders in the Digital Age. In Corporate Social Responsibility: Strategy, Communication, Governance (pp. 110-135). Cambridge University Press.

Freeman, E., & Moutchnik, A. (2013). Stakeholder management and CSR: questions and answers. *UmweltWirtschafts-Forum, 21*(1-2), 5-9.

Freeman, R. E. (1984). *Strategic management: A stakeholder approach*. Pittman.

Freeman, R. E. (1984). *Strategic Management: A Stakeholder Approach*. Pittman.

Freeman, R. E. (1994). The politics of stakeholder theory: Some future directions. *Business Ethics Quarterly, 4*(4), 409–421. doi:10.2307/3857340

Freeman, R. E., & Liedtka, J. (1991). Corporate social responsibility: A critical approach. *Business Horizons, 34*(July–August), 92–98. doi:10.1016/0007-6813(91)90012-K

Freeman, R. E., & Reed, D. L. (1983). Stockholders and stakeholders: A new perspective on corporate governance. *California Management Review, 25*(3), 88–106. doi:10.2307/41165018

Fresner, J., & Engelhardt, G. (2004). Experiences with Integrated Management Systems for Two Small Companies in Austria. *Journal of Cleaner Production, 12*(6), 623–631. doi:10.1016/j.jclepro.2003.09.013

Friedman, M. (1970). A Friedman doctrine: The social responsibility of business is to increase its profits. *The New York Times Magazine, 13*(1970), 32-33.

Friedman, M. (1970). The social responsibility of business is to increase its profits. *The New York Times Magazine*.

Friedman, M. (1970, September 13). The social responsibility of business is to increase its profits. *The New York Times Magazine*, 122-126.

Friedman, A. L., & Miles, S. (2002). Developing stakeholder theory. *Journal of Management Studies, 39*(1), 1–21. doi:10.1111/1467-6486.00280

Friedman, M. (1963). *Capitalism and freedom*. University of Chicago Press.

Frynas, J. G., & Yamahaki, C. (2016). Corporate social responsibility: Review and roadmap of theoretical perspectives. *Business Ethics (Oxford, England), 25*(3), 258–285. doi:10.1111/beer.12115

Fuller, T., & Tian, Y. (2006). Social and symbolic capital and responsible entrepreneurship: An empirical investigation of SME narratives. *Journal of Business Ethics*, *67*(3), 287–304. doi:10.100710551-006-9185-3

Galarraga, I. (2002). The use of eco-labels: A review of the literature. *European Environment*, *12*(6), 316–331. doi:10.1002/eet.304

Galbreath, J. (2008). The benefits of corporate social responsibility: An empirical study. *ANZAM Conference Proceedings (22nd Annual Conference. Auckland).*

Galbreath, J. (2012). Are boards on board? A model of corporate board influence on sustainability performance. *Journal of Management & Organization*, *18*(4), 445–460. doi:10.5172/jmo.2012.18.4.445

Galbreath, J. (2019). Drivers of green innovations: The impact of export intensity, women leaders, and absorptive capacity. *Journal of Business Ethics*, *158*(1), 47–61. doi:10.100710551-017-3715-z

Gallardo-Vázquez, D., Sánchez-Hernández, M. I., & Corchuelo-Martinez-Azua, M. B. (2013). Validación de un instrumento de medida para la relación entre la orientación a la responsabilidad social corporativa y otras variables estratégicas de la empresa. *Revista de Contabilidad*, *16*(1), 11–23. doi:10.1016/S1138-4891(13)70002-5

Gallego-Álvarez, I., Prado-Lorenzo, J. M., & García-Sánchez, I. M. (2011). Corporate social responsibility and innovation: A resource-based theory. *Management Decision*, *49*(10), 1709–1727. doi:10.1108/00251741111183843

Gallo, M. A. (2004). The family business and its social responsibilities. *Family Business Review*, *17*(2), 135–148. doi:10.1111/j.1741-6248.2004.00009.x

Gangi, F., Mustilli, M., & Varrone, N. (2019). The impact of corporate social responsibility (CSR) knowledge on corporate financial performance: Evidence from the European banking industry. *Journal of Knowledge Management*, *23*(1), 110–134. doi:10.1108/JKM-04-2018-0267

Garay-Tamajón, L., & Font, X. (2013). Corporate social responsibility in tourism small and medium enterprises evidence from Europe and Latin America. *Tourism Management Perspectives*, *7*, 38–46. doi:10.1016/j.tmp.2013.03.002

García, Q. (2016). *Historia de la RSC*. Retrieved from: https://mansunides.org/es/rsc/responsabilidad-social-corporativa/historia-rsc

García, F. N. (2012). *Responsabilidad social corporativa: teoría y práctica*. ESIC editorial.

Gargiulo, M., & Benassi, M. (1999). The dark side of social capital. In *Corporate social capital and liability* (pp. 298–322). Springer. doi:10.1007/978-1-4615-5027-3_17

Garriga, E., & Melé, D. (2004). Corporate social responsibility theories: Mapping the territory. *Journal of Business Ethics*, *53*(1-2), 51–71.

Garrigues, A. & Trullenque, F. (2008) Responsabilidad social corporativa: ¿papel mojado o necesidad estratégica? *Harvard Deusto Business Review*, 19-36.

Gasbarro, F., Annunziata, E., Rizzi, F., & Frey, M. (2017). The Interplay between Sustainable Entrepreneurs and Public Authorities: Evidence from Sustainable Energy Transitions. *Organization & Environment*, *30*(3), 226–252. doi:10.1177/1086026616669211

Gavetti, G. (2005). Cognition and hierarchy: Rethinking the microfoundations of capabilities' development. *Organization Science*, *16*(6), 599–617. doi:10.1287/orsc.1050.0140

Gavronski, I., Ferrer, G., & Paiva, E. L. (2008). ISO 14001 Certification in Brazil: Motivations and Benefits. *Journal of Cleaner Production*, *16*(1), 87–94. doi:10.1016/j.jclepro.2006.11.002

Gavronski, I., Klassen, R. D., Vachon, S., & Nascimento, L. F. M. (2011). A resource-based view of green supply management. *Transportation Research Part E, Logistics and Transportation Review*, *47*(6), 872–885. doi:10.1016/j.tre.2011.05.018

Gawer, A., & Cusumano, M. A. (2014). Industry Platforms and Ecosystem Innovation. *Journal of Product Development & Management Association*, *31*(3), 417–433.

George, G., Howard-Grenville, J., Joshi, A., & Tihanyi, L. (2016). Understanding and Tackling Societal Grand Challenges through Management Research. *Academy of Management Journal*, *59*(6), 1880–1895. doi:10.5465/amj.2016.4007

Gladwin, T. N., Kennelly, J. J., & Krause, T. (1995). Shifting paradigms for sustainable development: Implications for management theory and research. *Academy of Management Review*, *20*(4), 874–907. doi:10.5465/amr.1995.9512280024

Glavas, A. (2016). Corporate social responsibility and organizational psychology: An integrative review. *Frontiers in Psychology*, *7*, 1–13. doi:10.3389/fpsyg.2016.00144 PMID:26909055

Glavas, A., & Godwin, L. N. (2013). Is the perception of 'goodness' good enough? Exploring the relationship between perceived corporate social responsibility and employee organizational identification. *Journal of Business Ethics*, *114*(1), 15–27. doi:10.100710551-012-1323-5

Glavas, A., & Kelley, K. (2014). The effects of perceived corporate social responsibility on employee attitudes. *Business Ethics Quarterly*, *24*(2), 165–202. doi:10.5840/beq20143206

Glavas, A., & Mish, J. (2015). Resources and Capabilities of Triple Bottom Line Firms: Going over Old or Breaking New Ground? *Journal of Business Ethics*, *127*(3), 623–642. doi:10.100710551-014-2067-1

Gluch, P., Gustafsson, M., & Thuvander, L. (2009). An absorptive capacity model for green innovation and performance in the construction industry. *Construction Management and Economics*, *27*(5), 451–464. doi:10.1080/01446190902896645

Godelnik, R., & van der Meer, J. (2019). Sustainable Business Models in an Entrepreneurial Environment. In A. Aagaard (Ed.), *Sustainable Business Models* (pp. 239–276). Germany, Palgrave Macmillan. doi:10.1007/978-3-319-93275-0_9

Gómez-Bezares, F., Przychodzen, W., & Przychodzen, J. (2017). Bridging the gap: How sustainable development can help companies create shareholder value and improve financial performance. *Business Ethics (Oxford, England)*, *26*(1), 1–17. doi:10.1111/beer.12135

Gond, J., & Crane, A. (2010). Corporate social performance disoriented: Saving the lost paradigm? *Business & Society*, *49*(4), 677–703. doi:10.1177/0007650308315510

González Masip, J. (2018). Los grupos de interés y su importancia en la propuesta de valor de las empresas. *Boletín Económico de ICE*, (3096), 47-57.

González-Benito, J., & González-Benito, Ó. (2006). A review of determinant factors of environmental proactivity. *Business Strategy and the Environment*, *15*(2), 87–102. doi:10.1002/bse.450

González-Masip, J., Martín-de Castro, G., & Hernández, A. (2019). Inter-organizational knowledge spillovers: Attracting talent in science and technology parks and corporate social responsibility practices. *Journal of Knowledge Management*, *23*(5), 975–999. doi:10.1108/JKM-06-2018-0367

Goodpaster, K. E. (1991). Business ethics and stakeholder analysis. *Business Ethics Quarterly*, *1*(01), 53–73. doi:10.2307/3857592

Goodrick, E., & Salancik, G. R. (1996). Organizational Discretion in Responding to Institutional Practices: Hospitals and Cesarean Births. *Administrative Science Quarterly*, *41*(1), 1. doi:10.2307/2393984

Graafland, J., Van de Ven, B., & Stoffele, N. (2003). Strategies and instruments for organising CSR by small and large businesses in the Netherlands. *Journal of Business Ethics*, *47*(1), 45–60. doi:10.1023/A:1026240912016

Granovetter, M. (1995). Coase revisited: Business groups in the modern economy. *Industrial and Corporate Change*, *4*(1), 93–130.

Granovetter, M. S. (1985). Economic action and social structure: The problem of embeddedness. *American Journal of Sociology*, *91*(3), 481–510. doi:10.1086/228311

Grant, R. M. (1996). Toward a knowledge-based theory of the firm. *Strategic Management Journal*, *17*(S2), 109–122. doi:10.1002mj.4250171110

Grant, R. M., & Baden-Fuller, C. (1995). A knowledge-based theory of inter-firm collaboration. *Academy of Management Journal*, (1), 17–21.

Gratton, L., & Ghoshal, S. (2003). Managing Personal Human Capital: New Ethos for the 'Volunteer' employee. *European Management Journal*, *21*(1), 1–10. doi:10.1016/S0263-2373(02)00149-4

Gray, R. (2001). Thirty years of social accounting, reporting and auditing: What (if anything) have we learnt? *Business Ethics (Oxford, England)*, *10*(1), 9–15. doi:10.1111/1467-8608.00207

Grayson, D. (2006). Inspiring smaller firms with the responsible business mindset. In M. Epstein & K. Hansen (Eds.), *The accountable corporation: Corporate social responsibility* (pp. 279–298). Praeger.

Greening, D. W., & Turban, D. B. (2000). Corporate social performance as a competitive advantage in attracting a quality workforce. *Business & Society*, *39*(3), 254–280. doi:10.1177/000765030003900302

Gregerman, S. R., Lerner, J. S., Von Hippel, W., Jonides, J., & Nagda, B. A. (1998). Undergraduate student-faculty research partnerships affect student retention. *The Review of Higher Education*, *22*(1), 55–72. doi:10.1353/rhe.1998.0016

Grewatsch, S., & Kleindienst, I. (2017). When Does It Pay to be Good? Moderators and Mediators in the Corporate Sustainability–Corporate Financial Performance Relationship: A Critical Review. *Journal of Business Ethics*, *145*(2), 383–416. doi:10.100710551-015-2852-5

Griffin, J. J., & Mahon, J. F. (1997). The corporate social performance and corporate financial performance debate: Twenty-five years of incomparable research. *Business & Society*, *36*(1), 5–31. doi:10.1177/000765039703600102

Grodal, S., & O'Mahony, S. (2017). How does a Grand Challenge Become Displaced? Explaining the Duality of Field Mobilization. *Academy of Management Journal*, *60*(5), 1801–1827. doi:10.5465/amj.2015.0890

Guang, L. (2012). Natural resource based green supply chain management. *Supply Chain Management*, *17*(1), 54–67. doi:10.1108/13598541211212203

Guarnieri, P., & Gomes, R. C. (2019). Can public procurement be strategic? A future agenda proposition. *Journal of Public Procurement.*

Guerci, M., Longoni, A., & Luzzini, D. (2016). Translating stakeholder pressures into environmental performance e the mediating role of green HRM practices. *International Journal of Human Resource Management*, *27*(2), 262–289. doi:10.1080/09585192.2015.1065431

Guerola-Navarro, V., Oltra-Badenes, R., Gil-Gómez, H., & Stratu-Strelet, D. (2019). Eid@ Cloud: Integración De La Identificación Electrónica En Plataformas Europeas En La Nube De Acuerdo Con El Reglamento Eidas. *3C Empresa*, *8*(3).

Gulati, R. (1995). Social structure and alliance formation patterns: A longitudinal analysis. *Administrative Science Quarterly*, *40*(4), 619–652. doi:10.2307/2393756

Gulati, R. (1999). Network location and learning: The influence of network resources and firm capabilities on alliance formation. *Strategic Management Journal, 20*(5), 397–420. doi:10.1002/(SICI)1097-0266(199905)20:5<397::AID-SMJ35>3.0.CO;2-K

Guo, J., Sun, L., & Li, X. (2009). Corporate social responsibility assessment of Chinese corporation. *International Journal of Business and Management, 4*(4), 54–57. doi:10.5539/ijbm.v4n4p54

Gupta, M. C. (1994). Environmental management and its impact on the operations function. *International Journal of Operations & Production Management, 15*(8), 34–51. doi:10.1108/01443579510094071

Gupta, S., & Malhotra, N. (2013). Marketing Innovation: A Resource-Based View of International and Local Firms. *Marketing Intelligence & Planning, 31*(2), 111–126. doi:10.1108/02634501311312026

Guthrie, J., Petty, R., Yongvanich, K., & Ricceri, F. (2004). Using content analysis as a research method to inquire into intellectual capital reporting. *Journal of Intellectual Capital, 5*(2), 282–293. doi:10.1108/14691930410533704

Gutiérrez, L., Montiel, I., & Castillo, A. (2020). JBE virtual special issue: Responsible Innovation in Times of Crisis. *Journal of Business Ethics.*

Hafenbrädl, S., & Waeger, D. (2017). Ideology and the Micro-foundations of CSR: Why Executives Believe in the Business Case for CSR and how this Affects their CSR Engagements. *Academy of Management Journal, 60*(4), 1582–1606. doi:10.5465/amj.2014.0691

Hagen, R. (2002). Globalization, university transformation and economic regeneration: A UK case study of public/private sector partnership. *International Journal of Public Sector Management, 15*(3), 204–218. doi:10.1108/09513550210423370

Hahn, R., & Lülfs, R. (2014). Legitimizing negative aspects in GRI-oriented sustainability reporting: A qualitative analysis of corporate disclosure strategies. *Journal of Business Ethics, 123*(3), 401–420. doi:10.100710551-013-1801-4

Hahn, T., Figge, F., Aragón-Correa, J. A., & Sharma, S. (2017). Advancing Research on Corporate Sustainability: Off to Pastures New or Back to the Roots? *Business & Society, 56*(2), 155–185. doi:10.1177/0007650315576152

Half, R. (2019). *4 little known benefits of CSR for any company.* Retrieved from: https://www.roberthalf.com.hk/blog/employers/4-little-known-benefits-csr-any-company

Halila, F. (2007). Networks as a means of supporting the adoption of organizational innovations in SMEs: The case of Environmental Management Systems (EMSs) based on ISO 14001. *Corporate Social Responsibility and Environmental Management, 14*(3), 167–181. doi:10.1002/csr.127

Hall, J., & Wagner, M. (2012). Integrating Sustainability into Firms' Processes: Performance Effects and the Moderating Role of Business Models and Innovation. *Business Strategy and the Environment, 21*(3), 183–196. doi:10.1002/bse.728

Hall, R. (1992). The Strategic analysis of intangible resources. *Strategic Management Journal, 13*(2), 135–144. doi:10.1002mj.4250130205

Halme, M., Rintamäki, J., Knudsen, J. S., Lankoski, L., & Kuisma, M. (2018). When is there a sustainability case for CSR? Pathways to environmental and social performance improvements. *Business & Society.* Advance online publication. doi:10.1177/0007650318755648

Hambrick, D. C., Werder, A. V., & Zajac, E. J. (2008). New directions in corporate governance research. *Organization Science, 19*(3), 381–385. doi:10.1287/orsc.1080.0361

Hamel, G., & Heene, A. (1994). *Competence-Based Competition. The Strategic management series.* Wiley.

Hamilton, F., & Stiegert, K. (2000). Vertical coordination, antitrust law, and international trade. *The Journal of Law & Economics*, *43*(1), 143–156. doi:10.1086/467450

Hammann, E. M., Habisch, A., & Pechlaner, H. (2009). Values that create value: Socially responsible business practices in SMEs–empirical evidence from German companies. *Business Ethics (Oxford, England)*, *18*(1), 37–51. doi:10.1111/j.1467-8608.2009.01547.x

Hansen, S. D., Dunford, B. B., Boss, A. D., Boss, R. W., & Angermeier, I. (2011). Corporate social responsibility and the benefits of employee trust: A cross-disciplinary perspective. *Journal of Business Ethics*, *102*(1), 29–45. doi:10.100710551-011-0903-0

Harris, L. C., & Crane, A. (2002). The greening of organizational culture: Management views on the depth, degree and diffusion of change. *Journal of Organizational Change Management*, *15*(3), 214–234. doi:10.1108/09534810210429273

Harrison, J. S., & Freeman, R. E. (1999). Stakeholders, social responsibility and performance: Empirical evidence and theoretical perspectives. *Academy of Management Journal*, *42*, 479–487.

Hartman, D. (2019). *Desventajas de una empresa socialmente responsable*. Retrieved from: https://www.cuidatudinero.com/13102036/desventajas-de-una-empresa-socialmente-responsable

Hartmann, M. (2011). Corporate social responsibility in the food sector. *European Review of Agriculture Economics*, *38*(3), 297–324. doi:10.1093/erae/jbr031

Hart, S. (1995). A natural-resource-based view of the firm. *Academy of Management Review*, *20*(4), 986–1014. doi:10.5465/amr.1995.9512280033

Hart, S. L., & Dowell, G. (2011). Invited Editorial: A Natural-Resource-Based View of the Firm: Fifteen Years After. *Journal of Management*, *37*(5), 1464–1479. doi:10.1177/0149206310390219

Hart, S. L., & Milstein, M. B. (2003). Creating Sustainable Value. *The Academy of Management Executive*, *17*(2), 56–67. doi:10.5465/ame.2003.10025194

Hart, S. L., & Sharma, S. (2004). Engaging fringe stakeholders for competitive imagination. *The Academy of Management Perspectives*, *18*(1), 7–18. doi:10.5465/ame.2004.12691227

Hashim, R., Bock, A. J., & Cooper, S. (2015). The relationship between Absorptive Capacity and Green Innovation. *World Academy of Science, Engineering and Technology*, *9*(4), 1049–1056.

Haskel, J., & Westlake, S. (2017). *Capitalism without capital*. Princeton University Press. doi:10.2307/j.ctvc77hhj

Haugh, H. (2005). A research agenda for social entrepreneurship. *Social Enterprise Journal*, *1*(1), 1–12. doi:10.1108/17508610580000703

Haugh, H. M., & Talwar, A. (2016). Linking social entrepreneurship and social change: The mediating role of empowerment. *Journal of Business Ethics*, *133*(4), 643–658. doi:10.100710551-014-2449-4

Heald, M. (1957). Management's responsibility to society: The growth of an idea. *Business History Review*, *31*(4), 375–384. doi:10.2307/3111413

Heald, M. (1970). *The social responsibilities of business: company and community 1900–1960*. Pr. of Case Western Reserve Univ.

Heide, J. B., & Miner, A. S. (1992). The shadow of the future: Effects of anticipated interaction and frequency of contact on buyer-seller cooperation. *Academy of Management Journal*, *35*(2), 265–291. doi:10.5465/256374

Hejduk, I. K. (2005). On the way to the future: The knowledge-based enterprise. *Human Factors and Ergonomics in Manufacturing & Service Industries*, *15*(1), 5–14. doi:10.1002/hfm.20010

Helfat, C. E., & Peteraf, M. A. (2003). The dynamic resource-based view: Capability lifecycles. *Strategic Management Journal*, *24*(10), 997–1010. doi:10.1002mj.332

Helper, S. (1991a). *An exit-voice analysis of supplier relations. In Morality, rationality, and efficiency: new perspectives on socio-economics*. Sharp.

Helper, S. (1991b). How much has really changed between US automakers and their suppliers? *MIT Sloan Management Review*, *32*(4), 15.

Hervás-Oliver, J.-L., & Albors-Garrigos, J. (2009). The role of the firm's internal and relational capabilities in clusters: When distance and embeddedness are not enough to explain innovation. *Journal of Economic Geography*, *9*(2), 263–283. doi:10.1093/jeg/lbn033

Hiatt, S. R., Sine, W. D., & Tolbert, P. S. (2009). From Pabst to Pepsi: The Deinstitutionalization of Social Practices and the Creation of Entrepreneurial Opportunities. *Administrative Science Quarterly*, *54*(4), 635–667. doi:10.2189/asqu.2009.54.4.635

Hill, C. W., & Jones, T. M. (1992). Stakeholder-agency theory. *Journal of Management Studies*, *29*(2), 131–154. doi:10.1111/j.1467-6486.1992.tb00657.x

Hipkin, I., & Naudé, P. (2006). Developing effective alliance partnerships: Lessons from a case study. *Long Range Planning*, *39*(1), 51–69. doi:10.1016/j.lrp.2005.09.003

Hirschman, A. O. (1970). *Exit, Voice, and Loyalty. Responses to Decline in Firms, Organizations, and States*. Cambridge University Press.

Hitt, M. A., Ireland, R. D., & Hoskisson, R. E. (2007). *Strategic Management: Competitiveness and Globalization* (7th ed.). Thomson South-Western.

Hlady-Rispal, M., & Servantie, V. (2018). Deconstructing the way in which value is created in the context of social entrepreneurship. *International Journal of Management Reviews*, *20*(1), 62–80. doi:10.1111/ijmr.12113

Hodge, G. A., & Greve, C. (2007). Public–private partnerships: An international performance review. *Public Administration Review*, *67*(3), 545–558. doi:10.1111/j.1540-6210.2007.00736.x

Hoetker, G. (2005). How much you know versus how well I know you: Selecting a supplier for a technically innovative component. *Strategic Management Journal*, *26*(1), 75–96. doi:10.1002mj.453

Hoffman, A. J. (1999). Institutional Evolution and Change : Environmentalism and the U. S. *Chemistry & Industry*, *42*, 351–371.

Hoffmann, W. H., & Schlosser, R. (2001). Success factors of strategic alliances in small and medium-sized enterprises—An empirical survey. *Long Range Planning*, *34*(3), 357–381. doi:10.1016/S0024-6301(01)00041-3

Hollensbe, E., Wookey, C., Hickey, L., George, G., & Nichols, C. V. (2014). Organizations with Purpose. *Academy of Management Journal*, *57*(5), 1227–1234. doi:10.5465/amj.2014.4005

Hopkins, M. (2003). *The planetary bargain: CSR matters*. Earthscan.

Hoppmann, J. (2018). The Role of Interfirm Knowledge Spillovers for Innovation in Mass-Produced Environmental Technologies: Evidence from the Solar Photovoltaic Industry. *Organization & Environment*, *31*(1), 3–24. doi:10.1177/1086026616680683

Hormiga, E., Batista-Canino, R. M., & Sánchez-Medina, A. (2011). O papel do capital intelectual no sucesso de novos empreendimentos. *Revista Internacional de Empreendedorismo e Gestão*, *7*(1), 71–92.

Horzela, A. (2019). The Cluster as a Socially Responsible Entity. *Zeszyty Naukowe. Organizacja i Zarządzanie/Politechnika Śląska*, (140), 99-108. DOI: 10.29119/1641-3466.2019.140.9

Hoskisson, R. E., Hitt, M. A., Wan, W. P., & Yiu, D. (1999). Theory and research in strategic management: Swings of a pendulum. *Journal of Management*, *25*(3), 417–456. doi:10.1177/014920639902500307

Hoskisson, R., Hitt, M., Johnson, R., & Grossman, W. (2002). Conflicting voices: The effects of institutional ownership heterogeneity and internal governance on corporate innovation strategies. *Academy of Management Journal*, *45*(4), 697–716.

Howard-Grenville, J., Buckle, S. J., Hoskins, B. J., & George, G. (2014). Climate Change and Management. *Academy of Management Journal*, *57*(3), 615–623. doi:10.5465/amj.2014.4003

Hsu, J. L., & Cheng, M. C. (2012). What prompts small and medium enterprises to engage in corporate social responsibility? A study from Taiwan. *Corporate Social Responsibility and Environmental Management*, *19*(5), 288–305. doi:10.1002/csr.276

Huang, C.L., & Kung, F.H. (2011). Environmental consciousness and intellectual capital management: evidence from Taiwan's manufacturing industry. *Manag. Decis.*, *49*(9), 1405-1425.

Huang, P. S., & Shih, L. H. (2009). Effective environmental management through environmental knowledge management. *International Journal of Environmental Science and Technology*, *6*(1), 35–50. doi:10.1007/BF03326058

Huang, S. K. (2013). The Impact of CEO Characteristics on Corporate Sustainable Development: CSR Drivers, CSR CEO Characteristics, Hypotheses, Method [Discussion]. *Corporate Social Responsibility and Environmental Management*, *20*(4), 234–244. doi:10.1002/csr.1295

Huang, X., & Gardner, S. (2007). A stakeholder view of strategic management in Chinese firms. International Journal of Business Studies: A Publication of the Faculty of Business Administration. *Edith Cowan University*, *15*(1), 1–13.

Huang, X., & Watson, L. (2015). Corporate social responsibility research in accounting. *Journal of Accounting Literature*, *34*, 1–16. doi:10.1016/j.acclit.2015.03.001

Hussain, S. S. (1999). The ethics of 'going green': The corporate social responsibility debate. *Business Strategy and the Environment*, *8*(4), 203–210. doi:10.1002/(SICI)1099-0836(199907/08)8:4<203::AID-BSE204>3.0.CO;2-I

Husted, B. W. (2015). Corporate social responsibility practice from 1800–1914: Past initiatives and current debates. *Business Ethics Quarterly*, *25*(1), 125–141. doi:10.1017/beq.2014.1

Husted, B. W., Jamali, D., & Saffard, W. (2016). Near and dear? The role of location in CSR engagement. *Strategic Management Journal*, *37*(10), 2050–2070. doi:10.1002mj.2437

Husted, B. W., Montiel, I., & Christmann, P. (2016). Effects of local legitimacy on certification decisions to global and national CSR standards by multinational subsidiaries and domestic firms. *Journal of International Business Studies*, *47*(3), 382–397. doi:10.1057/jibs.2016.3

Huxham, C., & Vangen, S. (2013). *Managing to collaborate: The theory and practice of collaborative advantage*. Routledge. doi:10.4324/9780203010167

Ibrahim, N. A., & Angelidis, J. P. (1994). Effect of board members' gender on corporate social responsiveness orientation. *Journal of Applied Business Research*, *10*(1), 35. doi:10.19030/jabr.v10i1.5961

Ibrahim, N., & Angelidis, J. P. (1991). Effects of board members' gender on level of involvement in strategic management and corporate social responsiveness orientation. *Proceedings of the Northeast Decision Sciences Institute, 208*, 210.

Ince, I., & Hahn, R. (2018). How Dynamic Capabilities Facilitate the Survivability of Social Enterprises: A Qualitative Analysis of Sensing and Seizing Capacities. *Journal of Small Business Management*, 1–29.

Inkpen, A. C., & Tsang, E. W. K. (2005). Social capital, networks, and knowledge transfer. *Academy of Management Review, 30*(1), 146–165. doi:10.5465/amr.2005.15281445

Intermon, O. (2017). *Los diferentes tipos de responsabilidad social: del ámbito individual a las acciones gubernamentales*. Retrieved from: https://blog.oxfamintermon.org/los-diferentes-tipos-de-responsabilidad-social-del-ambito-individual-a-la-acciones-gubernamentales/?gclid=Cj0KCQiA0ZHwBRCRARIsAK0Tr-p6cDAHhJR-qypw3uOwNf_OaOFGXsoX-i0DMOXCQos4XFDx9LWuBDWkaAs-9EALw_wcB

Iqbal, N., Ahmad, N., Sheeraz, M., & Bashir, N. A. (2012). The impact of perceived corporate social responsibility (CSR) on job attitude and performance of internal stakeholders. *International Journal of Human Resource Studies, 2*(4), 77. Doi:10.5296/ijhrs.v2i4.2272

ISO/IEC 25010:2011 Systems and software engineering — Systems and software Quality Requirements and Evaluation (SQuaRE) — System and software quality models. https://www.iso.org/standard/35733.html

ISO/IEC 9126-1:2001 Software engineering — Product quality — Part 1: Quality model. This THIS STANDARD HAS BEEN REVISED BY ISO/IEC 25010:2011 https://www.iso.org/standard/22749.html

Ivanova, V., Poltarykhin, A., Szromnik, A., & Anichkina, O. (2019). Economic policy for country's digitalization: A case study. *Entrepreneurship and Sustainability Issues, 7*(1), 649–661. doi:10.9770/jesi.2019.7.1(46)

Jabbour, A. B. L. (2018). When titans meet – Can industry 4.0 revolutionise the environmentally-sustainable manufacturing wave? The role of critical sucess factors. *Technological Forecasting and Social Change, 132*, 18–25. doi:10.1016/j.techfore.2018.01.017

Jamali, D., Safieddine, A. M., & Rabbath, M. (2008). Corporate governance and corporate social responsibility synergies and interrelationships. *Corporate Governance, 16*(5), 443–459. doi:10.1111/j.1467-8683.2008.00702.x

Jamali, D., & Sidani, Y. (2008). Learning organizations: Diagnosis and measurement in a developing country context: The case of Lebanon. *The Learning Organization, 15*(1), 58–74. doi:10.1108/09696470810842466

Jamali, D., Zanhour, M., & Keshishian, T. (2009). Peculiar strengths and relational attributes of SMEs in the context of CSR. *Journal of Business Ethics, 87*(3), 355–377. doi:10.100710551-008-9925-7

Jamison, L., & Murdoch, H. (2004). *Taking the Temperature: Ethical Issues in the Supply Chain*. Institute of Business Ethics.

Jansen, J. J., Van Den Bosch, F. A., & Volberda, H. W. (2005). Managing potential and realized absorptive capacity: How do organizational antecedents matter? *Academy of Management Journal, 48*(6), 999–1015. doi:10.5465/amj.2005.19573106

Jansson, J., Nilsson, J., Modig, F., & Hed Vall, G. (2017). Commitment to Sustainability in Small and Medium-Sized Enterprises: The Influence of Strategic Orientations and Management Values: Commitment to Sustainability in SMEs. *Business Strategy and the Environment, 26*(1), 69–83. doi:10.1002/bse.1901

Jap, S. D. (2001). "Pie sharing" in complex collaboration contexts. *JMR, Journal of Marketing Research, 38*(1), 86–99. doi:10.1509/jmkr.38.1.86.18827

Jaw, B. S., & Liu, W. (2003). Promoting Organizational Learning and Self-Renewal in Taiwanese Companies: The Role of HRM. *Human Resource Management*, *42*(3), 223–241. doi:10.1002/hrm.10082

Jeffries, F. L., & Reed, R. (2000). Trust and adaptation in relational contracting. *Academy of Management Review*, *25*(4), 873–882. doi:10.5465/amr.2000.3707747

Jenkins, H. (2006). Small business champions for corporate social responsibility. *Journal of Business Ethics*, *67*(3), 241–256. doi:10.100710551-006-9182-6

Jenkins, H. (2009). A 'business opportunity' model of corporate social responsibility for small- and medium-sized enterprises. *Business Ethics (Oxford, England)*, *18*(1), 21–36. doi:10.1111/j.1467-8608.2009.01546.x

Jenkins, R. (2005). Globalization, corporate social responsibility and poverty. *International Affairs*, *81*(3), 525–540. doi:10.1111/j.1468-2346.2005.00467.x

Jenner, P., & Oprescu, F. (2016). The Sectorial Trust of Social Enterprise. Friend or Foe? *Journal of Social Entrepreneurship*, *7*(2), 236–261. doi:10.1080/19420676.2016.1158732

Jensen, M. C. (1994). Self-interest, altruism, incentives, and agency theory. *Journal of Applied Corporate Finance*, *7*(2), 40–45. doi:10.1111/j.1745-6622.1994.tb00404.x

Jensen, M. C., & Meckling, W. (1976). Theory of the firm: Managerial behaviour, agency costs, and ownership structure. *Journal of Financial Economics*, *3*(4), 305–360. doi:10.1016/0304-405X(76)90026-X

Jensen, N. M., Li, Q., & Rahman, A. (2010). Understanding corruption and firm responses in cross-national firm-level surveys. *Journal of International Business Studies*, *41*(9), 1481–1504. doi:10.1057/jibs.2010.8

Jeon, M. M., Lee, S., & Jeong, M. (2020). Perceived corporate social responsibility and customers' behaviors in the ridesharing service industry. *International Journal of Hospitality Management*, *84*, 1–10. doi:10.1016/j.ijhm.2019.102341

Jérez-Gómez, P., Cespedes-Lorente, J., & Valle-Cabrera, R. (2005). Organizational Learning and Compensation Strategies: Evidence from the Spanish Chemical Industry. *Human Resource Management*, *44*(3), 279–299. doi:10.1002/hrm.20071

Jia, M., & Zhang, Z. (2013). Critical mass of women on BODs, multiple identities, and corporate philanthropic disaster response: Evidence from privately owned Chinese firms. *Journal of Business Ethics*, *118*(2), 303–317. doi:10.100710551-012-1589-7

Jiang, B. (2009). Implementing supplier codes of conduct in global supply chains: Process explanations from theoretic and empirical perspectives. *Journal of Business Ethics*, *85*(1), 77–92. doi:10.100710551-008-9750-z

Jie, C. T., & Hasan, N. A. M. (2018). Predictors of employees' job satisfaction through corporate social responsibility (CSR) practices in Malaysian banking company. *Advanced Science Letters*, *24*(5), 3072–3078. doi:10.1166/asl.2018.11320

Jo, H., & Harjoto, M. A. (2011). Corporate governance and firm value: The impact of corporate social responsibility. *Journal of Business Ethics*, *103*(3), 351–383. doi:10.100710551-011-0869-y

Jo, H., & Harjoto, M. A. (2012). The causal effect of corporate governance on corporate social responsibility. *Journal of Business Ethics*, *106*(1), 53–72. doi:10.100710551-011-1052-1

Johannisson, B. (2016). Economies of Overview— Guiding the External Growth of Small Firms. *International Small Business Journal: Researching Entrepreneurship*, *9*(1), 32–44. doi:10.1177/026624269000900104

Johansen, T. S., & Nielsen, A. E. (2012). CSR in corporate self-storying—Legitimacy as a question of differentiation and conformity. *Corporate Communication: An International Journal*, *17*(4), 434–448. doi:10.1108/13563281211274130

John, A., Qadeer, F., Shahzadi, G., & Jia, F. (2019). Getting paid to be good: How and when employees respond to corporate social responsibility? *Journal of Cleaner Production*, *215*, 784–795. doi:10.1016/j.jclepro.2019.01.074

John, G. (1984). An empirical investigation of some antecedents of opportunism in a marketing channel. *JMR, Journal of Marketing Research*, *21*(3), 278–289. doi:10.1177/002224378402100305

Johnson, D., & Morgeson, F. (2005). Cognitive and Affective Identification in Organizational Settings. *Proceedings of the 65th Academy of Management Conference*. 10.5465/ambpp.2005.18780944

Johnson, H. (1971). *Business in contemporary society: framework and issues*. Wadsworth Pub.

Johnson, H. L. (1971). *Business in contemporary society: Framework and issues*. Wadsworth Pub. Co.

Johnson, M. P. (2015). Sustainability management and small and medium-sized enterprises: Managers' awareness and implementation of innovative tools. *Corporate Social Responsibility and Environmental Management*, *22*(5), 271–285. doi:10.1002/csr.1343

Jones, T. M. (1980). Corporate social responsibility revisited, redefined. *California Management Review*, *22*(3), 59.

Jones, C., Hesterly, W. S., & Borgatti, S. P. (1997). A General Theory of Network Governance: Exchange conditions and social mechanisms. *Academy of Management Review*, *22*(4), 911–945. doi:10.5465/amr.1997.9711022109

Jones, D. A., Willness, C. R., & Glavas, A. (2017). When Corporate Social Responsibility (CSR) Meets Organizational Psychology: New Frontiers in Micro-CSR Research, and Fulfilling a Quid Pro Quo through Multilevel Insights. *Frontiers in Psychology*, *8*, 8. doi:10.3389/fpsyg.2017.00520 PMID:28439247

Jones, J., York, J. G., Vedula, S., Conger, M., & Lenox, M. (2019). The Collective Construction of Green Building: Industry Transition Toward Environmentally Beneficial Practices. *The Academy of Management Perspectives*, *33*(4), 425–449. doi:10.5465/amp.2017.0031

Jones, T. M. (1995). Instrumental stakeholder theory: A synthesis of ethics and economics. *Academy of Management. Academy of Management Review*, *20*(2), 404–437. doi:10.5465/amr.1995.9507312924

Kamath, G. B. (2008). Intellectual capital and corporate performance in Indian pharmaceutical industry. *Journal of Intellectual Capital*, *9*(4), 684–704. doi:10.1108/14691930810913221

Kang, Y. S., Huh, E., & Lim, M. H. (2019). Effects of Foreign Directors' Nationalities and Director Types on Corporate Philanthropic Behavior: Evidence from Korean Firms. *Sustainability*, *11*(11), 1–18. doi:10.3390u11113132

Kang, Y., & Wood, D. J. (1995). Before-profit social responsibility: Turning the economic paradigm upside down. *Proceedings of the International Association for Business and Society*, *6*, 809-829. 10.5840/iabsproc1995672

Kaplan, R. S., & Norton, D. P. (1992). The Balanced Scorecard—Measures that drive performance. *Harvard Business Review*, *70*(1), 71–79. PMID:10119714

Kaplan, R. S., & Norton, D. P. (2006). *Alignment: Using the balanced scorecard to create corporate synergies*. Harvard Business Review Press.

Kaplan, S. (2020). Beyond the Business Case for Social Responsibility. *Academy of Management Discoveries*, *6*(1), 1–4. doi:10.5465/amd.2018.0220

Kapstein, E. B. (2001). The corporate ethics crusade. *Foreign Affairs*, *80*(5), 105–119. doi:10.2307/20050254

Kassen, M. (2018). E-participation actors: Understanding roles, connections, partnerships. *Knowledge Management Research and Practice*, *00*(00), 1–22. doi:10.1080/14778238.2018.1547252

Kassinis, G., & Vafeas, N. (2006). Stakeholder pressures and environmental performance. *Academy of Management Journal, 49*(1), 145–159. doi:10.5465/amj.2006.20785799

Kazemi, M., Nazemi, S., & Pooya, A. (2012). Intellectual capital: concepts, components and indicators: a literature review. *Management Science Letters, 2*.

Kechiche, A., & Soparnot, R. (2012). CSR within SMEs: Literature review. *International Business Research, 5*(7), 97. doi:10.5539/ibr.v5n7p97

Keeble, B. R. (1988). The Brundtland report: 'Our common future'. *Medicine and War, 4*(1), 17–25. doi:10.1080/07488008808408783

Keeble, J. J., Topiol, S., & Berkeley, S. (2003). Using indicators to measure sustainability performance at a corporate and project level. *Journal of Business Ethics, 44*(2-3), 149–158. doi:10.1023/A:1023343614973

Keenan, J., & Aggestam, M. (2001). Corporate governance and intellectual capital: Some conceptualizations. *Corporate Governance, 9*(4), 259–275. doi:10.1111/1467-8683.00254

Kendall, N. (1999). *Good corporate governance. Accountants' Digest, 40*. The ICA in England and Wales.

Kennedy, E. B., & Marting, T. A. (2016). Biomimicry Streamlining the Front End of Innovation for Environmentally Sustainable Products. *Research Technology Management, 59*(4), 40–47. doi:10.1080/08956308.2016.1185342

Kesting, T., Muros, V. G., & Vogt, H. (2018). Reflecting on the status quo of university business collaboration in Europe: An overview of current trends and challenges. *International Journal of Technology Management, 76*(1–2), 1–9.

Kianto, A., Sáenz, J., & Aramburu, N. (2017). Knowledge-Based Human Resource Management Practices, Intelectual Capital and Innovation. *Journal of Business Research, 81*, 11–20. doi:10.1016/j.jbusres.2017.07.018

Kilcullen, M., & Kooistra, J. O. (1999). At least do no harm: Sources on the changing role of business ethics and corporate social responsibility. *RSR. Reference Services Review, 27*(2), 158–178. doi:10.1108/00907329910275150

Kim, C. H., & Scullion, H. (2013). The effect of Corporate Social Responsibility (CSR) on employee motivation: A cross-national study. *Poznan University of Economics Review, 13*(2), 5-30.

Kim, C., Lee, C., & Kang, J. (2018). Determinants of firm's innovation-related external knowledge search strategy: The role of potential absorptive capacity and appropriability regime. *International Journal of Innovation Management, 22*(6). doi:10.1142/S1363919618500445

Kim, J. (2018). *A Multi-Step Model of Boundary Spanning and Absorptive Capacity: The Differential Impact of Board and Top Management Team Experience on the Development of Sustainability-Related Capabilities*. Arizona State University.

Kim, J. K. (2011). Effects of corporate social responsibility on BtoB relational performance. *International Journal of Business and Management, 6*(2), 24. doi:10.5539/ijbm.v6n2p24

Kim, S. (2019). The process model of corporate social responsibility (CSR) communication: CSR communication and its relationship with consumers' CSR knowledge, trust, and corporate reputation perception. *Journal of Business Ethics, 154*(4), 1143–1159. doi:10.100710551-017-3433-6

Kim, T. Y., Oh, H., & Swaminathan, A. (2006). Framing interorganizational network change: A network inertia perspective. *Academy of Management Review, 31*(3), 704–720. doi:10.5465/amr.2006.21318926

Kim, Y. J., Kim, W. G., Choi, H. M., & Phetvaroon, K. (2019). The effect of green human resource management on hotel employees' eco-friendly behavior and environmental performance. *International Journal of Hospitality Management, 76*, 83–93. doi:10.1016/j.ijhm.2018.04.007

King, B. (1996). The Use of Supermajority Voting Rules in Corporate America: Majority Rule, Corporate Legitimacy, and Minority Shareholder Protection, Delaware. *The Journal of Corporation Law*, *21*(3), 895.

Kiran & Sharma. (2011). Corporate Social Responsibility: A Corporate Vision. *International Journal of Contemporary Business Studies*, *2*(3), 58–67.

Kiron, D., Kruschwitz, N., Haanaes, K., & Reeves, M. (2015). Joining forces: Collaboration and leadership for sustainability. *MIT Sloan Management Review*, *56*(3).

Kiron, D., Unruh, G., Kruschwitz, N., Reeves, M., Rubel, H., & Mayer Zum Felde, A. (2017). *Corporate Sustainability at a Crossroads: Progress Toward Our Common Future in Uncertain Times*. MIT Sloan Mgt. Rev.

Kirpik, G., & Akdemir, B. (2019). Investigation of perceived organizational identification from different generations: TRC1 (Gaziantep, Adiyaman, Kilis) zone example of organized industrial enterprises. *Journal of Education and Practice*, *10*(22), 74–85. doi:10.7176/JEP

Klassen, R. D., & McLaughlin, C. P. (1996). The impact of environmental management on firm performance. *Management Science*, *42*(8), 1199–1214. doi:10.1287/mnsc.42.8.1199

Klassen, R. D., & Whybark, D. C. (1999). The impact of environmental technologies on manufacturing performance. *Academy of Management Journal*, *42*(6), 599–615.

Klassen, R. D., & Whybark, D. C. (1999). The Impact of Environmental Technologies on Manufacturing Performance. *Academy of Management Journal*, *42*(6), 599–615.

Klein, B., & Leffler, K. (1981). The role of price in guaranteeing quality. *Journal of Political Economy*, *89*(4), 615–641. doi:10.1086/260996

Kleine, A., & von Hauff, M. (2009). Sustainability-driven implementation of corporate social responsibility: Application of the integrative sustainability triangle. *Journal of Business Ethics*, *85*(S3), 517–533. doi:10.100710551-009-0212-z

Klein, N. (2000). *No Logo. Taking Aim at the Brand Bullies*. Flamingo.

Klettner, A., Clarke, T., & Boersma, M. (2014). The governance of corporate sustainability: Empirical insights into the development, leadership and implementation of responsible business strategy. *Journal of Business Ethics*, *122*(1), 145–165. doi:10.100710551-013-1750-y

Knudsen, J. S. (2011). Company delistings from the UN Global Compact: Limited business demand or domestic governance failure? *Journal of Business Ethics*, *103*(3), 331–349. doi:10.100710551-011-0875-0

Knudsen, J. S. (2013). The integration of corporate social responsibility (CSR) initiatives into business activities: Can lessons be learnt from gender diversity programmes? *International Journal of Business Governance and Ethics*, *8*(3), 210. doi:10.1504/IJBGE.2013.057376

Kok, P., van der Wiele, T., McKenna, R., & Brown, A. (2001). A corporate social responsibility audit within a quality management framework. *Journal of Business Ethics*, *31*(4), 285–297. doi:10.1023/A:1010767001610

Kolk, A., Van Tulder, R., & Welters, C. (1999). International codes of conduct and corporate social responsibility: can transnational corporations regulate themselves? *Transnational Corporations, 8*(1), 143-180.

Kolk, A., & Lenfant, F. (2016). Hybrid Business Models for Peace and Reconciliation. *Business Horizons*, *59*(5), 503–524. doi:10.1016/j.bushor.2016.03.014

Kolk, A., & Van Tulder, R. (2001). Multinationality and corporate ethics: Codes of conduct in the sporting goods industry. *Journal of International Business Studies*, *32*(2), 267–283. doi:10.1057/palgrave.jibs.8490952

Korhonen, J. (2003). Should we measure corporate social responsibility? *Corporate Social Responsibility and Environmental Management, 10*(1), 25–39. doi:10.1002/csr.27

Koryak, O., Mole, K. F., Lockett, A., Hayton, J. C., Ucbasaran, D., & Hodgkinson, G. P. (2015). Entrepreneurial leadership, capabilities and firm growth. *International Small Business Journal, 33*(1), 89–105. doi:10.1177/0266242614558315

Kotlar, J., De Massis, A., Frattini, F., & Kammerlander, N. (2020). Motivation gaps and implementation traps: The paradoxical and time-varying effects of family ownership on firm absorptive capacity. *Journal of Product Innovation Management, 37*(1), 2–25. doi:10.1111/jpim.12503

Kotler, P., & Lee, N. (2005). *Corporate social responsibility. Doing the most good for your company and your cause.* John Wiley & Sons, Inc.

Kotler, P., & Lee, N. (2005). *Corporate social responsibility: Doing the most good for your company and your cause*. Wiley.

Kotter, J. P. (1999). *John Kotter on What Leaders Really Do.* Harvard Business School Press.

Krause, D. R., Handfield, R. B., & Tyler, B. B. (2007). The relationships between supplier development, commitment, social capital accumulation and performance improvement. *Journal of Operations Management, 25*(2), 528–545. doi:10.1016/j.jom.2006.05.007

Kraus, S., Burtscher, J., Niemand, T., Roig-Tierno, N., & Syrjä, P. (2017). Configurational Paths to Social Performance in SMEs: The Interplay of Innovation, Sustainability, Resources and Achievement Motivation. *Sustainability, 9*(10), 18–28. doi:10.3390u9101828

Kraus, S., Ribeiro-Soriano, D., & Schüssler, M. (2018). Fuzzy-set Qualitative Comparative Analysis (fsQCA) in Entrepreneurship and Innovation Research – the Rise of a Method. *The International Entrepreneurship and Management Journal, 14*(1), 15–33. doi:10.100711365-017-0461-8

Kreps, D. M., & Wilson, R. (1982). Reputation and imperfect information. *Journal of Economic Theory, 27*(2), 253–279. doi:10.1016/0022-0531(82)90030-8

Krüger, P. (2009). *Corporate social responsibility and the board of directors. Job Market Paper.* Toulouse School of Economics.

Księżak, P. (2016). The Benefits from CSR for a Company and Society. *Journal of Corporate Responsibility and Leadership Contemporary Challenges in Corporate Social Responsibility, 3*(4), 53–65.

Kukalis, S. (2010). Agglomeration economies and firm performance: The case of industry clusters. *Journal of Management, 36*(2), 453–481. doi:10.1177/0149206308329964

Kulfas, M. (2003). El contexto económico. Destrucción del aparato productivo y reestructuración regresiva. *Empresas Recuperadas. Ciudad de Buenos Aires, Secretaría de Desarrollo Económico. Gobierno de la Ciudad de Buenos Aires.*

Kwon, I. W. G., & Suh, T. (2004). Factors affecting the level of trust and commitment in supply chain relationships. *The Journal of Supply Chain Management, 40*(1), 4–14. doi:10.1111/j.1745-493X.2004.tb00165.x

Kyffin, S., & Gardien, P. (2009). Navigating the Innovation Matrix: An Approach to Designled Innovation. *International Journal of Design, 3*, 57–69.

Laasch, O. (2018). Beyond the purely commercial business model: Organizational value logics and the heterogeneity of sustainability business models. *Long Range Planning, 51*(1), 158–183. doi:10.1016/j.lrp.2017.09.002

Labuschagne, C., Brent, A. C., & Van Erck, R. P. (2005). Assessing the sustainability performances of industries. *Journal of Cleaner Production, 13*(4), 373–385. doi:10.1016/j.jclepro.2003.10.007

Lai, C. S., Yang, C. F., & Wu, H. C. (2015). The influence of product-harm crises on consumer attribution and identification: The moderating effect of corporate social responsibility. *Procedia: Social and Behavioral Sciences*, *207*, 553–559. doi:10.1016/j.sbspro.2015.10.126

Lamberti, L., & Noci, G. (2012). The relationship between CSR and corporate strategy in medium-sized companies: Evidence from Italy. *Business Ethics (Oxford, England)*, *21*(4), 402–416. doi:10.1111/beer.12002

Landry, E. E., Bernardi, R. A., & Bosco, S. M. (2016). Recognition for sustained corporate social responsibility: Female directors make a difference. *Corporate Social Responsibility and Environmental Management*, *23*(1), 27–36. doi:10.1002/csr.1358

Lankoski, L., & Smith, N. C. (2018). Alternative Objective Functions for Firms. *Organization & Environment*, *31*(3), 242–262. doi:10.1177/1086026617722883

Larssaether, S., & Nijhof, A. (2009). Moral landscapes–understanding agency in corporate responsibility initiatives. *Corporate Social Responsibility and Environmental Management*, *16*(4), 228–236. doi:10.1002/csr.205

Lawrence, S. R., Collins, E., Pavlovich, K., & Arunachalam, M. (2006). Sustainability practices of SMEs: The case of NZ. *Business Strategy and the Environment*, *15*(4), 242–257. doi:10.1002/bse.533

Leal-Rodríguez, A. L., Roldán, J. L., Ariza-Montes, J. A., & Leal-Millán, A. (2014). From potential absorptive capacity to innovation outcomes in project teams: The conditional mediating role of the realized absorptive capacity in a relational learning context. *International Journal of Project Management*, *32*(6), 894–907. doi:10.1016/j.ijproman.2014.01.005

Lee, E. M., Park, S. Y., Rapert, M. I., & Newman, C. L. (2012). Does perceived consumer fit matter in corporate social responsibility issues? *Journal of Business Research*, *65*(11), 1558–1564. doi:10.1016/j.jbusres.2011.02.040

Lee, H., & Choi, B. (2003). Knowledge Management Enablers, Processes, and Organizational Performance: An Integrative Wiew and Empirical Examination. *Journal of Management Information Systems*, *20*(1), 179–228. doi:10.1080/07421222.2003.11045756

Lee, K. H., Herold, D. M., & Yu, A. L. (2016). Small and medium enterprises and corporate social responsibility practice: A Swedish perspective. *Corporate Social Responsibility and Environmental Management*, *23*(2), 88–99. doi:10.1002/csr.1366

Lee, M., & Jay, J. (2015). Strategic responses to hybrid social ventures. *California Management Review*, *57*(3), 126–147. doi:10.1525/cmr.2015.57.3.126

Lefebvre, M., & Singh, J. B. (1992). The content and focus of Canadian corporate codes of ethics. *Journal of Business Ethics*, *11*(10), 799–808. doi:10.1007/BF00872312

Lepoutre, J., & Heene, A. (2006). Investigating the impact of firm size on small business social responsibility: A critical review. *Journal of Business Ethics*, *67*(3), 257–273. doi:10.100710551-006-9183-5

Leppelt, T., Foerstl, K., & Hartmann, E. (2013). Corporate social responsibility in buyer-supplier relationships: Is it beneficial for top-tier suppliers to market their capability to ensure a responsible supply chain? *Business Research*, *6*(2), 126–152. doi:10.1007/BF03342746

Leventhal, G. S. (1980). What should be done with equity theory? In *Social exchange* (pp. 27–55). Springer. doi:10.1007/978-1-4613-3087-5_2

Levin, D. Z., & Cross, R. (2004). The strength of weak ties you can trust: The mediating role of trust in effective knowledge transfer. *Management Science*, *50*(11), 1477–1490. doi:10.1287/mnsc.1030.0136

Levinthal, D. A., & Fichman, M. (1991). History dependence in professional relationships: Ties that bind (No. 1991-33). Carnegie Mellon University, Tepper School of Business.

Levinthal, D. A., & Fichman, M. (1988). Dynamics of interorganizational attachments: Auditor-client relationships. *Administrative Science Quarterly*, *33*(3), 345–369. doi:10.2307/2392713

Levitt, T. (1958). The dangers of social-responsibility. *Harvard Business Review*, *36*(5), 41–50.

Lewis, B. W., Walls, J. L., & Dowell, G. W. S. (2014). Difference in degrees: CEO characteristics and firm environmental disclosure: Research Notes and Commentaries. *Strategic Management Journal*, *35*(5), 712–722. doi:10.1002mj.2127

Lichtenstein, D. R., Drumwright, M. E., & Braig, B. M. (2004). The effect of corporate social responsibility on customer donations to corporate-supported nonprofits. *Journal of Marketing*, *68*(4), 16–32. doi:10.1509/jmkg.68.4.16.42726

Lichtenthaler, U. (2009). Absorptive Capacity, Environmental Turbulence, and the Complementarity of Organizational Learning Processes. *Academy of Management Journal*, *52*(4), 822–846. doi:10.5465/amj.2009.43670902

Liebeskind, J. (1996). Knowledge, strategy, and the theory of the firm. *Strategic Management Journal*, *17*(2), 93–107. doi:10.1002mj.4250171109

Liebeskind, J., Oliver, A., Zucker, L., & Brewer, M. (1996). Social networks, learning, and flexibility: Sourcing scientific knowledge in new biotechnology firms. *Organization Science*, *7*(4), 428–443. doi:10.1287/orsc.7.4.428

Lim, K., Tseng, L., Tan, H., & Bui, D. (2017). Knowledge management in sustainable supply chain management: Improving performance through an interpretive structural modeling approach. *Journal of Cleaner Production*, *162*, 806–816. doi:10.1016/j.jclepro.2017.06.056

Liñán, F., & Santos, F. J. (2007). Does social capital affect entrepreneurial intentions? *International Advances in Economic Research*, *13*(4), 443–453. doi:10.100711294-007-9109-8

Lin, C., Baruch, Y., & Shih, W. (2012). Corporate social responsibility and team performance: The mediating role of team efficacy and team self-esteem. *Journal of Business Ethics*, *108*(2), 167–180. doi:10.100710551-011-1068-6

Linder, S., & Foss, N. J. (2018). Microfoundations of Organizational Goals: A Review and New Directions for Future Research. *International Journal of Management Reviews*, *20*, S39–S62. doi:10.1111/ijmr.12154

Lindgreen, A., & Swaen, V. (2010). Corporate social responsibility. *International Journal of Management Reviews*, *12*(1), 1–7. doi:10.1111/j.1468-2370.2009.00277.x

Lindgreen, A., Swaen, V., Maon, F., Andersen, M., & Skjoett-Larsen, T. (2009). Corporate social responsibility in global supply chains. *Supply Chain Management*.

Lindsey Hall, K. K., Baker, T. L., Andrews, M. C., Hunt, T. G., & Rapp, A. A. (2016). The importance of product/service quality for frontline marketing employee outcomes: The moderating effect of leader-member exchange (LMX). *Journal of Marketing Theory and Practice*, *24*(1), 23–41. doi:10.1080/10696679.2016.1089762

Li, S., Ragu-Nathan, B., Ragu-Nathan, T., & Subba Rao, S. (2006). The impact of supply chain management practices on competitive advantage and organizational performance. *Omega Int. J. Mang. Sc.*, *34*(2), 107–124. doi:10.1016/j.omega.2004.08.002

Liu, C. (2010). Developing green intellectual capital in companies by AHP. *2010 8th International Conference on Supply Chain Management and Information*, 1-5.

Liu, Y., Li, Y., Shi, L. H., & Liu, T. (2017). Knowledge Transfer in Buyer-Supplier Relationships: The role of transactional and relational governance mechanisms. *Journal of Business Research*, *78*, 285–293. doi:10.1016/j.jbusres.2016.12.024

Liu, Y., Luo, Y., & Liu, T. (2009). Governing buyer–supplier relationships through transactional and relational mechanisms: Evidence from China. *Journal of Operations Management*, *27*(4), 294–309. doi:10.1016/j.jom.2008.09.004

Lizcano, J. L., & Nieto, P. (2006). *La semántica de la responsabilidad social corporativa*. AECA.

Lockett, A., Moon, J., & Visser, W. (2006). Corporate social responsibility in management research: Focus, nature, salience and sources of influence. *Journal of Management Studies*, *43*(1), 115–136. doi:10.1111/j.1467-6486.2006.00585.x

London, K., & Siva, J. P. S. (2011). The role of reflexive capability in relation to intellectual capital in multi-international partnerships. *International Journal of Project Management*, *29*(7), 846–855. doi:10.1016/j.ijproman.2011.05.007

Longoni, A., & Cagliano, R. (2018). Sustainable Innovativeness and the Triple Bottom Line: The Role of Organizational Time Perspective. *Journal of Business Ethics*, *151*(4), 1097–1120. doi:10.100710551-016-3239-y

Lopez Hernandez, A. K., Fernandez-Mesa, A., & Edwards-Schachter, M. (2019). Team collaboration capabilities as a factor in startup success. *Journal of Technology Management & Innovation*, *13*(4), 13–23. doi:10.4067/S0718-27242018000400013

López-Fernández, M., Romero-Fernández, P. M., & Aust, I. (2018). Socially responsible human resource management and employee perception: The influence of manager and line managers. *Sustainability*, *10*(12), 4614–4623. doi:10.3390u10124614

Lopez-Gamero, M. D., Zaragoza-Saez, P., Claver-Cortés, E., & Molina-Azorín, J. F. (2011). Sustainable development and intangibles: Building sustainable intellectual capital2. *Business Strategy and the Environment*, *20*(1), 18–37. doi:10.1002/bse.666

López-Pérez, M. E., Melero, I., & Javier Sese, F. (2017). Management for sustainable development and its impact on firm value in the SME context: Does size matter? *Business Strategy and the Environment*, *26*(7), 985–999. doi:10.1002/bse.1961

Loureiro, S. M., Sardinha, I. M. D., & Reijnders, L. (2012). The effect of corporate social responsibility on consumer satisfaction and perceived value: The case of the automobile industry sector in Portugal. *Journal of Cleaner Production*, *37*, 172–178. doi:10.1016/j.jclepro.2012.07.003

Low, M. &Siegel, D. (2019). A bibliometric analysis of employee-centred corporate social responsibility research in the 2000s. *Social Responsibility Journal*. ahead-of-print. doi:10.1108/SRJ-09-2018-0243

Lozano, F. J., Lozano, R., Freire, P., Jiménez-Gonzalez, C., Sakao, T., Ortiz, M. G., Trianni, A., Carpenter, A., & Viveros, T. (2018). New perspectives for green and sustainable chemistry and engineering: Approaches from sustainable resource and energy use, management, and transformation. *Journal of Cleaner Production*, *172*, 227–232. doi:10.1016/j.jclepro.2017.10.145

Lubin, D. A., & Esty, D. C. (2010). The sustainability imperative. *Harvard Business Review*, *88*(5), 42–50.

Lucchini, A., & Moisello, A. (2019). Stakeholders' Pressure and CSR Engagement. A Case in the Apparel Sector. *American Journal of Industrial and Business Management*, *9*(01), 169–190. doi:10.4236/ajibm.2019.91012

Luce, R. A., Barber, A. E., & Hillman, A. J. (2001). Good deeds and misdeeds: A mediated model of the effect of corporate social performance on organizational attractiveness. *Business & Society*, *40*(4), 397–415. doi:10.1177/000765030104000403

Luke, B., & Chu, V. (2013). Social Enterprise versus Social Entrepreneurship: An Examination of the 'Why' and 'How' in Pursuing Social Change. *International Small Business Journal: Researching Entrepreneurship*, *31*(7), 764–784. doi:10.1177/0266242612462598

Lund-Thomsen, P., Lindgreen, A., & Vanhamme, J. (2016). Industrial Clusters and Corporate Social Responsibility in Developing Countries: What We Know, What We do not Know, and What We Need to Know. *Journal of Business Ethics, 133*(1), 9–24. doi:10.100710551-014-2372-8

Lund-Thomsen, P., & Nadvi, K. (2010). Clusters, Chains and Compliance: Corporate Social Responsibility and Governance in Football Manufacturing in South Asia. *Journal of Business Ethics, 93*(S2), 201–222. doi:10.100710551-010-0561-7

Lund-Thomsen, P., & Pillay, R. G. (2012). CSR in industrial clusters: An overview of the literature. *Corporate Governance: The International Journal of Business and Society, 12*(4), 568–578.

Luo, J., Kaul, A., & Seo, H. (2018). Winning us with trifles: Adverse selection in the use of philanthropy as insurance. *Strategic Management Journal, 39*(10), 2591–2617. doi:10.1002mj.2935

Luo, X., & Bhattacharya, C. B. (2006). Corporate social responsibility, customer satisfaction, and market value. *Journal of Marketing, 70*(4), 1–18. doi:10.1509/jmkg.70.4.001

Lutz, S. U. (2019). The European digital single market strategy: Local indicators of spatial association 2011–2016. *Telecommunications Policy, 43*(5), 393–410. doi:10.1016/j.telpol.2018.10.003

Lynes, J. K., & Andrachuk, M. (2008). Motivations for corporate social and environmental responsibility: A case study of Scandinavian airlines. *Journal of International Management, 14*(4), 377–390. doi:10.1016/j.intman.2007.09.004

Lyon, T. P., & Maxwell, J. W. (2008). Corporate social responsibility and the environment: A theoretical perspective. *Review of Environmental Economics and Policy, 2*(2), 240–260. doi:10.1093/reep/ren004

Lythreatis, S., Mostafa, A. M. S., & Wang, X. (2019). Participative leadership and organizational identification in SMEs in the MENA Region: Testing the roles of CSR perceptions and pride in membership. *Journal of Business Ethics, 156*(3), 635–650. doi:10.100710551-017-3557-8

MacGillivray, B. H. (2018). Beyond social capital: The norms, belief systems, and agency embedded in social networks shape resilience to climatic and geophysical hazards. *Environmental Science & Policy, 60*, 116–125. doi:10.1016/j.envsci.2018.07.014

Maclagan, P. (1998). *Management and morality*. Sage.

Madueño, J. H., Jorge, M. L., Sancho, M. P. L., & Martínez-Martínez, D. (2016). Responsabilidad social en las pymes: Análisis exploratorio de factores explicativos. *Revista de Contabilidad, 19*(1), 31–44. doi:10.1016/j.rcsar.2014.10.003

Mael, F., & Ashforth, B. E. (1992). Alumni and their alma matter: A partial test of the reformulated model of organizational identification. *Journal of Organizational Behavior, 13*(2), 103–123. doi:10.1002/job.4030130202

Mahoney, J. T., McGahan, A. M., & Pitelis, C. N. (2009). 'The interdependence of private and public interests'. *Organization Science, 20*(6), 1034–1052. doi:10.1287/orsc.1090.0472

Maignan, I. (2001). Consumers' perceptions of corporate social responsibilities: A cross-cultural comparison. *Journal of Business Ethics, 30*(1), 57–72. doi:10.1023/A:1006433928640

Mair, J., & Marti, I. (2006). Social entrepreneurship research: A source of explanation, prediction, and delight. *Journal of World Business, 41*(1), 36–44. doi:10.1016/j.jwb.2005.09.002

Malhotra, Y. (2003). *Measuring Knowledge Assets of a Nation Knowledge System for development*. Invited Research Paper Sponsored by the United Nations Department of Economic and Social Affairs. Keynote Presentation at the Ad Hoc Group of Experts Meeting at the United Nations Headquarters, New York, NY.

Malhotra, N., & Mukherjee, A. (2004). The relative influence of organisational commitment and job satisfaction on service quality of customer-contact employees in banking call centres. *Journal of Services Marketing*, *18*(3), 162–174. doi:10.1108/08876040410536477

Mallery, P., & George, D. (2003). *SPSS for Windows step by step: a simple guide and reference*. Allyn & Bacon.

Maloni, M. J., & Brown, M. E. (2006). Corporate social responsibility in the supply chain: An application in the food industry. *Journal of Business Ethics*, *68*(1), 35–52. doi:10.100710551-006-9038-0

Manning, P. (1982). Organizational work: Structuration of environments. *The British Journal of Sociology*, *33*(1), 118–134. doi:10.2307/589339

Marco-Lajara, B., Claver-Cortés, E., Zaragoza Sáez, P. D. C., & Úbeda García, M. (2015). Grado de aglomeración de los distritos turísticos españoles y procesos de internacionalización de empresas hoteleras. *Economía Industrial,* (397), 21-35.

Marcus, A., & Geffen, D. (1998). The dialectics of competency acquisition: Pollution prevention in electric generation. *Strategic Management Journal*, *19*(12), 1145–1168. doi:10.1002/(SICI)1097-0266(1998120)19:12<1145::AID-SMJ6>3.0.CO;2-B

Margolis, J. D., & Walsh, J. P. (2001). *People and profits? The search for a link between a company's social and financial performance*. Lawrence Erlbaum Associates. doi:10.4324/9781410600622

Margolis, J. D., & Walsh, J. P. (2003). Misery loves companies: Rethinking social initiatives by business. *Administrative Science Quarterly*, *48*(2), 268–305. doi:10.2307/3556659

Marín, A. (2004). Del Marketing con causa a la responsabilidad social de la empresa. *Research and Marketing*, *85*, 48–51.

Marín, L. J., & Rubio, A. (2008). La responsabilidad social corporativa como determinante del éxito competitivo: Un análisis empírico. *Revista Europea de Dirección y Economía de la Empresa*, *17*(3), 27–42.

Marin, L., & Ruiz, S. (2007). "I need you too!" Corporate identity attractiveness for consumers and the role of social responsibility. *Journal of Business Ethics*, *71*(3), 245–260. doi:10.100710551-006-9137-y

Marquis, C., Glynn, M. A., & Davis, G. F. (2007). Community Isomorphism and Corporate Social Action. *Academy of Management Review*, *32*(3), 925–945. doi:10.5465/amr.2007.25275683

Marrewijk, M. (2013). *Concepts and definitions of CSR and corporate sustainability: Between agency and communion*. Doi:10.1007/978-94-007-4126-3_32

Marsden, C. (2000). The new corporate citizenship of big business: Part of the solution to sustainability? *Business and Society Review*, *105*(1), 8–25. doi:10.1111/0045-3609.00062

Marshall, A. (1890/1920). *Principles of Economics*. MacMillan.

Marshall, A. (1920). *Principles of economics*. MacMillan, Londo.

Marshall, A., & Marshall, M. P. (1920). *The economics of industry*. Macmillan and Company.

Mårtensson, K., & Westerberg, K. (2016). Corporate environmental strategies towards sustainable development. *Business Strategy and the Environment*, *25*(1), 1–9. doi:10.1002/bse.1852

Martín de Castro, G. (2008). *Reputación empresarial y ventaja competitiva*. ESIC Editorial.

Martín De Castro, G., López, J. E. N., & Sáez, P. L. (2006). Business and social reputation: Exploring the concept and main dimensions of corporate reputation. *Journal of Business Ethics*, *63*(4), 361–370. doi:10.100710551-005-3244-z

Martín Rubio, I., & Andina, D. (2018). Smart Manufacturing in a SoSE Perspective. In Advances in Renewable Energies and Power Technologies. Vol 2 Biomass, Fuel Cess, Geothermal Energies and Smart Grids. Elsevier.

Martín-de Castro, G. (2014). Intellectual capital and the firm: Some remaining questions and prospects. *Knowledge Management Research and Practice*, *12*(3), 239–245. doi:10.1057/kmrp.2014.13

Martín-de Castro, G., Amores Salvadó, J., Navas-López, J. E., & Balarezo-Núñez, R. M. (2020). Corporate Environmental Reputation: Exploring its Definitional Landscape. *Business Ethics (Oxford, England)*, *29*(1), 130–142. doi:10.1111/beer.12250

Martín-de Castro, G., Amores-Salvadó, J., & Navas-López, J. (2016). Environmental management systems and firm performance: Improving firm environmental policy through stakeholders engagement. *Corporate Social Responsibility and Environmental Management*, *23*(4), 243–256. doi:10.1002/csr.1377

Martín-de-Castro, G., Navas-Lopez, J. E., Lopez-Saez, P., & Alama-Salazar, E. (2006). Organizational capital as competitive advantage of the organization. *Journal of Intellectual Capital*, *7*(3), 324–337. doi:10.1108/14691930610681438

Martínez Ávila, M., & Fierro Moreno, E. (2018). Aplicación de la técnica PLS-SEM en la gestión del conocimiento: Un enfoque técnico práctico. *RIDE Revista Iberoamericana para la Investigación y el Desarrollo Educativo*, *8*(16), 130–164. doi:10.23913/ride.v8i16.336

Martinez-Conesa, I., Soto-Acosta, P., & Palacios-Manzano, M. (2017). Corporate social responsibility and its effect on innovation and firm performance: An empirical research in SMEs. *Journal of Cleaner Production*, *142*(Part 4), 2374–2383. doi:10.1016/j.jclepro.2016.11.038

Martínez-del-Río, J., & Céspedes-Lorente, J. (2014). Competitiveness and Legitimation: The Logic of Companies going Green in Geographical Clusters. *Journal of Business Ethics*, *120*(1), 131–146. doi:10.100710551-013-1636-z

Martín, R. D. (2010). Tomando en serio al sector privado empresarial como actor de la ayuda: la responsabilidad social corporativa para el desarrollo. In A. Guerra, J. F. Tezanos, & S. Tezanos (Eds.), *La lucha contra el hambre y la pobreza* (pp. 265–297). Fundación Sistema.

Martin, R. L., & Osberg, S. (2007). Social entrepreneurship: The case for definition. *Stanford Social Innovation Review*, *5*(2), 28–39.

Massaro, M., Dumay, J., Garlatti, A., & Dal Mas, F. (2018). Practitioners' views on intellectual capital and sustainability: From a performance-based to a worth-based perspective. *Journal of Intellectual Capital*, *19*(2), 367–386. doi:10.1108/JIC-02-2017-0033

Matten, D., & Crane, A. (2005). Corporate citizenship: Toward an extended theoretical conceptualization. *Academy of Management Review*, *30*(1), 166–179. Advance online publication. doi:10.5465/amr.2005.15281448

Matten, D., & Moon, J. (2008). Implicit' and 'explicit' CSR: A conceptual framework for a comparative understanding of corporate social responsibility. *Academy of Management Review*, *33*(2), 404–424. doi:10.5465/amr.2008.31193458

Mayer, C. (2016). Reinventing the corporation. *Journal of the British Academy*, *4*, 53–72. doi:10.5871/jba/004.053

Mayer, R. C., Davis, J. H., & Schoorman, F. D. (1995). An integrative model of organizational trust. *Academy of Management Review*, *20*(3), 709–734. doi:10.5465/amr.1995.9508080335

May, W., Mason, C., & Pinch, S. (2001). Explaining industrial agglomeration : The case of the British high- fidelity industry. *Geoforum*, *32*(3), 363–376. doi:10.1016/S0016-7185(01)00004-5

Mazutis, D., & Eckardt, A. (2017). Sleepwalking into Catastrophe: Cognitive Biases and Corporate Climate Change Inertia. *California Management Review*, *59*(3), 74–108. doi:10.1177/0008125617707974

Mccann, B. T., & Folta, T. B. (2008). Location Matters: Where We Have Been and Where We Might Go in Agglomeration Research. *Journal of Management*, *34*(3), 532–565. doi:10.1177/0149206308316057

McDowell, W. C., Peake, W. O., Coder, L., & Harris, M. L. (2018). Building small firm performance through intellectual capital development: Exploring innovation as the "black box". *Journal of Business Research*, *88*, 321–327. doi:10.1016/j.jbusres.2018.01.025

McEvily, B., & Zaheer, A. (1999). Bridging ties: A source of firm heterogeneity in competitive capabilities. *Strategic Management Journal*, *20*(12), 1133–1156. doi:10.1002/(SICI)1097-0266(199912)20:12<1133::AID-SMJ74>3.0.CO;2-7

McGuire, J. W. (1969). The changing nature of business responsibilities. *Journal of Risk and Insurance*, *36*(1), 55.

McGuire, J. B., Schneeweis, T., & Branch, B. (1990). Perceptions of firm quality: A cause or result of firm performance. *Journal of Management*, *16*(1), 167–180. doi:10.1177/014920639001600112

McKendall, M., DeMarr, B., & Jones-Rikkers, C. (2002). Ethical compliance programs and corporate illegality: Testing the assumptions of the corporate sentencing guidelines. *Journal of Business Ethics*, *37*(4), 367–383. doi:10.1023/A:1015287823807

McWilliams, A., & Siegel, D. (2001). Corporate Social Responsibility: A Theory of the Firm Perspective. *Corp. Soc. Responsib. A Theory Firm Perspect.*, *26*, 117–127.

McWilliams, A., & Siegel, D. (2001). Corporate social responsibility: A theory of the firm perspective. *Academy of Management. Academy of Management Review*, *26*(1), 117–127. doi:10.5465/amr.2001.4011987

McWilliams, A., & Siegel, D. S. (2011). Creating and Capturing Value: Strategic Corporate Social Responsibility, Resource-Based Theory, and Sustainable Competitive Advantage. *Journal of Management*, *37*(5), 1480–1495. doi:10.1177/0149206310385696

McWilliams, A., Siegel, D. S., & Wright, P. M. (2006). Corporate social responsibility: Strategic implications. *Journal of Management Studies*, *43*(1), 1–18. doi:10.1111/j.1467-6486.2006.00580.x

Melé, D., Debeljuh, P., & Arruda, M. C. (2006). Corporate ethical policies in large corporations in Argentina, Brazil and Spain. *Journal of Business Ethics*, *63*(1), 21–38. doi:10.100710551-005-7100-y

Meski, O., Belkadi, F., Laroche, F., & Furet, B. (2019). Towards a knowledge-based framework for digital chain monitoring within the industry 4.0 paradigm. *29th CIRP 84 Design 2019*, 118-123.

Meuer, J., Koelbel, J., & Hoffmann, V. H. (2019). On the nature of corporate sustainability. *Organization & Environment*, *33*(3), 319–341. doi:10.1177/1086026619850180

Meuer, J., Koelbel, J., & Hoffmann, V. H. (2019). On the Nature of Corporate Sustainability. *Organization & Environment*.

Michelon, G. (2011). Sustainability disclosure and reputation: A comparative study. *Corporate Reput. Rev.*, *14*(2), 79–96. doi:10.1057/crr.2011.10

Milgrom, P., & Roberts, J. (1982). Predation, reputation, and entry deterrence. *Journal of Economic Theory*, *27*(2), 280–312. doi:10.1016/0022-0531(82)90031-X

Milgrom, P., & Roberts, J. (1986). Price and advertising signals of product quality. *Journal of Political Economy*, *94*(4), 796–821. doi:10.1086/261408

Milgrom, P., & Roberts, J. (1992). *Economics, organization and management*. Prentice Hall Inc.

Miller, C. C., Cardinal, L. B., & Glick, W. H. (1997). Retrospective reports in organizational research: A reexamination of recent evidence. *Academy of Management Journal*, *40*, 189–204. doi:10.2307/257026

Miller, J. (2002). The board as a monitor of organizational activity: The applicability of agency theory to non-profit boards. *Nonprofit Management & Leadership*, *12*(4), 429–450. doi:10.1002/nml.12407

Mintzberg, H. (2019). Please Welcome CSR 2.0. In Rethinking strategic management: Sustainable strategizing for positive impact (1st edition). Springer Berlin Heidelberg.

Miron, E., Erez, M., & Naveh, E. (2004). Do personal characteristics and cultural values that promote innovation, quality, and efficiency compete or complement each other? *Journal of Organizational Behavior*, *25*(2), 175–199. doi:10.1002/job.237

Missonier, S., & Loufrani-Fedida, S. (2014). Stakeholder analysis and engagement in projects: From stakeholder relational perspective to stakeholder relational ontology. *International Journal of Project Management*, *32*(7), 1108–1122. doi:10.1016/j.ijproman.2014.02.010

Mitchell, R. K., Agle, B. R., & Wood, D. J. (1997). Toward a theory of stakeholder identification and salience: Defining the principle of who and what really counts. *Academy of Management.the Academy of Management Review*, *22*(4), 853–886. doi:10.5465/amr.1997.9711022105

Mizruchi, M. S. (1996). What do interlocks do? An analysis, critique, and assessment of research on interlocking directorates. *Annual Review of Sociology*, *22*(1), 271–298. doi:10.1146/annurev.soc.22.1.271

Mohamed, S. T. (2001). The Impact of ISO 14,000 on developing World Businesses. *Renewable Energy*, *23*(3-4), 579–584. doi:10.1016/S0960-1481(00)00145-2

Mohr, J., & Spekman, R. (1994). Characteristics of partnership success: Partnership attributes, communication behavior, and conflict resolution techniques. *Strategic Management Journal*, *15*(2), 135–152. doi:10.1002mj.4250150205

Mohr, L. A., & Webb, D. J. (2005). The effects of corporate social responsibility and price on consumer responses. *The Journal of Consumer Affairs*, *39*(1), 121–147. doi:10.1111/j.1745-6606.2005.00006.x

Molina-Azorín, J. F. (2014). Microfoundations of strategic management: Toward micro–macro research in the resource-based theory. *BRQ Business Research Quarterly*, *17*(2), 102–114. doi:10.1016/j.brq.2014.01.001

Molina-Morales, F. X., Belso-Martinez, J. A., & Mas-Verdú, F. (2016). Interactive effects of internal brokerage activities in clusters: The case of the Spanish Toy Valley. *Journal of Business Research*, *69*(5), 1785–1790. doi:10.1016/j.jbusres.2015.10.056

Molina-Morales, F. X., & Martínez-Fernández, M. T. (2009). Too much love in the neighborhood can hurt: How an excess of intensity and trust in relationships may produce negative effects on firms. *Strategic Management Journal*, *30*(9), 1013–1023. doi:10.1002mj.766

Moneva, J. M., & Hernández-Pajares, J. (2018). Corporate social responsibility performance and sustainability reporting in SMEs: An analysis of owner-managers' perceptions. *International Journal of Sustainable Economy*, *10*(4), 405–420. doi:10.1504/IJSE.2018.095268

Montiel, I. (2008). Corporate social responsibility and corporate sustainability: Separate pasts, common futures. *Organization & Environment*, *21*(3), 245–269. doi:10.1177/1086026608321329

Montiel, I., Antolin-López, R., & Gallo, P. J. (2020). What on Earth should managers learn about corporate sustainability? A threshold concept approach. *Journal of Business Ethics*, *162*(4), 857–880. doi:10.100710551-019-04361-y

Montiel, I., Christmann, P., & Zink, T. (2019). The Effect of Sustainability Standard Uncertainty on Certification Decisions of Firms in Emerging Economies. *Journal of Business Ethics*, *154*(3), 667–681. doi:10.100710551-016-3350-0

Montiel, I., & Delgado-Ceballos, J. (2014). Defining and measuring corporate sustainability: Are we there yet? *Organization & Environment*, *27*(2), 113–139. doi:10.1177/1086026614526413

Montiel, I., Husted, B. W., & Christmann, P. (2012). Using private management standard certification to reduce information asymmetries in corrupt environments. *Strategic Management Journal*, *33*(9), 1103–1113. doi:10.1002mj.1957

Monzon, J. L., & Chaves, R. (2008). The European Social Economy: Concept and dimensions of the third sector. *Annals of Public and Cooperative Economics*, *79*(3-4), 549–577. doi:10.1111/j.1467-8292.2008.00370.x

Moon, H. C., Parc, J., Yim, S. H., & Park, N. (2011). An extension of Porter and Kramer's creating shared value (CSV): Reorienting strategies and seeking international cooperation. *Journal of International and Area Studies*, *28*(2), 49–64.

Moon, H.-C. H., & Parc, J. (2019). Shifting corporate social responsibility to corporate social opportunity through creating shared value. *Strategic Change*, *28*(2), 115–122. doi:10.1002/jsc.2252

Morgan, T., Anokhin, S., & Wincent, J. (2018). When the fog dissipates: The choice between value creation and value appropriation in a partner as a function of information asymmetry. *Journal of Business Research*, *88*, 498–504. doi:10.1016/j.jbusres.2017.11.032

Morrison, A., & Rabellotti, R. (2009). Knowledge and information networks in an Italian wine cluster. *European Planning Studies*, *17*(7), 983–1006. doi:10.1080/09654310902949265

Morrison, R. S. (1995). Validation of nursing management diagnoses. *Image—the Journal of Nursing Scholarship*, *27*(4), 267–271. doi:10.1111/j.1547-5069.1995.tb00886.x PMID:8530113

Moser, D. V., & Martin, P. R. (2012). A broader perspective on corporate social responsibility research in accounting. *The Accounting Review*, *87*(3), 797–806. doi:10.2308/accr-10257

Moulaert, F., & Nussbaumer, J. (2005). Defining the social economy and its governance at the neighbourhood level: A methodological reflection. *Urban Studies (Edinburgh, Scotland)*, *42*(11), 2071–2088. doi:10.1080/420980500279752

Moyano Fuentes, J., Jiménez Delgado, J. J., & Rodríguez Martínez, A. (2019). Territorial agglomerations and corporate social responsibility: The role of science and technology parks. *International Journal of Entrepreneurship and Innovation Management*, *23*(2), 180. Advance online publication. doi:10.1504/IJEIM.2019.10018520

Mozas, A. (2013). Emprendimiento y Economía Social. Presentación del número. *CIRIEC-España, Revista de Economía Pública. Social y Cooperativa.*, *78*, 7–9.

Mu, J., Peng, G., & Love, E. (2008). Interfirm networks, social capital, and knowledge flow. *Journal of Knowledge Management*, *12*(4), 86–100. doi:10.1108/13673270810884273

Muñoz, P., & Cohen, B. (2018). Sustainable Entrepreneurship Research: Taking Stock and Looking Ahead. *Business Strategy and the Environment*, *27*(3), 300–322. doi:10.1002/bse.2000

Muñoz-Pascual, L., Curado, C., & Galende, J. (2019). How does the use of informartion technologies affect the adoption of environmental practices in SMEs? A mixed-methods approach. *Review of Managerial Science*, *2019*, 1–28.

Muñoz-Pascual, L., Curado, C., & Galende, J. (2019). The triple bottom line on sustainable product innovation performance: A mixed methods approach. *Sustainability*, *11*(6), 1689. doi:10.3390u11061689

Muñoz-Pascual, L., & Galende, J. (2017). The Impact of Knowledge and Motivation Management on Creativity: Employees of Innovative Spanish Companies. *Employee Relations*, *39*(5), 732–752. doi:10.1108/ER-05-2016-0096

Muñoz-Pascual, L., & Galende, J. (2020). Ambidextrous Knowledge and Learning Capability: The Magic Potion for Employee Creativity and Sustainable Innovation Performance. *Sustainability*, *12*(10), 3966. doi:10.3390u12103966

Muñoz-Pascual, L., & Galende, J. (2020). Ambidextrous Relationships and Social Capability as Employee Well-Being: The Secret Sauce for Research and Development and Sustainable Innovation Performance. *International Journal of Environmental Research and Public Health*, *17*(9), 3072. doi:10.3390/ijerph17093072 PMID:32354118

Muñoz-Pascual, L., Galende, J., & Curado, C. (2019). Human Resource Management Contributions to Knowledge Sharing for a Sustainability-Oriented Performance: A Mixed Methods Approach. *Sustainability*, *12*(1), 161. doi:10.3390u12010161

Murillo, D., & Lozano, J. M. (2006). SMEs and CSR: An approach to CSR in their own words. *Journal of Business Ethics*, *67*(3), 227–240. doi:10.100710551-006-9181-7

Murray, K. B., & Montanari, J. B. (1986). Strategic management of the socially responsible firm: Integrating management and marketing theory. *Academy of Management Review*, *11*(4), 815–827. doi:10.5465/amr.1986.4284013

Murry, J. P. Jr, & Heide, J. B. (1998). Managing promotion program participation within manufacturer–retailer relationships. *Journal of Marketing*, *62*(1), 58–68.

Musa, M. H., & Mohamad, M. N. (2018). Importance of Green Innovation in Malaysian SMEs: Advantages and Future Research. *Int. Acad. J. Bus. Manag.*, *5*(01), 64–73. doi:10.9756/IAJBM/V5I1/1810010

Nagles, N. (2007). La gestión del conocimiento como fuente de innovación. *Revista Escuela de Administración de Negocios*, (61), 97-102.

Nanda, V., & Yun, Y. (1997). Reputation and financial intermediation: An empirical investigation of the impact of IPO mispricing on underwriter market value. *Journal of Financial Intermediation*, *6*(1), 39–63. doi:10.1006/jfin.1996.0208

Nejati, M., Quazi, A., Amran, A., & Ahmad, N. H. (2017). Social responsibility and performance: Does strategic orientation matter for small businesses? *Journal of Small Business Management*, *55*, 43–59. doi:10.1111/jsbm.12305

Nelson, R. R., & Winter, S. G. (1982). *An evolutionary theory of economic change*. Belknap Press.

Ng, A. C., & Rezaee, Z. (2015). Business sustainability performance and cost of equity capital. *Journal of Corporate Finance*, *34*, 128–149. doi:10.1016/j.jcorpfin.2015.08.003

Ngo, L. V., & O'Cass, A. (2013). Innovation and Business Success: The Mediating Role of Customer Participation. *Journal of Business Research*, *66*(8), 1134–1142. doi:10.1016/j.jbusres.2012.03.009

Ng, S. T., Wong, J. M. W., & Wong, K. K. W. (2013). A public private people partnerships (P4) process framework for infrastructure development in Hong Kong. *Cities (London, England)*, *31*, 370–381. doi:10.1016/j.cities.2012.12.002

Ng, T. W., Yam, K. C., & Aguinis, H. (2019). Employee perceptions of corporate social responsibility: Effects on pride, embeddedness, and turnover. *Personnel Psychology*, *72*(1), 107–137. doi:10.1111/peps.12294

Nicholls, A. (2006). *Social entrepreneurship: New models of sustainable social change*. OUP Oxford.

Nielsen. (2015). *Consumer versus Corporate Social Responsibility of Brands*. Retrieved from: https://www.nielsen.com/es/es/press-releases/2015/Cuatro-de-cada-diez-consumidores-pagarias-mas-por-prodcutos-de-empresas-socialmente-comprometidas/

Nieves, J., & Haller, S. (2014). Building Dynamic Capabilities Through Knowledge Resources. *Tourism Management*, *40*, 224–232. doi:10.1016/j.tourman.2013.06.010

Nonaka, I. (1994). A dynamic theory of organizational knowledge creation. *Organization Science*, *5*(1), 14–37. doi:10.1287/orsc.5.1.14

Nonaka, I., & Takeuchi, K. (1995). *The Knowledge Creating Company*. Oxford University Press.

Nunnally, J. C. (1978). *Psychometric Theory* (2nd ed.). McGraw-Hill.

O'Dwyer, B., & Owen, D. L. (2005). Assurance statement practice in environmental, social and sustainability reporting: A critical evaluation. *The British Accounting Review*, *37*(2), 205–229. doi:10.1016/j.bar.2005.01.005

Öberseder, M., Schlegelmilch, B. B., & Murphy, P. E. (2013). CSR practices and consumer perceptions. *Journal of Business Research*, *66*(10), 1839–1851. doi:10.1016/j.jbusres.2013.02.005

Öcal, A. T. (2007). *İşletmelerin sosyal sorumluluğu*. Beta.

Oeij, P. R., Kraan, K. O., & Vaas, F. (2010). *Impact of Social Innovation on Organisational Performance and Sickness Absence*. Paper presented at the XVII ISA World Congress of Sociology, Gothenburg, Sweden.

Oeyono, J., Samy, M., & Bampton, R. (2011). An examination of corporate social responsibility and financial performance: A study of the top 50 Indonesian listed corporations. *Journal of Global Responsibility*, *2*(1), 100–112. doi:10.1108/20412561111128555

Oficina Internacional del Trabajo. (2019). *Las mujeres en la gestión empresarial: argumentos para un cambio*. Ginebra.

Ogbeibu, S., Emelifeonwu, J., Senadki, A., Gaskin, J., & Kaivo-oja, J. (2020). Technological turbulence and greening of team creativity, product innovation, and human resource management: Implications for sustainaiblity. *Journal of Cleaner Production*, *244*(118703), 1–15. doi:10.1016/j.jclepro.2019.118703

Okoye, A. (2009). Theorising corporate social responsibility as an essentially contested concept: Is a definition necessary? *Journal of Business Ethics*, *89*(4), 613–627. doi:10.100710551-008-0021-9

Oliveira, L., Lima Rodrigues, L., & Craig, R. (2010). Intellectual capital reporting in sustainability reports. *Journal of Intellectual Capital*, *11*(4), 575–594. doi:10.1108/14691931011085696

Orlitzky, M., Schmidt, F. L., & Rynes, S. L. (2003). Corporate social and financial performance: A meta-analysis. *Organization Studies*, *24*(3), 403–441. doi:10.1177/0170840603024003910

Orlitzky, M., Siegel, D. S., & Waldman, D. A. (2011). Strategic corporate social responsibility and environmental sustainability. *Business & Society*, *50*(1), 6–27. doi:10.1177/0007650310394323

Ormiston, M. E., & Wong, E. M. (2013). License to Ill: The Effects of Corporate Social Responsibility and CEO Moral Identity on Corporate Social Irresponsibility. *Personnel Psychology*, *66*(4), 861–893. doi:10.1111/peps.12029

Ortega Carpio, M. L., & Román, A. (2018). *Anexo estadístico para el seguimiento de la agenda 2030 en españa*. Academic Press.

Ortiz-de-Mandojana, N., & Aragon-Correa, J. A. (2015). Boards and sustainability: The contingent influence of director interlocks on corporate environmental performance. *Business Strategy and the Environment*, *24*(6), 499–517. doi:10.1002/bse.1833

Ortiz-de-Mandojana, N., Aragón-Correa, J. A., Delgado-Ceballos, J., & Ferrón-Vílchez, V. (2012). The effect of director interlocks on firms' adoption of proactive environmental strategies. *Corporate Governance*, *20*(2), 164–178. doi:10.1111/j.1467-8683.2011.00893.x

Othman, A. A. E., & Hafez, M. G. (2019). A framework integrating corporate social responsibility for marketing architectural design firms in developing countries. Journal of Engineering. *Design and Technology*, *17*(6), 1174–1191. doi:10.1108/JEDT-11-2018-0202

Owen-Smith, J., & Powell, W. W. (2004). Knowledge networks as channels and conduits: The effects of spillovers in the Boston Biotechnology community. *Organization Science*, *15*(1), 5–21. doi:10.1287/orsc.1030.0054

Oyemomi, O., Liu, S., Neaga, I., & Alkhuraiji, A. (2016). How Knowledge Sharing and Business Process Contribute to Organizational Performance: Using the fsQCA Approach. *Journal of Business Research*, *69*(11), 4725–5546. doi:10.1016/j.jbusres.2016.04.116

Pablo, S.-I. H. J., Benito, Y.-A., & Juan, M.-G. (2019). Moderating effect of firm size on the influence of corporate social responsibility in the economic performance of micro-, small and medium-sized enterprises. *Technological Forecasting and Social Change*, 119774.

Pache, A. C., & Santos, F. (2012). Inside the Hybrid Organization: Selective Coupling as a Response to Competing Institutional Logics. *Academy of Management Journal*, *56*(4), 972–1001. doi:10.5465/amj.2011.0405

Pacheco, L. M., Alves, M. F. R., & Liboni, L. B. (2018). Green absorptive capacity: A mediation-moderation model of knowledge for innovation. *Business Strategy and the Environment*, *27*(8), 1502–1513. doi:10.1002/bse.2208

Paine, L. S. (1996). Moral thinking in management: An essential capability. *Business Ethics Quarterly*, *6*(4), 477–492. doi:10.2307/3857500

Paine, L. S. (2003). *Value Shift: Why Companies Must Merge Social and Financial Imperatives to Achieve Superior Performance*. McGraw-Hill.

Palacios-Marqués, D., García, M. G., Sánchez, M. M., & Mari, M. P. A. (2019). Social entrepreneurship and organizational performance: A study of the mediating role of distinctive competencies in marketing. *Journal of Business Research*, *101*, 426–432. doi:10.1016/j.jbusres.2019.02.004

Parkhe, A. (1993). Strategic alliance structuring: A game theoretic and transaction cost examination of interfirm cooperation. *Academy of Management Journal*, *36*(4), 794–829.

Park, S., & Levy, S. E. (2014). Corporate social responsibility: Perspectives of hotel frontline employees. *International Journal of Contemporary Hospitality Management*, *26*(3), 332–348. doi:10.1108/IJCHM-01-2013-0034

Paulík, J., Majková, M. S., Tykva, T., & Cervinka, M. (2015). Application of the CSR measuring model in a commercial bank in relation to their financial performance. *Economia e Sociologia*, *8*(4), 65–81. doi:10.14254/2071-789X.2015/8-4/5

Pava, M. L., & Krausz, J. (1997). Criteria for evaluating the legitimacy of corporate social responsibility. *Journal of Business Ethics*, *16*(3), 337–347. doi:10.1023/A:1017920217290

Pedersen, E. R. (2006). Making corporate social responsibility (CSR) operable: How companies translate stakeholder dialogue into practice. *Business and Society Review*, *111*(2), 137–163. doi:10.1111/j.1467-8594.2006.00265.x

Pedersen, E. R., & Andersen, M. (2006). Safeguarding corporate social responsibility (CSR) in global supply chains: How codes of conduct are managed in buyer-supplier relationships. *Journal of Public Affairs: An International Journal*, *6*(3-4), 228–240. doi:10.1002/pa.232

Peloza, J., & Shang, J. (2011). How can corporate social responsibility activities create value for stakeholders? A systematic review. *Journal of the Academy of Marketing Science*, *39*(1), 117–135. doi:10.100711747-010-0213-6

Peña, I. (2002). Intellectual capital and business start-up success. *Journal of Intellectual Capital*, *3*(2), 180–198. doi:10.1108/14691930210424761

Peña-Miranda, D. D., Arteaga-Ortiz, J., & Ramón-Cardona, J. (2019). Determinants of CSR application in the hotel industry of the Colombian Caribbean. *Sustainability*, *11*(18), 5045. doi:10.3390u11185045

Pérez López, S., Manuel Montes Peón, J., & José Vázquez Ordás, C. (2004). Managing knowledge: The link between culture and organizational learning. *Journal of Knowledge Management*, *8*(6), 93–104. doi:10.1108/13673270410567657

Perrini, F. (2006). SMEs and CSR theory: Evidence and implications from an Italian perspective. *Journal of Business Ethics*, *67*(3), 305–316. doi:10.100710551-006-9186-2

Perrone, V., Zaheer, A., & McEvily, B. (2003). Free to be trusted? Organizational constraints on trust in boundary spanners. *Organization Science*, *14*(4), 422–439. doi:10.1287/orsc.14.4.422.17487

Petersen, T. (1993). The economics of organization: The principal-agent relationship. *Acta Sociologica*, *36*(3), 277–293. doi:10.1177/000169939303600309

Petrash, G. (1996). Dow's journey to a knowledge value management culture. *European Management Journal*, *14*(4), 365–373. doi:10.1016/0263-2373(96)00023-0

Phillips, P., & Phillips, J. (2002). *Measuring Intellectual Capital: Twelve Case Studies from the Real World of Training*. American Society for Training and Development.

Phillips, R. (1999). On stakeholder delimitation. *Business & Society*, *38*(1), 32–34.

Podolny, J. M., & Page, K. L. (1998). Networks forms of organization. *Annual Review of Sociology*, *24*(1), 57–76. doi:10.1146/annurev.soc.24.1.57

Podsakoff, P. M., MacKenzie, S. B., Lee, J.-Y., & Podsakoff, N. P. (2003). Common method biases in behavioral research: A critical review of the literature and recommended remedies. *The Journal of Applied Psychology*, *88*(5), 879–903. doi:10.1037/0021-9010.88.5.879 PMID:14516251

Podsakoff, P. M., & Organ, D. W. (1986). Self-reports in organizational research: Problems and prospects. *Journal of Management*, *12*(4), 531–544. doi:10.1177/014920638601200408

Pojasek, R. B. (2007). A framework for business sustainability. *Environmental Quality Management*, *17*(2), 81–88. doi:10.1002/tqem.20168

Polletta, F. (1999). "Free spaces" in collective action. *Theory and Society*, *28*(1), 1–38. doi:10.1023/A:1006941408302

Poppo, L., Zhou, K. Z., & Ryu, S. (2008). Alternative origins to interorganizational trust: An interdependence perspective on the shadow of the past and the shadow of the future. *Organization Science*, *19*(1), 39–55. doi:10.1287/orsc.1070.0281

Porter, M. E. (1990). The Competitive Advantage of Nations. *Harvard Business Review*, *68*(2), 73–93.

Porter, M. E. (1998). Clusters and the new economics of competition. *Harvard Business Review*, •••, 77–90. PMID:10187248

Porter, M. E., & Kramer, M. R. (2006). Strategy and society: The link between competitive advantage and corporate social responsibility. *Harvard Business Review*, *84*(12), 78–92. PMID:17183795

Porter, M. E., & Kramer, M. R. (2006). The link between competitive advantage and corporate social responsibility. *Harvard Business Review*, *84*(12), 78–92. PMID:17183795

Porter, M. E., & Kramer, M. R. (2011). Creating Shared Value. *Harvard Business Review*, *89*, 62–77. doi:10.1108/09600039410055963

Porter, M. E., & van der Linde, C. (1995). Green and Competitive: Ending the Stalemate. *Harvard Business Review*.

Porter, M., & Kramer, M. (2002). The Competitive Advantage of Corporate Philanthropy. *Harvard Business Review. Collection Redefining Corporate Social*, *80*(12), 56–68. PMID:12510538

Porter, M., & Kramer, M. R. (2011). Creating shared value. *Harvard Business Review*, *89*(1/2), 62–77.

Porter, M., & van der Linde, C. (1995). *Green and competitive*. Harvard Business Review.

Portney, P. R. (2005). Corporate social responsibility: An economic and policy perspective. In B. L. Hay, R. N. Stavins, & R. K. Vietor (Eds.), *Environmental protection and the social responsibility of firms* (pp. 107–131). Resources for the Future.

Post, C., Rahman, N., & Rubow, E. (2011). Green governance: Boards of directors' composition and environmental corporate social responsibility. *Business & Society*, *50*(1), 189–223. doi:10.1177/0007650310394642

Potocan, V., Mulej, M., & Nedelko, Z. (2013). The influence of employees' ethical behavior on enterprises' social responsibility. *Systemic Practice and Action Research*, *26*(6), 497–511. doi:10.100711213-013-9299-3

Potrich, L., Cortimiglia, M. N., & de Medeiros, J. F. (2019). A systematic literature review on firm-level proactive environmental management. *Journal of Environmental Management*, *243*, 273–286. doi:10.1016/j.jenvman.2019.04.110 PMID:31102895

Potts, S., & Maluszewski, I. (2004). Ethics and Corporate Governance. *Corporate Governance*, *12*(2), 177–179. doi:10.1111/j.1467-8683.2004.00357.x

Powell, W. W., Koput, K. W., & Smith-Doerr, L. (1996). Interorganizational and the collaboration locus of innovation: Networks of learning in Biotechnology. *Administrative Science Quarterly*, *41*(1), 116–145. doi:10.2307/2393988

Prahalad, & Hart, S. (2002). The fortune at the bottom of the pyramid. *Strategy and Business*, 54-54.

Prentice, R. (2002). Enron: A brief behavioral autopsy. *American Business Law Journal*, *40*(2), 417–444. doi:10.1111/j.1744-1714.2002.tb00851.x

Preston, D. S., Chen, D. Q., Swink, M., & Meade, L. (2017). Generating supplier benefits through buyer-enabled knowledge enrichment: A social capital perspective. *Decision Sciences*, *48*(2), 248–287. doi:10.1111/deci.12220

Preston, L. E. (1988). *Social Issues and Public Policy in Business and Management: Retrospect and Prospect*. University of Maryland.

Preuss, L., & Perschke, J. (2010). Slipstreaming the larger boats: Social responsibility in medium-sized businesses. *Journal of Business Ethics*, *92*(4), 531–551. doi:10.100710551-009-0171-4

Prince of Wales Business Leadership Forum. (n.d.). *Website Resources, CSR Themes*. www.pwblf.org

Prutina, Ž., & Šehić, D. (2016). Employee's perceptions of corporate social responsibility: A case study of award recipients. *Ekonomska Misao i Praksa*, (1), 239–260.

Pucheta-Martínez, M. C., Bel-Oms, I., & Olcina-Sempere, G. (2018). The association between board gender diversity and financial reporting quality, corporate performance and corporate social responsibility disclosure. *Academia (Caracas)*, *31*(1), 177–194. doi:10.1108/ARLA-04-2017-0110

Puig, M., & Martínez, A. (2008). *La responsabilidad social en la administración pública. Un reto para el s.XXI.* Diputación de Barcelona. Retrieved from: https://www1.diba.cat/uliep/pdf/39527.pdf

Pujari, D. (2006). Eco-innovation and new product development: Understanding the influences on market performance. *Technovation, 26*(1), 76–85. doi:10.1016/j.technovation.2004.07.006

Pujari, D., Wright, G., & Peattie, K. (2003). Green and competitive: Influences on environmental new product development performance. *Journal of Business Research, 56*(8), 657–671. doi:10.1016/S0148-2963(01)00310-1

Pulic, A. (1997). *The physical and intellectual capital of Austrian banks.* Retrieved from http://www.vaic-on.net

Pulic, A. (2000). An accounting tool for IC management. *International Journal of Technology Management, 20*(5), 702–714. doi:10.1504/IJTM.2000.002891

Qian, F., Zhong, W., & Du, W. (2017). Fundamental Theories and Key Technologies for Smart and Optimal Manufacturing in the Process Industry. *Engineering, 3*(2), 154–160. doi:10.1016/J.ENG.2017.02.011

Quazi, A. M., & O'Brien, D. (2000). An Empirical Test of Cross-National Model of Corporate Social Responsibility. *Journal of Business Ethics, 25*(1), 33–51. doi:10.1023/A:1006305111122

Rahman, N., & Post, C. (2012). Measurement issues in environmental corporate social responsibility (ECSR): Toward a transparent, reliable, and construct valid instrument. *Journal of Business Ethics, 105*(3), 307–319. doi:10.100710551-011-0967-x

Rahman, S. (2011). Evaluation of definitions: Ten dimensions of corporate social responsibility. *World Review of Business Research, 1*(1), 166–176.

Rajasekar, D., & Deepa, S. R. (2017). Mandatory Corporate Social Responsibility in India and the Impact on Women Board of Directors: A Review. *International Journal of Civil Engineering and Technology, 8*(12), 400–409.

Ramanathan, R., Black, A., Nath, P., & Muyldermans, L. (2010). Impact of Environmental Regulations on Innovation and Performance in the UK Industrial Sector. *Management Decision, 48*(10), 1493–1513. doi:10.1108/00251741011090298

Ramos-González, M., Rubio-Andrés, M., & Sastre-Castillo, M. (2017). Building Corporate Reputation through Sustainable Entrepreneurship: The Mediating Effect of Ethical Behavior. *Sustainability, 9*(9), 1663. doi:10.3390u9091663

Raut, U. R., & Pawar, P. A. (2016). Analysis of the relationship between young retail frontline employees and their demographic profile: Skill development perspective. *International Journal of Commerce and Management Research, 2*(3), 124-128.

Rawhouser, H., Cummings, M., & Newbert, S. L. (2017). Social impact measurement: Current approaches and future directions for social entrepreneurship research. *Entrepreneurship Theory and Practice.*

Raynard, P., & Forstater, M. (2002). *Corporate social responsibility: Implications for small and medium enterprises in developing countries.* United Nations Industrial Development Organization.

Reder, A. (1994). *In pursuit of profit and principle: Business success through social responsibility.* GP Putnam's Sons.

Reed, R., & De Fillippi, R. J. (1990). Causal ambiguity, barriers to imitation, and sustainable competitive advantage. *Academy of Management Review, 15*(1), 88–102. doi:10.5465/amr.1990.4308277

Reimer, M., Van Doorn, S., & Heyden, M. L. M. (2018). Unpacking Functional Experience Complementarities in Senior Leaders' Influences on CSR Strategy: A CEO–Top Management Team Approach. *Journal of Business Ethics, 151*(4), 977–995. doi:10.100710551-017-3657-5

Reinhardt, F. L. (1998). Environmental product differentiation: Implications for corporate strategy. *California Management Review*, *40*(4), 43–73. doi:10.2307/41165964

Reputation Institute. (2018). *Global CR RepTrak® 100*. Retrieved from: https://ri.reputationinstitute.com/hubfs/_PDF/RepTrak/2018_Global_CR_100.pdf

Responsabilidad Social Corporativa. (2019). *La responsabilidad social empresarial*. Retrieved from: https://responsabilidad-social-corporativa.com/la-responsabilidad-social-empresarial/

Rettab, B., Brik, A. B., & Mellahi, K. (2009). A study of management perceptions of the impact of corporate social responsibility on organisational performance in emerging economies: The case of Dubai. *Journal of Business Ethics*, *89*(3), 371–390. doi:10.100710551-008-0005-9

Reuer, J. J., Zollo, M., & Singh, H. (2002). Post-formation dynamics in strategic alliances. *Strategic Management Journal*, *23*(2), 135–151. doi:10.1002mj.214

Reynolds, M. A. (2000). Professionalism, ethical codes and the internal auditor: A moral argument. *Journal of Business Ethics*, *24*(2), 115–124. doi:10.1023/A:1006179723979

Rezaee, Z. (2016). Business sustainability research: A theoretical and integrated perspective. *Journal of Accounting Literature*, *36*, 48–64. doi:10.1016/j.acclit.2016.05.003

Rhee, S. K., & Lee, S. Y. (2003). Dynamic change of corporate environmental strategy: Rhetoric and reality. *Business Strategy and the Environment*, *12*(3), 175–190. doi:10.1002/bse.356

Rhenman, E. (1968). *Industrial democracy and industrial management*. Tavistock Publications.

Ringle, C. M., Wende, S., & Becker, J. M. (2015). *SmartPLS 3*. Boenningstedt: SmartPLS GmbH.

Ring, P. S., & Van de Ven, A. H. (1994). Developmental processes of cooperative interorganizational relationships. *Academy of Management Review*, *19*(1), 90–118. doi:10.5465/amr.1994.9410122009

Robbins, S. P. (1994). *Management*. Prentice-Hall.

Roberts, D., & Woods, C. (2005). Changing the world on a shoestring: The concept of social entrepreneurship. *University of Auckland Business Review*, *7*(1), 45-51.

Roberts, P. W., & Dowling, G. R. (1997). The value of a firm's corporate reputation: How reputation helps attain and sustain superior profitability. *Corporate Reputation Review*, *1*(1), 72–76. doi:10.1057/palgrave.crr.1540020

Roberts, P. W., & Dowling, G. R. (2002). Corporate reputation and sustained superior financial performance. *Strategic Management Journal*, *23*(12), 1077–1093. doi:10.1002mj.274

Roberts, S. (2003). Supply chain specific? Understanding the patchy success of ethical sourcing initiatives. *Journal of Business Ethics*, *44*(2-3), 159–170. doi:10.1023/A:1023395631811

Robinson, J. (2006). Navigating Social and Institutional Barriers to Markets: How Social Entrepreneurs Identify and Evaluate Opportunities. In J. Mair, J. Robinson, & K. Hockerts (Eds.), *Social Entrepreneurship* (pp. 95–120). Palgrave Macmillan UK. doi:10.1057/9780230625655_7

Rodríguez, N. (2010). *Responsabilidad social y ONG*. Retrieved from: http://www.eexcellence.es/index.php/expertos-en-gestion/responsabilidad-social-y-ong

Rodríguez-Ariza, L., Aceituno, J. V. F., & Rubio, R. G. (2014). El consejo de administración y las memorias de sostenibilidad. *Revista de Contabilidad*, *17*(1), 5–16. doi:10.1016/j.rcsar.2013.02.002

Rodriguez-Fernandez, M. (2016). Social responsibility and financial performance: The role of good corporate governance. *BRQ Business Research Quarterly*, *19*(2), 137–151. doi:10.1016/j.brq.2015.08.001

Rodríguez-Piñero Royo, M. C. (2005). La responsabilidad social de la corporativa: una oportunidad y un desafío para todos. *Observatorio sobre la RSE y las Relaciones Laborales, Consejo Andaluz de Relaciones Laborales.* www.juntade-andalucía. es/empleo/carl/observatorio

Roman, R. M., Hayibor, S., & Agle, B. R. (1999). The relationship between social and financial performance: Repainting a portrait. *Business & Society*, *38*(1), 109–125. doi:10.1177/000765039903800105

Rossi, C., Cricelli, L., Grimaldi, M., & Greco, M. (2016). The strategic assessment of intelectual capital assets: An application within Terradure Srl. *Journal of Business Research*, *69*(5), 1598–1603. doi:10.1016/j.jbusres.2015.10.024

Rothenhoefer, L. M. (2019). The impact of CSR on corporate reputation perceptions of the public—A configurational multi-time, multi-source perspective. *Business Ethics (Oxford, England)*, *28*(2), 141–155. doi:10.1111/beer.12207

RSE. (2018). *10 ventajas de la RSE para las compañías.* Retrieved from: http://rse.elsalvador.com/articulos/10-ventajas-de-la-rse-para-las-companias/

Ruangviset, J., Jiraporn, P., & Kim, J. C. (2014). How does corporate governance influence corporate social responsibility? *Procedia: Social and Behavioral Sciences*, *143*, 1055–1057. doi:10.1016/j.sbspro.2014.07.554

Rubel, M. R. B., Kee, D. M. H., Quah, C. H., & Rimi, N. N. (2017). Ethical climate and employee turnover intention in the ready-made garment industry of Bangladesh. *Global Business and Organizational Excellence*, *36*(2), 61–73. doi:10.1002/joe.21770

Ruíz-Lozano, M., de los Ríos Berjillos, A., & Lara, S. M. (2016). ¿Son los códigos éticos un instrumento de gestión de la responsabilidad social? Un estudio exploratorio en Andalucía. *Intangible Capital*, *12*(2), 462–486. doi:10.3926/ic.702

Rumelt, R. (2011). *Good strategy bad strategy: The difference and why it matters.* Crown Business.

Rupp, D. E., Ganapathi, J., Aguilera, R. V., & Williams, C. A. (2006). Employee reactions to corporate social responsibility: An organizational justice framework. Journal of Organizational Behavior: The International Journal of Industrial. *Occupational and Organizational Psychology and Behavior*, *27*(4), 537–543. doi:10.1002/job.380

Rupp, D. E., & Mallory, D. B. (2015). Corporate social responsibility: Psychological, person-centric, and progressing. *Annual Review of Organizational Psychology and Organizational Behavior*, *2*(1), 211–236. doi:10.1146/annurev-orgpsych-032414-111505

Russo, A., & Perrini, F. (2010). Investigating stakeholder theory and social capital: CSR in large firms and SMEs. *Journal of Business Ethics*, *91*(2), 207–221. doi:10.100710551-009-0079-z

Russo, A., & Tencati, A. (2009). Formal vs. informal CSR strategies: Evidence from Italian micro, small, medium-sized, and large firms. *Journal of Business Ethics*, *85*(2), 339–353. doi:10.100710551-008-9736-x

Russo, M. V., & Fouts, P. A. (1997). A resource-based perspective on corporate environmental performance and profitability. *Academy of Management Journal*, *40*, 534–559.

Rutherfoord, R., Blackburn, R. A., & Spence, L. J. (2000). Environmental management and the small firm. *International Journal of Entrepreneurial Behavior & Research.*

Sachdev, S. B., & Verma, H. V. (2004). Relative importance of service quality dimensions: A multisectoral study. *Journal of Services Research*, *4*(1).

Sako, M., & Helper, S. (1998). Determinants of trust in supplier relations: Evidence from the automotive industry in Japan and the United States. *Journal of Economic Behavior & Organization*, *34*(3), 387–417. doi:10.1016/S0167-2681(97)00082-6

Salancik, G. R., & Pfeffer, J. (1978). A social information processing approach to job attitudes and task design. *Administrative Science Quarterly*, *23*(2), 224–253. doi:10.2307/2392563 PMID:10307892

Sangle, S. (2010). Empirical analysis of determinants of adoption of proactive environmental strategies in India. *Business Strategy and the Environment*, *19*(1), 51–63.

Santos, M. J. (2014). Theoretical contributions towards rethinking corporate social responsibility. *Management Research*, *12*(3), 288–307. doi:10.1108/MRJIAM-12-2013-0533

Sarkar, S., & Searcy, C. (2016). Zeitgeist or chameleon? A quantitative analysis of CSR definitions. *Journal of Cleaner Production*, *135*, 1423–1435. doi:10.1016/j.jclepro.2016.06.157

Sarkis, J. (2012). Models for Compassionate Operations. *International Journal of Production Economics*, *139*(2), 359–365. doi:10.1016/j.ijpe.2012.06.018

Sarstedt, M., Hair, J. F., Ringle, C. M., Thiele, K. O., & Gudergan, S. P. (2016). Estimation Issues with PLS and CBSEM: Where the bias lies! *Journal of Business Research*, *69*(10), 3998–4010. doi:10.1016/j.jbusres.2016.06.007

Saxenian, A., & Hsu, J. Y. (2001). The Silicon Valley–Hsinchu connection: Technical communities and industrial upgrading. *Industrial and Corporate Change*, *10*(4), 893–920. doi:10.1093/icc/10.4.893

Schad, J., & Bansal, P. (2018). Seeing the Forest and the Trees: How a Systems Perspective Informs Paradox Research: How a Systems Perspective Informs Paradox Research. *Journal of Management Studies*, *55*(8), 1490–1506. doi:10.1111/joms.12398

Schaltegger, S., & Burritt, R. L. (2010). Sustainability accounting for companies: Catchphrase or decision support for business leaders? *Journal of World Business*, *45*(4), 375–384. doi:10.1016/j.jwb.2009.08.002

Schaltegger, S., Hansen, E. G., & Lüdeke-Freund, F. (2016). Business Models for Sustainability: Origins, Present Research, and Future Avenues. *Organization & Environment*, *29*(1), 3–10. doi:10.1177/1086026615599806

Schaltegger, S., & Wagner, M. (2006). Integrative management of sustainability performance, measurement and reporting. *International Journal of Accounting. Auditing and Performance Evaluation*, *3*(1), 1–19. doi:10.1504/IJAAPE.2006.010098

Schaltegger, S., & Wagner, M. (2011). Sustainable Entrepreneurship and Sustainability Innovation: Categories and Interactions. *Business Strategy and the Environment*, *20*(4), 222–237. doi:10.1002/bse.682

Schaper, M. (2010). *Making Ecopreneurs: Developing Sustainable Entrepreneurship*. Gower/Ashgate Pub.

Schmidt, P., & Santos, J. L. (2002). *Avaliação de ativos intangíveis*. Atlas.

Schmitz, P., Francesconi, E., Hajlaoui, N., & Batouche, B. (2017, June). Towards a Public Multilingual Knowledge Management Infrastructure for the European Digital Single Market. In LDK Workshops (pp. 33-42). Academic Press.

Schneider, B., Parkington, J. J., & Buxton, V. M. (1980). Employee and customer perceptions of service in banks. *Administrative Science Quarterly*, *25*(2), 252–267. doi:10.2307/2392454

Schønning, A., Walther, A., Machold, S., & Huse, M. (2019). The Effects of Directors 'Exploratory, Transformative and Exploitative Learning on Boards' Strategic Involvement: An Absorptive Capacity Perspective. *European Management Review*, *16*(3), 683–698. doi:10.1111/emre.12186

Schramm, C. (2010). All Entrepreneurship is Social. *Stanford Social Innovation Review*, *7*, 20–22.

Schuler, D. A., & Cording, M. (2006). A corporate social performance–corporate financial performance behavioral model for consumers. *Academy of Management Review*, *31*(3), 540–558. doi:10.5465/amr.2006.21318916

Schwartz, M. (2001). The nature of the relationship between corporate codes of ethics and behaviour. *Journal of Business Ethics*, *32*(3), 247–262. doi:10.1023/A:1010787607771

Schwartz, M. S., & Carroll, A. B. (2003). Corporate social responsibility: A three-domain approach. *Business Ethics Quarterly*, *13*(4), 503–530. doi:10.5840/beq200313435

Schwartz, M. S., & Carroll, A. B. (2008). Integrating and unifying competing and complementary frameworks: The search for a common core in the business and society field. *Business & Society*, *47*(2), 148–186. doi:10.1177/0007650306297942

Scott, R. W. (1995). *Institutions and Organizations.* SAGE Publications.

Scott, W. R. (2003). *Organizations. Rational, Natural, and Open Systems* (5th ed.). Prentice-Hall.

Scott, W. R., & Davis, G. F. (2015). *Organizations and organizing: Rational, natural and open systems perspectives.* Routledge.

Searcy, C. (2012). Corporate sustainability performance measurement systems: A review and research agenda. *Journal of Business Ethics*, *107*(3), 239–253. doi:10.100710551-011-1038-z

Secchi, D. (2007). Utilitarian, managerial and relational theories of corporate social responsibility. *International Journal of Management Reviews*, *9*(4), 347–373. doi:10.1111/j.1468-2370.2007.00215.x

Seiffert, M. E. B. (2008). Environmental impact evaluation using a cooperative model for implementing EMS (ISO 14001) in small and medium-sized enterprises. *Journal of Cleaner Production*, *16*(14), 1447–1461. doi:10.1016/j.jclepro.2007.10.001

Selnes, F., & Sallis, J. (2003). Promoting relationship learning. *Journal of Marketing*, *67*(3), 80–95. doi:10.1509/jmkg.67.3.80.18656

Sethi, S. P. (1975). Dimensions of corporate social performance: An analytical framework. *California Management Review*, *17*(3), 58.

Setó-Pamies, D. (2015). The relationship between women directors and corporate social responsibility. *Corporate Social Responsibility and Environmental Management*, *22*(6), 334–345. doi:10.1002/csr.1349

Sforzi, F. (2008). Unas realidades ignoradas: de Marshall a Becattini. *Mediterráneo Económico*, (13), 43-54.

Sforzi, F. (2002). Los distritos industriales ante el reto de la globalización. *Geographicalia*, (41), 5–18. doi:10.26754/ojs_geoph/geoph.2002411364

Shahab, Y., Ntim, C. G., Chengang, Y., Ullah, F., & Fosu, S. (2018). Environmental policy, environmental performance, and financial distress in China: Do top management team characteristics matter? *Business Strategy and the Environment*, *27*(8), 1635–1652. doi:10.1002/bse.2229

Sharma, S., Sharma, J., & Devi, A. (2009). Corporate social responsibility: the key role of human resource management. *Business Intelligence Journal*, *2*(1), 205-213. doi: 10.1.1.514.7758

Sharma, S. (2000). Managerial interpretations and organizational context as predictors of corporate choice of environmental strategy. *Academy of Management Journal*, *43*(4), 681–697.

Sharma, S., & Henriques, I. (2005). Stakeholder influences on sustainability practices in the canadian forest products industry. *Strategic Management Journal*, *26*(2), 159–180. doi:10.1002mj.439

Sharma, S., & Vredenburg, H. (1998). Proactive corporate environmental strategy and the development of competitively valuable organizational capabilities. *Strategic Management Journal*, *19*(8), 729–753. doi:10.1002/(SICI)1097-0266(199808)19:8<729::AID-SMJ967>3.0.CO;2-4

Shaw, W. H., & Barry, V. (2015). *Moral issues in business* (6th ed.). Wadsworth.

Shea, C. T., & Hawn, O. V. (2019). Microfoundations of Corporate Social Responsibility and Irresponsibility. *Academy of Management Journal*, *62*(5), 1609–1642. doi:10.5465/amj.2014.0795

Sheehy, B. (2015). Defining CSR: Problems and solutions. *Journal of Business Ethics*, *131*(3), 625–648. doi:10.100710551-014-2281-x

Shen, N., Au, K., & Li, W. (2019). Strategic alignment of intangible assets: The role of corporate social responsibility. *Asia Pacific Journal of Management*. Advance online publication. doi:10.100710490-019-09681-1

Shevchenko, A., Lévesque, M., & Pagell, M. (2016). Why Firms Delay Reaching True Sustainability: Firms Delaying in Reaching True Sustainability. *Journal of Management Studies*, *53*(5), 911-935.

Shih, S. C., Hsu, S. H. Y., Zhu, Z., & Balasubramanian, S. K. (2012). Knowledge Sharing, a Key Role in the Downstream Supply Chain. *Information & Management*, *49*(2), 70–80. doi:10.1016/j.im.2012.01.001

Shin, I., Hur, W. M., & Kang, S. (2016). Employees' perceptions of corporate social responsibility and job performance: A sequential mediation model. *Sustainability*, *8*(5), 1–12. doi:10.3390u8050493

Shrivastava, P. (1995). Environmental technologies and competitive advantage. *Strategic Management Journal*, *16*(S1), 183–200. doi:10.1002mj.4250160923

Shuli, G., & Suwandee, S. (2017). Effect of corporate social responsibility on employee job performance: A case study of household products manufacturers in southern China. *Journal of Thai Interdisciplinary Research*, *12*(5), 57–63. doi:10.14456/jtir.2017.43

Simões, C., & Sebastiani, R. (2017). The nature of the relationship between corporate identity and corporate sustainability: Evidence from the retail industry. *Business Ethics Quarterly*, *27*(3), 423–453. doi:10.1017/beq.2017.15

Simon, H. A. (1993). Altruism and economics. *The American Economic Review*, *83*(2), 156–161.

Sinéad, R. (2014). Developing social capital in buyer-supplier relationships: The contingent effect of relationship-specific adaptations. *International Journal of Production Economics*, *151*, 89–89. doi:10.1016/j.ijpe.2014.01.008

Singhapakdi, A., Lee, D. J., Sirgy, M. J., & Senasu, K. (2015). The impact of incongruity between an organization's CSR orientation and its employees' CSR orientation on employees' quality of work life. *Journal of Business Research*, *68*(1), 60–66. doi:10.1016/j.jbusres.2014.05.007

Singhapakdi, A., & Vitell, S. (2007). Institutionalization of ethics and its consequences: A survey of marketing professionals. *Journal of the Academy of Marketing Science*, *35*(June), 284–294. doi:10.100711747-007-0030-8

Singh, K., & Mitchell, W. (1996). Precarious collaboration: Business survival after partners shut down or form new partnerships. *Strategic Management Journal*, *17*(S1), 99–115. doi:10.1002mj.4250171008

Sirsly, C. A., & Lamertz, K. (2007). When Does a Corporate Social Responsibility Initiative Provide a First-mover Advantage. *Business & Society*, *47*(3), 343–369. doi:10.1177/0007650307299221

Skandia. (1999). *Skandia annual report 1998*. Retrieved from http://www.skandia.com/financials/pdfs/e9712Human.pdf

Slack, R. E., Corlett, S., & Morris, R. (2015). Exploring employee engagement with (corporate) social responsibility: A social exchange perspective on organisational participation. *Journal of Business Ethics, 127*(3), 537–548. doi:10.100710551-014-2057-3

Slocombe, T. E., & Dougherty, T. W. (1998). Dissecting organizational commitment and its relationship with employee behavior. *Journal of Business and Psychology, 12*(4), 469–491. doi:10.1023/A:1025055122988

SMLC (Smart Manufacturing Leadership Coalition). (2011). *SMLC. Implementing 21st century smart manufacturing*. https://smartmanufacturingcoalition.org/sites/default/files/implementing_21st_century_smart_manufacturing_report_2011_0.pdf

Snell, R. S., Chak, A. M. K., & Chu, J. W. H. (1996). Codes of ethics in Hong Kong: espousal, evidence and impact. *Proceedings of the ANZAM*, 96.

Soler, L. E. V., & Celestino, D. J. C. O. (2007). Evaluating the scope of IC in firms' value. *Journal of Intellectual Capital, 8*(3), 470–493. doi:10.1108/14691930710774876

Somers, M. J. (2001). Ethical codes of conduct and organizational context: A study of the relationship between codes of conduct, employee behavior and organizational values. *Journal of Business Ethics, 30*(2), 185–195. doi:10.1023/A:1006457810654

Song, W., & Yu, H. (2018). Green Innovation Strategy and Green Innovation: The Roles of Green Creativity and Green Organizational Identity. *Corporate Social Responsibility and Environmental Management, 25*(2), 135–150. doi:10.1002/csr.1445

Sorenson, O., & Audia, P. G. (2000). The social structure of entrepreneurial activity: Geographic concentration of footwear production in the United States, 1940–1989. *American Journal of Sociology, 106*(2), 424–462. doi:10.1086/316962

Spence, L. J. (1999). Does size matter? The state of the art in small business ethics. *Business Ethics (Oxford, England), 8*(3), 163–174. doi:10.1111/1467-8608.00144

Spence, L. J. (2007). CSR and small business in a European policy context: The five "C" s of CSR and small business research agenda 2007. *Business and Society Review, 112*(4), 533–552. doi:10.1111/j.1467-8594.2007.00308.x

Spence, L. J., Coles, A.-M., & Harris, L. (2001). The forgotten stakeholder? Ethics and social responsibility in relation to competitors. *Business and Society Review, 106*(4), 331–352. doi:10.1111/0045-3609.00119

Spence, L., & Bourlakis, M. (2009). The evolution from corporate social responsibility to supply chain responsibility: The case of Waitrose. *Supply Chain Management, 14*(4), 291–302. doi:10.1108/13598540910970126

Spender, J. C. (1996). Making knowledge the basis of a dynamic theory of the firm. *Strategic Management Journal, 17*(S2), 45–62. doi:10.1002mj.4250171106

Spiller, R. (2000). Ethical Business and Investment: A Model for Business and Society. *Journal of Business Ethics, 27*(1/2), 149–160. doi:10.1023/A:1006445915026

Spinelli, S. Jr, & Adams, R. (2012). *New venture creation: entrepreneurship for the 21st century*. The McGraw-Hill Companies.

Srikantaiah, T. K., & Koenig, E. D. (2000). *Knowledge management: For the information professional*. Information Today, Inc.

Stahl, G. K., & Sully de Luque, M. (2014). Antecedents of Responsible Leader Behavior: A Research Synthesis, Conceptual Framework, and Agenda for Future Research. *The Academy of Management Perspectives*, *28*(3), 235–254. doi:10.5465/amp.2013.0126

Stevens, B. (1994). An analysis of corporate ethical code studies: Where do we go from here? *Journal of Business Ethics*, *13*(1), 63–69. doi:10.1007/BF00877156

Stevens, B. (1999). Communicating ethical values: A study of employee perceptions. *Journal of Business Ethics*, *20*(2), 113–120. doi:10.1023/A:1005869431079

Stewart, T. A. (1997). *Intellectual Capital: The New Wealth of Organizations*. Doubleday.

Stewart, T. A. (1998). *Capital intelectual: A nova vantagem competitiva das empresas*. Campus.

Stewart, T., & Ruckdeschel, C. (1998). Intellectual capital: The new wealth of organizations. *Performance Improvement*, *37*(7), 56–59. doi:10.1002/pfi.4140370713

Stigler, G. J. (1962). Information in the labor market. *Journal of Political Economy*, *70*(5), 94–105. doi:10.1086/258727

Stoian, C., & Zaharia, R. M. (2012). CSR development in post-communist economies: Employees' expectations regarding corporate socially responsible behaviour–the case of Romania. *Business Ethics (Oxford, England)*, *21*(4), 380–401. doi:10.1111/beer.12000

Strand, R. (2014). Strategic leadership of corporate sustainability. *Journal of Business Ethics*, *123*(4), 687–706. doi:10.100710551-013-2017-3

Strike, V. M., Gao, J., & Bansal, P. (2006). Being Good while Being Bad: Social Responsibility and International Diversification of US Firms. *Journal of International Business Studies*, *37*(6), 850–862. doi:10.1057/palgrave.jibs.8400226

Stuart, I., Deckert, P., McCutcheon, D., & Kunst, R. (1998). Case study: A leveraged learning network. *MIT Sloan Management Review*, *39*(4), 81.

Styles, C. (2006). Networking capability and international entrepreneurship: How networks function in Australian born global firms. *International Marketing Review*, *23*(5), 549–572. doi:10.1108/02651330610703445

Subramaniam, M., & Youndt, M. A. (2005). The influence of intellectual capital on the types of innovative capabilities. *Academy of Management Journal*, *48*(3), 450–463. doi:10.5465/amj.2005.17407911

Sukmadi, B. H. (2019). The Effect of Leadership and Ethics on Motivation in The Military. *International Humanities and Applied Sciences Journal.*, *2*(3), 49–57. doi:10.22441/ihasj.2019.v2i3.05

Su, L., & Swanson, S. R. (2019). Perceived corporate social responsibility's impact on the well-being and supportive green behaviors of hotel employees: The mediating role of the employee-corporate relationship. *Tourism Management*, *72*, 437–450. doi:10.1016/j.tourman.2019.01.009

Sullivan, P. (2001). *Value-driven Intellectual capital: How to convert intangible corporate Assets into market value*. Wiley.

Sullivan, P. (2001). *Value-driven Intellectual Capital: How to convert intangible corporate Assets into market value*. Wiley.

Sullivan, S. E., Carraher, S. M., Baker, L., Cochrane, D., & Robinson, F. (2009). The Entrepreneurial Dilemma: Grow or Status Quo? A Real Case. *The Journal of Applied Management and Entrepreneurship*, *14*(4), 37.

Surroca, J., Tribó, J. A., & Zahra, S. A. (2013). Stakeholder Pressure on MNEs and the Transfer of Socially Irresponsible Practices to Subsidiaries. *Academy of Management Journal*, *56*(2), 549–572. doi:10.5465/amj.2010.0962

Sveiby, K. E. (2007). *Methods for measuring intangible assets*. Retrieved from https://www.sveiby.com/articles/IntangAss/CompanyMonitor.html

Svensson, G., Wood, G., & Callaghan, M. (2006). Codes of ethics in corporate Sweden. *Corporate Governance: The International Journal of Business in Society, 6*(5), 547-566.

Swanson, D. L. (1999). Toward an integrative theory of business and society: A research strategy for corporate social performance. *Academy of Management Review, 24*(3), 506–521. doi:10.5465/amr.1999.2202134

Sweeney, L. (2009). *A Study of Current Practice of Corporate Social Responsibility (CSR) and an Examination of the Relationship between CSR and Financial Performance Using Structural Equation Modelling (SEM)* (PhD thesis). Dublin Institute of Technology.

Szekely, F., & Knirsch, M. (2005). Responsible leadership and corporate social responsibility: Metrics for sustainable performance. *European Management Journal, 23*(6), 628–647. doi:10.1016/j.emj.2005.10.009

Tang, Y., Qian, C., Chen, G., & Shen, R. (2015). How CEO hubris affects corporate social (ir)responsibility: CEO Hubris and CSR. *Strategic Management Journal, 36*(9), 1338–1357. doi:10.1002mj.2286

Tanis, M., & Beukeboom, C. J. (2011). Organizational identification and the communication of identity: Effects of message characteristics on cognitive and affective identification. *British Journal of Social Psychology, 50*(4), 784–791. doi:10.1111/j.2044-8309.2011.02036.x PMID:21749414

Tashman, P., & Raelin, J. (2013). Who and what really matters to the firm: Moving stakeholder salience beyond managerial perceptions. *Business Ethics Quarterly, 23*(4), 591–616. doi:10.5840/beq201323441

Tata. (n.d.). Retrieved on 06 December 2019 from https://www.tata.com/about-us/tata-group-our-heritage/tata-titans/jamsetji-tata

Taylor, P. J. (2005). Leading world cities: Empirical evaluations of urban nodes in multiple networks. *Urban Studies (Edinburgh, Scotland), 42*(9), 1593–1608. doi:10.1080/00420980500185504

Teece, D. J. (1986). *Profiting from technological innovation: Implications for integration, collaboration, licensing and public policy*. Academic Press.

Teece, D. J. (2000). Strategies for managing knowledge assets: The role of firm structure and industrial context. *Long Range Planning, 33*(1), 35–54. doi:10.1016/S0024-6301(99)00117-X

Teece, D. J. (2007). Explicating dynamic capabilities: The nature and microfoundations of (sustainable) enterprise performance. *Strategic Management Journal, 28*(13), 1319–1350. doi:10.1002mj.640

Teece, D. J. (2012). Dynamic Capabilities: Routines versus Entrepreneurial Action: Routines versus Entrepreneurial Action. *Journal of Management Studies, 49*(8), 1395–1401. doi:10.1111/j.1467-6486.2012.01080.x

Teece, D. J., Pisano, G., & Shuen, A. (1997). Dynamic capabilities and strategic management. *Strategic Management Journal, 18*(7), 509–533. doi:10.1002/(SICI)1097-0266(199708)18:7<509::AID-SMJ882>3.0.CO;2-Z

Tenbrunsel, A. E., Wade-Benzoni, K. A., Messick, D. M., & Bazerman, M. H. (2000). Understanding the influence of environmental standards on judgments and choices. *Academy of Management Journal, 43*(5), 854–866.

Tepthong, S. (2014). *Social entrepreneurship and organizational performance: combining the resource dependence and resource-based views*. National Institute of Development Administration.

Tesavrita, C., Suryadi, K., Wiratmadja, I. I., & Govindaraju, R. (2017). Intra-organizational and inter-organizational knowledge sharing in collaborative learning process: A conceptual framework for SME. *2017 4th International Conference on Industrial Engineering and Applications, ICIEA 2017*, 187–191. 10.1109/IEA.2017.7939204

Testa, F., Battaglia, M., & Bianchi, L. (2012). The diffusion of CSR initiatives among SMEs in industrial clusters: Some findings from Italian experiences. *International Journal of Technology Management*, *58*(1/2), 152–170. doi:10.1504/IJTM.2012.045793

Testa, F., Gusmerottia, N. M., Corsini, F., Passetti, E., & Iraldo, F. (2016). Factors Affecting Environmental Management by Small and Micro Firms: The Importance of Entrepreneurs' Attitudes and Environmental Investment. *Corporate Social Responsibility and Environmental Management*, *23*(6), 373–385. doi:10.1002/csr.1382

The Hofstede Centre. (2016). *The Hofstede Centre website*. Retrieved on 1 March 2016 from http://geert-hofstede.com/sweden.html

Tian, Q., & Robertson, J. L. (2019). How and when does perceived CSR affect employees' engagement in voluntary pro-environmental behavior? *Journal of Business Ethics*, *155*(2), 399–412. doi:10.100710551-017-3497-3

Tilley, F. (2000). Small firm environmental ethics: How deep do they go? *Business Ethics (Oxford, England)*, *9*(1), 31–41. doi:10.1111/1467-8608.00167

Tokgöz, N. (2012). *Genel İşletme*. Anadolu Üniversitesi Yayınları.

Tolukan, E., Şahin, M. Y., & Koç, M. (2016). The relationship of organizational identification levels of gymnastic trainers and the intention to leave the job. *Electronic Turkish Studies*, *11*(8), 377–398. doi:10.7827/TurkishStudies.9558

Tom, R. (n.d.). The Psychology of Procedural Justice: A Test of the Group-value Model. *Journal of Personality and Social Psychology*, *57*, 830–838.

Torreblanca, F. (2017). *Responsabilidad social corporativa en la estrategia de marketing*. Retrieved from: https://franciscotorreblanca.es/responsabilidad-social-corporativa-marketing/

Trevino, L. K., & Nelson, K. A. (1999). Managing Business Ethics. John Wiley & Sons.

Tsai, W., & Ghoshal, S. (1998). Social Capital and value creation: The role of intrafirm networks. *Academy of Management Journal*, *41*, 464–476.

Tseng, C. Y., & James Goo, Y. J. (2005). Intellectual capital and corporate value in an emerging economy: Empirical study of Taiwanese manufacturers. *R & D Management*, *35*(2), 187–201. doi:10.1111/j.1467-9310.2005.00382.x

Tsoutsoura, M. (2004). *Corporate social responsibility and financial performance*. Academic Press.

Tsui, A. S., Enderle, G., & Jiang, K. (2018). Income Inequality in the United States: Reflections on the Role of Corporations. *Academy of Management Review*, *43*(1), 156–168. doi:10.5465/amr.2016.0527

Turker, D. (2009). Measuring corporate social responsibility: A scale development study. *Journal of Business Ethics*, *85*(4), 411–427. doi:10.100710551-008-9780-6

Tuzzolino, F., & Armandi, B. R. (1981). A need-hierarchy framework for assessing corporate social responsibility. *Academy of Management Review*, *6*(1), 21–28. doi:10.5465/amr.1981.4287982

Tyler, T. R. (1989). The psychology of procedural justice: A test of the group-value model. *Journal of Personality and Social Psychology*, *57*(5), 830–838. doi:10.1037/0022-3514.57.5.830

Tyler, T. R., & Lind, E. A. (1992). A Relational Model of Authority in Groups. *Advances in Experimental Social Psychology*, 24.

Ulaga, W., & Eggert, A. (2006). Value-based differentiation in business relationships: Gaining and sustaining key supplier status. *Journal of Marketing*, *70*(1), 119–136. doi:10.1509/jmkg.2006.70.1.119

Ulrich, D. (1998). *Delivering results: A new mandate for human resource professionals*. Harward Business School Press.

United Nations. (1999, February 1). *Secretary-General address to the World Economic Forum in Davos* [Press Release SG/SM/6881]. New York: UN.

United Nations. (2020). *The United Nations website*. Retrieved on 22 May 2020 from https://www.un.org/sustainabledevelopment/es/development-agenda/

Unruh, G., Kiron, D., Kruschwitz, N., Reeves, M., Rubel, H., & zum Felde, A. M. (2016). Investing For a Sustainable Future. *MIT Sloan Management Review*.

Urban, B., & Joubert, G. C. D. S. (2017). Multidimensional and comparative study on intellectual capital and organisational performance. *Journal of Business Economics and Management*, *18*(1), 84–99. doi:10.3846/16111699.2016.1255990

Utting, P. (2000). *Business responsibility for sustainable development* (No. 2). Geneva 2000 Occasional Paper.

Uzzi, B. (1997). Social structure and competition in interfirm networks: The paradox of embeddedness. *Administrative Science Quarterly*, *42*(1), 35–67. doi:10.2307/2393808

Vachon, S., & Klassen, R. D. (2006). Extending green practices across the supply chain: The impact of upstream and downstream integration. *International Journal of Operations & Production Management*, *26*(7), 795–821. doi:10.1108/01443570610672248

Vachon, S., & Klassen, R. D. (2008). Environmental management and manufacturing performance: The role of collaboration in the supply chain. *International Journal of Production Economics*, *111*(2), 299–315. doi:10.1016/j.ijpe.2006.11.030

Valaei, N., Rezaei, S., & Wan-Ismail, W. K. (2017). Examining Learning Strategies, Creativity, and Innovation at SMEs using fuzzy set Qualitative Comparative Analysis and PLS Path Modeling. *Journal of Business Research*, *70*, 224–233. doi:10.1016/j.jbusres.2016.08.016

Van Den Bosch, F. A., Volberda, H. W., & De Boer, M. (1999). Coevolution of firm absorptive capacity and knowledge environment: Organizational forms and combinative capabilities. *Organization Science*, *10*(5), 551–568. doi:10.1287/orsc.10.5.551

Van den Brink, T. W. M., & van der Woerd, F. (2004). Industry specific sustainability benchmarks: An ECSF pilot bridging corporate sustainability with social responsible investments. *Journal of Business Ethics*, *55*(2), 187–203. doi:10.100710551-004-1901-2

van der Zwart, A. (2002). *Reputatie mechanisme in beweging: doelstreffend bij issues aan MVO?* (Master thesis). Erasmus University Rotterdam.

Van Marrewijk, M. (2003). Concepts and definitions of CSR and corporate sustainability: Between agency and communion. *Journal of Business Ethics*, *44*(2/3), 95–105. doi:10.1023/A:1023331212247

van Wijk, J., Zietsma, C., Dorado, S., de Bakker, F. G. A., & Martí, I. (2019). Social Innovation: Integrating Micro, Meso, and Macro Level Insights From Institutional Theory. *Business & Society*, *58*(5), 887–918. doi:10.1177/0007650318789104

Van Wijk, R., Jansen, J. J. P., & Lyles, M. A. (2008). Inter- and intra-organizational knowledge transfer : A Meta-analytic review and assessment of its antecedents and consequences. *Journal of Management Studies*, *45*(4), 830–853. doi:10.1111/j.1467-6486.2008.00771.x

VanVoorhis, C. W., & Morgan, B. L. (2007). Understanding power and rules of thumb for determining sample sizes. *Tutorials in Quantitative Methods for Psychology*, *3*(2), 43–50. doi:10.20982/tqmp.03.2.p043

Vázquez-Carrasco, R., & López-Pérez, M. E. (2013). Small & medium-sized enterprises and Corporate Social Responsibility: A systematic review of the literature. *Quality & Quantity*, *47*(6), 3205–3218. doi:10.100711135-012-9713-4

Vázquez-Maguirre, M., & Portales, L. (2014). La empresa social como detonadora de calidad de vida y desarrollo sustentable en comunidades rurales [Social enterprise as a generator of quality of life and sustainable development in rural communities]. *Pensamiento & Gestión,* (37), 255-284.

Vecchio, N. (2010). Réseaux de conseils d'administration et adoption de pratiques de gouvernance d'entreprise. *Revue Française de Gestion*, *202*(3), 145–161. doi:10.3166/rfg.202.145-161

Veleva, V. (2008). Product stewardship in the United States: the changing policy landscape and the role of business. *Sustainability: Science. Practice and Policy*, *4*(2), 29–35.

Velo, D. (2003). Corporate social responsibility in the global market. *European Union Review*, *8*(1–2), 29–42.

Villafañe, J. (2004). *La buena reputación*. Pirámide.

Villena, V. H., Revilla, E., & Choi, T. Y. (2011). The dark side of buyer–supplier relationships: A social capital perspective. *Journal of Operations Management*, *29*(6), 561–576. doi:10.1016/j.jom.2010.09.001

Villers, Ch., & Sharma, U. (2020). A critical reflection on the future of financial, intellectual capital, sustainability and integrated reporting. *Critical Perspectives on Accounting*, *79*(July), 101999. Advance online publication. doi:10.1016/j.cpa.2017.05.003

Vives, A. (2006). Social and Environmental Responsibility in Small and Medium Enterprises in Latin America. *Journal of Corporate Citizenship*, *21*(21), 39–50. doi:10.9774/GLEAF.4700.2006.sp.00006

Vogel, D. (2006). *The market for virtue: The potential and limits of corporate social responsibility* (2nd ed.). Brookings Institution Press. Retrieved from http://www.jstor.org/stable/10.7864/j.ctt6wpg2c

Vollenbroek, F. A. (2002). Sustainable Development and the Challenge of Innovation. *Journal of Cleaner Production*, *10*(3), 215–223. doi:10.1016/S0959-6526(01)00048-8

Von Weltzien Hoivik, H. (2011). Embedding CSR as a learning and knowledge creating process: The case for SMEs in Norway. *Journal of Management Development*, *30*(10), 1067–1084. doi:10.1108/02621711111182547

Von Weltzien Høivik, H., & Shankar, D. (2011). How can SMEs in a cluster respond to global demands for corporate responsibility? *Journal of Business Ethics*, *101*(2), 175–195. doi:10.100710551-010-0708-6

Vos, J., & Achterkamp, M. C. (2015). Bridging the transactional and relational view on management-stakeholder cooperation. *The International Journal of Organizational Analysis*, *23*(4), 652–663. doi:10.1108/IJOA-07-2013-0692

Waddock, S. (2004). Parallel universes: Companies, academics, and the progress of corporate citizenship. *Business and Society Review: Journal of the Center for Business Ethics at Bentley College*, *109*(1), 5–42. doi:10.1111/j.0045-3609.2004.00002.x

Waddock, S., & Graves, S. (1997). The corporate social performance - financial performance link. *Strategic Management Journal*, *18*(4), 303–319. doi:10.1002/(SICI)1097-0266(199704)18:4<303::AID-SMJ869>3.0.CO;2-G

Wagner, M. (2009). Innovation and Competitive Advantages from the Integration of Strategic Aspects with Social and Environmental Management in European Firms. *Business Strategy and the Environment, 18*(5), 291–306. doi:10.1002/bse.585

Waheed, A., Zhang, Q., Rashid, Y., & Zaman Khan, S. (2020). The impact of corporate social responsibility on buying tendencies from the perspective of stakeholder theory and practices. *Corporate Social Responsibility and Environmental Management, 27*(3), 1307–1315. doi:10.1002/csr.1885

Walley, N., & Whitehead, B. (1994). It's not easy being green. *Reader in Business and the Environment, 36*(81), 4.

Walls, J. L., & Berrone, P. (2017). The Power of One to Make a Difference: How Informal and Formal CEO Power Affect Environmental Sustainability. *Journal of Business Ethics, 145*(2), 293–308. doi:10.100710551-015-2902-z

Walls, L., Berrone, P., & Phan, H. (2012). Corporate governance and environmental performance: Is there really a link? *Strategic Management Journal, 33*(8), 885–913. doi:10.1002mj.1952

Walton, C. C. (1967). *Corporate social responsibilities*. Wadsworth Publishing Company.

Wang, C.N., Chang, Y.L., Huang, Q.H., & Wang, C.H. (2011). Assessment on intelectual capital management for Taiwanese pharmaceutical industry: using GRA and MPI. *Afr. J. Bus. Manag., 5*(7), 2950-2958.

Wang, G., Dou, W., Zhu, W., & Zhou, N. (2015). The effects of firm capabilities on external collaboration and performance: The moderating role of market turbulence. *Journal of Business Research, 68*(9), 1928–1936. doi:10.1016/j.jbusres.2015.01.002

Wang, H., Tong, L., Takeuchi, R., & George, G. (2016). Corporate social responsibility: An overview and new research directions. *Academy of Management Journal, 59*(2), 534–544. doi:10.5465/amj.2016.5001

Wang, J., Xue, Y., Sun, X., & Yang, J. (2020). Green Learning orientation, Green knowledge acquisition and ambidextrous Green innovation. *Journal of Cleaner Production, 250*, 119475. doi:10.1016/j.jclepro.2019.119475

Wang, Y., Xu, S., & Wang, Y. (2020). The consequences of employees' perceived corporate social responsibility: A meta-analysis. *Business Ethics (Oxford, England), 29*(3), 1–26. doi:10.1111/beer.12273

Wang, Z., & Huigang, L. (2014). Knowledge sharing, intellectual capital and firm performance. *Management Decision, 52*(2), 230–258. doi:10.1108/MD-02-2013-0064

Watts, P., & Holme, L. (1999). *Corporate social responsibility. Meeting changing expectations*. World Business Council for Sustainable Development.

Watts, P., & Holme, L. (2000). *Corporate social responsibility: Making good business sense*. World Business Council for Sustainable Development.

Weerawardena, J., & Sullivan-Mort, G. (2001). Learning, innovation and competitive advantage in not-for-profit aged care marketing: A conceptual model and research propositions. *Journal of Nonprofit & Public Sector Marketing, 9*(3), 53–73. doi:10.1300/J054v09n03_04

Weiss, J. W. (1994). Business ethics: A managerial, stakeholder approach (No. s 287). Belmont, CA: Wadsworth Publishing Company.

Wendra, W., Sule, E. T., Joeliaty, J., & Azis, Y. (2019). Exploring dynamic capabilities, intellectual capital and innovation performance relationship: Evidence from the garment manufacturing. *Business: Theory and Practice, 20*, 123–136. doi:10.3846/btp.2019.12

Werther, W. B. Jr, & Chandler, D. (2010). Strategic corporate social responsibility: Stakeholders in a global environment. *Sage (Atlanta, Ga.)*.

Westhues, M., & Einwiller, S. (2006). Corporate foundations: Their role for corporate social responsibility. *Corporate Reputation Review*, *9*(2), 144–153. doi:10.1057/palgrave.crr.1550019

Westley, F., & Antadze, N. (2010). Making a Difference: Strategies for Scaling Social Innovation for Greater Impact Frances Westley and Nino Antadze A. *Innov. J. Public Sect. Innov. J.*, *15*, 2–20.

Whetten, D. A., Rands, G., & Godfrey, P. (2002). What are the responsibilities of business to society? In A. Pettigrew, H. Thomas, & R. Whittington (Eds.), *Handbook of strategy and management* (pp. 373–408). Sage.

Whitaker, B. G., & Godwin, L. N. (2013). The antecedents of moral imagination in the workplace: A social cognitive theory perspective. *Journal of Business Ethics*, *114*(1), 61–73. doi:10.100710551-012-1327-1

White, G., Lee, A., Yuningsih, Y., Nielsen, C., & Bukh, P. N. (2010). The nature and extent of voluntary intellectual capital disclosures by Australian and UK biotechnology companies. *Journal of Intellectual Capital*, *11*(4), 519–536. doi:10.1108/14691931011085669

Wickert, C. (2016). "Political" corporate social responsibility in small-and medium-sized enterprises: A conceptual framework. *Business & Society*, *55*(6), 792–824. doi:10.1177/0007650314537021

Wiig, K. M. (1997). Integrating intellectual capital and knowledge management. *Long Range Planning*, *30*(3), 399–405. doi:10.1016/S0024-6301(97)90256-9

Wijethilake, C., & Lama, T. (2019). Sustainability core values and sustainability risk management: Moderating effects of top management commitment and stakeholder pressure. *Business Strategy and the Environment*, *28*(1), 143–154. doi:10.1002/bse.2245

Williamson, O. E., & Ouchi, W. G. (1981). The markets and hierarchies and visible hand perspectives. *Perspectives on organization design and behavior*, 347-370.

Williamson, D., Lynch-Wood, G., & Ramsay, J. (2006). Drivers of environmental behaviour in manufacturing SMEs and the implications for CSR. *Journal of Business Ethics*, *67*(3), 317–330. doi:10.100710551-006-9187-1

Williamson, O. E. (1983). Credible commitments: Using hostages to support exchange. *The American Economic Review*, *73*(4), 519–540.

Williamson, O. E. (1985). *The Economic Institutions of Capitalism: Firms, markets, relational Contracting*. Free Press.

Williams, R. J. (2003). Women on corporate boards of directors and their influence on corporate philanthropy. *Journal of Business Ethics*, *42*(1), 1–10. doi:10.1023/A:1021626024014

Wilson, M. (2003). Corporate sustainability: What is it and where does it come from. *Ivey Business Journal*, *67*(6), 1–5.

Winter, S. G. (2003). Understanding dynamic capabilities. *Strategic Management Journal*, *24*(10), 991–995. doi:10.1002mj.318

Winter, S. G. (2012). Capabilities: Their Origins and Ancestry: Capabilities: Their Origins and Ancestry. *Journal of Management Studies*, *49*(8), 1402–1406. doi:10.1111/j.1467-6486.2012.01081.x

Wirth, L. (2015). *La mujer en la gestión empresarial: Cobrando impulso*. Organización Mundial del Trabajo. Ginebra.

Wood, D. J. (1991). Corporate social performance revisited. *Academy of Management. Academy of Management Review*, *16*(4), 691–718. doi:10.5465/amr.1991.4279616

Wood, D. J. (2010). Measuring corporate social performance: A review. *International Journal of Management Reviews*, *12*(1), 50–84. doi:10.1111/j.1468-2370.2009.00274.x

Wood, D. J., & Logsdon, J. M. (2002). Corporate citizenship: From individuals to organizations. *The Ruffin Series*, *3*, 59–94.

Woodward, D., Edwards, P., & Birkin, F. (2001). Some Evidence on Executives Views of Corporate Social Responsibility. *The British Accounting Review*, *33*(3), 357–397. doi:10.1006/bare.2001.0165

World Commission on Environment and Development. (1987). *Our common future*. United Nations.

Wright, C., & Nyberg, D. (2017). An Inconvenient Truth: How Organizations Translate Climate Change into Business as Usual. *Academy of Management Journal*, *60*(5), 1633–1661. doi:10.5465/amj.2015.0718

Wry, T., & York, J. G. (2017). An Identity- Based Approach to Social Enterprise. *Academy of Management Review*, *42*(3), 437–460. doi:10.5465/amr.2013.0506

Wu, G. C. (2017). Effects of Socially Responsible Supplier Development and Sustainability-Oriented Innovation on Sustainable Development: Empirical Evidence from SMEs. *Corporate Social Responsibility and Environmental Management*, *24*(6), 661–675. doi:10.1002/csr.1435

Wu, M. L. (2006). Corporate social performance, corporate financial performance, and firm size: A meta-analysis. *The Journal of American Academy of Business, Cambridge*, *8*(1), 163–171.

Wunder, T. (2019). *Rethinking strategic management: Sustainable strategizing for positive impact* (1st ed.). Springer Berlin Heidelberg. doi:10.1007/978-3-030-06014-5

Wu, S. H., Lin, L. Y., & Hsu, M. Y. (2007). Intellectual capital, dynamic capabilities and innovative performance of organisations. *International Journal of Technology Management*, *39*(3/4), 279. doi:10.1504/IJTM.2007.013496

Wuyts, S., & Geyskens, I. (2005). The formation of buyer–supplier relationships: Detailed contract drafting and close partner selection. *Journal of Marketing*, *69*(4), 103–117. doi:10.1509/jmkg.2005.69.4.103

Xie, X., Fang, L., Zeng, S., & Huo, J. (2016). How does knowledge inertia affect firms' product innovation? *Journal of Business Research*, *69*(5), 1615–1620. doi:10.1016/j.jbusres.2015.10.027

Yamak, S. (2007). *Kurumsal sosyal sorumluluk kavramının gelişimi*. Beta Yayınları.

Yao, J., & Koga, C. (2017). Sustained competitive advantage and strategic intellectual capital management: Evidence from Japanese high performance small to medium sized enterprises. In J. Guthrie, J. Dumay, F. Ricceri, & C. Nielsen (Eds.), *The Routledge Companion to Intellectual Capital* (pp. 236–251). Routledge. doi:10.4324/9781315393100-15

Ybarra, J. A. (2000). La infomalización como estrategia productiva. Un análisis del calzado valenciano. *Rev. Estud. Reg.*, *57*, 199–217.

Yong, J. Y., Yusliza, M.-Y., Ramayah, T., & Fawehinmi, O. (2019). Nexus between Green intelectual capital and Green human resource management. *Journal of Cleaner Production*, *215*, 363–374. doi:10.1016/j.jclepro.2018.12.306

York, J. G., & Lenox, M. J. (2014). Exploring the sociocultural determinants of *de novo* versus *de alio* entry in emerging industries: Exploring Sociocultural Determinants. *Strategic Management Journal*, *35*(13), 1930–1951. doi:10.1002mj.2187

York, J. G., Vedula, S., & Lenox, M. J. (2018). It's Not Easy Building Green: The Impact of Public Policy, Private Actors, and Regional Logics on Voluntary Standards Adoption. *Academy of Management Journal*, *61*(4), 1492–1523. doi:10.5465/amj.2015.0769

Younis, H., Sundarakani, B., & O'Mahony, B. (2019). Green suppluy chain and corporate performance: Developing a roadmap for future research using a mixed method approach. *IIMB Management Review*. Advance online publication. doi:10.1016/j.iimb.2019.10.011

Yusoff, H., Lehman, G., & Mohd, N. (2006). Environmental engagements through the lens of disclosure practices: A Malaysian story. *Asian Review of Accounting*, *14*(1/2), 122–148. doi:10.1108/13217340610729509

Yusoff, Y. M., Nejati, M., Kee, D. M. H., & Amran, A. (2018). Linking green human resource management practices to environmental performance in hotel industry. *Global Business Review*, *21*(3), 1–18.

Yusoff, Y. M., Omar, M. K., Zaman, M. D. K., & Samand, S. (2019). Do all elements of Green intelectual capital contribute toward business sustainability? Evidence from the Malaysian context using the Partial Least Squares method. *Journal of Cleaner Production*, *234*, 626–637. doi:10.1016/j.jclepro.2019.06.153

Zaheer, A., & Bell, G. G. (2005). Benefiting from network position: Firm capabilities, structural holes, and performance. *Strategic Management Journal*, *26*(9), 809–825. doi:10.1002mj.482

Zaheer, A., & George, G. (2002). Absorptive capacity: A review, reconceptualization, and extension. *Academy of Management Review*, *27*(2), 185–203. doi:10.5465/amr.2002.6587995

Zaheer, A., McEvily, B., & Perrone, V. (1998). Does trust matter? Exploring the effects of interorganizational and interpersonal trust on performance. *Organization Science*, *9*(2), 141–159. doi:10.1287/orsc.9.2.141

Zaheer, A., & Venkatraman, N. (1995). Relational governance as an interorganizational strategy: An empirical test of the role of trust in economic exchange. *Strategic Management Journal*, *16*(5), 373–392. doi:10.1002mj.4250160504

Zaher, D. (2014). How to create a knowledge based organizational culture. *The JF Oberlin Journal of Business Management Studies*, *4*, 63–73.

Zahra, S. A., & Filatotchev, I. (2004). Governance of the entrepreneurial threshold firm: A knowledge - based perspective. *Journal of Management Studies*, *41*(5), 885–897. doi:10.1111/j.1467-6486.2004.00458.x

Zahra, S. A., Filatotchev, I., & Wright, M. (2009). How do threshold firms sustain corporate entrepreneurship? The role of boards and absorptive capacity. *Journal of Business Venturing*, *24*(3), 248–260. doi:10.1016/j.jbusvent.2008.09.001

Zahra, S. A., Neubaum, D. O., & Naldi, L. (2007). The effects of ownership and governance on SMEs' international knowledge-based resources. *Small Business Economics*, *29*(3), 309–327. doi:10.100711187-006-9025-y

Zahra, S. A., & Pearce, J. A. II. (1989). Boards of directors and corporate financial performance: A review and integrative model. *Journal of Management*, *15*(2), 291–334. doi:10.1177/014920638901500208

Zahra, S. A., Sapienza, H. J., & Davidsson, P. (2006). Entrepreneurship and Dynamic Capabilities: A Review, Model and Research Agenda. *Journal of Management Studies*, *43*(3), 917–955. doi:10.1111/j.1467-6486.2006.00616.x

Zaman, U., & Nadeem, R. D. (2019). Linking Corporate Social Responsibility (CSR) and affective organizational commitment: Role of CSR strategic importance and organizational identification. *Pakistan Journal of Commerce and Social Sciences, 13*(3), 704-726.

Zamudio, M. (2018). *Global Reporting Initiative (GRI): el lenguaje universal de la sostenibilidad.* Retrieved from: https://www.esan.edu.pe/conexion/actualidad/2018/08/20/global-reporting-initiative-gri-el-lenguaje-universal-de-la-sostenibilidad/

Zebryte, I., & Jorquera, H. (2017). Chilean tourism sector "B Corporations": evidence of social entrepreneurship and innovation. *International Journal of Entrepreneurial Behavior & Research.*

Zhang, Q., Cao, M., Zhang, F., Liu, J., & Li, X. (2019). Effects of corporate social responsibility on customer satisfaction and organizational attractiveness: A signaling perspective. *Business Ethics (Oxford, England)*, *29*(1), 20–34. doi:10.1111/beer.12243

Zhang, X. (2005). Critical success factors for public–private partnerships in infrastructure development. *Journal of Construction Engineering and Management*, *131*(1), 3–14. doi:10.1061/(ASCE)0733-9364(2005)131:1(3)

Zink, T. (2019). The Inevitable Labor and Environmental Crises and the Need for a New Economic System. *Journal of Management Inquiry*, *28*(3), 311–315. doi:10.1177/1056492619827382

Zobel, T. (2007). The 'pros' and 'cons' of joint EMS and group certification: A Swedish case study. *Corporate Social Responsibility and Environmental Management*, *14*(3), 152–166. doi:10.1002/csr.125

Zollo, M., & Winter, S. G. (2002). Deliberate Learning and the Evolution of Dynamic Capabilities. *Organization Science*, *13*(3), 339–351. doi:10.1287/orsc.13.3.339.2780

Zorpas, A. (2010). Environmental management systems as sustainable tools in the way of life for the SMEs and VSMEs. *Bioresource Technology*, *101*(6), 1544–1557. doi:10.1016/j.biortech.2009.10.022 PMID:19906527

Zyglidopoulos, S., Williamson, P., & Symeou, P. (2016). The corporate social performance of developing country multinationals. *Business Ethics Quarterly*, *26*(3), 379–406. doi:10.1017/beq.2016.41

About the Contributors

Gregorio Martín-de Castro is a Professor of Strategy and Business Sustainability. BA in Economics and Business Administration and Ph.D. in Management by Complutense University of Madrid. Post Graduate Diploma in Knowledge Management and Intellectual Capital by INSEAD and IUEE. He has been invited professor in different European and Latin American universities and research fellow and visiting scholar at RCC-Harvard University, MIoIR- University of Manchester, University of Southern California, University of California Los Angeles-UCLA, and The University of Edinburgh.

Jaime Juan González-Masip is Assistant Professor of Management and Corporate Social Responsibility at Rey Juan Carlos University (Spain) and at Alcalá University (Spain). He also was Assistant Professor at Complutense University of Madrid (Spain) from 2012 to 2018. He got his Ph.D. in Business Administration and CSR from Complutense University of Madrid in 2017. He earned the Best Doctoral Thesis Award of 2017 from the Economics and Business Faculty. He also holds a degree in Computer Science Engineering and a degree in Marketing. His main research interests include Corporate Social and Environmental Responsibility, Corporate Sustainability and Business Ethics.

* * *

María de la Soledad Agüera graduated in Advertising and Public Relations. Teacher of the Universidad Politécnica de Cartagena, developing this activity from the year 2001. Investigative activity framed inside the field of the sports sponsorship and the consumer behavior, publishing in the Yearbook of Investigative Young persons (AJICT), as well as realizing different presentations in International Congress of Physical Education, International Congress of Football Bases, International Congress EBES, Meeting of University Teachers of Marketing. Ph.D. thesis in Social Sciences carried out in the field of sports sponsorship.

Javier Amores-Salvadó is Associated Professor at Complutense University of Madrid. His research interest is focused on Organizations and Natural Environment (ONE) analysis from a number of perspectives such as management, innovation and strategy.

Remy Balarezo is an Assistant Professor of Strategy and Corporate Sustainability in the Business School at the Universidad de Piura (UDEP), Peru. He holds a PhD in management by Complutense University of Madrid. His research is focused on environmental certifications and environmental strategies.

Aletha Baumann is an Associate Professor of Psychology in the College of Liberal Arts and Social Sciences at the University of the Virgin Islands. She holds a Doctorate of Philosophy in experimental child psychology from the University of Iowa. Dr. Baumann teaches undergraduate and graduate courses in psychology and research, and conducts program evaluation and research consultation for various governmental and private agencies.

José Antonio Belso-Martínez is Associate Professor at the University Miguel Hernández, Spain. He graduated in Economics at the University of Alicante (Spain), and holds a PhD in Economics from University Miguel Hernández. He leads the AERT-Elx research group, and has also acted as coordinator of several research projects or contracts. His research is mainly focused on geography, innovation, planning and development, social innovation and business. His research has been awarded by Spanish academic organizations, and has been published in leading journals such as: Economic Geography, European Planning Studies, European Urban and Regional Studies, Urban Studies, Entrepreneurship and Regional Development, Journal of Business Research, Journal of Knowledge Management among others.

Enrique Claver-Cortés (PhD) is Professor of Business Administration and Strategic Management at the University of Alicante. His doctoral dissertation focused on corporate social responsibility, but his primary areas of research cover tourism management and strategic management. He is a member of the Tourism Research Institute at University of Alicante and the author of several books, book chapters and international articles related to strategic, tourism and human resource management. He has taken part in various public projects highlighting, amongst many others, the European project 'Next Tourism Generation Alliance', the competitive project for the creation of the Tourist Observatory of the Valencian Community (Spain) and other private projects. He is the Head of the Department of Management at the University of Alicante.

Isabel Díez-Vial is Associate Professor of Business Administration at Complutense University of Madrid where she co-coordinates the research group "Growth strategies". She obtained a Ph. D. Economics and Business Administration and a post doc as a Visiting Scholar, in the Haas School of Business, University of California Berkeley. Her research topics are clusters, science parks and networks. She has published in Journal of Management Studies, Technovation, Journal of Knowledge Managenement, Journal of Intellectual Capital, Journal of Small Business Management, Knowledge Management Research & Practice, Growth and Change, Review of Industrial Organization, The Journal of Technology Transfer, Journal of Business Economics and Management, European Planning Studies and European Management Journal, among others. She belongs to the Irujiko Nonaka Centre focused on knowledge management.

Jesús Galende (PhD) is Full Professor of Management at the Multidisciplinary Institute of Enterprise (IME), Department of Business Administration and Management, of the University of Salamanca (Spain). His main research topic focuses on innovation management and its relationships with other business areas, including human resource management. He has published numerous research papers in high impact scientific journals, such as Research Policy, Technovation, International Journal of Production Research, Journal of Business Research or Sustainability. He was visiting researcher at Management School of Lancaster University (UK). Actually, he is Dean at the Faculty of Economics and Business of the University of Salamanca.

Matilde García Pérez (PhD, University of Murcia) is a Professor of Management at the University of Murcia, Spain. She counts with several publications in the studies on nonprofit organizations and the social economy sector.

Hermenegildo Gil-Gómez is a full professor at Universitat Politècnica de València.

Cristian González-Zubieta is a researcher and doctoral candidate in Business Administration and Management at Complutense University of Madrid. His research is about Proactive Environmental Strategies and Corporate Governance.

Vicente Guerola-Navarro is an associate professor at Universitat Politècnica de València.

Kenny Hendrickson is an Associate Professor of Public Administration and Social Sciences, and the Director of the Master of Public Administration Program in the College of Liberal Arts and Social Sciences at the University of the Virgin Islands. He holds a Doctorate of Philosophy in Urban Studies and Public Affairs from the University of Akron in Ohio. His current research interests are centered on organizational authenticity and care, workplace performativity, discretion and professional decision making.

Daniel Jiménez-Jiménez is a Professor of Management at the University of Murcia, Spain. His work has been published in Industrial Marketing Management, Journal of Business Research, International Journal of Information Management, International Journal of Operations & Production Management, International Small Business Journal, Personnel Review and Journal of Knowledge Management, European Management Review, among others.

Anna López-Hernández is a researcher at Universitat Politècnica de València.

María José López-Sánchez received her MA in International Business Analysis from the Leicester University in 1994. Her work at the Business Confederation of the Province of Alicante and the Technological Institute of the Enterprise allows her to gain more than 10 years of experience giving assistance to SMEs on European financing funds. PhD in Economics from the University Miguel Hernández of Elche in 2014, where she works as a researcher and associate professor in the Department of Economic and Financial Studies. Her lines of research are related to territory, business clusters and innovation, social network analysis and social innovation (gender studies, social minorities…), on which she has coordinated and participated in several European and national research projects and published numerous articles and book chapters.

Bartolomé Marco-Lajara (PhD) is Professor at the University of Alicante. His research interests are strategic management and tourism management. He is the author of several books, book chapters and international articles related to teaching methodology and the areas above mentioned. He is a member of the Tourism Research Institute at the University of Alicante since its foundation and the main researcher of a European project 'Next Tourism Generation Alliance' and of the public competitive project for the creation of the Tourist Observatory of the Valencian Community (Spain). He has taken part in others public and private projects, such as the development of the strategic plan of the Alicante province for the period 2010-2020. He is the Assistant Dean of the Economics Faculty at the University of Alicante.

Irene Martín-Rubio is the Coordinator of Industrial Organization, Management and Economics at Technical and Industrial Design Center (ETSIDI) at Universidad Politécnica de Madrid.

Lucía Muñoz-Pascual (PhD) is Assistant Professor of Human Resource Management in the Business Administration and Management Department at Salamanca University. She received a PhD Degree in Business Administration from this university. Her main research topic is strategic human resource management and its influence on creativity and innovation. She has previously worked in multinational companies, such as Santander Bank and Bertelsmann. She is a visiting researcher at Lisbon University in Portugal and The George Washington University School of Business in Washington DC (USA). She has attended at various international conferences on Business Administration and Management. Since 2012, she has also been a coordinator for the Erasmus program at Salamanca University. In addition, since 2015 she has been a member of the Multidisciplinary Institute of Enterprise (IME) at Salamanca University. She is a regular coordinator for various teaching innovation projects, and she has published a number of research papers in high-impact scientific journals, such as Employee Relations, Journal of Business Research, Review of Managerial Science or Sustainability. Actually, she is Vice-Dean at the Faculty of Economics and Business of the Salamanca University.

Raul Oltra-Badenes is an associate professor at Universitat Politècnica de València.

Esther Poveda-Pareja (PhD Student) is an Assistant Professor at the University of Alicante. Her research interests are corporate social responsibility, strategic management and agglomeration economies. She is author of several articles and has presented papers in international conferences. She is graduated in an MBA and has a Business Degree.

María del Mar Ramos González is a Doctor of Economic and Business Sciences. She is currently a professor in the Faculty of Economics and Business Sciences at the CEU San Pablo University in Madrid, coordinator of the subject of Professional Ethics and Business Ethics, and teaches subjects in the area of business organisation. In 2008 she studied an Official Master in Humanities at the Francisco de Vitoria University (UFV of Madrid). She was a professor at the Universidad Europea de Madrid, UEM and at the Real Centro Universitario Escorial-Mª Cristina (Centre attached to the UCM). She continues a line of Research focused on Responsible and Sustainable Behavior of Companies. Among her most recent publications along with other authors include articles such as "Could innovative teams provide the necessary flexibility to compete in the current context?. Cuadernos de Gestión (2015); "Building Corporate Reputation through Sustainable Entrepreneurship: The Mediating Effect of Ethical Behavior" published in Sustainability MDPI, (2017); "Responsible management of human resources: good governance and corporate reputation" published in the Center for Financial Studies, CEF. Trabajo y Seguridad Social (2018) and "Exploring, sustainability, good governance and social responsibility in small and medium enterprises" published in Corporate Social Responsibility and Environmental Management (2019).

Mercedes Rubio Andrés, Doctor of Economic and Business Sciences (CEU), Degree in Business Administration and Master in Management Development (UAM), is professor in the Faculty of Economics and Business Sciences at the CEU San Pablo University in Madrid, coordinator of the subject of Human Resources Management, and she works in the area of business organisation. Among her most recent publications along with other authors include articles such as "The commitment of SMEs to CSR: advantages and obstacles", published in the College of Economists of Madrid, (2016); "Building Corporate Reputation through Sustainable Entrepreneurship: The Mediating Effect of Ethical Behavior" published in Sustainability MDPI, (2017); "Responsible management of human resources: good governance and corporate reputation" published in the Center for Financial Studies, CEF. Trabajo y Seguridad Social (2018) and "Exploring, sustainability, good governance and social responsibility in small and medium enterprises" published in Corporate Social Responsibility and Environmental Management (2019).

Miguel Ángel Sastre-Castillo is a professor of Business Organization. Graduate and PhD in Business Administration from the Complutense University of Madrid. He has been Director of the Division of Program Evaluation at the National Agency for Quality Evaluation and Accreditation ANECA. He is currently a member of the Academic Committee of the Ibero-American Network for Quality Assurance in Higher Education RIACES and is Director in Spain of the magazine ACREDITAS on Quality in Higher Education in Latin America. At the Complutense University of Madrid he has held the following management positions: Vice-rector for Economic Policy, Dean of the Faculty of Commerce and Tourism, and Vice-rector for Quality. At the same university, he directs the Human Resources Management Research Group. His main lines of research are human resources and entrepreneurship, in which he has published more than 40 academic articles in journals such as Corporate Social Responsibility and Environmental Management, Technological Forecasting and Social Change, International Journal of Emerging Markets, Employee Relations, Sustainability, Nonprofit Management & Leadership or Journal of Business Research, etc.

Doina Stratu Strelet is a researcher at Universitat Politècnica de València.

Robert Thompson is a student researcher in the College of Liberal Arts and Social Sciences at the University of the Virgin Islands. His current research interest is centered around corporate social responsibility, ethics, and employee performance.

Ignacio Tobaruela Delgado has been an associate professor Universidad Complutense de Madrid and Universidad Autónoma de Madrid, since 2012. Naval Architect by the Universidad Politécnica de Madrid, he has been Head of the Design, Engineering, Energy and Environmental Departments in several national and multinational firms.

Zeynep Merve Ünal is an Assistant Professor of management in the faculty of economics, administrative and social sciences at the Istanbul Gelisim University in Istanbul, Turkey. Her research interests include meaning, humor at workplace, spirituality, employee engagement, and person-job fit/person-organization fit. Zeynep has relevant ongoing research projects, either collaboratively or alone.

Ledian Valle-Mestre (PhD, University of Murcia) is a researcher at the University of Murcia. His research is based on entrepreneurship and social innovation relationships.

Index

R

S

T

V

W

www.ingramcontent.com/pod-product-compliance
Lightning Source LLC
LaVergne TN
LVHW060405300926
849162LV00006B/1347